Let's Speak Chickasaw
Chikashshanompa' Kilanompoli'

This book is published with the generous assistance of The Chickasaw Press, a division of the Chickasaw Nation, Ada, Oklahoma.

Let's Speak Chickasaw
Chikashshanompa' Kilanompoli'

Pamela Munro and Catherine Willmond

University of Oklahoma Press : Norman

Also by Pamela Munro and Catherine Willmond
  Chickasaw: An Analytical Dictionary (Norman, 1994)

Library of Congress Cataloging-in-Publication Data

Munro, Pamela.
  Let's speak Chickasaw, Chikashshanompa' kilanompoli' / Pamela Munro, Catherine Willmond.
      p.   cm.
  Includes bibliographical references and index.
  ISBN 978-0-8061-3926-5 (pbk. : alk. paper) 1. Chickasaw language—Grammar. I. Willmond, Catherine, 1922–
II. Title.
  PM801.M86   2008
  497'.3865—dc22
                                                                    2008005395

The paper in this book meets the guidelines for permanence and durability of the committee on Production Guidelines for Book Longevity of the Council on Library Resources, Inc. ∞

Copyright © 2008 by Pamela Munro and Catherine Willmond. Published by the University of Oklahoma Press, Norman, Publishing Division of the University. Manufactured in the U.S.A.

  2 3 4 5 6 7 8 9 10

Contents

Unit 8. New Types of Verbs

Unit 9. New Sentence Patterns

Unit 10. Adding More Nouns to Sentences

Unit 11. Irregular Verbs

Unit 12. "Have"

Illustrations

FIGURES

MAPS

Acknowledgments

The late Reverend Oliver Neal, who was greatly concerned with encouraging the preservation and study of the language of his people, originally introduced me to Catherine Willmond and inspired the writing of this book. *Let's Speak Chickasaw, Chikashshanompa' Kilanompoli'* is the result of years of study of Chickasaw, both in Los Angeles and in Oklahoma. This book grew out of lessons Mrs. Willmond and I prepared for an undergraduate Chickasaw linguistics class at UCLA in 1983, with increasingly revised versions of units 1–10 of the current book used in Linguistics 114 classes on American Indian linguistics, with a focus on Chickasaw, in 1994, 1995, 1996, 1998, 1999, 2002, Winter 2003, Fall 2003, Spring 2005, and Fall 2005. Later units were used in continuations following all but one of these classes, during which students had the opportunity to write and revise stories in Chickasaw under Mrs. Willmond's direction. Mrs. Willmond's contributions to knowledge of the Chickasaw language were recognized by her induction in August 2006 into the Chickasaw Nation Hall of Fame.

Chickasaw is a seriously endangered language, with at most a few hundred remaining speakers, virtually all of them well over the age of fifty. I am honored to have had the opportunity to learn about this wonderful language from Mrs. Willmond and many other gracious and insightful speakers in Oklahoma and Los Angeles, many of whom, sadly, are no longer alive. These additional Chickasaw speakers include the late Frankie Alberson, the late Adeline Brown, Vera Virgie Brown, the late Juanita Byars, the late Willie Byars, Onita Carnes, the late Mina Christie, the late Cora Lee Collins, the late Lizzie Frazier, Mary James, Luther John, the late Tecumseh John, the late Maybell Lacher, the late Caroline Milligan, the late Tennie Pettigrew, William Pettigrew, the late Eloise Pickens, the late Clarence Porter, the late Lee Fannie Roberts, the late Mary Ella Russell, the late Minnie Shields, the late Hattie Stout, Thomas Underwood, the late Adam Walker, the late Sue Walton, and Pauline Watson. Mrs. Christie and Mrs. Frazier deserve special thanks for sharing the stories that are reproduced at the end of units 18 and 19. These speakers represented areas of the Chickasaw Nation from Kingston in the south to Byng and Happyland (near Ada) in the north, and from Davis and Ardmore in the west to Fillmore and Wapanucka in the east; their ages at the time of our work together, between 1977 and the present, ranged from the late thirties to the late nineties. All were native speakers of Chickasaw with the exception of Mr. Byars, a native speaker of Choctaw who learned Chickasaw as a young man.

Still other speakers, including the late Yvonne Alberson, Edna Baken, Pauline Brown, the late Patsy Byars, Frank Christie, the late Jackson Collins, Hannah Corsello, Joyce Cripps, Josie Crow, JoAnn Ellis, the late Thomas Frazier, Geraldine Greenwood, Lorene Greenwood, Emily Howard, Jerry Imotichey, the late Amos James, Rose Jefferson, the late Jeff Johnson, the late Martha Johnson, the late Annie Orr, the late Dan

Pettigrew, the late Binum Pickens, the late Leola Porter, John Puller, Flora Reed, the late Veneta Stout, Fanny Underwood, and Jimmie Walker, made other helpful contributions and suggestions. Of course none of these people are in any way responsible for mistakes in the book.

My work has also involved the study of Choctaw, a language very closely related to Chickasaw. I am most grateful to the Choctaw speakers in Los Angeles, Oklahoma, and Mississippi who have helped me. These include the late Aaron Baker, the late Juanita Baker, Rosie Billy, Laura Carney, the late Gus Comby, Edith Gem, Jincy Ingram, Ollie Jack, Leona Jefferson, McDonnell Johnson, Levi Jones, Marie McKinney, Reba Meashintubby, Florence Nelson, the late Paul Perkins, the late Tillie Perkins, the late Steven Roberts, the late Semiah Robinson, the late Julia Thomas, Julia Tims, the late Henry Tubby, Gladys Wade, Frances Willis, and especially, the late Josephine Wade, the late Adam Sampson, and the late Buster Ned, who helped in many other ways as well.

In addition to these speakers, many others in Oklahoma, Texas, and California deserve my thanks for their encouragement, hospitality, and other types of support when it was most needed, especially Palma Aguirre, Susan Barber, Jerry Bennett, Martha and Kevin Bennett, Brenda Carnes, John Drayton, Matt Gordon, Brunetta Bernard Griffith, Joe Griffith, Heather Hardy, Becky Hoffman, Rhonda Hulsey, Felicia Ingram, Irene Marquez, Ramona Marquez, the late William A. (Mac) McGalliard, the late Wanda Ned, Jane Russell, Jerod Impichchaachaaha' Tate, Juanita Tate, Marilyn Trujillo, Joyce Wade, George Willmond, and all the other members of the Choctaw-Chickasaw Heritage Committee whom I have not named here.

A most important acknowledgement goes to the many authors of works on Choctaw and Chickasaw (some of which are described more fully later in this book) that have been of help in this research, particularly the late Reverend Jesse Humes and the late Mrs. Vinnie May (James) Humes, authors of the only book on Chickasaw written before our work, the invaluable *Chickasaw Dictionary* (1973). Works on Choctaw by the late Cyrus Byington, by T. Dale Nicklas and his former colleagues in the Choctaw Bilingual Education program at Southeastern Oklahoma State University (Durant), and by the late Allen Wright have also been of great use, as has technical work by Nicklas, Charles Ulrich, and George Aaron Broadwell. For full references to these works, please see the bibliography at the end of this book.

I am very grateful for the encouragement and support of the administration of the Chickasaw Nation of Oklahoma over the years. In particular I thank former Governor Overton James; Governor Bill Anoatubby; and present and former Chickasaw Nation employees including the late Yvonne Alberson, JoAnn Ellis, Emil Farve, Rhonda Hulsey, Cindy Huston, Geraldine Greenwood, J. Y. Tomlinson, and Gary White Deer, as well as the supportive and helpful staff at the Chickasaw Council House Museum in Tishomingo.

Many linguists have contributed to my understanding of Chickasaw and Choctaw, and thus to this book, though I cannot name them all here; my gratitude to them continues. Stephen R. Anderson worked with Mrs. Willmond and me on a 1978 class at UCLA that suggested the need for this book. Sameer Khan, Marcus Smith, Charles Ulrich, Cynthia Walker, Robert Williams, and Heather Willson have assisted with UCLA Chickasaw classes and provided considerable additional useful input and support. In addition Aaron Broadwell, Marion Bond, Tara Browner, John Dyson, Lynn Gordon, Marcia Haag, Jeanne Katzman, the late Peter Ladefoged, the late Robert Lang, Brook Lillehaugen, Allen Munro, J. P. Munro, Jay Shapiro, Doreen Szeto, and many UCLA Linguistics 114, 199, and 191B students gave encouragement, helpful comments, and other valuable contributions. Matthew Gordon's work on Chickasaw intonation was especially important. I am also grateful to people associated with other language revitalization projects, in particular Harold Crook of the Nez Perce Language Program; Juliette Blevins and Leanne Hinton of the Breath of Life Workshop; and Marcus Smith, Blake Cotton, and Kaylene Day of the Serrano Language Revitalization Project, who provided creative examples that we have adopted for Chickasaw. Thanks once more to all.

Work on this book, background research, and course development at UCLA have been supported by the Academic Senate, Department of Linguistics, American Indian Studies Center, and Instructional Development program of the University of California, Los Angeles, and by a grant from the National Science Foundation (*A Chickasaw Dictionary*, 1987–89). Additional support was provided by a grant from the National Science Foundation to Peter Ladefoged.

Pamela Munro
November 2007

About This Book

Let's Speak Chickasaw, Chikashshanompa' Kilanompoli' is a beginning course in the fundamentals of Chickasaw, a member of the Muskogean family of American Indian languages spoken today in Oklahoma and other locations around the United States by members of the Chickasaw Nation, one of the original Five Civilized Tribes of Oklahoma. This book introduces major types of words and sentences in Chickasaw, using a new, regular system for writing the language.

The units in this book are designed to be used in numerical order, since easier points are presented first as a foundation for the more difficult material that follows. The table of contents provides a useful guide to help you find things in the book.

You will learn more if you are able to imitate the pronunciation and usage of a teacher who knows Chickasaw well or if you can practice with another speaker of Chickasaw who will pronounce the words for you. The included CD with examples of pronunciation and spoken Chickasaw should prove helpful in this regard.

Each unit of this book includes from four to eight short lessons on single topics, accompanied by ten exercises. You will find that you will learn much more Chickasaw if you attempt each of the exercises. Even in you don't want to write out or say the answers, it is a good idea to look over each exercise briefly, since some of them introduce important additional information about the language. Each unit is followed by a list of the new grammatical terms it introduces, and each unit after unit 1 includes a summary listing of the new vocabulary items presented in that unit.

All units include dialogues or readings. Going over these over several times, especially out loud, and memorizing all or part of them if possible, will increase your understanding of how words and sentences are put together in Chickasaw. Many units also include "Beyond the Grammar" sections on the history of the Chickasaw language and people and of other related languages, along with various other points that have to do with the way in which the language is used. Selected units in the second half of the book include supplementary lessons on specialized topics in Chickasaw grammar. These provide an introduction to important aspects of the language, but mastery of the concepts they present is not required for later units.

Chickasaw words in the text are always written in **bold**, while their English translations are given in double quotation marks (" "). English words and words from other languages discussed as examples are given in *italics*. Pronunciations referred to that are not reflected in Chickasaw spelling and hypothetical words that are not actually used in the language are written in angled brackets (< >). Punctuation marks are used as in English, with two exceptions. We do not write hyphens (-) to break Chickasaw words at the end of a line of printing in this book, because the hyphen has two special meanings in Chickasaw spelling. One of these, as you will learn in unit 1, is to separate certain vowel sequences; the other is to separate the parts of a compound word such as **hattak-apa'** "man-eater", as you will learn in unit 18. The apostrophe (') is not a punctuation mark in Chickasaw but is a letter of the Chickasaw alphabet, as you'll see in unit 1.

You do not need any special background in grammar or linguistics to use this book. Grammatical terms used in the text are always written in SMALL CAPITALS the first time they appear. Definitions of all these terms are given in the glossary at the end of the book, with a reference to the unit in which they are introduced.

A number of other sections appear at the end of the book. Chickasaw-English and English-Chickasaw vocabularies include all the words introduced in the book. There are also charts, indexes, and summaries that you will learn more about in later units. A bibliography lists books and articles on Chickasaw. The table of contents at the beginning of the book is also a useful reference, since it includes a detailed list of the topics covered in each unit.

You can learn a lot about a language by working through an introductory book like this one. However, if you are seriously interested in learning to talk Chickasaw, you should find a speaker of the language who is willing to practice with you as you learn how to say more and more things from the book and go beyond what the book has to tell you.

The Chickasaw Nation covers an eighth or so of the area of the state of Oklahoma. Because Chickasaw is spoken by people living over such a wide area, there is considerable variation among speakers regarding how to pronounce certain words and how to put together certain types of sentences. This book is primarily based on the usage of older, conservative speakers from the southeastern part of the Chickasaw Nation. Some information is included that reflects the way people say things in other areas, but no work of this scope can hope to document all known variations. If you work with a Chickasaw teacher or if you already know some words yourself, you may find some disagreements between your teacher's or your own way of speaking and that described in the book. In such cases you should certainly go on saying your words and sentences in the familiar way that seems best to you or as your teacher says them, but you may find it interesting to see the different ways that other people would say the same thing. Of course we welcome any comments from readers concerning divergences from the usage we describe.

Work hard and enjoy studying Chickasaw. Good luck, and have fun!

Catherine Willmond (*left*) and Pamela Munro.

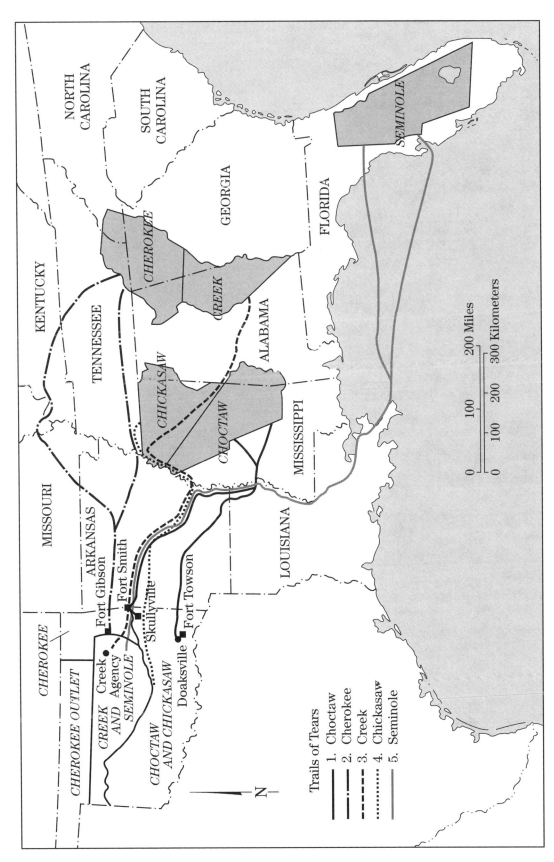

Removal of the Five Tribes

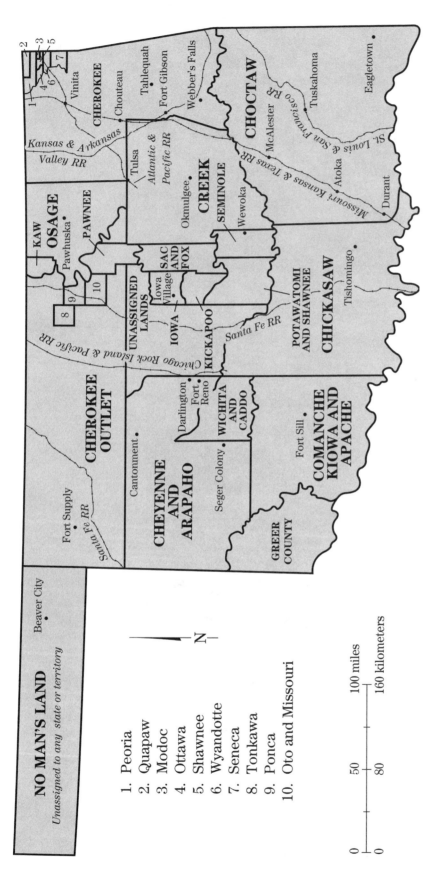

NO MAN'S LAND
Unassigned to any state or territory

Beaver City

N

1. Peoria
2. Quapaw
3. Modoc
4. Ottawa
5. Shawnee
6. Wyandotte
7. Seneca
8. Tonkawa
9. Ponca
10. Oto and Missouri

| 0 | 50 | 100 miles |
| 0 | 80 | 160 kilometers |

CHEROKEE OUTLET

CHEYENNE AND ARAPAHO

Fort Supply
Santa Fe RR

Cantonment

Seger Colony

Darlington
Fort Reno

WICHITA AND CADDO

Fort Sill

GREER COUNTY

COMANCHE KIOWA AND APACHE

KAW
OSAGE
PAWNEE
Pawhuska

Chicago Rock Island & Pacific RR

UNASSIGNED LANDS
SAC AND FOX
Iowa Village
IOWA
KICKAPOO
Santa Fe RR

POTAWATOMI AND SHAWNEE

CHICKASAW
Tishomingo

Kansas & Arkansas Valley RR

Tulsa
Atlantic & Pacific RR

Okmulgee

CREEK
SEMINOLE
Wewoka

Vinita
CHEROKEE
Chouteau

Tahlequah
Fort Gibson
Webber's Falls

CHOCTAW

St. Louis & San Francisco RR

McAlester
Atoka
Durant

Missouri Kansas & Texas RR

Tuskahoma

Eagletown

Indian Territory, 1886–1889

Let's Speak Chickasaw

Chikashshanompa' Kilanompoli'

The Sounds of Chickasaw

In the lessons in this unit you'll learn how to say a number of Chickasaw words and how to write them in the Chickasaw spelling system (or ORTHOGRAPHY).

Lesson 1.1 is an overview of pronouncing, writing, and spelling. Lesson 1.2 describes the vowels sounds of Chickasaw, and lesson 1.3 concerns syllables. Lesson 1.4 presents the consonant sounds, while Lesson 1.5 introduces the accents used in writing Chickasaw and several other important pronunciations. Lesson 1.6 covers other aspects of the Chickasaw sound and writing systems, including alphabetical order and borrowed words and sounds.

Lesson 1.1:
Learning to Pronounce and Write a New Language

Each language has its own set of sounds, and the rules for using letters of the alphabet to write those sounds differ somewhat from language to language. Many of the sounds of Chickasaw are about the same as sounds used in English, but some will seem quite unusual if you haven't heard them before.

We write Chickasaw with most of the same letters used for writing English. Many of the letters represent about the same sounds that they do in English, but other letters are used differently in Chickasaw, and you will need to learn their new meanings. It's especially important to listen to your teacher, to a Chickasaw tape recording, or to someone who speaks Chickasaw while you are first learning the sounds of the language. Remember to pronounce Chickasaw words using the Chickasaw sounds described in this unit—don't make the mistake of trying to use English pronunciations for Chickasaw words, or no one will understand you.

One difference between Chickasaw and English is that the Chickasaw spelling used in this book is much more regular than English spelling. This means that after you have learned all the rules of Chickasaw spelling, whenever you see a new Chickasaw word written according to these rules you will know how to pronounce it immediately, without having to look it up in a pronunciation guide or ask for help. It also means that when you master these spelling rules, each time you hear a new Chickasaw word that is unfamiliar to you, you will be able to write it down correctly.

Chickasaw, English, and all other languages have two main types of sounds, vowels and consonants. VOWEL sounds are made with your mouth open, with a continuous stream of air coming out without any obstruction. CONSONANT sounds are made with the stream of air coming from the lungs interrupted at some point by contact or constriction between the tongue and some other part of the mouth, between the two lips, or between other speech organs.

As each Chickasaw sound is presented during the lessons in this unit, listen carefully to your teacher's pronunciation and try to imitate the new sounds exactly. When you read the unit again after you have heard this demonstration, try to read each Chickasaw word aloud. If you are reading the examples and you forget the pronunciation of a particular sound, review the description of that sound earlier in the unit before you go on. You can listen to almost all the example words on the CD that accompanies this course.

Lesson 1.2:
Vowel Sounds

Many of the sounds in Chickasaw are pronounced just about the same as in English. Some examples of consonants that are pronounced and written similarly in both languages are *b, f, h, l, m, n, s, w,* and *y*. Three other consonants are almost (but not quite) the same in both languages—*k, p,* and *t*. We will use these familiar consonant sounds in words introducing the Chickasaw vowel sounds.

Chickasaw has three sets of vowel sounds: **a** vowels, **i** vowels, and **o** vowels. Each one is pronounced (and written) in three different ways, which means that Chickasaw has nine different vowels altogether. This may sound like a lot to you if you're thinking that English only has five vowels, *a, e, i, o,* and *u*. But in fact English has more vowel sounds than Chickasaw does. The letters *a, e, i, o,* and *u* actually represent about fifteen different vowel sounds in most varieties of American English.

The a vowels. The Chickasaw vowel **a** (written with one letter **a**), a SHORT VOWEL, is most commonly pronounced like the *a* at the end of the English word *sofa* or like the *u* in the word *but*. Sometimes people give it a more precise pronunciation, and it sounds more like the *a* in *father*. (You will learn more about these variations in pronunciation in unit 4.) Listen to your teacher pronounce the Chickasaw words **fala** "crow" and **aya** "to go". You'll hear that these words (like most words in Chickasaw) have STRESS (more emphasis, higher pitch) on the last vowel. Try to say the words just the way your teacher does. (Chickasaw words used in the text of this book are written in **bold**. English meanings are in quotation marks, and example words from English and other languages are in *italics*.)

The corresponding LONG VOWEL is **aa**, which takes longer to say than a short **a** and is written long or doubled. The two **a**'s of the LETTER COMBINATION **aa** together represent just one sound. Long **aa** is always pronounced like the *a* in English *father*. Listen as your teacher says some Chickasaw words with **aa**, such as **falaa** "to be long" or **yaa** "to cry". If you compare **fala** "crow" and **falaa** "to be long", you will hear why the vowel at the end of the first word is called short, while the vowel at the end of the second is called long—**aa** really takes longer to say than **a**.

The third type of vowel sound used in Chickasaw is a NASAL VOWEL. Nasal vowels are pronounced with the air released through the nose, rather than through the mouth as with ordinary vowels. We use nasal vowel sounds in English when pronouncing words like *can't* or *uh-uh* (meaning "no"). Other than this difference in how the air is released, Chickasaw nasal vowels sound about like the corresponding long vowel sounds. Chickasaw nasal vowels are written <u>underlined</u>. The Chickasaw nasal vowel <u>**a**</u> sounds a lot like the vowel of the English word *honk*, except that there is no real *n* sound. Here are examples of some words containing Chickasaw <u>**a**</u>: <u>**a**</u>**fala** "my crow", **pask**<u>**a**</u> "bread" (object form). Try to say these words just the way your teacher does. You will probably find that nasal vowel sounds are easier to make than you think.

Work on imitating the rhythm of your teacher's voice in pronouncing each new word. As you practice saying the **a** vowel sounds, notice that the nasal vowel <u>**a**</u> takes about the same amount of time to say as the long vowel **aa**—it is much longer than the short vowel **a**. All nasal vowels sound long like this.

When you are writing Chickasaw nasal vowels, it's important to remember to include the underlining. Chickasaw <u>**a**</u> is a very different sound from Chickasaw **a**. If you leave off the underlining under a nasal vowel, the word it's in is spelled wrong!

Exercise 1A. Practice pronouncing the following Chickasaw words: **taha** "to be finished", **wakaa** "to fly", **waaka** "to be spotted", **waaka̲** "cow" (object form), **ala** "to arrive", **lawa** "to be many", **paska** "bread", **naafka** "dress", **a̲naafka** "my dress", **a̲naafka̲** "my dress" (object form), **fama** "to be whipped", **laa** "to be plowed".

The Chickasaw vowels **i** and **o** also have short, long, and nasal varieties.

The i vowels. Short **i** is pronounced like the *i* in English *pit* or the *i* in *police*. (In unit 4 you will learn more about variations in vowel pronunciation.) **Iti** "mouth" and **bila** "to melt" are words containing Chickasaw short **i**. Try to imitate your teacher's pronunciation of these words. (At the end of a word, some English speakers feel that Chickasaw short **i** sounds more like the *e* of English *bet*. What do you think?)

The Chickasaw long **ii** sound, written with a double letter, occurs in words like **kii** "oh!" or **iila** "we have arrived". As your teacher pronounces these words, you will see that the **ii** in them sounds very much like the *i* in the English word *machine* and that it is considerably longer than the Chickasaw short **i** sound.

The nasal **i̲** sound in Chickasaw words like **i̲fala** "his crow" or **kili̲ha** or **kili̲ya** "to growl" is also longer sounding than the short **i**. Nasal **i̲** is just like a long **ii** pronounced with the air released through the nose. It sounds a lot like the vowel of English *seen*, but with no *n* sound.

Exercise 1B. Practice saying the following Chickasaw words: **ishi** "to take", **hika** "to stand up", **ilbak** "hand", **ikbi** "to make", **wiiki** "to be heavy", **kasbi** "yard", **tiwa** "to open", **ima** "to give", **impaska** "his bread", **i̲naafka** "her dress", **kiiyaa** "we cry", **i̲yaa** "to cry for him", **nakfish** "younger sibling", **impa** "to eat".

The o vowels. Short **o** is usually pronounced like the *o* in English *vote*, but it may occasionally sound like the *oo* in the English word *cook* or the *u* in the English word *put*. Listen as your teacher pronounces Chickasaw short **o** words like **omba** "to rain" and **koni** "skunk" and try to pronounce them the same way.

The Chickasaw long **oo** always sounds like the *o* in English words like *code*, and, as you would expect, it sounds longer than the short **o** sound. Imitate your teacher's pronunciation of examples like **ihoo** "woman" and **shooli** "to hug".

You can hear the nasal **o̲** sound in words like **po̲fa** "to smoke" and **o̲hika** "to step on". This vowel may sound a lot like the vowel of English *bone* pronounced without the *n*. While you say the nasal vowels in these and other words, you should be able to feel the air escaping from your nose (when you say other vowels, the air comes out only through your mouth). Like the other nasal vowels, these nasal **o̲**'s take longer to say than short vowel sounds.

Exercise 1C. Practice saying the following Chickasaw words: **losa** "to be black", **nosi** "to sleep", **lowak** "fire", **amo** "to mow", **anompoli** "to talk", **abooha** (or **aboowa**) "house", **hoyo** "to look for", **shooli** "to hug", **konta** "to whistle", **ho̲sa** "to shoot at", **po̲fala** "our crow", **hopoo** "to be jealous", **anaako̲** "me", **no̲wa** "to walk", **oblaashaash** "yesterday", **ooti** "to kindle".

Differences among vowel types. It is very important to pay attention to the kind of vowel sound you hear in a Chickasaw word, since the choice of short, long, or nasal vowel can often make a difference in meaning. Here are some sets of words containing different types of **a** vowels:

fala	"crow"
falaa	"to be long"
abi	"to kill"
aabi	"to paint, smear"
wakaa	"to fly"
waaka	"to be spotted"
takaali	"to get caught on"
pak<u>a</u>li	"to bloom"

Make sure you can pronounce these words (or the similar parts of these words) differently, so that your hearer can tell them apart.

A few special vowel combinations are described later in this unit, and lesson 1.5 gives more examples of contrasts between different types of vowels. You'll learn more about pronouncing vowels in unit 4.

Lesson 1.3:
Syllables

Each vowel sound that you hear in a word forms a SYLLABLE with certain surrounding consonants. A Chickasaw syllable may contain a long vowel, a short vowel, or a nasal vowel. Most Chickasaw syllables have a consonant at the beginning, and many also end with a consonant.

You will need to be able to divide Chickasaw words into syllables in order to pronounce them correctly and use them properly in sentences. Here's how:

- Each vowel sound is part of a different syllable. Thus, **fala** and **falaa** both have two syllables, even though **falaa** has three vowel letters, because the long **aa** letter combination represents just one vowel sound. When you are dividing a Chickasaw word into syllables, therefore, look for vowel sounds, not vowel letters.
- When possible, a syllable will begin with a consonant. The consonant just in front of each vowel in a word will generally be included in the same syllable with that vowel. Thus, we can divide **fa/la** and **fa/laa** into syllables (with syllable boundaries represented by slashes), including the consonants preceding each vowel in the syllables with the vowels that follow them.
- Any other consonant is then automatically included in the same syllable as the vowel in front of it, as with **a/nom/po/li**. Like vowel letter combinations, consonant letter combinations such as **sh** (which you will learn more about later in this unit) represent single sounds, so **ishi** is divided as **i/shi**.

Now, let's take a more complicated example, **oblaashaash**. It's best to begin dividing a word into syllables at the right side, at the end of the word, starting with the word's last vowel. The steps are as follows:

- Find the last vowel in the word **oblaashaash**: it's the second **aa**
- Put a slash before the consonant in front of that **aa**: it's the first **sh**, so we get **oblaa/shaash**
- Find the next vowel (from the right): it's the first **aa**
- Put a slash before the consonant in front of that vowel: **ob/laa/shaash**
- There's only one more vowel in the word, so you're done!

We don't have to worry about what syllable **b** and the second **sh** are in. When you put the slashes in as described above, **b** is automatically included in the first syllable and the final **sh** is automatically included in the last syllable. (Don't forget that **sh, ch,** and **lh** are letter combinations that name a single consonant.)

Exercise 1D. Divide each of the Chickasaw words in exercises 1A–1C into syllables, following the rules above.

After you've divided a number of words following the rules above, compare the syllables you've discovered. Some end with a short vowel, some end with a nasal vowel, some end with a long vowel, and some end with a consonant. A syllable that ends with a short vowel is called a LIGHT SYLLABLE. Every other Chickasaw syllable—all those that contain long or nasal vowels or that end in consonants—is a HEAVY SYLLABLE. If you listen to your teacher's pronunciation, you'll see that heavy syllables always receive more emphasis in pronunciation than light syllables do; they sound "heavier" or more prominent.

Even though two letters are needed to spell a long vowel sound like **aa**, the Chickasaw letter combination **aa** is only one sound and one syllable, so **aa** is never split up. It is possible for two separate vowel sounds to occur together in a Chickasaw word, however, as in

        aaima   "he gives it to him there"

This word has three syllables with three different vowels, **aa**, **i**, and **a**. When there is no consonant in front of a vowel, the syllable division slash goes in front of that vowel:

- Start at the end of the word. Find the last vowel in the word **aaima**: it's the short **a** at the end of the word
- Put a slash before the consonant in front of that **a**: it's the **m**, so we get **aai/ma**
- Find the next vowel (from the right): it's the **i**
- Look for the consonant in front of that vowel. There isn't one, so we put the slash in front of the vowel: **aa/i/ma**
- There's only one more vowel in the word, so you're done!

The sound at the beginning of a word is called an INITIAL sound, and the sound at the end of a word is called a FINAL sound. **Aaima** has an initial **aa** and a final **a**. **Koni** has an initial consonant, **k**, and a final **i**. Many more Chickasaw words end with vowels than with consonants. On the other hand, more Chickasaw words begin with consonants than with vowels.

Sometimes when two vowel sounds occur in a Chickasaw word with no consonant between them, they may be run together in speaking. Listen to your teacher say

        ibaa-aya   "he goes with him"

both slow and fast. When most Chickasaw speakers pronounce this word slowly, you can clearly hear four syllables, containing the vowels **i**, **aa**, **a**, and another **a**: **i/baa/a/ya**. In fast pronunciation, however, the long **aa** runs together with the following short **a**, and you'll probably hear the word with only three syllables, as **ibaaya**: **i/baa/ya**.

In this book we'll always write the full form of such words. We'll write words like **ibaa-aya** with a hyphen so that you will be able to tell that the long vowel comes before the short one. When the vowels next to each other are different, as in **aaima**, there is no need for a hyphen, since the division between the different vowel sounds, and the syllables, is clear.

You'll learn more about syllables, and about why it's important to learn the difference between light and heavy syllables, in unit 4.

Exercise lE. Look at each of the words you divided into syllables in exercise 1D and tell which syllables are heavy and which are light. (Remember, each syllable that contains a long or nasal vowel or that ends with a consonant is heavy.)

Lesson 1.4:
Consonant Sounds

Familiar consonant sounds. We'll begin with the consonant sounds that are pronounced and written almost the same in Chickasaw and English: **b, f, h, l, m, n, s, w,** and **y.** There are small differences in pronunciation between the way these are pronounced in Chickasaw and in English, of course. To improve your Chickasaw pronunciation, you should pay careful attention to the way your teacher makes these sounds and try to say them the same way.

The Chickasaw sound **b** (almost the same as in English *back*) appears in Chickasaw words like **bila** "to melt" and **abi** "to kill".

An **f** (pronounced just about as in English *fit*) is used in Chickasaw words like **fala** "crow" and **pofa** "to smoke".

The **h** sound (as in English *hick*) is used in words like **hosa** "to shoot at" and **ihoo** "woman". You'll learn more about special pronunciations with **h** later in this lesson.

The Chickasaw sound **l** (just about like the *l* in the English word *lick*) occurs in words like **lowak** "fire" and **ala** "to arrive".

The consonants **m** and **n** are like the Chickasaw nasal vowels in that they are pronounced with a release of air through the nose (you can feel it!). **M** and **n** are often referred to as NASAL CONSONANTS.

The **m** sound (as in English *mick*) is used in Chickasaw words like **miha** (or **miya**) "to try", **ima** "to give", and **ombataam**? "did it rain?".

An **n**, just about the same as the *n* of English *nick*, is used in Chickasaw words like **niha** "to be greasy", **ani** "to pour in", and **hakson** "cheekbone area".

The **s** sound (just about the same as in English *sick*) is used in Chickasaw words like **sishto** "rattlesnake" and **oksop** "bead".

There's a **w** (as in English *wick*) in Chickasaw words like **waa** "to be ripe" and **tiwa** "to open".

A **y** sound like that in English *yip* is used in Chickasaw words like **yaa** "to cry" and **aya** "to go". There's more about pronunciations with **y** in lesson 1.5.

Exercise 1F. Divide each example word in the preceding lesson into syllables. Which syllables are heavy? Say each word aloud. Have your teacher or another Chickasaw speaker or class member listen to the way you say the words. (You may feel silly at first saying these words out loud, but it's the best way to work on your pronunciation, and you should try to do this often.)

Four other Chickasaw consonant sounds are pronounced just about the same as their English counterparts—these are **k, p, t,** and the letter combination **ch.**

Chickasaw **k**, for instance, sounds just about like the English *k* in *nick*. If you compare the *k* in *nick* with the *k* in *kin*, you may hear a difference between these two English *k*'s—the *k* in *kin* is pronounced with a little puff of air (called ASPIRATION) following it, which is usually not heard following the *k* in *nick*. Chickasaw **k**'s are usually pronounced more like the *k* in English *nick* than like the *k* in English *kin*. They may have some aspiration (just as the *k* in *nick* may), but not as much as an initial *k* would have in English. Listen to your teacher.

K is a very common Chickasaw sound, used in Chickasaw words like **koni** "skunk", **hika** "to stand up", and **ilbak** "hand".

P, t, and the letter combination **ch** are also pronounced with less aspiration in Chickasaw than in English. Otherwise, though, these sounds are just about like their English counterparts.

Listen, for instance, as your teacher says **pisa** "to see", **apa** "to eat", and **oksop** "bead". Try to make the **p** sounds in these words sound Chickasaw, not English. Then try repeating your teacher's pronunciation of **t** in words like **tiwa** "to open", **ooti** "to kindle", and **ihooat** "woman" (subject form).

Ch is a letter combination that represents just one sound in both Chickasaw and English (as in the English word *chick*). Repeat the words **chaaha** "to be tall" and **oochi** "to draw (water from a well)" after your teacher. The word **oochi** only has three sounds—**oo**, **ch**, and **i**—even though it is written with five letters. How many sounds does the word **chaaha** have?

*Special pronunciations with **k***. Many sequences of two different consonants occur in Chickasaw words, and some of these have special pronunciations. When a **k** occurs before **l, m, n, w**, or **y**, it may sound like an English *g* (as in *snuggle*). You can hear this in the word **iklo** "he didn't get here". In fact you may even hear what sounds like an extra vowel sound when your teacher says **iklo**, right between the **k** and the **l**—the word might almost sound like <igilo> to you. (Spellings of things that might seem like Chickasaw words but that aren't correct are enclosed in angled brackets: < >.) Another example is in the word **haknip** "body". How does the **k** sound? What do you hear between the **k** and the **n**? Pronouncing these extra COPY VOWELS will make your Chickasaw sound more natural, even though we do not write the extra sounds as part of the word and they do not count as syllables. You'll hear copy vowels added to Chickasaw words most often when people are talking fast. Before consonants other than **l, m, n, w**, or **y**, a **k** sounds like **k**, not *g*, and there are no added copy vowels.

*Letter sequences with **n***. If you compare the *n*'s in the English words *rant, ranch*, and *rank*, you'll probably feel they are not quite the same—in English, and also in Chickasaw, the pronunciation of **n** varies according to the sound that follows it. Thus, the **n** in a Chickasaw word like **konti** "whistle" is different from the **n** in **chinchokmataa?** "are you well?", as well as from the **n** in the words **inkiliha** "to growl at" and **istokchank** "watermelon". Try to imitate your teacher's pronunciation.

Exercise 1G. Pronounce each of the following words: **onkof** "persimmon", **okla** "town", **tokfol** "dogwood", **chompa** "to buy", **kanchi** "to sell", **imaabachi** "to teach", **chaaha** "to be tall", **toklo** "two", **chokma** "to be good", **lakna** "to be yellow", **toksali** "to work", **fokha** "to put on (a dress)", **nokchito** "to behave oneself", **sipokni** "to be old".

Consonants that don't occur in English. Chickasaw has a few additional consonants and consonant combinations that are more different from the English sounds you are familiar with.

Sh is a Chickasaw sound that will remind you of English *sh* in a word like *ship*. However, if you listen to your teacher say words like **sholosh** "shoe" or **ishi** "to get", you'll hear that the Chickasaw **sh** sound has a bit more of a whistle to it than the English *sh* sound does. The Chickasaw **sh** is pronounced with the end of the tongue curled back, while the tongue is flatter and pointed toward the front of the mouth for English *sh*. Both in English and in Chickasaw, the letter combination **sh** represents just a single sound.

Like **ch** and **sh**, **lh** is a letter combination that represents a single Chickasaw sound. However, **lh** is a sound with no close counterpart in English. Listen to your teacher say **lhabanka** "to snore" and **hilha** "to dance". What does the **lh** sound like to you? It is something like a cross between an **l** and an **h**, or the way an English *l* sounds after a *k* sound in words like *Klondike*. You can practice making the **lh** sound by putting your tongue behind your top teeth (just as if you were going to say **l**) and making a breathy **h** sound. Practice will help you make a good Chickasaw **lh**. Imitate your teacher.

Some younger people who have trouble pronouncing the **lh** sound say <th> (as in English *thick*) instead of **lh** in Chickasaw words. You can do this too if you want to, but you will find that older Chickasaw speakers prefer the **lh** pronunciation and regard the use of the <th> sound as too much like English. It's worth taking the trouble to learn how to say **lh** correctly. Of course, once again you should follow your teacher's pronunciation.

H plus another consonant. Although Chickasaw **h** sounds just like English **h**, Chickasaw **h** can be pronounced between a vowel and a consonant. (This is different from English, where an *h* sound always has a vowel after it.) When **h** comes before **b**, **l**, **m**, **n**, **w**, or **y**, as in words like **tahli** "to finish" or **lohmi** "to hide", it may be pronounced with a following copy vowel, just as with **k**—so that "to finish" might sound like <tahali> to you. Some Chickasaw speakers pronounce syllables consisting of a vowel plus **h** the same as corresponding syllables with a long vowel. Thus, some people say <taali> instead of **tahli**, <loomi> instead of **lohmi**, and so on. Follow your teacher's pronunciation.

The sequence of **h** followed by **l** in **tahli** is very different from the letter combination **lh** in words like **hilha**. **Lh** is just one sound, while **hl** is a sequence of two different sounds.

H at the ends of words. Sometimes you might hear an **h** sound at the end of a Chickasaw word that is written with a final vowel. This pronunciation of **h** at the end of words is uncommon, so we do not write final **h** in this book. Listen to hear whether your teacher pronounces an **h** sound at the end of these words. If so, you should pronounce one there too, and you may write a final **h** if you like.

Exercise 1H. Pronounce the following Chickasaw words after your teacher: **talhpak** "basket", **ishto** "to be big", **holhchifo** "name", **bashpo** "knife", **anhi** "to wish", **cholhkan** "spider", **nalha** "to be shot", **hashaa** "to be angry", **palhki** "to be fast", **oshta** "four", **hofahya** "to be ashamed", **mahli** "wind", **achokmilhka** "to kneel", **tohbi** "to be white".

Then tell how many sounds (not letters!) each of these words has, according to its spelling—remember that letter combinations each represent just one sound.

The glottal stop sound. The last Chickasaw consonant sound is **'**, which is written with an apostrophe. This sound is called the GLOTTAL STOP. A glottal stop is the sound—or absence of sound, just a little catch in the throat—that you make in the middle of an English word like *uh-oh* (meaning "oops") or *uh-uh* ("no") by bringing together the folds of the glottis, the opening at the top of the larynx. English speakers use many glottal stops without being aware of them. If you say a name like *Annie Oakley* quickly, you'll probably notice that it sounds almost as though there is a *y* sound in between the *Annie* and the *Oakley,* but if you say the same name more slowly and precisely, you are making a glottal stop between the two words (you should be able to feel the catch in your throat). Similarly, you can say a phrase like *Aunt Alice* in two ways—quickly, so that the second word almost sounds as if it starts with a *t*, or more precisely, with a glottal stop at the beginning of the second word. Presence or absence of the glottal stop sound doesn't make much difference in English, so we have no regular way to spell this sound. In Chickasaw words, though, the glottal stop sound is very important and is written with the **'** letter (the apostrophe). A **'** sound is used at the end of many words for people, places, and things in Chickasaw, such as **ofi'** "dog" or **aachompa'** "store". It's also a common sound in the middle of Chickasaw words, such as **ikbi'lo** "it doesn't melt", **bo'li** "to beat up", or **sho̱'ka** "to kiss".

You're probably not used to paying a lot of attention to marks like **'** in a word, but the glottal stop can make a meaning difference in Chickasaw. Listen as your teacher says pairs of words like the following and repeat them after your teacher.

hilha "to dance"   hilha' "dancer", "a dance"
ikishko "he doesn't drink it"   ikishko' "let him drink it!"

As you can see, there's often a real difference in meaning between words with and without '. Leaving out the ' from the words in the second column would mean they were spelled wrong. Practice making the glottal stop sound yourself and listen for it when you hear people talking Chickasaw.

Double consonants. Just as Chickasaw vowels can be either long (written with two letters) or short, each of the consonant sounds introduced in this lesson other than ' can be either short, as in the examples already presented, or doubled (followed by another consonant just like it). Listen to the difference between the short and DOUBLE CONSONANTS in the following pairs of words:

fama "to be whipped"   fammi "to whip"
nalha "to be shot"   nalhlhi "to shoot"
iti "mouth"   itti' "wood"
aya "to go"   kayya "to be full"

Be sure you can hear the difference between the short and double consonants and practice pronouncing these words yourself. The double consonants consist of a sequence of two short consonants that takes longer to say than the corresponding short consonant sound. A double consonant sequence is thus two separate sounds, not a single letter combination—so, for example, **fammi** is divided into syllables as **fam/mi**. As this example shows, a syllable before a double consonant is always a heavy syllable. (If you've ever heard double consonants in another language—such as Italian, one European language that uses them—you may feel that Chickasaw double consonants are not as long as others. Don't worry—with practice you will learn to hear them well.)

One double consonant sometimes has a special pronunciation. A double **ll** often sounds like <dl>, especially in a long word or when someone is talking fast. Compare the short and double **l**'s in **ittihaalalli** "to marry"—most likely the **ll** at the end of the word will sound like a <dl> to you at least some of the time.

Exercise 11. Pronounce each of the following sets of words after your teacher. Repeat each one several times, trying to say it exactly the way your teacher does.

   taloowa "to sing" / **taloowa'** "song, singer"; **wakaa** "to fly" / **waaka** "to be spotted" / **waaka'** "cow"; **kiibi** "we kill him" / **kiibi'** "let's kill him"; **pali'** "flying squirrel" / **palli** "to be hot"; **tiwa** "to open" / **tiwwi** "to open (something)"; **kola** "to be dug" / **kolli** "to dig" / **kooli** "to break (something round)"; **chokfi** "rabbit" / **ofi'** "dog"; **ani** "to pour into a container" / **ani'** "fruit, produce"; **nita'** "bear" / **okshitta** "to close (something)"; **hoyo** "to look for" / **hoyya** "to drip"; **kawwi** "to break up for kindling" / **shawi'** "raccoon"; **bo'li** "to beat up" / **bohli** "to put down". The following four-way set is especially good to practice: **bo'li** "to beat up" / **bohli** "to put down" / **kolli** "to dig" / **kooli** "to break (something round)".

Not all Chickasaw consonant sounds can occur in every position in a word. The ' sound does not occur initially (at the beginning of a word), but it is the most common final consonant in many types of Chickasaw words. Only a few other consonants occur finally. Here are some examples: **f** occurs finally in only one word, **onkof** "persimmon"; **k**, as in **talhpak** "basket", is a common final consonant; **l** occurs finally in a few words, such as **tokfol** "dogwood"; **m** occurs finally in questions like **mallitaam**? "did he jump?"; **n** occurs finally in words like **cholhkan** "spider"; **p** occurs finally in words like **oksop** "bead"; **sh** is a common final consonant, as in **issosh** "bug"; and **t** occurs finally in certain forms of nouns and verbs, like **ihooat** "woman" (subject form).

Final **h** was discussed above, and final **y** will be covered in the next lesson. The other Chickasaw consonant sounds do not occur finally, except in words used to imitate noises.

Lesson 1.5:
Accents and Additional Special Pronunciations

Accents. You've already learned that most Chickasaw words have stress on the last syllable, and you've learned to listen for heavy syllables containing long or nasal vowels or vowels followed by more than one consonant. In addition, vowels in some Chickasaw verbs have a special pronunciation, shown with a special ACCENT mark.

The usual accent mark used on vowels in Chickasaw is a diagonal line pointing up to the right: ´ (an "acute accent"). In Chickasaw, accent marks are used almost exclusively on the vowels of certain heavy syllables in certain verbs (always either the next-to-last syllable or the syllable before that). The vowel with the accent mark is pronounced with a noticeable rise in the pitch of the voice and may sound louder or more prominent than the last vowel in the word. Accented vowels usually have the same sound as the corresponding unaccented long vowels: for instance, accented **á** always has the sound of English *a* in *father*, never the sound of English *a* in *sofa*. Accented vowels are never long, but they may be nasal.

The best way to practice hearing accents is to compare words with an accent with identical words that don't have one:

konta "to whistle"	kónta "still whistling"
mas<u>o</u>fa "to be bald"	mas<u>ó</u>fa "be balder"
impa "to eat"	ímpa "still eating"

The words on the left are pronounced with the usual Chickasaw stress on the last syllable. The words on the right, however, have louder, higher sounding next-to-last syllables. As you can see, the accent makes a difference in meaning, but words with and without an accent usually have related meanings. Since the meaning and pronunciation of words with accents usually is similar to those of words without accents, many people do not bother to write accent marks, but because they do make a difference, we will always write them in this book. Most words with accents are special types of verbs, which you'll begin learning about in unit 8.

The ng sound. The letter combination **ng** is used in Chickasaw in words like **chóngma** "to be better" and **hánglo** "to hear". In these words **ng** is always pronounced as in English words like *long* or *singer*. **Ng** only occurs following an accented vowel, before the sounds **m, l, n,** and **b**. You will learn more about words containing the **ng** sound in unit 8. Some Chickasaw speakers don't use the sound **ng**. They pronounce the words above as **chónkma** and **hánklo**.

Accented vowels plus yy. Chickasaw vowel sounds sometimes change their pronunciation when they are accented before a double **yy**. Usually, Chickasaw **ay** sounds like the *ai* in English *aisle*, as in **aya** "to go" and **kayya** "to be full". When its **a** is accented, **áyy** may also sound like the *ai* of *aisle,* but it is often pronounced like the *ay* of English *bay*, as in **áyya'sha** "they are there". The same *ay* in *bay* pronunciation is used when **ay** occurs at the end of a word or before a consonant other than **y**, as in **yakhookay** "thank you" or **ilaapakáyni** "by himself".

The sequence **óyyo** is often pronounced like <u> (like the sound of the *ou* in *Louie*), as in **fóyyokha** "to wear" (often pronounced like <fuyyokha>). Sometimes an **oyyo** sequence is pronounced like a long <uu> (so "to wear" might sound like <fuukha>). For some speakers, **óyyo** may even sound like a French *u* or a German *ü*—a sound that does not occur in English, pronounced like a Chickasaw **i** made with the lips pursed.

The vowel **i** does not change its pronunciation before **yy**, but an **íyyi** sequence is very often pronounced simply as **ii**, as in **bíyyi'ka** or <bíi'ka> "all the time".

The vowel sequence ia. Usually two short vowels are not written together in Chickasaw words. However, the sequence **ia** occurs in a few words, such as **ittialbi'** "lips". Many speakers pronounce **ia** in such words very much like the *e* sound in English words like *bet,* so this word might sound like <ittelbi'> to you. Some speakers may pronounce the two sounds separately, as Chickasaw **i** followed by Chickasaw **a**, while others may pronounce an **h** between the two sounds—for these speakers, "lips" is **ittihalbi'**. Follow your teacher's pronunciation.

Long nasal vowels. In some words, such as **ii** "yes", a nasal vowel is followed immediately by a short vowel, and often such a sequence sounds like an extra-long nasal vowel. These LONG NASAL VOWEL sequences are most common in accented verbs, such as **faláa** "to be longer" and **áa** "to go around". Usually these sequences of nasal plus plain short vowel are pronounced together, almost as one sound. But if you listen carefully, you may hear first the nasal vowel, then the short non-nasal vowel. A long nasal vowel is somewhat like a letter combination representing a single sound, but it really is a sequence of two similar sounds pronounced together.

The circumflex accent. There is a second type of accent, called a CIRCUMFLEX, that is used instead of the normal accent in a very small number of Chickasaw verbs. Compare these examples of vowels with and without the circumflex accent:

sakki "to catch up with"	sâkki "finally catch up with"
kochcha "to go out"	kôchcha "finally go out"
haklo "to hear, listen to"	hâklo "finally hear, finally listen to"

(These "finally" expressions are most commonly used with the word **kaniht** "finally".) Vowels with a circumflex accent start out with a strong rise in pitch and then have a fall in pitch; you may almost hear what sounds like a ' sound after these vowels. This accent is used only on certain verbs and is not at all common. You'll learn more about verbs that use the circumflex accent in the Advanced Chickasaw Grammar lesson in unit 20.

Exercise 1J. Practice saying the following words. Pay attention to the accents. **nokhánglo** "to be sad"; **passáa** "to spank"; **okshitta** "to close" / **(kaniht) okshîtta** "finally close"; **ayoppa** "to be happy" / **(kaniht) ayôppa** "finally get happy"; **chowaala'** "cedar"; **pichchaa** "barn"; **tiwa** "to open" / **tíwa** "still opening" / **(kaniht) tí'wa** "finally open"; **iila** "we have arrived" / **íla** "to be different"; **ikbi** "to make" / **ihíngbi** "make all the time" / **(kaniht) îkbi** "finally make".

Lesson 1.6:
More about Chickasaw Words

Chickasaw alphabetical order. You have now learned all of the vowel and consonant sounds that are used in Chickasaw. Just as with English, there is a special alphabetical order of the Chickasaw letters that is followed in dictionaries and other lists, such as the vocabulary at the end of this book. The alphabetical order of the Chickasaw sounds you have learned is **'**, **a**, **aa**, **a̱**, **b**, **ch**, **f**, **h**, **i**, **ii**, **i̱**, **k**, **l**, **lh**, **m**, **n**, **ng**, **o**, **oo**, **o̱**, **p**, **s**, **sh**, **t**, **w**, and **y**. As you can see, letter combinations have their own place in the Chickasaw alphabetical order. Accents on vowels are ignored in alphabetizing Chickasaw words, unless there is a word that looks exactly the same except for an accent. In that case the word without the accent comes first: thus, **konta** comes before **kónta** in the Chickasaw alphabet.

Borrowed words and sounds. Like all people, Chickasaw speakers have occasionally borrowed words from other languages with which they came in contact. Some examples of Chickasaw words that were originally borrowed from other languages include **saafki'** "sofkee (sour corn dish)" (borrowed from Creek), **ponta** "to borrow" (borrowed from French), **waaka'** "cow" (borrowed from Spanish), **tili'ko'** "flour" (borrowed from the Spanish "wheat"), and **tii'** "tea" (borrowed from English). Since many Chickasaw speakers know the

Choctaw language well, they often use Choctaw words in everyday Chickasaw conversation, and there are undoubtedly many words in modern Chickasaw that have been borrowed from Choctaw, just as some varieties of Choctaw probably contain words that originally were Chickasaw. Since the two languages are quite similar, it is sometimes hard to tell whether a word was originally Chickasaw or Choctaw.

The English language contains a number of sounds that are not normally used in Chickasaw, just as some Chickasaw sounds are not used in English. Some Chickasaw speakers use borrowed consonant sounds, such as **d**, **g**, **j**, **r**, **v**, and **z**, or borrowed vowel sounds like **e**, when pronouncing borrowed English words. Many words borrowed from English into Chickasaw have several pronunciations. Some speakers use borrowed sounds in these borrowed words, while others change the pronunciations so that they contain only standard Chickasaw sounds.

English word	Chickasaw word with borrowed sounds	Chickasaw word with standard sounds
dollar	daala'	taala'
vote	vooti	footi
car	kaar	kaa
professor	poffessa'	poffassa', poffissa'
window	winda'	winta'
read	riidi	riiti (still uses **r**)

As you can see, even the pronunciations that use the borrowed sounds are changed from the English originals. If your teacher uses these borrowed words, try to match your teacher's pronunciation. (Some Chickasaw speakers try to avoid using borrowed words, especially those with borrowed sounds, at all. These words are not on the CD that accompanies this course.)

The full Chickasaw alphabet, including all these borrowed sounds is **'**, **a**, **aa**, **a̲**, **b**, **ch**, **d**, **e**, **f**, **g**, **h**, **i**, **ii**, **i̲**, **j**, **k**, **l**, **lh**, **m**, **n**, **ng**, **o**, **oo**, **o̲**, **p**, **r**, **s**, **sh**, **t**, **v**, **w**, **y**, and **z**. The letters **c** (without a following **h**, in the Chickasaw letter combination **ch**), **q**, **u**, and **x** are never used in writing Chickasaw words (though they may be used in names of people and places that appear in Chickasaw sentences, as discussed below).

Names. Names might be thought of as another kind of borrowed word—they are usually not of Chickasaw origin, yet everyone uses them in normal conversation. (Some surnames of Chickasaw people, such as Imotichey, are of Chickasaw origin.) Generally personal names are written with their usual English spelling, but you may notice that Chickasaw speakers pronounce them a bit differently when they are speaking Chickasaw rather than English. For example, fluent Chickasaw speakers very frequently add a **'** sound to the end of English words ending in a vowel when they use these words in Chickasaw sentences.

Just as Chickasaw has borrowed words from English, English has borrowed words from Chickasaw, especially place-names such as *Tishomingo* (from Chickasaw **Tishohminko'**, the chief who led the Chickasaws on the Trail of Tears) and *Hauwani Creek* (from Chickasaw **hayowani'** "worm").

Terms and Concepts

ORTHOGRAPHY, VOWEL, CONSONANT, STRESS, SHORT VOWEL, LONG VOWEL, NASAL VOWEL, SYLLABLE, LIGHT SYLLABLE, HEAVY SYLLABLE, INITIAL, FINAL, NASAL CONSONANT, ASPIRATION, COPY VOWEL, GLOTTAL STOP, DOUBLE CONSONANT, ACCENT, LONG VOWEL, CIRCUMFLEX. All the new terms and concepts in each unit are defined in the Glossary of Grammatical Terms at the end of this book. Whenever you finish a unit, you should go over the list of terms and make sure you're familiar with each one; if not, review it in the unit. You can always check any term in the glossary if you feel uncertain about its meaning.

VOCABULARY

You do not need to try to memorize all the new words in this unit, although it would be good to go over them and try to learn some of them to prepare for what comes next. The Reading and Speaking section of this unit will give you an opportunity to practice what you've learned about pronouncing Chickasaw words.

Each unit after this one will include a list of all the vocabulary introduced in that unit, as well as a list of grammatical terms used for the first time in that unit (like the list given above).

READING AND SPEAKING

Greetings

Here's a chance to use what you've learned about reading Chickasaw. Repeat the following short dialogues after your teacher, then practice them with another student or someone who speaks Chickasaw. Go over each one until you can carry on these simple conversations without looking at your book.

Dialogues 1–9 were recorded on the CD that accompanies this course, performed by Catherine Willmond and Eloise Pickens:

1 (two speakers).
  —Chokma!   "Hello!"
  —Chokma!   "Hello!"

2 (two speakers).
  —Chokma!   "Hello!"
  —Chokmakáyni!   "Hello!"

3 (two speakers).
  —Chinchokma?   "Are you okay?"
  —Chokmakáyni!   "Fine!"

4 (two speakers).
  —Chinchokmataa?   "Are you okay?"
  —Ii, chokma.   "Yes, fine."

5 (three speakers).
  —Hachinchokmataa?   "How are you?" (addressed to more than one)
  —Chokma.   "Fine."
  —Ii, chokma.   "Yes, fine."

6 (two speakers).
  —Hallito!   "Hello!"

7 (two speakers).
  —Chinchokma?   "Are you okay?"
  —Ii, anchokma.   "Yes, I'm fine."

8 (two speakers).
  —Chinchokmataa?   "Are you okay?"
  —Ii, anchokma.   "Yes, I'm fine."

9 (two speakers).

  —Chinchokmataa?   "Are you okay?"

  —Ii, anchokma. Ishnaako?   "Yes, I'm fine. And you?"

  —Ii, anchokma.   "Yes, I'm fine."

10 (two speakers).

  —Chinchokma?   "How are you?"

  —Chokma. Ishnaako?   "Good. And you?"

  —Anchokma.   "I'm fine."

As you can see from the little dialogues above, most Chickasaw greetings use some form of the verb **chokma** "to be good", which was used as an example in this unit. Some Chickasaws regard the word **Hallito** as Choctaw, but many Chickasaws use it anyway. In dialogues 9 and 10, the word **ishnaako**? "and you?" may be replaced by **ishnaato**? by other speakers. Both **ishnaako** and **ishnaato** mean the same thing. Many speakers, however, regard **ishnaato** as Choctaw sounding.

If you listen to the questions that end in **–taa** (which you will learn more about in unit 4), you'll hear that their accent pattern is different from those of other Chickasaw words and phrases you've heard in this unit. Questions in **–taa** have their strongest stress on the last heavy syllable before **–taa**. Thus, **Chinchokmataa?** is pronounced with strongest stress on the **chok** syllable.

BEYOND THE GRAMMAR: CHICKASAW AND CHOCTAW ORTHOGRAPHIES

The spelling system, or orthography, used in this book is very similar to other systems that have been used for writing Chickasaw and Choctaw. These earlier ways of writing often had the disadvantages of inconsistency (certain words or sounds were written one way one time, another way another time) and incompleteness (differences in pronunciation that make a difference in meaning were not always represented in the spelling). The changes introduced in the new orthography used here were made so as to produce a spelling system that is more regular and easier to learn and remember, so that a user can correctly read any new word and correctly write down any word that is heard. The orthography used in this book was developed for a new dictionary, *Chickasaw: An Analytical Dictionary*, published in 1994 by the University of Oklahoma Press, and is the same as that used in this dictionary.

The consonant sounds are written about the same way in this book as in the earlier *A Chickasaw Dictionary* by the late Reverend Jesse J. Humes and Mrs. Vinnie May (James) Humes, the mother of former Chickasaw Nation Governor Overton James. The exception is that the Humeses' dictionary follows traditional practice in not writing the important glottal stop sound, which we write with ' in Chickasaw words in this book. Some of the vowel symbols used in this book also differ from those used in the *Chickasaw Dictionary*, whose spelling system is described more fully following unit 9.

There are a few other differences between the orthography in this book and that used in traditional Choctaw writings like the Bible, the Hymnbook, and the dictionary. In traditional Choctaw writing many double consonants are written short, and the **lh** sound is sometimes written **lh** and sometimes **hl**. This can be confusing, since **hl** also occurs as a sequence of two sounds in both Choctaw and Chickasaw, as in the word **tahli** "to finish". ' is never written in Choctaw, but many Choctaw words end in a final **h** sound that is not written in Chickasaw. As noted in the unit, you may occasionally hear an **h** sound at the end of Chickasaw words that do not end in ', but this **h** need not be written. In some orthographies for Chickasaw and Choctaw, nasal vowels are written in italics rather than underlined, and in others, nasal vowels are indicated with a small raised ⁿ following the vowel letter. There are also other differences between the way vowels are written in Choctaw and Chickasaw orthography.

If you go on to study more Chickasaw after you finish this book, or if you want to continue using the language, you will find it helpful to learn to use both the new *Chickasaw: An Analytical Dictionary* and the older *Chickasaw Dictionary*, as well as the different traditional and modern Choctaw writing systems. Hints on how to convert the spelling system used in this book to the older orthographies, as well as other information about other books on Chickasaw and Choctaw, are given in unit 9 and the bibliography.

Simple Sentences

In this unit you'll learn some Chickasaw nouns (lesson 2.1) and how to use them in a variety of sentences.

Lesson 2.2 presents the simplest Chickasaw sentences, while lesson 2.3 introduces the concept of subject and how to express "this" and "that". Lesson 2.4 discusses singular and plural. Simple sentences with verbs are described in lesson 2.5. Lesson 2.6 introduces commands, and lesson 2.7 sentences with "they" plural subjects.

Lesson 2.1: Nouns

A NOUN is a word used to name something—usually, a person, a place, or a thing. The English words *woman*, *town*, and *basket* are all nouns, and so are the Chickasaw words **ihoo** "woman", **okla** "town", and **talhpak** "basket".

Here are some Chickasaw nouns that you'll be able to use in sentences in this unit. Practice saying each one after your teacher.

ihoo	woman
hattak	person; man
nakni'	man, male
alikchi'	doctor
minko'	chief
Chikashsha	Chickasaw, Chickasaw person
Chahta'	Choctaw, Choctaw person
naahollo	white person, white man, non-Indian
nannalhpooba'	animal (typically, a domesticated animal)
issi'	deer
pinti'	mouse
ofi'	dog
okla	town
bala'	beans
talhpak	basket
itti'	tree, stick, log, wood

chow<u>aa</u>la', chow<u>a</u>hala'	cedar
paska	bread

Some of these words have more than one English translation. The word **itti'** is sometimes translated "tree", for instance, but other times "wood" or "stick" is a better English translation. Similarly, some English words have more than one Chickasaw translation. Most Chickasaw speakers use the word **hattak** to translate the English word "man", for example, both in the sense of "adult male person" and in the general sense of "mankind" or "people". For some speakers the basic meaning of **hattak** is "person"—either "man" or "woman"—so these speakers generally use the word **nakni'** to mean "adult male person". Many people use simply **hattak** to mean "man", though, so it can be a bit confusing.

> *Exercise 2A.* Learn the new words. It is important to develop a good Chickasaw vocabulary as soon as possible, so you should work at memorizing the new words in each unit as quickly as you can. You should be able to give the English translation for each Chickasaw word and to tell the Chickasaw equivalents of each English word.

Nakni' always means "male" as opposed to "female"—for instance, when speaking about the sex of animals. Some people say "man" with a PHRASE, or group of words used together: **hattak nakni'**. The exact meaning of this phrase is "male person" (the two parts are in the opposite order from their order in English). You can use **nakni'** after the name of any animal to specify the male of the species; thus, **issi' nakni'** means "male deer".

Hattak and **nakni'** are nouns, and **hattak nakni'** and **issi' nakni'** are NOUN PHRASES, because they are phrases (sequences of more than one word) used just like nouns. In this book we will usually not differentiate between single words and phrases used in the same way.

Chikashsha ihoo is a noun phrase that means "Chickasaw woman". (People often run these two words together and say **Chikashshihoo** or, occasionally, **Chikashshihoo'**.) To identify female animals, a special word, **tiik**, is used after the animal name. **Issi' tiik** is a noun phrase that means "female deer". In Chickasaw the word **tiik** is not used by itself without another preceding word.

Lesson 2.2:
Sentences with Nouns

A Chickasaw noun can be used all by itself as a complete SENTENCE. For example,

> Ihoo.

can mean "It's a woman" or "She's a woman"—you might say this to tell who was at the door or to describe how grown up some girl had gotten to be. If you were very surprised or agitated about this information, you could say

> Ihoo!

(an exclamation—notice that punctuation can be used to show the same kind of change in pronunciation in Chickasaw as in English). In any language a sentence contains all the words needed to express a complete thought—usually, to describe a situation or to report some event. In English most sentences have more than one word, but in Chickasaw many sentences consist of just one word.

There is no separate word in the Chickasaw sentences above to correspond with the English words "it" or "she" or "is". A Chickasaw noun like **ihoo** used by itself in this way makes an identificational statement, but no form of "be" (like "is" or "are") is included. When the people involved in a conversation understand who they are talking about, it's not necessary to say "he" or "she" or "it".

No word for "a" appears in the Chickasaw sentence. There is no exact word for "a" or "an" (or for "the") in Chickasaw. Thus, the sentence

Minko'.

might be translated as "He's a chief" or as "He's the chief", depending on the circumstances under which it was uttered.

As you learned in lesson 1.2, most Chickasaw words end with a stressed vowel with higher pitch than the rest of the word. This same pattern is used in most Chickasaw statements. When you speak Chickasaw, the pitch of your voice generally rises from the beginning to the end of the sentence, whether your sentence contains one word or many.

The sentences in this lesson are IDENTIFICATIONAL SENTENCES. An identificational sentence is mainly used to identify someone or something with the noun or name it contains. Such sentences are usually translated into English with "is" (or, as you'll see later, with "are").

Exercise 2B. Translate each of the following sentences into Chickasaw. Practice saying each one aloud. 1. It's a doctor. 2. He's the man. 3. It's a male mouse! 4. It's a tree. 5. It's a deer. 6. It's the bread. 7. He's a Chickasaw. 8. She's a white woman (**naahollo ihoo**). 9. It's a female dog. 10. It's a Chickasaw woman.

Now, give another translation for each of the Chickasaw sentences you wrote.

Lesson 2.3:
Subjects

The identificational sentences you saw in lesson 2.2 can be used alone to express a complete idea. However, these sentences suggest that you (the speaker) and the person you are talking to both have a clear notion of what you are talking about. You might say

Alikchi'.   "She's a doctor."

for example, after speaking of a particular woman or when gesturing at her.

What this kind of short sentence is missing is a SUBJECT word. The subject of a sentence is the noun that sentence is about. Of course there is an UNDERSTOOD subject for the sentence **Alikchi'**—namely, "she" or "it", the person or entity that the sentence is about. But this short sentence contains no separate word saying exactly who the subject is. In fact, as you will learn, most Chickasaw sentences do not contain a separate subject word.

Sometimes, putting in a separate subject word or phrase can make the sentence clearer, especially if you and your hearer don't have a clear understanding of what's being discussed. Here are some identificational sentences with subject phrases:

Alikchi' yammat ihoo.	"That doctor is a woman."
Ihoo yappat alikchi'.	"This woman is a doctor."
Itti' yappat chowaala'.	"This tree is a cedar."

In these sentences, **alikchi' yammat, ihoo yappat**, and **itti' yappat** are subject phrases. These subject phrases consist of a noun plus either **yammat** "that" or **yappat** "this". Chickasaw subject phrases always end in a **t**, like the **t** at the end of **yammat** and **yappat**. You'll learn other subject endings later.

Exercise 2C. Translate the following Chickasaw sentences into English. 1. Nannalhpooba' yappat pinti'. (This might suggest that the **pinti'** in question was a pet.) 2. Minko' yammat alikchi'. 3. Hattak yammat minko'. 4. Hattak yappat ihoo. 5. Issi' yammat issi' nakni'. 6. Alikchi' yappat Chikashsha.

Lesson 2.4:
Singular and Plural

English nouns change their form to show whether they are SINGULAR (referring to one thing) or PLURAL (referring to more than one thing). Here are some examples of singular and plural nouns in English: *dog/dogs, church/churches, man/men, ox/oxen.* Only a few English nouns have no difference between singular and plural—one example is *deer (one deer/two deer/lots of deer).* In Chickasaw, however, there is never a difference between the form of singular and plural noun words. Thus, **ihoo** can mean "woman" (as you've learned), and it can also mean "women"; **talhpak** can mean "basket", but it can also mean "baskets"; and **itti'** can mean either "tree" or "trees". Some nouns are most commonly translated in the plural, such as **bala'** "beans".

When you use **yappat** following a noun that refers to more than one thing, **yappat** will be translated as "these". Similarly, **yammat** means "those" when used with a plural noun. So **Ihoo yappat alikchi'** can mean either "This woman is a doctor" or "These women are doctors". As you can see, many other things in the English sentence change depending on whether you're talking about a singular or plural subject.

Yammat can be used without a preceding noun, in which case it means simply "that" or "that one" or (in the plural) "those". Similarly, **yappat** can be used without a noun to mean "this", "this one", or "these":

Yappat alikchi'.	"This is a doctor.", "This one is a doctor.", "These are doctors."
Yammat nakni', yappat ihoo.	"Those are men, these are women." (*or* "That is a man, this is a woman.")

Sentences like **Ihoo yappat alikchi'** "These women are doctors" and **Yappat ihoo** "These are women" are identificational sentences just like those in lesson 2.3, even though they are translated with "are" rather than "is". And longer noun phrases and names can also be used in these sentences, as follows:

Yammat issi' tiik.	"That is a female deer."
Yappat Bill.	"This is Bill."

Exercise 2D. i. Translate the following English phrases and sentences into Chickasaw. 1. animals 2. These animals are deer. 3. people 4. Those people are women. 5. Those trees are cedars. 6. This is bread. 7. Those are Chickasaws. 8. These women are Choctaws. 9. This doctor is a Chickasaw woman. 10. That is Mary.

ii. Each of the Chickasaw words and sentences you wrote in answer to i , except for number 10, can be translated back into English in at least one additional way. Give another translation for each one.

Practice saying each of the Chickasaw sentences you wrote for your teacher or another Chickasaw speaker.

Lesson 2.5:
Verbs

Most Chickasaw sentences contain VERBS, words that tell about some ACTION that the subject performs or that are used to describe the subject or tell what STATE the subject is in.

Here are some examples of Chickasaw verbs:

malli	to jump
n<u>o</u>wa	to walk
yaa	to cry
kil<u>i</u>ha	to growl
omba	to rain

Now, here are some examples of how you can use these verbs in sentences:

Minko' yappat malli.	"This chief is jumping.", "This chief jumps."
Ihoo yammat n<u>o</u>wa.	"That woman is walking.", "That woman walks."

As you can see, a single Chickasaw verb may sometimes be translated into English with one word (**malli** can mean "jumps" or "jump") and sometimes with more than one word (**malli** can mean "is jumping"). The verbs in these sentences refer to the PRESENT time, describing actions that are going on right now or that are generally true. In English we must use a present form of the verb *be* (such as *is* or *are*) plus another verb ending in +*ing* to refer to ongoing actions, but in Chickasaw the PLAIN verb with no ending is all you need.

The examples above are translated with singular subjects, but plural translations would be fine too:

Ihoo yammat n<u>o</u>wa.	"Those women are walking.", "Those women walk."
Hattak yappat yaa.	"These people are crying.", "These people cry."

A verb may be used alone, with the subject understood:

Yaa.	"He is crying." *or* "She is crying." *or* "They are crying." *or even* "It is crying."
Malli.	"She (*or* He *or* It) is jumping." *or* "They are jumping."

As you see, the exact English translation for one-word Chickasaw sentences with understood subjects depends a lot upon the particular situation in which the sentence is used.

In sentences like the following, there's no real subject, understood or not:

Omba.	"It is raining.", "It rains."

In English, we use a subject *it* with our verb *rain*—but if you think about it, this *it* doesn't mean much. There's no equivalent of this "it" in the Chickasaw sentence.

Exercise 2E. Translate these Chickasaw sentences. 1. Ihoo yammat yaa. 2. Minko' yappat n<u>o</u>wa. 3. Ofi' yappat kil<u>i</u>ha. 4. Pinti' nakni' yammat malli. 5. Chikashsha yammat n<u>o</u>wa. 6. Omba.

Practice saying each of these sentences aloud, then think of at least one more way to translate each one.

Each of the verbs you have just learned is used to refer to actions. Other Chickasaw verbs are used to refer to states of being. Here are some examples of Chickasaw verbs that refer primarily to states rather than to actions:

lhinko	to be fat
chonna	to be skinny
chokma	to be good
lakna	to be yellow, to be brown
ichchokwa	to be cold

(**Ichchokwa** isn't used about the weather or objects, just about people or animals feeling cold.) These new verbs can be used in sentences like

Hattak yammat lhinko.	"That man is fat.", "Those men are fat."
Talhpak yappat lakna.	"This basket is yellow.",
	"These baskets are yellow."
Alikchi' yammat ichchokwa.	"That doctor is cold.", "Those doctors are cold."

When sentences like these are used to refer to the present, their English translations include "is" (or "are", if the subject is plural).

> *Exercise 2F.* Translate each of the following Chickasaw sentences into English in as many ways as you can. 1. Chonna. 2. Pinti' yappat lakna. 3. Hattak yammat chokma. 4. Bala' yammat lakna. 5. Okla yappat chokma. 6. Naahollo ihoo yappat lhinko. 7. Chikashsha ihoo yammat chonna. 8. Ichchokwa.

Verbs like **malli**, **nowa**, and **yaa**, which refer to actions, are called ACTIVE verbs, while verbs that refer to states of being, like **chokma**, **lakna**, and **lhinko**, are called STATIVE verbs. This distinction is more important in Chickasaw than it is in English, so you should be sure that you understand the difference between these two types of verbs. Your teacher will discuss other examples of active and stative verbs with you.

Of course, sentences may be thought of as active or stative too. (Are the identificational sentences in lessons 2.2 and 2.3 active or stative?) Occasionally, the distinction between stative and active verbs depends on the speaker's intentions. If in saying "He was good" the speaker is just giving a description of a person's qualities, "was good" is stative—but if the sentence is used to mean that the person acted good, or did good, or behaved good, then "was good" is active. You will learn more about how active and stative meanings are indicated in Chickasaw in unit 3.

> *Exercise 2G.* Go back through the earlier lessons in this unit and read each Chickasaw sentence in it aloud. Tell whether each sentence is active or stative.

Lesson 2.6:
Commands

A Chickasaw verb can be used by itself as a COMMAND addressed to another person, as the following examples show:

Nowa!	"Walk!"
Malli!	"Jump!"
Kiliha!	"Growl!"

Just as in English, you have to raise your voice a bit, or make it sound more emphatic, when giving someone else a command in Chickasaw. Imitate your teacher's pronunciation. As in English, these simple commands consist of plain verbs with nothing added. The person to whom the command is addressed ("you") is understood, not mentioned, in both English and Chickasaw.

Although it is more common to use active verbs in commands, you can also order someone to be in a certain state:

Chokma!	"Be good!"

Of course, if the person has to make an effort in order to be good, then you might feel that this verb was being used to name an action. (It can get tricky!)

Exercise 2H. Practice giving commands in Chickasaw. Use each of the verbs you have learned, and see whether you are understood. Take turns with another student acting out the proper response to each other's orders. You'll discover that some verbs don't make very sensible commands. You can tell the sky **Omba!**, perhaps, but this doesn't make much sense addressed to another person. Since people don't have much control over their personal characteristics, it also doesn't make too much sense to tell someone **Chonna!** or **Lhinko!** What would these commands mean, if they meant anything?

Lesson 2.7:
The **Hoo±** Prefix

*The **hoo±** "they" plural prefix.* Although there is no way to show whether a Chickasaw noun is plural or not, it is possible to change the form of a verb to show that it has a plural subject. Study the following pairs of Chickasaw sentences:

Chokma.	"He is good.", "She is good.", "It is good.", "They are good."
Hoochokma.	"They are good."
Malli.	"He (*or* She *or* It) is jumping.", "They are jumping."
Hoomalli.	"They are jumping."

As you know, a plain Chickasaw verb may have either a singular or a plural subject. When you add **hoo±** to the front of a Chickasaw verb, however, this always means that the verb has a plural "they" subject, just as the above examples show. **Hoo±** may be used with any kind of "they" subject, but it is most commonly used on verbs with subjects that are human, or at least living creatures.

Of course, the plural subjects of the **hoo±** verbs in the four Chickasaw sentences above are understood, not explicitly mentioned. Subject nouns can be used with **hoo±** verbs too, as you can see in

Ihoo yammat hoochokma.	"Those women are good."
Ofi' yappat hoomalli.	"These dogs are jumping."

When a subject noun is used with a verb starting with **hoo±**, you know that that noun must refer to more than one person or thing, a group you could call "they", and you need to use a plural English noun to translate it.

Hoo± and other short elements that are attached to the front of a word are called PREFIXES. **Hoo±** and the other prefixes you'll learn later are not separate words, and you cannot use them alone in a Chickasaw sentence. All prefixes must be attached to a following word: for example, **hoo±** must always be attached to a verb. In this book, when we talk about any prefix or other word part that is not itself a separate word, we will write it with either an ordinary PLUS (+) sign or a PLINUS (±) sign following it, like the plinus sign used after **hoo±**. (You'll learn why we make a distinction between ± and + in lesson 4.3. For now, just think of them as two types of plus signs.) A ± or + follows a prefix to show that something else must be attached after the prefix in order for you to be able to pronounce it as part of a word. A Chickasaw prefix cannot be used as a word by itself; it always must be attached to something else.

Whenever **hoo±** comes before a vowel, you will hear that vowel pronounced after the long **oo** sound of the prefix (pronounced like a short **o**, but longer). Thus, **hooichchokwa** contains a sequence of **oo** plus **i**.

Hattak yammat hooichchokwa. "Those men are cold."

> *Exercise 2I.* Tell what each of the following Chickasaw sentences means. Then change each sentence so that its subject will be understood as plural by adding the prefix **hoo±** to the verb. Translate your new sentences into English. 1. Pinti' yammat malli. 2. Chowahala' yappat lakna. 3. Issi' nakni' yappat chokma. 4. Alikchi' yappat nowa. 5. Minko' yammat lhinko. 6. Ofi' yammat kiliha. 7. Ihoo yappat ichchokwa. 8. Chonna.

Hoo± with commands. There is one other place where the **hoo±** prefix is used by many Chickasaw speakers—with plural commands like

Hoomalli! "Jump!" (addressed to many)
Hooyaa! "Cry (all of you)!"

Some speakers do not use the **hoo±** prefix in plural commands, and others may pronounce it differently in this use. Follow your teacher's way of speaking.

Perhaps you are wondering how a Chickasaw speaker would be able to tell the difference between sentences like the following:

Hoomalli. "They are jumping."
Hoomalli! "Jump (you all)!"

These sentences sound similar, but the difference between them is in the tone or rhythm of the speaker's voice. Listen to your teacher and practice making the difference yourself. We will represent the special INTONATION (the tone or melody of the voice) for a command in this book with an exclamation point (!), so you'll know that

Hoomalli!

with an exclamation point, is an order addressed to many, while

Hoomalli.

with an ordinary period, is just a statement about what some group is doing.

Remember that you don't always have to use **hoo±**.

Malli.

alone usually refers to a singular subject ("He (*or* She *or* It) is jumping"), but it may refer to a plural subject too. So if everyone knew that you were talking about a group of people or animals, you could say **Malli** and mean "They are jumping." When you use **hoo±**, of course, the subject must be plural. Similarly,

Malli!   "Jump!"

is a command that could be addressed to any number of people. To make it clear that you're addressing a group, you can use **hoo±**.

> *Exercise 2J.* Make up five Chickasaw sentences using the words and sentence patterns you have learned in this unit. Tell what each sentence means. Read your sentences for your teacher or another Chickasaw speaker and correct any mistakes you have made.

Terms and Concepts

NOUN, PHRASE, NOUN PHRASE, SENTENCE, IDENTIFICATIONAL SENTENCE, SUBJECT, UNDERSTOOD, SINGULAR, PLURAL, VERB, ACTION, STATE, PRESENT, PLAIN, ACTIVE, STATIVE, COMMAND, PREFIX, PLUS, PLINUS, INTONATION.

VOCABULARY

alikchi' doctor
bala' beans
Chahta' Choctaw, Choctaw person
Chikashsha Chickasaw, Chickasaw person
Chikashshihoo, Chikashshihoo' Chickasaw woman
chokma to be good
chonna to be skinny
chowaala', chowahala' cedar
hattak person, man
ichchokwa to be cold (of a person)
ihoo woman
issi' deer
itti' tree, wood, stick, log
kiliha to growl
lakna to be yellow, to be brown
lhinko to be fat
malli to jump
minko' chief
nakni' man, male
nannalhpooba' animal (typically, a domesticated animal)

naahollo white person, white man, non-Indian
nowa to walk
ofi' dog
okla town
omba to rain
paska bread
pinti' mouse
talhpak basket
tiik female (used only after animal names; see lesson 2.1)
yammat that, that one, those (subject)
yappat this, this one, these (subject)
yaa to cry

The vocabularies following each unit in this book follow the same arrangement as the Chickasaw-English Vocabulary at the end of the book, which contains all the words you'll learn throughout the book. The entries in the end vocabulary also contain additional grammatical information and references to the units in which words are first introduced. Following the Chickasaw-English Vocabulary is an English-Chickasaw Vocabulary, which is helpful for looking up words. It does not contain as much information as the Chickasaw-English Vocabulary, however, so you should always check words you've found there in the Chickasaw-English Vocabulary.

Notice that Chickasaw alphabetical order puts each letter or letter combination separately. Thus, **yaa** is alphabetized after **yappat**, because **yaa** contains the letter combination **aa**, which follows **a** in the alphabet.

READING AND SPEAKING

Useful Questions

Here's how you can ask someone's name and introduce yourself.

—Nanta chiholhchifo? "What's your name?"
—Saholhchifoat Mary. "My name is Mary."

You'll learn more ways to ask someone's name and give your name in later lessons.
Below are some questions and answers that you can use to practice new words. Listen to your teacher's intonation as she or he reads these sentences to you.

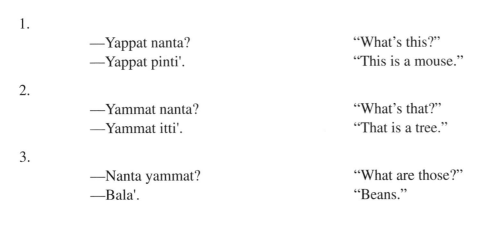

1.
   —Yappat nanta? "What's this?"
   —Yappat pinti'. "This is a mouse."

2.
   —Yammat nanta? "What's that?"
   —Yammat itti'. "That is a tree."

3.
   —Nanta yammat? "What are those?"
   —Bala'. "Beans."

4.

—Nanta yappat?	"What's this?
—Paska.	"Bread."

These little dialogues use identificational sentence patterns like the ones that you learned in lessons 2.2. and 2.3. You can make up many more similar question-and-answer pairs.

Nanta means "what". The first two questions above literally mean "This is what?" and "That is what?"— the subjects of these questions are the subject words **yappat** and **yammat**, which you learned earlier.

As the third and fourth questions show, you can change the order of the words in a "what is / what are" question.

Chickasaw questions can get complicated. You'll learn more about forming Chickasaw questions in lesson 4.4 and later units.

BEYOND THE GRAMMAR: THE CHICKASAWS AND THE CHICKASAW NATION

The Chickasaws originally lived on lands in northeastern Mississippi, northern Alabama, and southwestern Tennessee. Long ago they were known as a very warlike people. After early contacts with the Spanish, they were allied for some time with the English, who passed on a number of customs to the tribe. For instance, the Chickasaws are one of the few American Indian groups whose leader is a governor rather than a chief.

Along with several other groups of southeastern Indians, the Chickasaws were forced by the federal government to relocate from their ancestral lands to Indian Territory (Oklahoma) in the 1830s. The journey west was so difficult that it is often referred to as a Trail of Tears. Many people died on the trip, and most lost their possessions. Eventually, the tribe was established in the Chickasaw Nation in south-central Oklahoma. This sovereign state, whose first capital was in Tishomingo, had its own governor, legislature, constitution, laws, courts, and police force.

Oklahoma became a state in 1907, the culmination of a series of changes that began with the Dawes Act in 1887, by which land in Indian Territory was individually allotted to all Indians enrolled as tribal members. The governmental functions of the Indian nations were taken over by the state of Oklahoma, and Indians received land and U.S. citizenship.

Today there are no reservations in Oklahoma like those in other states. The Chickasaw Nation still provides many social, educational, and other services to the Chickasaw people. The present headquarters of the Chickasaw Nation is in Ada, and the current governor of the Chickasaw Nation, Bill Anoatubby, has served since 1987.

Stative and Active Verbs

In this unit, you'll learn how to change verbs to indicate different subjects like "I", "you", and "we".

The subject prefixes used on most active verbs (A prefixes) are described in lesson 3.1, and the "I" subject ending is presented in lesson 3.2. Lesson 3.3 presents the prefixes used on most stative verbs (S prefixes). Lesson 3.4 discusses singular and plural verbs and the **hoo±** "they" prefix. Lesson 3.5 introduces a group of verbs that can be used with either A or S markers. Lesson 3.6 describes how S prefixes are used on i-verbs. The subject markers used on some verbs are surprising (lesson 3.7). Lesson 3.8 explains how verbs are listed in the vocabulary.

Here are seven new active verbs you'll be able to use in this unit. Practice saying the new verbs after your teacher, imitating the rhythm of your teacher's voice.

impa	"to eat", "to have a meal"
konta	"to whistle"
owwatta	"to hunt"
taloowa	"to sing"
toyya	"to climb"
wakaa	"to fly"
lhabanka	"to snore"

Impa means "to do some eating". You don't use this word to tell what food was eaten.

Exercise 3A. Translate the following sentences into English. l. Minko' yammat konta. 2. Hattak yappat toyya. 3. Hoowakaa. 4. Nannalhpooba' yammat hooimpa. 5. Alikchi' yammat owwatta. 6. Chikashsha yammat hootaloowa. 7. Chahta' ihoo yammat lhabanka. 8. Hookonta.

Lesson 3.1:
Subject Prefixes

You've now seen a lot of sentences with noun subjects, but you've probably wondered how to put together sentences whose subject is yourself or the person you are talking to. To do this in English we use separate words (called PRONOUNS) like *I, you, we,* and so on. In Chickasaw, though, all you have to do is change the form of the verb a bit, usually by adding prefixes, to express these same ideas. In lesson 2.7 you learned how to express a "they" subject by using the prefix **hoo±**, as in

Hookonta. "They are whistling."

Here are some other forms of the verb **konta**, using new prefixes:

Ishkonta. "You are whistling."
Kiikonta. "We are whistling."
Hashkonta. "You all are whistling."

Unlike the prefix **hoo±**, which can be used to indicate a "they" subject with any Chickasaw verb, the new prefixes **ish±**, **kii±**, and **hash±** are only used with certain verbs, most of them active verbs like **konta**.

Ish± and **hash±** are both translated into English with the word "you". Use **ish±** when you are talking to one person (when "you" is singular), and **hash±** when you are talking to more than one (when "you" is plural—just as in English "you all" or "you guys"). Here are a few more examples:

Ishimpa. "You are eating."
Hashtoyya. "You all are climbing."
Ishyaa. "You are crying."

It's important to choose the right form of "you" in Chickasaw. Although any sentence using the prefix **hash±** can be translated into English with (plural) "you", for clarity we will use "you all" or "you guys" in this book to translate Chickasaw sentences with plural "you" forms.

Kii± means "we". Chickasaw speakers sometimes use the prefix **ii±** instead of **kii±** for "we". We will use both in this book:

Kiiwakaa. *or* Iiwakaa. "We are flying."

When either of these "we" prefixes comes before a vowel, its form changes, as the following examples illustrate:

Kilimpa. *or* Ilimpa. "We are eating."
Kilowwatta. *or* Ilowwatta. "We are hunting."

Kii± is replaced by **kil±** when the following verb starts with a vowel. Similarly, **ii±** is replaced by **il±**.

Another way to say "we" is with the prefix **kiloo±** (or **iloo±**). This special "we" prefix is used when the speaker is referring to a "we" that includes the addressee and at least one other person besides himself—a "we" that includes at least three people. We can call this an INCLUSIVE TRIPLURAL use. INCLUSIVE means that this "we" includes the hearer as well as the speaker, and TRIPLURAL means that it must refer to a group that is not just plural, but that contains at least three people. Here are some examples:

Kilooimpa. "We (more than two, including you) are eating."
Ilookonta. "We (more than two, including you) are whistling."

As the first example shows, the special inclusive triplural "we" prefixes **kiloo±** and **iloo±** do not change their form when they precede vowels. In this book we will often refer to inclusive triplural "we" as SPECIAL "we".

Unlike the "they" plural prefix **hoo±**, the new prefixes introduced in this lesson cannot be omitted. They must always be used when you want to express a "we", "you", or "you guys" subject.

Exercise 3B. Translate each of the sentences below into Chickasaw. Don't use the **kiloo±** or **iloo±** prefixes unless the translation specifically calls for them. When you have completed the exercise, read each sentence aloud.

l. We (two of us, including you) are walking. 2. You all are hunting. 3. You are climbing. 4. We (but not you) are climbing. 5. You are crying. 6. You all are singing. 7. We (more than two of us, but not you) are snoring. 8. We (more than two, including you) are jumping. 9. They are walking. l0. It is raining. (**Omba** is an example of a verb that is never used with a subject prefix.) 11. We (you and I) are crying. 12. We (more than two, including you) are walking.

Lesson 3.2:
"I" Subjects

Unlike "you" and "we" subjects, "I" subjects of Chickasaw active verbs like **yaa**, **toyya**, and **konta** are not shown with prefixes. Look at the following examples:

Yaali.	"I am crying."
Toyyali.	"I am climbing."
Kontali.	"I am whistling.

As you can see, what indicates the "I" subject of these verbs is the ENDING **+li**. Like the prefixes you have learned about, **+li** is not a separate word, and it cannot be used by itself—it must always be attached to an active verb. An ending is similar to a prefix except that it goes after the word it's attached to rather than before it. Unlike the plinus (±) prefixes you've learned up to now, **+li** is a plus (+) ending. The + comes before the ending **+li** to show that **+li** needs something else in front of it, just the way that the ± comes after prefixes like **hoo±**, **ish±**, **kii±**, and others to show that these need something else after them. You'll learn about the difference between ± and + in lesson 4.3.

In these Chickasaw sentences, the **+li** ending is the last syllable of its word. So **+li** always gets the stress in sentences like these—listen for this as your teacher says the "I" subject sentences above.

Exercise 3C. Each of the following verbs is missing its subject, but the missing subjects are given in English before each one. Change each verb so that it tells what its subject is. Then translate the sentences you make up and read each one aloud.

l. (I) n̲owa. 2. (we) wakaa. 3. (you all) kili̲ha. 4. (I) malli. 5. (you) yaa. 6. (they) toyya. 7. (we—relatively many) konta. 8. (you) taloowa. 9. (I) owwatta. l0. (we) impa.

Each answer should be a single word. Each of these words is a complete Chickasaw sentence.

The verb forms presented in unit 2 and in this unit, up through this lesson, are summarized in the chart on the next page. "He" here could also be "she" or "it".

	Singular subject	Plural subject
Subject is a noun or understood "he" or "they"	plain verb ("he . . .")	**hoo±**verb (or plain verb) ("they . . .")
Command (understood "you" subject)	plain verb	**hoo±**verb (or plain verb)
Subject includes the speaker	verb+**li** ("I . . .")	**kii±**verb, **ii±**verb ("we . . ."); **kiloo±**verb, **iloo±**verb ("more than two of us, including you" inclusive triplural "we")
Subject includes the hearer or hearers but not the speaker	**ish±**verb ("you . . .")	**hash±**verb ("you all . . .")

Lesson 3.3:
More about Stative Verbs

In lesson 2.5 you learned about two types of verbs used in Chickasaw and other languages, active verbs and stative verbs. Here are some new Chickasaw stative verbs:

homma	to be red
tohbi	to be white
nokhánglo	to be sad
chaaha	to be tall
palhki	to be fast
wiiki	to be heavy

Exercise 3D. Practice using the new verbs in the following sentences.
1. This basket is red. 2. That deer is white. 3. This woman is tall. 4. That mouse is fast. 5. Those people are heavy. 6. They are sad. Read each of the sentences you wrote aloud.

More subject prefixes. As you know (lesson 2.7), the **hoo±** prefix can be used on a stative verb, or any Chickasaw verb, to show that it has a plural noun subject or a plural understood "they" subject:

Hoochaaha. "They are tall."

A new set of prefixes is used to show other subjects of stative verbs like **chaaha**. Here are some examples of these new prefixes:

Sachaaha. "I am tall."
Chichaaha. "You are tall."
Pochaaha. "We are tall."
Hachichaaha. "You all are tall."

The **sa+** prefix is used on stative verbs like **chaaha** that a speaker uses to refer to him- or herself. **Sa+** means "I" when it indicates the subject of a stative verb:

Sanokhánglo.	"I am sad."
Sachokma.	"I am good."

The **chi+** prefix is used on stative verbs with "you" subjects:

Chipalhki.	"You are fast."
Chiwiiki.	"You are heavy."

The usual "we" prefix for stative verbs is **po+**:

Polhinko.	"We are fat."
Ponokhánglo.	"We are sad."

The prefix **hapo+** also means "we". The difference between **po+** and **hapo+** is the same as the difference between **kii±** and **kiloo±** that you learned about in lesson 3.1. Like **kiloo±**, the special "we" prefix **hapo+** is an inclusive triplural prefix; it refers to a group of at least three people and must include the hearer:

Hapochonna.	"We (more than two, including you) are skinny."
Hapochaaha.	"We (more than two, including you) are tall."

The plural "you" prefix, used when you are talking to more than one person, is **hachi+**:

Hachichokma.	"You all are good."
Hachiwiiki.	"You all are heavy."

Like the other subject prefixes you learned earlier, **sa+**, **chi+**, **po+**, **hapo+**, and **hachi+** cannot be used alone but must always be attached to another word. (In lesson 4.3 you'll learn why these new prefixes are followed by + rather than ±.) Like the other new subject prefixes, **sa+**, **chi+**, **po+**, **hapo+**, and **hachi+** cannot be omitted from a sentence the way the "they" prefix **hoo±** can.

Exercise 3E. i. Two of the new prefixes start with **ha**. Which ones? What do you think the **ha** on these prefixes means? Can you think of another prefix you learned earlier that includes **ha**?
　　ii. Read each of the following Chickasaw sentences aloud and then translate each one into English.
　　1. Sahomma. 2. Hapopalhki. 3. Chiwiiki. 4. Hachilhinko. 5. Powiiki. 6. Hapochokma. 7. Chinokhánglo. 8. Sachonna.

Lesson 3.4:
More about Plural Subjects

The prefixes **hash±**, **kii±** or **ii±** (as well as **kiloo±** or **iloo±**), **po+** (and **hapo+**), and **hachi±** indicate that the verbs they are attached to have plural subjects ("we" and "you all"). But these prefixes are different from the **hoo±** prefix you learned about in lesson 2.7. **Hoo±** also shows that a verb has a plural subject, as in the following examples:

Hootaloowa.	"They are singing."
Hattak yammat hootoyya.	"Those people are climbing."
Hoochonna.	"They are skinny."
Ofi' yappat hoolhinko.	"These dogs are fat."

However, the **hoo±** prefix only indicates a "they" plural subject and is never used along with any of the new prefixes introduced in this unit—it never appears on a verb that has another plural subject prefix such as **hash±** or **kii±**, **po±** or **hachi±**. **Hoo±** is also used by some speakers to make a plural command, as in **Hootaloowa!** "Sing, you guys!"

There are two important differences between **hoo±** and the prefixes introduced in this unit. First, **hoo±** can be left off a verb with a "they" subject when the meaning is clear. However, the other prefixes in this unit, and the **+li** ending, cannot be omitted this way. Second, all the new prefixes in this unit are associated with either active verbs or stative verbs, not both. **Hoo±**, however, can be used with both active and stative verbs, as the examples above illustrate.

> *Exercise 3F.* Each of the following Chickasaw sentences has a singular subject. Translate each sentence, then change each sentence so that it refers to the corresponding plural subject (if the sentence is a singular command, replace it with a plural command; if it refers to the speaker (with an "I" subject) change it to a form that refers to the speaker as a member of a group (with a "we" subject); if it has a singular "you" subject, change it to plural "you", and so on). If the sentence has a singular noun or understood subject, change the verb to include **hoo±**, but remember that you could also have said the sentence without using this prefix.
>
> 1. Issi' yammat malli. 2. Taloowa! 3. Salakna. 4. Ishkonta. 5. Pinti' yappat tohbi. 6. Wakaa. 7. Yaali. 8. Ishnowa. 9. Chichonna. 10. Nowali. 11. Ihoo yappat nowa. 12. Owwatta! 10. Toyyali. 13. Chipota yammat ichchokwa. 14. Kiliha.

Lesson 3.5:
S and A Markers

Below is a chart comparing the two sets of subject MARKERS (prefixes and endings) you have learned.

	S markers	*A markers*
"I" subject	sa+	+li
"you" subject	chi+	ish±
"we" subject	po+	kii±, ii±, kil±, il±
special "we" subject	hapo+	kiloo±, iloo±
plural "you" subject	hachi+	hash±

The elements in the first column that you just learned are called S markers; those in the second column, which you learned earlier in this unit, are called A markers. S markers are used to show the subjects of most stative verbs, and A markers are used to show the subjects of most active verbs.

As you know, "he" and "she" subjects don't need any extra marking on a verb. Any "they" subject can be marked on the verb with **hoo±**, regardless of whether the verb is stative or active. We use the term "special" here to refer to the inclusive triplural "we" forms.

All of these markers are prefixes except for the "I" ending +**li**. It's important for you to learn all these markers as soon as you can.

Exercise 3G. Each of the following items contains a sentence with an active verb followed by a stative verb in parentheses. Change the stative verb so that it has the same subject as the active verb. Read the new sentences you make up out loud. Then translate both sentences.

    Example. Nowali. (Palhki.)

    Answer. Nowali. Sapalhki. "I am walking. I am fast."

    1. Kiiyaa. (Nokhánglo.) 2. Hashmalli. (Palhki.) 3. Ishtoyya. (Chaaha.) 4. Kilooimpa. (Lhinko.) 5. Kontali. (Chokma.)

Stative and active meanings. In Chickasaw some verbs can be used with either S or A markers, depending on whether they describe a state of being or report an action. Here are some examples, using the verb **palhki**:

        Sapalhki.   "I am fast." (STATE)

        Palhkili.   "I go fast.", "I am going fast.", "I do it fast." (ACTION)

In these examples the same verb is used first with the S "I" prefix **sa**+ and then with the A "I" ending +**li**. The first sentence describes a state of being over which the speaker has little control, while the second reports an action the speaker brings about through his own initiative. These features are generally characteristic of the difference between stative and active verbs in Chickasaw.

    Here is another set of examples using the verb **chokma**:

        Hachichokma.   "You all are good." (STATE)

        Hashchokma.   "You all act good.", "You all are acting good." (ACTION)

The sentence with the S prefix **hachi**+ refers to a state, while the sentence with the A prefix **hash**± refers to an action.

    With some verbs, the English translation changes between the two uses:

        Chiwiiki.   "You are heavy: you (statively) displace weight." (STATE)

        Ishwiiki.   "You weigh yourself: you (actively) displace weight
                         (you step on a scale, for instance)." (ACTION)

These two uses of **wiiki** have something in common. Their different English translations make them seem less similar than they actually are.

Active meanings with "be". As you have seen in the examples above, the difference between a stative or an active use of a verb is often shown by a form of the verb "be" in the English translation: "I am heavy" (stative) versus "I weigh myself" (active), "You are good" (stative) versus "You act good" (active), and so on. The important thing here, though, is the meaning, not the English words. If you say to someone "You are really being good", you have used a form of "be", but what you mean is that the person's actions are good, or that he is deliberately keeping from acting bad. This is an active use of "good", and to say it in Chickasaw you would have to use an A prefix:

        Ishchokma.   "You are being good."

You can add "really" or "very" with the word **kaníhka**:

Kaníhka ishchokma.	"You are really being good."
Kaníhka chichokma.	"You are very good."

Controlled and not controlled actions. In each of the pairs of examples above, the verb with the A marker refers to an action (something the speaker controls or does because he or she wants to) and the verb with the S marker refers to a state (something the speaker does not control). Sometimes both verbs refer to actions:

Chokfiyammili.	"I hiccup (on purpose)." (CONTROLLED)
Sachokfiyammi.	"I hiccup (I can't help it)." (NOT CONTROLLED)

The difference here is between two types of action, CONTROLLED (done on purpose) and NOT CONTROLLED. Verbs like **chokfiyammi** have the same translation whether they are used with A or S markers, but the speaker's choice of marker can tell you whether the action was controlled or not. Verbs that work this way often refer to bodily functions that are usually not controlled, so S prefix use is more common with verbs like these.

Exercise 3H. i. For each of the following Chickasaw sentences, first determine whether it is used to refer to a state, a controlled action, or an action that is not controlled. Then translate it. Next change it to the opposite use, keeping the same subject. (Hint: Do this by changing from S to A or A to S markers.) Translate the second sentence. Finally, read both sentences aloud.

Example. Hachiwiiki.

Answer. Stative. "You all are heavy." / Hashwiiki. "You all are weighing yourselves."

1. Sachokma. 2. Kiloopalhki. 3. Iiwiiki. 4. Pochokfiyammi. 5. Ishpalhki. 6. Wiikili. 7. Pochokma. 8. Hachipalhki. 9. Chichokma. 10. Hashchokfiyammi.

ii. Sentences with noun subjects don't change their form to show a difference between controlled and not controlled uses. Give two different translations for each of the following and practice reading each sentence aloud.

11. Alikchi' yammat wiiki. 12. Ofi' yappat hoochokma.

Only certain verbs (like **chokfiyammi. palhki**, **wiiki**, and **chokma**) can be used with more than one set of subject markers in Chickasaw. Most Chickasaw verbs are only used with either A markers or S markers, not both.

Back to hoo±. The "they" prefix **hoo±** is neither an A marker nor an S marker. It can be used both with verbs that use A markers to mark their subjects and with verbs that use S markers.

Lesson 3.6:
I-Verbs

Here are four new verbs that take S prefixes. Like **ichchokwa** (lesson 2.5), these are I-VERBS because they start with **i**.

ishto	"to be big" (singular)
issikopa	"to be mean"
illi	"to die", "to be dead"
ilhpokonna	"to dream"

Ishto is only used with singular subjects (you'll learn later how to say that a plural subject is big). Thus,

Nannalhpooba' yammat ishto.

means only "That animal is big"—it can't refer to more than one animal. Because of this, you can't use **ishto** with the **hoo±** prefix. Other i-verbs can be used with **hoo±**, however:

Hooissikopa.   "They are mean."

When you add an S prefix to the front of an i-verb, the **i** at the front of the verb must DROP (it disappears from the verb and is neither written nor pronounced in the new word):

Polli.   "We are dead."
Chishto.   "You are big."
Salhpokonna.   "I dream."
Hachichchokwa.   "You all are cold."

Po+ plus **illi** equals **polli**, and so on. The **i** of an i-verb is never pronounced when an S prefix is used. After other prefixes, like **hoo±**, the **i** of an i-verb is unchanged.

> *Exercise 31.* i. Change each of the following verbs to show the subject given in parentheses. (Use only S subject markers, and remember to drop i's if necessary.) Read the new sentences you make aloud and then translate them.
> 1. ("we (not including you)") ichchokwa 2. ("you all") lakna 3. ("they") ilhpokonna 4. ("I") lhinko 5. ("we (at least three of us, including you)") illi 6. ("you") ilhpokonna 7. ("I") chaaha 8. ("I") ishto 9. ("we (you and I)") issikopa 10. ("you") illi
> ii. The following sentences are not good Chickasaw. Why?
> 11. Poshto. 12. Minko' yammat hooishto.
> You'll learn how to express these ideas correctly later on.

It's possible that you might hear some people say or write <poilli>, <chiishto>, <sailhpokonna>, and so on, without dropping the **i** of an i-verb. These pronunciations are considered incorrect by traditional speakers, and we will not use such forms in this book.

Lesson 3.7: Surprising Subjects

Illi "to die" and **ilhpokonna** "to dream" are the first examples you have seen of verbs that take S subjects not translated with the English verb "be". Most English speakers feel that dying and dreaming are actions, not states. These examples show that you may not always be able to guess whether a verb takes A or S markers simply from the meaning or from whether an action is involved.

In general S prefixes are used in Chickasaw on verbs referring to states, while A verbs are used on verbs referring to actions; S prefixes are used on verbs describing things that are or that just happen, while A markers are used on verbs describing things that people do; S prefixes are used on verbs referring to things that can't be controlled, while A markers are used on verbs referring to things that are controllable. And as you have seen, some verbs can be used with either S or A markers, depending on their meaning.

However, some verbs will surprise you when you learn what prefix they take. **Illi** "to die" refers to an action, yet it takes S prefixes; **lhabanka** "to snore" refers to a bodily function that is not controllable, yet it takes A markers. There are many other verbs that mark their subject in a surprising way: for instance, **chokkíllissa** "to be quiet" takes A markers, while **nokchito** "to rest, to behave oneself" takes S markers. Yet to most people being quiet probably seems like a state, while behaving oneself seems like an action.

Chokkíllissali.	"I am quiet."
Sanokchito.	"I rest.", "I behave myself."

These examples show that you cannot necessarily be sure that a verb is stative because it uses S prefixes, though this is usually the case, or that a verb is active because it uses A prefixes, though this is also usually the case.

We call **chokkíllissa** an A SUBJECT verb, because when this verb uses a marker for its subject, it will be an A marker (even though it expresses a state). **Nokchito** is an S SUBJECT verb, because it uses only S prefixes to mark its subject, even though it expresses an action. In most cases stative verbs are S subject verbs and active verbs are A subject verbs, but, as the examples here show, this is not always the case. You'll learn other verbs with surprising subjects as you study more Chickasaw.

Lesson 3.8:
Using the Vocabulary

The Chickasaw-English Vocabulary at the end of this book and the short vocabularies after each unit list verbs with a parenthesized abbreviation showing what kind of subjects they take:

malli to jump (A)
chaaha to be tall (S)
chokkíllissa to be quiet (A)
illi to die, to be dead (S)

It's best to learn this information each time you learn a new verb. One way to do this is to learn the "I" form of each verb along with it—thus, you could learn **mallili** "I jump" along with **malli**, and so on.

Here's the vocabulary entry for two verbs that can be used with more than one set of markers:

chokma to be good, nice (S); to act good (A)
chokfiyammi to hiccup (S / A)

When it means "to be good", **chokma** uses the (S) markers; when it means "to act good", **chokma** uses the (A) markers. (This vocabulary entry also tells you that **chokma** can mean "to be nice".) The entry for **chokfiyammi** only has one translation. The (S / A) after the verb shows a difference between not controlled and controlled uses.

Unlike **chokma** and **chokfiyammi**, however, most Chickasaw verbs are used with only one set of markers. For instance, **issikopa** "to be mean" is always an S subject verb, whether it is used to mean "be mean" (a state) or "act mean" (an action).

Here is a different kind of vocabulary entry:

omba to rain (—)

English sentences about rain, like *It is raining,* have a subject *it.* There's no corresponding word in Chickasaw, and you can't use subject prefixes on the verb **omba.** Verbs like this are listed in the vocabulary with (—), indicating that they don't take subject markers.

Now, here's an entry for another new verb:

tilhaa to run (plural subject) (A)

The vocabulary entry for the verb **tilhaa** tells you a number of different things. Along with the meaning, this entry gives additional important information—**tilhaa** means "run", but only when referring to a plural subject; you can't use **tilhaa** with a singular subject (you'll learn later how to say "run" with a singular subject). **Tilhaa** takes the A markers to show its subject, as you would expect, since "run" is a voluntary action:

Hashtilhaa. "You all are running."

The sentence

Minko' yammat tilhaa.

cannot mean "That chief is running", but only "Those chiefs are running", because **tilhaa** must always have a plural subject. A verb like **tilhaa** that must have a plural subject is not usually used with the **hoo±** plural prefix; you already know that the subject of **tilhaa** is plural, so **hoo±** is not necessary.

Exercise 3J. i. Look up the entries in the unit 3 vocabulary for the following new verbs: **ánta**, **hopoo**, **yimmi**. Make sure you understand each part of the dictionary entries. Does the set of subject markers used with any of these verbs surprise you? Tell the "I" subject form for each of these new verbs.

ii. Translate each of the following sentences into Chickasaw using the new verbs you have learned in this unit.

1. That woman is really jealous. 2. We are snoring. 3. You think so. 4. They are really good. 5. We (relatively many) are running. 6. These mice are quiet. 7. I am staying. 8. I am really jealous. 9. We are resting. 10. I dream. 11. You are dead. 12. You stay. 13. I believe it. 14. We are really tall. 15. You all are quiet. 16. Those Choctaws are running.

Terms and Concepts

PRONOUN, ENDING, MARKER, INCLUSIVE, TRIPLURAL, CONTROLLED, I-VERB, DROP, A SUBJECT, S SUBJECT.

VOCABULARY

ánta to stay (singular subject) (A)
chaaha to be tall (S)
chokfiyammi to hiccup (S/A)
chokkíllissa to be quiet (A)
chokma to act good (A)
homma to be red (S)
hopoo to be jealous (A)

illi to die, to be dead (S)
ilhpokonna to dream (S)
impa to eat, to have a meal (A)
issikopa to be mean (S)
ishto to be big (singular) (S)
kaníhka really, very
konta to whistle (A)
lhabanka to snore (A)
nokchito to rest, to behave oneself (S)
nokhánglo to be sad (S)
owwatta to hunt (A)
palhki to be fast (S), to go fast (A)
taloowa to sing (A)
tilhaa to run (plural subject) (A)
tohbi to be white (S)
toyya to climb (A)
wakaa to fly (A)
wiiki to be heavy (S), to weigh oneself (A)
yimmi to believe it, to think so (S)

READING AND SPEAKING

More Greetings and Farewells

Try practicing these dialogues.

1.

—Chinchokmataa?	"Hello—how are you!"
—Anchokma.	"I'm fine."
—Ayala'chi.	"I'm going."
—Chipísla'cho.	"I'll see you."

2.

—Hachinchokmataa?	"How are you all?"
—Ponchokma. Hachishnaako?	"We're fine. And you all?"
—Chokmahookay.	"Just fine."
—Kiliyya'chi.	"We're going."
—Onnakma iichipísa'cho.	"We'll see you tomorrow."

There's no word for "good-bye" in Chickasaw. People just say, "I'm going!"
Here are some more useful expressions:

—Bini'cha loshka!	"Sit down and tell lies!"
	(an invitation to gossip)
—Yakhookay.	"Thank you."

±Hookay (in **chokmahookay**) is an ending that some people regard as primarily Choctaw but that is occasionally used in Chickasaw conversation to indicate finality or formality. The same ending is part of the word **yakhookay**.

Counting in Chickasaw

Here's how to count to ten in Chickasaw:

chaffa	one
toklo	two
tochchí'na	three
oshta	four
talhlhá'pi	five
hanná'li	six
ontoklo	seven
ontochchí'na	eight
chakká'li	nine
pokkó'li	ten

Listen as your teacher says each number. You'll notice that many Chickasaw numbers have an accent. Practice so that you can count quickly and smoothly without hesitation. Try to memorize all the numbers. (In unit 10 you'll learn to count to twenty, and in unit 11 you'll learn higher counting numbers. Unit 12 explains how to use the numbers in sentences. For now, just use them for counting.)

Can you think of a good way to remember the Chickasaw numbers "seven" and "eight"? Compare them with the other numbers, and see if you can come up with a theory as to why they look the way they do.

Most speakers don't often count higher than ten in Chickasaw. There are a few higher numbers that everyone knows, though, such as **talhipa** "hundred". See how high your teacher feels like counting.

BEYOND THE GRAMMAR: THE MUSKOGEAN LANGUAGE FAMILY

Chickasaw and Choctaw belong to a group of related American Indian languages called the Muskogean language family. This family of languages also includes the Creek, Seminole, Mikasuki (or Miccosukee), Alabama, and Koasati languages, which are spoken in Oklahoma, Texas, Louisiana, Mississippi, and Florida. The Muskogean family also includes some languages that are now "extinct" (no longer spoken), including Hitchiti (a language spoken in Oklahoma that became extinct less than fifty years ago) and Apalachee (a language spoken hundreds of years ago in Florida).

The name of the language family is derived from the Creeks' name for themselves, pronounced in English as Muscogee (the Chickasaw word for "Creek" is **Mashkooki'**). All of the languages in the family have some characteristics in common, and some of the words in each language sound quite similar to words in the other languages. But each language is different, and each one has some words that speakers of other languages in the family would find hard to understand.

All of the Muskogean tribes originally lived in the southeastern part of the United States, but many of their people were moved westward to Indian Territory (the present state of Oklahoma) on Trails of Tears during the 1830s.

Like most Chickasaws and Choctaws, the majority of Creeks and Seminoles live in Oklahoma, though there are also a considerable number of Seminoles in Florida and some Creeks still live in their homeland in the Southeast. Most Mikasuki speakers live in Florida alongside the Seminoles there. The Alabamas and most Koasati speakers live in the vicinity of Livingston, Texas, on the Alabama-Coushatta Reservation. (Texas Koasatis use the name Coushatta.) Other Koasatis and Choctaws live in communities in Louisiana and Mississippi.

Rhythmic Patterns in Chickasaw Words

In this unit you'll learn how the pronunciation of Chickasaw vowel sounds in a word can change when prefixes and endings are added.

Lesson 4.1 presents the past ending **+tok**. Lessons 4.2 and 4.3 explain how lengthened vowels are pronounced and introduce the Chickasaw rhythmic lengthening rule. Chickasaw questions are presented in lesson 4.4, and lesson 4.5 describes how to use nouns as subjects.

| **Lesson 4.1:** The Past | If something happened in the past, we refer to it in English with a verb ending in +*ed*. Chickasaw verbs used to refer explicitly to the past end in **+tok**: |

Kontatok.	"She (*or* He *or* It) whistled."
Ishtoyyatok.	"You climbed."
Chokmatok.	"It was good."
Kilimpatok.	"We ate."
Hoowakaatok.	"They flew."
Ombatok.	"It rained."

Plain verbs like those you have seen up to now are said to be in the PRESENT, while verbs ending in **+tok** are in the PAST. The ending **+tok** goes at the very end of a Chickasaw verb, whether it is active or stative.

(Different forms of a verb that refer to different times are known as different TENSES. Some Chickasaw speakers use other past and present tense endings: for example, they may add ±**i'yo̱** or ±**i'** or ±**iy** after **+tok**, producing sentences like **Kontatoki'yo̱** or **Kontatokiy**. We will not use these variant forms in this book.)

If the verb has an "I" subject, the ending **+tok** comes after the ending **+li**:

Yaalitok.	"I cried."
Wakaalitok.	"I flew."

In all these **+tok** verbs, the **+tok** gets the stress, since it is the last thing in the word.

You can use the word **oblaashaash** "yesterday" in sentences like these. Most commonly it will go at the beginning of the sentence, as in **Oblaashaash yaalitok** "I cried yesterday." You may also hear **oblaashaash** at the end of a sentence like this.

> *Exercise 4A.* Translate the following past sentences after reading each one aloud.
> 1. Naahollo yammat kaníhka chaahatok. 2. Hashimpatok. 3. Oblaashaash ishmallitok. 4. Ihoo yappat ántatok. 5. Hopoolitok. 6. Ichchokwatok. 7. Oblaashaash Chahta' yammat owwattatok. 8. Kiitaloowatok. 9. Yaalitok oblaashaash. 10. Kiloochokkíllissatok.

As you listen to more spoken Chickasaw, you will realize that the Chickasaw ending +**tok** is not exactly equivalent to the English past ending +*ed*. In Chickasaw speakers often use a plain verb (without +**tok**) to refer to a past event, particularly one that has happened that same day. In a sense, when you add +**tok** to a Chickasaw verb referring to an event, you announce that the event referred to is not only past but done with. If you pay attention, you can find many examples of the use of plain verbs to refer to past events in people's Chickasaw conversation. However, we will assume in this book that the English past referring to a relatively recent event in the past should be translated into Chickasaw with +**tok**. (As you'll learn in unit 13, Chickasaw uses verbs with a different ending to refer to past events that happened a very long time ago, such as in one's childhood.)

Lesson 4.2:
Lengthened Vowels

Listen as your teacher pronounces the following words, each of which is a sentence in Chickasaw. You'll hear the stress on the last vowel of each word, but you'll also hear that some of the short vowels sound longer and more prominent than you might expect. These LENGTHENED VOWELS are written with a MACRON above them (ī ō ā) in the words below. (As you may recall from grade-school English spelling lessons, the macron, a small horizontal line above a vowel, is traditionally used to show that the vowel is long. English "long" vowels sound different from Chickasaw ones, of course.)

Kontalītok.	"I whistled."
Impalītok.	"I ate."
Nowalītok.	"I walked."
Bila.	"It is melting."
Bilātok.	"It melted."
Hika.	"He stands up."
Hikāli.	"I stand up."
Hikātok.	"He stood up."
Hikālitok.	"I stood up."
Hilha.	"He dances."
Hilhāli.	"I dance."
Ántalītok.	"I stayed."
Taloowalītok.	"I sang."
Tofāli.	"I spit."
Tofātok.	"He spat."
Chofāta.	"It is clean."
Lhayīta.	"It is wet."
Litīha.	"He is dirty."
Hopōba.	"She is hungry."

Chickasaw lengthened vowels sound longer than ordinary (nonlengthened) short vowels but generally not quite so long as long vowels. Syllables that contain lengthened vowels are heavy syllables. Like other heavy syllables, they receive more emphasis and give a special rhythm to the words in which they occur. Read each word above over to yourself, trying to imitate your teacher's pronunciation.

There is a real rhythm to Chickasaw words. Because of vowel lengthening, you almost never hear two short vowels in a row in a Chickasaw word. Compare the following pairs of words:

Chofāta. "It is clean."   Sachōfata. "I am clean."
Tikahbi. "He is tired."   Chitīkahbi. "You are tired."
Lhayīta. "She is wet."   Polhāyita. "We are wet."
Hopōba. "He is hungry."   Chihōpoba. "You are hungry."
Litīha. "He is dirty."   Polītiha. "We are dirty."
Hofahya. "She is ashamed."   Sahōfahya. "I am ashamed."

Listen to the differences in the rhythmic patterns of these words, according to which vowels are lengthened. The lengthened vowels are more prominent, and different vowels are lengthened in the various forms of the words above.

Exercise 4B. Practice saying each of the following words (written with macrons over the lengthened vowels) after your teacher. Try to make the lengthened vowels sound longer. What does each word mean? (As these words show, many Chickasaw words contain more than one lengthened vowel.)

sabīla	chofātatok	hashhikātok	chihōpoba
lhayītatok	polhāyita	polhāyitātok	chihōpobātok
chilītihātok	sachōfata	sachōfatātok	salhāyita
mallilītok	pohōpobātok	hilhātok	salhāyitātok

An important difference between the pronunciation of lengthened vowels and other short vowels in Chickasaw is that the pronunciation of lengthened vowels, like that of long vowels, varies less than that of short vowels. Lengthened **ā** always sounds like the *a* of the English word *father*, though nonlengthened short **a** can sound like the *a* of English *sofa*. Lengthened **ī** always sounds like the *i* of the word *police*, but non-lengthened **i** can sound like the *i* of *bit* or the *e* of *bet*. Lengthened **ō** always sounds like the *o*'s in *Ohio*, never like the *oo* of *cook* (which is sometimes the sound of nonlengthened short **o**).

You'll learn in this unit that it's always possible to tell which vowels, if any, will be lengthened in a Chickasaw word, so those vowels don't have to be written with macrons except as an aid for language learners. Macrons can be used over lengthened vowels as a pronunciation aid, as they are in this unit, but they are not part of the normal Chickasaw spelling system. You will soon find it easy to hear lengthened vowels in spoken Chickasaw, and lengthening vowels as you say Chickasaw words yourself will soon become automatic. But if it helps you to write lengthened vowels with macrons when you write Chickasaw words, you can do that.

Exercise 4C. Study the example sentences in this lesson (including exercise 4B) and write dictionary entries for the new words, **litiha** (some people say **litiya**), **lhayita, chofata, bila, hika, hilha, tofa, hofahya, tikahbi, hopoba**. For each word, give the meaning and tell which set of subject markers should be used with it. Put your entries in alphabetical order. (Note: **hika** refers to getting into a standing position, not to being in one. **Hika** also means "to step".) Then choose a sentence illustrating each word from the examples above and say it aloud.

Syllables: a review. When you say a word really slowly, you divide it into syllables—the Chickasaw word "clean", said very slowly, is **cho/fā/ta**, with three syllables (slashes (/) show how the word is divided).

Below is a review of how to divide a Chickasaw word into syllables, as explained in lesson 1.3. First, notice how many vowel sounds the word has. This is the number of syllables. Second, look at each vowel in turn, starting from the right (the end of the word). If it has a consonant in front of it, that consonant also belongs to the syllable containing the vowel you are looking at. For instance, consider the word **impalītok**. It has four vowels, so there are four syllables. Here's how we divide it into syllables:

- Find the last vowel in the word **impalitok**: it's the **o**
- Put a slash before the consonant in front of that **o**: it's the **t**, so we get **impali/tok**
- Find the next vowel (from the right): it's the second **i**
- Put a slash before the consonant in front of that vowel: **impa/li/tok**
- Find the next vowel (from the right): it's the **a**
- Put a slash before the consonant in front of that vowel: **im/pa/li/tok**
- There's only one more vowel in the word, so you're done!

Here are some other examples of how words are broken into syllables:

ho/poo/tok   chi/chaa/ha   mal/li/li   ish/toy/ya/tok

The syllable break (/) comes between the two **l**'s in **mallili** and the two **y**'s in **ishtoyyatok**. Remember that letter combinations representing a single sound (such as **ch**, **lh**, and **sh**) count as just one consonant, and long vowels each count as just one vowel. Never break a syllable in the middle of a letter combination. The second syllable of **chi/chaa/ha** begins with the letter combination **ch**, not with **h**. A long vowel is one vowel, not two, so you don't put a / between the two **a**'s in **chaa**. Long vowels thus work differently from double consonants.

A syllable never starts with more than one consonant, but some syllables may have more than one consonant at the end.

Words like **hoo/ilh/po/kon/na** show that if two separate vowel sounds come together in a word, the syllable division comes between them.

As you learned in lesson 1.3, syllables that end in a consonant or that contain long or nasal vowels are heavy syllables. Syllables with lengthened vowels are heavy syllables too.

Exercise 4D. i. Using slashes (/), show how each of the words in exercises 4A and 4B is divided into syllables. Be careful about letter combinations.

ii. Divide each of the following words into syllables and tell what each one means: alikchi', hattak, ishyaatok, kiloomalli, polhāyitātok, wiikili, nokhánglo, hashtilhaa, sachokma, talhpak, pobīlatok, iimallitok, nannalhpooba', kilimpatok, taloowalītok, chihōfahya, tofālitok.

Lesson 4.3:
Rhythmic Vowel Lengthening

Listen again to some examples of words containing lengthened vowels, like those in exercise 4B. Pay attention to the SHORT SYLLABLES—nonfinal syllables containing only a short vowel with no following consonant—especially in words where there is more than one short syllable in a row.

In the following examples, we have numbered the first of each RHYTHMIC LENGTHENING SEQUENCE of short syllables, each containing a short vowel and no final consonant, with 1, and so on, starting from the left. As the examples show, sometimes you start counting the short syllables at the beginning of a word, and sometimes you start later. For example, the first syllable of **toyyalitok** is heavy, so the first short syllable is **ya**, even though it is the second syllable of the word.

cho/fā/ta	sa/chō/fa/ta	sa/chō/fa/tā/tok	toy/ya/lī/tok
1 2	1 2 3	1 2 3 4	1 2

im/pa/lī/tok	ho/pō/ba	po/hō/po/ba	po/hō/po/bā/tok
1 2	1 2	1 2 3	1 2 3 4

The last syllable of the word isn't numbered in these examples, because final syllables are not considered short syllables. As the difference between **sachofata** and **sachofatatok** shows, however, when you add an ending, the old "final syllable" is no longer final, so it can be part of the rhythmic lengthening sequence.

Once you have identified the rhythmic lengthening sequences in a word, you can determine which vowels should be lengthened. Rhythmic lengthening follows a RULE that can be stated as follows:

THE VOWEL OF EVERY EVEN-NUMBERED SHORT SYLLABLE IN A RHYTHMIC LENGTHENING SEQUENCE IS LENGTHENED.

It is always the even-numbered short syllables whose vowels get lengthened.

Lengthened vowels are very common in Chickasaw. Some words contain as many as four (or more!) short syllables in a row, so such words have several lengthened vowels. As the examples show, adding an S prefix to a word can change the arrangement of short syllables, so that different vowels are lengthened than in the ORIGINAL form of the word before the prefixes were added.

> *Exercise 4E.* i. Number the short syllables in each of the examples in exercise 4B. Lengthened vowels should occur only in syllables to which you have given an even number.
>
> ii. **Foyopa** means "to breathe". "You breathe" is **Ishfoyopa**. How do you say "I breathe"?
> **Toksali** means "to work". "We work" is **Kiitoksali**. How do you say "I work"?
> **Chokoshkomo** means "to play". "I worked" is **Chokoshkomolitok**. What is "You guys work"?
> Say all these new words out loud, pronouncing the lengthened vowels.

The rule of RHYTHMIC LENGTHENING that you have just learned is regular, so we will not usually write macrons over lengthened vowels after this unit. However, there are a few more things to learn about how the rule works.

Rhythmic lengthening with A prefixes. You've seen examples of rhythmic lengthening in words containing S prefixes, the A ending **+li**, and the past ending **+tok**. Some new verbs will illustrate how the rule works in words with A prefixes:

achokmilhka	to kneel down (A)
anompoli	to speak, to talk (A)
okaami	to wash one's face (A)

When A prefixes are used with these verbs, syllable divisions and rhythmic lengthening don't work the way you might expect.

ish/o/kaa/mi	il/a/chok/milh/ka	kil/a/nom/po/li
1	1	1 1

You would probably expect that the **sh** of the prefix **ish±** would be included with **o** in the second syllable in the first example, but it's not: you don't say <i/sho/kaa/mi>. The other examples are the same. The final consonant of the A prefix (remember that **il±** and **kil±** are used instead of **ii±** and **kii±** before vowels) is not part of the following syllable. A prefixes are always pronounced as separate syllables; in other words, the syllable break comes right after them, as **ish±/**, **kil±/**, and so on. Because these prefixes all end in consonants (like **ish±** or **kil±**) or long vowels (like **kii±**), they are all heavy syllables. Both **kiloo±** and **iloo±** contain two syllables, the second of which is heavy.

Because the first word above is divided into syllables as **ish/o/kaa/mi**, not as <i/sho/kaa/mi>, this word doesn't contain any sequence of two short syllables. Therefore, there are no rhythmically lengthened vowels in this word. (If the word were divided as <i/sho/kaa/mi>, you'd expect that it would have a lengthened **o**, <i/shō/kaa/mi>, but this pronunciation is not correct.) **Kil/a/nom/po/li** shows that a word may contain two short syllables, but if they are not together, they do not form a rhythmic lengthening sequence.

You've seen that adding an S prefix to a word can cause its first vowel to be lengthened. Adding an A prefix to a word does not result in vowel lengthening, however.

This isn't just a difference between S and A markers, or between certain verbs that allow lengthening and other verbs that don't. Unlike the other A markers, the A ending **+li** can cause a preceding vowel in a verb to be lengthened. And the last syllable or syllables of the verbs whose first vowels can't be lengthened can be part of a rhythmic lengthening sequence when an ending like **+li** or **+tok** is added:

a/nom/po/lī/li	a/nom/po/lī/tok	o/kaa/mi/lī/tok	a/chok/milh/ka/lī/tok
1 1 2	1 1 2	1 1 2	1 1 2

What's important is the sequence of short syllables. Even though the **po** syllable in **anompolili** is the second short syllable in its word, it is the first one in its sequence. This word shows that if a short syllable is followed by a heavy syllable, that stops the rhythmic lengthening sequence. You must start counting short syllables all over again with the next short syllable, beginning a new rhythmic lengthening sequence.

Lengthening with + and ± markers. There's an important difference between prefixes or endings attached to the word with a plinus (±) sign and markers attached to the word with a plus sign (+). The A prefixes, as you know, are followed by ±, not by +. The + part of the ± symbol shows that these prefixes cannot be used alone, but have to be added to another word to be used in a Chickasaw sentence. But the - part of the ± symbol shows that these prefixes cannot be included in a rhythmic lengthening sequence. Adding a ± prefix or ending to a word never changes its rhythmic lengthening sequence. This is different from the way + markers (such as the S prefixes or the **+li** ending) work. Adding a + marker to a word can create a longer rhythmic lengthening sequence and result in different lengthened vowels and a new rhythmic pattern in the word. A + can come in the middle of a rhythmic lengthening sequence, but a ± never can.

Lengthening the final consonant of an A prefix. Listen to your teacher say **Ishanompoli** "You talk". The syllables are divided like this: **ish/a/nom/po/li**. When the syllable after an A prefix starts with a vowel and is not itself a heavy syllable, as in this word, you may notice that your teacher emphasizes or slightly lengthens the pronunciation of the final consonant of the A prefix. Thus, sometimes "You talk" may sound almost like <ishshanompoli>. Try to imitate your teacher's pronunciation.

*Lengthening with **hapo+** and **hachi+**.* There is just one more thing to learn now about how the rhythmic lengthening rule operates. Though you might think that the **hapo+** and **hachi+** prefixes would have their second vowels lengthened, this is not true. The **ha** syllable of these prefixes never is part of a rhythmic lengthening sequence. So when counting short syllables on words with these two prefixes, start counting with the syllable after **ha**:

ha/<u>chi/chō/fa/tā</u>/tok   ha/<u>po/lhā/yi</u>/ta

    1   2   3 4   1   2   3

Say these words aloud, making sure you lengthen the right vowels.

One way to remember this unexpected fact about **ha** prefixes is to think of them as **ha±chi+** and **ha±po+**. Then, if **ha±** is followed by a ±, this syllable cannot be part of a rhythmic lengthening sequence of short syllables. Alternatively, you can simply exclude the **ha** syllable from your short syllable count. The rhythmic lengthening sequences in each of the two example words above are underlined. This **ha** is never included in a rhythmic lengthening sequence.

> *Exercise 4F*. Give the **hachi+** and **hapo+** forms of each of the new stative verbs in exercise 4C. Tell what each new word means. Pronounce each word, lengthening the correct vowels.

Word building and rhythmic lengthening. Prefixes and endings that are joined to a plain verb with + create increasingly longer words, and often increasingly longer rhythmic lengthening sequences. Adding a + marker to the word can result in new lengthened vowels. But although prefixes and endings joined to a word with ± make a word longer, they don't change rhythmic lengthening sequences. Adding a ± marker to a word never results in new rhythmically lengthened vowels.

The rhythmic lengthening rule you have learned in this lesson is extremely important in Chickasaw—you need to keep it in mind in order to pronounce many words correctly. Because it is very regular, you will find it easy to learn. We will no longer write lengthened vowels with a macron after this unit, unless rhythmic lengthening is specifically being discussed. Review the rule carefully if you have any doubts about how it works. (There is a special section at the end of the book, Rhythmic Lengthening in Chickasaw, which summarizes all the information presented about this rule in this and later units. Later on, you may find it helpful to refer to this section.)

Lesson 4.4: Questions

In English we change around the verb of a sentence when asking for information with a QUESTION, so *He is jumping* becomes *Is he jumping?* In Chickasaw you can ask a question by putting **+taa** on the verb of the sentence.

Mallitaa?   "Is he jumping?"

A **+taa** question is one that can be answered by **ii** "yes" or **ki'yo** "no". Questions like these are called YES-NO QUESTIONS. (You'll learn about making negative statements—which could be used to answer a question negatively—in lesson 7.2 and unit 9 and about other types of questions in unit 17.)

Listen as your teacher asks the question above. Do you hear something unusual? Unlike all the other Chickasaw verbs you've heard up to now, this word does not have stress on the last vowel—instead, the stress is on the **mal** syllable. The verb of a Chickasaw **+taa** question like **Mallitaa?** has stress on its last heavy syllable before **+taa** rather than on its final syllable. **Mallitaa?** breaks into syllables as follows: mal/li/taa. **Li** is not a heavy syllable, so this question gets stress on the heavy syllable **mal**.

Now consider another example:

A/nom/po/lī/taa?   "Is he talking?"
1   1 2

The **li** syllable before **+taa** is an even-numbered short syllable in a rhythmic lengthening sequence, so it has a lengthened vowel. Any syllable with a lengthened vowel is heavy, so this **li** syllable (and any syllable containing a lengthened vowel before **+taa**) is stressed.

Normally we don't write stress in Chickasaw, but if you want to indicate it for clarity, as in exercise 4G below, you could put a double underline under the stressed syllable. For example, the questions discussed above could be written **Mallitaa?** and **Anompolitaa?**, with double underlines under the stressed syllables.

Exercise 4G. Divide each of the following questions into syllables and number the short syllables in order to determine which vowels are lengthened. Write a macron over each lengthened vowel. Put a double underline under the stressed syllable in each question verb. Practice saying each question aloud. Then make up a "yes" answer to each question, as in the examples. (Indicate the lengthened vowels in your answer, too.) What do the question and answer pairs mean?

Example. Chilhayitataa?
Answer. Chilhāyitātaa? Ii, salhāyita. "Are you wet?" "Yes, I am wet."
1. Hachichofatataa? 2. Okla yappat ishtotaa? 3. Ishmallitaa? 4. Anompolilitaa? 5. Kiitoyyataa? 6. Taloowalitaa? 7. Hashtofataa? 8. Kowi' yappat chofatataa? 9. Hachihofahyataa? 10. Potikahbitaa? 11. Alikchi' yammat okaamitaa? 12. Owwattalitaa? 13. Pochafatataa? 14. Ántataa?

In the question **Ántataa?** "Is she there?", the stressed vowel **á** is accented. In this verb the last heavy syllable in the word is the accented syllable. In some Chickasaw verbs you'll learn later, however, there is an accented vowel before the last heavy syllable before **+taa**. In these verbs the stress in **+taa** questions goes on the accented vowel.

Past questions. Chickasaw questions that refer to the past end in **+taam** rather than **+taa**. Below are a few examples.

Ishtotaam?   "Was he big?", "Was she big?", "Was it big?"
Oblaashaash ishtoksalītaam?   "Did you work yesterday?"
Hoobilātaam?   "Did they melt?"

The past question ending **+taam** works like **+taa**: it is not stressed itself, and stress goes on the last preceding heavy syllable. Thus, **Ishtotaam?** is stressed on the syllable **ish**, and **Ishtoksalitaam?** is stressed on the lengthened syllable **li**. Listen as your teacher asks these questions.

Questions without question endings. In Chickasaw as in English, you can sometimes ask a question simply by changing the intonation of a sentence, without changing the form or position of the verb. In English a speaker does this by raising the pitch of his or her voice at the end of the sentence, as in *He's jumping?* Since ordinary Chickasaw sentences normally have a rise in pitch at the end, Chickasaw questions have a fall in pitch at the end. This means that the last syllable of the verb of the question does not have stress. Instead, the stress goes on the last preceding heavy syllable (or on an accented syllable). Here are some examples of questions that do not use **+taa** or **+taam**:

Malli?	"He's jumping?"
Mallitok?	"He jumped?"
Malili?	"He's running?"

In the first two questions, the stress is on **mal**, the last heavy syllable before the final syllable. In the last one, the stress is on the lengthened vowel **li**.

Speakers feel differently about questions without +**taa** or +**taam**. Sometimes they seem appropriate, sometimes not. See what your teacher thinks. But remember that a Chickasaw question will have its main stress on a syllable before the last one of the verb. The question mark at the end of a Chickasaw question reminds you to put the main stress on a different syllable than in a statement.

Lesson 4.5:
Noun Subjects

Here are a few new nouns to use in Chickasaw sentences:

akanka' "chicken"	nita' "bear"
foshi' "bird"	fani' "squirrel"
osi' "eagle"	koni "skunk"
chipota "child; baby"	folosh "spoon"
chipota tiik "girl"	chipota nakni' "boy"
hashi' "sun"	

Practice saying each of these words after your teacher.

Exercise 4H. Make each of the following sentences into a question using ±**taa** or ±**taam**, keeping the same subject, verb, and time. Then give a "yes" answer to each question. Write macrons to indicate the lengthened vowels in your questions and answers and double underline the stressed vowel in each question verb. Practice each question-and-answer pair with another student, being careful to lengthen and stress the right vowels. Translate your questions and answers.

1. Oblaashaash hattak yammat toksalitok. 2. Fani' yappat toyya. 3. Nita' yammat achokmilhka. 4. Hashtilhaatok. 5. Foshi' yammat kontatok. 6. Koni yammat foyopatok. 7. Oblaashaash chipota tiik yappat okaamitok. 8. Akanka' yammat hopoba. 9. Folosh yappat chokma. 10. Hikalitok. 11. Ishhilha. 12. Minko' yappat tofatok. 13. Osi' yammat wakaa. 14. Chipota nakni' yappat chokoshkomotok. 15. Hashi' yappat toomi. (**toomi** "to shine")

You have already learned that nouns can be used as subjects when they are followed by the words **yappat** "this" (subject) and **yammat** "that" (subject). Both **yappat** and **yammat** end in ±**at**, which is the normal subject ending for Chickasaw nouns. The subject ending ±**at** can also be added directly to nouns:

Hattakat mallitok.	"The man jumped."
Ihooat yaa.	"A woman is crying."
Foloshat litiha.	"The spoon is dirty."
Foshi'at hookonta.	"Birds are whistling."
Hashi'at toomi.	"The sun is shining."

As the examples show, some Chickasaw subject nouns are translated into English with "the . . .", some are translated with "a . . .", and some do not have an added word like this. The subject ending ±at can be used in all these cases.

Adding ±at to a Chickasaw noun never results in a new rhythmically lengthened vowel, because ±at is a ± ending. You might guess that **foshi'at** would be divided into syllables as <fo/shī/'at> or that foloshat would be <fo/lō/shat>, with their second vowels lengthened. But this is not correct; adding ±at does not change the syllable division, and there are no lengthened vowels in these words:

fo/shi'/at   fo/losh/at
1   1

Unlike **hattak**, **ihoo**, and **foshi'**, some nouns change in the subject form, as you can see in the following sentences:

Minkaat nowatok.	"The chief walked."
Alikchaat impa.	"The doctor is eating."
Issaat mallitok.	"A deer jumped."

Compare the following nouns with their subject forms:

Plain noun word	*Noun ±at subject form*
minko'	minkaat
alikchi'	alikchaat
issi'	issaat
nannalhpooba'	nannalhpoobaat
o̱si'	o̱saat
okla	oklaat
chipota	chipotaat

Nouns like the ones in the table above are called VOWEL-LOSS NOUNS, because each one loses its last vowel (and ', if there is one at the end) in the subject form. In these nouns the last vowel or vowel-plus-' combines with ±at, forming the special ending ±aat.

Other nouns work differently:

Plain noun word	*Noun ±at subject form*
koni	koniat
talhpak	talhpakat
ihoo	ihooat
fani'	fani'at
ofi'	ofi'at
nita'	nita'at

Nouns like these just add ±at, with no other change. Practice saying all these subject forms after your teacher.

Exercise 4I. The following Chickasaw sentences include all the types of subjects you have learned about so far. Read each sentence out loud. Tell whether each subject is singular or plural. (In some cases the answer is "singular or plural", meaning that it could be either one, depending on how the sentence is used.) Remember that the main thing that shows whether the subject is singular or plural is the form of the verb of the sentence. Translate each sentence.

1. Chipota tiikat hoochokma. 2. Issi' naknaat malli. 3. Hashfoyopatok. 4. Oklaat chokma. 5. Ishkonta. 6. Wakaalitok. 7. Minko' yappat chonnatok. 8. Kilooimpa. 9. Nannalhpoobaat hootoyya. 10. Kilimpatok. 11. Ihooat konta. 12. Nita'at tilhaatok.

You don't need to memorize the subject forms shown in the tables above—you can figure them out yourself from the plain noun words. First of all, if the noun ends in any consonant other than ' or if it ends in a long vowel, all you do is add ±at, with no other change.

The nouns to be careful about are the ones that end in short vowels, with or without a following '. Some of these are vowel-loss nouns, but some are not. To determine this, you need to look at what comes before that final short vowel. If the next-to-last syllable in a noun of this type is heavy, it is a vowel-loss noun. If the next-to-last syllable is light, the noun is not a vowel-loss noun.

You've already learned how to identify light and heavy syllables. Look at the examples below.

min/ko'   is/si'   nan/nalh/poo/ba'   o̱/si'   chi/pō/ta

Each of these nouns has a heavy next-to-last syllable. In the nouns **minko'** and **issi'** this syllable ends with a consonant (either different from or the same as the following one), while in **nannalhpooba'**, **o̱si'**, and **chipōta** the next-to-last syllables contain a long, a nasal, and a lengthened vowel. Thus, each of these nouns is a vowel-loss noun: in the subject form, their final vowels (and ', if present) will be replaced by ±**aat**.

In the following nouns, the next-to-last syllables are all light:

ko/ni   o/fi'   fa/ni'   ni/ta'

These nouns are not vowel-loss nouns. Like nouns ending with long vowels or consonants other than ', these nouns simply add ±**at** in the subject form.

Exercise 4J. Tell what the subject form of each of the following Chickasaw nouns is. Then make up a sentence using each of your new subject words. Translate the sentences you make up.

1. nakni' 2. nita' 3. pinti' 4. ihoo 5. itti' 6. issi' 7. talhpak 8. okla 9. minko' 10. nannalhpooba' 11. akanka' 12. koni 13. Chahta' 14. fani' 15. alikchi' 16. naahollo.

Some variant pronunciations. Sometimes you'll hear a different syllable division with subject forms of non-vowel-loss nouns whose next-to-last syllable is light, such as **nita'**, **ofi'**, or **folosh**. Instead of **ni/ta'/at**, **o/fi'/at**, and **fo/losh/at**, you may also hear such words pronounced as **nit/a/'at**, **of/i/'at**, and **fol/o/shat**, with the consonant before the basic noun's last vowel pronounced at the end of the preceding syllable and the noun's final consonant pronounced in the same syllable as the ±**at** ending. In pronouncing subject forms like this, speakers sometimes emphasize or slightly lengthen the syllable-final consonants, so such words may sound almost like <nitta'at>, <offi'at>, <folloshat>. Listen for these variants.

Occasionally, speakers use subject forms of vowel-loss nouns like **issi'** or **okla** in which the last vowel is not lost—thus, they might use subject forms like **issi'at** or **okla-at** (do you see why we write this word with a hyphen?). However, most speakers regard such subject forms as less correct than the forms in which the last vowel is lost, and we will not use them in this book.

A spelling trick. You can often tell if the consonant sound before a final vowel or vowel-plus-' in a Chickasaw noun is single or double by the subject form of that noun. For example, **iti** "mouth" sounds a lot like **itti** "stick"; one difference is the final **'** in **itti'**, but you may find it hard to hear the difference in the number of **t**'s. However, the subject forms will help you out: **itti'** has the subject form **ittaat** (occasionally also **itti'at**), but **iti** has only the subject form **itiat** (never <itaat>). Because the subject form of **itti'** is **ittaat**, **itti'** is a vowel-loss noun. Therefore, **itti'** must have a double consonant before the last vowel (to make the next-to-last syllable heavy); because **iti** is not a vowel-loss noun, it must have a light next-to-last syllable, with just one **t** before the second **i**. This is a useful trick to remember when you're trying to figure out how to spell new words.

Terms and Concepts

PAST, TENSE, LENGTHENED VOWEL, SHORT SYLLABLE, RHYTHMIC LENGTHENING SEQUENCE, ORIGINAL, RULE, RHYTHMIC LENGTHENING, QUESTION, YES-NO QUESTION, VOWEL-LOSS NOUN.

VOCABULARY

akanka' chicken
achokmilhka to kneel down (A)
anompoli to talk, to speak (A)
bila to melt (S)
chofata to be clean (S)
chokoshkomo to play (A)
chipota child; baby
chipota nakni' boy
chipota tiik girl
fani' squirrel
folosh spoon
foshi' bird
foyopa to breathe (A)
hashi' sun
hika to stand up; to step (A)
hilha to dance (A)
hofahya to be ashamed (S)
hopoba to be hungry (S)
iti mouth
ii yes
ki'yo no
koni skunk
litiha to be dirty (S)
lhayita to be wet (S)
nita' bear

oblaashaash yesterday
okaami to wash one's face (A)
o̱si' eagle
tikahbi to be tired (S)
tofa to spit (A)
toksali to work (Λ)
toomi to shine (Noun)

READING AND SPEAKING

Conversations

Practice the following conversations with a friend.

1.

—Billmano? Imanompoli sabanna.   "Where is Bill? I want to talk to him."
—Abooha anonkaak ánta.   "He's in the house."

2.

—Maryat abooha anonka' ántataa?   "Is Mary in the house?"
—I̱i. Ánta.   "Yes. She's there."
—Chokma. Pisa sabanna.   "Good. I want to see her."

3.

—Marymano? Abooha anonka' ántataa?   "Where's Mary? Is she in the house?"
—Ki'yo, iksho.   "No, she's not around."
—Oo. Ayali!   "Oh. I'm going."

4.

—Ihoohmano?   "Where is the woman?"
—Akitha'no.   "I don't know."
—Ishpístaam?   "Have you seen her?"
—Ki'yo.   "No."

"Where is" questions in Chickasaw are formed with the ending ±**mano** (±**hmano** after a vowel) added to a noun. The "where is" ending ±**mano** is like +**taa** and +**taam** in that words with this ending are not stressed on their final syllable. Instead, the last heavy syllable before ±**mano** is stressed.

In this book we write endings attached directly to names, which follows traditional spelling practice. How does this look to you? If you would prefer, you can use a hyphen: **Bill-mano**, **Mary-at**. It doesn't really matter. (The name "Mary" is usually pronounced **Mari'** by traditional Chickasaw speakers, and you can spell it that way if you like. This pronunciation is important, because it means that the last heavy syllable of **Mari'mano** is the **ri'** syllable—this is the one that gets stressed in the question.)

In conversation 4, **Ishpístaam?** is translated "Have you seen her?". English translations like "has seen" for a Chickasaw past tense sometimes make more sense than the simple "saw" in a conversation. Chickasaw does not have a tense that exactly corresponds to English "has seen" (technically, the "present perfect"). You'll learn more about verbs like **ishpístaam** in unit 6.

Questions and Answers

Practice the following dialogues with a friend.

1.

    —Ittibaapishiat hikataam?   "Did his brother stand up?"
    —Ii, ittibaapishiat hikatok.   "Yes, his brother stood up."

2.

    —Ihoo yappat sashki'. Ihoo   "This woman is my mother. Is
    yammat chishki'to?   that woman your mother?"
    —Ii, yammat sashki'.   "Yes, that one is my mother."

3.

    —Sattibaapishiat hikataam?   "Did my brother stand up?"
    —Chittibaapishiat hikatok.   "Your brother stood up."

4.

    —Yappat chinakfishto?   "Is this one your younger sister?"
    —Ki'yo, yammakoot sanakfish.   "No, that one is my younger sister."

5.

    —Chittibaapishiat hikataam?   "Did your brother stand up?"
    —Sattibaapishiat hikatok.   "My brother stood up."

Remember that verbs in **+taa** and **+taam** are stressed on the last heavy syllable before the question ending. The same is true of questions ending in **-to** (Unit 17), as in dialogues 2 and 4.

The forms of **ittibaapishi** used in dialogues 1, 3, and 5 can mean either "brother" or "sister".

Dialogue 4 can only be used with the translation given between two female speakers. If two men used the same dialogue, it would refer to "younger brothers" rather than "younger sisters". The Chickasaw words for brothers and sisters are very different from English ones, as you can see. You will learn more about this and other things about POSSESSED nouns (nouns with a prefix to tell who has or "owns" them) in unit 7. For now, just practice the dialogues.

BEYOND THE GRAMMAR: THE CHOCTAWS

As you know, the Muskogean language most closely related to Chickasaw is Choctaw—many words and sentences sound almost exactly the same in Choctaw as they do in Chickasaw. You will learn more about the differences between Chickasaw and Choctaw words in the Beyond the Grammar section of unit 8.

The Choctaws originally occupied an area of the Southeast to the south and west of the Chickasaw area. There are still some Choctaws in Louisiana, and many still live in Mississippi. There is a large Choctaw reservation centered in Philadelphia, Mississippi, incorporating a number of different Choctaw communities. However, most Choctaws today live in the Choctaw Nation in Oklahoma, which occupies most of the southeastern quarter of the state. There are also Choctaw speakers in the Chickasaw Nation—one area with a large Choctaw-speaking population, for instance, is centered around Durwood, a small community located between Ardmore and Madill, Oklahoma.

The number of people of Choctaw ancestry today is quite large, much greater than the number of Chickasaws. Of course, there are also many of mixed Choctaw and Chickasaw blood. In Oklahoma the majority of

Choctaws under the age of forty do not speak their language, and there are few very young speakers, but in Mississippi almost all Choctaws on the Choctaw reservation speak the language, and there are Head Start programs for Choctaw toddlers who speak no English.

The history of the Choctaw people is comparable to that of the Chickasaws, which you learned about in the Beyond the Grammar section of unit 2. Like the Chickasaws, the Choctaws were removed to Indian Territory from their ancestral lands in the Southeast during the 1830s. The area they settled, which was known as the Choctaw Nation, functioned independently, like the Chickasaw Nation, until Oklahoma statehood in 1907. Currently, the Choctaws are governed by a chief, assisted by a tribal council. The Choctaw Tribal Council meets in the old Choctaw capitol city of Tuskahoma. The administrative center and new capitol of the Choctaw Nation is in Durant. Gregory Pyle has been chief of the Choctaw Nation of Oklahoma since 1997.

Objects

In this unit you'll learn how to add objects to Chickasaw sentences.

Lesson 5.1 introduces the concept of object and shows how object nouns appear in Chickasaw sentences. Lesson 5.2 explains how prefixes indicate non-noun objects. Lesson 5.3 describes one- and two-place verbs, and lesson 5.4 presents prefix combinations. Lesson 5.5 shows how object nouns change their form and how word order can change in sentences with objects. Reflexive verbs are presented in lesson 5.6, and lesson 5.7 shows how verbs change to refer to events that haven't happened yet.

Lesson 5.1: Sentences with Objects

Look at the following English sentences:

> The man kissed the woman.
> The chief is picking beans.
> The doctor spanked the baby.
> The girl is tickling the boy.
> This person speaks Chickasaw.

Unlike all the sentence translations we've seen so far, these have a verb and two PARTICIPANTS in the action. The first noun in each sentence, as you know, is the subject of that sentence. Following each English subject is the verb of that sentence, and after the verb is another noun that completes the idea of the verb by explaining who or what the verbal action or idea was directed at. A noun that completes the verb's idea in this way is called the OBJECT of that verb—thus, the object of the verb *kissed* in the first sentence is the woman, because the woman is the one who was kissed, and so on.

Here are some new Chickasaw verbs that are used with objects:

ayowa "pick", "gather"	bashaffi "cut"	bashli "operate on"
chinoffi "pinch"	chompa "buy"	halalli "pull"
holissochi "write"	hoppi "bury"	hotihna "count"
hoyo "look for"	kamoshli "tickle"	lohmi "hide"
nalhlhi "shoot"	nannabli "swallow"	passáa "spank"
sakki "catch up with"	sho̲ka "kiss"	

Hoyo and **bashli** are translated into English with two words, "look for" and "operate on"; **sakki** has a three-word translation. **Bashaffi** normally refers only to cutting with a knife.

Now, here are some examples of Chickasaw sentences using object nouns. The sentences below have the same meanings as the three English examples above; like them, they each have two involved participants. Look at each one carefully to be sure that you understand all the words.

> Hattakat ihoo sho̲'katok.
> Minkaat bala' ayowa.
> Alikchaat chipota passa̲atok.
> Chipota tiikat chipota naki' kamoshli.
> Hattak yappat Chikashshanompa' anompoli.

(You know from the title of this book that **Chikashshanompa'** means "Chickasaw language".) As in sentences you have seen in earlier lessons, the subject noun comes first and is marked with the subject ending **±at** (or **±aat**; see lesson 4.5). In these sentences the object noun is not marked at all.

The order of the phrases in the Chickasaw sentence is different from that in the English sentence. In both languages the subject phrase comes first in the sentence. In English the verb comes next, followed by the object phrase. In Chickasaw, however, the object follows the subject, with the verb at the end. In other words Chickasaw sentences use the order SUBJECT OBJECT VERB, while in English sentences the order of the object phrase and the verb is reversed. Although the orders are different, though, the meanings can be the same.

Here are some new nouns that you will be able to use in the first exercise:

Chikashshanompa'	"Chickasaw language"
holisso	"book", "paper", "letter", "document"
ishtalakchi'	"rope", "leash"
kowi'	"cat"
oka'	"water"
tali'	"rock"

Exercise 5A. Find the subject and object in each of the following English sentences. Then translate each sentence into Chickasaw.

1. That chief pulled the rope. 2. The cat is looking for water. 3. The woman shot the doctor. 4. The doctor operated on the chief. 5. The child cut the stick. 6. The white man swallowed the water. 7. The chief caught up with the doctor. 8. The woman is writing a letter. 9. The dog buried the rock. 10. The Choctaws hid the book. 11. The man is looking for the dog. 12. The woman is counting the books. 13. The white woman bought a chicken. 14. That man pinched the woman. 15. Does the chief speak Chickasaw? 16. The boy tickled the baby.

As you know, **yammat** "that" and **yappat** "this" may be used after a noun to form a subject phrase in sentences like

Ihoo yammat malli.	"That woman is jumping."
Hattak yappat malli.	"This man is jumping."

If you want to put "this" or "that" with an object noun, you have to use different forms of these words (since **yammat** and **yappat** include the subject ending ±**at**). The object forms of these words are **yamma̲** "that" and **yappa̲** "this", as in

Ihooat hattak yamma̲ sho̲'ka.	"The woman is kissing that man."
Hattakat chipota yappa̲ passáatok.	"The man spanked this child."
Alikchi' yammat minko' yappa̲ nalhlhitok.	"That doctor shot this chief."

The last vowel of both **yamma̲** and **yappa̲** is sometimes pronounced as **a** rather than **a̲**—in other words, you may also hear people say **yamma** or **yappa**.

If it is clear to the people you are talking with what you are referring to, you may leave out either the object phrase or the subject phrase or both. Here are some examples of Chickasaw sentences with understood objects:

Ihooat kamoshli.	"The woman is tickling him (*or* her *or* it)."
Kowi'at halallitok.	"The cat pulled it (*or* her *or* him)."

Now, here are some sentences with understood subjects:

Chipota kamoshli.	"She (*or* he) is tickling the child."
Minko' hoyotok.	"He (*or* she) looked for the chief."

There's never any difficulty understanding who is the subject and who is the object when one of these is omitted. Do you see why? The subject phrase will always end in ±**at**, and the object phrase won't. Thus, with **Ihooat kamoshli**, when you hear the ±**at** on **ihooat**, you know that the woman is the one who is doing the tickling. With **Chipota kamoshli**, on the other hand, when you hear that there's no ±**at** on **chipota**, you know that the child is the one being tickled.

When both speaker and hearer are familiar with what's going on and who's involved, a plain verb can be used alone, with both the subject and the object understood. In this case one word is enough to describe the whole situation:

Kamoshli.	"She (*or* he) is tickling him (*or* her *or* it)."
Hoyotok.	"He (*or* she) looked for her (*or* him *or* it)."

These sentences could also be interpreted as having plural subjects or objects.

Exercise 5B. i. Translate these sentences into Chickasaw. Read each one aloud.

1. She pinched him. 2. The girl pinched him. 3. She pinched the boy. 4. They are looking for this basket. 5. This child is counting them. 6. He shot a deer. 7. The doctor caught up with this man. 8. The man swallowed it. 9. She tickled the man. 10. The doctor wrote it.

ii. Give at least one additional English translation for each Chickasaw sentence.

Lesson 5.2:
Prefixes for Objects

If you want to name yourself or the person you are talking to as the object of the sentence, you must use an S prefix on the verb, as in the following examples:

Hattakat sahoyo.	"The man is looking for me."
Ihooat chihalallitok.	"The woman pulled you."
Alikchaat posho'ka.	"The doctor is kissing us."

The S prefix **sa+** in the first example means that the object of the verb **hoyo** is "me". There are no extra words in the sentence for "me", "you", or "us"—it is the S prefix that tells you who the object is.

Now, here are the same sentences with understood subject nouns:

Sahoyo.	"He is looking for me."
Chihalallitok.	"She pulled you."
Posho'ka.	"He is kissing us."

Once again, the S prefixes **sa+**, **chi+**, and **po+** in these sentences tell what the objects of these sentences are.

Lengthened vowels with object prefixes. Whenever an S prefix is added to the front of a verb that begins with a short syllable, the first vowel of the verb is lengthened, as you learned in lesson 4.3.

Sahōyo.	"He is looking for me."
Pohālalli.	"He pulls us."
Ihooat chibāshaffi.	"The woman cuts you."

As you've learned, the rhythmic lengthening process is regular, so you don't have to write macrons on lengthened vowels—just remember to say them!

Exercise 5C. i. Translate the following Chickasaw sentences into English.

l. Ofi'at kowi' yappa sho̲'katok. 2. Minkaat pohoyo. 3. Hattak nakni' yammat sakamoshlitok. 4. Ihoo yappat talhpak yamma̲ halallitok. 5. Chipota naknaat chibashaffi. 6. Ponalhlhi. 7. Paska nannablitok. 8. Chihoyotok. 8. Hattakat chisho̲'katok. 9. Chipota tiikat sakamoshlitok. 10. Alikchaat posakkitok. 11. Minkaat hapohotihnatok. 12. Hachichinoffi.

Practice saying each sentence aloud, making sure to lengthen all the right vowels.

ii. Turn each of the sentences in part i into a question. Put a double underline under the stressed vowel in each verb. Say each question aloud.

Lesson 5.3:
One- and Two-Place Verbs

S subjects and S objects. Probably you are curious about why the S prefix **sa+** sometimes means "me" but sometimes means "I":

Sahoyo.	"He is looking for **me**."
Sahomma.	"**I** am red."

The answer has to do with the nature of the verbs **homma** "to be red" and **hoyo** "to look for".

One- and two-place verbs. **Hoyo** "to look for" is a verb that must have both a subject and an object—two separate involved participants—to make sense. If you say just "I am looking for", it is incomplete. On the other hand, **homma** "to be red" is a verb that makes no sense with an object. "I am red it" makes no sense. Verbs like **hoyo, which** need both a subject and an object, are called TWO-PLACE VERBS. Verbs like **homma**, which have only a subject, are called ONE-PLACE VERBS.

A two-place verb always has an understood object, even if you don't see one in the sentence. Thus, the sentence **Hoyo** means "He is looking for her" (*or* "He is looking for it", *or* "She is looking for him", and so on), not just "He is looking for", because without an object, the sentence wouldn't make sense.

When an S prefix is used on a one-place verb like **homma**, the S prefix names the subject of that verb. When an S prefix is used on a two-place verb like **hoyo**, however, it names the object of the verb.

In a sentence like **Chichokma**, we know that the S prefix **chi+** must name a subject, because **chokma** "to be good" is a one-place verb—so the sentence means "You are good". However, in a sentence like **Chipassáa**, where the verb, **passáa** "to spank", is a two-place verb, we interpret the S prefix **chi+** as indicating the object—so "you" is the object, and the sentence means "He (*or* she) spanks you".

Vocabulary entries. If you see a sentence containing a verb with an S prefix and you don't know whether that verb is a one- or two-place verb, you won't be able to know whether the S prefix names the subject or the object of the verb. You will find that the Chickasaw-English Vocabulary at the end of this book provides helpful information. As you know, **homma** is listed in the vocabulary as follows:

homma to be red (S)

This vocabulary entry tells you not only the meaning of the verb **homma**, but that **homma** is a one-place verb that marks its subject with an S prefix. Two-place verbs are listed like this:

hoyo to look for (A,S)
kamoshli to tickle (A,S)

You can tell that these are two-place verbs, because the parentheses after each definition contain two items, A and S. The number of items in the parentheses matches the number of participants involved in the action the verb refers to.

A subjects of two-place verbs. As the entries above suggest, the subjects of **hoyo**, **kamoshli**, and the other two-place verbs you've learned so far can be indicated with A markers. Here are some examples of two-place verbs with the A ending **+li**:

Hattak yamma sho'kali.	"I am kissing that man."
Hoyolitok.	"I looked for her."
Chikamoshlilitok.	"I tickled you."

The last example shows that a two-place verb may have two different participant markers on it, one to indicate the subject (in this case, the A ending **+li**) and one to show the object (here, the S prefix **chi+**). A one-place verb can never have more than one participant marker.

A pronunciation note. When the A prefixes **ish±** and **hash±** are used before the verb **sakki** (or any verb that starts with **s**), most speakers will pronounce the expected <shs> sequence with **ss**: **Issakki** "You catch up with him", **Hassakki** "You all catch up with him". In general no Chickasaw word contains **sh** before **s**.

Noun objects. Some verbs don't make sense with S object prefixes. Two-place verbs like **holissochi** "to write" and **chompa** "to buy" can be used only with noun objects, not with S prefix objects. You can write a book or a letter, but you can't write a person. (The English sentence *I wrote him* doesn't really mean that the object *him* is what you wrote. In English this sentence is another way to say *I wrote to him*, which you'll learn how to express in Chickasaw in lesson 8.1.) In Chickasaw society, you can't buy a person either. Verbs of this type are listed in the vocabulary as follows:

> **holissochi** to write (A,Noun)
> **chompa** to buy (A,Noun)

These entries mean that you use an A marker for the subject, but that the object must be a noun and cannot be indicated by an object marker. Of course, like any noun object, the object of such verbs can be understood, so you can say, for example,

Chompalitok.	"I bought it."
Ishchompataa?	"Are you buying it?"

You've learned that **hilha** "to dance", **taloowa** "to sing", and **anompoli** "to speak, to talk" are one-place A subject verbs. These verbs can also be used with noun objects, as in

"Amazing Grace" taloowalitok.	"I sang 'Amazing Grace'"
Tango ishhilhataa?	"Are you dancing the tango?"
Chikashshanompa' anompolili.	"I speak Chickasaw."

We can list two uses for these verbs in the vocabulary: as one-place (A) verbs and as two place (A,Noun) verbs.

Another verb with two uses. Another verb that can be used both as a one-place verb and as a two-place verb is **hopoo**. You know that **hopoo** can be a one-place verb meaning "to be jealous (A)". It can also be a two-place verb meaning "to be jealous of (A, S)". Thus, **Sahopoo** means "He is jealous of me." Whenever an A prefix appears with **hopoo**, it refers to the person who is jealous, whether or not that person is jealous of someone in particular. An S prefix on the verb **hopoo** always refers to the object of the jealousy.

Surprising one-place verbs. Some verbs that you might guess could be used with objects (and that would thus be two-place verbs) are one-place verbs in Chickasaw. Here are two examples you already know:

> **impa** to eat (A)
> **owwatta** to hunt (A)

These Chickasaw verbs are only used about performing the actions of eating and hunting. The verbs only have one involved participant—you can't use them with objects specifying what was eaten or hunted.

> *Exercise 5D*. i. Translate each of the following sentences into Chickasaw.
>   1. That man shot you. 2. I am pulling it. 3. She cut us. 4. I am looking for you all. 5. He spanked me. 6. You all caught up with him. 7. We sang "Oh, Susanna!". (As with any name, you can simply write the name of the song in English.) 8. Do you speak Chickasaw?
>   ii. Translate each of the following sentences into English. (Some may have more than one possible translation.)
>   9. Chihopooli. 10. Hattakat pohopoo. 11. Ishhopoo. 12. Hopooli. 13. Chihopoo. 14. Iihopoo.

***Hoo±* with two-place verbs.** The **hoo±** prefix can be used with two-place verbs when you want to emphasize that a subject is plural:

Ihooat hattak hoosho̲'ka.	"The women are kissing the men."
	or "The women are kissing the man."
Hoopassáatok.	"They spanked him (*or* her *or* them)."
Hoochipassáatok.	"They spanked you."

As the last example shows, **hoo±** comes at the beginning of the verb, before any S prefix, if there is one. Remember that **hoo±** is only used with a noun or understood "they" subject. It can't be used with an A subject marker. **Hoo±** tells you that the subject is plural, but it does not tell you anything about the object.

Two-place i-verbs. As you know, the **i** at the beginning of a verb like **ishto** "to be big" drops after an S prefix, as in

Sashto.	"I am big."

The same thing happens when you use an S prefix to indicate the object on a two-place verb that starts with **i**, such as **itháana** "to know", as in

Satháana.	"He knows me."

Here are some other new two-place verbs that start with **i**:

ipita to feed (A,S)
isso to hit (usually used only with singular subjects) (A,S)
ishko to drink (A, S)
ittihaalalli to marry, to get married to (A, S̲)

If anyone ever needed to say "Drink me!" in Chickasaw, it would be **Sashko!** Although you may hear speakers use **isso** with plural subjects, this is not common.

Review: A prefixes on verbs starting with vowels. Remember that the first vowel of a verb starting with a vowel does not drop after an A prefix and that an A prefix does not count as part of a rhythmic lengthening sequence:

Ishowwattatok.	You hunted.
Bala' kilayowa.	We are picking beans.

Exercise 5E. Make a Chickasaw sentence from each subject, object, and verb, plus the endings **+tok**, **+taa**, or **+taam**, if indicated, as in the following example. Translate the sentences you make up.

> *Example.* (I, you) ittihalalli + tok.
> *Answer.* Chittihaalallilitok. "I married you."

l. (I, that bird) nalhlhi. 2. (this man, us) ithána + taa. 3. (you, this water) ishko + taam. 4. (she, me) isso. 5. (she, you all) ipita + taam. 6. (that doctor, you) ittihaalalli + tok. 7. (that woman, me) hoyo. 8. (he, us—special) hopoo. 9. (he, you all) bashaffi + taam. l0. (they, you) sho'ka + tok. 11. (he, you) isso + tok. 12. (he, me) sakki +taam. 13. (the doctor, you) bashli + taa. 14. (you, me) kamoshli + tok. 15. (she, us) chinoffi + tok. 16. (you, the chickens) hotihna + taam.

Lesson 5.4: Prefix Combinations

A and S prefixes on verbs. When an A prefix is used to tell the subject of a two-place verb, it comes before the S prefix that tells the object:

Kiichithána.	"We know you."
Hashpottihaalallitok.	"You all married us."

When the A prefix **ish±** comes before the S prefix **sa+**, the resulting PREFIX COMBINATION is **issa+**:

Issasho'katok.	"You kissed me."
Issathánataa?	"Do you know me?"

The final **sh** sound of the **ish±** prefix becomes an **s** before the **s** of the **sa+** prefix, and the result is a double **s**—listen for it as your teacher pronounces these sentences. The same thing happens with the prefix **hash±**—**hash±** plus **sa+** equals **hassa+**:

Hassasakkitok.	"You all caught up with me."

Never start a Chickasaw word with <ish±sa+> or <hash±sa+>. Just as you learned earlier, Chickasaw words do not contain the sequence of sounds <shs>.

Some combinations aren't used. In Chickasaw as in English, sentences like "I hit me", "you hit you", or "we hit us" don't make sense; you will never use an A subject marker and an S object prefix that refer to the same entity. There are a few other combinations that aren't used either.

As you know, there are both singular and plural "you" S prefixes that can be used to tell the object of sentences like the following:

Hachithánali.	"I know you all."
Chithánali.	"I know you (just one)."

However, the object prefix **hachi+** is not normally used following an A subject prefix. If you say the following sentence, then, you could be referring to knowing one person or knowing many:

Kiichithána.	"We know you."

Most speakers won't use the prefix **hachi**+ after **kii±** or **ii±**.

The special inclusive triplural S prefix **hapo±** "us" is also not used following the A prefixes **ish±** and **hash±**, but there's a good reason for this. Since **hapo±** refers to an "us" that includes the hearer "you", it doesn't make sense to use it with a "you" subject.

Similarly, the special "we" A prefix **kiloo±** can't be used before the S object prefix **chi**+ because, once again, this would be a combination of an A subject prefix that included the hearer "you" plus a "you" object prefix.

Exercise 5F. Translate the following sentences into Chickasaw.

1. You all know me. 2. They married us (more than two, including you). 3. We (more than two, including you) caught up with him. 4. We (more than two, not including you) tickled you. 5. I counted you all. 6. Did the rock hit you? 7. You operated on us (more than two, not including you). 8. Are you all kissing me? 9. We are looking for you all. 10. You all pinched us (two). 11. We (more than two, including you) know her. 12. I fed you.

Lesson 5.5:
The Object Ending ±**a**

In the two-place sentences you've seen so far, the object nouns have had no added ending. But often noun objects do have an object ending, ±**a**. Thus, instead of **Hattakat ihoo sho̱'katok**, you may hear

Hattakat ihoo**a** sho̱'katok.   "The man kissed the woman."

The meaning of this sentence with and without ±**a** on the object word is similar, but using ±**a** may call more attention to the object.

Adding ±**a** to a noun is similar to adding the subject ending ±**at**. If the noun ends in a consonant other than **'**, in a long vowel, or in an even-numbered short syllable, you add ±**a** directly to the end of the noun, but with a vowel-loss noun, whose next-to-last syllable is heavy and which ends in a short vowel or **'**, the final vowel and the **'** (if there is one) are replaced by ±**a** in the object form. The examples below illustrate both types of object forms:

Noun	*Object form*
hattak	hattak**a**
oka'	oka'**a**
koni	koni**a**
minko'	mink**a** (vowel-loss noun)
issi'	iss**a** (vowel-loss noun)
chipota	chipot**a** (vowel-loss noun)

In lesson 4.5 you learned about syllable division in subject forms of non-vowel-loss nouns with light next-to-last syllables. Object forms of these nouns work the same way. The object form of "water" may be pronounced as **o/ka'/a** or (very often) **ok/a/'a**. In this second pronunciation, the consonant before the last vowel in the basic form of the noun is pronounced at the end of a syllable, and the final consonant of the noun forms a syllable with the ending. Speakers sometimes emphasize or slightly lengthen the syllable-final consonants in such forms, so you may feel that the object form of "water" sounds like <okka'a>.

Exercise 5G. Add ±**a** to the object noun in each of the following sentences. Say each sentence aloud and tell what it means.

1. Chipota ishpassáataam? 2. Chahta' hashitháanataa? 3. Nita' yappat oka' ishkotok. 4. Kowi'at ofi' isso. 5. Naaholllo yammat talhpak halallitok. 6. Chikashsha kiihoyo. 7. Hattak yappat alikchi' itháanataa? 8. "Star Spangled Banner" ishtaloowataam? 9. Ihooat akanka' hotihnatok. 10. Chipota tiik kamoshli.

Lesson 5.6:
Word Order

Look at the different ways you can say "The man kissed the woman":

Hattakat ihooa sho'katok.
Hattakat sho'katok ihooa.
Ihooa hattakat sho'katok.
Ihooa sho'katok hattakat.

Subject-Object-Verb is by far the most common word order pattern in Chickasaw, but some other word orders do occur. Each of the sentences above means the same thing—there's no problem understanding them because of the ±**at** and ±**a** markers, which tell you clearly which noun is the subject and which is the object.

In almost any Chickasaw sentence, you can move the subject noun to the end, as in the fourth sentence above. You can also move an object noun marked with ±**a** to the end, as in the second sentence, or in front of the subject, as in the third sentence. Each of these changes puts some emphasis on the nouns that occur out of their expected order.

Occasionally, you might encounter two other patterns, in which both subject and object follow the verb (as in **Sho'katok hattakat ihooa, Sho'katok ihooa hattakat**), but these are extremely unusual and generally don't sound good to native speakers, so you should not try to make up sentences with these orders yourself.

You might think from these examples that any change in word order in a Chickasaw sentence is just fine, but this isn't true. If an object noun doesn't have the ending ±**a**, the only place for it is right in front of the verb. Thus, a sentence like <Ihoo hattakat sho'katok> or <Hattakat sho'katok ihoo> would not be good Chickasaw. Never use an object noun without ±**a** in sentences like these unless it is right before the verb. Without ±**a** on the object noun, there are only two correct ways to say "The man kissed the woman", both of which have the object noun right before the verb:

Hattakat ihoo sho'katok.
Ihoo sho'katok hattakat.

So whether or not the ±**a** is used is important!

So far we've only looked at changes in the order of words in sentences with objects, but you can also vary the order in sentences of the sort you learned in earlier units. Each of the first set of sentences below means "The dog growled", and each of the second set means "That woman is dancing":

Ofi'at kilihatok.
Kilihatok ofi'at.

Ihoo yammat hilha.
Hilha ihoo yammat.

In the second sentence of each set, the subject goes after the verb. Note that in the last example, the subject is a phrase, **ihoo yammat**. The words of a subject phrase or an object phrase consisting of more than one word must stay together when you change around the word order in a Chickasaw sentence.

Exercise 5H. After completing exercise 5G, give another word order for sentences 1, 2, 6, 8, and 9 and three additional word orders for sentences 3, 4, 5, 7, and 10.

Lesson 5.7:
Reflexive Verbs

Look at these sentences using the prefix **ili+**:

Ilisso.	"He hits himself."
Ilipassáalitok.	"I spanked myself."
Ishilihoppitaam?	"Did you bury yourself?"
Hashilithánataa?	"Do you all know yourselves?"

Verbs that contain **ili+** are REFLEXIVE—they say that their subject did the action of the original two-place verb to himself. **Ili+** tells you that the subject and object of the verb are the same (in a sense, there is only one involved participant). In English we have a number of different reflexive words ending in +*self* or +*selves*, but in Chickasaw **ili+** doesn't change depending on the subject. From the examples, you can see that **ili+** follows A prefixes. **Ili+** is not used on a verb with an S prefix.

If the original two-place verb starts with a vowel, just add **il+**, as in the first and fourth examples above.

When you put an A prefix on a reflexive verb, the last consonant of the prefix may sound almost double, as you learned in lesson 4.3. Thus, **Ishilihoppitaam** might sound like <ishshilīhoppitaam>. (The vowel of **ili+** is always lengthened when it precedes a single consonant.) Listen to your teacher.

The reflexive form of a verb with a "we" subject starts with **kilili+** or **ilili+** (pronounced **kil/i/lī** or **il/i/lī**), as you'd expect. The double sequence of **ilil** sounds awkward to many speakers, however, and people often tend to avoid using reflexive "we" sentences. Some Chickasaw verbs just don't sound good in the reflexive form. One example is **ipita** "to feed"—rather than saying "feed oneself", a Chickasaw speaker will simply say **impa** "eat", without using **ili+** (or **ipita**) at all.

Exercise 5I. Translate the following sentences into Chickasaw.
  1. He is looking for himself. 2. Did you pinch yourself? 3. I know myself. 4. We cut ourselves. 5. You all shot yourselves. 6. I fed myself. 7. The doctor is operating on himself. 8. Did you hit yourself?
  Read each of your sentences out loud.

Lesson 5.8:
The Future, Possibility, and Ability

The ±a'chi future ending. When you talk about something that hasn't happened yet but which you believe will happen, your statement refers to the FUTURE. Like past, future is a tense that can be marked on a verb. A future sentence in Chickasaw contains a verb with the ending ±**a'chi**:

Ishka'chi.	"He will drink."
Issakamoshla'chi.	"You are going to tickle me."
Homma'chi.	"It will be red."

Chickasaw future sentences using ±a'chi can be translated into English with either "will" or "going to". The last vowel of the verb in a future sentence is dropped before the future ending ±a'chi. Thus, ishko plus ±a'chi equals ishka'chi, and so on.

Listen carefully as your teacher pronounces the future sentences above. You will probably hear an added copy vowel between the ' and the ch of the ±a'chi ending, so that ishka'chi may sound like <ishka'achi>, and so on. You should try to put in these copy vowels the way your teacher does, but don't write them in the word. They do not count as extra syllables either.

When ±a'chi follows a verb that ends in a long vowel, the verb does not change. If it's appropriate, you can use onnakma "tomorrow" at the beginning of a future sentence.

Onnakma hopooa'chi.	"He will be jealous tomorrow."
Onnakma yaa-a'chi.	"She will cry tomorrow."

(Use a hyphen to separate the long aa and the short a in yaa-a'chi.)

The future ending ±a'chi goes after the A ending +li. The i of this ending drops the same way other short vowels before ±a'chi do. So future verbs with "I" subjects shown by an A marker end in +la'chi (never <+li+a'chi>):

Hopoola'chi.	"I will be jealous."
Chittihaalallila'chi.	"I will marry you."
Bashlila'chi.	"I am going to operate on him."

In a question about the future, +taa goes after ±a'chi:

Onnakma hooimpa'chitaa?	"Will they eat tomorrow?"
Mallila'chitaa?	"Am I going to jump?"

Listen as your teacher reads these questions. You might notice that the i of ±a'chitaa sounds like a lengthened vowel (which may seem a bit surprising). Try to imitate your teacher's pronunciation of the combination ±a'chītaa.

The ±a'ni possibility ending. Another Chickasaw verb ending that refers to events that have not occurred yet is ±a'ni, which is usually translated into English with the word "can":

Mallila'ni.	"I can jump."

This means that I have the potential, or perhaps the ability, to jump. ±A'ni may also be translated with "may":

Issa'ni.	"She may hit him."

These statements refer to events that could or might occur in the future, but about which the speaker is uncertain or unwilling to make a commitment.

Like ±a'chi, ±a'ni causes the preceding verb to drop its last vowel. ±A'ni comes after the A ending +li in a word, forming the combination +la'ni. ±A'ni comes before the question ending +taa, and when ±a'ni and +taa come together, most speakers pronounce the resulting combination as ±a'ntaa:

Illa'ntaa?	"Might he die?"

(Some speakers may pronounce the combination as ±a'nitaa.) As this example indicates, the best translation of ±a'ni in a question is often "might".

Talking about ability. English *can* also refers to ability. While the Chickasaw ending ±a'ni may refer to someone's ability to do something as well as the possibility that it may happen, the most common way to say this is with the ending ±a'hi followed by the AUXILIARY verb **bíyyi'ka**:

Chikashshanompa' anompolila'hi bíyyi'ka.   "I can speak Chickasaw."

An auxiliary or "helping verb" is used with another verb in a verb phrase to MODIFY (tell more about or clarify) the verb's meaning. In Chickasaw an auxiliary verb always comes after another verb. Unlike ±a'chi and ±a'ni, ±a'hi is usually not used by itself but generally needs to be followed by **bíyyi'ka.**

Exercise 5J. i. Put each of the following Chickasaw sentences into the future by adding ±a'chi. Translate the new sentences you make up.

1. Ihooat malli. 2. Chipota tiik yammat chaaha. 3. Fani'at sasso. 4. Minkaat Chikashsha yamma̲ hoyo. 5. Ihoo yappat chipota passa̱a. 6. Kiichitha̱nataa? 7. Alikchaat hilha. 8. Issi' kiloonalhlhi. 9. Ishhopoo. 10. Oka' ishishko.

ii. Translate the following sentences into Chickasaw.

1. Will you kiss me tomorrow? 2. I will spank you. 3. Is the man going to hit that woman? 4. Might they look for us? 5. The child can walk. 6. Will you be jealous? 7. They may kiss me. 8. He may operate on you tomorrow. 9. We can feed the dog. 10. Can you speak Chickasaw? 11. They are going to pinch me! 12. I can tickle myself.

Terms and Concepts

OBJECT, PARTICIPANT, TWO-PLACE VERB, ONE-PLACE VERB, REFLEXIVE, FUTURE, AUXILIARY, MODIFY.

VOCABULARY

ayowa to pick, gather (a food plant) (A,Noun)
bashaffi to cut (usually, with a knife) (A,S)
bashli to operate on (A,S)
Chikashshanompa' Chickasaw language
chinoffi to pinch (A,S)
chompa to buy (A,Noun)
halalli to pull (A,S)
holisso book, paper, letter, document
holissochi to write (A,Noun)
hopoo to be jealous of (A,S)
hoppi to bury (A,S)
hotihna to count (A,S)
hoyo to look for (A,S)
ipita to feed (A,S)
isso to hit (A,S) (usually used with only singular subjects)
ishko to drink (A, S)

ishtalakchi' rope, leash
ithána to know (A,S)
ittihaalalli to marry, to get married to (A, S)
kamoshli to tickle (A,S)
kowi' cat
lohmi to hide (A,S)
nannabli to swallow (A,S)
nalhlhi to shoot (A,S)
oka' water
onnakma tomorrow
passáa to spank (A,S)
sakki to catch up with (A,S)
sho'ka to kiss (A,S)
tali' rock

There are several ways to say "Chickasaw" (referring to the language). The shortest way, **Chikashshanompa'**, is given in the vocabulary list above. Another way is **Chikashshimanompa'** or **Chikashsha imanompa'**, both of which mean "the Chickasaws' language".

READING AND SPEAKING

Talking about Ownership

Practice the following sentence pattern and try substituting other subject nouns in for the ones used here.

Talhpakat ammi'.	"The basket is mine."
Ofi'at ammi'.	"The dog is mine."
Ittaat ammi'.	"The stick is mine."

Now practice these three dialogues:

1.

—Talhpakat chimmi'?   "Is the basket yours?"
—Ii, talhpakat ammi'.   "Yes, the basket is mine."

2.

—Pintaat hachimmi'?   "Is the mouse yours (pl.)?"
—Ki'yo, pintaat pommi' ki'yo.   "No, the mouse is not ours."

3.

—Paskaat immi'?   "Is the bread his?"
—Ii, immi'.   "Yes, it's his."

Again, you can make up more dialogues by substituting other subject nouns in the same patterns. You'll learn more about how to use these patterns in unit 7. You'll also learn more about possessive expressions and negative sentences using **ki'yo** in unit 7.

A Story about Old Times

Read the Chickasaw story below out loud, then use the supplementary vocabulary and grammar notes at the end to help you figure out its meaning. Try to understand it before you read the English translation at the end of this unit.

Koshibba'

Sashkaat abokkoli' ayahminattook. Koshibba' ayowahminattook. Koshibba' ishtalahminattook. Koshibba' hopoonihminattook. Koshibba' holhponi' kiipahminattook.

SUPPLEMENTARY VOCABULARY

abokkoli' woods, thicket
aya to go to (a place) (irregular verb—see note 3 below)
holhponi', see **koshibba' holhponi'**
hopooni to cook (A,S)
ishtala to bring, to bring home (irregular verb—see note 3 below)
koshibba' poke salad, pokeweed
koshibba' holhponi' cooked poke salad
kiipa we eat (something) (form of **apa**, an irregular verb—see note 3 below)
sashki' my mother (**ishki'** means "his mother" or "her mother")

NOTES

1. The sentences in the story about "Koshibba'" are in the REMOTE HABITUAL tense, indicated by the ending **+hminattook** (sometimes pronounced **+hnattook**). Speakers use this tense to talk about regular occurrences or situations in a long-ago time remote from the present. HABITUAL events are not one-time occurrences, but things that happen regularly, as a normal part of life. The best English translation of a **+hminattook** verb often uses "would" or "used to": thus, **kiipahminattook** means "we would eat it" or "we used to eat it". You'll learn about the nonhabitual remote past in unit 13.

2. **Sashki'** "my mother" is a POSSESSED noun, like the brother and sister terms in the dialogues in this unit. You will learn about possessed nouns in unit 7.

3. Chickasaw has fewer IRREGULAR verbs than English, but there are some: **aya** "to go", **ishtala** "to bring", and **apa** "to eat (something)" are three very common ones. Irregular verbs do not follow the regular rules you have learned concerning how prefixes and endings are used, as you can see from the "we" form of **apa**, which is **kiipa** (or **iipa**), not <kilapa> as you might have expected. You will learn more about using irregular verbs in unit 11. For now, it's best not to try to use irregular verbs yourself, unless your teacher explains how they work.

More about poke salad. Poke salad (also called pokeweed; sometimes pronounced "pork salad") is a green plant that grows wild in Oklahoma. It is cooked and eaten like spinach or other greens. (Maybe you are familiar with the song "Poke Salad Annie.")

More stories about old times. Each remaining unit in this book will include a short reading about old times in the Chickasaw Nation. The stories in the units are presented in somewhat simplified language. The versions of the stories as originally told by Mrs. Willmond are included in appendix B at the end of this book.

BEYOND THE GRAMMAR: THE FIVE CIVILIZED TRIBES

The Chickasaws and Choctaws are two of the Five Civilized Tribes of Oklahoma. The other three of the Five Civilized Tribes are the Creeks and the Seminoles, people who speak Muskogean languages related to Chickasaw (see the Beyond the Grammar section of unit 3), and the Cherokees, people who are culturally somewhat similar to the other tribes but who speak a language of the Iroquoian family, unrelated to the Muskogean languages.

Members of all five tribes originally lived in the southeastern United States. Descendants of the pre-Columbian Mound Builder culture, they were large and important groups with their own systems of government who lived in desirable areas that many white people wanted to open for settlement after the end of the War of 1812. In what the ethnologist John R. Swanton has called "a disgusting and disgraceful chapter in our national life," members of these five tribes were forcibly removed by the federal government from the Southeast to Indian Territory, the area that is now Oklahoma, during the 1830s. So many hardships were endured by members of the five tribes during the removal that the journey is now referred to as the Trail of Tears: many people died, families were split up, and most of the Indians lost all the property they had had in their old homes.

Once in Indian Territory, the members of each of these five tribes were settled in their own Indian nations in the eastern half of the present state of Oklahoma: along with the Chickasaw Nation, which you read about in the Beyond the Grammar section of unit 2, there were Choctaw, Cherokee, Creek, and Seminole Nations, each with its own government. Because of their organized systems of government and because they had widely adopted the Christian religion, these five tribes became known as the Five Civilized Tribes, a name still frequently heard today.

Oklahoma has many different Indian groups, almost all of whom were forcibly resettled there at different times. Today, some people feel that the term "civilized" might cause resentment among other groups, and certain branches of the Oklahoma state government prefer to use the designation "Five Tribes," as more politically correct.

The history of the Five Civilized Tribes and other Indians of the Southeast, both before and after the removal to Oklahoma, is fascinating. A good source for beginning to learn more about it is Swanton's *The Indians of the Southeastern United States* (1946).

Story Translation

Poke Salad

My mother would go to the woods. She would gather poke salad. She would bring the poke salad home. She would cook the poke salad. We would eat the cooked poke salad.

Unit 6

More about Verb Structure

In this unit you'll learn about a number of ways Chickasaw verbs change their form: some add prefixes in a new way, some drop their final vowels before endings, and some change to show causative meaning.

Lesson 6.1 describes how a-verbs work with S prefixes, and lesson 6.2 explains how some verbs drop their final vowels before certain endings. Lesson 6.3 describes the formation and use of Chickasaw causative verbs. Lesson 6.4 is about three-place verbs, and lesson 6.5 presents more about object marking and word order.

Lesson 6.1:
A-Verbs

Here are some new verbs, listed as they are in the Chickasaw-English Vocabulary at the end of this book. Since these verbs start with **a**, we call them A-VERBS.

ayoppa to be happy (S)
abika to be sick (S)
akmi to be frozen (S)

apila to help (A,S)
afama to meet (A,S)

Exercise 6A. i. As the vocabulary entries show, the new verbs vary according to what markers are used with them. For each new verb, tell whether it is a one-place verb or a two-place verb and how its subject and object (if any) will be marked. Then give some other verb you have learned in an earlier unit that works the same way. The last one is done for you:

Example. afama "to meet" is a two-place verb that marks its subject with an A marker and its object with an S marker. Another two-place (A,S) verb is passáa "to spank".

ii. Translate the following:

1. You are helping him. 2. She was sick. 3. We are meeting the doctor. 4. They are happy. 5. I will help the woman. 6. The bread is frozen.

A-verbs with A prefixes. As you learned in lesson 4.3, an A prefix is always followed by a syllable break. Listen to your teacher say the following a-verbs with A prefixes:

Hash/a/fa/ma/tok.   "You all met him."
Il/a/pi/la.   "We help her."

Since the consonant at the end of the A prefixes is not part of the following syllable, the rhythmic pattern of words like these does not change when the A prefix is added. The same vowels are lengthened in each word.

a/fā/ma — ish/a/fā/ma — hash/a/fā/ma/tok
a/pī/la — hash/a/pī/la — il/a/pī/la

As you know, adding an S prefix to a word can change the rhythmic lengthening sequence of short syllables in that word, causing different vowels to be lengthened. Adding an A prefix (or any ± marker) to a word never changes the word's rhythmic pattern of lengthened vowels. As you learned in lesson 4.3, however, when the syllable after an A prefix starts with a vowel and is not itself a heavy syllable, as in these words, a speaker may emphasize or slightly lengthen the pronunciation of the final consonant of the A prefix, so that **Ishafama** might sound like <ishshafāma>. Try to imitate your teacher's pronunciation.

Exercise 6B. Translate the following sentences into English.
1. Hooafamatok. 2. Ofi'at abikataa? 3. Alikchaat ayoppatok. 4. Ihoo yappa ishapilataam? 5. Chipotaat hooabikatok. 6. Hashapilataa? 7. Kilooafama. 8. Minko' yammat ayoppa'chi. 9. Chikashsha ishapilatok. 10. Hattak kilafama'ntaa?

A-verbs with S prefixes. Look at what happens when you use an S prefix with an a-verb:

Apopilatok.	"He helped us."
Achifamataam?	"Did he meet you?"
Asabika.	"I'm sick."
Apokmi.	"We are frozen."

As you can see from these examples, the S prefix goes after the **a** at the beginning of the verb—you have to split up **abika** "be sick", for instance, and put the S prefix **sa+** in between the initial **a** and the rest of the verb (**bika**). S-prefixes are always added after the initial **a** of an a-verb. Usually, adding an S prefix to an a-verb changes the verb's rhythmic pattern, but not always. Compare the following pairs of words, with and without S prefixes, as your teacher repeats them:

apīlatok — apōpilātok
afāmataa? — achīfamātaa?
abīka — asābika
akmi — apokmi

Try to practice saying each of these verbs with the S prefixes **sa+**, **chi+**, and **po+**.

The "you" plural S prefix **hachi+** and the inclusive triplural "we"/"us" S prefix **hapo+** are not used with a-verbs. Thus, a **chi+** prefix on an a-verb can show either a singular or plural "you", and a **po+** prefix on an a-verb shows all types of "we" or "us".

Exercise 6C. i. Translate each of the following Chickasaw sentences.

l. Apobika. 2. Achiyoppa. 3. Asapila. 4. Apofama. 5. Abika. 6. Achipila. 7. Apoyoppa. 8. Asafama. 9. Apopila. l0. Asayoppa.

ii. Now, translate each of the following sentences into Chickasaw.

l. He helps me. 2. She met us. 3. I am happy. 4. We are happy. 5. Will she meet us? 6. He helped us. 7. She will meet you. 8. Help me! 9. Are you sick? l0. He met me.

Practice saying each of the words in this exercise aloud.

Most a-verbs start with short **a**, but here are two with long **aa**:

> **aabi** to paint, smear (A,S)   **aabachi** to point at (A,S)

You hear the long **aa** in the plain verb and when the verb is used with an A marker:

> Ishaabitaam?   "Did you paint it?"
> Kilaabachītok.   "We pointed at it."

But with an S prefix, these verbs work just like a regular a-verb starting with short **a**:

> Asābitok.   "He painted me."
> Achībachītaam?   "Was she pointing at you?"

A-verbs with prefix combinations. The **a** at the beginning of an a-verb drops out when that verb has both an A and an S prefix:

> Hashpōfamātok.   "You all met us."
> Kiichīpila'chi.   "We will help you."

The same combinations of **ish±** or **hash±** plus **sa+** that you learned in lesson 5.4 are used with these verbs:

> Issāpila.   "You help me."
> Hassāfamātok.   "You all met me."

As you may have noticed, the rhythmic pattern of most a-verbs with A-S prefix combinations is different from what you might expect. Listen as your teacher says the words above, paying attention to the lengthened vowels.

The vowel of an S prefix is always lengthened when it's used on an a-verb that begins with a light **a** syllable. You should learn the following combinations of A plus S prefixes to use with two-place a-verbs that start this way:

> issā+   ishpō+   kiichī+   hassā+   hashpō+

Remember that the **hoo±** subject prefix isn't an A prefix—so the **a** at the beginning of an a-verb stays there after **hoo±**:

> Hooachīpilātok.   "They helped you."

Exercise 6D. Translate the following sentences into Chickasaw. Write all the lengthened vowels with macrons. Say each sentence aloud for your teacher.

1. Are you sick? 2. We might meet you. 3. They are happy. 4. Will you all help me? 5. He can help me. 6. I painted you. 7. We helped you. 8. Did I meet him? 9. They are frozen. 10. Did you help me? 11. They painted me. 12. You pointed at us.

Lesson 6.2:
Dropping Final Vowels in Verbs with Endings

Here are some more new verbs:

hosa to shoot at (A,S)
basha to be cut, to be operated on (S)
kamosha to be nauseated (S)
losa to be black (S)
nalha to be shot (S)

The final vowel drop rule. Listen as your teacher pronounces the following pairs of words (and be sure you can tell what they mean):

Losātaa? — Chilōstaa?	(not <chilosataa>!)
Hosa. — Hosli.	(not <hosali>!)
Bashātaam? — Sabāshtaam?	(not <sabashataam>!)
Nalhātok. — Ponālhtok.	(not <ponalhatok>!)

Each of the new verbs ends with **s**, **sh**, or **lh** plus a final vowel, and as you can see, these final vowels are dropped in some cases. The final vowels in the plain forms of these verbs are dropped whenever they come before the endings **+li**, **+tok**, **+taa**, or **+taam** and they are not lengthened by the rhythmic lengthening rule.

You might expect that "Are you black?" would be <chilōsataa?>. Instead, we say **Chilōstaa?** because the nonlengthened **a** is dropped between an **s** and the **+taa** ending. On the other hand, since **Losātaa?** "Is it black?" has the **a** at the end of the verb lengthened, that **a** will not drop. (When pronouncing these questions, did you remember to stress the last heavy syllable before **+taa**?) The verb **losa**, incidentally, is not generally used to mean that someone is a black person (for that, use **hattak losa'** "black person, African American").

The **ho** of **hosa** "to shoot at" is a heavy syllable, because it contains a nasal vowel. This means that the **a** of the following syllable can never be lengthened by the rhythmic lengthening rule, so this short **a** always drops before the endings **+li**, **+tok**, **+taa**, or **+taam**.

Hostaam? — Chihostaam?

Similarly, the second syllable of **kamosha** is lengthened, so it is a heavy syllable, which means that the short **a** of the last syllable of this verb will drop in a word like **kamoshtok**. However, when a prefix is added, it's the second vowel in a word like **sakamoshatok** that is lengthened. In that word the final **a** of the verb is lengthened too.

Kamōshtok. — Sakāmoshātok.

Here's a full statement of how this new vowel dropping rule works:

A NONLENGTHENED VOWEL AT THE END OF A VERB DROPS BETWEEN **s**, **sh**, OR **lh** AND ANY OF THE ENDINGS, **+li**, **+tok**, **+taa**, OR **+taam**, AS LONG AS THE **s**, **sh**, OR **lh** IS PRECEDED BY A VOWEL, **h**, OR **'**.

The last part of the rule explains why the vowels at the ends of the verbs in

Issotok.	He hit him.
Nalhlhili.	I shoot him.

do not drop. Even though the **o** of **isso** and the **i** of **nalhlhi** are not lengthened and they are between **s** and **+tok** and **lh** and **+li**, they do not drop, because neither the **s** of **isso** nor the **lh** of **nalhlhi** is preceded by a vowel or a vowel plus **h** or **'**.

Here are a few more new verbs:

aalhpí'sa to be right, to be correct, to do the right thing (A)
chokma'si to be pretty (S)
ilbashsha to be poor, pitiful (S)
kalakshi to be degraded (S)
nosi to be asleep, to fall asleep (S); to go to sleep, to sleep (A)

The new verbs are used in sentences like

Sakalakshitok.	I was degraded.
Chichokma'stok.	You were pretty.

As you can see, the final **i** in **kalakshi** does not drop before **+tok**, even though it is not lengthened and it follows a **sh**, because there is a consonant before that **sh** (a **k**). On the other hand, the final **i** of **chokma'si** does drop before **+tok**—it is not lengthened, and it is preceded by **'**. **Nosi** is a verb like **chokfiyammi** that uses A or S markers to show whether its action is controlled. With an S prefix, its final **i** will drop; otherwise, it remains (do you see why?):

Ishnositaam?	"Did you go to sleep?"
Chinostaam?	"Did you fall asleep?"

Exercise 6E. Translate the following sentences into Chickasaw. Write macrons over the lengthened vowels in your answers. Then read each of your sentences out loud, remembering to stress the last heavy syllable before the question endings **+taa** and **+taam** (if you like, you can write this stressed syllable with a double underline, but it is not required).

1. Was he operated on? 2. You shot at me. 3. Those men are poor. 4. We were degraded. 5. I was asleep. 6. I went to sleep. 7. You were right. 8. They are black. 9. You were shot. 10. She was pretty. 11. Are we poor? 12. I shot him.

Now, here are a few more new verbs:

ayoppánchi to like (A,S)　　　　　　**pilachi** to send (A,S)
aachi to say (A,Noun)　　　　　　　**kanchi** to sell (A,Noun)

Aachi and **kanchi** are like **holissochi** and the other (A,Noun) verbs discussed in lesson 5.3. The objects of these verbs can only be nouns, so they cannot be indicated with S prefixes. The object of **kanchi** can be any item you could sell. The kind of object you can use with **aachi** "to say" is a noun like **anompa** "word" or a direct quotation:

Anompa aachi.　　　　　　　　　　　"He is saying the word."
"Ihooat toyya," kilaachi.　　　　　　　"We say, 'The woman is climbing.'"

The ch/sh rule. Each of the new verbs ends with **chi**. Look at what happens when verbs like these come before **+li**, **+tok**, **+taa**, or **+taam** (and the **i** at the end is not lengthened):

Aashli.　　　　　　　　　　　　　　"I say it."
Aashtok.　　　　　　　　　　　　　　"He said it."
Pilāshtok.　　　　　　　　　　　　　"He sent it."
Pilāshli.　　　　　　　　　　　　　　"I send it."

Dropping the final vowel in these verbs is similar to what happens with verbs like **hosa** or **basha**, but in addition, the **ch** in each verb changes to **sh**. Just as before, the vowels can only be dropped if the syllable before them is heavy (and if those vowels would not be lengthened by the rhythmic lengthening rule):

Sapīlachītok.　　　　　　　　　　　　"He sent me (for instance, on an errand)."
Chipīlachīla'chi.　　　　　　　　　　　"I'll send you."

In examples like the last two, where the vowel at the end of the verb is lengthened, that vowel is not deleted and the **ch** does not become a **sh**.

Dropping a vowel with verbs that include nch. Now look at what happens with verbs like **ayoppánchi** or **kanchi** that end in a vowel plus **nch** plus a vowel:

Ayoppáshli.　　　　　　　　　　　　"I like her."
Achiyoppáshtok.　　　　　　　　　　"He liked you."
Kashli.　　　　　　　　　　　　　　"I am selling it."

The next-to-last syllable in a verb like this is always heavy, so the verb's final vowel always drops before **+li**, **+tok**, **+taa**, or **+taam**. When the vowel drops, as you know, the **ch** before it turns into **sh**. Something else happens too: the vowel plus **n** before the **ch** becomes a nasal vowel, so in these verbs, **anchi** becomes **ash** before **+li**, **+tok**, **+taam**, or **+taa**. Similarly, **inchi** can become **ish** and **onchi** can beome **osh**. Since the **á** of **ayoppánchi** is accented, the accent remains on this vowel when it becomes nasal in a word like **ayoppáshli**.

More about dropping vowels. Listen to your teacher say these sentences.

Kashlītok.	I sold it.
Aalhpí'slītaa?	Am I right?
Hoslītaam?	Did I shoot at him?

These words follow the final vowel drop rule: the last vowel of each verb drops just as you'd expect before **+li**. But these verbs have another ending (**+tok**, **+taa**, or **+taam**) after **+li**, and, as you can hear, the vowel of the **+li** suffix is lengthened.

It's easy to see what happens if you count short syllables in the rhythmic lengthening sequences in each word:

kan/chɨ/lī/tok	aalh/pí'/sɐ/lī/taa	ho/sɐ/lī/taam
1 2	1 2	1 2

The original forms of these words, before vowels drop and other changes occur, are given above, but the vowels that drop are written with a line through them. Counting the short syllables in the original forms of these words, you can see that, indeed, the vowels that drop are odd numbered, so they don't lengthen. But these odd-numbered short syllables still count as the first syllables of rhythmic lengthening sequences, so the **li** syllables that follow these syllables are even numbered and their vowels are lengthened.

Here is a summary of the changes you have learned about in this lesson. The symbol "V" is used to represent any vowel, and "<u>V</u>" a nasal vowel:

- Verbs with a heavy next-to-last syllable ending in a vowel, **h**, or **'** followed by **sV**, **shV**, or **lhV** drop their final vowel before **+li**, **+tok**, **+taa**, or **+taam**.
- Verbs with a heavy next-to-last syllable ending in a vowel, **h**, or **'** followed by **chV** drop their final vowel and change the preceding **ch** to **sh** before **+li**, **+tok**, **+taa**, or **+taam**.
- Verbs that end in **V**nch**V** change the **V**nch**V** to **<u>V</u>sh** before **+li**, **+tok**, **+taa**, or **+taam**.
- The **i** of a **+li** ending that follows a dropped vowel is lengthened before **+tok**, **+taa**, or **+taam**.

Remember, vowels only drop if they would not be lengthened by the rhythmic lengthening rule.

Exercise 6F. i. Pronounce each of the following sentences, then translate it into English.

1. Issahosa. 2. Chibasha. 3. Apoyoppánchi. 4. Pilachi. 5. Kilaachi. 6. Hashkanchi. 7. Ishisso. 8. Basha. 9. Hachipilachi. 10. Salosa. 11. Polbashsha. 12. Iinosi. 13. Hashaalhpí'sa. 14. Losa.

ii. Add **+tok** to each of the sentences in 1 (drop the last vowel of the verb, if necessary). Pronounce the new sentences and then translate them.

iii. Add **+taam** to each of the sentences in 1 (watch the final vowels). Translate them. Where does the stress go in the question verbs? Say each one out loud, using question intonation.

Lesson 6.3:
Causative Verbs

The causative ending. **+Chi** is an ending that is used to form new verbs. Here are some **+chi** verbs and the shorter verbs from which they were made:

abika to be sick	**abikachi** to make (someone) sick
homma to be red	**hommachi** to make (someone or something) red, to redden

hilha to dance	**hilhachi** to make (someone) dance
omba to rain	**ombachi** to make it rain
yopi to swim, bathe	**yopichi** to bathe (someone)

As the examples show, when you add **+chi** to a verb, the new verb you form adds "make" to the meaning of the old one. New verbs like these are called CAUSATIVE verbs. (**Yopichi** shows that "make" may not always be part of the translation.)

Verbs with **+chi** have an additional participant not involved in the event named by the original verb, as you can see by comparing the following examples:

Hilha.	"He dances."
Hilhachi.	"She makes him dance."

In the first sentence there is only one participant, the dancer. In the second there is an additional participant, the one who makes the dancer dance.

+Chi verbs are very common in Chickasaw, and you can add **+chi** to just about any Chickasaw verb to come up with a new idea that people will understand. However, some verbs are more often used with **+chi** than others. It is more usual to add **+chi** to one-place verbs than to two-place verbs, for instance, and certain verbs usually form their causative in other ways rather than with **+chi.**

Just as with other verbs ending in **chi**, the final vowel of these new **+chi** verbs may drop before the endings **+taam**, **+taa**, **+tok**, or **+li**. This vowel drops in a causative verb when the previous syllable is heavy, as in these examples:

Losashtok.	"He made it black."
Hilhashtok.	"She made him dance."
Hommachitok.	"He made it red.", "He reddened it."

Exercise 6G. i. Add **+chi** to each of the following verbs and tell what the new verbs mean.
    l. nowa 2. chokma 3. tohbi 4. ithána 5. ittihaalalli 6. nosi 7. palhki 8. konta 9. lakna 10. ayoppa.
    ii. Add **+tok** to each of the new verbs in part i, dropping final **i** and changing **ch** to **sh** where necessary. Say all the **+tok** forms aloud.

Some verbs use the ending **+chichi** instead of **+chi**. (This is IRREGULAR—these verbs don't follow the normal rules for use of prefixes and endings.) For example, here are the causative forms of **ishto** "to be big (singular subject)", **isso** "to hit", and **sho'ka** "to kiss":

    ishtochichi to make (someone or something singular) big
    issochichi to make (someone) hit
    sho'kachichi to make (someone) kiss

Since **ishto** refers only to the bigness of one subject, **ishtochichi** is only used to refer to making one thing big. Causative verbs are normally very regular in Chickasaw, but verbs that use the irregular ending **+chichi** are always listed in the vocabulary at the end of this book.

Causers and causees. A causative verb refers to someone (or something) causing the action or state of the original verb to occur. The CAUSER, the added participant who causes that action or state to occur, is the subject of the +**chi** verb. In the examples below, "I" is the causer in the first sentence and "you" and "we" are the causers in the next two. As these examples show, the causer is marked with an A prefix or ending:

Nowachilitok.	"I made him walk."
Ishhommachitaa?	"Are you making it red?"
Kiihilhashtok.	"We made him dance."

All +**chi** verbs have objects, corresponding to the CAUSEE, the person or thing who does the action or is in the state named by the original verb. The causees in the examples above are "him", "it", and "him"; the causees in the examples below are "me", "you", and "you":

Sahommachitok.	"He made me red."
Chinowachila'chi.	"I will make you walk."
Kiichihilhachitok.	"We made you dance."

There is no marker on the verb with a "him", "her", "it", or "they" causee object, of course. You use an S prefix to indicate other causee objects, regardless of whether the original verb would have had an S subject (as **homma** would) or an A subject (like **nowa**). As you'd expect, adding an S prefix can change the rhythmic pattern in the verb.

A +**chi** causative verb usually refers to someone making someone do something by physical force, often by physically manipulating the causee object.

Exercise 6H. Consider the situation described by the following Chickasaw sentences:

Example. Nanna aashtok. Nowalitok. "He said something. I walked."

(**Nanna** means "something.") Now, suppose that as part of what this person ("he") said, he actually forced me to walk. Then the situation could be described as follows:

Answer. Sanowachitok. "He made me walk."

Rewrite each of the following pairs of statements in the same way, assuming that in each case the first person not only said something but physically caused the second action. The subject of **aachi** "say" is the causer (the subject of the new +**chi** verb you'll use), and the subject of the second verb is the causee, the object (marked with an S prefix) of the new +**chi** verb. (Don't forget the irregular +**chichi** verbs introduced above.) Translate your answers into English.

l. Nanna ishaashtok. Kiimallitok. 2. Minkaat nanna aashtaa? Chihommataa? 3. Nanna kilaacha'chi. Lakna'chi. 4. Nanna aashlitok. Hashnowatok. 5. Nanna aachi. Ishsho'ka. 6. Nanna ishaashtok. Asayoppatok. 7. Nanna kilaashtaam? Achibikataam? 8. Nanna aashli. Hashisso. 9. Nanna ishaashtaam? Lhinkotaam?

Lesson 6.4:
Three-Place Verbs

Causatives formed from two-place verbs. You have just learned that an S prefix on a +**chi** causative verb can indicate the causee who is made to do something, the person who would have been the subject of the original verb. Thus, the **sa+** of

Sano̲wachitok.   "He made me walk."

indicates that "I" am the one who is caused to do something, "I" was made to walk. Similarly, the **sa+** of

Sassochishtok.

can mean that I was the one who was made to hit someone—so this sentence can be translated "She made me hit him."

However, this sentence can have another meaning—"She made him hit me." So an S prefix on a **+chi** form of an original two-place verb can refer either to the ORIGINAL OBJECT of the action that is caused to occur or (as we saw already) to the subject of that action. Thus, in **Sassochishtok** the prefix **sa+** can represent either the causee or the original object.

A sentence containing a causative of an original two-place verb in fact has two objects—the original object of the two-place verb and the new causee object, the one who performs the action of the original verb. In the examples you have seen so far, the two objects of causatives of original two-place verbs have been indicated by S prefixes or by understood nouns. Here are some example sentences using real noun words:

Alikchaat minko'a̲ ihoo   "The doctor made the chief kiss the woman."
  sho̲'kachishtok.
Hattaka̲ ofi' ishissochishtaam?   "Did you make the man hit the dog?"

As you see, in these sentences the noun that tells who did the action of the original verb comes before the noun that names the object of the original verb. This is the usual order you will hear people use, although the other order is not wrong, and you can use either one.

As you've learned, the object ending ±a̲ does not have to be used on all object nouns. However, in a sentence with two noun objects, you always need to put an ±a̲ ending on the first of the two objects, as in the two examples above.

Exercise 6I. Translate each of the following Chickasaw sentences into English:
  1. Ishpossochishtaam? 2. Ihooat chipota̲ hattak sho̲'kachicha'chi. 3. Oka' sashkochishtok. 4. Alikchaat minko'a̲ sasho̲'kachishtok. 5. Ofi' chissochishla'ni. 6. Chipota̲ yopishla'chi. 7. Foshi'a̲ ishanompolishtaam? 8. Asanompolishtok.

  Some of the sentences have more than one possible English translation, according to what you have just learned. Give another translation for those sentences.

Three-place verbs. A THREE-PLACE VERB is a verb with a subject and two objects. An example is **ipita** "to feed". You've seen this verb used with a subject (the person doing the feeding) and an object (the one fed), but you can also mention what is fed. As before, the ±a̲ ending goes on the first of these two objects.

Ihooat chipota̲ paska ipita.   "The woman is feeding the child bread."

Ipita is not a causative verb (it does not include **+chi**), but many three-place verbs are causative. When you form a **+chi** causative from an original one-place verb, you get a two-place verb: **no̲wa** "to walk" is a one-place verb, but **no̲wachi** "to make walk" is a two-place verb, with both a subject and an added object participant. When you form a causative from an original two-place verb, you get a three-place verb, since these **+chi**

verbs have a subject plus two different objects. You'll learn about more types of Chickasaw three-place verbs that are not causative beginning in lesson 8.1.

Causative verbs in the vocabulary. Most **+chi** causative verbs are not listed in the vocabulary, since their formation, use, and meaning are completely regular. Verbs that add **+chichi** are listed in the vocabulary. Here's an example:

issochichi to make hit (A,S,Noun)

The meaning "to make hit" is a short way of saying "to make (one object) hit (a second object)". We list the markers that can be used with this sort of three-place verb as (A,S,Noun). This means the verb may have an A marker to indicate its subject, an S marker to indicate one of its objects, and another object expressed with a noun word (Noun). Of course any of these three could simply be understood in a given conversational situation. As you saw earlier in this lesson, the S prefix can indicate either the first object, the one who is made to do something, or the second object, the one to whom something is done. So in a sense this causative verb (A,S,Noun) is short for (A,S,Noun *or* A,Noun,S). This is true of all three-place **+chi** verbs. See if you can figure out what the vocabulary entry for **sho'kachichi** is and check it in the vocabulary at the end of this unit.

There are no verbs listed in the vocabulary as (A,S,S) or, for that matter, (A,A) or (S,S). No Chickasaw verb can have two markers of the same set, so no verb can have both an A prefix and the A ending **+li**, and no verb (even one with two objects) can have two S prefixes. This means that it's not possible to say things like "He made me hit you" or "They made you all kiss us" with just one word in Chickasaw, since sentences like these would require one S prefix for the first object and another for the second. You will learn more about other restrictions on the number and type of markers that can occur on a single verb in later units.

A special note. Try making up some new causative verbs and see what your teacher thinks of them. However, don't try combining causative **+chi** with reflexive **ili+** on the same verb; most speakers don't feel this combination works well in Chickasaw.

Lesson 6.5:
More about Word Order and Object Marking

Here's a three-place verb sentence from lesson 6.4 that includes two noun objects:

Ihooat chipota paska ipita.   "The woman is feeding the child bread."

This sentence can have either object first. Most commonly, **chipota** would be first, because people are more interested in children than in bread. But the other order is not wrong. You could also say this the following way, and it would have the same meaning:

Ihooat paska chipota ipita.

It doesn't make sense to think about feeding a child to bread, so both versions of the sentence mean the same thing, no matter what order the objects come in. In both cases, as you learned earlier, the first of the two objects must include the ±a object marker.

Now, consider a different kind of example:

Ofi'a hattak ishissochishtaam?   "Did you make the man hit the dog?",
                                    "Did you make the dog hit the man?"

Hattaka ofi' ishissochishtaam?	"Did you make the man hit the dog?",
	"Did you make the dog hit the man?"

Here we have a sentence with a "you" subject (expressed with an A prefix on the three-place verb) and two noun objects. Again, there are two versions of the sentence, with the two objects in two different orders. In this example, however, either of the two objects could be the causee or the original object, so both versions of the sentence can have two translations. Speakers might tend to interpret the first noun as the causee (the hitter), but the other interpretation would also work. Once again, it is the first of the two objects that has the ±a ending.

Whenever there are two noun objects in a Chickasaw sentence, they can go in either order, regardless of their meaning or what kind of object they are. The object that is not immediately in front of the verb (in the examples above, the first object) must include an object marker, the ±a ending. The other object does not have an object marker—you don't get two ±a's in any sentence with just one verb.

In other words, the only place in the sentence where you can use an object without the ±a ending is right before the verb. This means that the following versions of the first example in this lesson are also good Chickasaw:

> Ihooat paska ipita chipota.
> Chipota ihooat paska ipita.
> Ihooat chipota ipita paska.
> Paska ihooat chipota ipita.

Be sure that you can explain all the parts of these sentences and how they follow the rule about the use of ±a.

Exercise 6J. Change each of the following sentences into a causative sentence by adding the causer in parentheses to the sentence (you will need to add **+chi**); remember vowel loss and the **ch/sh** rule. Translate the new sentences you make up.

Example. Foshi'at taloowa. ("I")

Answer. Foshi' taloowachili. "I make the bird sing."

1. Ihattakat abikatok. (ihoo) 2. Paskaat akmi. ("you") 3. Minkaat nita' hosa. ("we") 4. Ishhilha'chi. ("I") 5. Alikchaat chisho'ka. ("he")

Terms and Concepts

A-VERB, CAUSATIVE, CAUSER, CAUSEE, ORIGINAL OBJECT, THREE-PLACE VERB.

VOCABULARY

abika to be sick (S)
afama to meet (A,S)
akmi to be frozen (S)
anompa word; language
apila to help (A,S)
ayoppa to be happy (S)
ayoppánchi to like (A,S)
aabachi to point at (A,S)
aabi to paint, smear (A,S)

aachi to say (A,Noun)

aalhpí'sa to be right, to be correct, to do the right thing (A)

basha to be cut, to be operated on (S)

chokma'si to be pretty (S)

hattak losa' black person, African American

h‗osa to shoot at (A,S)

ilbashsha to be poor, pitiful (S)

ipita to feed (something) to (someone) (A,S,Noun)

issochichi to make hit (A,S,noun)

ishtochichi to make (someone or something singular) big (A,S)

kalakshi to be degraded (S)

kanchi to sell (A,Noun)

losa to be black (S)

nalha to be shot (S)

nanna something

nosi to fall asleep, to be asleep (S); to go to sleep, to sleep (A)

pilachi to send (A,S)

sh‗o'kachichi to make kiss (A,S,Noun)

yopi to swim, bathe (A)

Remember, most causative verbs aren't listed in the vocabulary, either here or at the end of the book, because they are formed regularly and have the expected "make . . ." meaning.

READING AND SPEAKING

Nani' Hoot Aya! (Go Fish!)

You can play the card game Go Fish in Chickasaw with an ordinary deck of cards. (If you're not familiar with the game, you can find the rules at http://en.wikipedia.org/wiki/Go_Fish.) To start with, here are the names of the cards:

holhtina' chaffa	ace
holhtina' toklo	two
holhtina' tochchí'na	three
holhtina' oshta	four
holhtina' talhlhá'pi	five
holhtina' hanná'li	six
holhtina' ontoklo	seven
holhtina' ontochchí'na	eight
holhtina' chakká'li	nine
holhtina' pokoli	ten
minko' oshi'	jack
minko' imihoo	queen
minko'	king

The numbers here are the same as those in unit 3, except that **pokoli** is used instead of **pokkó'li** "ten". (You'll learn another way to use the word **pokoli** in unit 11.)

Next, here are questions and answers you can use in playing the game.

Holhtina' talhlhá'pi toklo i̱'shli.	"I have a pair of fives."
Holhtina' oshta ishi̱'shtaa?	"Do you have a four?"
I̱i, i̱'shli.	"Yes, I do."
Ki'yo, iksamiksho.	"No, I don't."
Nani' hoot aya!	"Go fish!"
I̱'shli, yappa!	"I got it, here it is!"

Here's the new vocabulary:

holhtina' number
hoot aya! go look for it!
í'shi to hold, to have in one's hand (A,Noun)
nani' fish
yappa here it is (said when holding something out)

You'll learn more about verbs like **aya** and **iksamiksho** in units 11 and 12. For now, don't try to use them except in the sentences above.

A Story about Old Times

Below is another short reading about old times in the Chickasaw Nation, like the one at the end of unit 5. This story is simplified; the original story, as first told by Mrs. Willmond, is included in appendix B at the end of this book.

Read the Chickasaw story aloud. The supplementary vocabulary and grammar notes at the end will help you understand new words and sentence patterns. Try to understand the story before you read the English translation at the end of this unit.

Fani'

Hopaakikaashookano fani'at lawahminattook. Ankaat abokkoli' ayahminattook. Fani' abihminattook. Fani' ishtalahminattook. Sashkaat fani' anakshoolihminattook. Fani' hopoonihminattook. Fani' kiipahminatook.

SUPPLEMENTARY VOCABULARY

abi to kill (irregular verb—see note 3 below)
anakshooli to singe, burn the hair off (A,S)
anki' my father (**inki'** means "his father" or "her father")
hopaakikaashookano long ago
lawa to be many, to be numerous, for there to be a lot of (A)

NOTES

1. **Anki'** "my father" and **sashki'** "my mother" are both possessed nouns (they include prefixes that express the English word "my"), but as you can tell, they are formed differently. **Sashki'** (related to **ishki'** "his mother, her mother")

includes an S prefix, while **anki'** (related to **inki'** "his father, her father") includes a new kind of prefix called a D prefix, which you will learn about in lesson 7.3.

2. Like the sentences in the story in unit 5, the verbs here use the remote habitual ending **+hminattook**.

3. As noted following the story in unit 5, Chickasaw has some irregular verbs: **aya** "to go", **abi** "to kill", **ishtala** "to bring", and **apa** "to eat (something)", used here, are common ones. Irregular verbs do not follow the rules you have learned concerning how prefixes and endings are used, and it is best not to try using them until you learn more about how they work in unit 11.

More about eating squirrel. When a squirrel is prepared for cooking, its fur must first be singed off over a flame. Squirrel meat is usually prepared in a stew.

BEYOND THE GRAMMAR: THE ANCESTOR OF THE MUSKOGEAN LANGUAGES

Chickasaw and Choctaw are both languages belonging to the Muskogean family of American Indian languages, which also includes the languages Creek, Seminole, Mikasuki (or Miccosukee), Hitchiti, Alabama, and Koasati (or Coushatta).

A family is a group of related languages that are all descendents of a single ancestor language spoken long, long ago. The Muskogean languages all descend from a language known as Proto-Muskogean, which was spoken several thousand years ago. The Proto-Muskogean people who spoke this language must have lived in several neighboring villages, each of which probably had its own distinctive accent or way of speaking. Gradually, over a long period of time, the speech of these separate communities diverged so much that it was no longer possible to speak of one Proto-Muskogean language. The language had split into four distinct groups that became the ancestors of four modern groups of Muskogean languages. One branch of Proto-Muskogean became the ancestor of Chickasaw and Choctaw. Another was the ancestor of modern Creek and Seminole. A third was the ancestor of the Alabama and Koasati languages and also probably of the extinct language Apalachee. The last branch of Proto-Muskogean was the ancestor of Mikasuki and Hitchiti.

Every language has a history of development from an older ancestor form. The remote ancestor language from which English descends is called Proto-Indo-European. Just like Proto-Muskogean, Proto-Indo-European developed a number of distinct dialects that became separate languages. One of these descendants of Proto-Indo-European was Proto-Germanic, the more recent ancestor of English, and its close relatives, such as German, Dutch, and the Scandinavian languages.

Sometimes scholars are able to trace the development of a language back even further and find an earlier language from which a group of families descended. Many proposals have been made concerning earlier relationships of the Muskogean family, but none of these has yet been widely accepted.

Story Translation

Squirrel

Long ago there were a lot of squirrels. My father would go to the woods. He would kill squirrels. He would bring the squirrels home. My mother would singe the squirrels. She would cook the squirrels. We would eat squirrel.

Unit 7

Possession

In this unit you'll learn how possessive phrases like "my mother" or "the woman's book" are expressed in Chickasaw, either using the S prefixes you already know or with possessed forms of nouns, which are formed with the dative prefix **im±** and the new D prefixes. You'll also learn about one type of negative sentence.

Lesson 7.1 describes how S prefixes are used on possessed nouns. Lesson 7.2 presents negative sentences with **ki'yo**. Lesson 7.3 presents the dative prefix **im±** and the D prefixes, and lesson 7.4 explains the use of possessor nouns. Lesson 7.5 introduces possessive sentences containing forms of **immi'**. Words for relatives are described in lesson 7.6. Lesson 7.7 discusses some changes in nouns with dative prefixes, and lesson 7.8 shows how possessed forms of nouns are listed in the vocabulary.

Lesson 7.1: Possessive Expressions

When you use an English phrase like *my mother* or *the dog's leash*, you express POSSESSION—in these two expressions, or POSSESSIVE PHRASES, *mother* and *leash* are POSSESSED nouns, and *I* (shown by the word *my*) and *the dog* are POSSESSORS. In this unit you'll learn how to say things like "my mother" and "the dog's leash" in Chickasaw.

S possessive prefixes. Look at the different ways you can translate the word **ishki'** "mother" into English:

ishki'   "his mother", "her mother", "its mother", "their mother", "their mothers"

In Chickasaw it really doesn't make sense to think of a concept like "mother" without remembering that a mother must be possessed by someone. You already know that a verb with no added S or A prefix can be interpreted as having a "he", "she", "it", or "they" subject. Similarly, the noun **ishki'** can be interpreted as having a "his", "her", "its", or "their" possessor.

S prefixes can be used with nouns like **ishki'** to show different possessors:

sashki'	"my mother"
chishki'	"your mother"
poshki'	"our mother", "our mothers"
haposhki'	"our (inclusive triplural) mother", our (inclusive triplural) mothers"
hachishki'	"you all's mother", "you all's mothers"

The prefix **sa+** on **sashki'** tells you that the possessor is the person speaking. "My" is the possessive word corresponding to the subject word "I" and the object word "me", which, as you know, can both be indicated by **sa+**. Similarly, **chi+** indicates "your" in **chishki'**, **po+** indicates "our" in **poshki'**, and so on. As you can see, S prefixes in nouns like **ishki'** work just like S prefixes on i-verbs. If there is an **i** at the beginning of the word, you drop it off after any S prefix, so you say **sashi'**, never <saishki'>.

Like other Chickasaw nouns, these possessed nouns can be either singular or plural. It doesn't make sense for a person to have more than one mother, so **sashki'** and **chishki'** must be interpreted as singular. However, **hachishki'** can mean either "your mother" (if you're speaking to people with the same mother) or "your mothers" (if you're speaking to people with different mothers).

Many other Chickasaw nouns use S prefixes to show their possessors. Another example is **holhchifo** "name":

saholhchifo	"my name"
poholhchifo	"our name"
hachiholhchifo	"your (plural) name"

How would you say "your name" when talking to one person? What are some other English translations for the plain noun **holhchifo**?

Nouns that indicate their possessor with an S prefix are words for members of the family, parts of the body, or things closely associated with a person (such as "name"). Here are some more words that are used with S prefixes:

foni'	"bone"
holba'	"picture"
ilbak	"arm", "hand"
ishkin	"eye"
iyyi'	"leg", "foot"
nakfish	"younger sister (of a female)", "younger brother (of a male)"
nipi'	"flesh"

Each of these words is already in POSSESSED FORM, like **ishki'** and **holhchifo**. Nouns that are in possessed form express a relationship between the item named and another participant (the possessor). This means that each of these words can be interpreted on its own as having a "his", "her", "its", or "their" possessor or that they can be used with S prefixes. Thus, **foni'** can be translated "his bone", "her bone", "its bone", or "their bone"; "my bone" is **safoni'**; and so on. (An S prefix on **foni'** changes the rhythmic lengthening sequence, of course. "My bone" is pronounced **safōni'**, with a lengthened ō.) Any word that is in possessed form includes the idea of an associated possessor in its meaning. If there is no other prefix to tell you who the possessor is, then the possessor must be "his", "her", "its", "their", or a noun.

The S possessor used with **holba'** tells who the picture is of—thus, **saholba'** "my picture" is "a picture of me". You'll learn more about using **nakfish** and the other Chickasaw words for brothers and sisters in lesson 7.6.

Exercise 7A. Translate each of the following English possessive phrases into Chickasaw.
  1. my foot 2. your eye 3. our picture, a picture of us 4. his flesh 5. their eyes 6. you-all's arms 7. a picture of her 8. my mouth 9. our bones 10. my younger sister (a woman is talking)

Lesson 7.2:
Negative Sentences

Ki'yo means "no" in Chickasaw—you can use it to answer a question negatively, just as you can answer a question positively with **ii** "yes". In addition, **ki'yo** can be used at the end of almost any Chickasaw sentence to make it NEGATIVE or to deny that what it says is true. Here are some examples:

Chipass<u>á</u>ali.	"I am spanking you."
Chipass<u>á</u>ali ki'yo.	"I am not spanking you."
Sashkaat malli.	"My mother is jumping."
Sashkaat malli ki'yo.	"My mother is not jumping."
Chiholhchifoat Jim.	"Your name is Jim."
Chiholhchifoat Jim ki'yo.	"Your name is not Jim."

In these sentences, then, **ki'yo** means "not". **Ki'yo** goes after the verb in sentences like the first two that end in verbs. In identificational sentences with two nouns (like those you learned about in lesson 2.3), **ki'yo** goes after the second noun.

> *Exercise 7B.* Make each of the following sentences negative by adding **ki'yo**. Translate the sentences you make up.
> 1. Hachittibaapishi'at chokma'si. 2. Iyy<u>a</u> bashaffilitok. 3. Poholhchifo ith<u>á</u>na. 4. Sashkinat losatok. 5. Chishkaat hattak yamma sh<u>o</u>'ka. 6. Haponakfishat ishto. 7. Nipi'at homma. 8. Ihoo yappat chiholba' hoyotok. 9. Salbak ishisso. 10. Holhchifoat hoochokma'si.

Using **ki'yo** is not the most common way to make Chickasaw sentences negative, however, as you'll learn in unit 9.

Lesson 7.3:
The Dative Prefix and the D Prefixes

The dative prefix im±. Chickasaw words like **bashpo** "knife" that refer to ordinary objects that people own or to other items in the world don't work like **ishki'**.

As we've seen, a noun like **ishki'** "mother" expresses the idea of "his mother" or "her mother". This isn't true of a noun like "knife" or most other Chickasaw nouns, however, since these are not necessarily possessed. Unlike words like **ishki'**, these nouns are not always possessed and don't express relationships.

For a noun like **bashpo** to be used in a possessive phrase, it must be in possessed form. Possessed forms not only refer to an item in the world, such as a "knife" or a "mother", but also tell you something about the relationship of an additional participant (the possessor) and this noun. When you want to mention the owner of a noun like **bashpo**, you need to put it in possessed form, showing the involvement of an additional participant (the possessor) with that noun.

To put an ordinary noun like **bashpo** into possessed form, you need to add a special DATIVE prefix, **im±**, which creates a possessed form and shows the involvement of an extra participant with the noun.

imbashpo	"knife" (possessed form)

Imbashpo is a possessed form that, like **ishki'**, is interpreted as having a "his", "her", or "their" possessor.

imbashpo	"his knife", "her knife", "their knife"

(**Imbashpo** could also mean "its knife", but it's harder to think of how that interpretation would be used.)

Here's a table that shows how all this works:

noun	unpossessed form	possessed form	translation
"mother"	—	ishki'	"his mother" (etc.)
"knife"	bashpo	imbashpo	"his knife" (etc.)

There is no unpossessed form of "mother" in Chickasaw, but **bashpo** "knife" is unpossessed, because it is fine to talk about a knife without thinking about its possessor. "Mother" is **ishki'**, a possessed form that can be translated as "his mother", "her mother", or "its mother". The possessed form of "knife" is **imbashpo** (formed by adding a dative prefix to the unpossessed form), which can be translated as "his knife", "her knife", or (maybe!) "its knife". The translations of the possessed forms include a mention of the extra participant (the same way a plain verb with no added markers can be translated with a "he", "she" or "it" subject).

D prefixes. Here's a complete list of words for different people's knives:

ambashpo	"my knife"
chimbashpo	"your knife"
pombashpo	"our knife"
hapombashpo	"our (inclusive triplural) knife"
hachimbashpo	"your (plural) knife"

These words contain the new D prefixes **a+**, **chi+**, **po+**, **hapo+**, and **hachi+**. These prefixes aren't hard to learn, since—except for the "my" prefix—they are just like the S prefixes you already know. (Remember that **hapombashpo** refers to a special "our" that includes at least three people, including the hearer.) In the examples above, the D prefixes are added to the possessed form **imbashpo**. Since that possessed form begins with an **i**, the **i** drops after the D prefixes, the same way the **i** of an i-verb drops after an S prefix (unit 3). D prefixes are only used before the dative prefix **im±**. Thus, the D-plus-dative prefix combination forms a unit within a possessed form.

Unlike S prefixes, the dative prefix and D-plus-dative prefix combinations usually show ownership of ordinary objects that can be acquired or given away, such as **oka'** "water", **issi'** "deer", **itti'** "stick", **ofi'** "dog", and **pinti'** "mouse". Most Chickasaw nouns have a dative prefix in their possessed form, with additional possessors shown with D prefixes:

imoka'	"his water"
amissi'	"my deer"
chimitti'	"your stick"
pomofi'	"our dog"
hachimpinti'	"you guys's mouse"

*Pronouncing words with **im±** and D prefixes.* Listen as your teacher says the following possessed nouns aloud:

imofi'	"her dog"
chimoka'	"your water"
pomihoo	"our wives"

Like A prefixes, the dative prefix and the D-plus-dative combinations are ± prefixes; they are not broken between syllables, and adding the dative prefix to a word doesn't result in new lengthened vowels. The syllable divisions in the three words above go like this:

im/o/fi'   chim/o/ka'   pom/i/hoo

When you count short syllables to determine which vowels will be rhythmically lengthened, the presence of a dative prefix on the word makes no difference to the syllable count. You don't lengthen the vowel after a dative prefix. In fact a dative prefix or a D-plus-dative prefix combination on a word whose first syllable consists of a single short vowel may have its **m** emphasized or almost doubled (just as the final consonant of an A prefix can be, as you learned in lesson 4.3). Thus, **imofi'** might sound almost like <immofi'>. Listen to the way your teacher says these words.

Exercise 7C. i. Pronounce each of the Chickasaw possessed nouns below and then give two or more translations for each one:
    1. ilbak. 2. imoka'. 3. iyyi'. 4. imbashpo. 5. impaska. 6. holba'. 7. imihoo. 8. holhchifo.
    ii. Translate the following Chickasaw possessed nouns:
    1. ampaska. 2. pomitti'. 3. sashkin. 4. chimpinti'. 5. hachilbak. 6. pomoka'. 7. pomissi'. 8. amofi'.

The D prefixes **po+**, **hapo+**, and **hachi+** show that a possessed noun has a plural possessor ("our", regular or special, or plural "your"). These prefixes tell you that the possessor is plural, not that the possessed noun is plural. **Pombashpo** "our knife", for instance, is a knife, or knives, that we own. Just as with any Chickasaw noun, possessed nouns are usually interpreted as singular, but they may also be plural:

Pombashpo hoyotok.   "He looked for our knife.", "He looked for our knives."

*Changing the form of **im±** and the D-plus-dative prefixes.* The dative prefix and the D-plus-dative prefix combinations do not always end in **m**, although they always contain a nasal consonant or a nasal vowel (review these terms in unit 1, if necessary).

Before a word that starts with a vowel or with the consonants **p** or **b**, the dative prefix ends in **m** , as you just learned.

Before a word starting with **t**, **ch**, or **k**, you use a different form of the dative prefix, **in±**. This means that the D prefixes in such words will be followed by **n**, not **m**:

    antalhpak   "my basket"
    chinchow<u>a</u>ala'   "your cedar"
    inkoni   "her skunk"

You will probably hear that the **n**'s in these words are pronounced slightly differently from each other depending on the sounds that follow them, as discussed in lesson 1.4. Try to imitate your teacher's pronunciation.

> *Exercise 7D*. i. **Chokka'** means "house". How would you say "my house", "your house", "his house", "our house"?
>
> ii. Translate the following Chickasaw expressions into English and then say each one aloud.
>
> 1. pontali' 2. chinkowi' 3. haponchowaala' 4. intalhpak 5. anchipota 6. chinkoni 7. hachinchokka' 8. ponchipota (**inchipota** means "his child, her child"—just as in English, this expression is used to refer to a son or daughter).

Before words that begin with the nasal consonants **m** and **n**, the dative prefix is **i±** (with a nasal vowel):

iminko'	"his chief"
inita'	"her bear"
inannalhpooba'	"your animal"

When you add a D prefix to possessed forms that start with a nasal vowel, the **i** drops and the vowel of the D prefix becomes nasal. Thus, **a+** plus **i±** gives a "my" prefix combination **a±**, and so on:

aminko'	"my chief"
ponita'	"our bear"
chinannalhpooba'	"your animal"

A nasal vowel is also used in dative and D prefixes that come before nouns beginning with any consonant pronounced with a continuous flow of air out of the mouth—**f**, **h**, **s**, **sh**, **l**, **lh**, **w**, and **y**. Here are some examples:

fani' "squirrel"	afani' "my squirrel"
waaka' "cow"	powaaka' "our cow"
holisso "book"	iholisso "his book"

Relationship and body-part words with dative prefixes. In addition to tools, pets, and other objects, some words describing relationships and body parts also show their possessor with a dative prefix. An example is **imihoo** "wife", which is formed from **ihoo** "woman" with a dative prefix. As this word shows, translations often depend on what we know about the meaning of a word. **Imihoo** can be translated "his wife" or "their wives", but the translations "her wife" or "its wife" would be far less likely.

Although most body parts indicate their possessor with an S prefix, there are some that include a dative prefix in their possessed form. One example is **salakha'** "liver". In a possessed phrase, you use the dative prefix or a D-plus-dative combination. Thus, "his liver" is **isalakha'** and "my liver" is **asalakha'**.

Differences in meaning between dative and S prefixes. Sometimes you will see a dative or D-plus-dative combination on a noun that you know is usually used with S prefixes:

aholba'	"my picture"

Saholba' means "my picture" in the sense of "a picture of me". **Aholba'**, on the other hand, is used to refer to a picture that I own. Other similar examples involve words for parts of the body:

nipi'	"meat (of any kind)"
sanipi'	"my flesh (of my body)"
<u>a</u>nipi'	"my flesh (that I own)", "my meat"

Suppose you had a leg of some animal you planned to cook—you could call it **amiyyi'** "my leg". If you meant your own leg, you would say **sayyi'**.

Exercise 7E. i. Remember that when a dative prefix is used with **ihoo** "woman", the result, **imihoo**, means "wife". What do you think **<u>i</u>hattak** means?

    ii. **Naafokha** (or, for short, **naafka**) means "dress". How do you say "her dress"? "My dress"?

    iii. Translate the following into Chickasaw.

    1. my house 2. your squirrel 3. our child 4. your picture (that you own) 5. your picture (of you) 6. their dress (two ways) 7. our chief 8. your (pl.) meat 9. your liver 10. her bird 11. my eagle 12. our flesh (of our bodies)

Below is a chart of the three sets of Chickasaw markers you now know:

A	*S*	*D (used with dative* im±*)*
+li	sa+	a+
ish±	chi+	chi+
kii±, ii±, kil±, il±	po+	po+
kiloo±, iloo±	hapo+	hapo+
hash±	hachi+	hachi+

Make sure you know what each line of the chart refers to (for instance, the first line contains the markers used by the speaker to refer to himself or herself—as "I", "me", or "my") and how they can be translated. Review the uses of each set of markers. Don't forget that the D prefixes are always used before the dative prefix **im±**, which also has the variant forms **in±** and **i±**.

Lesson 7.4:
Possessor Nouns

When you use a "his", "her", or "their" possessive word, you often want to name the possessor. This is done by putting the possessor noun directly in front of the possessed form of the possessed noun, as in the following examples:

minko' ishki'	"the chief's mother"
nita' foni'	"a bear's bone"
ofi' inchokka'	"the dog's house"
ihoo <u>i</u>naafka	"the woman's dress"

Possessed nouns like **ishki'** or **foni'** are always in possessed form (and take S prefixes). Other possessed nouns, like **inchokka'** and **<u>i</u>naafka**, have to include a dative prefix.

The possessor can even be a possessed noun itself:

sashki' imofi'	"my mother's dog"
sashki' imofi' inchokka'	"my mother's dog's house"

A noun phrase that contains both a possessor word and a possessed noun is called a possessive phrase. If you want to use a word like "this" or "that" with such an expression, it goes at the end:

ofi' inchokka' yamma	"that dog's house", "that house of the dog's"

The subject and object endings go at the very end of possessed noun phrases:

Sashki' imofi'at malili.	"My mother's dog is running."
Ofi' inchokka' yammat ishto.	"That house of the dog's is big."
Hattak inchipota passáatok.	"She spanked the man's child."

Exercise 7F. Translate each of the following sentences into English.
1. Sattibaapishi' ilbakat homma. 2. Chishki' holbaat chokma'si ki'yo. 3. Fani' inchokkaat itti'; kowi' inchokkaat talhpak. 4. Minko' imbashpaat losa. 5. Issi' holhchifoat Bambi. 6. Aholissaat chokma. 7. Hattak yammat ihoo imalikchi' ki'yo. 8. Salbakat chofata.
(Pronunciation note: in Chickasaw, a name like **Bambi** is pronounced with a final ' sound, and you may include the ' in the spelling of the word if you wish.)

Lesson 7.5:
Possessive Sentences with **Immi'**

Suppose you want to make a statement about who something belongs to—in English, you could say something like "That knife is mine" or "That is my knife". Chickasaw expressions of the first type use forms of the word **immi'** (which you saw examples of in the Reading and Speaking section of unit 6):

Bashpo yammat immi'.	"That knife is his.", "That knife is hers.", "That knife is theirs."
Bashpaat ammi'.	"The knife is mine."
Bashpo yappat chimmi'.	"This knife is yours."
Bashpaat pommi'.	"The knife is ours."
Bashpo yappat hachimmi'.	"This knife is you all's."
Bashpo yammat hapommi'	"That knife is ours (inclusive triplural)."

As you can see from the examples, the forms of the new word **immi'** "his, hers, theirs" change according to who the possessor is—**ammi'** means "mine", **chimmi'** means "yours", and so on. **Immi'** includes a dative prefix, and the other words are formed by adding the D prefixes you have just learned. You'll find it helpful to learn these new words.

Immi' is like a possessed noun, and as with any possessed noun, you may put the name of the possessor immediately before this word:

Bashpo yammat alikchi' immi'.   "That knife is the doctor's."

Exercise 7G. Change each of the following sentences containing a form of **immi'** to a sentence with a possessed noun with a dative prefix (and a D prefix if necessary), as in the example below. Translate both the original sentence and the new one.

Example. Issi' yammat ammi'. "That deer is mine."

Answer. Yammat amissi'. "That is my deer."

1. Ofi' yammat pommi'. 2. Itti' yappat chimmi' ki'yo. 3. Pinti' yappat hachimmi'. 4. Ofi' yappat ammi'. 5. Bashpo yammat chimmi'. 6. Oka' yappat immi'. 7. Chokka' yammat sashki' immi'. 8. Yappat minko' immi'.

Now translate these sentences:

9. Ihooat chimihoo ki'yo. 10. Yammat hachimbashpo.

Lesson 7.6:
More Words for Relatives

A number of words referring to relatives are used only with a dative prefix or a D-plus-dative prefix combination. An example is **inki'** "father", which can also be interpreted as "his father", "her father", or "their father". To express other possessors, add a D prefix before the dative prefix **in±**: **anki'** is "my father", **chinki'** is "your father". Such words are similar to **ishki'** and **holhchifo** in that they are always in possessed form. The dative prefix in a word like **inki'** cannot be removed; there is no word <ki'>.

Other such dative prefix words are for brothers and sisters. You saw the word **nakfish**, which is used to say "younger brother" or "younger sister" in lesson 7.1. The meaning of the word is a bit more specific—it actually means "younger brother" (of a male) or "younger sister" (of a female). In other words, the interpretation of a word like **sanakfish** varies according to the sex of the person you hear using it—it means "my younger sister" if a woman is speaking, but "my younger brother" when used by a man. Similarly, **ihoo nakfish** means "the woman's younger sister", while **hattak nakfish** means "the man's younger brother". **Chinakfish** is how you say "your younger sister" if you're talking to a woman, but if you were talking to a man, this word would be interpreted as "your younger brother".

The corresponding term for the older sibling ("big brother" or "big sister") of the same sex is **intikba'**, which includes a dative prefix and is always in possessed form. **Chintikba'** means "your older brother" when you're talking to a man but "your older sister" when you're talking to a woman.

Two other words with dative prefixes are used to refer to siblings of the opposite sex, with no older/younger distinction. **Intiik** means "sister" (of a man), and **inakfi'** means "brother" (of a woman). Thus, **anakfi'** always means "my brother", but you would use this word only if you were a woman. **Chintiik** means "your sister" if you are talking to a man; in talking to a woman, you simply don't use this word.

All these terms can be used in exactly the same way to refer to first cousins, as well as to brothers and sisters. So a girl would call her younger female first cousin **sanakfish**, and so on.

The Chickasaw system of referring to brothers and sisters is complicated and very different from English. Some people do not use all these brother and sister terms in the way we have just described, and you should follow your teacher's usage. If you are unsure of what word to use in some case, you can use the general word **ittibaapishi**, which means either "brother" or "sister" ("sibling", in other words). Sometimes this word has a religious connotation—it might be used among members of a church, for example.

Exercise 7H. i. One of the following expressions would be inappropriate for a woman to use—which one? Why? Translate each of the remaining expressions as if a woman was talking.

1. sanakfish 2. ạnakfi' 3. antikba' 4. antiik 5. sattibaapishi

ii. Change the prefix on each expression in i to a "your" prefix. Then tell what each expression would mean if addressed to a man. Some will be inappropriate—tell which ones and explain why.

iii. What, if anything, is wrong with the following possessive expressions?

1. ihoo intiik 2. chipota ittibaapishi 3. hattak nakni' ịnakfi'.

Translate any of these that are good Chickasaw and tell how to improve any that are wrong.

Lesson 7.7:
Changes in Nouns with Dative Prefixes

A few nouns change in unexpected ways when used with dative prefixes. For instance **abooha** means "house", but "his house" is **imambooha**. (Any time a dative prefix comes before a word that begins with a short vowel plus **b**, an **m** is added between the vowel and the **b**.) **Chokka'** and **abooha** both mean "house", incidentally, and can be used in many of the same ways. But **chokka'** can also mean "home", while **abooha** can be used to refer to other buildings or parts of buildings that house people—sometimes you will hear **abooha** translated simply as "building", other times as "room".

Dropping i plus a consonant. Words that start with **i** plus a double consonant or **i** plus **sh** plus another consonant, followed by at least two more syllables, have more than one pronunciation. Here are some examples:

ittibaapishi *or* tibaapishi	"brother, sister"
issoba *or* soba	"horse"
ishtalakchi' *or* shtalakchi'	"leash"

Ittibaapishi starts with an **i** plus two **t**'s and has three more syllables after that. **Issoba** "horse" has two **s**'s after the **i** and two more syllables. **Ishtalakchi'** "leash" has two consonants, **sh** and **t**, after the **i**, with three following syllables. The alternative forms of these words are made by dropping the initial **i**. If two different consonants remain at the beginning of the word after the **i** is dropped (as in **shtalakchi'**), nothing more is changed, but if the new, shorter word starts with a double consonant, that consonant becomes a single one.

Most words that have these alternative shorter pronunciations start with **i** plus a double consonant. If the two consonants after the **i** are different, the first one must be **sh**. In other words, there is no short way to say **imbashpo** or **ilbak**. Speakers use these shorter pronunciations often. Here's a surprising example:

Issathána. *or* Sathána.	"You know me."

This variation may seem confusing, since the short version **Sathána** also means "He knows me". However, in a particular situation the hearer will almost certainly know what the speaker means.

The part of the rule concerned with the number of syllables in such words is important, as you'll see if you compare the new words and their alternative pronunciations with shorter nouns like **issi'** "deer" or **itti'** "stick". Both these words start with **i** plus two consonants, but they don't have an alternative shorter form, because only one syllable follows these two consonants. In general you don't shorten a word if the result would be only one syllable long. (However, some speakers allow short forms of words that end in consonants. These people use **shkin** as an alternative pronunciation of **ishkin**, **tish** as an alternative pronunciation of **ittish** "medicine", and **sosh** as an alternative pronunciation of **issosh** "bug".) Now look at this new word:

itti'chanaa *or* ti'chanaa   "wagon"

"Wagon" comes from an expression meaning "rolling wood" and contains **itti'** "wood, stick", which by itself cannot shorten. But since the full word "wagon" has four syllables, the shorter alternative pronunciation is possible.

Words like **issi'**, **itti'**, and **ittish** add dative prefixes just as you have learned:

itti' "stick, wood"	imitti' "his stick, his wood"
issi' "deer"	chimissi' "your deer"
ittish "medicine"	amittish "my medicine"

However, possessed forms of the longer nouns that can drop their initial **i** are different:

issoba, soba "horse"	isoba "her horse"
ishtalakchi', shtalakchi' "leash"	ishtalakchi' "its leash"
itti'chanaa, ti'chanaa "wagon"	inti'chanaa "his wagon"

As the examples show, these nouns add the dative prefix not to the long form, but to the shorter alternative form. Most speakers feel that it is not good Chickasaw to say things like **amissoba**—for these speakers, "my horse" is always **asoba**. However, some people do say **amissoba**. You should follow your teacher's usage.

When adding a dative prefix to a noun that begins with **i** plus two consonants (either a double consonant or **sh** plus another consonant) plus two or more syllables, drop the **i** (and change any following double consonant to a single consonant) before adding the dative prefix. The dative prefix used is the appropriate one for the consonant the alternative form of the word starts with: a nasal vowel prefix before **s** or **sh** and an **n** form of the prefix before **t**, for instance.

Exercise 71. Translate each of the following possessive expressions with a Chickasaw sentence. Then say the same thing another way, as in the example, and translate. If there is an alternative pronunciation for a word in your new sentence, tell what it is. Practice saying each expression.

Example. Ihoo inti'chanaa'.

Answer. This means "It's the woman's wagon." Another way to say it is Itti'chanaa-at ihoo immi'. "The wagon is the woman's". Itti'chanaa can also be pronounced ti'chanaa.

1. Pomambooha. 2. Minko' isoba. 3. Ofi' ishtalakchi'. 4. Chinti'chanaa. 5. Alikchi' imambooha. 6. Ashtalakchi'. 7. Hachisoba. 8. Chimissosh.

Sometimes dative prefixes are not used when the possessor noun is not a person or animal. For instance, you can say **chokka' abooha** "the rooms of the house", but <chokka' imambooha> would sound wrong to most Chickasaw speakers. Another way of thinking about this is that the room is like a part of the house's body (an S possession relationship), while a dative possessed form like **imambooha** refers to ownership.

Lesson 7.8:
Possessed Forms in the Vocabulary

Most Chickasaw nouns can be made into possessed forms by adding a dative prefix. When you find a Chickasaw noun in the vocabulary, you can assume that it is used this way unless it is followed by the symbol (SP), which indicates that possession of this noun is expressed with S prefixes. Here is an example:

---

iyyi' foot, leg (SP)

Irregular dative prefix forms are listed in the vocabulary. The following vocabulary entry, for example, tells you that the dative possessed (DP) form of **abooha** is **imambooha**.

abooha house, building, room (DP = imambooha)

As you have learned, some nouns always have a dative prefix (they are always in possessed form) or change their meaning when they are used with a dative prefix. An example is **imihoo** "wife", in which a dative prefix is used on **ihoo** "woman". Such nouns are listed in the vocabulary in their dative prefix form along with their special meaning, as in

imihoo wife (DP)

When you see (DP) after the definition of a noun, you know that the **im±** or **in±** or **i±** at the beginning of that noun is a dative prefix. To express other possessors, you add a D prefix; thus, to make the "my" form, you add **a+** before the dative prefix **im±**:

amihoo   "my wife"

Sometimes the change in meaning is subtle. **Inchipota** means "her child" or "his child"; in other words, it refers to a son or daughter. Without the dative prefix, as you know, **chipota** still means "child", but it just refers to a young human being.

When the definition of a noun is followed by either SP or DP in its vocabulary entry, you know that it is a possessed noun. The vocabulary form of such nouns can always be translated with a possessive word ("her", "his", "its", or "their"). Thus, although **iyyi'** is translated as "foot, leg" in the sample entry above, since **iyyi'** is an SP word, you know that it can also mean "his foot", "her leg", "their legs", and so on. Similarly, although **imihoo** is translated as "wife", you know that it can be used to mean "his wife" or "their wives".

The short vocabulary in this book doesn't include all nouns, of course. Here are some general rules for deciding what prefix to use to indicate the possessor on a new noun. First, look at the noun word. If it already appears to include a dative prefix (as with **inki'** or **inakfi'**), then you can assume that the noun will express other possessors by adding D prefixes. Otherwise, think about the meaning of the noun. If it's a word for a body part or a family member, you should assume that it probably uses S prefixes. In all other cases, you should assume that it needs to add a dative prefix to make its possessed form and that other possessors will be expressed by adding D prefixes. You won't be right in every case, but you will be right most of the time.

> *Exercise 7J*. Write a vocabulary entry for each of the following words, using the principles described above. 1. bashpo 2. ishki' 3. ittibaapishi 4. naafokha 5. inakfi' 6. inki' 7. ihattak 8. chokka' 9. nipi' 10. nakfish 11. salakha' 12. itti'chanaa. Compare your vocabulary entries with the actual ones in the vocabulary below. Tell what the "my" form is for words 2, 3, 5, 6, 7, 9, and 10.

Terms and Concepts

POSSESSION, POSSESSIVE PHRASE, POSSESSOR, POSSESSED, POSSESSED FORM, NEGATIVE, DATIVE.

VOCABULARY

abooha house, building, room (DP = imambooha)
bashpo knife
chokka' house, home
foni' bone (SP)
holba' picture (of the possessor) (SP)
holhchifo name (SP)
ilbak arm, hand (SP)
imihoo wife (DP)
immi' his, hers, theirs (DP)
inchipota child (son or daughter) (DP)
inki' father (DP)
intikba' older sister (of a female), older brother (of a male) (DP)
intiik sister (of a male) (DP)
issoba horse
issosh bug, insect
ishki' mother (SP)
ishkin eye (SP)
itti'chanaa wagon
ittibaapishi brother, sister (SP)
ittish medicine
iyyi' leg, foot (SP)
ihattak husband (DP)
inakfi' brother (of a female) (DP)
ki'yo not
nakfish younger sister (of a female), younger brother (of a male) (SP)
naafokha, naafka dress
nipi' meat; flesh (SP)
salakha' liver (DP = isalakha')

NOTES

1. "DP" after a noun in possessed form identifies it as containing a dative prefix. To express "my", "your", or "our" forms, add a D prefix before the dative prefix.

"SP" after a noun in possessed form means that it takes S possessive prefixes.

You can make the possessed form of any noun not identified as DP or SP, or without a DP form in parentheses, by adding a dative prefix. This makes the word into a DP form; to express a different possessor, add the appropriate D prefix.

READING AND SPEAKING

A Story about Old Times

Below is another short reading about old times in the Chickasaw Nation. (This is a simplified version of Mrs. Willmond's first telling of the story, which you can read in appendix B.) Read the Chickasaw story aloud and use the supplementary vocabulary and grammar notes at the end to help you figure out the meaning. Try to understand the story before you read the English translation on the next page.

Aaittanaa'

Hopaakikaashookano Hattak Api' Hommaat lawahminattook. Aaittanaa' ayahminattook. Holisso Holitto'pa' ittimanompolihminattook. Chahta' iholisso ittimanompolihminattook. Aba' anompa ishtanompoli'at Chahta' imanompa' toshoolihminattook. Chahta' intaloowa'o taloowahminattook. Himmaka' nittakookano naahollo intaloowa' bíyyi'ka.

SUPPLEMENTARY VOCABULARY

aba' anompa ishtanompoli' preacher
aaittanaa' church
bíyyi'ka it's all (see note 3 below)
Hattak Api' Homma' Indian person
himmaka' nittakookano nowadays
Holisso Holitto'pa' Bible
ittimanompoli to read (A,Noun)
taloowa' song, hymn
toshooli to explain something in (a language), to translate (something) (A,Noun)

NOTES

1. Like the sentences in earlier readings, most of the verbs here use the remote habitual ending **+hminattook**.

2. As noted following the readings at the end of units 5 and 6, Chickasaw has some irregular verbs: **aya** "to go" is one of these. Irregular verbs do not follow the rules you have learned concerning how prefixes and endings are used. It is best not to try using irregular verbs until you learn about them in unit 11.

3. **Bíyyi'ka** is an unusual type of verb. When used after a noun, as in the last sentence above, it means "it's all" and is used to mention the only type of thing that is found in a situation; thus, **naahollo intaloowa' bíyyi'ka** means "it's all white people's songs".

More about possessive phrases. Chickasaw possessive phrases are sometimes translated without English possessives. Thus, **Chahta' iholisso** literally means "the Choctaws' book" (or "the Choctaw's book", but here the meaning is plural), but a better translation might be "the Choctaw book". Similarly, **Chahta' imanompa** means "the language of the Choctaws", but you can translate it simply as "Choctaw". **Chikashsha Iyaakni'** "the land of the Chickasaws" is used to mean "Chickasaw Nation".

Sometimes the D possessive prefix is omitted in such phrases; thus, the COMPOUND word **Chahtanompa** is another way to refer to the Choctaw language, just as the Chickasaw language may be called either **Chikashshanompa** or **Chikashsha imanompa**. (A compound is a single word formed of two separate words. Don't try to drop D prefixes on your own in such phrases—follow the patterns used by your teacher or other Chickasaw speakers.) Pronunciation of such words may change slightly; thus, many speakers say **Chikashshanompa'** or **Chahtanompa'** with a final ' that is not present in the simple word **anompa**. You will learn more about Chickasaw compound words in unit 18.

More about the story. As you will read in the Beyond the Grammar sections of this unit and unit 9, the Choctaw language was written down long before Chickasaw. The Bible was translated into Choctaw more than one hundred years ago, but only short passages have been translated, relatively recently, into Chickasaw. Consequently, even when a whole congregation natively spoke Chickasaw, they would hear the Bible and sermons in Choctaw and would sing hymns in Choctaw in church. For this reason, most Chickasaw speakers are familiar with Choctaw, though the reverse is not true.

Story Translation

Church

Long ago there were a lot of Indians. They would go to church. They would read the Bible. They would read the Choctaw book. The preacher would explain it in Choctaw. They would sing Choctaw hymns. Nowadays it's all white people's hymns.

Hooki' Pooki'

You probably know how to sing the Hokey Pokey song in English (if not, you can find the tune and words at http://www.niehs.nih.gov/kids/lyrics/hokey.htm). Below are the words to the **Hooki' Pooki'** in Chickasaw, with an English translation. Because Chickasaw words tend to be longer than English ones, you might have to add a few extra beats to fit the words to the music. Experiment and find the rhythm that sounds best to you.

Chilbaka oshtishwihli,	You put your hand out,
Chilbak ishfalammichi,	You bring your hand back,
Chilbaka oshtishwihli,	You put your hand out,
Kanihka ishilhko'cha'chi.	You're really gonna shake it.
Ishhilha Hooki' Pooki'a,	You dance the Hokey Pokey,
Ishilifilito'chi,	You turn yourself about,
Yappako ishyahmi!	You're doing this!
Chiyyi'a oshtishwihli,	You put your foot out,
Chiyyi' ishfalammichi,	You bring your foot back,
Chiyyi'a oshtishwihli,	You put your foot out,
Kanihka ishilhko'cha'chi.	You're really gonna shake it.
(chorus)	
Chishkobo' oshtishwihli,	You put your head out,
Chishkobo' ishfalammichi,	You bring your head back,
Chishkobo' oshtishwihli,	You put your head out,
Kanihka ishilhko'cha'chi.	You're really gonna shake it.
(chorus)	
Chihatipa oshtishwihli,	You put your backside out,
Chihatip ishfalammichi,	You bring your backside back,
Chihatipa oshtishwihli,	You put your backside out,
Kanihka ishilhko'cha'chi.	You're really gonna shake it.
(chorus)	
Ishnaakoot oshtishhi'kacha,	You yourself step forward and
Anowa' ishfalama'chi.	Then you're gonna go back.

Ishnaakoot oshtishhi'kacha,	You yourself step forward and
Kan<u>i</u>hk<u>a</u> ishilhko'la'chi.	You're really gonna shake.

(chorus)

You can make up more verses using other body parts if you like!

SUPPLEMENTARY VOCABULARY

an<u>o</u>wa' again

falama to return, go back (A)

falammichi to return (something), bring (something) back, take (something) back (A,S)

hatip hip; backside (SP)

Hooki' Pooki' Hokey Pokey

ilifilito'chi to turn (oneself) around (A)

ilhko'chi to shake (something), to move (something) (A,S)

ilhko'li to shake (oneself), move (oneself) (A)

ishkobo' head (SP)

ishnaakoot you (subject, contrastive—see note 2 below)

wihli to hold (something) out (A,S) (used with **osht±**—see note 1 below)

yahmi to do (A,Noun)

yappak<u>o</u> this (object, contrastive—see note 2 below)

NOTES

1. Many of the verbs in the song are used with **osht±**, which indicates that an action is done "that way". **Osht±** is a PREVERB, like a prefix, but it is added before any other prefixes. The **t** at the end of **osht±** drops before any other consonant. You'll learn more about using preverbs in units 13 and 19.

2. **Ishnaakoot** is a contrastive subject PRONOUN, used to emphasize a "you" subject with a verb that still has a "you" subject prefix. **Yappak<u>o</u>** is also a contrastive object form, of "this". You'll learn more about pronouns in unit 9.

BEYOND THE GRAMMAR: EARLIER STUDENTS OF CHOCTAW AND CHICKASAW

There have always been learners of Choctaw and Chickasaw, of course—each generation of Choctaw and Chickasaw children has learned these languages from their parents just as children always do.

In the days before white men began their exploration of North America and made their initial contacts with the Muskogeans, speakers of these and other neighboring languages often learned each others' languages, because of intermarriage and in order to make trade and travel easier. Such multilingual Indians later served as guides and translators for the earliest white explorers.

There are some very old records of the Chickasaw and Choctaw languages, but the earliest useful recordings were made in the nineteenth century. The most serious early students of Choctaw and Chickasaw were Christian missionaries, who wanted to learn the languages so that they could preach to the Indians and convert them. Such people often spent years living among the Indians, studying their language. Most of this missionary activity was concentrated on the Choctaws. Nineteenth-century missionaries developed a writing system for Choctaw that was very similar to the one used in this book. The most important of these missionaries was the Reverend Cyrus Byington, a Presbyterian minister. Byington was primarily responsible for translating the Bible into Choctaw and for translating some familiar hymns and writing others. (For more about this, see the Beyond the Grammar section of unit 10.) He also wrote a brief grammar of Choctaw, which was published in 1871, and an extensive dictionary, which was first published in 1915 and is still widely used by Choctaw people and linguists.

The most important other early scholar who contributed to our knowledge of the way Choctaw used to be spoken was Allen Wright, a native speaker of Choctaw who wrote another popular dictionary of the language. It was Wright who coined the name "Oklahoma", from the Choctaw words **oklah** "people" and **homma** "red", to refer to the "red people's" state. The corresponding Chickasaw phrase would mean "red town".

After the development of a standard writing system and publication of the Bible and dictionaries, the Choctaw language was used for a number of legal purposes in Indian Territory.

Because the early missionaries and other scholars concentrated on Choctaw, the Chickasaw language was never used for hymns or Bible translations, and, as you read in this unit, Chickasaw speakers relied on the Choctaw books for their religious services. Today, many Chickasaw speakers still feel that Choctaw is a written language, but Chickasaw is only a spoken one. Because of books like this one, *Chickasaw: An Analytical Dictionary* by Munro and Willmond, and the Humeses' *Chickasaw Dictionary* (see the Beyond the Grammar sections of units 1 and 10), however, this no longer is true—Chickasaw speakers can now learn to write their own language.

Unit 8

New Types of Verbs

In this unit you'll learn about how the dative prefix is used on verbs and about some other new types of Chickasaw verbs.

Dative prefixes are used to indicate both objects (lesson 8.1) and subjects (lesson 8.2); lesson 8.3 shows how these verbs are listed in the vocabulary, and lesson 8.4 explains how dative prefixes are used with S subject verbs. Lessons 8.5 and 8.6 show how Chickasaw verbs make the HN grade. Lesson 8.7 presents the **li** deletion rule.

Lesson 8.1:
Dative Prefixes on Verbs

As you learned in lesson 7.3, a dative prefix added to a noun puts it into the possessed form; thus, the possessed form of **tali'** "rock" is **intali'**. (The **in±** form of the dative prefix **im±** is used because **tali'** starts with a **t**; if you're not sure of how to choose the right dative prefix, review lesson 7.3.) Adding a dative prefix to a word usually shows that an additional participant is involved with that word. A noun with a dative prefix must have a possessor, so a noun like **intali'** "his rock, her rock, its rock, their rock" has two participants involved, the rock itself and the possessor.

Dative object prefixes. Dative prefixes are also used on Chickasaw verbs—again, to show the involvement of an additional participant with the action. In most cases this added participant is someone the action was done for. Thus, **hilha** means "dance" and **ihilha**, with a dative prefix, means "dance for"; **taloowa** is "sing" and **intaloowa** is "sing for", as in examples like

Ihilhatok.	"He danced for her."
Intaloowa'chi.	"She will sing for him."

(You learned about how to change the form of the dative prefix **im±** in lesson 7.3.) There are two participants in these sentences, the one performing the action of the verb and the person the action is performed for. The performer is the subject and the added participant is an object. Almost any Chickasaw verb can be used with a dative prefix that tells a "for" object, an additional participant. We call such objects D OBJECTS or dative objects to distinguish them from the objects you learned about in lesson 5.2, which we can call S OBJECTS. When an S object is "me", "you", "him", "her", "it", "us", or "them", it is marked with an S prefix. When a D object is one of these, it is marked with a D prefix before the dative prefix on the verb.

Adding a D object changes the number of participants the verb tells about. **Hilha** is a one-place verb; with the D object, **ihilha** is a two-place verb. Similarly, **taloowa** "sing" is a one-place verb and **intaloowa** "sing for" is a two-place verb. Noun subjects or objects can be used with dative object verbs, just as with any other two-place verb:

Alikchaat ihoo ihilhatok.	"The doctor danced for the woman."
Hattaka ihilhalitok.	"I danced for the man."
Ihooat intaloowa'chi.	"The woman will sing for him."

You can express other types of objects (like "for me", "for you", and "for us") by adding the same D prefixes you learned in lesson 7.3 in front of the dative prefix on the verb in sentences like those above. Here are some examples:

Ahilhatok.	"She danced for me."
Chintaloowala'chi.	"I will sing for you."
Hashpohilha'chi.	"You all will dance for us."

Again, see lesson 7.3 for a reminder about how to combine D prefixes with the dative prefix, especially before the consonants **f**, **h**, **s**, **sh**, **l**, **lh**, **m**, **n**, **w**, and **y**, where the D-plus-dative combination ends with a nasal vowel. The D-plus-dative combination **a±** in the first sentence tells you that the speaker is involved in the action. We know that this is a D object prefix, so this prefix adds the meaning "for me" to the sentence. In the second sentence the D-plus-dative combination **chin±** expresses the meanings "for" (from the included dative prefix) plus "you". The third example includes the D-plus-dative combination **po±**, meaning "for us". This example also has an A prefix, which tells its subject. A prefixes come before the dative prefix (or any D prefix) on a verb.

Adding the dative prefix **im±**, **in±**, or **i±** to a verb changes the verb so that it has a "for" object. With no added D prefix, that "for" object can be translated as "for him", "for her", "for it", or "for them". If you want to use a different "for" object, the D prefix goes before the dative prefix on the verb.

> *Exercise 8A.* Translate the following Chickasaw sentences, which have "for" objects expressed with dative or D-plus-dative prefixes.
> 1. Chihilhatok. 2. Hattakat hachihilha'chi. 3. Chimimpalitok. 4. Antaloowataa? 5. Hachiyaali. 6. Anowatok. 7. Foshi'at powakaatok. 8. Ankaat issoba anchompatok. 9. Ishintaloowatok. 10. Oka'at pombilatok.

Prefix combinations with D-plus-dative prefix combinations. When the A prefixes **ish±** and **hash±** come before the D prefix **a+** followed by the dative prefix, new prefix combinations are used, as in the following examples:

Issahilha'chitaa?	"Will you dance for me?"
Hassamanompola'ni.	"You all may speak for me."

In other words the **ish±** or **hash±** plus the D prefix **a+** becomes **issa+** or **hassa+**. These combine with the dative prefix to form the combinations **issam±**, **issan±**, or **issa±** and **hassam±**, **hassan±**, or **hassa±**. Learn these new prefix combinations. Another way to think of this is to notice that an extra **s** is added before the D prefix **a+** when an A prefix comes before it.

You learned in lesson 5.4 that the plural S prefixes **hachi+** and **hapo+** aren't used after A prefixes—**chi+** and **po+** are used instead. Similarly, the plural D prefixes **hachi+** and **hapo+** aren't used after an A prefix. Thus, **ha** is not used after an A prefix:

Kiichintaloowatok.	"We sang for you.", "We sang for you all."

"To" objects. A dative object is not always a "for" object. Another common translation for a dative object, especially with verbs referring to communication, uses the English word "to". In the sentences below either translation might be correct, but one is probably more appropriate in any given situation. With some verbs only one translation may seem right.

Chintaloowali.	"I sing for you." *or* "I sing to you."
Pomanompolitok.	"He talked for us." *or* "He talked to us."

Two- and three-place D object verbs. When you add a dative prefix to a one-place verb, you get a two-place verb. If you start with a two-place verb, adding a dative prefix gives you a three-place verb—for instance, **ishko** "to drink" is a two-place verb, but the dative prefix verb **imishko** is a three-place verb: it has a subject (the one who does the drinking) and two kinds of object, a D object (the one for whom something is drunk) and a noun object (the original object), which tells what is drunk:

Ishka oka' imishkotok.	"He drank the water for his mother."

In this sentence the subject is understood "he", the D object is **ishki'** "his mother", and the other object is **oka'** "water". Once again, adding the dative prefix to the original two-place verb **ishko** adds a participant involved in the action. To show a different object, add the appropriate D prefix before the dative prefix.

Here are some more examples of sentences with three-place D object verbs:

Hattak yammat ofi' ampilacha'chitaa?	"Will that man send the dog to me?"
Talhpak chihoyola'chi.	"I will look for the basket for you."

Three-place D object verbs can have two noun objects, too:

Talhpaka ihoo ihoyola'chi.	"I will look for the basket for the woman."

Just as you learned in lessons 5.6 and 6.5, the object noun that is not immediately before the verb must have the ±**a** object ending, but the two object nouns may come in either order.

Three-place verbs with two noun objects can often be interpreted in two ways:

Ihooa alikchi' ihoyola'chi.	"I will look for the woman for the doctor.", "I will look for the doctor for the woman."
Alikcha ihoo ihoyola'chi.	"I will look for the woman for the doctor.", "I will look for the doctor for the woman."

Each of the two sentences above can have either of the two translations given. Either of the two nouns can come first in the sentence, and, in both cases, both nouns can be interpreted as either the original object or the D object. In a given situation, the speaker's intended meaning will almost always be completely clear to the hearer.

Object prefixes with three-place D object verbs. You've already learned that a Chickasaw verb can never have more than two markers to indicate its subject and one object. Since the subject and D object of the new three-place verbs are specified with markers, you can't add another prefix to tell what the second object is. You can use A and S markers together, of course, on two-place verbs such as

Chihoyoli.	"I am looking for you."
Chipilachili.	"I am sending you."

but you can't add a dative object like "for him" to these sentences. We can say

Ihoyoli.	"I am looking for it for him."
Impilashli.	"I am sending it to him."

but there's no way to put "you" into these sentences in place of "it", because to do this you'd have to add another prefix.

No Chickasaw verb can have three markers, and, in fact, no Chickasaw verb can have both a dative prefix and an S prefix. This means that there's no way to say "I am looking for you for him" or "He is sending me to you" with one simple Chickasaw sentence. When there is a dative prefix (because you want to specify the addition of a "to" or "for" participant in the sentence), the only other kind of object you can put in the sentence is a noun.

Here's another way to say the same thing. You can only add a dative prefix to a two-place verb if that verb's object is a noun. The original object in a sentence with a three-place D object verb must be a noun and can never be indicated by a prefix.

Exercise 8B. Translate the following sentences into Chickasaw.

1. The woman sang for her husband. 2. I am crying for my dog. 3. The bird will not sing for the cat. 4. The child drank for the doctor. 5. Are you going to work for that man? 6. You sang for me. 7. I sent the woman to the chief. 8. Did you say the word to your younger sister? (Assume that you are talking to a woman.) 9. My mother could sing to the man's mother. 10. The child will not drink for us. 11. We sent the woman something. 12. She helped the child for me. 13. I will climb for you. 14. I am looking for the basket for you. 15. They run for us. l6. The woman will hit him for me.

Lesson 8.2:
D Subject Prefixes

As you learned in lesson 7.6, some nouns (such as **inki'** "father") always include a dative prefix. There are verbs like this, too. One example is **intakho'bi** "to be lazy". This verb always has a dative prefix; <takho'bi> is never used alone:

Ihooat intakho'bi.	"The woman is lazy."

In the next example, the D prefix **a+** is added before the dative prefix **in±** of the verb to show a reference to the speaker, the subject "I".

Antakho'bi.	"I am lazy."

Verbs like **intakho'bi** are D SUBJECT verbs (in contrast with the A and S subject verbs you've learned earlier). With verbs like this, the dative prefix does not express an added participant; there's no one else involved with the state of being lazy besides the person who is lazy.

Here are two more D subject verbs:

> **imilhlha** to be scared; to be wild
> **inchokmishto** to be healthy

Each includes a dative prefix, and both, like **intakho'bi**, cannot be used without the prefix. Many (but not all) D subject verbs are one-place stative verbs that refer to feelings or states that are not controlled.

Chokma "good" is a verb you already know that can be used with a D subject. As you learned in lesson 3.5, with an S prefix **chokma** means "be good", while with an A marker it means "do good". With a dative prefix, **inchokma** means "feel good". To express a different subject, add the appropriate D prefix before the dative prefix on the verb:

> Inchokmatok.   "He felt good."
> Anchokma.   "I feel good."

As you know, most verbs can only be used with one set of markers. **Chokma** is probably the only one-place verb that makes sense with subjects marked in three different ways.

The **hoo±** plural prefix comes before a dative prefix, as shown by the following:

> Hooinchokmishto.   "They are healthy."

Exercise 8C. Translate the following sentences into Chickasaw.
1. My father feels good. 2. Are you lazy? 3. She is healthy. 4. The bear is wild. 5. You all are really healthy. 6. You were not lazy. 7. We felt good. 8. My younger brother is scared. (Assume a man is talking.)

Lesson 8.3:
Dative Prefix Verbs in the Vocabulary

Verbs that take D subject prefixes are listed in the Chickasaw-English Vocabulary with the **im±**, **in±**, or **i±** dative prefix included, so you'll find them all in the **i**'s. Here are the vocabulary entries for the four D subject verbs you've just learned:

> **inchokma** to feel good (D)
> **intakho'bi** to be lazy (D)
> **imilhlha** to be scared; to be wild (D)
> **inchokmishto** to be healthy (D)

The (D) after each verb means that to show an "I", "you", or "we" subject, you must use an appropriate D prefix at the beginning of the verb.

D object verbs in the vocabulary are also listed with the dative prefix included. Vocabulary entries for some D object verbs we've just seen would look like the examples below. First, some two-place D object verbs:

imanompoli to talk to, to talk for (A,D)
ihilha to dance for (A,D)

The (A,D) after **imanompoli** and **ihilha** means that their subjects are shown with an A marker, while their objects are D objects. Next, some three-place D object verbs:

imishko to drink (something) for (A,D,Noun)
ihoyo to look for (someone or something) for (A,D,Noun)
impilachi to send (someone or something) to (A,D,Noun)

Each of the three-place verbs is followed by (A,D,Noun). This means that in addition to the A subject and the D "for" or "to" object, each verb may also have a noun object. Just as with D subject verbs, D object verbs can be used with D prefixes added before the dative prefix on the verb. Most D object verbs are not listed in the vocabulary, however, because they are completely regular. You can form many more D object verbs on your own.

Some verbs have an irregular form or an unexpected translation when used with a dative prefix (they don't follow the normal rules we've given). For example, **atobbi** means "to pay (something)". Its dative prefix form, **imaatobbi** "to pay (something) to" is listed in the vocabulary because the first vowel of the original verb turns into a long **aa** when the prefix **im±** is added:

Imaatobbili.   "I pay it to him."

Similarly, the dative prefix form of **aabachi** "to point at" will be listed in the vocabulary, because with a dative prefix this verb has a completely different meaning:

imaabachi to teach (A,D); to teach (a subject) to (A,D,Noun)

As you know, several of the D subject verbs you've learned are never used without their dative prefix. **Ihollo** "to love" is a two-place D object verb with an A subject and a D object, which, similarly, is never used without its dative prefix—<hollo> cannot be used on its own:

Chiholloli.   "I love you."

We do not list dative prefix verbs in the vocabulary unless they occur only in the dative prefix form (like **intakho'bi** or **ihollo**) or their meaning or form is unexpected. Remember, you can add a dative prefix to almost any verb to express a "to" or "for" object.

Exercise 8D. Translate the following sentences into Chickasaw.
  1. The doctor will not send the book to me. 2. I kissed the woman for the chief. 3. We are really lazy. 4. Do you love that woman? 5. Did you all send me the mouse? 6. You really love me. 7. I will speak to you. 8. You danced for the chief. 9. Hit him for me! 10. We say it to him. 11. Did you pay it to me? 12. That woman teaches me Chickasaw (teaches Chickasaw to me).

Lesson 8.4:
D Objects with S
Subject Verbs

A D object (usually translated with "for", "to", "at", or "of") can be added to many verbs that normally take S subjects:

abika to be sick	**imambiika** to be sick for
issikopa to be mean	**imissikopa** to be mean to
hashaa to be angry	**ihashaa** to be angry at
hofahya to be ashamed	**ihofahya** to be ashamed of

Imambiika follows the **m** addition rule you learned in lesson 7.7 and contains an unexpected long vowel: we don't say <imambika>.

Occasionally, the meaning of the plain verb changes a bit when the dative prefix is added:

nokhánglo to be sad	**inokhánglo** to be sorry for
palhki to be fast	**impalhki** to be too fast for

In each of these cases, the dative prefix indicates an added object, so the new verbs are two-place verbs. Now, compare the following one place sentences with S subjects and two-place sentences with added D objects:

Asabikatok. "I was sick."	Imambiikalitok. "I was sick for him."
Chissikopa. "You are mean."	Issamissikopa. "You are mean to me."
Ponokhánglo. "We are sad."	Kilinokhánglo. "We are sorry for her."

When there is a D object in a sentence, the subject is indicated with an A marker. As you learned earlier, no Chickasaw verb can have both a D and an S prefix. So when you add a D object to a verb that normally is used with an S subject, you have to use an A marker for the subject, not an S prefix.

Another verb where you can add a D object and change an S to an A is **yimmi** "to believe, think so". **Yimmi** can also be either a one-place (S) verb, as you have learned, or a two-place (S,Noun) verb, with a nonhuman noun object:

Sayimmi.	"I think so."
Imanompa sayimmi.	"I believe his word."

You can use a human object with **yimmi** or say "believe in" with a D object:

Issayimmitaa?	"Do you believe me?"
Chihoowa iyimmili.	"I believe in God."
Iichiyimmitok.	"We believed in you."

More vocabulary entries. Adding a D object to an S subject verb is almost as regular and simple as adding a D object to an A subject verb—but not quite, because you have to remember to use A subjects with these new verbs. So all the new D object verbs formed from original S subject verbs are included in the vocabulary, following this example:

imambiika to be sick for (A,D)

Of course the (A,D) means that the subject of **imambiika** (the one who gets sick) is shown with an A marker, and the object (the one for whom this is done) with a D. With a few verbs a human subject wouldn't make sense, so their subject is specified as a noun:

imishto to be big for (singular subject) (Noun,D)

Exercise 8E. i. Write vocabulary entries for the new verb **hashaa** and for the new D object verbs **ihashaa, ihofahya, imissikopa, inokhánglo,** and **impalhki.**

ii. Change each of the following sentences by adding to it the D object given in parentheses. (The subjects should stay the same, although how they are specified may change.) Translate the new sentences you make.

Example. Sahashaa. (at you)

Answer. Chihashaali. I'm angry at you.

1. Sanokhánglotok. (for the chief) 2. Naafokha yappat ishto. (for my sister) 3. Achibikataam? (for me) 4. Hattak imofi'at issikopa. (to you all) 5. Chipalhki. (for us) 6. Hachihashaatok. (at her) 7. Sattibaapishiat abikatok. (for you) 8. Ponokhánglotok. (for you) 9. Chiyimmitaa? (in the chief) 10. Sassikopa'ntok. (to you)

Lesson 8.5:
The HN Grade

Here are some new verbs that you'll use in this lesson:

kiliha to growl (A)　　　　　　**kochcha** to go out of (A,Noun)
okshitta to close (A,Noun)　　**waaka** to be spotted (S)
tahli to finish (A,Noun)　　　　**ikbi** to make (A,S)

HN grades. You've already learned some Chickasaw verbs that have accents: **ithána, nokhánglo, passáa, ánta, ayoppánchi,** and **aalhpí'sa** and the number words in unit 3. These words, like all Chickasaw verbs with accents, are GRADE FORMS. The grade system is a series of processes by which Chickasaw verbs change in regular ways in order to express differences in meaning. In this lesson you'll learn how to make the HN grade from the BASIC (original, unaccented) form of a verb. Listen to your teacher say the following examples of verbs and their HN grade forms.

Basic verb	*HN grade form*
foyopa "to breathe"	foyohómpa
pilachi "to send"	pilahánchi
ipita "to feed"	ipihínta
kalakshi "to be degraded"	kalahánkshi
basha "to be operated on"	bahás̲ha
hilha "to dance"	hihíl̲ha
nosi "to sleep"	nohós̲i
hoyo "to look for"	hohóyo
afama "to meet"	afahám̲a

As you can see, HN grades get their name because they contain **h** (H) and a nasal (N) consonant or vowel.

The meaning of HN grade verbs. HN grades are used to refer to activities that are repeated or that someone keeps on doing; thus, **Talohówali** might be translated "I sing and sing" or "I keep singing". HN grade forms are often used with the auxiliary verb **bíyyi'ka**:

Talohówali bíyyi'katok.	"I sang all the time."
Chipassaháa bíyyi'ka.	"He spanks you all the time."
Chokoshkohómo bíyyi'ka'chi.	"She's going to play all the time."
Sahopohómba bíyyi'ka.	"I get hungry all the time."

The HN grade form, with subject and object markers attached, goes in front of **bíyyi'ka**. If you want to use an ending like **+tok**, **+taa**, or **±a'chi**, referring to the time or certainty of the whole sentence, it goes at the very end, after **bíyyi'ka**.

You will hear HN grades used in a variety of other ways if you listen to Chickasaw speakers. One thing you'll notice is that HN grades almost always refer to actions, not states. Thus, when you use the HN grade of a basically stative verb like **hopoba**, as in the last example above, the translation will probably refer to the action of "getting hungry" rather than to the state of "being hungry".

Forming HN grades. To make an HN grade, you have to change the next-to-last syllable of the basic verb. First, add **h** after the next-to-last vowel of the basic verb. (This vowel is called the CHANGING VOWEL.) Then, put an accented nasal copy of that vowel after the **h**. The form of this nasal copy depends on what follows the changing vowel in the basic verb. Look at the examples above. In some cases the added nasal copy is a nasal vowel, while in others the added vowel is followed by a nasal consonant (**m** or **n**).

If a **p** or a **b** follows the changing vowel, the added vowel must be followed by **m**—thus, **foyopa** adds **hóm** before the **p** to make the HN grade form **foyohómpa**. If the changing vowel is followed by **t** or **ch**, the added vowel must be followed by **n**—thus, **ipita** adds **hín** before the **t** to make the HN grade form **ipihínta**, and the HN grade of **pilachi** is **pilahánchi**. In most cases the same thing happens if the changing vowel is followed by **k**—so the HN grade of **kalakshi** is **kalahánkshi**.

If almost any other sound follows the changing vowel, the added accented vowel will be a nasal vowel. So you add **há** to **basha** to make the HN grade **bahásha**, **hí** to **hilha** to make the HN grade **hihílha**, **hó** to **nosi** to make **nohósi**, and so on. In each case the changing vowel is followed by **h** plus an accented nasal copy of that vowel. This happens whenever the changing vowel is followed by **f**, **s**, **sh**, **l**, **lh**, **w**, or **y** and also when this vowel is followed by a single **m**, **n**, or **h** or by **mm** or **nn**. (All this may sound like the rules for the form of dative prefixes that you learned in lessson 7.3. These same processes are used in several ways in Chickasaw.)

Exercise 8F. Make the HN grades of the following verbs. (Do you know what each verb means?)
1. palhki. 2. nalha. 3. bila. 4. hopoba. 5. toyya. 6. lhayita. 7. achokmilhka. 8. issikopa. 9. losa. 10. anompoli. 11. imaabachi. 12. tofa.

More about HN grade formation. A few types of verbs change slightly before making the HN grade. If the changing vowel of the basic verb is long, for example, you usually shorten it before following the rules above:

waaka "to be spotted"	wahánka
okaami "to wash one's face"	okahámi
hopooni "to cook"	hopohóni

Once in a while, however, a long changing vowel will stay long in the HN grade:

aabi "to paint"   aahámbi

Most HN grades are completely regular. Irregular HN grades like **aahámbi** are listed in the Chickasaw-English Vocabulary at the end of this book.

In most cases nothing happens if the changing vowel is followed by a doubled consonant. Thus, the HN grade of **kochcha** is **kohónchcha**, and the HN grade of **yimmi** is **yihími**. If the changing vowel is followed by **pp**, **bb**, **tt**, or **kk**, however, you shorten that doubled consonant before making the HN grade:

ayoppa "to be happy"   ayohómpa
okshitta "to close"   okshihínta
sakki "to catch up with"   sahánki

If the changing vowel is followed by **h** or **'** plus another consonant, you drop that **h** or **'** before following the rules above:

hofahya "to be embarrassed"   hofaháya
tahli "to finish"   taháli
tohbi "to be white"   tohómbi
aalhpí'sa "to be right"   aalhpihísa

Tohbi minus its **h** is <tobi>, with **b** after the changing vowel. When you make an HN grade from this form, you need to add **hóm** after this vowel. The HN grade **aalhpihísa** shows that an accented changing vowel is treated just like a plain one and that you can usually apply these rules even to other grade forms.

If the changing vowel is already nasal or if it's followed by **m** or **n** plus another consonant (other than a second **m** or **n**), a nasal is already there, so you don't need to add another one. The vowel before the **h** in the HN grade is a short, plain form of the changing vowel, and the same nasal vowel or vowel-plus-**m**-or-**n** that occurs in the basic verb comes after the **h**:

kiliha "to growl"   kilihíha
omba "to rain"   ohómba
konta "to whistle"   kohónta

This works even if you start with a grade form with an accented changing vowel. The HN grade of **ánta** is **ahánta**, and the HN grade of **ayoppánchi** is **ayoppahánchi**.

The HN grade of **sho'ka** follows the rules. The changing vowel is nasal already. But you have to drop the **'** in the HN grade, which means that that changing vowel will come before a **k**. Before **k** the added syllable of the HN grade must end in **n**, so this added syllable will be **hón**, and the HN grade is **shohónka**.

If the basic verb ends with a long vowel, the HN grade ends in a short version of this long vowel, plus **h**, plus an accented long nasal copy of the same vowel. For example, **yaa** ends in long **aa**. Its HN grade ends in short **a** plus **h** plus **áa**: **yaháa**. **Passáa**, which ends in a long nasal vowel, makes its HN grade similarly: **passaháa**. One way to think of what is happening here is to consider that in verbs of this type the changing vowel is the first part of the final long or long nasal vowel. Thus, the changing vowel of **yaa** is the first **a** of the final long **aa**, and the changing vowel of **passáa** is the **á**. **Hopoo** is somewhat irregular: its HN grade is **hopohówa**.

Finally, if the changing vowel is followed by **kb, kl, km, kn, kw**, or **ky**, the **nk** you'd expect in the HN grade turns into **ng**. Instead of <chohónkma> for the HN grade of **chokma**, you replace the **nk** with **ng**, so you say **chohóngma**. Similarly, the HN grade of **ikbi** is **ihíngbi**. Some speakers may not use **ng** in these forms, so you may hear HN grades like **chohónkma** or **ihínkbi**. Follow your teacher's usage.

Exercise 8G. Make the HN grades of each of the following verbs:
1. taloowa. 2. aachi. 3. atobbi. 4. tikahbi. 5. intakho'bi. 6. nalhlhi. 7. chonna. 8. impa. 9. wakaa. 10. lakna. 11. wiiki. 12. lohmi. 13. chompa. 14. holissochi. 15. i̱hollo. 16. ichchokwa. 17. **falaa** "to be long". 18. akmi.

Then put **bíyyi'ka** after each new HN grade and translate the sentences you make up.

Lesson 8.6: Using HN Grades

Basic forms and the HN grade. As you know, the HN grade is made from the basic form of the verb. The basic form of a verb is the one for which you could give a dictionary definition, including "to . . .", with information about subject and object markers, such as (D) or (A,S). Once you make an HN grade, you can add on endings such as **+li, +tok, +taa, ±a'chi**, and so on:

Anompohólili bíyyi'ka.	"I talk all the time."
Kilihíhatok.	"He growled all the time."

The basic form from which the HN grade verb **anompohólili** is made is **anompoli**, not **anompolili**. You can tell this because the changing vowel of **anompohólili** is the next-to-last vowel of **anompoli** (o), not the next-to-last vowel of **anompolili** (i). Similarly, the basic form from which the HN grade verb **kilihíhatok** is made is **kiliha**, not **kilihatok**—its changing vowel is **i̱**, not **a**.

A few prefixes and endings are included in the basic forms from which HN grades are made, however. Compare the next two sentences. The HN grade in the first is made from the basic form **losa** "to be black", while the second is from the causative basic form **losachi** "to make black". Unlike other endings, the causative ending **+chi** is included in the basic form from which the HN grade is made. The changing vowel of a causative verb is the vowel before the causative ending:

Lohósa bíyyi'ka.	"It gets black all the time."
Losahánchi bíyyi'ka.	"He makes it black all the time."

If a verb is very short and its next-to-last syllable includes an S prefix, the changing vowel is the vowel of the S prefix:

Sahásso bíyyi'ka. "He hits me all the time."

Lengthened vowels in HN grades. Compare the following words:

Basic verbs	*HN grades*
ho/pō/ba	ho/po/hóm/ba *or* hop/o/hom/ba
a/fā/ma	a/fa/há/ma *or* af/a/há/ma

---

i/pī/ta   i/pi/hín/ta *or* ip/i/hín/ta
sa/bī/la   sa/bi/hí̱/la *or* sab/i/hí̱/la
chi/nō/si   chi/no/hó̱/si *or* chin/o/hó̱/si

(Do you know what each verb means?) The basic verbs all contain lengthened vowels, but the corresponding vowels are not lengthened in the HN grades. The changing vowel of an HN grade is never lengthened. In fact, in words like those above, in which the syllable before the changing vowel is light, it may sound as if the consonant before the changing vowel has moved over into the preceding syllable, as shown in the alternative syllable divisions above. When this happens, you may hear the consonant before the changing vowel as slightly emphasized or lengthened—so **hopohómba** might sound like <hoppohómba> to you. Listen to your teacher and see what you think.

This fact that changing vowels of HN grades are not lengthened does not mean that HN grade verbs never contain lengthened vowels. Other vowels in an HN grade can be lengthened—just not the changing vowel.

         Sahōpohomba.   "I get hungry all the time."

Dropping vowels in HN grade verbs. Using an HN grade changes the rhythmic pattern of the verb: the next-to-last syllable of an HN grade is always heavy. Sometimes this means that the vowel drop process you learned about in lesson 6.2 will occur in an HN grade even though it does not happen in the original verb:

         Hilhali.   "I dance."
         Hihí̱lhli.   "I dance all the time."

The syllable before the ending **+li** is heavy in **Hilhāli** (it has a lengthened vowel). In the HN grade verb **Hihí̱lhli**, however, **+li** is preceded by a nonlengthened short vowel. Since that vowel follows an **lh**, it drops. The vowel drop rule applies when the last vowel of an HN grade is preceded by **s, sh, lh** or (with the ch/sh rule) **ch**, and the HN grade is followed by the ending **+li, +tok, +taa,** or **+taam**. Review the rule in lesson 6.2 if you need to.

An overview of HN grade formation and use. Below is a summary of the facts about HN grade formation and usage that you have learned in this lesson.

- The HN grade is made by adding a nasal syllable after the changing vowel of a basic verb (which may include **+chi** but not other endings). This syllable starts with **h** and includes an accented copy of the changing vowel. The accented copy is followed by **m** if the following consonant is **b** or **p** and by **n** if the following consonant is **ch, t,** or (usually) **k**. In other cases the copy is a nasal vowel.
- If the changing vowel is long, it is shortened in the HN grade.
- If the changing vowel is followed by **bb, pp, tt,** or **kk,** this double consonant is undoubled in the HN grade.
- An **h** or **'** after the changing vowel and before another consonant is dropped before making the HN grade.
- If the changing vowel is already nasal or followed by **m** or **n** plus a consonant other than **m** or **n,** no additional nasal is added.
- If the last vowel of the basic verb is long or if the verb ends in a long nasal vowel, the HN grade ends with a short, plain copy of this vowel, plus **h,** plus an accented long nasal vowel.
- If the changing vowel is followed by **k** plus **b, l, m, n, w,** or **y,** the HN grade includes **h,** plus an accented copy of the changing vowel, plus **ng.**
- The changing vowel is never lengthened in the HN grade.

- Since the next-to-last syllable of an HN grade is always heavy, the vowel drop rule can apply when the last vowel of an HN grade is preceded by **s**, **sh**, **lh**, or (with the ch/sh rule) **ch** and the HN grade is followed by the ending **+li**, **+tok**, **+taa**, or **+taam**.

By following these rules, you can put almost any verb into the HN grade. Try forming the HN grade of other verbs you know. You may find, however, that Chickasaw speakers think some verbs don't sound too good in this form.

Exercise 8H. Translate the following sentences into Chickasaw, using an HN grade in each one. 1. Is he being good all the time? 2. We are dying all the time! 3. We are hitting you all the time. 4. They are drinking water all the time. 5. Do you sell horses all the time? 6. We pay you all the time. 7. They bury people all the time.

Lesson 8.7:
The Final **li** Deletion Rule

*Losing a **li** syllable.* A special process affects verbs that end in **li**—not the A subject ending **+li**, but a **li** that is part of the verb itself. Many verbs you know end in a **li** syllable, such as **anompoli** "talk", **ittihaalalli** "marry", **nannabli** "swallow", and **tahli** "finish". Here are a few more:

malili to run (singular subject) (A)	**bínni'li** to sit (singular subject) (A)
kisili to bite (A,S)	**halili** to touch (A,S)
lhiyohli to chase (A,S)	**shooli** to hug (A,S)

When the past ending **+tok** is added to verbs that end in **li**, some of them lose this final **li** syllable:

Shootok.	"He hugged her." (not <shoolitok>)
Malitok.	"He ran." (not <malilitok>)
Tahtok.	"He finished it." (not <tahlitok>)
Bínni'tok.	"He sat." (not <bínni'litok>)

Other verbs ending in **li** do not lose that syllable before **+tok**, however:

Toksalitok.	"He worked."
Nannablitok.	"He swallowed it."
Mallitok.	"He jumped."

Can you see the difference? It's a little tricky. A final **li** syllable of a verb will drop before **+tok** if it is preceded by a heavy syllable ending in a vowel, **h**, or **'**.

The syllables before **li** in the first group of verbs above are heavy: **shooli** has the heavy syllable **shoo**, with a long vowel; **malili** has the heavy syllable **lī**, with a lengthened vowel; and **tahli** and **bínni'li** have the heavy syllables **tah** and **ni'**, which end in **h** and **'**. On the other hand, the verbs in the second group are different. **Toksali** has a light syllable (**sa**) before **li**. The syllables before **li** in **nannabli** and **malli** are heavy (**nab** and **mal**), but they end in consonants other than **h** or **'**.

If you divide each of these verbs into syllables as you have learned, you'll see that all this is true. The **li** syllables that drop before **+tok** are syllables whose vowels are not lengthened by the rhythmic lengthening rule and that are preceded by vowels, **h**, or **'**. The **li** syllables that do not drop either have rhythmically lengthened vowels or are preceded by consonants other than **h** or **'**. Take a minute to see how this works in the examples above.

The A suffix **+li** is never deleted by this or any other rule, even when its vowel is not lengthened. Thus, you say

Toksalilitok.   "I worked."

Even though this word contains a **li** syllable with a nonlengthened **i** before **+tok**, that **li** does not drop, because it is the A suffix **+li**. Only **li**'s that are actually part of the verb itself drop because of **ii** deletion.

Exercise 8I. Change each of the following Chickasaw sentences to refer to the past by adding **+tok**. Remember to drop final **li** syllables when appropriate (if a heavy syllable ending in a vowel, **h**, or **'** precedes **li**, and if **li** is not the A subject suffix). Translate the new sentences.
1. Kiloomalli. 2. Ishnannabli. 3. Hootoksali. 4. Toksalili. 5. Hopooli. 6. Ishshooli. 7. Hashtahli. 8. Ishbínni'li. 9. Nannablili. 10. Malili. 11. Hopoonili. 12. Hoohalili. 13. Hashittihaalalli. 14. Lhiyohli. 15. Hilhali. 16. Kiilookisili.

Li deletion with other endings. The **li** deletion rule you have just learned affects **li** syllables before other endings that begin with **t**—not just **+tok**, but also **+taa** and **+taam**. So just as **li** drops when you add **+tok** to a verb like **malili**, **li** also drops before **+taa** and **+taam**:

Ishmalītok.   "You ran."
Ishmalītaa?   "Are you running?"
Ishmalītaam?   "Did you run?"

Li deletion with different forms of the same verb. As you know, when an S prefix is added to a verb, the rhythmic pattern of that verb can change.

halīli — sahālili   kisīli — chikīsili

Now look at what happens when **+tok**, **+taa**, or **+taam** is added:

halītok — sahālilītok   kisītaam? — chikīsilītaam?

The same **li** syllables that drop off the end of **halili** and **kisili** remain when these verbs include S prefixes. When there is an S prefix on the verb, the vowel of the **li** syllable is lengthened, since it is an even-numbered short syllable, so it won't drop:

ha/lī/l̵i/tok   sa/hā/li/lī/tok
1 2 3   1 2 3 4

Even-numbered short syllables, like the second **li** of **Sahalilitok**, have their vowels lengthened. (Review the rhythmic lengthening rule in lesson 4.3 if you need to.) The vowels of odd-numbered short syllables are not lengthened. If a **li** at the end of a verb (not the ending **+li**) is an odd-numbered short syllable, it is dropped, as shown here by the line through that syllable.

Li deletion with HN grades. Earlier in this lesson you learned to make the HN grade of words like **toksali** and **sahalili**: these are **toksaháli** and **sahalihíli**. Now compare what happens when you add **+tok** to these basic and HN grade forms:

Toksalitok. "He worked."	Toksahátok. "He worked and worked."
Sahalilitok. "He touched me."	Sahalihítok. "He kept touching me."

A verb-final **li** syllable of an HN grade form always drops before **+tok** and the other **t** endings, because that **li** syllable will always be preceded by a heavy syllable ending in a nasal vowel. (The next-to-last syllable of an HN grade is always heavy.)

There is something extra to notice, too. When you delete **li** from **Toksahálitok**, the nasal vowel **á** of the HN grade doesn't change, even though it's before a **t**. Listen carefully as your teacher says these words.

Exercise 8J. Translate the following sentences, remembering lengthened vowels and **li** deletion.
1. Are you working and working? 2. Did the child touch you? 3. Did she run? 4. I married him. 5. Did you finish it? 6. Did we work? 7. Did the mouse jump? 8. Were you sitting down? 9. The chief kept touching the rock. 10. He swallowed the meat. 11. Will they chase you? 12. He hugs me all the time.

For most Chickasaw speakers, **li** deletion applies before all + endings that begin with **t, ch**, or **n** other than the causative ending **+chi**. Some Chickasaw speakers may apply the **li** deletion rule somewhat differently from the way we have described it here, however. You should follow your teacher's usage. There's more information about how **li** deletion works in the Advanced Chickasaw Grammar section in unit 20.

Accented vowels and stress in **+taa** *and* **+taam** *questions.* In lesson 4.4 you learned that an accented vowel is stressed in a **+taa** or **+taam** question even if there is another heavy syllable later in the word. This is true in questions containing words like **bínni'li** and **bíyyi'ka**, in which the accented vowel does not appear in the last heavy syllable of the word.

Bínni'taa?	"Is he sitting?"
Hihílha bíyyi'kataam?	"Was he dancing all the time?"

In the words **bínni'taa** (the final **li** of **bínni'li** drops before **+taa** because of **li** deletion) and **bíyyi'kataam**, stress falls on the accented syllable (as shown here with double underlining) even though there is another, later heavy syllable before the question ending. Listen for the stress as your teacher pronounces the questions above.

Terms and Concepts

D OBJECT, S OBJECT, D SUBJECT, GRADE FORM, BASIC VERB, CHANGING VOWEL.

VOCABULARY

atobbi to pay (A,Noun)
bínni'li to sit, be in a sitting position (singular subject) (A)
bíyyi'ka all the time (auxiliary)
Chihoowa God
falaa to be long (Noun)

halili to touch (A,S)
hashaa to be angry (S)
hopooni "to cook" (A,S)
ikbi to make (A,S)
imambiika to be sick for (A,D)
imaabachi to teach (A,D); to teach (something) to (A,D,Noun)
imaatobbi to pay (something) to (A,D,Noun)
imilhlha to be scared; to be wild (D)
imissikopa to be mean to (A,D)
imishto to be big for (singular subject) (Noun,D)
impalhki to be too fast for (A,D)
inchokma to feel good (D)
inchokmishto to be healthy (D)
intakho'bi to be lazy (D)
ihashaa to be angry at (A,D)
ihollo to love (A,D)
ihofahya to be ashamed of (A,D)
inokhánglo to be sorry for (A,D)
iyimmi to believe (someone), to believe in (A,D)
kiliha to growl (A)
kisili to bite (A,S)
kochcha to go out of (A,Noun)
lhiyohli to chase (A,S)
malili to run (singular subject) (A)
okshitta to close (A,Noun)
shooli to hug (A,S)
tahli to finish (A,Noun)
waaka to be spotted (S)
yimmi to believe (something) (S,Noun)

Most verbs with dative object prefixes aren't listed in the vocabulary, because their meaning and form are regular.

Bíyyi'ka is an auxiliary verb with several uses. As you learned in lesson 5.8, it is also used after verbs with the "can" ending **±a'hi.**

READING AND SPEAKING

Days of the Week

Nittak means "day". Here are the traditional Chickasaw names for the days of the week.

Nittak Ammo'na' Monday
Nittak Atokla' Tuesday
Nittak Atochchi'na' Wednesday
Nittak Hollo' Aaiklanna' Wednesday

Nittak Ayyoshta' Thursday
Nittak Ishtalhlha'pi' Friday
Nittak Hollo' Nakfish Saturday
Nittak Hollo' Sunday

Some people use other names for Saturday and Sunday, although the two above are most common:

Nittak Ishhanna'li' Saturday
Nittak Ishtontoklo' Sunday

If you compare these day names with the numbers that you learned at the end of unit 7, you can see where many of these names came from. Ordinal number modifiers usually begin with **a** (or **ayy** before a vowel) or **isht** (or **ish** before a consonant) added to a number: thus **atochchi'na'** means "third" (Wednesday is the third day of the week, if you start with Monday) and **ishtalhlha'pi'** means "fifth" (Friday is the fifth day). Sometimes there are other changes: "second" is **atokla'**, even though "two" is **toklo**, and **ammo'na'** "first" looks no more like **chaffa** than the English word *first* looks like *one*.

Nittak Hollo' is the most common way to say "Sunday"; literally, this means "sacred day". **Nittak Hollo' Aaiklanna'**, a word some speakers use for "Wednesday", literally means "half (way to) Sunday". Why do you think Saturday can be called **Nittak Hollo' Nakfish**?

In older times Chickasaw speakers probably had their own words for the months of the year, but no one uses any of these any more—months are referred to in English in Chickasaw conversation. Some speakers use the English names for the days of the week, as well.

Here is how to use the days of the week in sentences. If the day you're referring to is in the future, add ±**kma** to the end of the name of the day.

Nittak Atokla'kma taloowala'chi.   "I'll sing on Tuesday."

If the day you're referring to is in the past, add ±**aash** to the end of the name of the day:

Nittak Atokla'aash taloowalitok.   "I sang on Tuesday."

A Story about Old Times

Below is another short reading about old times in the Chickasaw Nation (Mrs. Willmond's original, more complicated version is given in appendix B). Read the Chickasaw story aloud, using the supplementary vocabulary and grammar notes at the end to help you figure out the meanings. Try to understand the story before you read the English translation at the end of the unit.

Nittak Hollishto'

Hopaakikaash Nittak Hollishto' ookma Appo'si' inchokka' kiliyyahminatook. Nittak Hollishto' ookma nanna habinachihminattook. Ankaat itti'chanaa ishtayahminattook. Onnakmako falamat kiimintihminattook.

SUPPLEMENTARY VOCABULARY

Appo'si' Grandmother, Granny (see note 1 below)
falamat minti to come back (A) (see note 4 below)
habinachi to give (something) to (someone), usually as a present (A,S,Noun)
ishtaya to bring (irregular verb—see note 3 below)
kiliyya we go (form of **aya**, an irregular verb—see note 3 below)
minti to come (A)
Nittak Hollishto' Christmas
Nittak Hollishto' ookma on Christmas
onnakmako the next morning
ookma see Nittak Hollishto' ookma

NOTES

1. **Appo'si'** "Grandmother" or "Granny" is a special type of possessed noun, used by a speaker to address or refer to his or her own grandmother. It does not include a prefix or other marker otherwise used to mean "my". (The ordinary term for "his grandmother" is **ippos'si'**; thus, "my grandmother" is **sappo'si'**.)

2. Like the sentences in earlier readings, the verbs here use the remote habitual ending +**hminattook**.

3. As noted following the readings at the end of units 5–7, Chickasaw has some irregular verbs: **aya** "to go" and **ishtaya** "to bring", used here, are common ones. Irregular verbs do not follow the rules you have learned concerning how prefixes and endings are used, as you can see from the word **kiliyya** "we go" (you might have expected <kilaya>). It is best not to try using irregular verbs until you've read unit 11.

4. **Falamat minti** "to come back" works in an unusual way—the A prefix goes on the second word of this verb phrase, and the first one does not change.

More about the story. Mrs. Willmond grew up in a log cabin her father built near McMillan, Oklahoma, a town that no longer appears on maps—it was located near the Marshall-Carter county line, a few miles south of US Highway 70 (off a road now signposted as McMillan Road), about halfway between the towns of Madill and Ardmore. Her grandmother lived east of Fillmore, Oklahoma, in eastern Johnston County. Today it takes only about an hour to drive from McMillan to Fillmore in a car, but it could be a long day's journey with a horse and wagon. (For more about log cabins, see the story about old times following unit 10.)

Days and sacred days. As you learned earlier in this unit, "Sunday" is **Nittak Hollo'**, which originally meant "sacred day". **Nittak Hollishto'** "Christmas" literally means "big sacred day".

Story Translation

Christmas

Long ago on Christmas we would go to Granny's house. On Christmas they would give things as presents. My father would bring the wagon. The next day we would come back.

New Sentence Patterns

In this unit you'll learn about how to form Chickasaw negative verbs and about contrastive endings and "want" sentences.

Lesson 9.1 describes the formation of negative verbs using the unaccomplished prefix **ik±** and the negative ending **±o**, lesson 9.2 introduces the N prefixes, and lesson 9.3 explains how endings are added to negative verbs. Some verbs are always negative (lesson 9.4). Lesson 9.5 presents the contrastive noun endings, which are also used on pronouns (lesson 9.6). Lesson 9.7 introduces sentences using **banna** "to want".

Lesson 9.1:
Negative Verbs

In lesson 7.2 you learned how to make sentences negative with the word **ki'yo**. Another way to make Chickasaw sentences negative is by changing their verbs:

Lakna. "It is brown."   Iklakno. "It is not brown."
Sholaffi. "He is scratching her."   Iksholaffo. "It is not scratching her."
Isso. "She hits it."   Ikisso. "She does not hit it."

The negative sentences on the left have two changes to their verbs. First, the UNACCOMPLISHED prefix **ik±** is added at the front of the verb (since the verb refers to something that hasn't happened or been accomplished), and second, the final vowel of the verb is replaced by the negative ending **±o**. (If the plain verb ends in **o** already, you don't see a change.) Verbs like those in the second column that have the negative ending **±o** are called NEGATIVE VERBS. A negative active verb can have two types of translations—so, for example, **ikisso** could be "She is not hitting it" as well as "She does not hit it".

If a verb has an S, dative, or D prefix, the unaccomplished prefix **ik±** goes in front of the other prefix, right at the beginning of the verb. Check each of these examples to be sure that you see the unaccomplished prefix and the negative ending on each negative verb.

Sasso. "He is hitting me."   Iksasso. "He isn't hitting me."
Chichokma. "You are good."   Ikchichokmo. "You are not good."
Chihollo. "He loves you."   Ikchihollo. "He doesn't love you."

When the unaccomplished prefix comes before the D prefix **a+**, you have to add an extra **s** before that prefix:

Iksanchokmo.   "I don't feel good."
Iksahollo.   "He doesn't love me."

You know that an extra **s** is also added when an A prefix comes before the D prefix **a+**. Whenever the D prefix **a+** comes after either an A or an N prefix, it becomes **sa+**.

Exercise 9A. Make each of the following sentences negative in two ways, as in the example. Translate your negative sentences.
  Example. Hattakat chihofahya.
  Answer. Hattakat chihofahya ki'yo. Hattakat ikchihofahyo. "The man is not ashamed of you."
  1. Sahomma. 2. Kowi'at minko' sholaffi. 3. Amisso. 4. Chipota tiik yappat inchokmishto. 5. Popalhki. 6. Ihooat malli. 7. Chilhpokonna. 8. Chipota naknaat amaatobbi. 9. Pintaat malli. 10. Hattak yammat nannabli. 11. Chahta' isoba-at salhiyohli. 12. Chipotaat alikchi' imittish lohmi.

Now look at these regular and negative verbs:

Hilha. "She is dancing."   Ikhi'lho. "She is not dancing."
Yopi. "He is swimming.",   Ikyo'po. "He is not swimming.",
  "He is taking a bath."   "He is not taking a bath."
Hilhachi. "He makes her dance."   Ikhilha'cho. "He doesn't make her dance."
Holbachi. "She photographs him."   Ikholba'cho. "She doesn't photograph him."

These examples show what happens in the negative of a basic verb that ends in a vowel plus a single consonant plus another vowel, such as **hilha**, **yopi**, **hilhachi**, or **holbachi** ("to photograph"). (Remember that the **lh** and **ch** each represent just one consonant.) With these verbs, a **'** goes into the negative verb before the last consonant.

Negative verbs like these differ from the corresponding non-negatives in three ways—they include the unaccomplished prefix **±ik**, the **±o** ending, and the added **'**. Here are some more examples:

Chilosa. "You are black."   Ikchilo'so. "You are not black."
Malili. "It is running.   Ikmali'lo. "It is not running."
Sassikopa. "I am mean."   Iksassiko'po. "I am not mean."
Ponkiliha. "He growls at us."   Ikponkili'ho. "He doesn't growl at us."

Here is how you make the negative of a verb that ends in **mb**, **mp**, **nt**, **nch**, or **nk** plus a vowel:

Konta. "He whistles."   Ikko'to. "He doesn't whistle."
Impa. "She is eating."   Iki'po. "She is not eating."
Omba. "It is raining."   Iko'bo. "It isn't raining."

Like other verbs, these add **ik±** and **±o**. In addition, you change the vowel plus **m** or **n** in the next-to-last syllable of the verb to a nasal vowel—here, **on** becomes **o**, **im** becomes **i**, and **om** becomes **o**. Then, since at this point there is only one consonant before the last vowel, you put in a **'**.

If the next-to-last vowel of a verb is long, it will shorten in the negative:

Aachi. "He says it."   Ika'cho. "He doesn't say it."
Taloowa. "She sings."   Iktalo'wo. "She doesn't sing."
Baafa. "He stabs him."   Ikba'fo. "He doesn't stab him."

The unaccomplished prefix **ik±** comes before the plural subject prefix **hoo±**:

Ikhoochokmo.   "They aren't acting good."
Ikhoosasso.   "They aren't hitting me."

As you can see, the last verb has three different prefixes, **ik±**, **hoo±**, and **sa+**.

Exercise 9B. Translate the following sentences using negative verbs like those in the examples.
    1. They are not swimming. 2. We are not fat. 3. The man is not touching the woman. 4. He is not sending money to me. (**ta'osso** = "money") 5. The birds are not singing to the cat. 6. I am not scared. 7. We aren't heavy. 8. They do not whistle. 9. The doctors are not kissing us. 10. He's not talking to her. 11. She is not hugging me. 12. The horse is not spotted. 13. They aren't buying a house. 14. She doesn't wash her face.

Lesson 9.2:
N Prefixes

Negatives of verbs with A subjects use different prefixes for "I", "you", and "we" subjects. Compare these sets of sentences with "you" and "I" subjects:

Ishisso. "You hit him."   Chikisso. "You didn't hit him."
Yopili. "I swim."   Akyo'po. "I don't swim."
Hashimpa. "You all eat."   Hachiki'po. "You all don't eat."

These verbs add **±o** and **'** where necessary just like the negative verbs you saw in the last lesson. However, these negative verbs don't use the unaccomplished prefix **ik±**, and instead of A markers, they have N prefixes.
    Here are the N prefixes that correspond to the "I" and "you" A markers:

A Marker	*N Prefix*
+li	ak±
ish±	chik±
hash±	hachik±

In each case the N prefix looks like a D-plus-dative prefix combination with a final **k** instead of **m**. The N prefixes substitute for **ik±** on negative verbs formed with **±o** and **'**.
    With "we" subjects the situation is a little different:

A Marker	*N Prefix*
ii±, kii±	kii±
il±, kil±	kil±
iloo±, kiloo±	kiloo±

As you learned in lesson 3.1, A "we" prefixes have two variants, one with **k** and one without. The N "we" prefixes sound just like the A "we" prefixes that start with **k**. (There are no N "we" prefixes that start with **i**— a "we" verb that starts with **i** is never negative.) Again, however, the N "we" prefix substitutes for unaccomplished **ik±** on a negative verb. (The similarity between the A and N "we" prefixes can seem very confusing to English speakers. Remember, though, that a negative verb will always end in **±o**, so most of the time there's no difficulty recognizing whether or not a verb is negative.)

N prefix combinations. All of the new N prefixes are only used with A subject verbs. Like the unaccomplished prefix **ik±**, all these other N prefixes come before any S, dative, or D prefixes in the verb word. When any N prefix comes before the D prefix **a+**, an extra **s** is added before the prefix.

Chiksasso.	"You aren't hitting me."
Hachikpompila'cho.	"You all aren't sending it to us."
Kiichihali'lo.	"We aren't touching you."
Chiksamisso.	"You aren't hitting him for me."

The **a** at the beginning of an a-verb with an S prefix drops after unaccomplished **ik±** or an N prefix. Compare the following non-negative and negative a-verbs with S prefixes.

Apobika. "We are sick."	Ikpobi'ko. "We're not sick."
Achipilali. "I help you."	Akchipi'lo. "I don't help you."
Asakmi. "I am frozen."	Iksakmo. "I'm not frozen."

You learned in lesson 6.1 that the **a** of an a-verb does not drop after the plural subject prefix **hoo±**. This is also true when the verb is negative:

Hooasafama. "They meet me."	Ikhooasafa'mo. "They don't meet me."
Hoochiholbachi. "They photograph you."	Ikhoochiholba'cho. "They don't photograph you."

Any prefix vowel that is lengthened in the non-negative will be lengthened in the negative, even if the preceding **a** is deleted. So just as you say **asābika** and **achīpilāli**, you'll say **iksābi'ko** and **ikchīpi'lo**. (This works the same as with combinations of A prefixes before S prefixes on a-verbs, as explained in lesson 6.1.)

Like A prefixes and the dative prefix, the unaccomplished prefix **ik±** and the N prefixes are **±** prefixes, and they always end a syllable. So we say **ik/a/bī/ka'/cho** "he isn't making her sick", for instance, with the **k** of the unaccomplished prefix ending its own syllable. An **ik±** or N prefix syllable is always a heavy syllable. As with the A and dative prefixes, before a syllable consisting of a single short vowel the unaccomplished and N prefixes may sound as if they contain emphasized or double consonants, so you might hear "he isn't making me sick" as <ikkabīka'cho>. Listen carefully as your teacher reviews the pronunciation of all the negative words above.

Exercise 9C. Translate each of the following negative sentences. Then tell another way to say each one in Chickasaw.

1. Ikhooasapi'lo. 2. Chiktoyyo. 3. Toyyali ki'yo. 4. Achikmi ki'yo. 5. Akchisso. 6. Chikchokmo. 7. Hashposho̲'kachichi ki'yo. 8. Kilanompoli ki'yo. 9. Kilooisso. 10. Chiksampila'cho.

You have now learned all the sets of Chickasaw markers used for subjects and objects. Below is a complete chart for reference—make sure you know what each line of the table refers to and how to use each set of prefixes.

	A	S	D *used with* **im±**	N *substitute for* **ik±**
"I", "me"	+li	sa+	a±	ak±
"you" (singular)	ish±	chi+	chi±	chik±
"we", "us"	kii±, ii±, kil±, il±	po+	po⊥	kii±, kil±
special "we", "us"	kiloo±, iloo±	hapo+	hapo±	kiloo±
"you" (plural)	hash±	hachi+	hachi±	hachik±

When using the chart for reference, remember that D prefixes are always used with a form of the dative prefix **im±** and that N prefixes always substitute for the unaccomplished prefix **ik±** (on a verb that would take A prefixes when non-negative). As you know, too, both S and D prefixes can also be used to indicate possessors; these translations are not given in the chart.

Some exceptional negatives. Verbs that end in a long vowel form their negatives in a special way, as shown by

Hopoo. "He's jealous."	Ikhopo'o. "He's not jealous."
Yaa. "He cries."	Ikya'o "He does not cry."
Tilhaa. "They run."	Iktilha'o. "They don't run."

These verbs change their last single vowel to ±o and then add ' before the ±o. Words like **ikhopo'o** and **iktilha'o** appear to contain two short syllables before the ', but that's not how they are pronounced. There are no lengthened vowels, because, as you know, adding a ± ending can never change the rhythmic lengthening sequences in a word. The syllable divisions sound like

ik/ho/po/'o *or* ik/hop/o/'o	ik/ti/lha/'o *or* ik/tilh/a/'o

The second version of each pair is the more common pronunciation, with the consonant before the ' pronounced at the end of a syllable. You may almost feel that such words sound as though the middle consonant in the verb is doubled, somewhat like <ikhoppo'o> or <iktilhlha'o>. Listen to the way your teacher says these words, and imitate his or her pronunciation.

This change only happens in verbs with a single short syllable before the final long vowel of the basic non-negative verb. In cases like the following, where there are two short syllables before that final long vowel, syllable division and lengthening work just as you'd expect:

Iksahōpo'o.	"He's not jealous of me."

Try to pronounce all these words exactly as your teacher does.

Negatives of grade forms. Look at the following pairs of sentences:

Pisa. "He looks at it."	Písa. "He sees it."
Haklo. "He listens to it."	Hánglo. "He hears it."

Because they are accented, you can tell that the verbs **písa** "see" and **hánglo** "hear" are grade forms, related to the basic verbs **pisa** "look at, catch sight of" and **haklo** "listen to". These are N GRADE forms, which are similar to HN grades, but without the **h**. You'll learn more about N grades in unit 15.

The difference in meaning between these pairs of related verbs is similar to the difference in their English translations—the verbs in the first column refer to actions, and the verbs in the second column refer to states. Sometimes you may also hear **pisa** and **haklo** translated by English "see" and "hear", since in English those verbs can refer to the action of initially seeing or hearing something, as well as to the state of seeing or hearing, which is what **písa** and **hánglo** refer to.

However, there is only one negative form corresponding to each pair of verbs:

>Ikpi'so. "He doesn't look at it.", He doesn't catch sight of it.", "He doesn't see it."
>Ikhaklo. "He doesn't listen to it.", "He doesn't hear it."

Ikpi'so and **ikhaklo** are the regular negatives you'd expect for **pisa** and **haklo**. The accent and nasalization in **písa** and **hánglo** don't show up in the negative. Accented grade forms usually aren't used in negative verbs. Usually the negative used for a grade form is the negative of the corresponding basic verb, as in

Talohówa. "He sings and sings."	Iktalo'wo. "He doesn't sing (and sing)."
Ayoppánchi. "He likes her."	Ikayoppa'cho. "He doesn't like her."
Ithána. "She knows him."	Ikitha'no. "He doesn't know him."

On the other hand, some accented grade forms are kept in the negative:

Nokhánglo. "He is sad."	Iknokhánglo. "He isn't sad."
Ánta. "He stays."	Ikánto. "He doesn't stay."
Passáa. "She spanks him."	Ikpassáo. "She doesn't spank him."

There's a special rule about making the negative of a grade form. If the negative is made from the accented grade form rather than the basic form, you do not need to add ' as you would in making a normal negative of a basic, unaccented verb. Thus, you don't say <iká'to> or <ikpassá'o>. Although **nokhánglo**, **ánta**, and **passáa** follow this rule, the fact that they keep their grade form in the negative is irregular, and you just have to memorize this.

Exercise 9D. Translate the following sentences using verbs with the negative ending ±**o**.
1. We don't spank you. 2. I don't stay. 3. She doesn't talk to you all. 4. I'm not jealous of you. 5. We don't listen to her. 6. You don't see us. 7. We aren't sad. 8. She doesn't like me.

Lesson 9.3:
Endings on Negative Verbs

The negative auxiliary **ki'yo** can be used with a preceding verb referring to any time:

Hilhatok ki'yo.	"He didn't dance."
Hilha'chi ki'yo.	"He's not going to dance."

But when endings like **+tok** and **±a'chi** follow a negative verb, things work differently. Negative verbs use the special negative past ending **+kitok**:

Ikhi'lhokitok.   "He did not dance."

The **ki** of **+kitok** might remind you of **ki'yo**. As you can hear, the ending **+kītok** is always pronounced with a lengthened ī vowel. This happens because **±o** always follows a heavy syllable, so **ki** is always an even-numbered short syllable.

+Kitaa (**+kītaa**) and **+kitaam** (**+kītaam**) are used in questions formed from negative verbs:

Ikhi'lhokitaa?   "Isn't he dancing?"
Ikhi'lhokitaam?   "Didn't he dance?"

These combinations are always stressed on the **ki** syllable, with its lengthened vowel.

Negative verbs add **+ka'chi** in the future:

Ikhi'lhoka'chi.   "He isn't going to dance."

You can think of this ending as having two parts—the same **+ki** that occurs before the **+tok** of **+kitok** or the **+taa** of **+kitaa**, plus the normal future ending **±a'chi**. As you know, any short vowel drops before the ending **±a'chi**, so **+ki** plus **±a'chi** is **+ka'chi**. A similar ending is **+ka'ni**, which contains the same **+ki** plus **±a'ni**:

Ikhi'lhoka'ni.   "He can't dance."

Exercise 9E. Make each of the following Chickasaw sentences negative using **ik±** or an N prefix plus **±o**. Then translate each one. Remember to use **+ki** when necessary! Practice saying each negative verb.
   1. Foshi'at kowi' intaloowa'chi. 2. Polhinko. 3. Asabikatok. 4. Ishyopitok. 5. A̲hattakat hopooa'chi. 6. Hattakat hachishootok. 7. Ombatok. 8. Po̲minka nipi' hooimpilashtok. 9. Achiyoppáshla'chi. 10. Ilimpatok. 11. Polhiyohla'chi. 12. Naahollaat ta'osso lohmitok.

Perhaps you are wondering why there are two different ways to form negative sentences in Chickasaw. These two kinds of negatives often have different meanings. Usually, the meaning of a **ki'yo** negative is more stative than that of a negative verb ending in **±o**—**ki'yo** is used more often with stative verbs, and when it is used with active verbs, the meaning may refer more to a continuing state or situation than to an event. The best way to get a feeling for these distinctions is to observe the way native speakers of Chickasaw use **ki'yo** and **±o** negatives in everyday conversation. Your teacher may have ideas on this difference.

Endings on ki'yo. As you know, the auxiliary **bíyyi'ka** follows a verb with its subject and object markers, and endings like **+tok**, **±a'chi**, and so on are added to **bíyyi'ka**. **Ki'yo** is an auxiliary too, and endings like **+tok** and **±a'chi** can be used on **ki'yo** instead of on the verb before **ki'yo**. When you use **+tok**, **±a'chi**, and so on with **ki'yo**, you have to add **+ki** or **+k** just as you do after an **±o** negative verb:

Hilhali ki'yoka'chi.   "I won't be dancing."

This sentence means about the same as **Hilhala'chi ki'yo**. To make a question from a **ki'yo** sentence, you have to add **+kitaa** or **+kitaam** at the end, after **ki'yo**:

Hilha ki'yokitaa?   "Isn't he dancing?"

Lesson 9.4:
Verbs That Are Always Negative

There are some Chickasaw verbs that always include **ik±** and **±o**, even though they're not usually translated with "not". Most verbs like this refer to negative sorts of things—two examples are **ikimalhpi'so** "to be sad, unhappy" and **ikayyo'bo** "to be bad". Both these verbs contain the unaccomplished prefix **ik±**, the negative ending **±o**, and '. **Ikimalhpi'so** has a D subject, and **ikayyo'bo** an S subject. Here are some examples of how these verbs are used:

Iksamalhpi'so.   "I am sad."
Ikchimalhpi'sokitaam?   "Were you sad?"
Ikhooayyo'bokitok.   "They were bad."
Ikpoyyo'bo.   "We are bad."

As you can see, these verbs work like other negative verbs. The D and S subject prefixes go after **ik±**, just as you have learned, with the **a** of **ikayyo'bo** deleted between **ik±** and any S prefix. The plural subject prefix **hoo±** goes after the **ik±** on these verbs, and the verbs are used with the negative past and future endings **+kitok** and **+ka'chi** and the negative question endings **+kitaa** and **+kitaam**.

Iksho is a verb used to talk about the lack or nonexistence of something:

Oka'at iksho.   "There is no water."
Fani'at iksho.   "There are no squirrels."

Certainly, the first sentence is a statement about water—or the lack of it. What there is none of is the subject of **iksho**. Even when you are referring to a plural subject, you never use **hoo±** with **iksho**.

Iksho is a negative verb—it includes the unaccomplished prefix **ik±** and the negative ending **±o**, and it uses the other special negative endings:

Ikshoka'chi.   "There won't be any."
Oka'at ikshokitaam?   "Wasn't there any water?"

"Any" is used in translating many **iksho** sentences, especially when there's an understood subject.

With a human subject (marked by an S prefix), **iksho** means "not be around":

Alikchaat iksho.   "The doctor isn't around."
                                   (*also* "There aren't any doctors.")
Iksakshokitok.   "I wasn't around."
Ikchiksho.   "You aren't around."

Putting an S prefix on **iksho** is very irregular! What happens is this—**iksho** starts with **i**, so you'd expect to get <saksho>, and so on. But since **iksho** contains **ik±**, which has to come before **sa+**, an extra **ik±** goes on the front. You should memorize the words **iksaksho**, **ikchiksho**, and **ikpoksho**.

Exercise 9F. Translate the following sentences into Chickasaw using the new verbs.
1. There was no bread. 2. We will not be sad. 3. It is not bad. 4. I will not be around. 5. There is no bread. 6. The woman's child will be bad. 7. Aren't there any spoons? 8. The chief wasn't around.

Lesson 9.5:
Using Nouns Contrastively

As you know, you can call attention to the object of a Chickasaw sentence by adding ±**a** to it:

> Ank<u>a</u> ish<u>i</u>hollotaa?   "Do you love my father?"

Sometimes you want to be even more emphatic, however. In English we usually show emphasis by intonation or changes in the structure of the sentence—for instance, to make it clear that you didn't hit the cat, you might say, "I hit the <u>dog</u>," or maybe "It was the <u>dog</u> that I hit." Both of these types of English sentence suggest a contrast with something else (either might be completed, for example, by ". . . not the cat."). The Chickasaw CONTRASTIVE ending ±**ako** expresses the same meaning:

> Ofi'ak<u>o</u> issolitok.   "I hit the <u>dog</u>.", "It was the <u>dog</u> that I hit."
> Chimihooak<u>o</u> <u>i</u>holloli.   "I love <u>your wife</u>.", "It's <u>your wife</u> that I love."

(Underlining in the English translation indicates that the speaker puts emphasis on the underlined words. In writing Chickasaw you don't need to use underlining, because you use the contrastive ending.) The last example shows that ±**ako** can indicate a contrast with normal expectations—we feel that someone would love his own wife, so a statement about loving someone else's wife contrasts with what is expected.

In vowel-loss nouns, ±**ako** combines with the noun's final vowel (and **'**, if there is one) to form ±**aako**:

Noun	*Vowel-loss noun plus* ±***ako***
itti'	ittaak<u>o</u>
anki'	ankaak<u>o</u>
chipota	chipotaak<u>o</u>

Vowel-loss nouns are nouns ending with a vowel or **'** that have a heavy next-to-last syllable. Other nouns simply add ±**ako**.

±**Akoot** is a subject contrastive ending used when you want to emphasize or contrast a subject noun in sentences like

> Ofi'akoot sakisilitok.   "The <u>dog</u> bit me.", "It was the <u>dog</u> that bit me."
> Chishkaakoot hilha.   "<u>Your mother</u> is dancing.", "It's <u>your mother</u> who's dancing."

As the second example shows, ±**aakoot** is used with vowel-loss nouns.
You shouldn't try to use two contrastive nouns in the same sentence.

Exercise 9G. Tell the form of each of the following nouns when used with the endings ±**at**, ±**a**, ±**akoot**, and ±**ako**, as in the example. (Think about whether it's a vowel-loss noun or not.)

Example. issi'

Answer. issaat, iss<u>a</u>, issaakoot, issaak<u>o</u>

Then make up and translate a sentence, using either a subject or object contrastive ending for each noun. (For example, you could say Hattakat issaak<u>o</u> nalhlhitok. "It was the <u>deer</u> that the man shot.", using the object contrastive ending.)

1. chintikba' 2. fani' 3. chipota nakni' 4. **tii'** ("tea") 5. oka' 6. bashpo 7. poyyi' 8. koni 9. nannalhpooba' 10. kowi' 11. ta'osso 12. itt<u>i</u>sh

---

Lesson 9.6:
Pronouns

A PRONOUN is a separate word for a subject or object normally indicated only by a verb prefix or ending, in other words a separate word meaning "I", "me", "you", "we", or "us". Chickasaw pronouns usually include either ±**akoot** (in subject forms) or ±**ak<u>o</u>** (in object forms), since they are used almost entirely to show emphasis or contrast. Here is a list of Chickasaw pronouns for you to learn:

Subject pronouns	*Object pronouns*
anaakoot "I"	anaak<u>o</u> "me"
ishnaakoot "you (singular)"	ishnaak<u>o</u> "you (singular)"
poshnaakoot "we"	poshnaak<u>o</u> "us"
haposhnaakoot "(special) we"	haposhnaak<u>o</u> "(special) us"
haishnaakoot "you (plural)"	hashnaak<u>o</u> "you (plural)"

These pronouns are used for emphasis, or to show contrast, in sentences like

Anaakoot <u>i</u>holloli.	"<u>I</u> love him.", "<u>I</u>'m the one that loves him."
Ishnaak<u>o</u> chipislitok.	"I saw <u>you</u>.", "It's <u>you</u> that I saw."

The verbs of these sentences still have all the regular markers. In the first sentence the verb is marked for an "I" subject with the A ending +**li** even though there is an "I" subject pronoun; in the second, the presence of the "you" object pronoun doesn't make any difference to the presence of the S object prefix **chi+** on the verb. The verb of a Chickasaw sentence must always have any necessary markers referring to the subject and object, regardless of whether pronouns are used.

English speakers may feel that sentences like **Chipislitok** that consist of only one word sound incomplete, and new speakers of Chickasaw sometimes try to make their sentences more like English ones by adding pronouns, even when no emphasis is needed. This isn't right, however. The Chickasaw pronoun words should only be used when you really want to emphasize or make a contrast.

Usually you don't need to emphasize more than one thing (at the very most) in any single sentence. Therefore, sentences that include more than one pronoun are extremely rare in Chickasaw.

To emphasize or contrast "he", "she", "they", "them", "her", or "him", you use contrastive forms of the "that" and "this" words you learned in lesson 2.3:

	Subject	*Object*
"that"	yammakoot	yammak<u>o</u>
"this"	yappakoot	yappak<u>o</u>

Both subject words can be translated into English by "he", "she", or "they", while the object words can mean "them", "her", or "him". Use a "this" word to refer to someone who is relatively near you and a "that" word to refer either to someone who is relatively farther away or whose location is unimportant. Each word is used, like other pronouns, only when you want to emphasize or make a contrast:

Yammakoot ilhpokonna.	"<u>She</u> is dreaming.", "<u>She</u>'s the one that's dreaming."
Yappakoot hootoyya.	"<u>They</u> (the near ones) are climbing."
Yammak<u>o</u> imaashlitok.	"I said it to <u>him</u>.", "I said it to <u>that one</u>."

As the last example shows, "that" contrastive forms can also be translated "that one", while "this" contrastive forms can be translated "this one".

You can also use these contrastive forms after a noun:

Ihoo yammak<u>o</u> issola'chi.	"I'm going to hit <u>that woman</u>."
Alikchi' yappakoot sath<u>á</u>na.	"<u>This doctor</u> knows me."

Remember that any marking for subject or object goes at the end of the whole subject or object phrase. If you want to end the subject phrase with a contrastive word like **yappakoot**, you put this after the plain form of the noun. In other words, you would never put anything after a noun subject word like **alikchaat**.

Exercise 9H. Translate the following sentences into Chickasaw, using contrastive forms.
1. She talked to <u>me</u>. 2. Were you looking for a <u>spoon</u>? 3. <u>That woman</u> is not pretty. 4. <u>She</u> (relatively nearby) was really good. 5. He did not make her hit <u>you</u>. 6. <u>We</u> aren't around. 7. <u>This basket</u> is black. 8. Are <u>you guys</u> running? 9. The man's father hugged <u>us</u>. 10. <u>I</u>'m the one that's jumping. 11. The <u>cat</u> scratched me. 12. They chased <u>us</u>.

Lesson 9.7:
Using **Banna** "Want"

Banna "want" is an (S,Noun) verb, like **yimmi** (lesson 8.4):

Ofi' sabanna.	"I want a dog."
Tii' chibannataa?	"Do you want tea?"

But unlike **yimmi**, **banna** is never used with a D prefix, and **banna** can never be used with pronoun objects ("me", "us", "you"). (In other words, you can't translate "I want you" into Chickasaw using **banna**.) There's no way to add another object prefix onto a verb whose subject is marked with an S prefix.

*"Want to" sentences with **banna**.* You can also use **banna** to make a sentence with another verb:

Hilha sabanna.	"I want to dance."
Yimmi chibannataa?	"Do you want to believe?"

Foshi'at taloowa banna ki'yo.	"The bird doesn't want to sing."
Tii' ishko chibannataa?	"Do you want to drink tea?"

The verb expressing what the subject wants to do goes right in front of **banna**.

In this sentence pattern, there is never any subject marker on the verb in front of **banna** if that verb is one that should have an A or S subject. However, there may be object marking on the verb in front of **banna**:

Achibikachi sabanna.	"I want to make you sick."
Poyimmi chibannataa?	"Do you want to believe in us?"

When the verb in front of **banna** takes a D subject, you can either mark that verb for the same subject as **banna** or leave it in the **im±/in±/i±** form:

Chinchokmishto chibannataa?,	"Do you want to be healthy?"
Inchokmishto chibannataa?	

Another way to say the same thing as the simple **banna** sentences above is to put the **±a'ni** ending after the verb in front of **banna**:

Achibikacha'ni sabanna.	"I want to make you sick."
Yimma'ni chibannataa?	"Do you want to believe?"

Since the **±a'ni** ending can mean "could", you might think of sentences like this as equivalent to "I wish I could make you sick", and so on.

Exercise 9I. Translate the following sentences into English.
1. Chipotaakoot yaa banna ki'yo. 2. Foshi'at wakaa banna. 3. Chokma'sa'ni sabanna. 4. Inchokma chibanna ki'yokitaa? 5. Pontakho'bi pobannatok. 6. Hattak yammakoot ihoo yappa itti-haalalli hoobanna. 7. Chimissikopa sabanna ki'yo. 8. Hattak yammat sasso banna. 9. Alikchaat sabashli bannatok. 10. Ta'osso kaníhka sabanna. 11. Chipotaat chokoshkomo hoobanna. 12. Sahol-bachi hachibannataa?

"Want someone to" sentences. Each of the English translations of the **banna** sentences above includes "want to", "wants to", or "wanted to". In a "want to" sentence, the person doing the wanting wants to do or be something him- or herself. In other "want" sentences like the following, however, the wanter wants someone else to do something:

Achibika'ni sabanna.	"I want you to be sick."
Kiihalila'ni chibannataa?	"Do you want us to touch it?"

These sentences are "want someone to" sentences. In this pattern the first verb (telling the desired action or state) always has its subject marked (as in a simple sentence) and always ends in **±a'ni**. As before, the wanter is indicated with an S prefix on **banna**.

Here's a "want someone to" sentence where the subject of the "wanted" action is a noun. The wanted event is expressed with a complete sentence (ending in ±a'ni, and marked with a broken underline) in front of **banna**.

Alikchaat taloowa'ni sabanna.   "I want the doctor to sing."

Now, here's a "want someone to" sentence with two nouns:

Ihooat hattakat hilha'ni banna.   "The woman wants the man to dance."

Below is a diagram of the "want someone to" pattern:

SUBJECT	SUBJECT	"wanted" VERB	**banna**
of **banna**—the "wanter"	of "wanted" verb	**±a'ni**	
±at/akoot	**±at/akoot**		
Ihooat	hattakat _____ hilha'ni		banna.

If you're going to mention both the subject of **banna** and the subject of the other verb with nouns, the **banna** subject comes first. In the example above, the first noun, **ihoo**, is the subject of **banna**, while **hattak** is the subject of **hilha**. The second subject goes with the verb that directly follows it, and the first subject goes with **banna**.

When you want some event to occur, this event is the object of your wanting. You know that Chickasaw objects normally go in the middle of the sentence, between the subject and the verb. In the example above, the man's dancing is what's wanted, so the whole object sentence **hattakat hilha'ni** (double underlined in the example above) goes right between the first subject (**ihooat**) and its verb (**banna**). This object sentence has its own subject (**hattakat**, marked with the ±at subject ending) and a verb (**hilha**, marked with **±a'ni**).

Compare these two sentences:

Alikchaat paska sapita'ni sabanna.   "I want the doctor to feed me bread."
Alikchaat paska sapita'ni banna,   "The doctor wants to feed me bread."
Alikchaat paska sapita banna.

These sentences look similar, but they have quite different meanings. The key is the forms of **banna** that they use. In the first, a "want someone to" sentence, the speaker is the subject of **banna** (you can tell this from the **sa+** prefix on **banna**) and the doctor is the subject of the object sentence, **alikchaat paska sapita'ni**. The second pair of sentences are both "want to" sentences with the doctor as their subject. As you can see, it's important to pay attention to the prefix on **banna** if you want to understand a Chickasaw "want" sentence.

> *Exercise 9J.* Combine each of the following pairs of sentences into a "want someone to" sentence, as in the example. Translate the new sentences.
>   *Example.* Hattakat ofi' issa'ni. Ihooat ikbanno.
>   *Answer.* Ihooat hattakat ofi' issa'ni ikbanno. "The woman doesn't want the man to hit the dog."
>   1. Foshi'at intaloowa'ni. Sanakfishat banna. 2. Issasho'ka'ni. Sabanna. 3. Oklaat chokma'sa'ni. Minko' yammakoot bannatok. 4. Kiihilha'ni. Poshkaat banna. 5. Hikala'ni. Alikchaat banna. 6. Minkaat sabaafa'ni. Iksabanno.

Things can get even more complicated. Consider these additional sentences:

Alikchaat ihooat sapita'ni banna.   "The doctor wants the woman to feed me bread."

Ihooat alikchaat sapita'ni banna.   "The woman wants the doctor to feed me bread."

These "want someone to" sentences each have two nouns, so it's clear who's doing what: the first noun is the wanter, the second is the subject of the wanted action. But if it was clear that a woman was involved, a speaker might say these corresponding shorter sentences:

Alikchaat sapita'ni banna.   "The doctor wants her to feed me bread."
Alikchaat sapita'ni banna.   "She wants the doctor to feed me bread."

The same Chickasaw sentence is used in each case (and it's the same as one of the ways to say "The doctor wants to feed me bread"!). In the first case, the speaker is thinking of "doctor" as the wanter, the subject of the **banna** sentence; in the second, the speaker knows that "doctor" is the subject of the wanted sentence, whose verb is **ipita** "feed".

All these different interpretations may seem confusing, since in English we tend to spell things out much more explicitly. Chickasaw speakers like to omit nouns from their sentences, and many Chickasaw sentences have several possible interpretations. In a given conversational situation, however, things are usually completely clear.

Terms and Concepts

UNACCOMPLISHED, NEGATIVE VERB, CONTRASTIVE, PRONOUN.

VOCABULARY

anaakoot I (contrastive)
anaak<u>o</u> me (contrastive)
banna to want (S,Noun)
baafa to stab (A,S)
haklo to listen to, to hear (A,S)
hánglo to hear (A,S)
haposhnaakoot we (special form) (contrastive)
haposhnaak<u>o</u> us (special form) (contrastive)
hashnaakoot you (plural subject, contrastive)
hashnaak<u>o</u> you (plural object, contrastive)
holbachi to photograph, take a picture of (A,S)
iknokhánglo not to be sad (S)—negative of nokhánglo
ikánto not to stay (A)—negative of ánta
ikayyo'bo to be bad (S)
ikimalhpi'so to be sad, unhappy (D)
ikpass<u>á</u>o not to spank (A,S)—negative of pass<u>á</u>a
iksho not to be there, not to be around (S) (irregular verb: iksaksho, ikchiksho, ikpoksho)
ishnaakoot you (subject, contrastive)

ishnaako you (object, contrastive)
pisa to look at, to catch sight of, to see (A,S)
písa to see (A,S)
poshnaakoot we (contrastive)
poshnaako us (contrastive)
ta'osso money
tii' tea

Only negative verbs that don't follow the regular patterns given in this unit are listed.

READING AND SPEAKING

"Happy Birthday" in Chickasaw

Here's how we sing "Happy Birthday" in Chickasaw. Try it!

> Chimafammi chokma!
> Chimafammi chokma!
> Chimafammi chokma, _____(name)_____!
> Chimafammi chokma!

(You can hear the tune at http://www.101kidz.com/music/happybday1.mid.) **Afammi** means "year"; thus, **chimafammi chokma** is "your good years" (you'll learn more about modifying verbs like this in unit 12).

A Story about Old Times

Below is another short reading about old times in the Chickasaw Nation (Mrs. Willmond's original version is given in appendix B). Read the Chickasaw story aloud, using the supplementary vocabulary at the end to help you figure out the meanings. Try to understand the story before you read the English translation on the next page.

Tashpishofa

Hopaakikaashookano Chikashshaat tanchi' waachihminattook. Ilaapakáynit tanchi' hosihminattook. Yammako tashpishofa ikbihminattook. Shokha' abihminattook. Shokha' nipi'a ibaanihminattook. Hopoonihminattook. Yammako "tashpishofa" hochifohminattook. Himmaka' áyya'shookano nannakat pilla' alhtaha bíyyi'ka. Tanchi' ishchompa. Nipi' ishchompa. Aaholhponi' ishchompa. Yammak ishaahopoon'achi. Lowak nannakya ishoota'chi kı'yo. Talı' pallı' bíyyi'ka. Ishaahopoona'chi himmaka' nittakookano.

SUPPLEMENTARY VOCABULARY

alhtaha to be ready, to be already prepared (of a food, for example) (Noun)
aaholhponi' pot
aahopooni to cook (something) in, cook (something) on (a stove, for example) (A,Noun,Noun)
himmaka' áyya'shookano these days
hochifo to name (someone) (A,S); to name (someone or something) (a name) (A,S,Noun)
hosi to pound (corn) in a wooden mortar (A,Noun)

ibaani to add (something) to (something) (A,Noun,Noun)

ilaapakáynit by himself, by herself, by themselves (see note 1 below)

lowak fire

nannakat things (subject) (see note 2 below)

nannakya any (see note 3 below)

ooti to kindle (a fire), start (a firc), for warmth or cooking (A,Noun)

pilla' just

tali' palli' appliance

tanchi' corn

tashpishofa pishofa (a Chickasaw dish)

waachi to grow, cultivate (a plant) (A,Noun)

NOTES

1. **Ilaapakáynit** "by himself, by herself, by themselves" is used to show that a subject performed an action without assistance.

2. **Nannakat** is a special form of **nanna** "something" used as the subject of a following verb. In the story above, the best translation of **nannakat** is "things" or "everything".

3. **Nannakya** means "any" and is used to emphasize the object of a negative verb.

4. **Aahopooni** "to cook (something) in" is a special type of three-place verb containing the prefix **aa±** that tells what an action was done in. You'll learn more about **aa±** verbs in lesson 10.4.

As with most of the old-time stories you have read, most of the verbs in this story use the remote habitual ending **+hminattook**. The story shows that the auxiliary **bíyyi'ka** "all the time" (lesson 8.5) can be used after verbs that are not in the HN grade.

As noted earlier, Chickasaw has some irregular verbs, such as **abi** "to kill". Irregular verbs do not follow the rules you have learned concerning how prefixes and endings are used, and it is best not to try using them yourself until you learn more about how to use them in unit 11.

More about Pishofa. Pishofa (**tashpishofa** in Chickasaw) is a tasty corn and pork stew served at traditional Chickasaw gatherings. The corn used is a dried white corn, rather similar to hominy. Traditionally, pishofa is cooked slowly outdoors in a very large iron cauldron over an open fire. Nowadays, however, people also make pishofa on top of the stove or in a slow cooker.

Story Translation

Pishofa

Long ago the Chickasaws would grow corn. They would pound the corn themselves in a mortar. They would make it into pishofa. They would kill a hog. They would add the pork to it. They would cook it. They named that "pishofa". These days things are just already prepared all the time. You buy the corn. You buy the meat. You buy the pot. You'll cook it in that. You won't kindle any fire. It's all appliances. You cook on them nowadays.

BEYOND THE GRAMMAR: SOME DIFFERENCES BETWEEN CHICKASAW AND CHOCTAW

There are many differences between the Chickasaw and Choctaw languages, even though the two languages are really very similar and a speaker of one language can often understand a speaker of the other quite well.

Perhaps the easiest kind of differences to recognize are differences in words. Some Chickasaw and Choctaw words are completely different, as these examples show:

Chickasaw	Choctaw	English translation
bala'	tobi	"bean"
chipota	alla	"child"
chofak	ishtipa	"fork"
chokoshkomo	washohah	"to play"
haksi	tasiboh	"to be crazy"
ímmayya	ishahlih	"to be more than"
okla *or* aachompa'	tamaha	"town"
sho'ka	ahpalih	"to kiss"

A larger number of words are similar but not quite the same, as in these cases:

Chickasaw	Choctaw	English translation
chokma	achokmah	"to be good"
fohi'	fowi *or* foyi	"bee"
ihoo	ohoyo	"woman"
ilbak	ibbak	"hand"
ishno'	chishno	"you"
ishto	chitoh	"to be big"
malili	balilih	"to run"
takolo	takkon	"peach"
waaka'	waak	"cow"

The words for "you" are noncontrastive forms comparable to the pronouns you learned in this unit.

Looking at these words, you may notice a number of other differences. There are no glottal stops in the Choctaw words, because glottal stop is not written in Choctaw (although most Choctaw speakers do pronounce glottal stops after words written with final vowels). Words such as verbs that would end in a vowel in Chickasaw are written and pronounced with a final **h** in Choctaw.

A number of the prefixes and endings you know are different in Choctaw. The S prefix **po+**, for instance, is **pi+** in Choctaw, so to say "He knows us", for example, you say

Pithánah. *or* Pikhánah.

(notice the final **h**!), not

Pothána.

as in Chickasaw. (Different Choctaw speakers pronounce the verb "know" differently.) The future ending ±**a'chi** is ±**aachi** in Choctaw—compare the Choctaw and Chickasaw ways to say "He will run":

Chickasaw	Choctaw
Malila'chi.	Balilaachih.

When you hear Choctaws speaking, you may feel that their speech has a different rhythm from that of Chickasaw speakers. There are additional differences between the two languages as well. If you know any Choctaws, you can ask them to tell you their ways to say some of the things you have learned. Maybe you'll find some differences no one has noticed yet.

Unit 10

Adding More Nouns to Sentences

This unit will help you learn several ways to use more nouns in Chickasaw sentences.

Lesson 10.1 presents the way o-verbs work with S prefixes. Lesson 10.2 describes the **on±** "on" prefix, lesson 10.3 the **ibaa±** "along with" prefix, and lesson 10.4 the **aa±** location prefix, as well as positional verbs and verbs that don't take location prefixes. Lesson 10.5 introduces the special object ending **±ak**, and lesson 10.6 describes the use of locational nouns. Lesson 10.7 summarizes the way S prefixes are used on words starting with vowels. Lesson 10.8 presents reciprocal verbs.

Lesson 10.1: O-Verbs

Below are some O-VERBS (which all begin with **o**):

okcha to be awake, to wake up (S)   **okchali** to wake (someone) up (A,S)
okchamali to be blue, to be green (S)   **okcháa** to be alive (S)
ollali to laugh (A); to laugh at (A,S)   **oktosha** to snow (—)

Okcha and **okchali** both mean "wake up"; **okcha** is a one-place verb, and **okchali** is a two-place verb with an object. As in many other languages, "green" and "blue" are expressed with just one verb, **okchamali**, in Chickasaw. An o-verb you already know is **okaami** "to wash one's face"; its causative is **okaamichi**, another o-verb. The object of this verb is the person whose face is washed.

O-verbs work with A prefixes, with the dative prefix **im±** (or with D prefixes), with the unaccomplished prefix **ik±**, or with N prefixes the same way other verbs do:

Ishollalitok.   "You laughed."
Amokchali!   "Wake him up for me!"
Ikokaami'cho.   "She isn't washing his face."

Exercise 10A. Translate the following sentences into English.
1. Kowi'at okchatok. 2. A̲naafkaat ikokchama'lo. 3. Ihoo yammat inchipota̲ okaamichitok. 4. Ofi'at okcháataa? 5. Naahollo yamma̲ ilollalitok. 6. Chimihooa̲ ishokchala'chitaa? 7. Chipota̲ ikchimokcha'lo. 8. Okoshacha'chi.

The following sentences show how the S prefixes **sa+**, **po+**, and **chi+** work on o-verbs. As you can see, the combinations are a bit unexpected:

Asokch<u>á</u>a.   "I am alive."
Apollalitaam?   "Did he laugh at us?"
Achokaamichitok.   "She washed your face."

There are two ways for you to learn how to use an S prefix on an o-verb. You could simply memorize the new combinations of the S prefixes you know plus the following o-verb. This would be like learning a new set of S prefixes, each consisting of **a** plus the consonant of the regular S prefix you know:

<sa+ o-verb> = as+ o-verb
<chi+ o-verb> = ach+ o-verb
<po+ o-verb> = ap+ o-verb

But there's another way you could think about this process. When an S prefix comes before an o-verb, two things happen: **a** is added to the beginning of the word, and the vowel of the prefix drops. Here's how it works:

<chi + o-verb>   (start with S prefix plus o-verb)
<a+ chi + o-verb>   (then add **a** at the beginning)
a + ch + o-verb   (finally, drop the vowel before the **o**)

Dropping the vowel of the prefix before the **o** is regular, just the way you drop the vowel at the end of a verb before ±**a'chi**. So the only new thing you need to learn is that o-verbs with S prefixes have an extra **a** before the prefix. (**A** comes before the S prefix on an a-verb, too, though those do not work exactly the same way. However, as with a-verbs, the plural S prefixes beginning with **ha** are not used with o-verbs.)

When there is an A prefix in front of the S prefix on the o-verb, the extra **a** does not show up. (Again, this is similar to what happens with a-verbs.)

Issokchalitok.   "You woke me up."
Kiichollali.   "We are laughing at you."

However, the extra **a** is used after the subject prefix **hoo±**:

Hooasokchali.   "They are waking me."

Exercise 10B. Translate the following sentences into Chickasaw using o-verbs. Practice saying each one aloud. 1. I am blue (in color). (Unlike English *blue*, Chickasaw **okchamali** cannot mean "sad".) 2. Are you awake? 3. The doctor woke us up. 4. The children are laughing at us. 5. It rained for you guys. 6. You are not alive. 7. That woman's dress is green. 8. I am really laughing. 9. My mother's eyes are blue. 10. We are not awake.

Lesson 10.2:
The **on±** "on" Prefix

In lesson 8.1 you learned how the dative prefix **im±** can be used to add "to" or "for" objects to Chickasaw sentences. In this unit you'll learn several additional ways to add new nouns to sentences. For instance, **on±** can add an "on" noun:

omba to rain	**onomba** to rain on
tofa to spit	**ontofa** to spit on
bínni'li to sit	**ombinni'li** to sit on
malli to jump	**o̱malli** to jump on

It's easy to remember that **on±** means "on" in English (even though, of course, Chickasaw **on±** is not pronounced like English *on*). As the examples show, **on±** changes its form similarly to the way **im±** and the D prefixes do, according to the first sound of the following word. **On±** is used before vowels and before **k**, **t**, and **ch** (as you know, the **n**'s vary slightly in pronunciation); **om±** is used before **p** and **b**; and **o̱±** is used before all other sounds.

Like **im±** and **ik±** and the A and N prefixes, **on±** always forms a syllable by itself. So **onomba** "it rained on him" must be divided into syllables as **on/om/ba**. Sometimes, in fact, as with other ± prefixes before vowels, you may hear what sounds like a doubled **n** sound: <onnomba>. Listen to your teacher's pronunciation and imitate it.

Like the dative prefix **im±**, **on±** adds an extra participant, forming two-place verbs from one-place verbs; a sentence with an **on±** verb has an extra noun that's not present in the corresponding sentence without **on±**:

Hattakat tofatok.	"The man spat."
Hattakat ofi' ontofatok.	"The man spat on the dog."
Chipotaat mallitok.	"The child jumped."
Chipotaat topa o̱mallitok.	"The child jumped on the bed."

The sentences without **on±** are one-place sentences that can't have extra nouns added. With **on±**, the sentence has an "on" object (like **ofi'** or **topa** "bed") that works like any other object noun. Most **on±** verbs are not listed in the vocabulary, because their meaning and use is regular. They have an A subject (the one who performs the action) and an S object (the one on whom the action is done). Because all **on±** verbs are o-verbs (whether they start with **o** or **o̱**), they work in the special way you have just learned with S object prefixes.

Issontofatok.	"You spat on me."
Apo̱malli.	"He is jumping on us."

On± is usually not translated "onto". **O̱malli** tells the location of the jumping rather than its direction.

Exercise 10C. Change each Chickasaw sentence below into an **on±** sentence using the object in parentheses, as in the example. Translate the new sentences.

    Example. Kowi'at no̱watok. (the bed)

    Answer. Kowi'at topa o̱nowatok. "The cat walked on the bed."

    1. Foshi'at bínni'li. (my husband) 2. Ombatok. (me) 3. Alikchaat tofatok. (the money) 4. Ofi'at malli. (us) 5. Ishmallitok. (the house) 6. Tofala'chi. (you) 7. Chipotaat hootoyyatok. (us) 8. Hilhalitok. (the table). (**aai'pa'** = "table")

Lesson 10.3:
The ibaa± "with" Prefix

Look at the following sentences containing the prefix **ibaa±**:

Ihooa ibaamalilili.	"I'm running with the woman."
Ihooat sabaamalili.	"The woman is running with me."

Just like **im±** and **on±**, **ibaa±** adds an extra participant, someone who is participating "with" or "along with" someone else. When you add the prefix **ibaa±** onto a verb, you add a "with" object to the sentence—from the one-place verb **malili** "run", you can make the two-place verb **ibaamalili** "run with".

An **ibaa±** verb always has an A subject and an S "with" object, regardless of what kind of subject the original verb has. For instance, when you add **ibaa±** to **ayoppa** "be happy", you get a two-place (A,S) verb "be happy (along) with", even though (as you know) by itself **ayoppa** takes an S subject:

> Chipota ishibaa-ayoppatok.   "You were happy along with the child."

(Notice that when **ibaa±** comes before a verb starting with **a**, we use a hyphen to break up the string of three **a**'s. Listen to your teacher say this word. Because **ibaa±** ends in a long vowel, no short vowel is ever deleted after this prefix.) It works the same way when you add **ibaa±** to a D subject verb like **intakho'bi**. The new **ibaa±** verb also has an A subject and an S object:

> Issabaaintakho'bitok.   "You were lazy with me."

Ibaa± expresses a "with" or "along with" of accompaniment, or sometimes helping, never a "with" that means "using" (you'll learn about expressing this "with" in unit 13). Almost always, an **ibaa±** object is a human or other living creature. As the sentences above show, A prefixes come before the **ibaa±**. So do **ik±** and the N prefixes.

You can add **ibaa±** to an original two-place verb and get a new three-place verb with an **ibaa±** object, too. The **ibaa±** object tells someone who did the action along with the subject or helped the subject to do the action:

Hattaka fani' ibaahostok.	"She shot at the squirrel along with the man."
Hattaka chibaahostok.	"She shot at the man along with you."

The first sentence means that the man helped her shoot at the squirrel; the second means that you helped her shoot at the man. In both cases, two people are shooting, and only one thing is being shot. As you know, when there are two noun objects in front of a Chickasaw verb, they can come in either order and be interpreted either way. But only the first one of these two objects can have **±a** on it. Usually the **ibaa±** object word will come first, but not always. So, in fact, the first sentence above could mean "She shot at the man along with the squirrel"—as long as the squirrel was helping her shoot. (You could also say **Fani'a hattak ibaahostok.**) When there's an S prefix on an **ibaa±** verb like **ibaahosa**, though, that S prefix can only tell you who helped the subject perform the action. The second sentence above can't mean that you were shot at.

Exercise 10D. Write these sentences in Chickasaw. 1. He is singing with my father. 2. I ate with her brother. 3. The doctor will not jump with you all. 4. The deer was shot with the bear. 5. The horse was sick along with the dog. 6. Will you dance with me? 7. I could be happy with you. 8. We will drink with the chief. 9. I did not meet the woman with you. 10. We were sad with you.

Lesson 10.4:
Verbs That Specify Locations

Here are some words for places:

Oklahomma' Oklahoma
aalhponi', aaholhponi' kitchen
aachompa' town, store
pichchaa barn
kasbi yard

Naahollo Iyaakni' Texas
aanosi' bedroom; hotel
holiss-aapisa' school
aaittanaa' church
aaimpa' abooha dining room.

Place words often include the location prefix **aa±**, which you'll learn more about in this lesson—**aanosi'**, for instance, includes the verb **nosi** and means "place to sleep"; **aaimpa'** "restaurant" includes **impa** and means "place to eat"; **aaimpa' abooha** is a "room that's a place to eat". **Aachompa'** includes the verb **chompa** "to buy". This is a newer word for "town" than **okla**. When it makes sense, you can use a dative prefix to make a possessed form of these words just as you'd expect, and D prefixes can be used along with the dative prefix to tell who the possessor is: **amaanosi'** means "my bedroom", and **chiholiss-aapisa'** is "your school". (You'll learn more about nouns that include **aa±** and the use of the hyphen in this kind of word in unit 18.) **Yaakni'** means "land" or "world". What does **Naahollo Iyaakni'** mean? This word dates from the time when Oklahoma was Indian Territory and Texas wasn't.

*The **aa±** location prefix.* The prefix **aa±** is used on most verbs that tell the "in" or "at" location where some event occurred, as in

Oka' hooaayopitok.
Oklahomma' kilaahilhatok.
Holis-saapisa' aanosilitok.
Aaimpa' abooha kilaaimpa.

"They swam in the water."
"We danced in Oklahoma."
"I slept at school."
"We eat in the dining room."

You may not think of a location as a participant in the action, exactly, but **aa±** is like **im±**, **on±**, and **ibaa±** in creating a new verb that can be used in a sentence that contains an additional noun. The **aa±** prefix makes a verb that adds a location to the sentence.

Aa± goes at the front of the plain form of the verb. As the examples above show, **hoo±** and the A prefixes go in front of **aa±**. So do **ik±** and the N prefixes:

Aalhponi' kilaai̱'po.

"We don't eat in the kitchen."

No vowel is deleted after **aa±**. When **a** or **aa** follows **aa±**, you can write a hyphen:

Aaittanaa' aa-apilatok.

"She helped him at church."

Sometimes the **aa-a** sequence will be run together, especially when someone's speaking quickly, and you may not hear both syllables. But they're really there!

The location noun used with an **aa±** verb is an object. So **aa±** verbs like **aahilha** and **aayopi** that are formed from one-place verbs are two-place verbs—their subject is the subject of the one-place verb, and their object is a location noun.

With an original two-place verb, like **apila** in the last example or **isso** in the next one, **aa±** adds an extra location object in addition to the original object:

Okla aasapistok.	"She saw me in town."
Aanosi' ikaasassokitok.	"He didn't hit me in the bedroom."
Chokk<u>a</u> aachintaloowatok.	"He sang for you in the house."
Holiss-aapisa' aa-asafama'chi.	"She's going to meet me at school."
Oklahomma' kilaachihoyotok.	"We looked for you in Oklahoma."
Aalhponi' aa-asokaamichitok.	"She washed my face in the kitchen."
Aaittanaa' ishaapop<u>í</u>staam?	"Did you see us at church?"

As these examples show, **aa±** comes before an S, dative, or D prefix on the verb, as well as before the **a** at the beginning of an a-verb or an o-verb with an S prefix.

*Special combinations with **aa±**, a "you" subject, and a "me" object.* When **aa±** is used with a verb with a "you" subject prefix (**ish±** or **hash±**) and a "me" object prefix, the combinations work differently.

Although usually **aa±** comes before an S or D prefix, **ish±** or **hash±** plus the D prefix **(s)a+** plus the dative prefix **im±** (combining as **issam±** or **hassam±**) comes before **aa±**:

Holiss-aapisa' issamaahilhataa?	"Are you dancing for me at school?"
Kasbaak<u>o</u> hassamaataloowa.	"You all are singing to me in the <u>yard</u>."

Things are stranger when you combine **aa±** with **ish±** or **hash±** plus the S prefix **sa+** (combining as **issa+** or **hassa+**). In this case the **issa+** or **hassa+** combination comes first, followed by **aa±**, followed by another **sa+** before the verb.

Holiss-aapisa' issa-aasapisa'chitaa?	"Will you see me at school?"
Aaimpa' abooha issa-aasafamatok.	"You hit me in the dining room."

Probably it's best just to memorize these special combinations.

Aa± plus iksho. The verb **iksho** combines with **aa±** like this:

Pintaat abooh<u>a</u> aaiksho.	"There are no mice in the house."

Since you know that the **ik** at the beginning of **iksho** is like the unaccomplished prefix, you might think that **aa±** would go after this **ik**. But **aa±** goes in front of **iksho.** Once again, this verb does not work like other **ik±** verbs.

Exercise 10E. Translate the following sentences into Chickasaw using **aa±**. 1. The chief is eating in the bedroom! 2. We bought meat at the store. 3. I'll look for you at church. 4. The child doesn't want to sleep in his bedroom. 5. Dance in the yard! 6. You all will talk to me in the barn. 7. There's no bread in the basket. 8. That woman is going to work in Oklahoma.

Locations with weather verbs. A few verbs do not use **aa±** to refer to a location. For instance, to tell a location with a verb referring to weather conditions like **omba** "to rain" or **mahli** "to be windy", you don't use **aa±** and the location becomes the subject of the sentence:

Oklahomma'at ombatok.   "It rained in Oklahoma."
Naahollo Iyaaknaat mahli.   "It's windy in Texas."

This may remind you of English sentences like *Oklahoma was rainy* or *Texas is windy,* but the meaning is a little different.

Many other verbs whose main meaning is to tell location don't use **aa±** either. For example, **ánta** can take a location object without adding **aa±**:

Chokka' ánta.   "He is staying in the house."

Positional verbs. **Bínni'li** and other POSITIONAL verbs work similarly:

Chokka' bínni'li.   "He is in the house (sitting)."
Chokka' tí'wa.   "He is in the house (lying down)."
Chokka' híkki'ya.   "He is in the house (standing up)."

Tí'wa, **híkki'ya**, and **bínni'li** tell you what position a subject was in, in a location. These verbs never refer to getting into a position, only to being in it. (In contrast, **hika** "to stand up" refers only to assuming a position, not to being in it.)

Each of these positional verbs refers only to a singular subject. Most positional verbs have three different forms, depending on how many the subject refers to. In addition to the singular forms above, there are DUAL forms, used when the subject is exactly two, and TRIPLURAL forms, used when the subject is three or more:

chí'ya to sit (A); to be in (a location, sitting) (A,Noun) (dual subject)
binohmáa to sit (A); to be in (sitting) (A,Noun) (triplural subject)
káyya'a to lie (A); to be in (a location, lying) (A,Noun) (dual subject)
kahat máa to lie (A); to be in (lying) (A, Noun) (triplural subject)
hí'li to stand (A); to be in (a location, standing) (A,Noun) (dual subject)
hiyohmáa to stand (A); to be in (standing) (A,Noun) (triplural subject)

There are many different sets of positional verbs in Chickasaw, but these three are among the most common, and they are the ones most often used to refer to people. All positional verbs have singular, dual, and triplural subject forms, but most other verbs don't have these different forms. (You know one verb, "run", which has two forms, singular **malili** and plural **tilhaa**, which refers to two or more.) Positional verbs are stative verbs, and they have "surprising subjects" (unit 3) indicated with A markers.

Triplural positional verbs always include the auxiliary **máa**, which may be pronounced either separately (as in **kahat máa**) or attached to the end of the preceding word. With "they" subjects, there's nothing unusual about these verbs:

Ihoo yammat topa kahat máa.   "Those women are lying in the bed."
Chipotaat hiyohmáatok.   "The children were standing (in a standing position)."

(Never use **hoo±** with a triplural or plural subject verb.) **Binohmáa** and **hiyohmáa** are short forms of **binoht máa** and **hiyoht máa**. When you need an A or N prefix, it goes on **máa**, and you use the full form of the preceding word, ending in **t**:

Chokka' binoht hashmáa.	"You all are sitting in the house."
Kahat kiimáatok.	"We are lying down (in a lying position)."
Hattakat hiyoht ikmáokitok.	"The men weren't standing."

(The negative form of **máa** is **ikmáo**.) The Chickasaw A, S, D, and N plural prefixes are used with both dual and triplural subject verbs.

Two other singular subject positional verbs are commonly used to show the location of various kinds of objects or to talk about their existence:

wáyya'a to exist, be located (see below)   **tálla'a** to exist, be located (see below)

Wáyya'a is used to give the location of things that are thought of as having a relatively flat top and open space at the bottom. You can use this word to refer to the location of a car (**kaar,** in Chickasaw), a four-legged animal, a table, or an upside-down cup (**ishtaka'fa'**), all of which are seen as having an open area underneath. **Tálla'a** is the opposite—it refers to the location of things such as an upside-down table, a rightside-up cup, or a house, each of which is thought of as having a flat bottom with an open area above this. These words are very commonly used in Chickasaw but may sound rude when used to refer to people. Like the other positional verbs, **wáyya'a** and **tálla'a** take a location object, and they aren't used with **aa±**:

Kaarat okla wáyya'a.   "The car is in town", "There's a car in town."

Now, listen as your teacher says these forms of **wáyya'a**, **tálla'a**, and **káyya'a**:

Wáyya'atok.	Tálla'atok.	Káyya'atok.	Káyya'ali.

According to the rhythmic lengthening rule, you would expect the third **a** in these words to be lengthened, but, as you can hear, it is not. A vowel following a glottal stop is never rhythmically lengthened in Chickasaw. You can think of the ' in words like those above as like **'h**: in fact, some speakers say **káyya'a**, **wáyya'ha**, and **tálla'ha**. In these words the ' ends a heavy syllable (**kay/ya'/ha/tok**), so there is no reason to expect that the third **a** should be lengthened.

Exercise 10F. Tell where each of the following events takes place by adding the location in parentheses to the sentence. Some sentences will use **aa±** and some won't. Translate each sentence. 1. Taloowalitok. (aalhponi') 2. Ishánta'chi. (anchokka') 3. Chipotaat káyya'a. (inki' imaanosi') 4. Oktosha. (Naahollo Iyaakni') 5. Minkaat hiyohmáa. (okla yammako) 6. Ihooat ikhooyo'po. (oka') 7. Chihattak chikshọ'kokitok. (pichchaa) 8. Iichissa'chi. (kasbi) 9. Hashchí'ya. (aaittanaa'). 10. Iiholissochitok. (holiss-aapisa') 11. Alikchaat ittish lohmitok. (inchokka') 12. Sashkaat sashootok. (aalhponi') 13. Ankaarat wáyya'a (pichchaa). 14. Ishtaka'faat tálla'a. (aaịpa')

Make sure that you review the note on the stress in **+taa** and **+taam** questions using accented verbs like **bínni'li**, **tálla'a**, **wáyya'a**, and **kayya'a** at the end of lesson 8.7.

"Here" and "there". When an **aa±** verb is used without a location noun (with its location noun understood, in other words), the English translation will usually use the word "there":

Aahilhalitok.   "I danced there."

Or you can use the words **yammak** "there" or **yappak** "here":

Yammak aahilhalitok.	"I danced there, in that place."
Yappak aahilha!	"Dance here!"

Lesson 10.5:
The Special ±ak Object Ending

Yammak and **yappak** are related to the "that" and "this" words you already know, such as **yammat** and **yappat**. The new words contain a special object ending, ±**ak**, that can be used in place of ±**a** on many object nouns. It is common on location objects, but you will hear it used on many other noun objects of two- and three-place verbs in Chickasaw. Like ±**a**, ±**ak** is used to draw a little attention to the noun that it follows. Here are some examples:

Holiss-aapisa'ak aaimpa.	"She eats at school."
Ihooak ayyopáshli.	"I like the woman."
Oklahommaak ánta.	"He is staying in Oklahoma.", "He is in Oklahoma."
Ankaak imanompola'chi.	"He will talk to my father."

As the last two examples show, with a vowel-loss noun, the final vowel (and the following ', if there is one) combines with the ending ±**ak** to form ±**aak**.

There is never more than one ±**ak** in a sentence. It is rare for ±**ak** to be used in a sentence containing another object noun with the ±**a** ending or any contrastive object noun, although you may hear ±**ak** used on an object that comes after a contrastive subject:

Sashkaakoot yammak aahilha.	"<u>My mother</u> is dancing there."

> *Exercise 10G.* Use ±**ak** nouns to translate the objects in each of the following sentences. Some of the verbs use **aa±** and some don't. (Assume that objects are right-side up in their normal position.) 1. We sang at school. 2. I talked to the Chickasaw woman. 3. I am not staying at your house. 4. We (two) are sitting in the bedroom. 5. You all are standing there. 6. Our house is there. 7. It rained on my car. 8. Your car is at the church. 9. I was lying here. 10. The dog is here.

Lesson 10.6:
Locational Nouns

Sometimes you want to specify a location more precisely than just by using "in" or "at". In English we can do this with words like "behind", "on" (or "on top of"), and "under". In Chickasaw you can specify precise locations with LOCATIONAL NOUNS referring to a part of an object, such as

pakna' top	**nota'** bottom
anonka' inside	**ashaka'** rear, back
tikba' front	**apootaka'** side

Another word for "inside" is **anonkaka'**.

Locational nouns are used following another noun to specify a precise location with regard to that noun. Here are some examples using **chokka'** "house":

chokka' pakna'	"the top of the house"
chokka' nota'	"the bottom of the house"
chokka' anonka'	"the inside of the house"
chokka' a̱shaka'	"the back of the house"
chokka' tikba'	"the front of the house"
chokka' apootaka'	"the side of the house"

Normally, locational nouns are not used after nouns referring to living creatures.
    Locational noun phrases are often used as objects of **aa±** verbs, as in

    Chokka' anonka' aahilhatok.   "He danced at the inside of the house."

Sentences containing locational noun phrases can usually also be translated into English with phrases beginning with "on", "behind", "inside", "under", and so on. So the last example also means "He danced inside the house". The four locational nouns you have learned can have the following additional translations:

pakna' on, on top of	**nota'** under
anonka' inside, in	**a̱shaka'** (or **a̱shka'**) behind, in back of
tikba' in front of	**apootaka'** beside, next to

So, for instance, **pichcha̱a a̱shaka'** can mean either "behind the barn" (a location relative to the barn) or "the back of the barn" (an actual part of the barn)—two quite different things, depending on how the speaker uses the Chickasaw phrase.
    Sometimes only one translation works. The locational noun phrase **tali' nota'** can mean either "the bottom of the rock" or "the underside of the rock". Look at this sentence, though:

    Tali' nota'ak bínni'li.   "She is sitting under the rock."

In this case "She is sitting on the bottom of the rock" wouldn't make much sense—the "under" translation is better. (The locational noun phrase in this sentence has the special object ending **±ak**.) Similarly, the following sentence doesn't mean "they are sitting on the back of the house".

    Abooha a̱shaka' chí'ya.   "They (two) are sitting behind the house."

    Locational noun phrases can also be used as subjects:

Talhpak paknaat losa.	"The top of the basket is black."
Topa nota'at litiha.	"Under the bed is dirty.", "It's dirty under the bed."

As the second example shows, the locational noun phrase is not necessarily always the subject in English. But you should make the locational noun phrase the subject in Chickasaw if the verb you are using has the location as its real subject.
    The actual location can be understood:

Pakna' aahilhatok.	"He danced on top of it."
A̱shaka'at homma.	"The back of it was red.", "It was red in back of it."

150

Exercise 10H. Find the locational noun phrases in the following sentences and translate each sentence into English, choosing the translation that makes most sense to you.

Example. Ihooat imambooha a̲shaka'a̲ inchipota aapassa̲atok.

Answer. imambooha a̲shaka'a̲. "The woman spanked her son at (or in) the back of her house" *or* "The woman spanked her son behind her house".

1. Alikchaat itti'chanaa nota'ak aanositok. 2. Itti̲sha aaittanaa' a̲shaka' aalohmilitok. 3. Kowi'at abooha anonka' tí'wa. 4. Chishkaakoot itti' a̲shaka'ak híkki'yataam? 5. Ishtaka'faat chimaai̲'pa' pakna' tálla'a. 6. Holiss-aapisa' a̲shaka' binoht iima̲a. 7. Issoba-at pichcha̲a anonkaak wáyya'a. 8. Aai̲'pa' paknaat okchamali.

Lesson 10.7:
S Prefixes on Words Starting with Vowels

Prefixes on locational nouns. To say things like "under me" or "behind us", you use an S prefix on the locational noun:

sanota' "under me"
hachipakna' "on top of you guys"

You can say **asanonka'** for "inside me" (some speakers feel that **asanonkaka'**, with an extra **ka**, is a better way to say this). The S prefix goes into the word after the initial **a**, just as in an a-verb.

Nouns starting with o. There are only a few nouns that start with **o** and mark their possessor with an S prefix. Two of these are **oshi'** "son" and **oshiitiik** "daughter". S prefixes marking the possessors of such words work just like S prefixes on o-verbs. When an S prefix goes on a noun beginning with **o**, there is an **a** in front of the prefix consonant and the vowel of the S prefix drops:

asoshi' "my son"
aposhiitiik "our daughter"

Summary. When you add S prefixes to a word starting with a vowel, you do one of the following:

- If the word starts with a plain, short **i**, the **i** is dropped and the S prefix goes in its place. Example: <sa+ishto> = **sashto**.
- If the word starts with **a**, the S prefix goes between that **a** and the rest of the word. Example: <sa+abika> = **asabika**. The same is true of words that start with long **aa** in their original form; with these words, too, the **a** before the prefix is short. Example: <sa+aabi> = **asabi**. (The location prefix **aa±** remains long before an S prefix.)
- If the word starts with **o**, put the S prefix consonant at the front of the word and put an **a** in front of that. (Example: <sa+okcha> = **asokcha**, since the S prefix consonant is **s**.)
- If the word starts with any other vowel, you usually do the same thing as with words that start with **o**: put the S prefix consonant at the front of the word and put an **a** in front of that. (Example: <sa+o̲malli> = **aso̲malli**, since the S prefix consonant is **s**.)

All the examples of the last rule you saw earlier in this lesson were verbs that started with **o̲**, but words like **í̲la** "to be different" use S prefixes the same way:

Asíla.   "I am different."
Achílataa?   "Are you different?"

Exercise 10I. Combine each of the following words with the S prefix indicated and translate the new verbs you form. 1. (chi+) nota' 2. (po+) íla 3. (sa+) ollali 4. (chi+) aabachi 5. (sa+) pakna' 6. (sa+) oshiitiik 7. (sa+) ohilha 8. (chi+) ashaka' 9. (hachi+) íla 10. (chi+) anonkaka' 11. (hapo+) ilhpokonna 12. (po+) ishkin 13. (chi+) onomba. 14. (po+) íla.

Lesson 10.8:
Reciprocal Verbs

The **itti+** prefix makes a RECIPROCAL "each other" verb:

Hooilisho'katok.   "They kissed themselves."
Hooittisho'katok.   "They kissed each other."

A reflexive **ili+** verb's subject does some action to himself, as you learned in lesson 5.6. An **itti+** verb has a plural subject, and the subjects act on one another.

Itti+ becomes **itt+** before a verb starting with a vowel:

Ittabikachitok.   "They made each other sick."
Ittontofatok.   "They spat on each other."
Ittibaahilhatok.   "They danced with each other."
Ittintaloowatok.   "They sang for each other."

As these examples show, **itti+** comes before the prefixes **on±**, **ibaa±**, and **im±**.

The **it** of the **itti+** prefix usually drops after any A or N prefix or after the unaccomplished prefix **ik±**. **Hash±** plus **itti+** is **hashti+**; **ii±** or **kii±** plus **itti+** is **iiti+** or **kiiti+**; **ik±** plus **itti+** is **ikti+**; and **hachik±** plus **itti+** is **hachikti+**:

Hashtisho'katok.   "You kissed each other."
Kiititha'no.   "We don't know each other."

(Speakers don't always follow this rule. So you may hear people say things like **Hashittisho'katok** or **Kilittitha'no**, too.)

There are many special Chickasaw expressions that include **itti+** verbs but are not translated with "each other" or that have an unexpected meaning. For instance, **itti+** plus **halalli** "to pull", usually pronounced and written **ittihaalalli**, means not just "to pull each other" but (as you know) "to marry".

Ittihaalalli is special because it can be used like an ordinary two-place (A,S) verb, as well as like other reciprocal **itti+** verbs. It can have a singular subject, it takes S object prefixes, and usually the **it** at the beginning does not drop after an A or N prefix. Alternatively, you can use it as a one-place (A) reciprocal verb.

Chittihaalalli sabanna.   "I want to marry you."
Ilittihaalalla'chi.   "We are going to get married."

(Some speakers might say **iitihaalalla'chi** here, too.)

Another unusual **itti+** verb is **ittimanompoli** "to read". Can you imagine how this meaning developed from **itti+** plus **imanompoli** "talk to"? Like **ittihaalalli**, this verb can also be used with a singular subject. **Ittimanompoli** can be used with an additional dative prefix (as **imittimanompoli**), if you want to say "read to".

Exercise 10J. Translate the following sentences into Chickasaw. 1. My father wants to read to me. 2. The people hugged each other. 3. The animals bit each other. 4. You all will laugh at each other. 5. The Chickasaws did not chase each other. 6. Will you marry me? 7. We are operating on each other. 8. The children are washing each other's faces. 9. Do you all know each other? 10. We did not pay each other. 11. I read to my mother. 12. The white people sent each other money.

Terms and Concepts

O-VERB, POSITIONAL, DUAL, TRIPLURAL, LOCATIONAL NOUN, RECIPROCAL.

VOCABULARY

anonka', anonkaka' inside (locational noun); inside, in (SP, see note 1 below: with prefix, often anonkaka')

apootaka' side (locational noun); beside, next to

aachompa' town, store

aaimpa' restaurant

aaimpa' abooha dining room

aaittanaa' church

aai'pa' table

aalhponi', aaholhponi' kitchen

aanosi' bedroom

a̲shaka' rear, back (locational noun); behind, in back of (SP)

binohmáa to sit (A); to be in (sitting) (A,Noun) (triplural subject)

chí'ya to sit (A); to be in (a location, sitting) (A,Noun) (dual subject)

hí'li to stand (A); to be in (a location, standing) (A,Noun) (dual subject)

híkki'ya to stand (A); to be in (a location, standing) (A,Noun) (singular subject)

hiyohmáa to stand (A); to be in (standing) (A,Noun) (triplural subject)

holiss-aapisa' school

ishtaka'fa' cup

ittimanompoli to read (A,Noun)

ittihaalalli to marry (A,S); to get married (A)

i̲la to be different (S)

kahat máa to lie (A); to be in (lying) (A,Noun) (triplural subject)

kasbi yard

káyya'a, káyya'ha to lie (A); to be in (a location, lying) (A,Noun) (dual subject)

kaar car

mahli to be windy (—); to have wind (of a location) (Noun); wind (noun)

Naahollo I̲yaakni' Texas

nota' bottom (locational noun); under (SP)

okcha to be awake, to wake up (S)

okchali to wake (someone) up (A,S)

okchamali to be blue, to be green (S)

okcháa to be alive (S)

okaamichi to wash (someone's) face (A,S)

Oklahomma' Oklahoma

oktosha to snow (—)

ollali to laugh (A); to laugh at (A,S)

oshi' son (SP)

oshiitiik daughter (SP)

pakna' top (locational noun); on, on top of (SP)

pichcha̱a barn

tálla'a to exist (Noun); to be located in (a location) (Noun,Noun) (of a noun thought of as having an opening at the top)

tí'wa to lie (A); to be in (a location, lying) (A,Noun) (singular subject)

topa bed

wáyya'a to exist (Noun); to be located in (a location) (Noun,Noun) (of a noun thought of as having an opening to the bottom)

yaakni' land; world

NOTES

1. The S prefixes that go on locational nouns are similar to the S possessive prefixes on possessed nouns, so the fact that these nouns are used with S prefixes is indicated with (SP) after the nouns.

Some speakers use **wáyya'a** with a human A subject to tell a person's location in a joking way. This type of sentence may sound quite rude to many people, so you probably should not use the verb this way yourself until you really feel comfortable with the language.

Does your teacher pronounce **aai'pa'** and **aaimpa'** differently? If not, of course, you should follow your teacher's pronunciation, but if so, make sure you can pronounce the difference. You'll learn more about words like this in unit 18.

READING AND SPEAKING

Telling Time

In order to tell time, you need to be able to count to twelve. In unit 3 you learned to count to ten. Here are the Chickasaw numbers from ten to twenty:

awa-chaffa	eleven
awa-toklo	twelve
awa-tochchí'na	thirteen
awa-oshta	fourteen
awa-talhlhá'pi	fifteen
awa-hanná'li	sixteen
awa-ontoklo	seventeen
awa-ontochchí'na	eighteen
awa-chakká'li	nineteen
pokoli toklo	twenty

Not all Chickasaw speakers use these numbers, but many do. Almost no one uses any numbers higher than twenty, but you will learn about how to form these in the Advanced Chickasaw Grammar section of unit 11.

Now, here's how to talk about time:

Hashi' kanalli katohmi?	"What time is it?"
Hashi' kanalli chaffa.	"It's one o'clock."
Hashi' kanalli tochchí'na.	"It's three o'clock."
Hashi' kanalli awa-toklo.	"It's twelve o'clock." etc.

Unit 12 includes more about using numbers in sentences.

A Story about Old Times

Below is another short reading about old times in the Chickasaw Nation (Mrs. Willmond's original version is in appendix B). Read the Chickasaw story aloud, using the supplementary vocabulary to help you figure out its meaning. Try to understand the story before you look at the English translation at the end of this unit.

Itti' Ittabaana' Abooha

Hopaakikaashookano hattakat ilaapakáynit chokka' ikbihminattook. Itti' ittabaana' abooha ikbihminattook. Ilaapakáynit itti' hoocha'lihminattook. Abokkoli' anonka'a itti' aa-ayowahminattook. Itti' katolhlhihminattook. Itti'chanaaa itti' anihminattook. Itti' shaalihminattook. Itti' yammako chokka' ikbihminattook. Aahashtahli' chompahminattook. Aahashtahli' abihlihminattook. Mishsha' fónkha áyya'shookano aahashtahli'a amposhi' shokawwa'li' nannakya ikabihlokihminattook. Okkisoshi'o ikbihminattook. Himmaka' nittakookano itti' ittabaana' abooha nannakya iksho. Itti' basha' abooha bíyyi'ka, lokfi' nona' abooha bíyyi'ka, yammakilla himmaka' nittakookano.

SUPPLEMENTARY VOCABULARY

abihli to put (two or a small number of objects) in (A,S,Noun)
amposhi' shokawwa'li' glass
ani to put (many objects or a liquid) into (a container) (irregular verb—see note 2 below)
aahashtahli' window
cha'li to chop, to chop down (A,Noun)
itti' basha' abooha frame house
itti' ittabaana' abooha log house, log cabin
katolhlhi to cut, cut up (A,Noun)
lokfi' nona' abooha brick house
mishsha' fónkha áyya'shookano in still earlier times
okkisoshi' little door
shaali to haul (A,Noun)
yammakilla just that, just those

NOTES

1. As in earlier stories, most of the verbs here use remote habitual +**hminattook**.
2. As noted earlier, Chickasaw has some irregular verbs, such as **ani** "to put in". Irregular verbs do not follow the rules you have learned concerning how prefixes and endings are used. You'll learn how to use them in unit 11.
3. **Amposhi' shokawwa'li'** "glass" originally referred only to a drinking glass, but it now can be used to refer to the material, as used in windows, for example.

BEYOND THE GRAMMAR: USING CHICKASAW AND CHOCTAW DICTIONARIES

You already know how to use the vocabulary at the back of this book, which includes many of the words you might want to look up. Several other dictionaries of Chickasaw and Choctaw will help you learn about additional words that aren't in the vocabulary—but you have to learn a few tricks to be able to use them effectively.

The dictionary that will probably seem easiest for you to use at this point is *Chickasaw: An Analytical Dictionary* (University of Oklahoma Press, 1994) by Pamela Munro and Catherine Willmond, the authors of *Chikashshanompa' Kilanompoli'*. Because it uses exactly the spelling system that you already know, you won't have to learn any new rules. The only thing you need to be aware of to start using it is that it employs some different abbreviations to tell about verb subject and object markers from the ones that are used in this book. Instead of A markers, *Chickasaw: An Analytical Dictionary* refers to I markers; S prefixes are called II prefixes; and D prefixes are called III prefixes. Once you learn these new terms, you won't have any trouble using this dictionary.

The only other dictionary of Chickasaw is *A Chickasaw Dictionary* by Vinnie May (James) Humes and the Reverend Jesse Humes, published by the Chickasaw Nation. (Mrs. Humes was the mother of former Chickasaw governor Overton James.) This book, which goes from English to Chickasaw, includes a number of interesting old words, but is sometimes a bit difficult to use because the spelling system is not always consistent. For instance the letter *u* is used to represent the sounds of both short **a** and short **o**. *A Chickasaw Dictionary* does not write the Chickasaw ' sound, and you may find other differences. The authors give pronunciation hints that may be helpful, however, and you can always ask a speaker of Chickasaw about the pronunciation of a word. (Some speakers claim that some of the words in the Chickasaw Dictionary are actually Choctaw, not Chickasaw, but opinions vary on this subject. The definitions in this dictionary are very brief, and there is no grammatical information to show how words are used in sentences. Although part-of-speech identifications such as "noun" and "verb" are included, these usually refer to the English words listed and do not always match the Chickasaw.)

Several good Choctaw dictionaries were written during the nineteenth century, but only the *Dictionary of the Choctaw Language* by the missionary Cyrus Byington (see the Beyond the Grammar section of unit 7) is now generally available. This dictionary was originally published by the Bureau of American Ethnology, part of the Smithsonian Institution in Washington, D.C., and has been reprinted several times. The Central Council of Choctaws in Oklahoma City published the most widely distributed reprint, in two volumes: Choctaw-English (with a green cover) and English-Choctaw (with a blue cover). Both these volumes usually have pictures of the late Choctaw chief David Gardner on the front, and both include pages of photographs of well-known Choctaws.

Byington's dictionary uses roughly the same spelling system that we use for Chickasaw, with a few important differences. Occasionally, Byington didn't notice double consonants, so he wrote some of these with single letters. The glottal stop sound ' does not occur in the middle of Choctaw words as it does in Chickasaw, so you won't see this letter in the dictionary. Most of the differences between Byington's *Dictionary* and our book involve vowel sounds. Nasal vowels, for example, are written with a small raised *n* after the vowel rather than underlined. The chart on the next page gives some other correspondences for you to be aware of. The *ạ* with a dot underneath it represents the short **a** sound, which is written in some other older Choctaw books with a *v* (sometimes this letter is in italics, sometimes not). The dotted *ạ* was added by some scholars who edited Byington's book without knowing as much Choctaw as he did.

Byington's *Dictionary*	*Chikashshanompa' Kilanompoli'*
a	**aa** *or* **a**
ạ	**a**
o	**oo** *or* **o**
u	**o**
e	**ii**
i	**ii** *or* **i**

Another change these editors made involved the **lh** sound. Byington used both *lh* and *hl* to represent this sound. The editors changed all the *hl*'s in the book to *ł* (an *l* with a line through it, or slashed *l*), which, they wrote, should be pronounced like our **lh**. However, some of the *hl*'s that they changed represent sequences of **h** plus **l**, rather than the letter combination **lh**, as in the word **mahli** "wind", which does not contain the **lh** sound. So a slashed *ł* in Byington's dictionary may represent either **lh** or **hl**.

As Byington's dictionary, which was first published in 1915, was written well over a hundred years ago, it contains many old words that are no longer used, even in Choctaw. Since many of the words in Choctaw and Chickasaw are the same (as explained in the Beyond the Grammar section of unit 9), however, you can often find a word you're looking for in Byington's dictionary. Before using any word you find in this dictionary, however, you should check with a Chickasaw speaker to make sure the word you've found really is used in Chickasaw and to see if you've figured out the pronunciation correctly.

Some modern works on Choctaw, including the *Introduction to Choctaw* by Betty Jacob, T. Dale Nicklas, and Betty Lou Spencer and *Choctaw Language and Culture: Chahta Anumpa* by Marcia Haag and Henry Willis, use spelling systems quite similar to Byington's. There are also many more technical works on Choctaw grammar written for linguists.

Story translation

Log Houses

Long ago people would build houses themselves. They would build log houses. They would chop trees down themselves. They would get trees in the woods. They would cut the trees up. They would put the logs in wagons. They would haul the logs. They would make those logs into a house. They would buy windows. They would put the windows in. In still earlier times they didn't put any glass in windows. They would make little doors. Nowadays there aren't any log houses. It's all frame houses, it's all brick houses, there are just those nowadays.

Unit 11

Irregular Verbs

In this unit you'll learn about a number of Chickasaw irregular verbs and about how to form a type of complex sentence containing more than one verb.

Lesson 11.1 presents the irregular verb "be", and lesson 11.2 introduces the irregular short verbs. Lesson 11.3 describes "when" sentences containing dependent verbs. The Advanced Chickasaw Grammar unit covers formation of higher numbers, which are used very seldom by Chickasaw speakers.

| **Lesson 11.1:** "Be" in Chickasaw | Here are some new nouns you will be able to use in this unit: |

Chalakki' "Cherokee"
Hattak Api' Homma' *or* Hattak Nipi' Homma' "Indian"
ink<u>a</u>na' "friend" (DP)
Mashkooki' "Creek"
Shimmanooli' "Seminole"
nannimaabachi' "teacher"
naalhtoka' "policeman"
Oshpaani' "Mexican, Hispanic person"

"(DP)" means that **ink<u>a</u>na'** "friend" (or "his or her friend") contains a dative prefix. To express other possessors, add the proper D prefix before the dative prefix **in±** at the beginning of the word. Thus, **ank<u>a</u>na'** means "my friend", and so on.

Irregular verbs. As you've learned, a few Chickasaw verbs are irregular—they do not follow the rules you've learned for adding prefixes and endings. The most irregular verb in Chickasaw is "be". As you learned in unit 2, with a noun or understood subject there is no word "be" or any form like "is" or "are" at all:

Ihoo.   "It (*or* She) is a woman."
Ihooat alikchi'.   "The woman is a doctor."

The verb "be". You would probably guess that since "be" refers to a state, it would be used with the S prefixes. However, how can you add a prefix onto a verb that's not there? With an S prefix subject, you use the form <ya>:

saya "I am"	chiya "you are"	poya "we are"

(We write <ya> in <>'s as a reminder that <ya> is not a word by itself. <Ya> must always have an S prefix to be used in a Chickasaw sentence.) These words are used in sentences like

Mashkooki' poya.	"We are Creeks."
Naalhtoka' saya.	"I am a policeman."

Unlike all the other Chickasaw verbs you have learned so far, these new "be" words are not complete sentences and do not make sense when used by themselves. They must always be used with a preceding noun.

The new "be" verbs can be used with endings like **+tok**, **+taam**, and **±a'chi**:

Alikchi' sayatok.	"I was a doctor."
Minko' chiyataam?	"Were you a chief?"
Nannimaabachi' poya'chi.	"We will be teachers."

"Be" without a prefix. "Be" changes when it's used in a sentence with an ending but no S prefix. Take a sentence like

Hattakat ponkana' ki'yo.	"The man isn't our friend."

You might think you would use <yatok> to put this sentence in the past, but you don't. With an ending but no S prefix, "be" is <oo> (again, we write this word in angled brackets because it must be used with an ending; it can't be used alone):

Hattakat ankana' ootok ki'yo.	"The man wasn't my friend."
Ihooat minko' ootaam?	"Was the woman a chief?"

With the ending **±a'chi** and no prefix, there's no visible form of "be":

Minkaat chinkana' a'chi.	"The chief is going to be your friend."

What happens here? Maybe the vowel <oo> deletes before the vowel-initial ending **±a'chi**, though we know this doesn't usually happen with long vowels. Maybe this is <a> plus **±a'chi**. Or maybe it is just another, different form of "be" to learn. (The ending **±a'ni** might work similarly, but this ending isn't normally used in "be" sentences.)

The prefix **hoo±** is never used with any form of "be", and "be" is never used with an N prefix. You'll learn another way to ask "Is it a . . . ?" questions (without "be") in unit 17.

Exercise 11A. Translate each of the following sentences into English. 1. Chalakki' chiyataa? 2. Hattak inkana' saya. 3. Shimmanooli' poya. 4. Chahta' ki'yo. 5. Ihoo hachiyatok. 6. Hattak losa' poya. 7. Hattak Api' Homma' ootok. 8. Hattak yammakoot Oshpaani' ootok ki'yo. 9. Minko' saya'chi. 10. Chikashsha poya ki'yo.

Lesson 11.2:
Short Verbs

"Be" is the most irregular verb in Chickasaw: sometimes it isn't used at all, and its form can change completely, from <ya> to <oo>. The other Chickasaw irregular verbs are all SHORT VERBS—verbs consisting of a short vowel, a single consonant, and another short vowel. All short verbs are irregular. Here are three of them:

ala to arrive, to get here (A)
apa to eat (something) (A,S)
abi to kill (A,S)

Apa is a two-place verb, used when you want to mention the thing that's eaten or to say "eat it". **Impa** "to eat" is a one-place verb.

Exercise 11B. Look at the following examples of the new short verbs with A and N prefixes. Try to see what the new patterns are and then answer the questions below.

With A prefixes

Ishla. "You arrive, You get here."
Hashpa. "You all eat it."
Kiibi. "We kill him."
Ki'bo. "We don't kill him."

With N Prefixes

Aklo. "I do not arrive."
Ikpo. "He is not eating it."
Chikbo. "You don't kill him."

i. What happens to the new verbs when they are used with A prefixes? With **ik±** or N prefixes (and the **±o** ending)? Try to give a general answer to this question.

ii. Translate the following: 1. He is eating it. 2. She arrives. 3. Your friend doesn't kill it. 4. We eat it. 5. She kills the snake. (**sinti'** = "snake") 6. You kill it. 7. It is not arriving. 8. I don't eat snakes. 9. I don't kill it. 10. You don't eat it. 11. You all get here. 12. We arrive.

Nothing unexpected happens when the new short verbs are used with the A subject ending **+li**, with no ending (for a "he", "she", "it", or "they" subject), with the plural subject prefix **hoo±**, or with the special "we" prefix **kiloo±**:

Abili.	"I kill it."
Abi.	"She kills it."
Hooabi.	"They kill it."
Kilooabi.	"We (relatively many) kill it."

Shortening short verbs. When the new short verbs are used with A or N prefixes (other than **kiloo±**), however, their initial **a** drops, as you saw in exercise 11B:

Ishbi.	"You kill it."
Kiila.	"We arrive."
Ikpo.	"He doesn't eat it."
Chikbo.	"You don't kill it."
Ki'lo.	"We don't arrive."

You'd expect that these verbs would be used with the "we" prefixes **il±** or **kil±**, since each of them starts with a vowel in its dictionary form. When the initial **a** of these verbs drops, however, these new short verbs act as if they started with consonants. With an N prefix and the negative ending **±o**, the last vowel of these short verbs drops, too—so the middle consonant is the only thing left of the verb!

Short verbs with S prefixes. The **a** at the beginning of these three new short verbs also drops when an S object prefix is used:

Sapa.	"He's eating me."
Chibila'chi.	"I'm going to kill you."

This is different from they way S prefixes work with other a-verbs (you learned about this in unit 6).

Now, look at where the ' goes in negative short verbs with prefixes:

Iksa'bo.	"He isn't killing me."
Akchi'poka'chi.	"I won't eat you."

The ' always goes right in front of any single consonant in front of **±o**. As you saw above, the long vowel at the end of the N "we" prefix **kii±** shortens before the ':

Ki'pokitok.	"We didn't eat it."

The special "we" N prefix **kiloo±** is not used on negative short verbs.

An unusual reciprocal verb. **Ittibi** means "to fight". It's formed by adding the reciprocal prefix **itti+** to **abi**, but the result is not <ittabi> as you'd expect. Like **ittihaalalli** "to marry" (unit 10), **ittibi** can be used with a singular object, as well as like other reciprocal verbs.

Exercise 11C. Translate the following sentences into Chickasaw. Some use short verbs, some don't.
1. He's not here. (He has not arrived). 2. Are you here? (Did you get here?) 3. Did she eat you? 4. Did the Creek eat? 5. They killed us. 6. We are dead. 7. They are here, They have arrived. 8. You all are going to kill me. 9. We fought. 10. He fought me. 11. We (relatively few) didn't kill the hog. (**shokha'** = "hog") 12. We didn't get here. 13. I ate. 14. I ate it.

Short verbs with dative prefixes. With dative and D prefixes, the short verbs **ala**, **apa**, and **abi** also behave in an unexpected way. Here are some dative prefix forms of **ala** and **apa**:

Imappalitok.	"I ate it for him."
Chimallatok.	"He came to you, He arrived for you."

After the dative prefix, the single consonant of **apa** and **ala** becomes a doubled consonant. When these words are divided into syllables, **im/ap/pa/li/tok** and **chim/al/la/tok**, you can hear that the syllable after the dative prefix is a heavy syllable. With **abi** things are different. After the dative prefix, **abi** becomes <ambi>.

   Imambitok.   "He killed it for her."

When an N prefix is added to one of these short verbs with dative or D-plus-dative prefixes, the results are just as you'd expect:

   Ikimappo.   "He's not eating it for her."
   Chiksama'bokitok.   "You didn't kill it for me."

Imalla and **imappa** work like other verbs with two consonants before the last vowel—there's no added ' in the negative form. **Imambi** works like other verbs that end in a nasal consonant plus **b**, **ch**, **k**, **p**, or **t** plus a vowel—' is added, and the vowel-plus-nasal consonant is replaced by a nasal vowel.

Exercise 11D. Add either a noun and a dative prefix or a D-plus-dative prefix combination to each of the following Chickasaw sentences. (Not all of them use short verbs. Keep in mind the rules about object marking.) Then translate the new sentences you make up.
 Example. Alikchaat shokha' abitok. (for the woman)
 Answer. Alikchaat ihooa shokha' imambitok. "The doctor killed the hog for the woman."
 1. Chipotaat nipi' apatok. (for his mother) 2. Kiila'chi. (to you) 3. Chipotaat impatok. (for his father) 4. Hattakat nita'a abitok. (for the chief) 5. Foshi'at hootaloowa. (for you all) 6. Abikatok. (for us) 7. Ishlataam? (for your sister) 8. Fani' akbokitok. (for my friend) 9. Paska kiipa ki'yo. (for the doctor) 10. Hashhilha'ntaa? (for us)

Two more short verbs. Here are two more new short verbs:

   ani to put into a container (especially, to pour) (A,S), to set fruit,
    to have fruit on it (of a plant) (Noun)
   amo to mow, harvest (grass), to give a haircut to (A,S)

Each of these new verbs has two quite different meanings. (Not all Chickasaw speakers use the second meaning of **amo**, however. Follow your teacher's usage.) These new short verbs use endings, **hoo±**, the dative prefix **im±**, and D prefixes in the same way as the first three short verbs:

   Amo.   "He is cutting it."
   Anili.   "I pour it."
   Hooamotok.   "They mowed it."
   Chimannila'chi.   "I'll pour it for you."
   Imammotok.   "He mowed it for her."

The verb **ani**. Now, look at the way **ani** works with A prefixes:

   Ishanni.   "You pour it."
   Ilannitok.   "We poured it."

After an A prefix, **ani** has the same <anni> form used after the dative prefix. With an N prefix, you can either use this same <anni> form or use the regular form **ani**. (Of course, the final **i** of the verb drops before negative ±**o**.)

Ika'nokitok, Ikannokitok.	"It did not set fruit.", "He didn't pour it."
Aka'no, Akanno.	"I don't pour it."

These two different negative forms of **ani** both mean the same thing.

The verb amo. **Amo** is also used in two different ways with A and N prefixes. Some people drop the **a** (as with the short verbs **ala**, **apa**, and **abi**), and some double the consonant (as with **ani**). Compare these two sets of examples:

Like ala, apa, or abi		*Like ani*
ishmo	"you mow"	ishammo
ikmo	"he doesn't mow"	ikammo
kiimo, iimo	"we mow"	kilammo, ilammo
ki'mo	"we don't mow"	kilammo

See which forms your teacher prefers. Most likely, he or she will use only forms from one of these two columns, but some people may use some from one column and some from the other.

Exercise 11E. i. What are the Chickasaw short verbs you have learned so far? Explain the differences in how these verbs are used with the prefixes you know.

ii. Translate these Chickasaw sentences into English. 1. Oka' issamannitaam? 2. Hattakat ihoo imallatok. 3. Tii' kilanna'chi. 4. Chipotaat ishka nipi' imappa'chi. 5. Nita minko' ishimamba'ntaa?

iii. Translate the following three sentences and then give another way to say each one.

6. Takolo ika'no. (**takolo** = "peach") 7. Ankanaat hashshok ikmokitok. (**hashshok** = "grass") 8. Ishma'ni pobanna.

The verb aya. The Chickasaw verb "go" is **aya**. As the following examples of **aya** show, it is also an irregular verb.

Ayali.	"I go."
Aya.	"He goes."
Ishiyya.	"You go."
Kiliyya.	"We go."
Hashiyya.	"You all go."

Whenever there is an A prefix before the verb "go", it changes from **aya** to <iyya>.

A different form, <ayya>, is used when "go" has a dative, unaccomplished, or N prefix. (In a negative sentence, you also need to add the ending ±**o**.)

Chimayyali.	"I go to you."
Akayyo.	"I don't go."

The basic verb **aya** is used with other prefixes like **hoo±** and **ibaa±**:

Hooayatok.	"They went."
Kilíbaa-ayatok.	"We went with him."

In the last example there is an A prefix, but you still use **aya**, because the A prefix is not right in front of "go".
Objects with aya. **Aya** can take a place as its object:

Holiss-aapisa' ishiyyataa?	"Are you going to school?"

(You don't need to use **aya** with an **aa±** prefix.)
You need a dative prefix on the verb to say "go to" a person:

Chishkaak ishimayyataa?	"Are you going to your mother?"

Practice saying all the forms of "go" after your teacher.

> *Exercise 11F.* I. Translate these sentences into Chickasaw. 1. They will go to town. 2. They will go to the chief. 3. You didn't go to Oklahoma. 4. You all can go to us. 5. The deer goes to the child. 6. I will go with my father. 7. The men want to go with each other. 8. We can go. 9. Did you go to Texas? 10. I went yesterday.

The verbs ishi and í'shi. **Ishi** means "take", "get", or "pick up (something)":

Ishi!	"Pick it up!"
Ishilitok.	"I took it."
Hooisha'chi.	"They will get it."
Ibaaishitok.	"He got it with her."

Like **aya**, **ishi** changes its form after an A prefix, after the unaccomplished prefix **ik±**, or after an N prefix. After an A prefix, use **íshi**:

Ishíshi.	"You are taking it."
Kilíshtok.	"We took it."

With **ik±** or an N prefix, add **'** and **±o**:

Akí'shokitok.	"I didn't take it."
Kilí'shoka'chi.	"We won't get it."

Ishi with a dative prefix. With a dative object prefix, you use the verb **ishi** no matter what other prefix is used. **Imishi** "to take for" is divided into syllables as **i/mi/shi**—in other words, the **m** of **im±** does not have to end a syllable. Listen as your teacher pronounces the following sentences, paying attention to the lengthened vowels:

Amīshtok.	"He took it for me."
Issamīsha'chitaa?	"Will you get it for me?"
Akimi'shokitok.	"I didn't take it for him."

"Keep", "hold". **Íʼshi** means "to keep" or "to hold" (some people use it to mean "to have" when referring to actual physical possession). This verb is not a short verb, though it is related to **ishi**, so its forms are all regular. Make sure you can hear the difference between pairs of sentences like the following:

Kilíshi.	"We are taking it."
Kilíʼshi.	"We are keeping it."

The first sentence uses the **íshi** form of **ishi** "take"; the second, **íʼshi** "keep".

With a noun subject or a +**li** "I" subject, the two verbs sound more different:

Ishi.	"He's taking it."
Íʼshi.	"He's keeping it."
Ishili.	"I'm taking it."
Íʼshli.	"I'm keeping it."

The negative of **ishi** sounds just like the negative of **íʼshi**. This isn't usually confusing in a conversation:

Akíʼshokitok.	"I didn't take it.", "I didn't keep it."

> *Exercise 11G*. Read the following Chickasaw sentences out loud and then translate them. 1. Hashíʼshtaa? 2. Hattakat talhpaka̲ ihoo imishtaam? 3. Ishtaka'fa̲ íʼshi chibannataa? 4. Kowi' íʼshlitok. 5. Ofi' ishíshtaa? 6. Nipi'ako̲ ishilitok. 7. Minkaat holisso ishitok. 8. Alikchaat itti̲sh íʼshi. 9. Paska chikíʼshokitok. 10. Bashpo íʼshtok. 11. Anka̲naat amishtok. 12. Folosh ikíʼshok'achi.

The verb ima. **Ima** "to give to" is always a three-place verb—it always includes a dative prefix. Listen as your teacher says the following Chickasaw sentences:

Hattakat ihoo ofi' imātok.	"The man gave the woman a dog.",
	"The man gave a dog to the woman."
Bashpo ishīmataam?	"Did you give the knife to him?"
Nipi' chimāla'chi.	"I'll give you the meat."

You learned in unit 4 that an A prefix can't be split up by the process of syllable division, and in unit 7 you learned that the same is true of the dative prefix **im±**. Normally, each of these prefixes forms a heavy syllable by itself, and you begin counting short syllables in a rhythmic lengthening sequence after the end of one of these prefixes. This regular rule is broken for the verb **ima**. Both the dative prefix that is included in the verb and any added A prefix may be divided up by the regular rules of syllable division that you learned in units 1 and 4:

i/mā/tok	i/shī/ma	chi/mā/li	ha/shī/ma	ki/lī/ma
1 2	1 2	1　2	1　2	1 2

In each case syllable counting starts at the very beginning of the word, whether there is an A prefix or not, and the even-numbered short syllables are rhythmically lengthened. As you know, **im±** and the A and dative prefixes are normally ± prefixes, which means that they don't count as part of a rhythmic lengthening sequence of short syllables. With **ima** these prefixes act like + prefixes: they can be divided into separate syllables, and they count as part of the rhythmic lengthening sequence.

However, short-syllable counting still does not include the **ha±** of the D prefixes **hapom±** and **hachim±**:

hachi/mā/li   hapo/mā/tok
  1 2   1 2

And of course, if the A prefix forms a heavy syllable by the regular rule, short-syllable counting starts after that prefix:

kii/chi/mā/tok   has/sa/mā/ta
    1 2   1 2

Short verbs with o. There are two short verbs that start with **o**: **ona** "to get there" and **ola** "to crow, to make a noise". (**Ona** "get there" is roughly the opposite of **ala** "get here". **Ola** refers mainly to animals making their characteristic noises but may also refer to the sound of musical instruments.) These verbs are irregular, like **ima**, in the way they work with **im±** and the A and D prefixes. Listen to the following examples:

Hashōnatok.	"You all got there."
Amōla'chi.	"He will crow for me."

We'd expect the A prefix **hash±** or the D prefix **am±** to form their own separate, heavy syllables. Instead, they are divided by the rule of syllable division, serving as the first short syllables in rhythmic lengthening sequences. With **ona** and **ola**, as with **ima**, an added A, dative, or D prefix acts like a + prefix rather than a ± prefix.

ha/shō/na/tok   a/mō/la'/chi
1 2 3   1 2

When **ona** or **ola** has both an A prefix and a dative prefix, the A prefix acts like a ± prefix, but the dative prefix is included in the rhythmic lengthening sequence:

Ishimonataam?   (ish/i/mō/na/taam)   "Did you get there for him?"
                            1 2

With **ik±** and the N prefixes, all three of these new verbs work just as you'd expect:

Chiksa'mokitok.	"You didn't give it to me."
Ako'noka'chi.	"I'm not going to get there."
Ikhoo-o'lo.	"They aren't crowing."

You've now seen ten Chickasaw short verbs: **abi**, **ala**, **amo**, **ani**, **apa**, **aya**, **ima**, **ishi**, **ola**, and **ona**. Every language has some irregular verbs, which are often among the most common verbs in the language. In Chickasaw these short verbs (except for **amo** and **ola**) are very common verbs that you will hear and need to use every day, so you must memorize the way each one works.

Exercise 11H. Translate the following sentences into Chickasaw. 1. The rooster didn't crow yesterday (**ak̲anakni'** = "rooster"). 2. We gave it to him. 3. Did you get there? 4. Did you get (there) to him? 5. Did she get (here) to him? 6. I will pour it for you. 7. He didn't mow it. 8. Kill me! 9. I ate it for her. 10. We went with you. 11. Did you get it? 12. Are you giving it to me?

Lesson 11.3:
Building Longer Chickasaw Sentences

In lesson 9.7 you learned about sentences that use **banna** "want" with another verb. In this lesson you'll learn another way to make Chickasaw sentences that have more than one verb. One verb in such a sentence is the MAIN VERB, and all the others are DEPENDENT VERBS. The main verb is the one that is marked for present, past, future, "can", and so on, like the verb in a sentence with only one verb. Dependent verbs are marked to show their relationship to the main verb.

Hilhalihmat taloowalitok.	"After I danced, I sang."
Alikchaat itt̲ish ishihmat ayatok.	"After the doctor got the medicine, he went."

In these sentences the second verb is the main verb. (Usually, the main verb comes last in Chickasaw.) The main verb could be used by itself as a complete sentence, but the dependent verb, which comes before the main verb, doesn't have one of the sentence endings you've learned before. In the sentences above, the dependent verbs have the ending ±**hmat**. ±**Hmat** means something like "after": it shows that the first action started before the second one.

Two kinds of "after". In both of the examples above, the subjects of the main and the dependent verb are the same: the speaker is the subject of both verbs in the first sentence, and the doctor is the subject of both verbs in the second. ±**Hmat** is only used when both the dependent verb and the main verb have the same subject. If the subjects of the two verbs are different, you use the ending ±**hma**:

Ishhilhahma taloowalitok.	"After you danced, I sang."
Itt̲ish ishilihma alikchaat ayatok.	"After I got the medicine, the doctor went."

We're using a comma (,) after the dependent sentence in the English but not in the Chickasaw. This is because Chickasaw speakers usually don't use as long a pause after their dependent sentence as English speakers do. However, if you want to write a comma in Chickasaw, that's fine.

Both ±**hmat** and ±**hma** mean "after". (Another translation is "when" So the first sentence also means "When you danced I sang.") Both endings are added to verbs with all their normal subject and object markers. In each case the dependent verb's ending tells you whether its subject is the same as (±**hmat**) or different from (±**hma**) that of the main verb. Although the dependent verb has come first in all the examples you've seen so far, this is not always the case:

Taloowalitok hilhalihmat.	"I sang after I danced."
Alikchaat ayatok itt̲ish ishilihma.	"The doctor went after I got the medicine."

As you can see, when the two verbs change position, the nouns naming their participants stay with those verbs: **alikchaat** goes with **ayatok** and **itt̲ish** goes with **ishilihma** in the example above.

In the examples we've seen so far, the verbs have shown clearly who their subjects were. Now, look at the following examples, with the subjects understood:

Taloowahmat hilhatok.	"After he sang, he danced."
Taloowahma hilhatok.	"After he sang, he danced."

Here's something interesting. The two different Chickasaw sentences have the same English translation. Do they mean the same thing, then? Think about it. They don't, because the first Chickasaw sentence tells you (with ±hmat) that the same person who sang danced, while the second one says (with ±hma) that the person who sang was not the same as the one who danced. You might express the difference in English by pointing or by changing the intonation you use, but the English words don't show the difference the way they clearly do in Chickasaw.

Pronunciation with ± endings. Listen to your teacher say **hilhahmat**. When a word ending in an even-numbered short syllable comes before a ± ending that starts with a consonant, like ±hmat, you may hear a different rhythmic pattern from what you expect. **Hilhahmat** may be pronounced **hi/lhah/mat**, according to the regular rules of syllable division you learned in units 1 and 4. Alternatively, it may be pronounced as **hilh/ah/mat**, with the consonant before the ± ending pronounced at the end of the preceding syllable, perhaps even sounding double, almost like <hilhlhahmat>.

Whenever a Chickasaw syllable ending with a consonant comes before a syllable beginning with a vowel, the consonant at the end of the first syllable often sounds longer. This is just like what you've learned about the final consonants of the A, D, N, and **on±** prefixes, all of which are consonant-final prefixes that, because they are ± prefixes, are pronounced as their own separate syllables.

The new rule is this:

WHEN AN EVEN-NUMBERED SHORT SYLLABLE COMES BEFORE A ± ENDING THAT STARTS WITH A CONSONANT, THE LAST CONSONANT BEFORE THE ± ENDING MAY BE PRONOUNCED AS PART OF THE SYLLABLE THAT PRECEDES IT.

Try to imitate your teacher's pronunciation of words like **hilhahmat**.

Exercise 111. Read the following Chickasaw sentences and underline the dependent verb in each one. Make sure you understand what its ending means, then translate the sentences into English. 1. Ishtaloowahmat ishhilhatok. 2. Ishhilhatok taloowalihma. 3. Kiitaloowahmat kiihilhatok. 4. Nipi' ishpahmat oka' ishishkotok. 5. Chalakki' ihooat paska chompahmat inchokka ayatok. 6. Chissohma ishyaataam? 7. Hachimamboohaak alalihmat hachimanompolilitok. 8. Hassamanompolitok hachimamboohaak alalihma.

"After" in the future. Look at these new sentences using ±kmat and ±kma:

Taloowalikmat hilhala'chi.	"After I sing, I'll dance."
Taloowalikma sashkaat hilha'chi.	"When I sing, my mother will dance."

Listen as your teacher says **taloowalikma**. Because the new endings are ± endings starting with consonants, this word may be pronounced **ta/loo/wa/lik/ma** or **ta/loo/wal/ik/ma**.

The new sentences are similar to the sentences with **±hmat** and **±hma** you just learned about. The dependent verbs have an ending that means "after" or "when": **±kmat** is used when the subject of the dependent verb is the same as that of the main verb, and **±kma** is used when the subjects are different. The difference is that the new sentences don't refer to the past. Although we can still use *after* in these English sentences, neither the singing nor the dancing has happened yet. The new endings show the same kind of relationship between the dependent and main verbs as in the **±hmat/±hma** sentences, but they reflect the fact that their verbs refer to events that aren't yet over. Here's a chart showing how all four endings work:

	Event is over	*Event isn't over*
Subjects the same	±hmat	±kmat
Subjects different	±hma	±kma

Dependent verbs with the **±kmat/±kma** ending aren't always translated with "after" or "when". Sometimes they mean "if", as in the following example:

Pisalikmat asayoppa'chi.   "If I see him, I'll be happy."

The same sentence could, of course, mean "When I see him I'll be happy" (*or* "After I see him I'll be happy"). Using "if" in English makes it seem a little less likely that the seeing referred to will occur, but the same uncertainty is expressed by Chickasaw **±kmat/±kma**, so "if" is a fine translation for the Chickasaw.

Here's another example:

Pisalikmat asayoppa.   "When I see him, I'm happy".

This sentence means that what's true now was also true in the past, yet we still use the **k** ending, not the **h** one. This Chickasaw sentence emphasizes the prediction about the future, not the comment about the past.

This system of marking whether the reference (or meaning) of the two subjects is the same or whether it switches between the main and dependent verb is called SWITCH-REFERENCE. Usually, a dependent verb that shows a same subject ends in **t**, and a dependent verb that shows a different subject ends in a nasal vowel. Switch-reference is the main way that verbs are joined together in Chickasaw. You will learn other ways of using switch-reference in later units.

Exercise 11J. Translate the following sentences into Chickasaw. You will need to identify the main and dependent verbs in the English translation, then choose the right switch-reference ending for the Chickasaw dependent verb. 1. After I ate, I went to sleep. 2. After you got the basket, you gave it to me. 3. When you get the basket, will you give it to me? 4. If you find the basket, my sister will be happy. 5. I woke up when the rooster crowed. 6. When you go to Oklahoma, look for my friend. 7. After we kill the hog, we'll eat it. 8. If you see the teacher, give her this book.

Terms and Concepts

IRREGULAR, SHORT VERB, MAIN VERB, DEPENDENT VERB, SWITCH-REFERENCE.

VOCABULARY

abi to kill (A,S) (short verb—see this unit)

ak<u>a</u>nakni' rooster

ala to arrive, to get here (A) (short verb—see this unit)

amo to mow, harvest (grass), to give a haircut to (A,S) (short verb—see this unit)

ani to put into a container (especially, to pour) (A,Noun), to set fruit, to have fruit on it (of a plant) (Noun) (short verb—see this unit)

apa to eat (something) (A,S) (short verb—see this unit)

aya to go (A), to go to (a place) (A,Noun) (short verb—see this unit)

Chalakki' Cherokee

hashshok grass

Hattak Api' Homma', Hattak Nipi' Homma' Indian

ima to give to (A,D,Noun) (short verb—see this unit)

ink<u>a</u>na' friend (DP)

ishi to get, to take, to pick up (A,S) (short verb—see this unit)

ittibi to fight (A); to fight, fight with (A,S)

í'shi to keep, to hold, to have in one's hand (A,Noun)

Mashkooki' Creek

nannimaabachi' teacher

naalhtoka' policeman

ola to crow, to make a noise (A) (short verb—see this unit)

ona to get there (A), to get to (a place there) (A,Noun) (short verb—see this unit)

Oshpaani' Mexican, Hispanic

Shimmanooli' Seminole

sinti' snake

shokha' hog

tak<u>o</u>lo peach

<ya>, <oo> to be (S) (irregular verb—see this unit)

Full lists of the irregular forms of the short verbs listed here are included in the Chickasaw-English Vocabulary at the end of this book.

READING AND SPEAKING

The readings included in units 11–20 of this book are more challenging than those given for units 5–10. If you're studying Chickasaw, you should try your best to understand the reading for each unit based on the vocabulary and notes provided in the context of the current unit. If you need more help or if you are mainly interested in the readings as a window on Chickasaw culture, translations are provided in Appendix C.

A Trip to Texas

The following reminiscence is Mrs. Willmond's story of a trip she took with several linguists to the Alabama-Coushatta Indian Reservation in Huntsville, Texas in 1983 or 1984. Mrs. Willmond was particularly struck on that occasion by how the Alabama language (a Muskogean language fairly closely related to Chickasaw but not spoken in Oklahoma), which she had not heard before, seemed to have things in common with Chickasaw, Choctaw, and Creek, and maybe other languages, but was not the same as any one of them.

Haatokm̲a himmak̲a yappak̲o hachimaashla'chi.

Pam iitáwwa'at 1983-84 fokhakaash̲o Naahollo I̲yaakni' kiliyyattook.

Haatokoot ilonahm̲a Hattak Api' Homma' bíyya'kahoot áyya'shattook.

Alibaamo' aachih̲o ootilimanompolittook. Chikashshahookano yammak̲o "Hattak Yoshoba'" aachi. Anompa talhlhá'pih̲o anompolihoot áyya'shattook!

Ootilibaaittanahattook.

Yappakílla aashla'chi. Yappat alhpí'sa.

As you'll see, Mrs. Willmond's story makes use of several of the irregular verbs you learned in this unit. Below are the new vocabulary words (and new uses of familiar words), as well as notes on the sentence patterns in the story.

SUPPLEMENTARY VOCABULARY

aachi to call (someone something) (A,Noun,Noun)
alhpí''sa to be enough (Noun)
Alibaamo' Alabama Indian
áyya'sha to be there (pl. subj.) (A)
fokhakaash̲o about (used with a date)
haatokm̲a well, OK (used to begin a story)
haatokoot and then (same-subject)
Hattak Yoshoba' Lost Tribe, Lost People
himmaka' now
ittanaha to have a church service (A) (used with **ibaa±** in the story)
iitáwwa'at see **táwwa'a**
ootimanompoli to go to talk to (A,D) (includes preverb **oot±**—see note 7 below)
táwwa'a (used to say "and"—you'll learn more about this in unit 19—as in **Pam iitáwwa'at** "Pam and I")
yappakílla only this

NOTES

1. The story refers to a time in the REMOTE PAST (more than a year ago). This is indicated with the ending ±**ttook**. You'll learn more about this ending in unit 13.

2. **Himmaka'** "now" looks like a noun and, like a noun, can be used with the object ending ±**a**.

3. **Táwwa'a** is used to say "and", which is complicated in Chickasaw (you can look ahead at unit 19 if you want to find out more about this). **Pam iitáwwa'at** means "Pam and I".

4. In the Reading and Speaking section of unit 8, you learned that ±**aash** can be added to time words to say "on" or "in" a date in the past. You can also use this ending with a past year, as in **1983aash** "in 1983". (Chickasaw speakers pronounce **1983** just as in English.) A variant of this ending is ±**aash̲o**. **1983 fokhakaash̲o** means "in about 1983"; **1983–84 fokhakaash̲o**, as in the story, means "in about 1983 or '84".

5. **Haatokoot** means "and then". This word includes a same-subject ending, so it's only used between two sentences or paragraphs with the same subject. The corresponding different-subject "and then" is **haatok̲o**.

6. **Hattak Api' Homma' bíyyi'kahoot áyya'shattook** means "it was all Indians there". The ±**hoot** focus subject ending shows that the ones who were all Indians were there.

7. **Ootimanompoli** includes the PREVERB **oot±** "go and". A preverb is the first item in its word; it goes before any subject or object prefixes, as in the words **ootilimanompolittook** and **ootilibaaittanahattook**. You'll learn more about using preverbs in unit 13.

8. **Alibaamo' aachih̲o** means "the ones they call the Alabamas". There is no word for "the ones"—that part is just understood. The focus object ending ±**h̲o** shows that this word is an object in the sentence. You'll learn more about this type of modifying phrase in unit 20.

9. ±**Hookano** is an ending that shows that the preceding noun or noun phrase is of continuing importance in a long passage. Listen, and you'll hear speakers use this ending in conversation.

ADVANCED TOPICS IN CHICKASAW GRAMMAR

Units in the second half of this book include supplementary lessons in advanced Chickasaw grammar. Later units will not require that you have mastered the concepts these lessons contain, but these units will introduce you to important specialized topics.

ADVANCED CHICKASAW GRAMMAR 1

Counting Higher in Chickasaw

In the Reading and Speaking section of unit 3, you learned the Chickasaw numbers from one to ten, and the Reading and Speaking section of unit 10 presented the numbers from ten to twenty:

chaffa	one
toklo	two
tochchí'na	three
oshta	four
talhlhá'pi	five
hanná'li	six
ontoklo	seven
ontochchí'na	eight
chakká'li	nine
pokkó'li	ten
awa-chaffa	eleven
awa-toklo	twelve
awa-tochchí'na	thirteen
awa-oshta	fourteen
awa-talhlhá'pi	fifteen
awa-hanná'li	sixteen
awa-ontoklo	seventeen
awa-tochchí'na	eighteen

awa-chakká'li	nineteen
pokoli toklo	twenty

This Advanced Chickasaw Grammar lesson will tell you how to form these higher numbers—you may be able to amaze the Chickasaw speakers you know, and it's not really too hard . . .

Numbers from eleven to ninety-nine. As the numbers above may have suggested to you, Chickasaw uses a decimal (ten-based) system, like English. Words for the decade numbers include **pokoli** followed by the multiple of ten:

pokoli toklo	twenty
pokoli tochchí'na	thirty
pokoli oshta	forty, etc.

Pokoli is related to **pokkó'li** "ten", but this word is never used by itself.

To form a more complex number, add **awa±** plus the unit's number:

pokoli tochchí'na awa-chaffa	thirty-one
pokoli ontoklo awa-oshta	seventy-four
pokoli hanná'li awa-hanná'li	sixty-six, etc.

As you can see, **awa±** means something like "and", but it's not used to mean "and" in other types of sentences, only in number expressions. (You'll learn about other ways to say "and" in units 15 and 19.) **Awa±** is a ± marker, but because people think of it as a very separate item, we've written it with a hyphen before the following number. A following vowel is never deleted after **awa±**. Listen carefully to how your teacher pronounces these numbers.

You might expect that Chickasaw numbers from "eleven" to "nineteen" would begin with **pokkó'li** "ten", but instead, only **awa±** is used, as you learned in unit 10 (we might think of the "ten" part as understood).

"One hundred" and higher. The word for "hundred" is **talhipa**. As in English, this is not a complete number by itself—it must be used with another number that gives the number of hundreds:

talhipa chaffa	one hundred
talhipa talhlhá'pi	five hundred
talhipa chakká'li	nine hundred

To add onto a "hundred" expression, you follow the "hundred" expression with +**cha**:

talhipa toklocha awa-tochchí'na	two hundred thirteen
talhipa ontochchí'nacha pokoli oshta	eight hundred forty
talhipa oshtacha pokoli toklo awa-hanná'li	four hundred twenty-six

(+**Cha** also means something like "and". You'll learn more about other uses of this marker in lesson 15.)

"Thousand" is **talhipa sipokni'**. (Can you guess the literal meaning of this expression?) As with **talhipa**, you use "thousand" with a following number:

talhipa sipokni' chaffa	one thousand
talhipa sipokni' toklo	two thousand
talhipa sipokni' chakká'li	nine thousand

And again, as with **talhipa** expressions, you use **+cha** following the "thousand" expression if you want to add on:

talhipa sipokni' talhlhá'picha pokoli hanná'li awa-oshta	five thousand sixty-four
talhipa sipokni' chakká'cha talhipa ontochchí'nacha pokoli toklo awa-talhlhá'pi	nine thousand eight hundred twenty-five

The full pattern, then, is as follows:

talhipa sipokni' number **+cha**	thousands
talhipa number **+cha**	hundreds
pokoli number	tens
awa± number	ones

No Chickasaw word for "million" or any higher number has ever been recorded. If you like, you can try to figure out how such ideas would be expressed. But you won't hear Chickasaw speakers count anywhere near this high very often.

Unit 12

"Have"

In this unit you'll learn about how to say "have" in Chickasaw and about focus endings, which can be used in modifying phrases. You'll also learn about using numbers in sentences.

Lesson 12.1 presents the basic "have" sentence pattern. Lesson 12.2 introduces the focus endings. Lesson 12.3 describes the use of Chickasaw number verbs, and lesson 12.4 presents more "have" sentence patterns. Lesson 12.5 explains the use of modifying verbs; lesson 12.6 describes the use of numbers as modifying verbs and introduces a new "have" pattern. The Advanced Chickasaw Grammar section is about positional verbs and "where is" questions.

Lesson 12.1:
"Have" Sentences

Wáyya'a and tálla'a. In unit 10 you learned **wáyya'a** and **tálla'a**, two of the most common Chickasaw verbs that refer to existence in a location:

Aai'paat wáyya'a.	"There is a table."
Aboohaat tálla'a.	"There is a house."

As you know from unit 10, **wáyya'a** is used with a singular subject thought of as having a flat top with an opening underneath, and **tálla'a** with a singular subject thought of as having a flat bottom with open space above.

"Have" sentences. Here's a new type of sentence:

Chipotaat aai'paat iwáyya'a.	"The child has a table."
Ihooat aboohaat intálla'a.	"The woman has a house."

In Chickasaw "have" sentences, the word corresponding to the subject of the English sentence comes first and is marked with ±**at**, like other Chickasaw subjects. But what is special about "have" sentences is that the next word, corresponding to the object of the English sentence, is also marked with ±**at**.

The first part of a Chickasaw "have" sentence is the subject, which is marked with ±**at**, like other Chickasaw subjects. The next part is the "HAVE" OBJECT—the thing possessed—which is also marked with the ending ±**at**. Finally, the verb of a "have" sentence has a dative prefix. Such sentences follow the new "have" sentence pattern:

SUBJECT±at/±akoot	"HAVE" OBJECT±at	DATIVE PREFIX±VERB
Chipotaat	aai'paat	iwáyya'a.

The verb is selected according to the characteristics of the "have" object; thus, **wáyya'a** is the proper verb for use with the "have" object "table" (something thought of as having its opening below), and **tálla'a** is right for use with the "have" object "house" (something thought of as having its opening at the top, possibly because Chickasaw houses once had smoke-holes at the top). A dative prefix is added to make the "have" verbs **iwáyya'a** and **intálla'a**.

You can see that "have" sentences are different from the other sentences with subjects and objects that you've been using since unit 5, in terms of the ending on the "have" object noun. Another difference is especially important to remember. As you learned in unit 5, an ordinary object noun marked with **±a** can come in almost any position in the sentence. This is not true, however, for a "have" object. "Have" objects must always go right in front of the "have" verb.

> *Exercise 12A.* Translate the following Chickasaw "have" sentences. 1. Sashkaakoot itti'chanaa-at iwáyya'a. 2. Ankaat chokkaat intálla'a'chi. 3. Minkaat issoba-at iwáyya'atok. 4. Alikchi' yammat ofi'at iwáyya'ataa? 5. Hattakat ishtaka'faat intálla'atok. 6. Chipota yappakoot kowi'at iwáyya'a.

Here are some "have" sentences with subjects marked with D prefixes added before the dative prefix in the "have" sentence pattern. Sentences like these don't include a separate subject word before the "have" object:

Issaat chiwáyya'ataa?	"Do you have a deer?"
Aai'paat iwáyya'a'chi.	"He's going to have a table."

"Have" sentences are D subject sentences, so even if the subject isn't expressed with a separate word, you can tell what it is from the D prefix on the verb. These sentences show that you have to pay attention to keep from being fooled by a "have" object—although the nouns at the beginning of these sentences end in **±at**, they are not subjects, but "have" objects!

"HAVE" VERBS are listed in the Chickasaw-English Vocabulary as in the following example:

iwáyya'a to have (sg. "have" object thought of as having an opening on the bottom) (D,Noun±at)

The (D,Noun±at) following the meaning of the verb means that **iwáyya'a** has a D subject and that its object must be a noun word followed by the ending **±at**. The definition tells you that the object of this "have" verb must be a singular noun of the type that could be the subject of the positional verb **wáyya'a**. As with other D subject verbs, the dative prefix is listed as part of a "have" verb, and D prefixes can be added in sentences with "I", "you", and "we" subjects.

> *Exercise 12B.* Following the example, make up and translate a Chickasaw "have" sentence for each of the following subjects and "have" objects, using the new "have" sentence pattern. You will have to decide, in each case, whether **iwáyya'a** or **intálla'a** is the right "have" verb to use.
> *Example.* chipota, pinti'
> *Answer.* Chipotaat pintaat iwáyya'a. "The child has a mouse."
> 1. sashki', aai'pa' 2. chipota, itti'chanaa 3. ahattak, kaar 4. ihoo, issoba 5. ofi', chokka' 6. "I", talhpak 7. "you", ishtaka'fa 8. chinki', abooha 9. "we", nita' 10. nannimaabachi', amposhi' (**amposhi'** = "dish") 11. Chikashsha ihoo, aaombiniili' (**aaombiniili'** = "chair") 12. sanakfish, aashoppala' (**aashoppala'** = "lamp")

More about "have" subjects and objects. As the "have" sentence pattern shows, ±**akoot** can be used to emphasize the subject of a "have" sentence, just as it can emphasize any sentence subject:

Hattakakoot chokkaat intálla'a.   "The <u>man</u> has a house."

In this sentence ±**akoot**, rather than the regular subject ending ±**at**, marks the emphasized subject.

There is no way to emphasize a Chickasaw "have" object with ±**akoot** or ±**ako**, however. "Have" objects must be marked with ±**at**. Also, while understood subjects can be left out of "have" sentences, "have" objects must always be included. There's no such thing as an understood "have" object in Chickasaw. Finally, in Chickasaw it doesn't make sense to add **yammat** or **yappat** after a "have" object. Usually, a "have" object is just a plain noun word with ±**at** added.

More positional verbs. In unit 10 you learned that positional verbs have separate forms used with singular, dual, and triplural subjects. **Wáyya'a** and **tálla'a** are positional verbs, and they also have dual and triplural forms:

wáyyo'wa to exist (Noun), to be in (a place) (Noun,Noun) (dl. subject thought of as having an opening on the bottom)

wayowat máa to exist (Noun), to be in (a place) (Noun,Noun) (pl. subject thought of as having an opening on the bottom)

tállo'wa to exist (Noun), to be in (a place) (Noun,Noun) (dl. subject thought of as having an opening on the top)

talowat máa to exist (Noun), to be in (a place) (Noun,Noun) (pl. subject thought of as having an opening on the top)

"Have" verbs with dual and triplural objects. You can make "have" verbs by adding D prefixes to these verbs. The new "have" verbs are used with dual and triplural "have" objects. Compare the following sentences:

Minko' inchokkaat tállo'watok.   "The chief's two houses existed."
Minkaat chokkaat intállo'watok.   "The chief had two houses."

See how it works? With the positional verb, the noun being located is the subject, but in the "have" sentence, with the dative prefix added, that noun is the "have" object. So a verb like **intállo'wa** is always used with a dual "have" object, and you can express an idea like "had two houses" without using a separate word meaning "two".

The dative or D prefix used with the plural object verbs goes on the first word of the verb phrase, not on **máa**:

Chahtaat aaombiniilaat iwayowat máa.   "The Choctaw has chairs."
Ishtaka'faat hapontalowat máa.   "We all have cups."

Once again, you follow the regular "have" sentence pattern, with the "have" object marked with ±**at** and placed right before the "have" verb with its dative prefix. As before, if the subject is understood, it can be omitted—if the subject is "I", "you", or "we", you'll know this from the D prefix on the "have" verb; if the "have" verb starts with a form of the dative prefix **im**±, without an added D prefix, you'll know the sentence has a "he", "she", "it", or "they" subject.

Exercise 12C. Translate the following "have" sentences into English. 1. Ankaakoot aai'paat iwáyya'atok. 2. Nannimaabachi'akoot aboohaat intálla'a. 3. Chipotaat kowi'at iwáyyo'wa. 4. Sashkaat ishtaka'faat intalowat máatok. 5. Issoba-at chiwayowat máataa? 6. Chokkaat hachintállo'wataa?

Lesson 12.2: Focus

The subject focus ending. Look at these Chickasaw sentences:

Konihoot shoha.	What smells bad is a skunk.
Kowi'oot sakisilitok.	What bit me was a cat.

(**Shoha** is an S subject verb meaning "to smell bad" or "to stink".) The subjects of these two sentences have a new type of subject ending, a FOCUS ending. This ending emphasizes the identification of the subject—not in contrast to some other possible subject, as with a contrastive ending, but somewhat the way you do with English sentences like the "what" translations above. (The English translations are more complicated than the Chickasaw sentences, you may notice. The Chickasaw focus ending just adds the focus idea to the normal sentence, without changing everything around.) The Chickasaw subject focus ending is ±**hoot**, which becomes ±**oot** after any consonant, including a '.

Object focus. Now, here are some examples with the object focus ending:

Ihooho pisalitok.	"What I saw was a woman."
Chikashshanompa'o anompoli.	"What he's speaking is Chickasaw."

The object focus ending is ±**ho** after a vowel and ±**o** after any consonant, including '. These endings work the same way as the subject focus endings.

Have you noticed that the three subject endings you've learned, ±**at**, ±**akoot**, and ±**hoot**, all end in **t**? Final **t** is the sign of a Chickasaw subject ending. (It also appears on the subject "this" and "that" words, **yappat** and **yammat**.) Similarly, object endings like ±**a**, ±**ako**, and ±**ho**, as well as the object "this" and "that" words **yappa** and **yamma**, all end in a nasal vowel. A nasal vowel is the sign of a Chickasaw object ending. (The special object ending ±**ak** doesn't end in a nasal vowel, but it is quite different from the other object endings.)

You can focus a "have" subject by using ±**hoot** or ±**oot**:

Chipotahoot aai'paat iwáyya'a.	"The one that has a table is a child."
Hattakoot chokkaat intálla'a.	"The one that has a house is a man."

("What" wouldn't sound too good in these English translations. You can change the translation of a focus noun any way that makes sense to you, or sometimes even express the focus idea in English just by emphasizing the focus noun with your voice, as with contrastive nouns. Remember, though, that the focus ending is used to identify, not to contrast.) You can't focus on a "have" object in Chickasaw, however. This should make sense to you, since Chickasaw "have" objects can't be contrastive either.

Focus and contrast are both important ideas. For this reason, they can't easily be combined in the same sentence. If you use a focus subject, you won't use a contrastive object, and vice versa.

Exercise 12D. Translate the following sentences that use the new focus endings. 1. Minko' intiikat naafkah<u>o</u> hoyo. 2. Nannimaabachi'oot kaarat <u>i</u>wáyya'a. 3. Nipi'oot shohatok. 4. Talhpak<u>o</u> pobanna. 5. Holiss<u>o</u> hachibannataa? 6. Nita'oot minko' abitok.

Lesson 12.3:
Number Verbs

Counting numbers. You learned the Chickasaw numbers from one to ten in the Reading and Speaking section of unit 3. Practice saying them again now.

chaffa "one"	toklo "two"
tochchí'na "three"	oshta "four"
talhlhá'pi "five"	hanná'li "six"
ontoklo "seven"	ontochchí'na "eight"
chakká'li "nine"	pokkó'li "ten"

Number verbs. Surprising as it may sound, the Chickasaw numbers are all verbs: **toklo** means "to be two in number", **tochchí'na** means "to be three in number", and so on. You can use these number verbs in sentences like

| Hattakat toklo. | "The men are two in number.", "There are two men." |
| Kiloshtatok. | "We were four in number.", "There were four of us." |

Often a translation with "there" sounds better in English. Notice that the number verbs take A subject markers to tell who is referred to. Note, too, that a sentence like

| Kiitoklo. | "We are two in number.", "There are two of us." |

never refers to age; it can't mean "We are two years old". **Kiitoklo** is what you might say in a restaurant when asked how many are in your party, for example.

(In the Advanced Chickasaw Grammar section of unit 11, you learned how to form numbers higher than twenty. Any number can be used as a verb, but we won't practice numbers higher than ten this way here.)

To say "just" or "only" with a number (implying that more would have been expected), you add ±'si to number verbs ending in **a**. With other number verbs, drop the last vowel of the number verb and add the ending ±o'si:

Tochchí'na'si.	"There are only three."
Hashhanna'lo'stok.	"There were just six of you."
Tak<u>o</u>laat chaffa'si.	"There is only one peach."

These "just"/"only" endings go after the number verb but before other endings like +**tok** or +**taa**. Of course the **i** of ±'**si** or ±**o'si** is in an odd-numbered short-vowel syllable, so it drops before +**tok**, +**taa**, and +**taam.**

The ±**o'si** ending is most common (as you might guess) with lower numbers. With **chaffa**, it's much more common to use the ending than to leave it off. So in sentences, you'll hear **chaffa'si** used more often than **chaffa.**

Exercise 12E. Practice using Chickasaw number verbs in the following sentences. 1. Will there be three of you? ("you" must be plural) 2. There are only eight baskets. 3. There will be ten. 4. There may be nine children. 5. We are six in number. 6. There was only one lamp. 7. There are four women. 8. There were just two of us. 9. Are there five of you? 10. There are only seven of us.

"Have" sentences with number verbs. The number verbs from "one" to "three" can be used in "have" expressions to say that someone has from one to three items. Here are some examples:

Hattak yammat chokkaat intochchí'na.	"That man has three houses."
Chipotaat talhpakat inchaffa'si.	"The child has only one basket."
Issoba-at pontoklotok.	"We had two horses."

The number "have" sentence pattern is like the one used with positional verbs like **tálla'a** and **wáyya'a**:

SUBJECT±at/±akoot/±hoot	"HAVE" OBJECT±at	DATIVE PREFIX±NUMBER VERB
Hattak yammat	chokkaat	intochchí'na.

As the last sentence above shows, you can change the dative prefix on the number verb to a D prefix to indicate an "I", "you", or "we" subject, just as with positional verbs:

Kowi'at chintoklotaa?	"Do you have two cats?"
Aai̲'paat ponchaffa'si.	"We have one table."

In each case the number verb tells how many "have" objects there are (from "one" to "three"). These "have" objects are like the other "have" objects you saw earlier, in that a "have" object noun must be included in each "have" sentence, and this "have" object cannot be followed by any ending but ±**at**. Like other "have" objects, these can only come in one position in the sentence, right before the verb.

If you think about it, a "have" object is always possessed, even though it doesn't have a dative prefix to indicate this. (The possessor, of course, is the subject of the "have" sentence.) Nouns whose meaning changes when they are possessed usually have the special possessed meaning in "have" sentences:

Hattakat ihooat intoklo.	"The man has two wives."

Normally, this new "have" sentence pattern isn't used with number verbs higher than "three". However, you may hear speakers using it with higher number verbs on occasion. You'll learn another way to use numbers in "have" sentences later in the unit.

Exercise 12F. Translate each of the following sentences into English. 1. Ankaakoot ishtaka'faat inchaffa'si. 2. Chipota yappat tali'at intochchí'na. 3. Ofi'at pontoklo'si. 4. Itti'chanaa-at hachintoklotaa? 5. Aai̲'paat pontochchína'si. 6. Ittaat anchaffa'si. 7. Alikchi' yammat itti̲shat intochchí'na. 8. Aboohaat hachinchaffa'staa?

Lesson 12.4:
More "Have" Sentence Patterns

"Have" sentences with possessed objects. The "have" objects you've seen so far have had no prefixes. If the "have" object is a possessed noun, it may have a prefix:

Hattak naknaat intikbaat intoklo.	"The man has two older brothers."
Pontikbaat pontoklo.	"We (women) have two older sisters."
Chipotaat holhchifoat intochchí'na.	"The child has three names."
Poholhchifoat pontoklo.	"We have two names."
Chilbakat chinchaffa'staa?	"Do you have only one hand?"

If the "have" object is a noun that always includes a dative prefix (like **intikba'** and various other words for relatives introduced in lesson 7.6), it keeps its prefix in a "have" sentence. Here is the patterns for sentences with noun subjects:

SUBJECT±at/±akoot/±hoot	im±"HAVE" OBJECT±at	im±VERB
Hattak naknaat	intikbaat	intoklo.

and here is the pattern for sentences with understood "I", "you", and "we" subjects, with a D prefix added before the dative **im±** prefixes on both the "have" object and the verb:

D PREFIX+**im±**"HAVE" OBJECT±at	D PREFIX+**im±**VERB
Pontikbaat	pontoklo.

If the "have" object is a noun that marks its possessor with an S prefix (like **holhchifo**), things work a bit differently. With a noun subject, there's no S prefix on the possessed noun; a sentence like the third one above follows the ordinary "have" pattern. When the subject is "I", "you", or "we", you get both an S prefix on the possessed noun and a D-plus-dative prefix combination on the verb, as in the last two example sentences above. In this kind of sentence both the prefix on the "have" object and the matching D prefix on the verb help you identify the subject:

S PREFIX+"HAVE" OBJECT±at	D PREFIX+**im±**VERB
Pohlhchifoat	pontochchí'na.

"Have" sentences with plural subjects. When the subject of a "have" sentence is a plural noun (understood or not), speakers sometimes use **hoo±** before the dative prefix on the verb:

Kowi'at hooinchaffa'si.	"They have just one cat."
Chipotaat talhpakat hoointálla'a.	"The children have a basket."

The **hoo±** on the verb tells you that the sentence has a plural subject (a plural possessor). The verb still tells you something about the "have" object, however.

New positional verbs. **Ánta** "stay, be there, be located, live" is a positional verb, so it has a form for dual subjects, **áshwa**, and a form for triplural subjects, **áyya'sha**. Unlike the other positional verbs you have learned, these verbs don't specify the bodily orientation of their subjects, so you can use them when you're not sure about this. Here are some examples of how these verbs are used:

Ankaat ántatok.	"My father was there."
Hashą́shwataam?	"Were you (two) there?"
Kiláyya'shtok.	"We were there."

"Have" with a human object. With a dative prefix or a D-plus-dative prefix combination, the new verbs can be used to say "have" with a human "have" object:

Ankaat amánta.	"I have a father."
Ihooat chimántataa?	"Do you have a wife?"
Ittibaapishiat imáyya'sha.	"He has brothers and sisters."

You use **imánta** to say someone has one relative, **imą́shwa** to say he has two relatives, and **imáyya'sha** to say he has more than two relatives or that more than two human "have" objects are involved. Otherwise, these new verbs use the same "have" sentence patterns you've already learned. With a "have" object like **inki'** that always includes a dative prefix, you will have a prefix both on the "have" object and on the verb; with a "have" object like "wife", a word that can occur without a dative prefix, no prefix is used on the object. With a "have" object like **ittibaapishi** that takes an S possessive prefix, you'll only see the prefix when the possessor is "our", "your", or "my". Once again, though, the "have" verb you choose is selected according to the number of the "have" object—in the second example above, the subject is singular, but you still use the verb **imáyya'sha**.

"Have" objects with imáyya'sha. **Imáyya'sha** is an important "have" verb. It's not only used with plural "have" objects, but also with "have" objects that form a shapeless mass, such as water, sand (**shinok**), or money:

Ta'ossaat amáyya'sha.	"I have money."
Hattakat shinokat imáyya'sha.	"The man has sand."

In addition, you may hear "have a husband" or "have a wife" expressed with **imáyya'sha** even though there's only one "have" object:

Ihooat chimáyya'shtaa?	"Do you have a wife?"

Exercise 12G. I. Translate these sentences into Chickasaw. 1. The women have a wagon. 2. Those people have cups. 3. The woman has two older sisters. 4. The chief has a wife. (you could say this one two ways) 5. We all (relatively many) were there. 6. Do you have water? 7. Do you have three younger brothers? (addressing a man) 8. I have just one sister. (a man is talking) 9. That woman has children. 10. They (two) may be there. 11. We have money. 12. The men have sand.

"Not to have". **Ikimiksho** is a "have" verb that means "not to have" or "to not have". This new verb is a form of **iksho**, including a dative prefix. **Imiksho** is the most common way to say that someone does not have something, as in

Ta'ossaat iksamiksho.	"I have no money."
Ofi'at chokkaat ikhooimikshokitok.	"The dogs had no home."

As in any "have" sentence, the "have" object of **ikimiksho** is always marked with **±at**. As the first example shows, the D prefix **am±** is **sam±** after the first **ik±** of **ikimiksho**, just as after any N prefix. The plural noun subject prefix **hoo±** goes after this **ik±**.

In most cases Chickasaw speakers prefer sentences with **ikimiksho** rather than negatives of ordinary "have" sentences.

Exercise 12H. Make each of the following Chickasaw sentences negative by using **ikmiksho**. Then translate the new sentences. 1. Alikchaat ittishat hooimáyya'sha. 2. Sanakfishat ishtaka'faat intálla'a. 3. Itti'chanaa-at awáyya'a. 4. Kowi'at chiwáyya'ataam? 5. Oka'at pomáyya'shatok. 6. Minkaat aboohaat intálla'a.

Other "have" sentence patterns. Most other positional verbs can be used as "have" verbs following the patterns you have studied in this unit. The verb you choose depends on the position or orientation of the "have" object. Here's an example:

Chipotaat holissaat intí'wa.   "The child has a book."

The "have" verb here is formed by adding a dative prefix to the singular positional verb **tí'wa** "to lie". This is appropriate, because we think of books as characteristically lying down flat. If you knew that the book in question was standing up, however, you would use another "have" verb. Many different verbs are used to express "have" in Chickasaw, as you'll hear if you listen to Chickasaw conversation. Most Chickasaw "have" sentences, whatever verb they use, follow the same patterns you have learned in this unit.

Lesson 12.5: Modifying Verbs

In English a words like *red* or *big* can be used in two ways, as part of a verb phrase, in sentences like *Her dress is red* and *You are really big*, or as part of a noun phrase, in sentences like *I bought a red dress* and *A big cat bit me*. In the second type of phrase, the words *red* and *big* MODIFY the meanings of the nouns by telling us more about them. Up to now, you've only used Chickasaw verbs like **homma** or **ishto** in verb phrases, but they can be used as part of noun phrases, too, as in

Naafka hommaho chompalitok.   "I bought a red dress."
Kowi' ishtohoot sakisilitok.   "A big cat bit me."

In these sentences, **homma** and **ishto** are MODIFYING VERBS: they tell us some useful additional information about the noun phrases **naafka** and **kowi'**. It's not just any dress, but it's a red dress; it's not just any cat, but it's a big cat. Modifying verbs modify, specify, or help identify the meaning of the noun they are used with.

You already know everything about how these modifying verbs work. First of all, just like the words **yammat**, **yappat**, and so on, modifying verbs follow the plain form of the noun they refer to. Next, modifying verbs are followed by focus endings: **±hoot** for a subject noun phrase, **±ho** for an object noun phrase. As you know, subject and object marking always goes at the end of a noun phrase: the whole noun phrase **naafka hommaho** is the object of the verb **chompalitok** in the first sentence above, and the whole noun phrase **kowi' ishtahoot** is the subject of the verb **sakisilitok** in the second example.

Most verbs that are used as modifying verbs are stative verbs that take S subjects. Here are some new verbs that you'll be able to use in the exercise:

champoli "to be sweet, good tasting" (S)

haloppa "to be sharp" (S)

hichito "to be big" (plural subject) (S)

himitta "to be young" (S)

iskanno'si "to be little, small" (singular subject) (S)

s̲a̲wa'si "to be little, small" (plural subject) (S)

sipokni "to be old" (S)

Both "big" and "little" have different forms for singular and plural subjects.

Exercise 12I. Find the modifying verbs in the Chickasaw sentences below and then translate each sentence. 1. Minkaat chokka' tohbih̲o̲ k̲ashtok. 2. Ihoo sipoknihoot oblaashaash amanompolitok. 3. Paska chokmah̲o̲ apalitok. 4. Chipota iskanno'sih̲o̲ pís̲litok. 5. Hattak hichitohoot hoosalhiyohtok. 6. Bashpo haloppah̲o̲ chibannataa? 7. Hattak sipoknih̲o̲ ishith̲á̲nataa? 8. Paska champolih̲o̲ kiipatok. (**Paska champoli'** can refer to any sweet baked goods—cake, cookies, pie, etc.) 9. Ofi' s̲a̲wa'sihoot tilhaa. 10. Alikchi' oshiitiik himittahoot tak̲o̲lo champolih̲o̲ amatok.

Lesson 12.6:
Numbers as Modifying Verbs

Modifying number verbs. Numbers are often used as modifying verbs:

Tali' tokloh̲o̲ hoyolitok.	"I was looking for two rocks."
Hattak tochchí'nahoot apopilatok.	"Three men helped us."

Lawa "to be many, for there to be a lot of" is an A subject verb that is used just like the number verbs: as a main verb, a "have" verb, and a modifying verb.

Kiilawa.	"We are many.", "There are a lot of us."
Ank̲a̲naat paskaat i̲lawa.	"My friend has a lot of bread."
Hattak lawahoot taloowa.	"Many people are singing."

"Have" with numbers higher than "three". A special "have" sentence pattern containing a modifying number verb and **imáyya'sha** is used to say "have" with higher numbers than "three". Here are some examples of how this works.

Ihooat issoba oshtahoot imáyya'sha.	"The woman has four horses."
Ankaakoot kaar talhlhá'pihoot imáyya'sha.	<u>My father</u> has five cars."

The pattern in these sentences is

SUBJECT±at/±akoot/±hoot	"HAVE" OBJECT PHRASE±hoot	im±áyya'sha.
	("HAVE" OBJECT NUMBER VERB±**hoot**)	
Ihooat	issoba oshtahoot	imáyya'sha.

Like other "have" sentences you have seen, these sentences include a "have" object that looks like a subject and a "have" verb with a dative prefix. The "have" object phrase in these number sentences, however, is different from other such phrases you have seen up to now—it consists of the "have" object word (with no ending) followed by a number verb plus the subject focus ending ±**hoot**. As you know, usually the ending on a "have" object is ±**at**, but because these "have" object phrases contain a number modifying verb, they must end in ±**hoot**.

As with other "have" sentences, the subject can be omitted from these sentences. In sentences like the following, you can figure out who the subject is by the form of the D prefix on the "have" verb **imáyya'sha**.

Holisso pokkó'lihoot chimáyya'sha.	"You have ten books."
Chipota chakká'lihoot pomáyya'sha'chi.	"We will have nine children."
Tak<u>o</u>lo oshtahoot hooimáyya'shtok.	"They had four peaches."

Combining modifying verbs. If you want to use both a number modifying verb and another modifying verb, here's the pattern to use:

NOUN	MODIFYING VERB	NUMBER VERB±**hoot**/±**h<u>o</u>**

Use the plain form of both the noun and the first modifying verb, as in

Ofi' lakna tokloh<u>o</u> p<u>i</u>slitok.	"I saw two brown dogs."
Alikchi' chokma oshtahoot alatok.	"Four good doctors arrived."

Occasionally, you will hear speakers omit the ±**h<u>o</u>** from an object number modifier, but it's usually there if you ask them to repeat the sentence slowly.

Now, suppose you want to add a "that" or "this" word like **yammat**, **yappat**, **yamma**, and so on. These words go at the very end of the phrase, after plain forms of the noun, the modifying verb, and the number verb. The ending on the "this" or "that" word should be the right one for the whole phrase.

NOUN	MODIFYING VERB	NUMBER VERB	"THIS"/"THAT"
ofi'	lakna	toklo	yamm<u>a</u>

The first example below shows the complete pattern. The next two examples show that you can omit one of the middle verbs from the pattern, too:

Ofi' lakna toklo yamm<u>a</u> p<u>i</u>slitok.	"I saw those two brown dogs."
Ihoo ontochchí'na yappat <u>i</u>mpa.	"These eight women are eating."
Chipota tikahbi yammat hoonosi.	"Those tired children are sleeping."

Exercise 12J. Translate the following sentences containing modifying verbs into Chickasaw. 1. We saw many big bears. 2. My mother made these seven pretty dresses. 3. Five women are looking for the big dogs. 4. A young child danced in the yard. 5. There are many Chickasaws in Oklahoma (translate this one as though it said "staying in"). 6. The doctor has seven cups. 7. I know nine Cherokees. 8. The sharp knives are lying on the table (assume there are two knives, but don't use the word "two"). 9. Our mother has eight cats. 10. A sweet peach is good. 11. Ten old doctors got the medicine. 12. Does that hungry man have a car?

Terms and Concepts

"HAVE" OBJECT, "HAVE" VERB, FOCUS, MODIFY, MODIFYING VERB.

VOCABULARY ("HAVE" VERBS ARE LISTED SEPARATELY BELOW.)

amposhi' dish, plate

áyya'sha to stay, be there (A); to be located, live in (a place) (A,Noun) (tpl. subj.)

aaombiniili' chair

aashoppala' lamp, light

áshwa to stay, be there (A); to be located, live in (a place) (A,Noun) (dl. subj.)

chaffa to be one in number (A)

chakká'li to be nine in number (A)

champoli to be sweet, good tasting (S)

haloppa to be sharp (S)

hanná'li to be six in number (A)

hichito to be big (pl. subj.) (S)

himitta to be young (S)

ikimiksho not to have (D,Noun±at)

iskanno'si to be little, small (sg. subj.) (S)

lawa to be many, to be numerous, for there to be a lot (A)

ontochchí'na to be eight in number (A)

ontoklo to be seven in number (A)

oshta to be four in number (A)

paska champoli' cake, cookie, pie

pokkó'li to be ten in number (A)

sawa'si to be little, small (pl. subj.) (S)

sipokni to be old (S)

shinok sand

shoha to stink, smell bad (S)

tállo'wa to exist (Noun); to be located in (a place) (Noun,Noun) (dl. subj. thought of as having an opening on the top)

talowat máa to exist (Noun); to be located in (a place) (Noun,Noun) (tpl. subj. thought of as having an opening on the top)

talhlhá'pi to be five in number (A)

tochchí'na to be three in number (A)

toklo to be two in number (A)

wayowat máa to exist (Noun); to be located in (a place) (Noun,Noun) (tpl. subj. thought of as having an opening on the bottom)

wáyyo'wa to exist (Noun); to be located in (a place) (Noun,Noun) (dl. subj. thought of as having an opening on the bottom)

"HAVE" VERBS INTRODUCED IN THE UNIT (If you've learned the "have" sentence pattern, you won't need to learn each of these verbs separately. Many other "have" verbs are used in Chickasaw.

imánta to have (a relative) (sg. human "have" object) (D,Noun±at)

imáyya'sha to have (relatives) (tpl. human "have" object) (D,Noun±at)

imáshwa to have (relatives) (dl. human "have" object) (D,Noun±at)

imontochchí'na to have eight (D,Noun±at)

imontoklo to have seven (D,Noun±at)

imoshta to have four (D,Noun±at)

impokkó'li to have ten (D,Noun±at)

inchaffa to have one (D,Noun±at)

inchakká'li to have nine (D,Noun±at)

intálla'a to have (D,Noun±at) (sg. "have" obj. thought of as having an opening on the top)

intállo'wa to have (D,Noun±at) (dl. "have" obj. thought of as having an opening on the top)

intalowat máa to have (D,Noun±at) (tpl. "have" obj. thought of as having an opening on the top)

intalhlhá'pi to have five (D,Noun±at)

intí'wa to have (D,Noun±at) (sg. lying "have" obj.)

intochchí'na to have three (D,Noun±at)

intoklo to have two (D,Noun±at)

ihanná'li to have six (D,Noun±at)

ilawa to have many, to have a lot of (D,Noun±at)

iwayowat máa to have (D,Noun±at) (tpl. "have" obj. thought of as having an opening on the bottom)

iwáyya'a to have (D,Noun±at) (sg. "have" obj. thought of as having an opening on the bottom)

iwáyyo'wa to have (D,Noun±at) (dl. "have" obj. thought of as having an opening on the bottom)

READING AND SPEAKING

The Haggadah in Chickasaw

Mrs. Willmond was asked to express part of the Jewish Passover Seder ceremony (traditionally referred to as the Haggadah) into Chickasaw as part of a project designed to foster intercultural understanding, published in 2007 as 300 Ways to Ask the Four Questions, *by Murray Spiegel and Rickey Stein (http//:whyisthisnight.com). Mrs. Willmond's Chickasaw version serves as a reminder of the importance of Passover in Judeo-Christian culture. (The translation is provided in Appendix C.)*

Katihmihta himmaka' oklhilihookano oklhili ílaka ittimíla?

Oklhili ílahookano paska shatabli' paskikshatablo' tawáaho iipahminatookya himmaka' oklhilihookano paskikshatablo' illaho iipa'chi.

Oklhili ílahookano nannokchamali' iláyyo'ka mómaho iipahminatookya himmaka' oklhilihookano alba homi' illaho iipa'chi.

Oklhili ílahookano iitakaffihminatok ki'yohookya himmaka' oklhilihookano hitokla' iitakaffa'chi.

Oklhili íllahookano kanihmit iibiniilihookya ilimpahminatookya himmaka' oklhilihookano aaombiniili' atáyya'at iibiniilikmakoot ilimpa'chi.

Oklhili íllahookano kanihmit ilimpahminatookya himmaka' oklhilihookano aai̲'pa' holiito'pa' ilaaimpa'chi.

SUPPLEMENTARY VOCABULARY

alba weed
alba homi' bitter weed
atáyya'at leaning back against
aai̲'pa' holiito'pa' holy table
aai̲'pa' table
biniili to sit down, take a sitting position (A)
himmaka' oklhili tonight
hitokla' twice
homi to be bitter (Noun)
iláyyo'ka to be various, separate, different (A)
illa only
ittimíla to be different from (A,S)
íla to be other, different (S)
kanihmit doing it somehow, doing it any old way
katihmihta̱ why
mó̱ma to be all (A)
nannokchamali' greens, vegetables
oklhili night
paska shatabli' bread made with yeast (light bread, leavened bread)
paskikshatablo' bread made without yeast (unleavened bread)
takaffi to dip (something) (A,Noun)
tawá̱a both (to be both together)

NOTES

1. As you learned in unit 12, modifying verbs are normally followed by the subject or object focus endings ±**hoot** and ±**ho̱**. Sometimes, however, they are used with ±**kat** (for subjects) and ±**ka** (for objects), as with **oklhili íllaka̱** "other nights". You'll learn more about the usual use of these endings as switch-reference markers in unit 13.
2. **Tawá̱a** "both . . . and" is related to **táwwa'a**, which is used to express "and". These words follow two words that would be linked by "and" in English. You'll learn more about expressing "and" in unit 19.
3. +**Hminatok** is a nonremote habitual ending, like the remote habitual introduced in the Reading and Speaking section of unit 5 but not referring to remote past time.
4. ±**Hookya** is an ending that means "but" (you'll learn more about this in unit 16; the **kya** in this ending may sound to you like <kiya> or <giya>, since the ending is usually pronounced with an echo vowel). The combination of +**hminatok** and ±**hookya** is +**hminatookya**. (±**Hookya** becomes ±**ookya** after a consonant.)
5. Dependent verbs that tell more about how an action was done often appear before a main verb with a +**t** ending. T-verbs like **atáyya'at** "leaning back" are often translated with English verbs ending in –*ing*. (**Kanihmit**, translated here

as "somehow, any old way", is also a t-verb, which more literally means "doing it somehow, doing it any old way".) You'll learn more about uses of t-verbs in unit 13.

6. ±Kmakoot is a same-subject dependent sentence marker used for noncompleted events (somewhat comparable to ±kmat).

7. A puzzle about this passage is why the verb **biniili** "to take a seat, sit down" is used, even though Mrs. Willmond is referring to "we" generally, since usually this verb requires a singular subject (as you'll see in unit 19). That's the way it works, though!

ADVANCED CHICKASAW GRAMMAR 2: MORE ABOUT POSITIONAL VERBS AND "WHERE IS" QUESTIONS

Six sets of positional verbs were introduced in lesson 10.4 and in this unit:

ánta to stay, be there (A); to be located, live in (a place) (A,Noun) (sg. subj.)
áshwa to stay, be there (A); to be located, live in (a place) (A,Noun) (dl. subj.)
áyya'sha to stay, be there (A); to be located, live in (a place) (A,Noun) (tpl. subj.)

bínni'li to sit (A); to be in (a location, sitting) (A, Noun) (sg. subj.)
chí'ya to sit (A); to be in (a location, sitting) (A,Noun) (dl. subj.)
binohmáa to sit (A); to be in (a location, sitting) (A,Noun) (tpl. subj.)

híkki'ya to stand (A); to be in (a location, sitting) (A, Noun) (sg. subj.)
hí'li to stand (A); to be in (a location, standing) (A,Noun) (dl. subj.)
hiyohmáa to stand (A); to be in (standing) (A,Noun) (tpl. subj.)

tí'wa to lie (A); to be in (a location, lying) (A,Noun) (sg. subj.)
káyya'a to lie (A); to be in (a location, lying) (A,Noun) (dl. subj.)
kahat máa to lie (A); to be in (a location, lying) (A, Noun) (tpl. subj.)

tálla'a to exist (Noun); to be located in (a location) (Noun,Noun) (of a sg. subj. thought of as having an opening at the top)
tállo'wa to exist (Noun); to be located in (a place) (Noun,Noun) (dl. subj. thought of as having an opening on the top)
talowat máa to exist (Noun); to be located in (a place) (Noun,Noun) (tpl. subj. thought of as having an opening on the top)

wáyya'a to exist (Noun); to be located in (a location) (Noun,Noun) (of a sg. subj. thought of as having an opening on the bottom)
wáyyo'wa to exist (Noun); to be located in (a place) (Noun,Noun) (dl. subj. thought of as having an opening on the bottom)
wayowat máa to exist (Noun); to be located in (a place) (Noun,Noun) (tpl. subj. thought of as having an opening on the bottom)

There are many other sets in Chickasaw. Here are four more:

fóyyokha to be inside (A,Noun) (sg. subj.)
albí'ha, albí'ya to be inside (A,Noun) (dl. subj.)

albihat máa, albiyat máa to be inside (A,Noun) (tpl. subj.)

láppa'li to be sticking onto (A,Noun) (sg. subj.)
láppohli to be sticking onto (A,Noun) (dl. subj.)
lapoht máa, lapoot máa to be sticking onto (A,Noun) (tpl. subj.)

pátta'a to be lying spread out on the floor (A); to be lying spread out on the floor in (a location) (A,Noun) (sg. subj.)
patkáyya'chi to be lying spread out on the floor (A); to be lying spread out on the floor in (a location) (A,Noun) (dl. subj.)
patkachit máa to be lying spread out on the floor (A); to be lying spread out on the floor in (a location) (A,Noun) (tpl. subj.)

tákka'li to be hanging, be crouched down, be squatting (A); to be hanging, be crouched down, be squatting in (a location) (A,Noun) (sg. subj.)
tákkohli to be hanging, be crouched down, be squatting (A); to be hanging, be crouched down, be squatting in (a location) (A,Noun) (dl. subj)
takoht máa to be hanging, be crouched down, be squatting (A); to be hanging, be crouched down, be squatting in (a location) (A,Noun) (tpl. subj.)

All sets of Chickasaw positional verbs work like the ones you've already learned about, although some are more common than others. All of them have separate singular, dual, and triplural subject forms, and in almost every case the triplural subject verb uses the triplural auxiliary **máa**. All of them can also be used to talk about the location or existence of their subjects, or (with dative prefixes) as "have" verbs, following the patterns in this unit.

Perhaps you recall the **±hmano** "where is" (or "where are"; **±mano** after consonants) question ending introduced in the Reading and Speaking section of unit 4. If you use a full sentence to answer a **±hmano** question, it must contain a positional verb. Here are some examples of "where is" dialogues.

—Ofi'mano?   —"Where is the dog?"
—Aai'pa' nota' tí'wa.   —"He's lying under the table."

—Chinki'mano?   —"Where is your father?"
—Aachompa' ánta.   —"He is in town."

—Anta'ossohmano?   —"Where is my money?"
—Shokcha fóyyokha.   —"It's in the bag."

—Naafkahmano?   —"Where are the dresses?"
—Chokka' anonka' takoht máa.   —"They are hanging in the house."

—Akka' patalhpo'mano?   —"Where is the rug?"
—Yammako pátta'a.   —"It's lying spread out on the floor over there."

Chickasaw speakers normally feel that answers to **±hmano** questions that don't contain a verb sound incomplete. Try practicing other **±hmano** dialogues with your friends!

Unit 13

Building Longer Sentences

In this unit you'll learn another way to say "with", and you'll learn how to refer to events that happened long ago. You'll also learn new switch-reference endings and how to say "bring", "take", and "begin". The unit includes an Advanced Chickasaw Grammar section.

Lesson 13.1 introduces the **isht±** "with" preverb, a new type of prefix that works differently from the other prefixes you have learned. Lesson 13.2 presents the **±ttook** remote past ending. The **±kat** and **±ka** switch-reference endings are introduced in lesson 13.3. Lesson 13.4 shows how to say "bring" and "take" with **isht±** and a motion verb. Lessons 13.5 and 13.6 present t- verbs and their use with **ishtaya** "begin". The Advanced Chickasaw Grammar lesson introduces some new types of negative sentences with **ki'yo**.

Lesson 13.1: The **Isht±** "with" Prefix	In unit 10 you learned to use the **ibaa±** prefix on verbs to say "along with". Another prefix, **isht±**, means "with" in the sense of "by means of" or "using":

    Hattakat ihooa tali' ishtissotok.   "The man hit the woman with a rock."

In this example, **tali'** "rock" is the INSTRUMENT with which the hitting was done. Though **isht±** and **ibaa±** both mean "with", if you think about the kind of "with" you want to express, you shouldn't have trouble deciding which prefix to use. If the sentence tells what object was used to accomplish the action, use **isht±**.

    Adding **isht±** to a one-place verb like **impa** makes a new two-place verb; adding **isht±** to a two-place verb like **apa** makes a new three-place verb:

    Chipotaat folosh ishtimpa'ni ki'yo.   "The child can't eat with a spoon."
    Chipotaat chofaka nipi' ishtapatok,   "The child ate the meat with a fork."
    Chipotaat nipi'a chofak ishtapatok.

(**Chofak** is "fork".) Remember, when there are two object nouns in a Chickasaw sentence, the one that is not directly before the verb has the object ending **±a**. The two object nouns in such sentences can occur in either order, but the first one must have an object ending.

Isht± is a special type of prefix called a PREVERB. Preverbs work differently from other prefixes. They are always the first thing in their words, coming before all of the other prefixes you have learned, even A and N prefixes:

Bashpo ishtishbashaffitaam?	"Did you cut it with a knife?"
Salbak ishtakí'shokitok.	"I didn't take it with my hands."

Look at the examples—**isht±** comes first every time.

Another way in which preverbs like **isht±** are different from other prefixes is that the D prefix **a+** is unchanged after **isht±** (it does not become **sa+**, as it would after an A or N prefix), as in the following. (**Ishholissochi'** means "pen" or "pencil".)

Ishholissochi' ishta̱holissochitok.	"He wrote to me with a pen."

Instrument object nouns used with **isht±** verbs work just like other objects. Here are three different ways to say "I hit the chief with a hammer" using the new word **naaishbo'wa'**:

Naaishbo'wa̱ minko' ishtissolitok.
Minka̱ naaishbo'wa' ishtissolitok.
Naaishbo'waako̱ minko' ishtissolitok.

Can you think of other ways to say the same thing?

Exercise 13A. Add **isht±** to the verbs of the following Chickasaw sentences so that you can add the instrument objects in parentheses to the sentences. Don't forget to use the object ending **±a** in sentences with two object nouns. Translate the new sentences you make up.

Example. Chokaano abilitok. (holisso) (**chokaano** means "fly", and in this sentence, **holisso** could mean "newspaper")

Answer. Holissa̱ chokaano ishtabilitok. "I killed the fly with a newspaper."

1. Hattak yamma̱ issa'chi (itti'). 2. Chipotaat ishki' i̱holissochi. (ishholissochi') 3. Ihooat ihattak issotok. (**ishpiha'** = "broom") 4. Ishpihtaam? (ishpiha'); (**pihli** = "to sweep" (A,Noun)) 5. Hattakat ashiila apatok. (folosh); (**ashiila** = "stew"). 6. Alikchaat amofi' antakchi. (ishtalakchi') (**takchi** = to tie (A,S), used with a dative and D prefix) 7. Choklhan akhali'lokitok. (amitti') (**choklhan** = "spider") 8. Sashkaat chipota okaamichi. (oka')

In each of the examples you've seen so far, **isht±** comes before a vowel. When **isht±** comes before a consonant, here is what happens:

Ishpiha' ishpihtaam?	"Did she sweep it with a broom?"
Tali' ishchikissokitok.	"You didn't hit him with a rock."
Shawi'a̱ itti' ishhoobo'li.	"They are hitting the raccoon with a stick."

(**Bo'li** means for one person "to hit more than once" or "to beat up" or for many people "to hit". **Shawi'** means "raccoon".) Before a consonant the "with" prefix is **ish±**, not **isht±**. When **isht±** comes before the **p** of the verb **pihli** in the first example, or the **ch** of the N prefix **chik±** in the second example, or the **h** of the **hoo±**

prefix in the last one, the **t** at the end of **isht±** drops out. Before a consonant, then, the "with" prefix sounds exactly like the A prefix **ish±**.

Ishpihtaam?	"Did you sweep it?"
Ishpihtaam?	"Did she sweep it with it?"
Ishbo'li.	"You beat him up."
Ishbo'li.	"He beats him up with it."

When **isht±** (**ish±**, in other words) comes before the S prefix **sa+**, some (but not all) speakers pronounce the resulting combination as **issa+** (which sounds just like the combination of the A prefix **ish±** plus **sa+**). Other speakers, however, pronounce the "with" prefix plus **sa+** as **ishsa+**.

Hattakat tali' issasso *or* ishsasso.	"The man hit me with a rock."

Three types of "with". You've already learned two ways to say "with" using **isht±** and **ibaa±**. There's a third way to say "with" using the location prefix **aa±**, which you learned about in unit 10. Here are some examples of **aaikbi** "to make with, make from":

Shokhoshi' yammat imambooha	"That pig made his house with sticks.",
itti' aaikbitok.	"That pig made his house from sticks."

(**Shokhoshi'** means "pig".) The "with" in "make with" doesn't tell you about an instrument, but rather about a material that becomes something else.

In other words, Chickasaw distinguishes three different types of "with", and you need to think about this while expressing "with" in Chickasaw. When you can substitute "from" or "out of" for "with", Chickasaw uses **aa±** to express "with". When you can substitute "along with" or "together with" for "with", Chickasaw uses **ibaa±** to express "with". When you can substitute "by means of" for "with", Chickasaw uses **isht±** to express "with".

Exercise 13B. Translate the following sentences that contain "with". Pay attention to which type of "with" is involved, choosing **isht±** (**ish±** before consonants), **ibaa±**, or **aa±**, as appropriate. 1. You touched it with a stick. 2. You didn't touch it with your hand. 3. The child writes with a pen. 4. Did you make bread with flour? (**tili'ko'** = "flour") 5. She wants to talk with her hands. 6. I want to run with my son. 7. Are you going to hit me with a broom? 8. That man wants to talk with my husband. 9. You didn't make it with a hammer. 10. You swept the house with a broom. 11. My older sister hit the cat (several times) with a stick. (say this as if a woman is talking) 12. The doctor cut the man's arm with his knife. 13. My mother made a dress with a sack. (**shokcha** = "sack") 14. My mother made a dress with a needle. (**naaishtalhcho'wa'** = "needle")

"About". **Isht±** can have another meaning, too. With the following verbs **isht±** (or **ish±** before consonants) adds the meaning "about" to the sentence:

ishtanompoli "to talk about"	ishhashaa "to be angry about"

Ishtanompoli is an (A,S) verb. First comes **isht±**, then comes the S prefix on the verb **anompoli**. As with any S prefix on an a-verb, the prefix **chi+** comes after the **a** at the beginning of the verb.

Ishtachinompoli.   "He's talking about you."

When you add **isht** to an S subject verb, two things can happen. **Ishhashaa** has an S subject (like **hashaa**) and can be used with a Noun object:

Holisso ishpohashaa.   "We're angry about the book."

When you put **isht** on the S subject verb **ilhpokonna** "to dream", the new verb **ishtilhpokonna** is an (A,S) verb. The person who dreams is an A subject, and the one that's dreamed about can be shown with an S prefix after **isht±**. As with any i-verb, the **i** of **ilhpokonna** drops after this S prefix:

Ishchilhpokonnali.   "I dream about you."

Isht± verbs with more complex meanings. The meaning "about" is regular when you put **isht±** on a verb like **anompoli**, which refers to conversation, or a verb like **hashaa** or **ilhpokonna**, which refers to emotion or mental activity. In some cases, however, the meaning of an **isht±** verb seems a bit more complicated. The following verbs show how the meaning of one complicated verb is built up:

bohli to lay down, put down (A,S)
ombohli to lay down on, put down on (A,S,Noun)
ishtombohli to accuse, blame (A,S) [isht ombohli]

(Make sure you can pronounce the difference between **bo'li** and **bohli**.) In English you can talk about laying blame on someone, and **ishtombohli** expresses a similar idea in Chickasaw. What you need to remember is that the person doing the blaming or accusing is the A subject, and the person being blamed is the S object. Probably this verb originally referred to blaming someone "about" something, but nowadays you only mention the person blaming and the person being blamed, as in

Alikchaat ishtasombohtok.   "The doctor blamed me."

At the end of the vocabulary entry for **ishtombohli**, you'll see "[isht ombohli]" in brackets, showing how this verb can be broken up into two parts. This information is included in all vocabulary entries that include **isht±**, in order to remind you that prefixes go after **isht±**, at the beginning of the verb. Most verbs that include **isht±** are not listed in the vocabulary, however, because adding **isht±** to a verb is usually completely regular, and such verbs do not need to be learned specially.

Exercise 13C. Translate the following sentences into English. 1. Ihoo yammat ishhooasanompola'chi. 2. Sattibaapishiat ofi' yappako ishhashaa. 3. Chipotaat to'wa' ishchokoshkomo. 4. Chipotaat kowi' ibaachokoshkomo. 5. Hattak sipoknihoot imihoo ishtaloowa. 6. Ankaat kaníhka ishhashaa. 7. Ishtissanompolitaam? 8. Holiss-aapisa' ishtanokfillilitok. (**anokfilli** = "think") 9. Ishhassombohtaam? 10. Ishtachinompoli sabanna ki'yo. 11. Ihoo yammat tili'ko' ishhooanompolitok. 12. Ankaat ishtasombohtok sanakfishat shokhoshi'a honkopahma.

Chickasaw has several other preverbs that work like **isht±**. Preverbs all end in **t**, and they must all go before any other prefix on their verb. You'll see a few more preverbs in some of the readings in later units.

Lesson 13.2:
The ±**Ttook** Remote Past

As you learned in unit 4, a plain verb can refer either to the present or to the very recent past, while a verb with the +**tok** past ending refers to past time that is viewed as distinct from the present but not necessarily that long ago.

Hattakat ofi' isso.	"The man is hitting the dog.",
	"The man hit the dog (just now)."
Hattakat ofi' issotok.	"The man hit the dog (a bit longer ago; it's over)."

To say that something happened even longer ago, you can use the ending ±*ttook*:

Hattakat ofi' issottook.	"The man hit the dog (long ago)."

±**Ttook** marks the REMOTE PAST—this tense ending refers to a time long, long ago that is remote from the present. It's helpful to remember that the long **oo** and double **tt** of the longer ±**ttook** ending indicate a longer ago past time than the recent +**tok** past.

Isso, **issotok**, and **issottook** can all be translated "he hit him", with the English past. Usually, the past is shown by +**tok**, so **issotok** is the most usual way to say "he hit him". If the hitting seems very recent or has just happened, you may say **isso**. If it happened several years ago or longer, **issottook** is right. The ±**ttook** remote past is always used to refer events that took place before the speaker was born or in his or her childhood. Listen to the way your teacher uses these different past forms.

Pronouncing verbs with the ±ttook ending. +**Tok** and ±**ttook** look similar, but it's not hard to hear the difference between them. Compare the past and remote past forms of verbs like **hilha** or **sapilachi**, ending in even-numbered short syllables:

hi/lhā/tok	sa/pī/la/chī/tok
hilh/at/took	sa/pī/lach/it/took

With the +**tok** ending, the vowel of the even-numbered short syllable at the end of these verbs is rhythmically lengthened. With the ±**ttook** ending, this vowel is never lengthened, because ±**ttook** is a ± ending that begins with a consonant. As you learned in unit 11, when such endings follow an even-numbered short syllable, the last consonant before the ending may be pronounced as part of the syllable in front of it and may even sound almost double: thus, you might hear the last two examples as <hilhlhattook> or <sapilachchittook>.

In examples like the following the rule does not apply, because the last vowel before ±**ttook** is not an even-numbered short syllable.

Malilittook.	"She ran (long ago)."
Wakaattook.	"It flew (long ago)."

As the first of these new examples shows, an odd-numbered **li** syllable is not deleted before ±**ttook**. There are several reasons for this. The **li** deletion rule (unit 6) only applies to **li** syllables before endings like +**tok**, +**taa**, and +**chi** within a rhythmic lengthening sequence. As you know, although ± markers make words longer, they do not create longer rhythmic lengthening sequences. So the rhythmic lengthening sequence in **malilittook** is no longer than the one in **malili**; **±ttook** is not included in the rhythmic lengthening sequence. **Li** deletion only works before + endings, and **±ttook** is not a + ending. Finally, although **±ttook** starts with **t**, just like **+tok** and **+taa**, the **li** deletion rule only works before certain + endings that start with a single **t**, **ch**, or **n**. **±Ttook** starts with a double **t**.

The same **+ki** ending that goes between **±o** and other endings like **+tok** and **+taa** is used before **±ttook** in negative remote past sentences:

> Ikayyokittook.   He didn't go (long ago).

Exercise 13D. Translate each of the following sentences into Chickasaw two ways, using the **+tok** past and the **±ttook** remote past, and explain the differences in meaning. Then divide each verb into syllables using /'s, with capitals for lengthened vowels, following the pronunciation rules you've learned in units 4 and 11. Say each sentence aloud for your teacher. 1. The bird sang to us (relatively many). 2. The doctor wrote with a pen. 3. I hit the woman with a broom. 4. I did not want you to work in the house. 5. The man took the basket. 6. I went to Oklahoma.

Lesson 13.3:
New Switch-Reference Endings

Look at the following sentences, which include new switch-reference endings:

> Sachaahakat ith**á**nali.   "I know I'm tall."
> Chichaahak**a** ith**á**nali.   "I know you're tall."

The new endings **±kat** and **±ka** are used on dependent verbs that function as the objects of main verbs like **ith**á**na** "to know". What do I know? I know that I'm tall—so the sentence *I'm tall* works like an object of *know*, and you can use **±kat** on the dependent verb **sachaaha**. As with the switch-reference endings you learned in unit 11, you decide whether to use **±kat** or **±ka** after comparing the subjects of the dependent and main verbs. When the two subjects are the same, as in the first example, you use **±kat**; when the two subjects are different, you use **±ka**.

Many verbs are used with **±kat** or **±ka** dependent verb objects. Sometimes the translation will include English "that" (the first sentence above could be restated as "I know that I'm tall", for instance), and sometimes it won't, as in

> Issoba-at mallik**a** p**í**slitok.   "I saw the horse jump," I saw the horse jumping. "

Because **±kat** and **±ka** are ± endings, they cannot be part of a rhythmic lengthening sequence. A dependent verb like **hilhakat** doesn't have any lengthened syllables and may even sound like <hilhlhakat> to you.

Exercise 13E. Translate the following sentences into English. 1. Holisso yapp**a** ittimanompolilikat ith**á**nali. 2. Alikchaat itt**i**sh chimak**a** ishith**á**nataa? 2. Ihooat inchipot**a** pass**á**ak**a** hashp**í**staam? 3. Ki'yo, pass**á**ak**a** kiipi'sokitok. 4. Minkaat taloowak**a** h**á**nglolittook. 5. Hattak yamm**a** ith**á**nalikat anokfillili. 6. Ihoo yammat chokma'sik**a** ishanokfillitaa?

"Remember" and "forget". Two new verbs are **nokfónkha** "to remember", which takes an S subject, and **imalhkaniya** "to forget", which takes a D subject:

Ihoo sanokfónkha.	"I remember the woman."
Hattaka amalhkaniyattook.	"I forgot the man (long ago)."

These verbs can't be used with object prefixes. Thus, there's no way to say "I remember you" or "He forgot me" with a single verb in Chickasaw. One way to express such ideas using two verbs is discussed below.

The new verbs are often used with dependent verbs ending in ±**kat** or ±**ka**:

Chichaahaka sanokfónkha.	"I remember that you're tall."
Chahta' ooka chinokfónkhataam?	"Did you remember that she's Choctaw?"

(**Oo** is the form of "to be" that's used in sentences with an ending but no prefix, as you learned in unit 11.)

Combination endings with ±kat and ±ka. Look at the following examples:

Sachaaha'chikat ithánali.	"I know I'll be tall."
Ishla'chika amalhkaniyatok.	"I forgot that you were going to arrive."

A dependent verb that includes ±**a'chi** before ±**kat** or ±**ka** refers to something that is, or would have been, in the future at the time of the main verb. See how it works? The first example has a present main verb, so the dependent verb just refers to the ordinary future. The second is trickier. In the past, it says, I forgot that at that time (when I forgot) your arrival was in the future.

Dependent verbs like this can also include +**tok**:

Holisso yappa ittimanompolilikat ithánali.	"I know that I am reading this book."
Holisso yappa ittimanompolilitokat ithánali.	"I know that I read this book."
Hattakat ihooat taloowatoka ithána.	"The man knows that the woman sang."
Ithánalitokat amalhkaniyatok.	"I forgot that I knew her."
Tili'ko' chompalitokat amalhkaniyatok.	"I forgot that I had bought the flour."

The interpretation of these dependent verbs depends on the time of the main verb. When the main verb is present, a dependent verb ending in +**tokat** or +**toka** refers to the past. When the main verb is past, the dependent verb refers to a time before the time of the main verb. (Just as a plain verb can sometimes express the recent past, a ±**kat** or ±**ka** verb can sometimes refer to a time before that of the main verb.) The combination of +**tok** plus ±**kat** or ±**ka** is pronounced with only one **k** (don't say <+tokkat>). However, +**tokat** includes a ± marker (it's either +**to**±**kat** or +**tok**±**at**), so the **o** of this ending will never be rhythmically lengthened.

Dependent verbs containing ±**ttook** work the same way:

Taloowattooka ishithánataam?	"Did you know that she sang (long ago)?"

There's only one **k** in **±ttookat** and **±ttooka̱**.

Chickasaw speakers might use one of these combination endings to express what English speakers would say as "I remember you". One possibility would be

Chipíslitokat sanokfónkha. "I saw you, I remember it." *or*
"I remember that I saw you."

Negatives with ±kat and ±ka̱. Look at these sentences in which one of the new endings is used after a negative verb:

Akhi'lhokat itha̱nali. "I know I'm not dancing."
Iksatha'noka̱ chimalhkaniyataa? "Did you forget he doesn't know me?"

There's no **+ki** syllable between **±o** and the new endings. **+Ki** is used between **±o** and following endings beginning with **t** (like +tok, +taa, and ±ttook) but not before ±kat, ±ka̱, or most other endings. However, you do need to use **+ki** when a negative verb comes before combination endings like **+tokat** or **±ttooka̱**:

Akhi'lhokitokat itha̱nali. "I know I didn't dance."

What's important is which ending comes immediately after the negative verb. You must add **+ki** between **±o** and **+tok** or **±ttook**.

Exercise 13F. Translate the following sentences into English. 1. Chi̱holissa̱ chinokfónkhataam? 2. Oblaashaash hattak holhchifoa̱ pomalhkaniyatok. 3. Chikashsha chiyaka̱ amalhkaniyatok. 4. Chipotaat abikaka̱ ikponokfokhokitok. 5. Ishtaloowa'chikat chikitha'no. 6. Abooha akpihlokitokat itha̱nali. 7. Ofi'at illika̱ ishpístok. 8. Ofi'at illitoka̱ ishitha̱nataa? 9. Ofi'at illittooka̱ chimalhkaniyataam? 10. Anka̱naat sabaachokoshkoma'chika̱ sanokfónkha. 11. Chinka̱naat sabaachokoshkoma'chika̱ sanokfónkhatok. 12. Chipotaat yaa'chika̱ kilitha̱na.

When the main verb has a noun subject. Look at what happens when the main and dependent verbs both have noun subjects:

Sashkaat issoba-at mallika̱ pístok. "My mother saw the horse jump."

As you know, Chickasaw uses the sentence order SUBJECT OBJECT VERB. If the **±ka̱** dependent verb plus its subject and object (which we might think of as a full dependent sentence) is the object of the main verb here, it isn't surprising that the dependent sentence **issoba-at mallika̱** comes between the main verb **pístok** and its subject,-**sashkaat**. The sentence pattern is similar to the "want someone to" pattern (unit 9):

MAIN VERB SUBJECT	DEPENDENT VERB SUBJECT	DEPENDENT VERB±**ka̱**	MAIN VERB
Sashkaat	issoba-at	mallika̱	pístok.

DEPENDENT SENTENCE

It's also correct to take the dependent sentence and put it either at the front or the end of the whole sentence, as follows:

Issoba-at mallika sashkaat pístok, "My mother saw the horse jump."
Sashkaat pístok issoba-at mallika.

(Such a change in word order, incidentally, is not possible with the "want someone to" sentences you learned about in lesson 9.7.) As you'd expect from what you already know, the dependent verb and its subject (and object, if there is one) stay together in all new sentences like this.

The examples above may remind you of unit 11 sentences like

Issoba-at mallihma sashkaat pístok. "When the horse jumped, my mother saw it."

("It" here could be the horse, the jumping, or something else.) A dependent verb with ±**hma** (or the other switch-reference endings you learned about in unit 11) tells about an event that is separate from the main verb. A dependent verb with ±**ka** or ±**kat**, on the other hand, tells about an event that is connected with the main verb, as its object. That's why a ±**ka** dependent verb can come between the main verb and its subject. But this sentence pattern is not possible with ±**hma** or ±**kma** dependent verbs.

> *Exercise 13G.* Translate the following sentences into English. Then find a new way to say each one, using the same words but a different word order, as in the example. Remember to keep the parts of the dependent sentence together when you change things around.
>
> *Example.* Minkaat imalhkaniyatok hattak imofi'at illika.
>
> *Answer.* "The chief forgot that the man's dog had died." Minkaat hattak imofi'at illitoka imalhkaniyatok. *or* Hattak imofi'at illitoka minkaat imalhkaniyatok.
>
> 1. Sanakfishat ankaat abikaka nokfónkhatok. 2. Ihooat ithána ihattakat fani' abitoka. 3. Alikchi' sipokni yammat chipotaat ittish lohmitoka imalhkaniyatok. 4. Nannimaabachi'at ikitha'nokitok sashkaat taloowa'chika. 5. Ankanaat itti'chanaa-at iwáyya'aka hattakat ithánataa? 6. Sashkat shokcha ishika amalhkaniyatok.

Lesson 13.4:
Isht± on Motion Verbs

"Bring" and "take" verbs. Most MOTION VERBS, which express the subject's movement, have a special meaning when used with the "with" preverb **isht±**:

Nipi' ishtayatok. "He went away with the meat.", "He took the meat."
Chipota ishtalala'chi. "I'll get here with the child.", "I'll bring the child."

When you use **isht±** on a motion verb, it means either "bring" or "take", in the manner of the particular motion verb. Thus, **ishmalli** means "to bring" (or "take") while jumping:

Foshi'at itti' ishmalli. "The bird is jumping with the stick", "The bird is taking the stick (jumping)."

A subjects and S objects of these **isht±** "bring" and "take" verbs, like those of other **isht±** verbs, are marked on the verb that follows **isht±**:

Ishtishiyyataam? "Did you take it?"
Ishpomallitok. "He's taking us (jumping)."

These **isht±** verbs refer to taking something from one location to another, not just getting something—to express that kind of taking, you use **ishi**.

As you know, many motion verbs are irregular short verbs—this is why we say **ishtishiyya**. S objects of verbs like **ishtaya**, **ishtala**, and **ishtona** work like any other objects of a-verbs and o-verbs:

Ishtasalatok.	"He brought me."
Ishtachiya'chi.	"He'll take you."
Ishtaponatok.	"He took us (there)."
Ishtiksayyokitok.	"He didn't take me."

(This follows the regular rules, not the special rules you learned in unit 11 for S objects of short verbs like **abi**. When a short verb has a prefix, it acts less like a short verb.) **Ishtaya** becomes **ishtayya** before the A ending **+li** and in the negative **ikayyo**; "you take" is **ishtishiyya** or **ishhashiyya**.

<table>
<tr><td>

Lesson 13.5:
Saying "Begin" with **Ishtaya**

</td><td>

Ishtaya *"begin"*. Ishtaya can also mean "to begin, start":

</td></tr>
</table>

Ishtaya.	"He's beginning, starting."

Here's how you tell the kind of action or state that was begun:

Impat ishtayyali.	"I begin to eat."
Holisso ittimanompolit ishtishiyyataa?	"Are you starting to read the book?"
Hopoot ishhashiyya.	"You guys are starting to be jealous."
Sabo't ishtishiyya!	"You're starting to beat me up!"
<u>A</u>hilhat ishtaya.	"She's starting to dance for me."

The verb that names this action, with the new ending **+t**, goes at the front of the sentence, before the form of **ishtaya** that tells you who the subject is.

T-verbs. Verbs with the **+t** ending are called T-VERBS. As the last two examples above show, a t-verb may have an S or D object prefix, but it can never have an A subject prefix. An A subject marker must go on **ishtaya**.

Ishtaya with S and D subject verbs. When **ishtaya** is used with a verb that takes an S or D subject, the subject prefix goes on the t-verb:

Sabannat ishtaya.	"I'm starting to want it."
Chintakho'bit ishtayataa?	"Are you beginning to be lazy?"

With an S or D subject t-verb, the **ishtaya** verb never has a subject marker.

A dative prefix or any S or D prefix (whether it marks subject or object), then, goes on the t-verb, while all A markers go on **ishtaya**.

Stative t-verbs. A stative t-verb followed by **ishtaya** often sounds better translated with "get" than with "begin" or "start":

| Satikahbit ishtaya. | "I'm beginning to be tired.", "I'm getting tired." |
| Hopoot ishtayyali. | "I'm beginning to be jealous.", "I'm getting jealous." |

Usually, **ishtaya** is not used in the negative when it means "begin", "start", or "get".

Exercise 13H. Translate the following sentences into English. 1. Are you going to take me? 2. He is starting to play with the paper. 3. They began to play with the child. 4. I got lazy yesterday. 5. The woman is beginning to sing in the bedroom. 6. We brought him here (long ago). 7. The tree is getting yellow. 8. Is your mother beginning to make bread? 9. The doctor was beginning to touch me (long ago). 10. Don't start to talk about it. 11. The child is beginning to write in the school. 12. We are beginning to dance with you all.

Lesson 13.6:
More about T-Verbs and **Ishtaya** Sentences

Dropping vowels before +t. The new ending +**t** works similarly to other + endings such as +**tok** or +**taa**. When a verb ending with a heavy syllable that ends with a vowel, **h**, or ' followed by a single **s**, **sh**, or **lh** and a non-lengthened short vowel comes before +**t**, the final short vowel of that verb is dropped in the t-verb.

| Fani' host ishtayatok. | "He began to shoot at the squirrel." |

The next-to-last syllable of **hosa**, from which the t-verb **host** is made, is heavy; this syllable is followed by a single **s** plus a short vowel, so that final vowel drops in the t-verb.

In t-verbs made from verbs ending in a heavy syllable plus a single **ch** plus a short vowel, the last vowel of the verb drops and the **ch** changes to **sh** before +**t**.

| Aasht ishtishiyyataa? | "Are you starting to say it?" |
| Chokka' inkasht ishtiliyya. | "We are beginning to sell houses to her." |

The t-verbs here are made from the verbs **aachi** and **inkanchi**. A vowel plus **n** becomes a nasal vowel when a **ch** after it becomes **sh**; thus, the **anch** of **inkanchi** becomes **ash** in the t-verb. (You can review the vowel drop rule in unit 6.)

Li deletion before +t. When a verb ending in a **li** syllable that follows a heavy syllable ending in a vowel, **h**, or ' comes before +**t**, that **li** syllable is dropped. You can review this rule in unit 8.

Sashoot ishtishiyya.	"You're starting to hug me."
Piht ishtayyala'chi.	"I'll start to sweep."
Malit ishtayatok.	"He started to run."

The next-to-last syllable of **sashooli** is heavy, because it includes a long vowel. The next-to-last syllable of **pihli** is heavy, because it ends in **h**. The next-to-last syllable of **malili** is heavy, because it contains a lengthened vowel. The **li** syllables following all these heavy syllables are dropped in the t-verb. However, a **li** syllable after a heavy syllable ending in a consonant other than **h** or ' does not drop:

| Mallit ishtiliyya. | "We're starting to jump." |

As you know from unit 8, adding an S prefix to a verb ending in **li** can change the rhythmic pattern of that word:

Halit ishtaya.   "He begins to touch it."

Sahalilit ishtaya.   "He begins to touch me."

Since **halili** ends in a **li** syllable that follows a heavy syllable, this verb becomes **halit** when +**t** is added. However, the **li** at the end of **sahalili** follows a light syllable, so it does not delete before +**t**.

Hoo± with *ishtaya* sentences. In a "start" sentence, the plural subject prefix **hoo±** may go either on the t-verb or on **ishtaya** (after **ish±**):

Ihooat hoohilhat ishtaya,   "The women are starting to dance."

Ihooat hilhat ishhooaya.

Exercise 131. Use **ishtaya** to add "begin" or "get" to each of the following sentences, making all necessary changes, as in the examples. Translate each of the new sentences you make up.

Example. Apali.

Answer. Apat ishtayyali. "I'm beginning to eat."

Example. Sachaaha.

Answer. Sachaahat ishtaya. "I'm getting tall."

1. Ishtaloowa. 2. A̱soba-at palhki. 3. Issabaachokoshkomo. 4. Abooha hashpihli. 5. Chinchokka' iliyya. 6. Ofi'at chipota kisili. 7. Iitahli. 8. Kanı̱hka chichokma. 9. Kanı̱hka ishchokma. 10. Hattak yamma̱ amalhkaniya. 11. Chipotaat paska hooapa. 12. Paska̱ tili'ko' kilaaikbi.

Special t-verbs. There are many special t-verbs that combine with the verb which follows them to make a phrase. Here are three of these, the verbs they are derived from, and verb phrases in which they are often used:

special t-verb	derived from	used in verb phrase
apat	apa "to eat"	apat pisa "to taste"
malit	malili "to run"	malit kaniya "to run away" (singular subject)
pist	pisa "to see"	pist aya "to go see"

Here are some examples of sentences using these new verb phrases.

Paska apat pisalitok.   "I tasted the bread."

Chipotaat malit kaniyataam?   "Did the child run away?"

Chipist kiliyya'chi.   "We will go see you."

As in the **ishtaya** sentences you learned earlier, the A subject of each phrase is marked on the last verb, but the S object of a whole phrase like "go see" is marked on the preceding t-verb, **pist**.

Irregular t-verbs. Some t-verbs work irregularly. The usual t-verb from **pisa** "to see" is **pisat**, but you will hear **pist** more often, especially in phrases like **pist aya**. **Pist** is sometimes pronounced (and written) as one word with the following verb. In this case a speaker may drop the final **t** in **pist** when it comes before a consonant.

Pist chikayyokitok, Pischikayyokitok.   "You didn't go see him."

So you might think of **pist±** as a kind of ± prefix. Here's the vocabulary entry:

> pist aya, pistaya to go see (A,S) [pist aya]

This entry uses brackets around [pist aya] just the way the **isht±** verbs explained earlier do, to show you that any subject markers will go on **aya**, not on **pist**. The A (or N) marking goes on **aya**, while the S marking goes on **pist**.

> *Exercise 13J.* Translate the following sentences into Chickasaw. 1. Did you taste the meat? 2. They went to see you all. 3. I want to run away. 4. I will run away. 5. You do not want to taste the peach. 6. Did you go to see me? 7. We went to see all of you. 8. You came to see me (long ago).

The way the **t** on **pist** or **pist±** drops may remind you of **isht±**, which, in fact, originally came from a special t-verb derived from **ishi** "take". The normal t-verb of **ishi** is **ishit**:

> Ittish ishit ishtayyala'chi.   "I'll start to take the medicine."

When you think about it, probably you can see how the t-verb's original meaning of "taking" or "holding" might have developed into the "with" meaning of **isht±**. Of course, **isht+** is very different from the other t-verbs you have learned about. **Isht±** is always pronounced and written as part of the following verb word, and S objects of **isht±** verbs are marked on those verbs after **isht±**, never on **isht±** itself.

Terms and Concepts

INSTRUMENT, PREVERB, REMOTE PAST, DEPENDENT SENTENCE, MOTION VERB, T-VERB.

VOCABULARY (additional "bring" and "take" verbs can be formed as described in the unit)

anokfilli to think (A)
apat pisa to taste (A,Noun)
ashiila soup
bo'li to hit (more than once); to beat up; (pl. subj.) to hit (A,S)
bohli to lay down, put down (sg. obj.) (A,S)
chofak fork
choklhan, cholhkan spider
chokoshkomo to play (A)
imalhkaniya to forget (D,Noun)
ishhashaa to be angry about (S,Noun)
ishholissochi' pen, pencil
ishpiha' broom
ishtala to bring (here) (A,S) [isht ala]
ishtaya to begin (used with preceding t-verb) (A); to bring, take (A,S) [isht aya]
ishtilhpokonna to dream about (A,S) [isht ilhpokonna]
ishtombohli to accuse, blame (A,S) [isht ombohli]
ishtona to take (over there) (A,S) [isht ona]
kaniya to go away (sg. subj.) (A)

malit kaniya to run away (sg. subj.) (A)
naaishbo'wa' hammer
naaishtalhcho'wa' needle
nokfónkha to remember (S,Noun)
ombohli to lay (sg. obj.) down on, put (sg. obj.) down on (A,S,Noun)
pihli to sweep (A,Noun)
pistaya, pist aya to go see (A,S) [pist aya]
shokcha bag, sack
shokhoshi' pig
shawi' raccoon
takchi to tie; to tie up (A,S)
tili'ko' flour

READING AND SPEAKING

Hattak Api' Hommaat Okloshi' Ilayyo'kakat Lawa

We wrote this story in Chickasaw inspired by a Choctaw "creation story" told by a woman named Pisatuntema ("Emma") in 1909.[1] (The translation is provided in Appendix C.)

Hopaakikaashookano Chihoowaat hattak lawaho ikbittook. Hattak mómakat Chikashsha ookat, Chikashshanompa anompolikat, ittimithánattook. Hattak yammat yaakni' anonkaka' aamintikat, lokfi' lakna' aaiksaattook. Hattak íla' nannakya ikshokittook.

Nittak chaffaka mómakat shotik pisakat, yappat nanna ooka ittimasilhhattook. Shotik ona bannahootokoot, tali' ishta'lacha, onchaba ikbit ishtayattookookya oklhilika nosika mahlikat tali'a hattak oyilhlhichit tahlittook.

Hattakat ikillohookya, nittaki ittimanompolit ishtayakat, mómakat imilhlhattook—himónali' anompa íla' anompolikat, iktimitha'nokittook.

Kani'mikat Chikashshanompa anompolittook: yammakoot Chikashsha attook, Chikashsha Iyaakni' tobattook. Kani'mikat anompaat ittihooba chohmiho anompolittook: yammakoot Chahta' attook, Chahta' Iyaakni' tobattook. Hattak ila' áyya'shakat anompa yamma ikimitha'nokat ittibit ishtayattook.

Hattak mómakat ittifilamo'littook. Chikashsha Chahta' táwwa'at ittimilinka'sittookookya, ila' mómakat hopaakichit ayattook—kani'mikat falammi ayahma, kani'mikat hashaakochcha' ayahma, kani'mikat hashaaobya' ayattook. Mómakat iyaakni' íla' tobattook. Yammakaatooko Hattak Api' Hommaat okloshi' ilayyokakat lawa.

1. The original story (whose heroes are Choctaw, not Chickasaw) appears in *The Choctaw of Bayou Lacomb, St. Tammany Parish, Louisiana,* by David I. Bushnell, Jr., Smithsonian Institution, Bureau of Ethnology Bulletin 48. Washington, D.C.: Government Printing Office, 1909, p. 30.

SUPPLEMENTARY VOCABULARY

aaiksaa to be made from (S,Noun)

aaminti to come from (A,Noun)

Chahta' Iyaakni' Choctaw Nation

falammi north

hashaakochcha' east

hashaaobya', hashaaobyaka' west

himónali' suddenly

hopaakichi to go far off (A)

ittihooba chohmi to be just about the same (Noun)

ittimasilhha to ask each other (A)

ittimithána to understand each other (A)

ittifilamo'li to separate from each other (A)

ittimilinka'si to be close to each other (A)

kani'mi to be some, to be several (A)

lokfi' mud

nannakya iksho not to exist at all (S) (see note 1 below)

nittak chaffaka one day

nittaki in the morning

okloshi' tribe

oklhilika at night

onchaba mountain

oyilhlhichi to knock (something) down on (someone or something) (A,S,Noun)

shotik sky

tahli completely (auxiliary) (see note 6 below)

táwwa'at (expresses "and")

toba to become (A,Noun)

yammakaatooko that's why

NOTES

1. **Nannakya iksho** is a stronger way than **iksho** to say "to not exist". Usually the noun used as the subject of this expression is not marked with the subject ending ±**at**, as in **Hattak íla' nannakya ikshokittook** "There were no other people at all."

2. The different-subject marker ±**ka** is often used in time expressions, such as **nittak chaffaka** "one day" or **oklhilika** "at night". In fact, since the words in these expressions are verbs, this usage makes sense, since the time expression doesn't have the same subject as the following sentence. But you can just memorize such phrases, if you like.

3. Verbs that refer to numbers, such as **móma** "to be all" and **kani'mi** "to be some, to be several", can be used with ±**kat** (for subjects) or ±**ka** (for objects) to mean "all of them", "some of them", and so on. Thus, **hattak mómakat** means "all the people" (subject) and **mómakat** on its own means "all of them" (subject), but both of these phrases could be used to mean "everyone" (subject).

4. ±**Hootokoot** is a same-subject switch-reference ending that means "because".

5. +**Cha** is a special same-subject switch-reference ending that means "and". It works differently from all other switch-reference endings (except its different-subject counterpart +**na**), as you'll learn in unit 15.

6. **Tahli** is used as an auxiliary meaning something like "completely" following a t-verb. You'll learn more about this sentence pattern in unit 14.

7. **Anompaat ittihooba chohmiho** means "a language that was just about the same" (object). You'll learn more about this type of modifying phrase in unit 20.

8. **Hattak api' hommaat okloshi' ilayyo'kakat lawa** means "the Indians have many separate tribes", expressed with a special "have" sentence pattern.

ADVANCED CHICKASAW GRAMMAR 3: NEW TYPES OF **KI'YO** NEGATIVE SENTENCES

Study the following sets of **ki'yo** negative sentences:

Haklo ki'yo.	"He doesn't hear it."
Haklo' ki'yo.	"He can't hear it (maybe he's deaf)."
Hakla' ki'yo.	"He never hears it (maybe he doesn't listen)."
Malilili ki'yo.	"I don't run."
Malilili' ki'yo.	"I can't run (maybe I'm in a wheelchair)."
Malilila' ki'yo.	"I never run (maybe I'm lazy)."

The first sentence in each set is the kind of **ki'yo** negative you learned about in unit 7: the negative word **ki'yo** comes after a complete verb. The next two sentences in each set use new patterns.

In the second sentence of each set, a ' comes after the verb before **ki'yo** (this verb may have the A ending **+li**, but it cannot have another ending after that). Such sentences are usually translated with "can't". They show that the subject of the sentence isn't able to perform the action or be in the state named by the verb.

In the third sentence of each set, the last vowel of the verb before **ki'yo** (which, again, may have the A ending **+li** but cannot have another ending after that) is replaced by ±**a'**. This type of sentence means that the subject of the sentence never performs the action or is in the state named by the verb for any reason. It may be because of lack of ability, but it's more likely because the subject chooses not to do this. Usually such sentences are translated with "never".

The meanings of these two new types of negative sentences overlap. The first type of sentence can also be translated with "never" (since if you can't do something, you never do it), and the second can also be translated with "can't". Use the first type when you're specifically drawing attention to the subject's lack of physical ability and the second when you're emphasizing the idea of "never".

Notice that when a verb ends with **a**, the two new patterns come out the same—except, of course, when the verb has a **+li** ending.

Ishimpa' ki'yo.	"You can't eat", "You never eat".
Impali' ki'yo.	"I can't eat (I'm fed through a tube)."
Impala' ki'yo.	"I never eat (I'm too busy)."

Unit 14

New Types of Subjects and Objects

In this unit you'll learn several new "have" sentence patterns and some new types of negatives. You'll also learn about expressing completion. The Advanced Chickasaw Grammar section presents more types of possessor/subject sentences.

Lesson 14.1 discusses sentences with color verbs used as "have" verbs. Lesson 14.2 covers the interpretations of sentences whose verbs include both **ibaa±** "with" and causative **+chi**. Lesson 14.3 introduces possessor/subject sentences. "Not yet" negative sentences are presented in lesson 14.4. Lesson 14.5 shows how to express completion with t-verbs and the **tahli** and **taha** auxiliaries.

Lesson 14.1: "Have" Sentences with Color Verbs	

As you learned in unit 12, there's no single verb that means "have" in Chickasaw. Instead, expressing "have" means using some other verb, with a completely different meaning, in a new sentence pattern. Saying "have" with a color verb, as in the following examples, uses another new sentence pattern:

Ihooat ishkinat lakna.	"The woman has brown eyes."
Poshnaakoot polbakat losa.	"We have black hands."

In these sentences the "have" sentence pattern is

SUBJECT±at/±akoot/±hoot	"HAVE" OBJECT±AT	COLOR VERB
Ihooat	ishkinat	lakna.

Just as in the "have" sentences in unit 12, the "have" object is marked with **±at**. Like other "have" objects, this one must go right before the verb. However, with color verb "have" sentences there is never a dative or D prefix on the verb.

With S possessor nouns like **ishkin** and **ilbak**, as in the sentences above, you mark the possessor (the same person as the subject) on the "have" object. This is also true with "have" object nouns that use a dative prefix in the possessed form:

Chipotaat imofi'at homma.	"The child has a red dog."
Sashkaat inaafkaat tohbi.	"My mother has a white dress."

With a color "have" verb, the "have" object noun always has the proper possessive marking to go with the subject of the sentence, even when that subject is understood, as in

Chishkinat losa.   "You have black eyes."
Chinaafkat tohbi.   "You have a white dress."

In these sentences the subject "you" is understood, but the "have" objects **chishkinat** and **chinaafkaat** are marked for "you" possessors. There is no prefix on the verb.

> *Exercise 14A.* Translate each of the following Chickasaw sentences into English using the new sentence pattern. 1. Kowi'at iyyaat tohbi. 2. Hattak yammakoot isoba-at losa. 3. Poshnaakoot pomamboohaat lakna. 4. Minkaat imbalaafkaat okchamali. (**balaafka'** = "pants") 5. Foshi'at fanalhchaat homma. (**fanalhchi'** = "wings")

Two translations. Because there is no prefix on a "have" color verb, some of these sentences can be a little confusing. Consider a sentence like

Hishi'at lakna.

Hishi', which takes S prefixes, means "fur". This sentence can have two English translations—either "Its fur is brown", with an understood possessor, or "It has brown fur", with an understood subject. Now, look at these longer sentences:

Nita' hishi'at lakna.   "The bear's fur is brown."
Nita'at hishi'at lakna.   "The bear has brown fur."

The longer sentences make it clear whether or not **lakna** is being used as a "have" verb. When there is a subject marked with ±at, ±akoot, or ±hoot (or any other subject marking) in front of the possessed noun, as in the second sentence, you know there should be a "have" in the translation. When the possessor does not have a subject ending, as in the first sentence, the translation should include a possessive phrase. The first sentence might be used to make a statement specifically concerning the fur, while the second suggests that the speaker is more interested in the bear. But when the subject or possessor is understood, you can't be sure. (Don't let this worry you too much—after all, how much real difference in meaning is there between "It has brown fur" and "Its fur is brown"? Often, it's fine to say either one.)

If the possessed noun in a sentence like these has a subject ending other than ±at, is followed by **yammat** or **yappat**, or comes in a position other than immediately in front of the verb, the sentence is not a "have" sentence:

Hishi'akoot lakna.   "<u>Its fur</u> is brown."
Inaafka yammat homma.   "That dress of hers is red."
Okchamali chishkinat.   "Your eyes are blue."

Remember, a "have" object must end in ±at (and only ±at) and must come right in front of the verb.
    The "they" plural subject prefix **hoo±** is not used on "have" color verbs.

New S prefix nouns. Here are some new nouns that use S possessive prefixes:

ibichchala' "nose"	ipashi' "hair"
hakshop "skin"	haksibish "ear"
shakba' "upper arm"	iyyinto'lhka' "knee"
ilbakchosh "fingernail"	iyyakchosh "toenail"
ishkobo' "head"	ittakoba' "stomach, belly"

Ipashi' only refers to the hair on a person's head or to a horse's mane. Hair on the body, on the other hand, is called **hishi'**, so **hishi'** means not only "fur", but "body hair". This word is also used in expressions like

foshi' hishi' "feather"	itti' hishi' *or* itti'shi' "leaf"

Like **hishi'**, **hakshop** has a broad meaning:

itti' hakshop "bark"	holisso hakshop "book cover"

When **hishi'** is used to mean "body hair", speakers usually precede it by the name of the body part whose hair is referred to, as in

sayyi' hishi'	"my leg hair"
chilbak hishi'	"the hair on your arm"

Such phrases work like any other possessed phrase in which the possessor is itself a possessed noun.

Exercise 14B. i. Translate the following. 1. my stomach. 2. the man's nose. 3. your head. 4. our knees. 5. your (plural) skin. 6. my fingernails. 7. our (special) toenails. 8. my mother's ear.

ii. Give two translations for each of the following sentences. 9. Sapashaat losa. 10. Chishkinat okchamataa? 11. Inaafokhaat tohbi. 12. Pobichchala'at hommatok.

iii. The following sentences have only one English translation. Explain why, then translate them. 13. Sapashaakoot losa. 14. Hishi'oot lakna. 15. Okchamali pomamboohaat. 16. Issi' hishi'akoot tohbi.

Lesson 14.2:
Ibaa± Causative Verbs

Unlike other three-place **ibaa±** verbs, those that include the causative ending **+chi** can have several different meanings:

Ihooa hattak ibaahilhashlitok.	"I made the man dance with the woman."

The English translation here can be interpreted in two different ways, and so can the Chickasaw sentence. Let's start by assuming that the first noun in the example sentence, the woman, is the **ibaa±** object. Then this sentence can be interpreted in the same two ways the English one can: it can mean either that the woman helped me make the man dance, or that I made the man and the woman dance together. (Think about it, and you'll see that the English sentence really has these two quite different meanings.) Only when **ibaa±** is added to a causative verb do you get these two different meanings for an **ibaa±** object.

The reason that causative **ibaa±** verbs have these two interpretations is a little tricky, but kind of neat, too. Suppose you start with a causative verb like **hilhachi** "make dance", a two-place verb. As you know, when you add an **ibaa±** object to a two-place verb like **hosa**, the **ibaa±** object tells you someone who helps the subject perform the action of the verb. By this interpretation, the example sentence above would mean that the woman helped me make the man dance.

On the other hand, suppose we start with the one-place verb **hilha** and add **ibaa±** to get the two-place verb **ibaahilha** "dance with". Then the only interpretation is that the **ibaa±** object is someone who dances with the subject. Now, if we add **+chi** to this two-place **ibaa±** verb, the new subject of **ibaahilhachi** is the causer, the one who makes **ibaahilha** happen. The one who dances, the subject of **ibaahilha**, is the causee. And the one that the causee dances with, the **ibaa±** object, counts as the original object of the three-place causative verb (you can review how this works in unit 8 if you need to)—so in this case, I make the man dance with the woman, together. Any time you have a causative verb with the **ibaa±** prefix and the **+chi** ending, there are two ways to interpret the meaning of the **ibaa±** object. Either it can tell you someone who did the causing with the subject, or it can tell you an additional object who was caused to do the action of the original verb.

+Chi sentences like the following also have several interpretations:

Ihooa issabaahilhashtok.   "You made me dance with the woman.",
     "You made the woman dance with me."

Maybe I helped you make the woman dance, maybe you made me dance with her. See if you can work it out.

As you learned in unit 5, it is always possible to change the order of two object nouns in a Chickasaw sentence. So our original sentence **Ihooa hattak ibaahilhashlitok** has even more different interpretations if you think of the man as the **ibaa±** object. What are they?

Exercise 14C. Translate each of the following Chickasaw sentences with three-place **ibaa+** verbs into English. Most sentences have a second interpretation. If you can, tell what it is. 1. Anchipota amofi' ibaayopishlitok. 2. Alikchaat chipota ihoo ibaayaashtaam? 3. Ahattaka anakfi' ibaaissolitok. 4. Alikchi' yammakoot inka hattak ibaaimanompolitok. 5. Chishka chinaafokha ishibaaikbitaam? 6. Minkaat hattak yamma imihoo ikibaasho'kokitok. 7. Issaako sanakfish ibaanalhlhilitok. 8. Hattaka ofi' ibaanowachila'chi. 9. Chishkaat ihooa pobaahilhacha'chi. 10. Ihooat foshi' sabaataloowachitok.

Lesson 14.3:
Possessor/Subjects

Look at these sentences:

Chipota imofi'at mallitok.   "The child's dog jumped."
Ihoo ihattakat chaaha.   "The woman's husband is tall."

Sentences like these have a possessed noun subject and a one-place verb. There is another way to talk about the same things, especially when you want to draw attention to the possessor:

Chipotaat ofi'at imallitok.   "The child's dog jumped.",
     "The child had his dog jump."

Ihooat hattakat inchaaha.

"The woman's husband is tall.",
"The woman has a tall husband."

The new examples show a new kind of "have" sentence pattern. You can change a sentence with this pattern—

POSSESSOR	**im±SUBJECT±at/±akoot/±hoot**	VERB
Chipota	imofi'at	mallitok.

to a sentence with this new pattern—

POSSESSOR/SUBJECT±at/±akoot/±hoot	"HAVE" OBJECT±at	**im±VERB**
Chipotaat	ofi'at	<u>i</u>mallitok.

In the new pattern, the original possessor noun becomes a subject (we can call this a POSSESSOR/SUBJECT, since it is both a possessor and a subject), while the original subject becomes a "have" object. The dative prefix (which of course may be **im±**, **in±**, or **i±**) goes on the verb, instead of on the possessed noun.

As you can see, "have" may be used in the translation (with the possessor as the translation's subject), or the translation may remain the same as for the original sentence (with the possessed noun as the subject).

Exercise 14D. Each of the following sentences has a possessed noun subject. Translate the sentence and then change it to the new "have" pattern, as in the example.

Example. Ihoo <u>i</u>foshi'at taloowa.

Answer. "The woman's bird is singing." Ihooat foshi'at intaloowa.

1. Minko' <u>i</u>soba-at malitaa? 2. Ofi' <u>i</u>shtalakchaat litiha. 3. Alikchi' imihoot yaa ki'yo. 4. Hattak imamboohaat hichito. 5. Hattak imamboohaat ishto. 6. Anki' inkaarat palhki. 7. Ihoo inchipotaat ayoppa. 8. Sanakfish impaskaat ikchampo'lo. (HINT: remember that a dative prefix always goes after the unaccomplished prefix.)

In this new sentence pattern there is always an emphasis on the possessor/subject, which can, of course, be marked with **±akoot** or with **±hoot**:

Alikchi'oot chokkaat imishto.

"The one who has a big house is the doctor."

The same sentence pattern can be used with an "I", "you", or "we" subject. You can use an emphatic pronoun to express the possessor/subject, as in the following sentence. In this pattern, the D prefix on the verb matches the subject:

Ishnaakoot issoba-at chintilhaa.

"<u>You</u> have your horses running."

It's actually more common not to emphasize these possessor/subjects so much. In a sentence like the following, the "you" possessor subject is understood, but we know that "you" is the subject because of the D prefix on the verb:

Issoba-at chintilhaa.

"You have your horses running."

Perhaps you find "have" translations like "The child had his dog jump" or "You have your horses running" a bit odd—this type of "have" sentence is more common in Chickasaw than in English. Using these translations may help you understand how the possessor is made into a subject in the new Chickasaw sentence pattern. But all sentences in this new pattern can also be translated in the same way as the original sentences, with possessed noun subjects.

Possessor/subject sentences normally don't mean that the subject necessarily caused the event of the sentence, although this type of "have" sentence might be interpreted that way in English. The possessor/subject pattern simply puts emphasis on the subject.

Exercise 14E. Translate the following possessor/subject sentences into English. 1. Ihooat hattakat inchaaha. 2. Hattakat anchaaha. 3. Chipotaat foshi'at intaloowa'chi. 4. Foshi'at chintaloowa'chi. 5. Alikchaat chokfaat imallitok. (**chokfi** = "rabbit") 6. Hattak yammat nashobaat imishto. (**nashoba** = "wolf") 7. Minkakoot chipotaat ikimi'pokitok. 8. Chipotaat ikpomi'pokittook.

The one-place verbs that can be used with D prefixes in this new pattern may be either original A subject or S subject verbs. (You can't use this new pattern with a one-place D subject verb. And color verbs always use the special pattern you learned earlier in this unit, so they cannot be used in this new pattern either.) The "have" objects in the possessor/subject pattern are always nouns with ±**at** added, which, like all "have" objects, must go right in front of the verb.

Look at these examples:

Asoba-at tilhaa.	"My horses are running."
Issoba-at antilhaa.	"My horses are running.",
	"I have horses running."

In the first sentence, the use of the plural-subject verb **tilhaa** means that the subject **asoba-at** refers to more than one horse. The second sentence uses the new pattern, with an "I" possessor/subject and with a D prefix on the verb rather than on the possessed noun. **Tilhaa** still refers to **issoba-at**, so there must still be more than one horse. You could also say **Anaakoot issoba-at antilhaa**, with an emphatic subject pronoun added.

In this new sentence pattern, there usually is no dative prefix on the "have" object. But if the "have" object has an S possessive prefix, or if it is a word (like **inki'** "father") that always has a dative prefix in the possessed form, the "have" object will have a prefix:

Ishnaakoot chipashaat chintapatok.	"Your hair was cut.",
	"You got your hair cut."

(**Tapa** means "to be cut" or, more specifically, "to have the end or head cut off".) It would be wrong to use the "his" possessive form **ipashaat** in this sentence—you have to say **chipashaat** "your hair".

Exercise 14F. Translate the following sentences into Chickasaw. Then practice saying each sentence out loud. 1. The man has a big house. 2. I have a sick husband. 3. Do you have a fast horse? 4. The doctor made the woman sick for the chief. 5. Those men painted our house for us. 6. These women have big feet. 7. My mother has a dirty dress. 8. The bird had its beak (say "nose") cut. 9. We have fast feet. 10. I have clean hands.

Lesson 14.4:
Negative Sentences with ±ísha

There are still a few more things to learn about negative sentences. Compare these ordinary negative sentences with some "not yet" sentences:

Iki̱'po.	"He's not eating."
Iki̱'pokísha.	"He's not eating yet."
Chaaha ki'yo.	"She's not tall."
Chaaha ki'yokísha.	"She's not tall yet."

±Ísha is a special ending that is only used in negative sentences. It follows a negative verb (either one with an N prefix and ±o, like those you learned about in unit 9, or a verb plus the auxilary ki'yo). As you learned in unit 9, when any ending is added to a negative verb, the extra ending +ki (or simply +k before a vowel) must go between the negative verb and the following ending. This means that whenever you hear ±ísha, you'll hear +k before it, as in the examples above. Otherwise, though, ±ísha works like other endings (such as ±a'chi, for example) that can be used after a negative verb, and a negative verb plus ±ísha has the same meaning as an English "not yet" sentence.

Other endings may follow ±ísha:

Akchipi'sokíshtok.	"I hadn't seen you yet."
Iki̱'pokíshaka̱ ithánali.	"I know he didn't eat yet."

> *Exercise 14G.* Translate the following "not yet" sentences into Chickasaw. 1. The woman didn't dance yet. 2. The water isn't frozen yet. 3. We didn't get there yet. 4. The child didn't drink yet. 5. My mother knows that you didn't dance yet. 6. He hadn't yet danced (long ago). 7. My rabbit isn't jumping yet. 8. The wolf didn't eat you yet.

Lesson 14.5:
Completion

Special auxiliary verbs are used in Chickasaw sentences to indicate completion or totality of an action or state. Here are some examples:

Apat ishtahtok.	"You ate it all up."
Satikahbit taha.	"I'm all tired out.", "I'm completely tired."

These sentences use the auxiliary verbs **tahli** and **taha**. By themselves, the verbs refer to finishing: **tahli** means "to finish" and **taha** means "to be finished, to be worn out, to be used up".

Ishtahli.	"You're finishing it."
Paskaat taha.	"The bread is used up."
Sataha.	"I'm worn out."

These new verbs have several uses as auxiliaries. You'll learn about the most common one, expressing completion or totality, in this unit.

Completion with active verbs. **Tahli** is used to express the successful completion of an action or the totality of its accomplishment following an A-subject active verb, most often a two-place A-subject verb. COMPLETION means succeeding in finishing the action completely or affecting all the objects of the action. Here are some examples of how this works:

Taloowat tahtok.	"He finished singing.", "He sang it completely."
Popassáat ishtahli.	"You're spanking us all."
Paska apat tahlilitok.	"I ate up the bread."
Abit tahlila'chi.	"I'm going to kill them all."

In this pattern a t-verb (like those you learned about in unit 13) of the first verb comes before **tahli**. If there is an object prefix, either S or D, it normally goes on the first verb. The A subject marker goes on **tahli**. Here's the pattern that's used with A prefixes:

OBJECT + VERB + **t**	A	± **tahli**
PREFIX	PREFIX	

completion pattern for active verbs with **tahli**

If the A marker is the ending **+li**, it follows **tahli**, as in the third and fourth examples. If you use other prefixes that change the meaning of the verb, such as **aa±**, **ibaa±**, or **on±** or the preverb **isht±**, these all go on the first verb, just as S or D object prefixes do. In general, only A markers go on **tahli**.

As you can see, there are a number of different ways to translate completion sentences into English. You can use the words "finish" or "completely", or you can use "all" referring to the object. With many English verbs, it makes sense to add "up" to express the idea of completion.

When there is a subject prefix on **tahli**, as in the second example above, it's easy to tell that a t-verb is followed by a separate verb. When the t-verb immediately precedes **tahli**, however, as in the first and third examples, such a combination will often sound like a single word: <taloowattahtok>, <abittahlila'chi>. You may even have trouble hearing two **t**'s in these words: perhaps they will sound like <taloowatahtok> or <abitahlila'chi> to you. If you want to write these words like this, just remember that the middle **t** (or **tt**) separates two rhythmic lengthening sequences. In this book we will always write **tahli** and **taha** auxiliaries as separate words.

Exercise 14H. Translate the following **tahli** sentences into English. 1. Pobo't ishtahtok. 2. Ofi'at hachikisilit tahtok. 3. Holisso ittimanompolit ishtahtaam? 4. Impat iitahla'chi. 5. Paska apat iitahla'chi. 6, Sashki' iholisso mómaho sho't tahlilitok. (**sho'li** = "to carry", **móma** "to be all"—works like a modifying number word)

A slightly different pattern is used for some completion sentences containing short verbs. There is nothing unusual about the last example above, **Abit tahlila'chi**, or about the last sentence in exercise 14H, **Paska apat iitahla'chi**. These sentences use the regular pattern, with the A subject prefix for the whole sentence on **tahli**. When a short verb like this has an object that must be marked with an S prefix or a D and dative prefix combination, however, a different pattern is used, as these examples show:

Abit hachitahlila'chi.	"I'm going to kill you all."
Nashobaat apat potahla'chi.	"The wolf is going to eat us all."
Apat pontahtok.	"He ate it for all of us."

The difference here is that the object prefix (an S prefix or a D plus dative prefix combination) goes on **tahli** rather than on the first verb, as in the following pattern:

VERB + **t**　　A　　±　　OBJECT　　+ **tahli**
　　　PREFIX　　　　PREFIX

completion pattern for short active verbs with **tahli**

Once again, if the A marker is the ending **+li**, it simply follows **tahli.**

These kinds of sentences are not too common, because the only short verbs that make much sense with an S object are **abi** "to kill" and **apa** "to eat", and most people don't talk about completely killing or eating people very often!

Most speakers do not follow this new rule with "bring" and "take" verbs containing **isht±** plus a short motion verb (like those you learned about in unit 13). With these verbs, the S object prefix stays on the first verb for most speakers:

Ishtishpoya'chi.	"You'll take us."
Ishtapoyat ishtahla'chi.	"You'll take us all."

Some speakers may say **Ishtayat ishpotahla'chi**. Follow your teacher's usage.

Exercise 14I. Translate the following completion sentences into Chickasaw using a t-verb plus **tahli**. (Remember **li** deletion.) 1. The chief kisses all the women. 2. We kissed all the chiefs. 3. The bear ate up the rabbit. 4. Did you tear up the paper? (**lhilaffi** = "to tear" (A,S) 5. The doctor will kill us all! 6. I brought you all. 7. The dog bit you all. 8. The wolf ate you all.

Completion with stative verbs. The second completion pattern uses the auxiliary **taha** with a stative verb, usually a one-place S-subject or D-subject verb. Here are some examples:

Satikahbit taha.	"I'm completely tired.", "I'm all tired out."
Losat tahatok.	"It got all black."
Ponchokmishtot taha'chi.	"We'll get completely healthy."

Sentences like these may use the word "completely" in their translation, but it is just as common to hear "all". Such sentences refer to the achievement of a completely affected state, so they are often translated with "get".

As with the active sentences, **taha** sentences have a t-verb before the auxiliary. The D or S subject prefix, if there is one, goes on the t-verb. Here's the pattern:

SUBJECT + VERB + **t**　　　**taha**
　　　　　PREFIX

completion pattern for stative verbs with **taha**

Since the t-verb always comes right before **taha**, you may feel even more strongly than with the **tahli** sentences that these t-verb plus **taha** phrases are pronounced as a single word, perhaps with only one **t** sound. However, in this book we will write all such verb phrases with two words.

Exercise 14J. Turn each of the following Chickasaw sentences into a new sentence that expresses completion. Add **tahli** to active sentences and **taha** to stative sentences. Remember to change the verb of the original sentence into a t-verb, and remember that an A subject must be marked on **tahli**. Translate the new sentences you make up. 1. Ishmalili. 2. Chisipokni. 3. Chipota hoyooshtok. (Assume that **chipota** refers to more than one child.) 4. Oka'a ishkolitok. 5. Antakho'bi. 6. Salhiyohtok. 7. Issalhiyohtok. 8. Nampakalaat lakna. (**nampakali'** = "flower")

Terms and Concepts

POSSESSOR/SUBJECT, COMPLETION.

VOCABULARY

balaafokha' / balaafka' pants
chokfi rabbit
fanalhchi' wings (SP)
foshi' hishi' feather
haksibish ear (SP)
hakshop skin, outer covering (SP)
hishi' fur; body hair (SP) (as "body hair", usually follows name of the body part whose hair is referred to)
ibichchala' nose (SP)
ilbakchosh fingernail (SP)
ipashi' hair of the head; mane (of a horse) (SP)
ishkobo' head (SP)
ittakoba' stomach, belly (SP)
itti' hakshop bark (of a tree)
itti' hishi', itti'shi' leaf (of a tree)
iyyakchosh toenail (SP)
iyyinto'lhka' knee (SP)
lhilaffi to tear, rip (sg. obj.) (A,S)
móma to be all (A)
nampakali' flower
nashoba wolf
shakba' upper arm (SP)
sho'li to carry (A,S)
taha to be finished, used up, worn out (for instance, no longer wearable), all raggedy (S); completely (auxiliary)
tahli to finish (A,Noun); completely (auxiliary)
tapa to be cut; to have the end or head cut off (S)

READING AND SPEAKING

Tishohminko'

We wrote this to commemorate Chief Tishomingo, who is pictured on the Great Seal of the Chickasaw Nation. In this reading and others later in the book, English words used in the Chickasaw text are italicized. (The translation is provided in Appendix C.)

The old courthouse in Tishomingo, Oklahoma (the former capitol of the Chickasaw Nation), now a Chickasaw Nation museum. Photograph by Steven Baker.

Tishohminkaat Chikashsha iminko' attook. Missipi' ántattook. Holhchifaat "minko' intisho" aachi.

Tishohminkaat sipoknit tahahma naahollaat Chikashsha oothooímmayya'chittook. 1832aash naahollaat aachikat Chikashshaat Pantataka nannalhpisa' holisso aailhafa'chika aachittook. Tishohminkaat minko' ilayyo'kaako nannalhpisa' holisso ibaailhafittook.

Nannalhpisa' holisso imanompa kanihmo'si 12at aachikat, afammi mómaka Tishohminkaat daala' talhipa chaffaka isha'chitoka aachittookookya nannalhpisa' holissaat anowa' aachikat Chikashshaat iyaakni' aaissa'shcha hashaaobyaka' aya'chi imaachittook.

Ikalhchibo'soka Chikashsha lawahoot inchokka' ifilammit Oklahomma' ayattook. Yaháat ittan-nahówattook. Naahollimanompaat aachikat *"Trail of Tears"* hochifo. 1840aash Tishohminkaat Oklahomma' iko'nokíshcha illittook. (Daala' talhipa chaffaka ishittookchi?)

Chikashsha Iyaakni' in*capital* ámmo'nakat Tishomingoak attook. Tishomingo aachikat, Tishohminko'ako aholhchi'fottook. *Tishomingo County Mississippi*at anowa' Tishohminko'ako aholhchi'fottook. Tishohminko' holbaat *Great Seal of the Chickasaw Nation* í'ma. Hattakat Tishohminko' nokfóyyokhakat ímmo'ma.

SUPPLEMENTARY VOCABULARY

aholhchi'fo to be named after (A,S)
ámmo'na to be first (A)
anowa' again; also
aachi to mean (something) (Noun,Noun)
aaissachi to leave (A,S)
daala' dollar
ikalhchibo'soka not too long after, a while later
imanompa kanihmo'si article (of a document) (DP)
ímmo'ma still (auxiliary—used with preceding t-verb)
í'ma to be located on (something) as an integral part (for instance, of a picture painted on a wall) (A,Noun)
ifilammi to leave behind (A,D)
ilhafi to sign (a document) (A,Noun)
Missipi' Mississippi
nannalhpisa' holisso treaty
Naahollimanompa' English
nokfóyyokha to really remember (A,S)
ootímmayya'chi to beat, conquer (A,D) (includes preverb **oot±**)
Pantatak Pontotoc, Mississippi; Pontotoc, Oklahoma
tisho assistant (usually, to an Indian doctor or shaman) (old word)
Tishohminko' Tishomingo (Chickasaw chief); Tishomingo, Oklahoma
yaháat ittanohówa to pass by crying (tpl. subj.) (A) (traditional way to refer to the journey on the Trail of Tears)

NOTES

1. To say that someone says something, it is common to follow the subject word with the same-subject dependent word **aachikat** or another "say" verb, plus a quotation or report of what was said, plus a main verb form of **aachi**. In this pattern the two "say" verbs FRAME the quotation or what was said. You'll learn more about this pattern in unit 20.

2. The combination of future **±a'chi** plus past **+tok, ±a'chitok**, means "was supposed to", as in **Tishohminkaat daala' talhipa chaffaka isha'chitok** "Tishomingo was supposed to get one hundred dollars". You'll learn more about this pattern in unit 16.

3. **Tishohminkaat Oklahomma' iko'nokíshcha illittook** means "Tishomingo had not yet reached Oklahoma and he died" or, more idiomatically in English, "Tishomingo died before reaching Oklahoma".

4. The **±hchi** ending (**±chi** after consonants) means "maybe" or "I wonder". You'll learn more about this ending in unit 20.

5. The "still" auxiliary, **ímmo'ma**, is used with a preceding t-verb.

6. The Advanced Chickasaw Grammar section of unit 11 explains how to form higher numbers, like 12 and 1840, in Chickasaw. Most Chickasaw speakers pronounce any number higher than 10 or 20 as in English.

ADVANCED CHICKASAW GRAMMAR 4: MORE POSSESSOR/SUBJECT SENTENCES

In this unit you learned about possessor/subject sentences like

Chipotaat ofi'at imillitok.	"The child's dog died."
Ihooat hattakat inchaaha.	"The woman's husband is tall."

which express about the same meaning as sentences like

> Chipota imofi'at illitok.
> Ihoo ịhattakat chaaha.

The possessor/subject sentence pattern is

POSSESSOR/SUBJECT±at/±akoot/±hoot	"HAVE" OBJECT±at	D PREFIX±VERB
Chipotaat	ofi'at	imillitok.

There is a second possessor/subject sentence pattern that you may hear speakers use in a similar way. Here are some examples of sentences in this pattern:

> Chipotaat imofi'at illitok.
> Ihooat ịhattakat chaaha.

The new possessor/subject sentence pattern is

POSSESSOR/SUBJECT±at/±akoot/±hoot	POSSESSED "HAVE" OBJECT±at	VERB
Chipotaatimofi'at	imofi'at	illitok.

The only difference between the new type of possessor/subject sentence and the original sentences (in the second group of examples above) is that the possessor has a subject ending. Otherwise, the new sentences still have their subject marked as a possessed noun (with a D prefix, if necessary) and their verb unchanged (without a D prefix). The difference is in what the subject is—in the sentence **Chipota imofi'at illitok**, the subject is **chipota imofi'** "the child's dog", while in the sentence **Chipotaat imofi'at illitok**, the subject is **chipota** "the child".

Like the first type of possessor/subject sentence you learned, this new type of sentence puts a strong emphasis on the possessor/subject noun, and that noun works just like any other subject: it can be moved to the end of the sentence, it can be marked with any subject ending, and so on.

Imofi'at illitok chipotaat.	"The child's dog died.",
	"The child had his dog die."
Chipotaakot imofi'at illitok.	"The <u>child</u> had his dog die."

The "have" object in this new type of sentence is like other "have" objects. It must be marked with **±at**, and it can only occur immediately before the verb. As these examples show, "have" may be used in the translation (with the possessor as the translation's subject), or the translation may remain the same as for the original sentence (with the possessed noun as the subject), just as with other possessor/subject sentences.

As with the first possessor/subject sentence pattern, the verb of this new sentence type must be a one-place verb that takes either an A or an S subject. The new possessor/subject sentence pattern is not quite as common as the one you learned in unit 14. Some verbs are more commonly used in one pattern, and some in the other. In fact, some verbs are never used in possessor/subject patterns. Listen to Chickasaw speakers and practice using both patterns.

Unit 15

Hortatives and "More"

In this unit you'll learn another new set of switch-reference endings. You'll learn about how to form and use hortative sentences. And you'll learn how to form a new grade, the N grade, as well as how to use it in comparative sentences. The unit includes an Advanced Chickasaw Grammar section.

Lesson 15.1 introduces the switch-reference endings **+cha** and **+na**, which work differently from other switch-reference endings. Lesson 15.2 presents the negative hortative ending **±nna** and the non-negative hortative ending **±a'shki**, and lesson 15.3 shows how non-negative hortatives are formed with the unaccomplished prefix **ik±**. Lesson 15.4 presents the N grade, and lesson 15.5 describes the comparative sentence pattern.

Lesson 15.1:
The Switch-Reference
Endings **+cha** and **+na**

The switch-reference endings you learned in units 11 and 13, along with most other Chickasaw switch-reference endings, end in **t** for same subject or a nasalized vowel for different subject. However, there are two switch-reference endings that are different: **+cha** and **+na**. Here are some sentences with these endings:

Ihooat mallicha taloowatok.	"The woman jumped and sang."
Ihooat mallina hattakat taloowatok.	"The woman jumped and the man sang."

+Cha is a new same-subject ending, and **+na** is a new different-subject ending. These are most often translated with "and", although you may hear other translations for them. The two verbs in such sentences may refer to things that happened at the same time, or the **+cha /+na** event may slightly precede the main verb event.

Just as with other switch-reference endings, dependent verbs ending in **+cha** and **+na** must have their own subject markers. This is true even with **+cha** verbs, which are often translated into English with the repeated subject omitted:

Ishmallicha ishtaloowatok.	"You jumped and you sang.", "You jumped and sang."
Ishmallina hattakat taloowatok.	"You jumped and the man sang."

One difference between +**cha** and +**na** and other switch-reference endings is that the new endings cannot be combined with endings like +**tok**, ±**ttook**, and ±**a'chi**. Verbs with +**cha** and +**na** are interpreted as referring to the same time as the main verb they are used with:

Mallicha taloowatok.   "He jumped and sang."

Mallicha taloowa'chi.   "He's going to jump and sing."

As in sentences with other switch-reference endings, a question ending only goes on the main verb:

Chintakho'bicha chihopobataa?   "Are you lazy and hungry?"

> *Exercise 15A.* Translate the following sentences into English. 1. Hattakat owwattacha fani'a abitok. 2. Sanakfishat sassona yaalitok. 3. Chipota tiikat imofi' sho'kana ishkaat ihashaatok. 4. Hattak issikopahoot satakchicha ayatok. 5. Okkisa' ishokshittacha ishbínni'tok. (**okkisa'** = "door")

The new endings change when they come after a verb with the A ending +**li**. Look at these examples:

Mallilit taloowalitok.   "I jumped and I sang."

Mallili ishtaloowatok.   "I jumped and you sang."

+**Li** plus +**cha** becomes +**lit**, and +**li** plus +**na** becomes +**li**. (You may think that **mallilit** looks like a t-verb, but there is a difference. A markers are never used on t-verbs, so you would never see a t-verb ending in +**li** plus +**t**.)

A similar thing happens when +**cha** and +**na** are used after negative verbs:

Chikmallot chiktalo'wokitok.   "You didn't jump and you didn't sing."

Chikmallo aktalo'wokitok.   "You didn't jump and I didn't sing."

Negative ±**o** plus +**cha** is ±**ot**, and ±**o** plus +**na** is ±**o**.

Here are some new verbs you'll be able to use in the exercises.

akiilawa to belch, burp (S / A)

haksi to be drunk, get drunk; to be crazy (S)

hotolhko to cough (S / A)

hoyahno to sweat (S)

impalli to feel hot (D)

ihimonha to wait for (A,D)

palli to be hot (S)

to'li to play ball (A)

yokachi to catch, grab (pl. obj.) (A, S)

yollichi to shake, shiver, tremble (S)

habishko to sneeze (S / A)

himonha to wait (A)

howita to vomit (S / A)

imilhlhali to scare (A,D)

inkapassa to feel cold (D)

kapassa to be cold, get cold (S)

páa to whoop (A)

yanha to have a fever (S)

yokli to catch, grab (sg. obj.) (A,S)

Palli is the word to use when talking about objects or the weather being hot, but it is usually better to use **impalli** when referring to people's temperature. **Yokli** is used about catching or grabbing one thing (a singular object), while **yokachi** refers to catching or grabbing more than one thing (a plural object).

> *Exercise 15B.* Combine each of the following pairs of sentences, using **+cha** or **+na** as appropriate, following the examples. (Remember that **+tok, ±a'chi,** and **±ttook** aren't used with **+cha** and **+na.**) Translate the new sentences.
>
>   *Example.* Chipotaat inkapassatok. Yollichitok.
>
>   *Answer.* Chipotaat inkapassacha yollichitok. "The child felt cold and shivered."
>
> (The two sentences have the same subject, so **+cha** is used to connect them. The first verb no longer needs to have the ending **+tok.**)
>
>   *Example.* A̱hattaka̱ fammila'chi. Ikayoppoka'chi.
>
>   *Answer.* A̱hattaka̱ fammili̱ ikayoppoka'chi. "I'll whip my husband and he won't be happy."
>
> (The two sentences have different subjects, so **+na** is used on the first verb, without **±a'chi.**)
>
>   1. A̱hattakat owwatta. Pá̱a. 2. Minkaat kochchatok. Anka̱ pisatok. 3. Hashi'at palli. Sahoyahno. 4. Ofi'at illitok. Iihoppitok. 5. Chihabishko. Chihotolhko. 6. Anka̱na' i̱himonhalitok. Satikahbitok. 7. Chipotaat iki'pokitok. Hopobatok. 8. Sayanhatok. Ampallitok. 9. Minkaat haksitok. Howitatok. 10. Hattakat to'tok. Pá̱atok.

Now, look at these new examples of other **+cha** and **+na** verbs:

    Chipotaat paska a'pacha ollalitok.   "The child ate the bread and smiled."

    Chipotaat paska a'pana ishkaat ollalitok.   "The child ate the bread and his mother smiled."

When you add **+cha** or **+na** to a verb with only one consonant before its last vowel, you need to add ' before that consonant. (This is the same thing that happens to verbs with the negative ending **±o**, as you learned in unit 9.) With a verb that ends in a vowel plus **mb, mp, nch, nk,** or **nt** plus a vowel, the first vowel becomes nasal and is followed by **'b, 'p, 'ch, 'k,** or **'t:**

    Chipotaat i̱'pacha ollalitok.   "The child ate and smiled."

    Chipotaat i̱'pana ishkaat ollalitok.   "The child ate and his mother smiled."

These same things happen when such verbs include the A ending **+li:**

    Paska a'palit ollalilitok.   "I ate the bread and smiled."

As with negative verbs, no ' is added following an accented vowel:

    Talohó̱wana apoyoppatok.   "He was singing and we were happy."

Li deletion occurs in the **+cha** or **+na** form of any verb whose basic form ends in a vowel, **h,** or ' plus **li.** Since ' must be added between a vowel and **li,** the syllable before **li** is always heavy in any such verb followed by **+cha** or **+na.**

    Ofi' ishlhiyohcha ishyoklitok.   "You chased the dog and caught it."

    Chipotaat mali'cha mallitok.   "The child ran and jumped."

Remember that **li** deletion does not affect the A ending +**li**:

Mali'lili̱ ishmallitok.   "I ran and you jumped."

Vowel deletion occurs in the +**cha** or +**na** form of any verb whose basic form ends in a vowel, **h**, or ' plus **s**, **sh**, **lh**, or **ch**, plus another vowel. (Remember that **ch** becomes **sh** when it comes before a consonant.) Once again, because of the added ', the next-to-last syllable is always heavy in such +**cha** or +**na** forms.

Ishhi'lhna taloowalitok.   "You danced and I sang."
"Boo!" a'shna amilhlhatok.   "He said 'Boo!' and I got scared."

In the last example, a ' is added to **aachi**, giving <a'chi> (the long vowel shortens, just as in negative verbs); before +**na**, the final **i** of the verb drops, giving <a'chna>; and **ch** becomes **sh** before the following consonant **n**.
    The same thing happens even when the ending is +**cha**:

"Boo!" a'shcha amilhlhalitok.   "He said 'Boo!' and scared me."

Two **ch**'s may occur in a row in basic nouns and verbs such as **kochcha**, but when **ch** comes before **ch** (as in +**cha**) because of vowel deletion, the first **ch** always becomes **sh**.
    +**Cha** and +**na** (or their short forms combined with +**li** or ±**o**) are always the last ending in their words.

Exercise 15C. Translate the following sentences into Chickasaw, using +**cha** and +**na**. Use ' when needed in verbs before +**cha** and +**na**. Remember that +**cha** and +**na** never combine with endings like +**tok** and ±**a'chi**, but that **li** deletion and vowel deletion may be necessary, depending on the form of the +**cha**/ +**na** verb. 1. I sneezed and coughed. 2. You got drunk and went to sleep. 3. You got drunk, and I left. 4. He scared us, and we went to our house. 5. We played ball and whooped. 6. You worked, and they waited for you. 7. He sent me a letter, and I read it. 8. We sold the horse, and you bought it. 9. I caught the bird, and it sang to me. 10. I caught the birds and killed them.

Lesson 15.2:
Two Hortative Endings

Negative commands with the negative hortative ending. To tell someone not to do something, you use a negative command with the new ±**nna** ending:

Ishissonna!   "Don't hit it!"
Hashishkonna!   "Don't drink (you guys)!"
Chitikahbinna!   "Don't be tired!"

A negative command must have a "you" subject marker.
    Since ±**nna** is a ± ending, it does not form part of a rhythmic lengthening sequence, and verbs that end in even-numbered short syllables may have their final consonants syllable-final and slightly lengthened before ±**nna**:

Ishhilhanna!   "Don't dance!" (ish/hilh/an/na)
Ishchokoshkomonna!   "Don't play!" (ish/cho/kosh/kom/on/na)

A verb that expresses the wish that something should or should not be allowed to happen is called a HORTATIVE. A verb ending in ±**nna** is a negative hortative—for instance, when we give a negative command like **Ishhilhanna**! we're actually saying something like "You shouldn't dance!" You can tell that this translation must be closer to the actual Chickasaw meaning, because the verb has a "you" subject prefix, unlike English commands and the normal non-negative Chickasaw commands you learned about in unit 2. Chickasaw has several different kinds of hortatives.

±**Nna** can also be used on negative hortatives with other subjects:

Ihooat hilhanna!	"The woman shouldn't dance!"
Chipotaat hooayanna!	"The children shouldn't go!"

As you can see, these are certainly not commands—they are usually translated with "should not" or "shouldn't". They express a negative meaning but do not include **ik**±, **ki'yo**, ±**o**, or N prefixes.

With a "we" subject, the meaning of a negative hortative is "let's not":

Kiito'linna!	"Let's not play ball!"
Kiliyyanna!	"Let's not go!"

In general, speakers don't use the negative hortative ending with "I" subjects.

Positive hortatives. One type of positive hortative uses the ending ±**a'shki**.

Taloowa'shki!	"He should sing!"
Ishhilha'shki!	"You should dance!"
Ayala'shki!	"I must go!"

Just as with ±**nna**, verbs with the ±**a'shki** ending must have subject markers. ±**A'shki** verbs are usually translated with "should" or "must".

±**A'shki** may remind you of ±**a'chi**—both endings refer to things that haven't happened yet, and they sound quite similar, too. But ±**a'shki** is quite different from ±**a'chi**. Unlike ±**a'chi**, ±**a'shki** cannot combine with other endings such as ±**kat** or ±**ka**. Also, it expresses a very strong emotion. ±**A'chi** simply makes a prediction about the future, while ±**a'shki** expresses the speaker's very strong feeling about how things ought to be. To some speakers, ±**a'shki** may sound almost religious in its intensity. Don't use this ending unless you really mean it!

Both ±**nna** and ±**a'shki** are always the last ending in their words.

Exercise 15D. Each of the following sentences uses either ±**nna** or ±**a'shki**. Translate each sentence, then change its meaning by replacing the ±**nna** with ±**a'shki** or ±**a'shki** with ±**nna**. Translate the new sentence. 1. Chinki' ishihimonha'shki! 2. Chipotaat anchokka' ayanna! 3. Ampaska ishpa'shki! 4. Yamma hashishkonna! 5. Hattakat chipota imilhlhalinna! 6. Kiito'la'shki! 7. Ishakiilawanna! 8. Hattakat Oklahomma' aya'shki.

Lesson 15.3:
Unaccomplished Hortatives

Another type of Chickasaw hortative uses the unaccomplished prefix **ik±** and is translated with "let":

Chipotaat ikanompoli'! "Let the child talk!"

This sentence may surprise you. Although it includes an unaccomplished prefix, it does not express a negative idea (you need **±o** to do that). Unaccomplished prefixes are used on two types of sentences referring to events that have not happened, either events whose truth the speaker is denying (negatives with **±o**) or events that the speaker would like to see accomplished ("let" hortatives like those above).

You can substitute N prefixes for **ik±** in hortative sentences like

Holisso akpisa'! "Let me see the book!"
Kiihilha'! "Let us dance!", "Let's dance!"
Ihoo kilapila'! "Let's help the woman!"

Each example has an N prefix referring to the subject of the sentence, the person mentioned after "let" in the English translation. Remember that the form of the "we" (or "let's") N prefix, **kil±/kii±**, changes depending on the sound that follows it. "Let's" or "Let us" has two meanings in English—it can mean "allow us to . . ." or "shall we . . ." Both these ideas can be expressed with Chickasaw **kil±/kii±** hortatives. (Finally, you can understand how to form sentences like **Chikashshanompa' Kilanompoli'**, the title of this book!)

In addition to their meaning, there are two other differences between these "let" hortatives and the **±o** negatives you learned about in unit 9. First, hortatives with unaccomplished or N prefixes do not have a ' added when a single consonant precedes the final vowel. (This only happens in negative verbs with **±o** and, as you learned in lesson 15.1 above, in **+cha** and **+na** verbs.) Next, there is a **±'** ending on the hortatives. This **±'** is a "let" hortative ending (not connected with the ' in the middle of **±o** negative verbs), used only on unaccomplished hortative verbs. (Some speakers do not use the **±'** ending; rather, they pronounce "let" hortatives with a plain final vowel. We will use **±'** on all "let" hortatives in this book, but you should follow your teacher's usage if it is different.)

Exercise 15E. Translate the following "let" hortative sentences into Chickasaw. Each sentence should have an unaccomplished or N prefix and a final **±'**. 1. Let her dance! 2. Let's play ball! 3. Let me eat! 4. Let him get drunk! 5. Let's drink this water! 6. Let me go out! 7. Let's hit the chief! 8. Let me talk to the doctor!

Like other hortatives, these new unaccomplished hortatives do not combine with endings like **±a'chi**, **+tok**, **±ttook**, or **+ta**; the **±'** at the end of these sentences is always the last thing in its word.

You can use object prefixes on unaccomplished hortatives—just follow the regular rules you learned in unit 9 for combining N prefixes with S or D object prefixes.

Akchintaloowa'! "Let me sing for you!"
Kiichipila'! "Let us help you!"

"Let them" hortatives begin with **ikhoo±**:

Ikhoohilha'! "Let them dance!"

As you know, negatives of sentences with S or D subjects all start with **ik±**:

Iksanokhánglo.   "I'm not sad."
Ikpontakho'bo.   "We're not lazy."

Similarly, unaccomplished hortatives of S and D subject verbs start with **ik±too**:

Iksanokhánglo'!   "Let me be sad!"
Ikpontakho'bi'!   "Let's be lazy!"

Iksanokhánglo, as you know, means "I'm not sad". A comparison of **iksanokhánglo** and **iksanokhánglo'** shows that the final **±'** in a "let" hortative is very important with verbs whose basic form ends in **o**. Can you think up another similar pair of sentences? (You'll find one in exercise 15F.)

There are no "let" hortatives beginning with the N prefix **chik±**, corresponding to A subject verbs with "you" subjects. (To say "you should" do something, use an **±a'shki** hortative or a command like those you learned about in unit 2.) However, you can use unaccomplished hortatives with S or D "you" subjects. These have about the same meaning as ordinary commands:

Ikchihopoba'!   "Be hungry!, Get hungry!"
Ikchintakho'bi'!   "Be lazy!"

Sentences like this, and also some of the other S and D subject **ik±** hortatives, seem a bit odd to some speakers. These sentences may sound more natural if you add the word **hookmat**, **mikmat**, or **haatokmat** to the sentence either before or after the hortative word. This is something like saying "OK" or "Go ahead" in the corresponding English sentence:

Ikchintakho'bi' hookmat!   "Go ahead, be lazy!"
Mikmat iksahopoba'!   "OK, let me be hungry!"

Follow your teacher's usage on sentences like these.

Exercise 15F. Translate the following sentences into English. Some are "let" hortatives, and some are negatives. 1. Chikmallo. 2. Akmalli'. 3. Hattakat ikhasha'o. 4. Hattakat ikhashaa'. 5. Kilisso'. 6. Kilisso. 7. Ankaat iksafammo. (**fammi** = "to whip"). 8. Ankaat iksafammi'. 9. Chipotaat ikmo'. 10. Chipotaat ikmo.

Unaccomplished hortatives can't be formed with verbs that are always negative, such as **ikcha'ho** "to be short" or **iksamalhpi'so** "to be sad".

Lesson 15.4:
The N Grade

In unit 8 you learned to make Chickasaw HN grade forms. In this unit you'll learn to recognize and form verbs in another Chickasaw grade form, the N grade. You already know a number of verbs in the N grade, including **ánta**, **ayoppánchi**, **hánglo**, **ithána**, **nokhánglo**, **passáa**, and **písa**. If you look at these verbs, you'll see that each one contains an accented vowel that is either nasalized or followed by **n** or **m**. (So far, this sounds like the description of an HN grade. However, there is no added **h** in an N grade.)

The meaning of N grades. The N grade of an active verb usually refers to ongoing activity that happens at the same time as another event or that the speaker views as "still" happening. Listen for this use of N grade forms when you hear people speaking Chickasaw. N grades are more commonly used with stative verbs. With stative verbs that describe a quality, an N grade is often used to express a relative COMPARATIVE meaning. Thus, **chóngma** means "to be better"—when the verb is used on its own, it means relatively or comparatively better, not specifically better than something else:

Sachóngma.   "I'm better."

(You'll learn more about comparatives in the next section of this unit.) Many of the N grade verbs that you have already learned, like **ayoppánchi, hánglo, itháana, nokhánglo,** and **píisa,** are two-place verbs referring to mental states that are the result of mental events (**píisa** "to see (be seeing)" can be the result of **pisa** "to catch sight of", **hánglo** "to hear" can be the result of **haklo** "to listen to", and **itháana** "to know" can be the result of **ithana** "to get to know, to realize" (a new verb)).

Forming N grades. Here are some more examples of N grades. Make sure you know what each of the basic verbs means.

Basic verb	*HN grade form*
foyopa	foyómpa
pilachi	pilánchi
ipita	ipínta

Basic verb	*HN grade form*
kalakshi	kalánkshi
losa	lóosa
okchamali	okchamáli
tohbi	tóhbi

Making an N grade is very similar to making an HN grade. All you have to do is to make the next-to-last syllable of the basic verb nasal. Just as in HN grades, the changing vowel is the next-to-last vowel of the basic verb. The changing vowel is always accented in an N grade, and it either becomes nasal or has **m** or **n** added after it. One difference between N and HN grades, as you may have noticed, is that verbs like **tohbi** keep their **h** in the N grade.

If a **p** or a **b** follows the changing vowel, the changing vowel must be followed by m—thus, **foyopa** adds **m** before the **p** to make the N grade form **foyómpa**. If the changing vowel is followed by **t** or **ch**, the added vowel must be followed by **n**—thus, **ipita** adds **n** before the **t** to make the N grade form **ipínta**, and the N grade of **pilachi** is **pilánchi**. In most cases the same thing happens if the changing vowel is followed by **k**—so the N grade of **kalakshi** is **kalánkshi**.

If almost any other sound follows the changing vowel, the changing vowel will be nasal. So the N grade of **losa** is **lóosa**, the N grade of **okchamali** is **okchamáli**, and so on. This happens whenever the changing vowel is followed by **f, s, sh, l, lh, w,** or **y,** and also when this vowel is followed by a single **m, n,** or **h** or by **mm** or **nn**. (These are the same as the rules for the form of dative prefixes that you learned in unit 7 and for forming HN grades in unit 8.)

> *Exercise 15G.* Form the N grades of the following verbs. 1. palhki. 2. nalha. 3. bila. 4. hopoba. 5. toyya. 6. lhayita. 7. achokmilhka. 8. issikopa. 9. champoli. 10. anompoli. 11. imaabachi. 12. tofa.

More about N grade formation. Some verbs change slightly before making the N grade, generally the same way as with the HN grade. If the changing vowel of the basic verb is long, for example, you shorten it before following the rules above:

waaka	wánka
chaaha	cháha
okaami	okámi

In most cases nothing happens if the changing vowel is followed by a doubled consonant. Thus, the N grade of **kochcha** is **kónchcha**, and the N grade of **yimmi** is **yímmi**. If the changing vowel is followed by **pp**, **bb**, **tt**, or **kk**, however, you shorten that doubled consonant before making the N grade:

ayoppa	ayómpa
okshitta	okshínta
sakki	sánki

If the changing vowel is already nasal, or if it's followed by **m** or **n** plus another consonant (other than a second **m** or **n**), a nasal is already there, so you don't need to add another one—the only difference between the basic form and the N grade will be the accented changing vowel.

kiliha	kilíha
omba	ómba
konta	kónta

If a verb has a **'** before its final consonant, you drop this sound before making the N grade in the usual way:

intakho'bi	intakhómbi

As you can see, what follows the changing vowel depends on the consonant that comes after the **'** in the basic form. The N grade of **intakho'bi** has an added **m**, because its last consonant is **b**.

If the basic verb ends with a long vowel, the N grade ends in an accented long nasal version of this vowel. For example, the N grade of **yaa** is **yáa**, and the N grade of **hashaa** is **hasháa**.

Finally, if the changing vowel is followed by **kb, kl, km, kn, kw**, or **ky**, the **nk** you'd expect in the N grade turns into **ng**. Instead of <chónkma> for the N grade of **chokma**, you replace the **nk** with **ng**, so you say **chóngma**. Similarly, the N grade of **ikbi** is **íngbi**. (Some speakers may not use **ng** in these forms, so you may hear N grades like **chónkma** or **ínkbi**. Follow your teacher's usage.)

> *Exercise 15H.* Form the N grades of each of the following verbs: 1. taloowa. 2. aachi. 3. atobbi. 4. tikahbi. 5. intakho'bi. 6. nalhlhi. 7. chonna. 8. impa. 9. wakaa. 10. lakna. 11. wiiki. 12. lohmi. 13. chompa. 14. holissochi. 15. ihollo. 16. ichchokwa. 17. falaa. 18. hopoba.

Most N grades are formed completely regularly, but a few verbs have irregular N grades. The most common one is **ishto**, which has the irregular N grade **chínto**. (Some people also say **íshto**, but **chínto** is better.)

Lesson 15.5: Comparative Sentences

Chickasaw COMPARATIVE sentences that express "than"—in which one thing is compared specifically to another—use the verb **ímmayya**. By itself, **ímmayya is a**n A subject, D object verb meaning "to be ahead of":

Hattakat ámmayya.   "The man is ahead of me."

The D prefix in **ímmayya** has **m** before **m** (just as in **immi'** "his") and is accented.

Here are two examples of comparative sentences with **ímmayya**:

Hattakat chaahakat ihoo ímmayya.   "The man is taller than the woman."
Amofi'at issikopakat chimofi' ímmayya.   "My dog is meaner than your dog."

Comparative sentences with noun subjects and objects use a new sentence pattern:

SUBJECT±at/±akoot/ . . .	COMPARED VERB±kat	OBJECT	**ímmayya**
Hattakat	chaahakat	ihoo	ímmayya.
Amofi'at	issikopakat	chimofi'	ímmayya.

The subject of a Chickasaw comparative sentence is the same as the subject of an English comparative sentence (it may have any subject ending, such as ±**at**, ±**akoot**, and so on). The object of the Chickasaw sentence is the one that comes after "than" in the English sentence (it may have no ending or it may have an object ending). The COMPARED VERB expressing the quality being compared, comes next. In a sentence like this, the compared verb never has any subject marking and is followed by ±**kat**. The last thing in a comparative sentence is **ímmayya**.

To express a sentence with an "I", "you", or "we" subject, you do not need a separate subject word. To express a sentence with a "me", "you", or "us" object, you do not need a separate object word. The compared verb is the same as in the pattern above, with no marking other than ±**kat**. All you have to do is to change **ímmayya**: this comparative verb must have an A prefix indicating the sentence's subject, and a D prefix must be used before dative **im±** to indicate a "me", "you", or "us" object. Thus, the comparative verb **ámmayya** shows that the first sentence has a "me" object (shown by the D prefix **a+**).

Hattakat chaahakat ámmayya.   "The man is taller than me."
Ishtokat chímmayyala'chi.   "I will be bigger than you."
Issikopakat chimofi' ímmayyali.   "I am meaner than your dog."

As the second example above shows, endings like ±**a'chi** go on **ímmayya**. The compared verb doesn't have a subject marker. And if there is a noun subject or object, it goes in the position you'd expect from the basic pattern.

Exercise 151. Translate the following Chickasaw comparative sentences into English. 1. Ihoo yammat chokma'sikat chímmayya. 2. A̱holissaat chokmakat chi̱holissa ímmayya. 3. Hopookat hattak yamma̱ ímmayyali. 4. Hopobakat iichímmayya'chi. 5. Sashkaat sipoknikat ámmayya. 6. Ankaat ishtokat chinki' ímmayya. 7. Hashaakat pómmayya. 8. Tikahbikat chímmayyali.

The compared verb never has a A, S, or D subject marker, no matter who the subject is. These compared verbs are not like the same-subject ±**kat** verbs you've seen up till now—all regular switch-reference verbs always have subject marking, but compared verbs don't.

In all of the examples above, the compared verb is an ordinary basic verb. N grades are often used in comparative sentences, too:

Chóngmakat ímmayyali.	"I'm better than him."
Chipotaat hasháakat ámmayyatok.	"The child was angrier than me."
Yappat chíntokat yammạ ímmayya.	"This one is bigger than that one."

There is not too much difference between these two types of comparatives. The second kind may emphasize the comparison a bit more, but you will hear both types of comparative sentences used.

> *Exercise 15J.* Translate each of the following comparative sentences into Chickasaw in two ways, once with a plain compared verb, once with an N grade compared verb. 1. Our dog is meaner than your dog. 2. My book is redder than my younger sister's [brother's] book. (Use "sister" if you're female, "brother" if you're male.) 3. This peach is sweeter than that peach. 4. That man is taller than that woman. 5. That stick is longer than this one. 5. Is your knife sharper than that one? 6. I am poorer than that old man.

All the comparative sentences discussed here use stative verbs. But there are also comparative sentences using active verbs, such as "I ate more pancakes than Jim", and more complicated sentences with stative verbs, such as "My daughter likes corn more than beans". If you listen to Chickasaw speakers, you can figure out how to express these more complex patterns, too.

Terms and Concepts

HORTATIVE, COMPARATIVE, COMPARED VERB.

VOCABULARY

akiilawa to belch, burp (S / A)
chínto bigger (irregular N grade of **ishto**)
fammi to whip (A,S)
habishko to sneeze (S / A)
haksi to be drunk, get drunk; to be crazy (S)
haatokmat go ahead, OK (in "let" hortative sentences)
himonha to wait (A)
hotolhko to cough (S / A)
howita to vomit (S / A)
hoyahno to sweat (S)
hookmat go ahead, OK (in "let" hortative sentences)
imilhlhali to scare (A,D)
ímmayya to be ahead of (A,D); to be more than (preceded by compared verb plus ±**kat**) (A,D)
impalli to feel hot (D)
inkapassa to feel cold (D)

ithana to get to know (A,S); to realize, learn (A, N)
ihimonha to wait for (A,D)
kapassa to be cold, get cold (S)
mikmat go ahead, OK (in "let" hortative sentences)
okkisa' door; gate
palli to be hot (S)
páa to whoop (A)
to'li to play ball (A)
yanha to have a fever (S)
yokachi to catch, grab (pl. obj.) (A,S)
yokli to catch, grab (sg. obj.) (A,S)
yollichi to shake, shiver, tremble (S)

READING AND SPEAKING

The Lord's Prayer in Chickasaw

This expression of the Lord's Prayer is by the late Eloise Pickens, with input from Mrs. Willmond. (The translation is provided in Appendix C.)

Pinki' Chihoowa aba' bínni'lihma chiholhchifoat holittó'pa'shki.

Chimaapihlichikaat ala'shki.

Yaakni' nannaayámmohmikat Aba' Yaakni' nannaayámmohmika ittíllawwa'shki.

Himmaka' nittak kilimpa'chika ishpopihínta'shki.

Nanna ilahiika' ishponkashoffikat, íla áyya'shaka nanna ahiika'ilinkashoffika ittíllawwa'shki.

Nanna ikaachokmoka kiliyya' chikpomanhoka'shki.

Nanna ikaachokmoka ishaapolhakoffihíncha'shki.

Aapihlichika' mikmat nannishtaayalhlhi' micha' nannishtaaholiitó'pakaat chimmit bílli'yacha bílli'ya'shki.

Yámmohma'shki.

SUPPLEMENTARY VOCABULARY

aba' above
Aba' Yaakni' Heaven
ahiika to incur a debt; to go into debt (A) (see note 4 below)
aalhakoffichi to save from (A,S)
aapihlichika' kingdom (DP)
bílli'yacha bílli'ya forever and ever (see note 6 below)
holiittó'pa to be precious, holy, sacred (S)—G grade of holiitopa

inanhi to wish something for (someone) (A,D)

inkashoffi to forgive (A,D); to forgive (someone) for (A,D,Noun)

ittíllawwi to be equal to, to be the same as (A,S)

micha' and (see note 5 below)

mikmat and (see note 5 below)

nanna ikaachokmoka where things are bad

nannaayámmohmi to be some way in (a place) (A,Noun) (includes **nanna** "things", used as a preverb)

nannishtaaholiitó'paka' glory

nannishtaayalhlhi' power

Pinki' Chihoowa God our Father

yámmohmi to be like that (A)

NOTES

1. **Pinki' Chihoowa** is a traditional way to say "God our Father". **Pinki'** is a Chickasaw version of the Choctaw for "our father" (because Chickasaws are familiar with the Choctaw Bible—see the Beyond the Grammar section of unit 7). **Pinki' Chihoowa aba' bínni'li** means "God our Father who sits above". Some Chickasaws might say **Ponki' Chihoowa** here, but this does not sound right to Mrs. Willmond. Another possibility would be **Inki' Chihoowa**, but that seems further from the meaning of the prayer.

2. Sentences with the hortative ending ±a'shki often suggest a religious context.

3. **Nannaayámmohmi** includes **nanna** "things" which acts like a preverb—thus, subject and object prefixes will follow **nanna**.

4. **Nanna ilahiika'** means "the things we incur as debts" or "our debts".

5. **Mikmat** and **micha'** are sometimes used to mean "and", but these words are not common in Chickasaw conversation.

6. **Chimmit bílli'yacha bílli'ya** means "it will be yours forever and ever".

ADVANCED CHICKASAW GRAMMAR 5: MORE ABOUT SPECIFYING LOCATION

In unit 10 you learned about using locational nouns in phrases like

chokka' tikba'	"the front of the house", "in front of the house"
tali' nota'	"the underside of the rock", "under the rock"
aai'pa' pakna'	"the top of the table", "on top of the table"
kaar apootaka'	"the side of the car", "beside the car", "next to the car"
talhpak anonka'	"the inside of the basket", "in the basket"
holisaapisa' ashaka'	"the back of the school", "in back of the school"

As you learned in unit 10, the Chickasaw phrases here refer to actual parts of items, but they can also be used to specify locations relative to those items.

Here are some examples of how locational noun phrases are used to specify location in Chickasaw sentences:

Chokka' tikba' bínni'lili.	"I am sitting in front of the house."
Issosha tali' nota' aahoyotok.	"He looked for the bug under the rock."
Holissaat aai'pa' pakna' tí'watok.	"The book is (lying) on top of the table."
Hattakat kaar apootaka' híkki'ya.	"The man is standing next to the car."
Ta'ossa talhpak anonka' ishanitaam?	"Did you put the money in the basket?"

Kowi'a holissaapisa' ashaka' kilaapístok.   "We saw the cat in back of the school."

A locational noun phrase, like other nouns and noun phrases, can be used to specify a location with a positional verb like **bínni'li, tí'wa,** and **híkki'ya.** Most other verbs used with locational nouns need a prefix like locational **aa-** (or the "on" prefix **on-**), although some, like **ani** "to put in", include a locational idea and so don't need a prefix. The locational noun phrases in these sentences consist just of a noun plus a locational noun:

NOUN	LOCATIONAL NOUN
chokka'	*tikba'*
tali'	*nota'*
aaipa'	*pakna'*
kaar	*apootaka'*
talhpak	*anonka'*
holissaapisa'	*ashaka'*

Locational nouns can't be used this way to specify a location relative to a person or animal, however. When you want to specify location relative to a living creature, in a sentence like *I am sitting in front of the girl, The woman was standing next to you,* or *We saw the cat behind the dog,* Chickasaw speakers generally use sentences like the following:

Chipota tiikat aabínni'lika tikba' bínni'lili.	"I am sitting in front of the girl."
Ihooat ishaahíkki'yaka apootaka' híkki'yatok.	"The woman was standing next to you."
Kowi'a ofi'at aatí'waka ashaka' kilaapístok.	"We saw the cat in back of the dog."

The locational noun phrases in these sentences are more complicated. In addition to the living creature you want to specify location relative to ("the girl", "you", and "the dog") and the locational noun, they also contain a positional verb. Here's the pattern:

SUBJECT	**aa±**	POSITIONAL VERB	**±ka**	LOCATIONAL NOUN
chipota tiikat	*aa±*	*bínni'li*	*±ka*	*tikba'*
ish±	*aa±*	*híkki'ya*	*±ka*	*apootaka'*
ofi'at	*aa±*	*tí'wa*	*±ka*	*ashaka'*

The "subject" in these locational noun phrases corresponds to the noun at the end of the English phrase: **chipota tiik** is the "subject" within the phrase **chipota tiikat aabínni'lika tikba'**, but in English we say *in front of the girl*; "you" are the "subject" within the phrase **ishaahíkki'yaka apootaka'**, but in English we say *next to you,* and so on. **Chipota tiikat** includes the subject ending **±at,** and **ish±** is the A marker for a "you" subject.

As you can see, the person or animal is the subject of a positional verb in the locational noun phrase, which tells you the person or animal's position. So, more complete translations of the sentences above would be "I am sitting in front of where the girl is sitting", "The woman was standing next to where the girl was standing", and "We saw the cat in back of where the dog was lying". This means, then, that the last sentence would be different if the dog was standing or sitting:

Kowi'a ofi'at aathíkki'yaka ashaka'
    kilaapístok.

"We saw the cat in back of where
    the dog was standing."

Kowi'a ofi'at aabínni'lika ashaka'
    kilaapístok.

"We saw the cat in back of where
    the dog was sitting."

You don't need to include the positional verb in your English translation, but it is part of the meaning of the Chickasaw sentences.

Although the pattern given above shows the subject before the positional verb in the locational noun phrase, the pattern will be different if the subject is "I", since the A subject marker +**li** is an ending:

Ihooat ahíkki'yalika apootaka'
    híkki'yatok.

"The woman was standing next to me."
    ("The woman was standing next to
    where I was standing.")

Because the positional verb is a dependent sentence with a different subject from the main sentence, it ends in the different-subject switch-reference marker ±**ka**. Because the positional verb is referring to a location "where", it includes the **aa**± locational prefix. Usually, as you know, **aa**± is not used on positional verbs. It's important to remember that this type of locational noun phrase works differently.

Here are some more sentences with locational noun phrases specifying location relative to people and animals. Can you figure out what they mean?

Hattakat chipota aatí'walika apootaka' hoyotok.
Alikchi' toklohoot minkaat aabínni'lika tikba' chí'ya.
Johnat aahíkki'yaka binoht kiimáa.

If you have trouble, take the locational noun phrases (**aatí'walika apootaka'**, **minkaat aabínni'lika tikba'**, and **Johnat aahíkki'yaka**) and match them up with the parts of the pattern given above.

If you listen to Chickasaw speakers, you'll hear other variations on this pattern.

Unit 16

"But" . . . and More about Verbs

In this unit you'll learn about Chickasaw verb pairs. You'll learn how to add "from" objects to sentences and more about adding prefixes to short verbs. You'll also learn some more ways to talk about possibility and how to say "but".

Lesson 16.1 explains how to form and use verb pairs. In lesson 16.2 you'll learn about more ways to talk about people's names. Lesson 16.3 presents the "from" object prefixes **aa±** and **imaa±**. Lesson 16.4 tells more about how endings are used with short verbs. Lesson 16.5 introduces the "but" ending **±hookya**, lesson 16.6 explains how to talk about past obligations and possibilities, and lesson 16.7 shows how to express conclusions with "must". Lesson 16.8 is about "too much". The Advanced Chickasaw Grammar section of this unit explains more about verb pair relationships.

Lesson 16.1:
Verb Pairs

Many Chickasaw verbs are members of VERB PAIRS related in meaning, appearance, and use in regular ways. Here are some verb pairs you already know:

V1	*V2*
basha "to be operated on"	bashli "to operate on"
taha "to be finished"	tahli "to finish"
okcha "to wake up, be awake"	okchali "to wake (someone) up"
nalha "to be shot"	nalhlhi "to shoot"

And here are some new ones:

bashafa "to be cut"	bashaffi "to cut (usually, with a knife)"
fama "to be whipped"	fammi "to whip"
kola "to be dug"	kolli "to dig"
tiwa "to open (of a door)"	tiwwi "to open (a door)"

We call the two members of a Chickasaw verb pair V (for Verb) 1 and V2. Usually the V1 is a one-place verb that takes an S subject (this is true in each of the cases above). The V2 is almost always a two-place verb used to say that its A subject causes someone else (the S object) to experience the V1 state (again, this is true in each case above). As the last example shows, sometimes the meanings of a V1 or V2 are not exactly what you'd expect. For example, **tiwa** doesn't refer to a door being open but rather to the action of a door opening or coming open by itself.

> *Exercise 16A.* Translate the following Chickasaw sentences. 1. Okissa'at tiwatok. 2. Kiikollittook. 3. Hattakat fani' nalhlhitok. 4. Fani'at nalhataam? 5. Asokchatok. 6. Chipota famma'chi. 7. Sanakfishat ilbaka̱ bashaffitok. 8. Ofi'at famatok. 9. Kowi'at shanti' okchalitok. (**shanti'** = "rat") 10. Shantaat okchatok.

More verb pairs. The V1–V2 pairs above illustrate the most common relationship between such verbs, in which the V1 ends in **a** and the V2 ends in a doubled version of the consonant before the **a**, or the V1 plus **i**, or in **li**. But there are many other types of verb pairs. Here are some more examples:

V1	*V2*
bila "to melt (by itself)"	biliili "to melt (something)"
holiitopa "to be sacred, precious"	holiitobli "to make sacred, consider precious"
chofata "to be clean"	chofalli "to clean"
talakchi "to be tied up"	takchi "to tie"
holhchifo "to be named"	hochifo "to name"
alhtoka "to be elected"	atookoli "to elect"
fokha "to be inside (something) (used of a singular subject)"	fokhi "to put (a singular object) inside (something)"
lhabocha "to be mashed"	lhaboshli "to mash"

The Advanced Chickasaw Grammar section of this unit will help you to recognize many different types of relationships between V1–V2 pairs.

Using verb pairs in sentences. Usually, a V1 takes an S subject. Here are some examples:

Safamatok.	"I was whipped."
Ikchitalakcho.	"You aren't tied up."

A V2 usually takes an A subject and an S object, as in these sentences:

Issafammitok.	"You whipped me."
Akchitakchokitok.	"I didn't tie you up."

However, this pattern isn't the only one. Here's an example of a verb pair in which the V1 takes an A subject:

wakaa "to fly"	wakiili "to make (something) fly"

Exercise 16B. Translate the following sentences into Chickasaw. 1. We could whip you. 2. The women cleaned the table. 3. I was tied. 4. They did not tie me. 5. We put the rabbit in the bag 6. The bird is flying. 7. I was not elected. 8. The knife is in the boat. (**piini'** = "boat") 9. The snow is melting. (**okti'** = "snow (a noun)") 10. You will not melt the snow. 11. The children were whipped. 12. The meat is finished, all gone. 13. I flew the plane (made the plane fly). (**piini' wakaa'** = "plane") 14. The chiefs elected me. 15. The bottle is clean. (**kitoba** = "bottle")

You'll learn other V1–V2 patterns as you study more Chickasaw. It's good to learn verb pairs—they are very common in Chickasaw, and you will hear speakers use them frequently. However, because there are so many different ways for V1's and V2's to be related, you probably shouldn't try to make them up yourself.

Lesson 16.2:
Naming

The V1 **holhchifo** "to be named", a verb that sounds like the noun "name", is used with an S subject. Usually, an actual name is mentioned in the sentence before the verb.

| Mary saholhchifo. | "I am named Mary." |

There are several ways to ask and answer the question "What's your name?" in Chickasaw. You can make the noun **holhchifo** the subject of the question or your answer, using a "be" sentence like those in unit 2 and the patterns in the Reading and Speaking section of that unit:

| Chiholhchifoat nanta? | "What is your name?" |
| Saholhchifoat Bill. | "My name is Bill." |

(**Nanta** means "what". You'll learn more about other ways to use this word in unit 17.) Or you can use the new verb, as in the first example:

| Bill saholhchifo. | "I am named Bill." |

Here's another similar sentence, using the name as the subject:

| Billat saholhchifo. | "Bill is my name." |

You'd be more likely to use this one if someone had been talking about the name Bill already (as in the English translation), rather than to answer the question.

The V2 **hochifo** "to name" can also be used either with or without a name, in addition to its A subject and S object:

| Chipota kiihochi'fokitok. | "We didn't name the baby." |
| Mary chihochifola'chitaa? | "Shall I name you Mary?" |

Exercise 16C. Translate the following sentences into Chickasaw. 1. We named the dog Losa' ("Black One"). 2. What's the chief's name? 3. The chief's wife's name is Pauline. 4. Her name isn't Mary. (use **ki'yo**) 5. What are you guys's names? 6. Our name is Brown.

Lesson 16.3:
"From" Objects

You've already learned how to add prefixes to verbs to express "to" or "for" objects (with **im±**, unit 8), "on" objects (with **on±**, unit 10), "along with" objects (with **ibaa±**, unit 10), "at" objects (with **aa±**, unit 10), and instrument "with" or "about" objects (with **isht±**, unit 13). In this section you'll learn how to express "from" objects using **imaa±** and **aa±**.

Here are some new verbs that can be used with "from" objects:

> hobachi to copy, imitate (A,S)
> honkopa to steal, kidnap (A,S)
> ponta to borrow (A,Noun)

Each of these verbs is a two-place verb that can be used with a subject and object:

Chihobachila'chi.	"I'll copy you."
Chipota kiihonkopatok.	"We kidnapped the child."
Holisso ishpontattook.	"You borrowed the book (long ago)."

Each verb can take a "from" object, as in the following sentences:

Holisso aahobashla'chi.	"I'll copy from the book."
Ta'ossa *bank* kilaahonkopatok.	"We stole money from the bank."
Ta'ossa *bank* ishaapontattook.	"You borrowed money from the bank."

(Most Chickasaw speakers use the English word *bank* pronounced just as in English in Chickasaw sentences. The word is written in italics in the examples to remind you not to pronounce it like a Chickasaw word.) As you can see, when you want to express a "from" object, you add **aa±** (the same prefix that can show an "at" object) to the verb. This turns the two-place verbs **honkopa** and **ponta** into three-place verbs **aahonkopa** and **aaponta**. **Aahobachi** looks like a two-place verb in the example above, but it could be a two-place verb if you mention the word or other item that was copied. (The **aa±** "from" objects here are somewhat like the **aa±** "with" objects that you learned about in lesson 13.1.)

When you express "from" with the **aa±** prefix, the "from" object must be INANIMATE—a nonliving thing or an institution. If the "from" object is ANIMATE (usually, if it is a person), you must use a different "from" prefix, **imaa±**:

Chimaahobashla'chi.	"I'll copy from you."
Minka ta'osso kilimaahonkopatok.	"We stole money from the chief."
Holissa issamaapontattook.	"You borrowed a book from me."

A verb with an animate "from" object needs the prefix **imaa±**. If the animate "from" object is "me", "you", or "us", you substitute the appropriate D prefix for the **im** of **imaa±**.

Some speakers use the **im±** prefix to express "from" plus an animate object with some verbs. These speakers might say **ihonkopa** rather than **imaahonkopa** for "steal from", for example. For other speakers, **ihonkopa** means "steal for", not "steal from", and this is how we will use the verb in this book. Follow your teacher's usage.

Exercise 16D. Translate the following sentences into Chickasaw. 1. I borrowed a dress. 2. My mother made a dress from a sack. 3. We stole bread. 4. Did you steal a dog from the doctor? 5. Don't copy from me! 6. My child borrowed from the Chickasaw Nation. (**Chikashsha Iyaakni'** = the Chickasaw Nation, the land of the Chickasaws) 7. We copied from the book. 8. They copied the

Lesson 16.4:
More about Prefixes on Short Verbs

In unit 11 you learned about the Chickasaw short verbs, which work differently from other verbs with a lot of the prefixes you've learned (especially the A and S prefixes). These short verbs can combine with many of the other prefixes you've learned, including the **imaa±** "from" prefix. When they do, the result is often a more regular verb than the original short verb.

Imaaishi means "take from". Like **imishi**, it is an (A,D,Noun) verb.

      Imaaishilitok.   "I took it from him."

As you learned in unit 11, **ishi** is replaced by **íshi** in some forms. However, neither **imishi** nor **imaaishi** is ever replaced by **í'shi**.

You know that **apa** is a two-place short verb meaning "to eat (something)" (it is used with an object telling what was eaten), while **impa** is a one-place verb meaning "to eat". But you can add prefixes to **impa** to make it into a two-place verb. **Aaimpa** means "to eat in (a location)", **ibaaimpa** means "to eat with (someone)", and **onimpa** means "to eat on (something)". Each of these is a two-place "eat" verb that does not tell the thing eaten. **Aa-apa**, **ibaa-apa**, and **onapa** are three-place "eat" verbs. What does each of these mean?

When you use **aa±**, **ibaa±**, or **on±** on a short verb, the new verb doesn't work like a short verb any more, just like any other verb that starts with **aa**, **i**, or **on**.

Exercise 16E. Make up a sentence with each of the following new verbs, using a subject or object prefix, (or both,) in each of your sentences: **aaimpa**, **ibaaimpa**, **onimpa**, **aa-apa**, **ibaa-apa**, and **onapa.** Then make up a second sentence for each verb using a noun subject and at least one noun object. Translate all of your sentences. Read each one aloud.

Lesson 16.5:
"Too Much"

Here are some "too much" sentences:

Ahattakat impa' salami.	"My husband eats too much."
Ihoo yammat anompoli' salami.	"That woman talks too much."
Anompolili' salami ki'yo!	"I don't talk too much!"

A Chickasaw "too much" sentence consists of a normal sentence (including all the usual subject and object markers on the verb) in the present tense, with a ±' at the end, followed by the auxiliary **salami**. Any other verb endings go after **salami**:

Ishishko' salaminna!	"Don't drink too much!"
Shokhaat impa' salama'chi.	"The hog is going to eat too much."
Oblaashaash impali' salamitok.	"I ate too much yesterday."
Ishn<u>o</u>wa' iksala'mokitok.	"You didn't walk too much."

With stative verbs, **salami** is usually translated with "too" rather than "too much":

Paskaat champoli' salami.	"The bread is too sweet."
<u>A</u>naafkaat ishto' salami.	"My dress is too big."

Here are some examples of **salami** used with sentences that have objects (the second one is a joke Chickasaw speakers like to make, based on the similarity of the "too much" word **salami** and the English word *salami,* which is pronounced **salami'**, with an added **'**, in Chickasaw):

Oka' homi' ishko' salami.	"He drank too much whiskey."
Salami' kiipa' salami.	"We ate too much salami."
Ahi' ishpa' salami.	"You ate too many potatoes."

Notice that with objects that can be counted it will sound best to use "too many" in the translation.

> *Exercise 16F.* Here are some Chickasaw sentences. Turn each one into a "too much" sentence by ading **salami**, then translate it into English, as in the examples.
> *Example.* Ishhilha.
> *Answer.* Ishhilha' salami. "You dance too much."
> *Example.* Anchipotaat holisso ittimanompoli.
> *Answer.* Anchipotaat holisso ittimanompoli' salami. "My child reads too many books."
> 1. Ofi'at kowi' lhiyohli. 2. Oka'at palli. 3. Ishtofa. 4. Chipota naknaat topa <u>o</u>malli. 5. Kowi"at foshi' yokachi. 6. Hashyaa.

Lesson 16.6: "But"

In English we use separate words to connect two ideas that contrast with each other, such as *but* or *although*. In Chickasaw, however, this concept is expressed with a verb ending, as in the following examples:

Holisso imaapontala'chihookya ittimanompolila'chi ki'yo.
  "I'm going to borrow the book from her but I'm not going to read it."
Ihoo yammat anompoli' salamihookya ayopp<u>á</u>shli.
  "That woman talks too much but I like her."

These sentences use the "but" ending **±hookya**, which is attached to the verb of the first sentence of the two you're connecting. The **kya** in this ending may sound to you like <kiya> or <giya>; the ending is usually pronounced with an echo vowel.

±Hookya connects two complete sentences, which may have their own tense endings. After a past ending like **+tok** or **±ttook**, the ending is pronounced as **±ookya**:

Holisso imaapontalitokookya aktimanompo'lokitok.
    "I borrowed the book from her but I didn't read it."

The Chickasaw ending ±**hookya** is different from any other complex sentence ending you've learned. It connects two complete sentences (in the first example above, these are **Holisso imaapontala'chi** "I'm going to borrow the book from her" and **Akittimanompo'loka'chi** "I'm not going to read it"), but there is no switch reference marking on either of the verbs of these sentences. You use the same form, ±**hookya**, whether the two sentences have the same subject or different subjects.

Ahattakat lhinkohookya ayoppa.   "My husband is fat but he's happy."
Ahattakat lhinkohookya asayoppa.   "My husband is fat but I'm happy."

> *Exercise 16G.* Take each of the sentences you wrote in answer to exercise 16E and think of a way that you could expand it by adding a "but" sentence. Connect the two sentences with ±**hookya**. Read the sentences you come up with aloud. What does each one mean?

Lesson 16.7:
Obligations and Possibilities

A "has to" ending. ±**Kmaka'chi** is a verb ending that expresses about the same idea as English "has to" or "have to", referring to an obligation.

Inchokka' kanchikmaka'chi.   "She has to sell her house."
Kiliyyakmaka'chi.   "We have to go."

Past obligations and possibilities. You can talk about obligations or possibilities that existed in the past by combining ±**a'chi** and ±**a'ni** with +**tok**.
    ±**A'chi** plus +**tok** equals ±**a'chitok** and is usually translated "was supposed to" (or, with a plural subject, "were supposed to").

Impala'chitok.   "I was supposed to eat."
Hattakat hoya'chitok.   "The man was supposed to look for her."

The **i** of ±**a'chitok** sounds like a lengthened vowel, just like the **i** of the combination ±**a'chitaa**, which you learned about in unit 5. Try to imitate your teacher's pronunciation of the combination ±**a'ch_tok**.
    ±**A'ni** plus +**tok** equals ±**a'ntok**. This combination means "could have" or "might have" and is used about an event that did not take place:

Impala'ntok.   "I could have eaten (but I didn't)."
Omba'ntok.   "It might have rained (but it didn't)."

The **i** of ±**a'ni** deletes before +**tok** just the same way that the same **i** deletes before +**taa**, as you saw in unit 5.

> *Exercise 16H.* Read aloud and then translate each of the sentences below. Then turn each sentence into a reference to past obligation or possibility by adding +**tok**. Finally, translate the new sentences.
> 1. Ishhilha'chi. 2. Pohángla'ni. 3. Achipila'chi. 4. Ikpopi'soka'ni. 5. Ihooat bala' hopoona'chi. 6. Chipotaat nampakali' ama'ni.

You can make the same kind of reference to obligations or possibilities in the remote past by using ±**ttook** instead of +**tok**.

> Hilhala'chittookookya akhi'lhokittook.
> "I was supposed to dance (long ago) but I didn't dance."

In this example the new "but" ending ±**hookya** comes after the remote past obligation sentence **Hilhala'chittook**. (In the combination ±**a'chittook**, you won't hear any lengthening of the **i,** since ±**ttook** is a ± ending.)

Exercise 16I. Translate each of the following sentences into Chickasaw. 1. He has to marry her. 2. You might have been jealous of me. 3. He might have known her (long ago). 4. They were supposed to hug me. 5. The chief has to kill the horse. 6. The doctor was supposed to look for the paper (long ago). 7. We could have run. 8. The cedar could have hit you. 9. The squirrel might have bitten this child. 10. The people were supposed to come (long ago).

Lesson 16.8:
Drawing Conclusions

Sometimes you aren't sure about whether something is true, so you just say what you conclude on the basis of what you know at the time, often using the word *must*, as in English sentences like

> *You must be a doctor.*
> *He must have gone.*
> *That man must be going to kiss me.*
> *The woman must have been supposed to dance.*

Chickasaw sentences corresponding to these use the ending ±**ha'ni**. This ending is somewhat similar to ±**a'ni** (unit 5) in both its meaning and its use.

±**Ha'ni**, however, goes at the very end of a Chickasaw verb word, after every other ending. Here are some examples of Chickasaw sentences using ±**ha'ni**. (Note that when ±**ha'ni** follows a consonant, its **h** is dropped.)

> Alikchi' chiyaha'ni.   "You must be a doctor."
> Ayatoka'ni.   "He must have gone."
> Hattak yammat sasho̲'ka'chiha'ni.   "That man must be going to kiss me."

You can even use ±**ha'ni** after one of the obligation / possibility endings introduced in lesson 16.5.

> Ihooat hilha'chittooka'ni.   "The woman must have been supposed
>   to dance (long ago)."
> Inchokka' kanchikmaka'chiha'ni.   "She must have to sell her house."

Exercise 16J. Translate these sentences from Chickasaw to English. 1. Ihoo yappat alikchi' imihoo ootoka'ni. 2. Chipotaat hootaloowatoka'ni. 3. Omba'chiha'ni. 4. Hattak yammat minko' atookolittooka'ni. 5. Chintiikat ahi' lhaboshlitoka'ni. 6. Ahi'at lhabochattooka'ni. 7. Chipota̲ Jim hoohochifa'chiha'ni. 8. Amalhkaniyatoka'ni.

Terms and Concepts

VERB PAIR, V1, V2, PASSIVE, INANIMATE, ANIMATE.

VOCABULARY

alhtoka to be elected (S)
atookoli to elect (A,S)
bashafa to be cut (of a long subject) (S)
biliili to melt (something) (A,S)
Chikashsha Iyaakni' the Chickasaw Nation
chofalli to clean (A,S)
fama to be whipped (S)
fokha to be inside (singular subject); to put on (clothes) (A,Noun)
fokhi to put (singular object) inside (A,S,Noun)
hobachi to copy, imitate (A,S)
hochifo to name (A,S); to name (someone) (a name) (A,S,Noun)
holiitopa to be sacred, precious (S)
holiitobli to make sacred, consider precious (A,S)
holhchifo to be named (S); to be named (a name) (S,Noun)
honkopa to steal, kidnap (A,S)
imaaishi to take (something) from (someone) (A,D,Noun)
kitoba bottle
kola to be dug (Noun)
kolli to dig (A,Noun)
lhabocha to be mashed (Noun)
lhaboshli to mash (A, Noun)
nanta what
okti' snow
piini' boat
piini' wakaa' airplane, plane
ponta to borrow (A,Noun)
salami too much (aux.)
shanti' rat
talakchi to be tied up (S)
tiwa to open (of a door) (Noun)
tiwwi to open (a door) (A,Noun)
wakiili to make (something) fly (A,S)

Not all the new verbs discussed in the unit that use the new prefix **imaa±** (or the familiar prefixes **aa±, ibaa±,** or **on±**) are listed in the vocabulary. Additional verb pairs are given in the Advanced Chickasaw Grammar section of this unit.

READING AND SPEAKING

The Scott Family Comes Home

Mrs. Willmond told this story of a family confusion long ago. (The translation is provided in Appendix C.)

Emile Scott imihoo cho'mat aachompa' ayat tahatokoot,
falamat alat tahahm<u>a</u>,
inchokka' alat tahahmat,
abooha chokkowa'chitokak<u>o</u>,
kaniya'mat ánta aho'bana,
pisa bannakat,
kochcha' hiyohm<u>á</u>ana
abooha anonka' pilla ántahootokoot,
ittikalhalha'chik<u>a</u>
hánglohmat,
kochcha' áyya'shna,
naalhtoka' hoya'chitokakoot,
naalhtoka' ikhoyyok<u>í</u>shna—
akanka'oot ántatokchincha!

Ak<u>a</u>nakni'at ántatokchincha!

Winda'<u>a</u> mallitakaat ootkochchacha olattook! (aachi).

Ithanahmat, "Aa! Akanka'oot ánta. Kanookya iksho," aa'shcha abooha tiwwicha chokkowat tahattook (aachi).

SUPPLEMENTARY VOCABULARY

ahooba to look like, resemble, seem like (A,S) (see note 6 below)
aa oh
aachi they say (used to indicate that the speaker is reporting)
chokkowa to go in (A)
cho'mi to be (more than two) together (A) (see note 1 below)
ittikalhalha'chi to make a banging noise (A)
kanahookya, kanookya everyone; (in a negative sentence) no one (see note 10 below)
kaniya' someone (see note 5 below)
kochcha' outside
mallittakaali to jump back, jump off (A)
taha (auxiliary used with motion verbs with a tpl. subj.)
winda' window

NOTES

The first part of this story is one very long sentence. To make it easier for you to follow, it is written here with each verb on a separate line.

1. **Cho'mi** is used to indicate that a group of more than two individuals is working together. As you'll learn in unit 19, it works like **táwwa'a**, which you've already seen in these readings. **Emile Scott imihoo cho'mat** means that a group including Emile Scott, his wife, and others (the children?) is a subject.

2. **Ayat taha** means "they (triplural) go". You'll learn about this special use of **taha** with motion verbs in unit 19.

3. **Falama** "to return" is often used as a t-verb, for instance in **falamat aya** "to go back".

4. The complex endings ±**a'chitokako** (different subject) and ±**a'chitokakoot** (same subject) mean "be about to".

5. The usual Chickasaw word for "someone" is **kana**, and **kaniya'** normally means "somewhere", as you'll learn in unit 17. However, **kaniya'** can also mean "someone" (subject form **kaniya'mat**), as in this story.

6. **Ahooba** means "to look like, resemble, seem like". This verb may be used (like **banna**) with a preceding verb without an ending, as in **Kaniya'mat ánta ahooba** "It seems like someone is in there".

7. **Hoyo** has an irregular negative form, **ikhoyyo.**

8. The ending +**tokchincha** indicates that the speaker (or someone else that the speaker sympathizes with in telling a story, as here) has made a judgment or conclusion.

9. **Aachi** can be used to mean "they say", indicating that the speaker is reporting someone else's words.

10. **Kanahookya** or **kanookya** means "everyone" in a positive sentence; in a negative sentence, as in the story, it means "no one". You'll learn more about this use of ±**ookya** in unit 19.

BEYOND THE GRAMMAR: AMERICAN INDIAN LANGUAGE CLASSIFICATION

As you learned in unit 6, Chickasaw is a member of the Muskogean family of languages, as are Choctaw, Creek, Seminole, Alabama, Koasati, and Mikasuki (and the extinct language Hitchiti).

Scholars have been working for many years to try to figure out what relationship there is, if any, between families of languages like Muskogean and other American Indian language families.

In the first such proposal, made in 1929, Edward Sapir proposed that Muskogean should be included in a large group of theoretically related languages called Hokan-Siouan, which included (among others) the Hokan languages of California and the Pacific Coast and the Siouan family.

In 1965 Charles and Florence Voegelin argued that Muskogean was part of a different group called Macro-Algonkian, which included (among others) the Algonkian languages of the Northeast. This followed a proposal by Mary Haas, who had studied Creek and other Muskogean languages for many years, relating Algonkian to Muskogean and four other smaller southeastern groups, Natchez, Tunica, Chitimacha, and Atakapa, known together as the Gulf languages.

In 1987 Joseph Greenberg put forward a new classification by which Muskogean and the other Gulf languages were included in the Penutian group, which includes languages from northern California to Central America.

These suggestions are all interesting, but the fact that each is so completely different from the others supports the idea that if the Muskogean languages are related to any other linguistic group, such a relationship is extremely distant at best.

ADVANCED CHICKASAW GRAMMAR 6: MORE ABOUT VERB PAIRS

V1–V2 relationships. Below is the first set of verb pairs given in lesson 16.1:

basha "to be operated on"	bashli "to operate on"
taha "to be finished"	tahli "to finish"
okcha "to wake up, be awake"	okchali "to wake (someone) up"
nalha "to be shot"	nalhlhi "to shoot"
bashafa "to be cut"	bashaffi "to cut (with a knife)"
fama "to be whipped"	fammi "to whip"
kola "to be dug"	kolli "to dig"
tiwa "to open (of a door)"	tiwwi "to open (a door)"

You can see several different relationships in the form of these pairs. Usually, the V1 ends in a single consonant plus **a**, and often the V2 ends in **li**. However, as **nalhlhi** shows, many V2's end in a double consonant (the same as the last consonant in the V1) plus **i**. The single-double consonant pairs you'll see in different Chickasaw verb pairs are **b-bb, f-ff, l-ll, lh-lhlh, m-mm, n-nn, w-ww**.

There are a number of other possible relationships between V1–V2 pairs. Compare **taha / tahli** or **basha / bashli** with **okcha / okchali**. In many pairs the same consonant comes before both the V1 ending **a** and the V2 ending **li** (as in the first two cases), but in some pairs (like the last one) there's a vowel before **li**. In some pairs the vowel in the V2 looks different from any vowel in the V1:

bila "to melt (by itself)"	biliili "to melt (something)"
falaa "to be long"	faliili "to lengthen"

These examples show that although most V1–V2 relationships are fairly regular, you can't always predict one form from the other.

Sometimes the final consonant of the V1 changes when **li** is added in the V2. If a V1 ends in **pa**, the V2 will usually end in **bli**:

tapa "to be cut off at the top", "to be cut in two"	tabli "to cut the top off", "to cut in two"
holiitopa "to be sacred, precious"	holiitobli "to make sacred, consider precious"

If the V1 ends in **ta**, the V2 will usually end in **lli** (some speakers pronounce this like <dli>):

chofata "to be clean"	chofalli "to clean"

And if a V1 ends in **cha**, the V2 will usually end in **shli**:

lhabocha "to be mashed"	lhaboshli "to mash"

Sometimes a V1 has an **l** or **lh** after its first vowel:

talakchi "to be tied up"	takchi "to tie"
almo "to be mowed"	amo "to mow"
holhchifo "to be named"	hochifo "to name"

L is used before vowels or before **b, m, n, l,** or **w** (perhaps also **y**); **lh** is used before **ch, f, k, p,** and **t** (and possibly other consonants such as **h, lh, s,** and **sh**). While the examples you've seen so far have probably convinced you that the difference in meaning between the two members of a verb pair can be unpredictable, the **l / lh** in these examples almost always corresponds to a PASSIVE meaning (like *be tied up, be mowed, be named*), expressed in English with *to be* plus a verb usually ending in *-ed*.

This use of **l** or **lh** in a V1 may be combined with another V1–V2 pattern, such as final **a** versus final double consonant plus **i** pattern, or the final **a** versus final **li** pattern:

alhtoka "to be elected"	atookoli "to elect"
olhkomo "to be mixed"	okommo "to mix"

The second example shows that vowels may change from short to long or from long to short between a V1 and V2. As the third example shows, occasionally a consonant may change from single to double between a V1 and a V2.

Here is an example of a V1 with a passive meaning and a sentence with the corresponding V2:

Minkaat alhtokatok.	"The chief was elected."
Minko' kilatookolitok.	"We elected the chief."

In addition to sentences like those above, English allows you to tell who did the action of a passive verb by using *by* as in *The chief was elected by us.* Chickasaw passive V1's don't allow you to mention the one who did the action, however. There's no way to add anything like "…by us" to the first example sentence above.

In a few pairs the only difference between the V1 and the V2 is that the V1 ends in **a** and the V2 ends in **i**:

fokha "to put on (clothing)"	fokhi "to put (a singular object) inside (something)"

These meanings may seem quite different to you. Can you see the relationship between them?

As with **wakaa**, the subject of the V1 **fokha** is specified with an A prefix.

Alikchaat balaafka fokha.	"The doctor is putting on pants."
Balaafka fokhali.	"I am putting on pants."
Kowi'a shokcha fokhilitok.	"I put the cat in the sack."

Fóyyokha means "be inside" or "wear":

Alikchaat balaafka fóyyokha.	"The doctor is wearing pants."
Balaafka ishfóyyokhataa?	"Are you wearing pants?"
Kowi'at shokcha fóyyokha.	"The cat is in the sack."

This verb is the Y grade of **fokha**, a type of verb you'll learn more about in unit 18. As you can see, even though this verb has a stative meaning, it still uses an A subject marker.

There are a few other V1–V2 patterns, but most of them are variants of those you've just seen. You'll learn a few other V1–V2 patterns as you study more Chickasaw.

It's good to learn verb pairs—they are very common in Chickasaw, and you will hear speakers use them frequently. However, because there are so many different ways for V1's and V2's to be related, it's better for you to learn each pair than to try to make them up yourself.

Unit 17

Questions and Question Words

This unit will introduce you to a number of new question patterns and the Chicksaw question words, as well as to "some" / "any" words.

Lesson 17.1 presents two types of questions that don't use verbs, and lesson 17.2 introduces the most basic Chickasaw question words. Lesson 17.3 presents "when" questions, and lesson 17.4, focus questions. In lesson 17.5 you'll learn about Chickasaw question verbs; the use of these to say "how" and "why" is covered in lesson 17.6. Lesson 17.7 introduces "some" and "any" words.

Lesson 17.1:
Questions without Verbs

"Where is . . ." questions with ±mano. In the Reading and Speaking section of lesson 4 and the Advanced Chickasaw Grammar section of unit 12, you learned that adding ±**mano** (after consonants, including ') or ±**hmano** (after vowels) to a noun or name makes a "where is" or "where are" question:

Ofi'mano?	"Where is the dog?"
Konihmano?	"Where are the skunks?"
Chiholissohmano?	"Where is your book?"
Mari'mano?	"Where is Mary?"
Itti' iskánno'sihmano?	"Where's the little tree?"

The "where is" endings ±**mano** and ±**hmano** can only be added to nouns or names, or to nouns plus modifying verbs, as in the last example. These endings cannot be used on pronouns like **ishno'** "you", or following "this" and "that" words. There is no verb in these questions, and you can't add a verb to them. Although the noun and names in these questions seem like subjects, they don't include ±**at** or any other subject endings. Answers to ±**hmano**/±**mano** questions must include positional verbs.

As you know, Chickasaw questions, unlike other types of sentences, do not have stress on their last vowel. Verbs ending in +**taa** or +**taam** are accented on any preceding accented vowel, if there is one, or on the last preceding heavy syllable. Nouns don't have accented vowels, so ±**mano** questions are accented on their last heavy syllable, which is always the last syllable of the noun. The stressed syllables in the questions above are indicated with double underlines (though we won't usually write these). Practice saying these questions.

The answer to a ±**mano** question is usually a simple locational statement with a positional verb, like

Aachompaak áyya'sha.	"They are in town."
Abooha anonka' tí'wa.	"It's (lying) in the house."
Aai'pa' nota' wáyya'a.	"It (an animal) is (standing) under the table."
Yammako bínni'li.	"She's sitting over there."

Of course, a speaker could say

Akitha'no!	"I don't know!"

An answer to a ±**mano** question must be a full sentence. **Aachompaak**, **Abooha anonka'**, or **Aai'pa' nota'** would not be a complete answer. You'll learn more about positional verbs in the Advanced Chickasaw Grammar section of this unit.

"Is it . . ." questions with ±to. Another type of simple question that is formed from a noun or name is an "is it" question, such as

Ofi'to?	"Is it a dog?"
Chikashsha Iminko'to?	"Is it the Chickasaw governor?", "Is he the Chickasaw governor?"
Chipota nakni' inchokfihto?	"Is it the boy's rabbit?"
Mari'to?	"Is it Mary?", "Is she Mary?"

These questions use the endings ±**to** (after consonants) and ±**hto** (after vowels), which are added to the end of the noun. Once again, the last syllable of the noun gets the stress (indicated here with a double underline, though, again, we won't usually write this). Once again, these questions do not use verbs.

You can add a subject to these questions:

Bill Anoatubbyat Chikashsha Iminko'to?	"Is Bill Anoatubby the Chickasaw governor?"
Hattak yammat Iksa'to?	"Is that man a Christian?"

±**To** / ±**hto** questions can be answered with **ii** "yes" or **ki'yo** "no". You can leave it at that or continue with a confirmation sentence that follows the is-a-noun sentence pattern you learned in unit 2.

Ii, Bill Anoatubbyat Chikashsha Iminko'.	"Yes, Bill Anoatubby is the Chickasaw governor."

Exercise 17A. i. For each of the following nouns, make up a "where is" question. Read each of your questions out loud, making sure the accents are right.

1. Sally (in Chickasaw, you'll normally pronounce this name with a final ', as if it was spelled **Sali'**) 2. Chikashsha Iminko' 3. chishki' 4. to'wa' 5. holisso 6. onkof ("persimmon") 7. asholosh (**sholosh** = "shoes") 8. alikchi' inchokka' 9. minko' inkaar 10. nannimaabachi'

ii. Now, make up an "is it" question for each of the nouns in part i. Again, read each question aloud.

iii Find another Chickasaw student to practice using these questions with. Take turns asking and answering the questions.

Lesson 17.2:
Question Words

Question words and question word questions. Here are the three most basic Chickasaw QUESTION WORDS:

nanta	"what"
kata	"who"
katiya', katiyaak	"where"

And here are some examples of these question words in QUESTION WORD QUESTIONS. Question word ques-tionss are used to ask for specific information, not just a "yes" or "no" answer.

Nanta <u>ish</u>patok?	"What did you eat?"
Kata ishima<u>nom</u>poli?	"Who are you talking to?"
Katiyaak ishiy<u>ya</u>'chi?	"Where are you going to go?"
Katiya' <u>a</u>ya?	"Where is he going?"

The first thing you'll notice when you hear these questions is the sound of the verb. As with **+taa/+taam** questions, the stress in these questions doesn't go on the last syllable. Instead, it goes on the last heavy syllable before the end of the word, or, if there is an accented syllable, on that syllable. In a two-syllable verb like **aya** that has no heavy syllables, the stress goes on the first syllable. In this lesson we indicate the stress with a double underline (although this is not a part of regular spelling, and we will not continue to write it here).

Subject and object question endings. **Kata** and **nanta** can be subjects of question word questions, as in the following examples:

Katahaat hattak <u>is</u>sotok?	"Who hit the man?"
Nantahaat chikisi<u>li</u>tok?	"What bit you?"

Because **kata** and **nanta** are subjects, they need subject endings. Question words used as subjects use the special subject question ending ±**haat**.

When a question word is used as an object, it can have the object question ending ±**hta**, sometimes pro-nounced ±**hta**. (After a consonant, ±**haat** is ±**aat**, and ±**hta** is ±**ta** or ±**ta**.) Here are some examples:

Hattakat katah<u>ta</u> <u>is</u>sotok?	"Who did the man hit?"
Ihooat katiyaak<u>ta</u> ay<u>a</u>'chi?	"Where is the woman going to go?"
Chipotaat nantah<u>ta</u> apa <u>ban</u>na?	"What does the child want to eat?"

The question object ending is sometimes omitted in the same types of sentences in which the normal ±**a** object ending may be omitted, when the question word object is immediately before a verb, as in the first examples in this lesson or the following ones:

Katiyaak a<u>ya</u>tok?	"Where did he go?"
Alikch<u>a</u> nanta im<u>a</u>tok?	"What did she give to the doctor?"

More about "where". As you know, when you want to add a word specifying location to a one-place verb, you need to add the prefix **aa±** onto the verb:

Abooa anonka' aahi<u>lh</u>alitok.   "I sang in the house."

The same is true with questions—if you ask a "where" question using a verb that doesn't normally include a location idea, then you need to add **aa±**:

Katiyaakt<u>a</u> ishaahi<u>lh</u>atok?   "Where did you dance?"

Exercise 17B. Each of the following Chickasaw sentences has one word or phrase in italics. Replace that italicized word or phrase by a question word to make a question word question, as in the examples. (Pay attention to whether the question words you add are subjects or objects.) Translate your questions and read them aloud. Make sure you accent the right vowel in the verbs of your questions.

Example. Chipota naknaat *ofi'* lhiyohtok.

Answer. Chipota naknaat nantaht<u>a</u> lhiyohtok? "What did the boy chase?"

With a sentence like the following, you might want to make an additional change. Which of the two answers below seems more sensible to you?

Example. Nannimaabachi'at sapístok.

Answer. Katahaat sapístok? "Who saw me?" *or* Katahaat chipístok? "Who saw you?"

1. *Sapontaki'at* sakisilitok. (**sapontaki'** = "mosquito") 2. Ihooat *aachomp<u>a</u>* bala' aachompa'chi. 3. *Ihooat* aachompa bala' aachompa'chi. 4. Ihooat aachompa *bala'* aachompa'chi. 5. *Aaittanaa'* kiiaataloowa'chi. 6. Chipota tiikat nampak<u>a</u>li'<u>a</u> *ishki'* imatok.

The original sentences you started with could be used as answers to the questions you made up, if you want to practice them in dialogues with your fellow students.

Word order in question word questions. You have probably noticed an unusual thing about the questions in this lesson. In English we almost always put question words at the beginning of questions, but this is not true with Chickasaw questions. There are several other ways a speaker might have asked the last question:

Alikch<u>a</u> nantaht<u>a</u> imatok?
Nantaht<u>a</u> alikchi' imatok?
Nantaht<u>a</u> alikch<u>a</u> imatok?
Nanta imatok alikch<u>a</u>?
Nantaht<u>a</u> imatok alikch<u>a</u>?

As you can see, the second noun in this sentence, **alikchi'**, can go either before or after the verb, but **nanta** can only be before the verb. In Chickasaw questions, question words may go anywhere a noun in a corresponding nonquestion may go, as long as they are before the verb. Question words may not go after the verb of a question.

Both **alikchi'** and **nanta** must have an object ending if they are not directly before the verb. It's fine to use both of these object endings in the same sentence.

Unlike yes-no questions, question word questions can use **+tok**, and they don't need to use **+taa.**

Exercise 17C. i. Translate the following questions into Chickasaw. 1. What are you eating? 2. What ate the mouse? 3. Who saw you? 4. Who did you see? 5. Where did he sing? 6. Where do you want to go? 7. What are you making? 8. Who is your brother going to marry? 9. What scared the girl? 10. Who gave you that book?

ii. Some of the questions in part i have alternative word orders. Give these alternate possibilities.

Lesson 17.3: "When" Questions

Asking "when" questions. There are several ways to say "when" in Chickasaw. The important thing is whether you are asking "when" about an event that has already taken place (past "when") or an event that occurs regularly or has not yet occurred (nonpast "when").

Here are some examples of nonpast "when" questions:

Katiya fokhakmak ishona'chi?   "When will you get there?"
Chinkaat katiya fokhakmak   "When does your father go to town?"
    aachompa' aya?

These nonpast "when" questions use **katiya fokhakmak.** The corresponding past "when" is **katiya fokhakaash,** as in

Katiya fokhakaash ishonatok?   "When did you get there?"
Chinkaat katiya fokhakaash   "When did your father go to town
    aachompa' ayattook?   (long ago)?"

(**Katiya fokhakaash** is sometimes pronounced as **katiya fokhakaasht, katiya fokhakaashta,** or **katiya fokhakaashta.**) We are not marking the stress on the verbs of these questions, but the rule is the same as for the questions in lesson 17.2—the stress does not go on the last syllable of the verb, but rather on the last preceding accented or heavy syllable, just as in yes-no questions with +**taa** or +**taam**. For verbs with no heavy syllables (like **aya**), stress goes on the first syllable.

There are two other ways to say "when", with nonpast **katihkmak** and past **katihkaash** (sometimes pronounced as **katihkaasht, katihkaashta,** or **katihkaashta**). These words are used just the same way as **katiya fokhakmak** and **katiya fokhakaash.** Like the question words you learned in lesson 17.2, these new "when" words cannot go after the verb in a question.

Answering "when" questions. **Onnakma** means "tomorrow", and **oblaashaash** means "yesterday". As you saw in the Reading and Speaking section of unit 8, if you want to say "on Tuesday" (for example) referring to the future you use **Tuesdayakma**, with the ending ±**akma.** "On Tuesday" in the past is **Tuesdayaash**, with the ending ±**aash.** Here are some examples:

Tuesdayakma onala'chi.   "I'll get there on Tuesday."
Tuesdayaash onalitok.   "I got there on Tuesday."

Thus, you can use a time word (either a Chickasaw time word or a borrowed one) with ±**akma** to refer to a time in the future and with ±**aash** to refer to a time in the past. (You can review the Chickasaw names for the days of the week in the Reading and Speaking section at the end of unit 8. Most speakers, however, use English words for the days of the week in casual conversation.) It works the same way with borrowed names of months, as in

Mayakma Oklahomma' aya'chi.   "He is going to Oklahoma in May."

Although Chickasaw people formerly had their own names for months, these are not used by speakers today.

Exercise 17D. Give a "when" question that each of the following statements might be used to answer. Then translate each question-and-answer pair, as in the example.

Example. Wednesdayaash alikchi' pistayalitok.

Answer. Katiya fokhakaash alikchi pistishiyyatok? "When did you go see the doctor?" "I went to see the doctor on Wednesday."

1. Marchaash alalittook. (**ala** "to arrive" can also mean "to be born".) 2. Ihooat Nittak Hollo'akma aaittanaa' aya'chi. 3. Oblaashaash ta'osso hayooshlitok. 4. Onnakma ankaat minko' imanompola'ci. 5. Saturdayakma chompa sabanna. 6. Nittak Hollo'aash holisso yappa habinalitok. (**habina** = "to get as a present")

Lesson 17.4:
Focus Questions

In English we can put extra stress or emphasis on a noun to show that it is contrastive or focused, but in Chickasaw, as you know, a speaker shows that a noun is contrastive or focused by using special endings. To indicate focus on nouns in questions, you can use the question endings that you learned in lesson 17.2, subject ±**haat** and object ±**hta** (after consonants, ±**aat** and ±**ta**). Here are some examples:

Chimofi'at nani' ap<u>a</u>taa?	"Is your dog eating a fish?"
Chimofi'at nani't<u>a</u> apa?	"Is your dog eating a <u>fish</u>?"
Chimofi'aat nani' <u>a</u>pa?	"Is <u>your dog</u> eating a fish?"

The first question is just an ordinary yes-no question like the ones in unit 4. The next two are FOCUS QUESTIONS, yes-no questions with either the subject or the object focused by using the question object and subject endings instead of the regular subject and object endings. When you hear a speaker ask these questions, you'll hear that the last syllable of the verb word is not stressed. Stress goes on the last heavy syllable before the last syllable (unless there is an accented syllable, in which case that one is stressed), or, in the case of **apa** (which has no heavy syllables), on the first syllable, as indicated in the examples by double underlining (which we don't normally write). Focus questions like the second two examples do not use ±**taa** at the end of the verb.

Here is an ordinary question compared with two past focus questions:

Chimofi'at nani' ap<u>a</u>taam?	"Did your dog eat a fish?"
Chimofi'at nani't<u>a</u> apam?	"Did your dog eat a <u>fish</u>?"
Chimofi'aat nani' apam?	"Did <u>your dog</u> eat a fish?"

The first question is an ordinary past yes-no question with the past question ending ±**taam** that you learned in unit 4. The focus questions are just like the nonpast focus questions, except that their verbs end with ±**m**. Once again, in all of these questions stress is not on the last syllable of the verb.

The order of the words in a focus question can change, but a noun with a question subject or object ending, just like a question word, cannot come after the verb. Thus, the following are additional ways to say "Did your dog eat a <u>fish</u>?":

Nani't<u>a</u> chimofi'at apam?
Nani't<u>a</u> apam chimofi'at?

Listen for Chickasaw speakers using focus questions. You'll probably hear object focus questions more often than subject focus questions.

Exercise 17E. Read each of the following focus questions aloud. Decide what element is focused in each one and then translate it into English. Underline the focused item (and remember to pronounce it with extra stress), as in the examples in this lesson. 1. Johnaat Oklahomma' ayam? 2. Nittak Hollo'aash naafkahta ishhabinam? 3. Chishkaat alikchi'ta ittihaalalla'chi? 4. Issoshaat tili'ko' áyya'sha? 5. Foshi'at chishki'ta intaloowam? 6. Pali'ta ishpísam? (**pali'** = "flying squirrel")

Lesson 17.5:
Using Question Verbs

In English our question words are short and simple: *who, what, where, when, why, how, which,* plus longer expressions like *how many* and *what kind of.* In Chickasaw, however, most question words—including all those you have not yet learned—are actually verbs, or complex expressions derived from verbs.

Katimpi "which" *and* *katohmi* "how many". Let's look at two additional Chickasaw question words, **katimpi** "which" or "which one" and **katohmi** "how many". One use of **katohmi** is to ask the time, as you learned in the Reading and Speaking section of unit 10. These new question words can be used on their own, as in the following examples:

Katimpihta ittihaalalla'chi?	"Which one is she going to marry?"
Katohmihaat chipístok?	"How many saw you?"

In addition these new question words can be used as noun modifiers, as you can see in the following pairs of questions:

Ofi' katimpihaat chikisilitok?	"Which dog bit you?"
Ofi' katohmihaat chikisilitok?	"How many dogs bit you?"
Chipota tiikat paska champoli' katimpihta apa'chi?	"Which cookie is the girl going to eat?"
Chipota tiikat paska champoli' katohmihta apa'chi?	"How many cookies is the girl going to eat?"

As you learned in unit 12, words used to modify a noun come after it, just as **katimpi** and **katohmi** do in the examples. The subject noun phrases **ofi' katimpi** "which dog" and **ofi' katohmi** "how many dogs" in the first pair of questions are marked with the question subject ending ±**haat**, and the object noun phrases **paska champoli' katimpi** "which cookie" and **paska champoli' katohmi** "how many cookies" in the second pair of questions are marked with the question object ending ±**hta**.

As you know from unit 12, words used as modifiers in noun phrases are stative verbs, and **katimpi** and **katohmi** are no exception to this rule. Although we can translate **katimpi** as "which" and **katohmi** as "how many" in the examples above, in fact, **katimpi** is a verb meaning "to be which one" or "to be which ones", and **katohmi** is a verb meaning "to be how many". In the following questions, **katimpi** and **katohmi** are used with the verb endings +**tok** and +**a'chi**.

Chahta' yammat katimpitok?	"Which of those Choctaws was it?"
Chahta' yammat katohma'chi?	"How many of those Choctaws are there going to be?"

It might surprise you that **katimpi** and **katohmi** are verbs, but this explains why these words can be used with verb endings like **+tok** and **±a'chi**. Notice how the translations work. The most natural way to express these sentences in English is by saying "which of" or "how many of" plus the subject.

Even though they are stative verbs, **katimpi** and **katohmi** are surprising subject A subject verbs. Here are some examples of how they can be used with plural subject markers:

Hashkatimpitok?	"Which of you guys was it?"
Kiikatohma'chi?	"How many of us are there going to be?"

> *Exercise 17F.* Translate the following English sentences into Chickasaw. 1. Which girl sang? 2. Which doctor did you go and see? 3. How many of you are there? 4. Which chief went to Texas? 5. How many bugs did your child find? 6. Which horses did he buy? 7. Which of us was it? 8. How many books is the boy holding?

Now, here's how you use **katimpi** and **katohmi** in more complicated questions with "you" and "us". First, some questions where the "which" or "how many" phrase works like a subject. In these examples, **katimpi** and **katohmi** are followed by the question subject ending **±haat**:

Hashkatimpihaat hashiyya'chi?	"Which of you guys are going?"
Kiikatohmihaat kiliyya'chi?	"How many of us are going?"

And now, some questions where the "which" or "how many" phrase works like an object. Here, **katimpi** and **katohmi** are followed by the question object ending **±hta**:

Kiikatimpihta popístok?	"Which of us did he see?"
Hashkatohmihta hachipístok?	"How many of you guys did he see?"

Because **katimpi** and **katohmi** are verbs, when you use them with A subject markers in more complicated sentences like these, they need to have switch-reference markers. **±Haat** is used when the "which" or "how many" phrase is a subject; **±hta** is used when the **katimpi** or **katohmi** phrase expresses the object of the following verb. In each case the following verb or verb phrase must include an appropriate "we"/"you guys" subject marker or "us"/"you guys" object marker.

Thus, for example, in the last sentence above, **hashkatohmi** expresses "how many of you guys". This phrase is the object of the following main verb **pístok**, so that verb has the S object prefix **hachi+** and the question object ending **±hta** goes on **hashkatohmi.** Look at the other examples and make sure you can explain how they work.

> *Exercise 17G.* Complete the following Chickasaw sentences by adding the equivalent of the English phrase in parentheses. Then translate each full sentence into English, as in the example.
> *Example.* (How many of you guys) hilha hachibanna?
> *Answer.* Hashkatohmikat hilha hachibanna? "How many of you guys want to dance?"
> 1. Minkaat (which of us) potháana? 2. (How many of you guys) minko' hashitháana? 3. (How many of us) aya pobanna? 4. Nannimaabachi'at (how many of you guys) holisso hachimatok? 5. (Which of us) minko' kiliholissocha'chi? 6. (Which of you guys) ṭashpishofa hashikba'hi bíyyi'ka? (**ṭashpishofa** is pishofa, a Chickasaw dish made from corn and pork—see the Reading and Speaking section of unit 9) 7. Ofi'at (which of you guys) hachilhiyohtok? 8. (How many of us) holisso ittimanompolit kiitahtok?

Katihmi and katihchi. Here are some examples of the question verb **katihmi**:

Nantahaat katihmi?	"What's happening?"
Nantahaat chikatihmi?	"What's happening to you?", "What's wrong with you?"
Nantahta ishkatihma'chi?	"What are you going to do?"

As these examples show, **katihmi** can mean either "to happen" or "to happen to, to be wrong with" (with **nantahaat** "what" as its subject) or "to do" (with **nanta** "what" as its object).

Before endings starting with **t** or **ch**, katihmi becomes **katih-**:

Nantahaat katihtok?	"What happened?"
Nantahaat chikatihtok?	"What happened to you?", "What was wrong with you?"
Nanta ishkatihtok?	"What did you do?"

Katihchi means "to do (what) to", as in

Ishkatihshtok?	"What did you do to him?"
Nanta sakatihcha'chi?	"What is he going to do to me?"

As these examples show, you don't necessarily have to use **nanta** "what" in a sentence with **katihchi** the way you do with **katihmi**. Speakers sometimes use **nanta**, but sometimes they don't.

Exercise 17H. Translate the following sentences into Chickasaw. 1. What happened? 2. What happened to your child? 3. What's going to happen to me? 4. What did the doctor do to you? 5. What is the Chickasaw governor going to do? 6. What's wrong with the cat?

Lesson 17.6:
"Why" and "How"

"Why". Here are some questions that use **katihmita** "why":

Katihmihta ishiyya?	"Why are you going?"
Katihmihta alikchaat chipota issotok?	"Why did the doctor hit the child?"

It's usually best to put **katihmihta** at the beginning of the sentence.

"How". There are two common ways to express "how" in Chickasaw, **katiht** and **katihsht** or, sometimes, **katihchihaat**.

Katiht is usually used for "how" questions where you feel that it's unlikely that the event in question could happen or could have happened. Often these might be expressed with "how on earth" in English. Here are some examples:

Katiht ayatok?	"How did he go?", How was he able to go?"
Katiht Oklahomma' ishona'chi?	"How are you going to get to Oklahoma?"
Katiht iksaashla'chi?	"How could I make it?"
Katiht ihooat iksaacha'chi?	"How's the woman going to make it?"

The first two questions, for example, might be asked if you felt that there was no way the person could make the trip. The second two might suggest that the person had no money, no sewing machine, or otherwise no way of doing the project. (Occasionally, you might hear **katihmihaat** instead of **katiht** in this sort of question.)

Katihsht and **katihchihaat** are generally used where you believe that an event will or did happen, but you want to know the manner, style, or procedure in which it is or will be accomplished:

Katihsht ishiksaashtok?	"How did you make it?"
Katihchihaat ishyahmishtok?	"How did you do it?"
Katihsht paska ishiksaachi?	"How do you make bread?"
Katihchihaat yamihshla'chi?	"How should I do it?"
Katihsht abitok?	"How (in what way) did he kill it?"

The first question, for example, might ask in what style a dress was made or what specific procedure was used to accomplish something. The last one might ask whether a gun or poison, for example, was used to kill an animal.

Sometimes you will hear people using A subject markers on **katihchihaat**, matching those that are used on the following verb, as in

Katihshlihaat yamihshla'chi?	"How should I do it?"
Ishkatihchihaat ishiksaashtok?	"How did you make it?"

Saying "say how" and "say what". "Say how" and "say what" don't use any of the words just mentioned, but instead are expressed with the special verb **nantokaachi** "to say how, to say what", as in

Chishkaat nantokaachi?	"How does your mother say it?"
Anompa yappa ishnantokaashtaam?	"How did you say this word?"
Nantokaashtaam?	"What did he say?", "How did he say it?"

> *Exercise 171.* Translate the following Chickasaw "how" and "why" questions into English. 1. Katihmihta hattakat ofi' abitok? 2. Katiht illitok? 3. Katihsht ishtishonatok? 4. Katihmihta yammako ishaashtok? 5. Katihchihaat alikchaat inka lhakoffichitok? (**lhakoffi** = "to cure") 6. Katihsht tashpishofa ishiksaachi? 7. Kiinantokaashtaam? 8. Chahtaat nantokaashtok?

Saying "how" and "why" in Chickasaw is complicated, and speakers often vary in terms of how they express these question words. Listen carefully to other speakers you know, and you'll learn more about saying "how" and "why".

Lesson 17.7:
"Some" and "Any" Words

Words like English *someone, something,* and *somewhere* are used to refer to people and things that we know must exist, but that we cannot identify. Here are some examples of Chickasaw sentences with corresponding words:

Alikchaat kana pístok.	"The doctor saw someone."
Anchipotaat nanna apatok.	"My child ate something."
Kaniya' kiliyyatok.	"We went somewhere."

The "some . . ." words in these examples are **kana** "someone", **nanna** "someone", and **kaniya'** "somewhere". Take a look at these words—they are exactly the same as the question words you learned at the beginning of this unit but with **n** substituted for **t**, as the following chart shows. We can consider the question words in the chart on the next page as T-WORDS, and the "some" words you'll learn about in this lesson as N-WORDS:

t-words	*n-words*
kata "who"	**kana** "someone"
nanta "what"	**nanna** "something"
katiya' "where"	**kaniya'** "somewhere"

The "some" n-words words in the examples above are all objects used right before the verb of their sentences, so they do not need endings. Subject "some" words use the "some" subject ending ±**hmat**, as in the following examples:

Kanahmat sassotok!   "Someone hit me!"
Nannahmat chikisilitaam?   "Did something bite you?"

If you use object "some" words in sentence positions other than right before the verb, they need the "some" object ending ±**hma** (±**ma** after **kaniya'**)—and, like all object endings, this one can also be used on objects in the normal object position. Here are some examples:

Alikchaat nannahma pístok   "The doctor saw someone."
Anchipotaat apatok nannahma.   "My child ate something."
Kaniya'ma kiliyyatok.   "We went somewhere."

Sometimes Chickasaw "some" words are translated with "any" in English. Thus, "some" words could also be considered "any" words. One place this happens is in questions:

Kaniya' ishiyyataam?   "Did you go anywhere?"
Kanahma ishpístaa?   "Do you see anyone?"

We also use "any" in English in negative sentences. You'll learn how to express this type of "any" in unit 19. For now, don't try to put the new n-words in this lesson into negative sentences.

> *ExeICse 17J.* Translate the following Chickasaw sentences into English. 1. I found something. 2. Did you find anything? 3. Did anything bite you? 4. They went somewhere yesterday. 5. The dog is chasing something, but I can't see it. 6. Someone lived here (long ago).

Terms and Concepts

QUESTION WORD, QUESTION WORD QUESTION, FOCUS QUESTION, T-WORD, N-WORD.

VOCABULARY

ala to be born (A)
Chikashsha Iminko' the Chickasaw governor (the governor of the Chickasaw Nation)
habina to get (something) as a present (A,Noun)
Iksa' Christian
kana someone, somebody
kaniya' / kaniyaak somewhere
kata who
katihchi to do what to (A;S); to do (what) to (A;S;Noun = **nanta**)
katihkaash / katihkaasht / katihkaashta / katihkaashta when (past)
katihkmak when (nonpast)
katihmi to happen (Noun = **nantahaat**); to happen to, be wrong with (Noun = **nantahaat**; S); to do (what)
    (A;Noun = **nanta**) (becomes **katih-** before endings starting with **t** or **ch**)
katihmihaat how
katihmihta why
katihsht / katihchihaat how, in what way (see lesson 17.6)
katiht how, how on earth (see lesson 17.6)
katimpi which; to be which (A)
katiya' / katiyaak where
katiya fokhakaash / katiya fokhakaasht / katiya fokhakaashta / katiya fokhakaashta when (past)
katiya fokhakmak when (nonpast)
katohmi how many; to be how many (A)
nanna something
nanta what
nantokaachi to say how (A, Noun); to say what (A)
onkof persimmon
pali' flying squirrel
sapontaki' mosquito
sholosh shoes
tashpishofa pishofa (Chickasaw dish made from corn and pork; see the Reading and Speaking section of unit 9)

READING AND SPEAKING

Selections from the Universal Declaration of Human Rights

*In honor of the fiftieth anniversary of the United Nations, the Office of the High Commissioner for Human Rights solicited translations of the Universal Declaration of Human Rights (originally written in 1947) into a wide range of world languages. We provided a Chickasaw translation of the declaration (or more properly retold it, since producing an exact translation would have been difficult), selections from which are given below. There are thirty articles (**anompa kanihmo'si**) in all; you can read the complete Chickasaw declaration online at http://www.unhchr.ch/udhr/lang/cic.htm, and the original English version at http://www.unhchr.ch/udhr/lang/eng.htm. (A translation of this retelling is provided in Appendix C.)*

Hattak Móma Iholisso

Ishtaa-aya Ámmo'na Holisso

Hattakat yaakni' áyya'shakat mómakat ittíllawwi bíyyi'ka. Naalhpisa'at hattak mómakat immi'. Alhínchikma hattak mómakat ishtayoppa'ni. . . .

Hattak yaakni' áyya'shakat mómakat yammookano ittibaachaffahookmaka'chi nannakat aalhpí'sa bíyyi'ka'chika. . . .

Anompa Kanihmo'si 1

. . . Hattak mómakat ittíllawwi bíyyi'kacha nanna mómaka ittibaachaffa'hitok.

Anompa Kanihmo'si 2

Hattakat pisa ittimilayyokhacha kaniya'o aamintihookya mómakat ittíllawwi bíyyi'ka. Hattakat yaakni' kaniya'o aamintihookya ittíllawwi bíyyi'ka.

Anompa Kanihmo'si 3

Hattakat hattak yoka'shcha aba'nikat imaalhpí'sa ki'yo. Hattakat holiitopa bíyyi'ka.

Anompa Kanihmo'si 4

Hattak yoka'at ikshoka'ni.

. . . Anompa Kanihmo'si 8

Hattakat nanna ikchokmoho hattak iyahmohmikma naapiisa' alhihaakoot hattak yamma apila'chi.

. . . Anompa Kanihmo'si 16

1. Hattakat ihoo táwwa'at kaniya'o ittihaalalli bannakmat ittihaalalla'nikat imaalhpí'sa.
2. Ittihaalalli ikbannokmat ittihaalalla' ki'yo kaniya'ookya. . . .

. . . Anompa Kanihmo'si 18

Kanahaat nanna aayimmikat ittimilayyokha bíyyi'kahookya, nannaho ayoppachi bannakmat ayoppacha'ni.

Anompa Kanihmo'si 19

Nannaho anokfilli chibannakmat ishanokfilla'ni. Nannaho holissochi chibannakmat ishholissocha'ni. Holisso nannaho ittimanompoli chibannakmat ishtimanompola'ni.

. . . Anompa Kanihmo'si 26

Chipota mómakat holissaapisa' aya'nikat imaalhpí'sa, ta'osso nannikimikshohookya. Kana mómakat nanna aaithana' aya bannakmat aya'ni. . . .

. . . Anompa Kanihmo'si 29

1. Kana mómakat ittapilakmakilla.
2. Hattakat naalhpisa' ikbi, hattak apila bannahoot. Naalhpisa' kobaffa' ki'yo.
3. Anompa kanihmo'si yappat alhkaniya' ki'yo.

SUPPLEMENTARY VOCABULARY

alhiha' bunch (see note 7 below)

alhkaniya to be forgotten (S)

ayoppachi to worship; to praise (A,S)

aayimmi to believe in (something) (S,Noun)

alhínchi to be enacted, made true (Noun)

hattak yoka' slave, prisoner

imaalhpí'sa to have the right to (D) (see note 8 below)

immi' (used to say "belong to"—see note 3 below)

Ishtaa-aya Ámmo'na Holisso Preamble (where the document first begins)

ittibaachaffa to agree with each other about (A,Noun)

iyahmohmi to do (something) to (someone) (A,D,Noun)

kana móma everyone

kaniya'ookya everyone (see note 9 below)

nanna some; any (see note 5 below)

nanna aaithana' educational institution, place to learn

nanna ikchokmo something bad

nannakat what (subject—see note 5 below)

naalhpisa' law

naapiisa' lawmaker

pisa ittimilayyokha to look different from each other (A)

yokachi to imprison (pl. obj.) (A,S)

NOTES

1. The use of **bíyyi'ka** throughout the declaration, beginning with Ishtaa-aya Ámmo'na Holisso, is highly emphatic. Although this word is most commonly translated as "always" or "all the time", "truly" seems like a better translation here.

2. **Hattak yaakni' áyya'shakat** (Ishtaa-aya Ámmo'na Holisso) means "people of the nations" or "people who live in the nations" (we know this must be plural because of the use of the triplural subject positional verb **áyya'sha**). This is a modifying phrase pattern slightly different from those you'll learn about in unit 20.

3. **Naalhpisa'at hattak mómakat immi'** "The laws belong to all people" (Ishtaa-aya Ámmo'na Holisso) uses a "have" sentence pattern, with two things marked as subjects.

4. **±Hookmaka'chi** (Ishtaa-aya Ámmo'na Holisso) is a "must" ending.

5. Sometimes the n word **nanna** acts as if it was a verb, taking the same subject dependent sentence ending **±kat**, as in **nannakat aalhpí'sa bíyyi'ka'chi** "what is going to be truly right" (Ishtaa-aya Ámmo'na Holisso). Another meaning **nanna** can have is "some", as in **Holisso nannaho ittimanompoli chibannakmat ishtimanompola'ni** "If you want to read some book you can read it" (Anompa Kanihmo'si 19). In a negative sentence this use of **nanna** usually becomes "any", as in **ta'osso nanna ikimiksho** "they don't have any money".

6. Here's a sentence that uses n-words in an unusual way: **Kanahaat nanna aayimmikat ittimilayyokha bíyyi'ka** (Anompa Kanihmo'si 18). This means "The things people believe in may truly be different from each other". Here, the n-words **kana** and **nanna** are translated with the words "people" and "thing" rather than words like "someone" or "something".

7. **Alhiha'** "bunch" (Anompa Kanihmo'si 8) is used only about groups of people, as you'll learn in unit 19.

8. **Imaalhpí'sa** "to have the right to" (Anompa Kanihmo'si 16) is used with a preceding same-subject dependent verb ending in **±kat**.

9. As noted in unit 16's Reading and Speaking section, **kaniya'** can sometimes mean "someone" as well as "somewhere". You'll see this in Anompa Kanihmo'si 16. Similarly, **kaniya'ookya** can mean "everyone" or, in a negative sentence, "anyone".

10. **±Hookya** normally means "but", but in Anompa Kanihmo'si 26, it means "even if": **Chipota mómakat holis-saapisa' aya'nikat imaalhpí'sa, ta'osso nannikimikshohookya** "All children have the right to go to school, even if they don't have any money".

11. **±Kmakilla** (Anompa Kanihmo'si 29) means something like "should".

ADVANCED CHICKASAW GRAMMAR 7: QUESTION WORDS IN DEPENDENT SENTENCES

English sentences like *I know who you saw* or *The woman asked me what I found* use question words in dependent sentences. Here are some examples of how you say this kind of thing in Chickasaw:

Kanaho ishpísaka ithánali.	"I know who you saw."
Nannaho píslikat ithánali.	"I know what I saw."
Ihooat nannaho hayooshlika amasilhhatok.	"The woman asked me what I found."
Ihooat kanahoot sassotoka amasilhhatok.	"The woman asked me who hit me."

In Chickasaw you use an n-word (not a t-word, surprisingly) to express the English question words in these dependent sentences. The n-words used to express the question word ideas in these sentences have focus endings. However, although speakers usually use focus endings on n-words used in this way, you'll occasionally encounter other endings on these words.

All the t-words you've learned in this lesson, including the question verbs, have n-word equivalents. Here's an example with **nannokaachi**, the n-word equivalent of **nantokaachi** "to say how":

Nannokaachika ithánali.	"I know how she says it."

You'll find many examples of n-words in dependent sentences in the Reading and Speaking sections of this book. For example, in the Christmas story that follows unit 20, you'll see the following example:

Chihoowaat nannaho hapomoktanihínchikma iloopisa'shki.	"We should see what God has revealed to us."

Unit 18

New Types of Nouns and Verbs

In this lesson you'll learn how to form a number of new types of Chickasaw nouns and verbs.

Lesson 18.1 shows how to form several different types of nouns from verbs. Lesson 18.2 concerns compound nouns. Lesson 18.3 introduces the "in" or "into" verb prefix **okaa-**. Lesson 18.4 shows how to connect sentences with the "because" endings **±hootokoot** and **±hootoko**. The Y grade is presented in lesson 18.5, and lesson 18.6 discusses exclamations. The Advanced Chickasaw Grammar section presents more types of compounds.

Lesson 18.1:
Making Nouns from Verbs

Nouns can be formed from many Chickasaw verbs by adding a ±' ending. Here are some examples:

> **ani'** "produce, crop, fruit" (from **ani** "to bear fruit")
> **impa'** "food" (from **impa** "to eat")
> **hilha'** "dance" or "dancer" (from **hilha** "to dance")

As you see, nouns formed by adding the ±' ending to a verb can refer either to the subject of the verb or to an object affected or created by the verb. The second type of meaning is more common. Thus, **hilha'** can mean either "dancer" (the one who dances) or "dance" (what is created by dancing). Although it might be possible to use **impa'** to mean "eater", the usual meaning is "food", and so on.

Because the ±' is a ± ending, you may hear nouns formed with this ending with the same type of rhythmic pattern you've seen with other ± endings. Thus, **hilha'** will usually be pronounced **hilh/a'**, with the syllable break before the final vowel.

> *Exercise 18A.* Choose ten verbs from the vocabulary. Add ±' to each one. Pronounce the new nouns and tell what you think they should mean. Then try each one out on a fellow student or a Chickasaw speaker. Were you right?

Chickasaw nouns adding the ±' ending to a verb often include the **aa±** or **isht±** prefixes.
Here are some examples of **aa±** nouns you have already learned:

aaimpa' "restaurant" (from **aa±** plus **impa ±'**)
aanosi' "bedroom" (from **aa±** plus **nosi ±'**)
aaholhponi' "kitchen" , "pot" (from **aa±** plus **holhponi** "to be cooked" **±'**)

As you can see, a noun formed from a verb with the **aa±** prefix refers to a location where the verb's action can be performed—eating is done at a restaurant, sleeping is done in a bedroom, things get cooked in a kitchen, and so forth.

Now, here are some nouns derived from **isht±** verbs:

ishbashli' "kitchen knife" (from **isht±** plus **bashli ±'**)
ishholbachi' "camera" (from **isht±** plus **holbachi ±'**)

Nouns formed from verbs with the **isht±** preverb refer to instruments used to perform the action named by the verb. A knife is an item to cut with, a leash is an item with which something is tied, and a hammer is an item with which something becomes hammered. As you know from unit 13, when **isht±** is added to the front of a verb that starts with a consonant, it becomes **ish±**. Sometimes these nouns include **nanna** "something" or the short form **naa±**:

naaishbo'wa' "hammer" (from **naa±** plus **isht±** plus **bo'wa** ("to be hammered") **±'**)

As the examples show, nouns containing the **aa±** and **isht±** prefixes are often formed from the V1 member of a verb pair (lesson 16.1). You'll find that it is easy to make up new nouns using these patterns. All the new words in this section are listed in the Chickasaw-English Vocabulary at the end of this book, but the vocabulary contains only a small fraction of the possible new words that can be made in this way.

Exercise 18B. i. Here are three more **isht±** nouns you already know. Tell what each means and explain how it is formed:
  ishholissochi'; **ishpiha'** (**piha** = "to be swept"); **ishtalakchi'**
  ii. Here are some additional **aa±** nouns you've seen. Can you explain how they are formed?
  aaombiniili'; **aachompa'**; **aahashtahli'** "window" (**hashtahli** = "to be bright")
  iii. Now, here are some new nouns made from verbs. Try to figure out what each one means and explain how it is formed:
  abika'; **aahilha'**; **aaholloppi'** (**holloppi** = "to be buried"); **ishchokoshkomo'**; **ishfama'**; **ishliichi'** (**liichi** = "to plow"); **ishtalhchifa'** (**alhchifa** = "to be washed"); **ishtiwa'**; **taloowa'**
  You can check the meanings of these words in the vocabulary at the end of this lesson.

One thing you'll notice about the new types of nouns in this section is that sometimes an extra **'** appears before the last consonant of the verb when they are formed. Here are some examples:

hilha'chi' "top (toy)" (from **hilhachi** "to make (something) dance" **±'**)
ishtaka'fa' "cup" (from **isht±** **takafa** "to be dipped up" **±'**)
ishtasha'na' "lock" (from **isht±** **ashana** "to be locked" **±'**)
aai'pa' "table" (from **aa±** **impa ±'**)

Note that when this **'** is added before the **p** of **impa**, the **im** becomes **i̱**, the same way it does in the negative word **iki̱'po**.

It's not easy to predict which nouns will get this extra '. For example, **aai'pa'** "table" has the extra ' (at least for many speakers), while **aaimpa'** "restaurant" does not. Just listen for the added ' when you hear people using new nouns from verbs. Any new noun presented in this unit that has this extra ' is listed in the vocabulary, even if its meaning is predictable.

Lesson 18.2: Compounds

With a two-place verb, you can make a COMPOUND noun—a noun formed from more than one word—referring to the two-place verb's subject. Look at these compound nouns:

> **hattak-apa'** "man-eater, cannibal"
> **hattak-abi'** "man killer, murderer"
> **hashshok-ishtamo'** "grass cutter, scythe"

We write a hyphen (-) to connect the parts of a Chickasaw compound, just as in many English compounds. As you can see, the Chickasaw and English words have exactly the same structure—first the object (**hattak** or *man*), then the verb (**apa** or *eat*, **abi** or *kill*), followed by an ending that makes the whole thing into a noun (±' or *–er*). (Not all compound nouns contain a noun plus a verb. The Reading and Speaking section of unit 7 introduces another type of compound noun.)

The hyphen written in a Chickasaw compound word reminds you that the two parts of the compound are kept separate in pronunciation. A new syllable always starts after the hyphen: **hat/tak-/a/pa'**. (Alternatively, you could write these compounds as two words, as **hattak apa'** or **hashshok ishtamo'**, for example. We'll usually use the one-word spelling with the hyphen in this book, but both are correct. You do need to use either the space or the hyphen, however; if you write these words as a single word with no hyphen, the spelling will not reflect the pronunciation correctly.) When compound words appear in an alphabetical list, the hyphen is ignored in alphabetical order.

Here are some more examples:

> **issoba-honkopa'** "horse thief"
> **ofi'-abi'** "dog killer"
> **kowi'-sho'ka'** "cat kisser"

Just as in English, you can easily make up new compounds, and people can understand them even if they are a little silly. Many such examples are just made-up words. They don't need to be listed in the vocabulary, but any speaker will understand them and other words formed the same way.

Listen to your teacher say the three compounds above. The chances are that you may hear your teacher use two different pronunciations for such words, depending on how fast he or she is talking. The two parts of the word may be kept separate—**kowi' sho'ka', issoba honkopa', ofi' abi'** (almost as if they were different parts of a sentence)—or the first word may be pronounced with a special intonation pattern, with a heavy accent on the next-to-last syllable and the last vowel starting its own syllable. In this special COMPOUND ACCENT pattern, the three words may sound like this:

> is/sob/a-/hon/ko/pa'   of/i'-/a/bi'   kow/i'-/sho'/ka'.

Using the compound accent pattern is a bit like adding a ± ending onto the first word of the compound.

The two parts of a compound are always kept separate by the hyphen, but when the first part of the compound ends in a vowel, the compound accent pattern is usually used. Listen carefully to your teacher.

Exercise 18C. Pronounce each of the following compounds carefully, using the compound accent pattern where appropriate. Tell what each one means. Draw lines to show how the new words are divided into syllables. Tell what words go together to form the compounds.

　　1. onkof-apa' 2. ahi'-apa' 3. tii'-ishko' 4. chomak-howasa' (**chomak** = "tobacco"; **howasa** = "to chew") 5. chomak-pofa' (**pofa** = "to smoke") 6. shawi'-abi'

　　You will not find all of the compound words in this lesson listed in the Chickasaw-English Vocabulary at the end of this book—they are only listed in cases where their meanings are specialized or unexpected.

If the noun before the verb in a compound is a vowel-loss noun, its final vowel or vowel-plus-' drops when the following verb starts with a vowel. See how this works in the examples below:

> **sint-apa'** "snake eater" (from **sinti'** plus **apa ±'**)
> **iss-abi'** "deer killer" (from **issi'** plus **abi ±'**)

The verb of the compound may include an **aa±** or **isht±** prefix:

> **ta'oss-aa-alhto'** "small bank, money box" (from **ta'osso** plus **aa±** plus **alhto** "to be shut up in, to be placed inside" plus **±'**)
> **holiss-aapisa'** "school" (from **holisso** plus **aa± pisa ±'**)

(At school we look at books. . . .) You may hear some compounds like this in which the vowel does not drop, but that is not common. The first example will remind you that another way hyphens are used in Chickasaw spelling is to separate letters like **aa** from **a**, as explained in lesson 1.

When you pronounce compounds like these in which a vowel or vowel-plus-glottal stop has been lost, remember that the hyphen in the spelling tells you to begin a new syllable. So you say **sint-/a/pa'**, and so on.

Sometimes a final short vowel or vowel-plus-glottal stop is dropped from the object noun in a compound even though that vowel is not odd numbered. Here's an example:

> **of-abi'** "dog killer" (from **ofi'**- **abi ±'**)

Since the **i'** (final vowel-plus-glottal stop) of **ofi'** is even numbered, you would not expect it to drop—but in a compound like this, it might. If you listen, you'll hear people pronounce other compounds in this way. The **f** in **of-abi'** may sound lengthened, almost as if the word were <offabi'>. Listen to your teacher.

"Big" and "little" compounds. The words **ishto'** (ishto "big" plus **±'**) and **oshi'** "son" can be used in compounds with other nouns to refer to big and little varieties of those nouns. Here are some examples:

> **topa** "bed": **topa-ishto', top-ishto'** "big bed"; **top-oshi', topa-oshi'** "little bed, crib"
> **chokka'** "house": **chokk-ishto'** "big house"; **chokk-oshi'** "little house"
> **kowi'** "cat": **kow-ishto', kowi'-ishto'** "mountain lion"; **kow-oshi'** "kitten"

In **oshi'** compounds the last vowel of the first noun usually drops, and this can also happen with **ishto'** compounds. **Oshi'** compounds are very common in Chickasaw, especially in reference to small or young animals. Sometimes these words have special meanings that are worth remembering:

> **abooha / aboowa** "house": **aboowoshi'** "bathroom, outhouse"
> **shokha'** "hog": **shokhoshi'** "pig"

Exercise 18D. i. List ten nouns that you already know. Then, for each noun, choose an appropriate verb and make up a new compound from that noun plus that verb. Don't forget the final ' at the end of the verb. Pronounce each new word and tell what you would expect it to mean. Then try your new compounds out on another student or a Chickasaw speaker. Does everyone agree on their meaning?

ii. Form an **oshi'** compound from each animal name below, as in the example. In every case the last vowel of the first noun drops before **oshi'**. Tell what each new word means. Say the new words aloud, remembering the new pronunciation rules.

Example. nita'

Answer. nit-oshi' "bear cub"

Issi'; ofi'; foshi'; nannalhpooba'; pinti'; koni; issoba; fani'; waaka'; shawi'. (How would you say "bull"?) It's easy to make up these new "little" words. Most of them are not listed in the Chickasaw-English Vocabulary.

Lesson 18.3:
Okaa± "into, inside, in"

Like **im±**, **aa±**, **on±**, **ibaa±**, and **isht±**, **okaa±** is a verb prefix that allows you to add an additional participant to the sentence. **Okaa±** means "into", "inside", or "in". Here are some pairs of sentences that show how the **okaa±** prefix is used (make sure you can find the **okaa±** in the second sentence in each pair):

Ishhikanna!	"Don't step!"
Oka' ishokaahikanna!	"Don't step in the water!"
Ihooat tofatok.	"The woman spat."
Ihooat ishtaka'fa' okaatofatok.	"The woman spat into the cup."
Oktaat bila'chi.	"The ice is going to melt."
Oktaat tii' okaabila'chi.	"The ice is going to melt in the tea."
Sahowitatok.	"I vomited."
Shokcha okaahowitalitok.	"I vomited into the sack."

The last example shows that when a verb with an S subject gets an added object participant, its subject changes to an A subject.

In some cases the meaning or translation of a verb will change when it is used with the **okaa±** prefix. Most of the new **okaa±** verbs above are not listed in the English-Chickasaw Vocabulary, because their meaning is predictable. The following one is, however.

Hattakat sabaafatok.	"The man stabbed me."
Hattakat sashkin okaabaafatok.	"The man stuck his finger in my eye."

As you can see, **okaa±** verbs are o-verbs.

Exercise 18E. Translate the following Chickasaw sentences into English. 1. Chipotaat oka' okaamallitok. 2. Sashkin okaabaafanna! 3. Hattak ishkin ishokaabaafatok. 4. Hattakat chishkin okaabaafattook. 5. Oka' okaahíkki'yali.

Áyya'sha means "be in", so you wouldn't think it would need to be used with **okaa±**. However, in a sentence like the following, **okaa±** is used with **áyya'sha** to emphasize that the subject is actually completely inside.

Iss<u>o</u>shat tili'ko' okaa-áyya'sha.   "There are bugs in the flour."

Listen, and you'll learn more about when Chickasaw speakers use **okaa±** and other such location prefixes.

Lesson 18.4:
"Because"

"Because" is expressed in Chickasaw with a new set of switch-reference endings which work like the ones you learned about in lessons 11 and 13. Here are three pairs of same- and different-subject "because" examples that show how the new endings **±hootokoot** and **±hootoko** work:

Satikahbihootokoot nosila'chi.	"Because I'm tired I'm going to sleep."
Ombahootok<u>o</u> nosila'chi.	"Because it's raining I'm going to sleep."

Asayoppa hattak ishkin
   okaabaafalitokootokoot.
	"I am happy because I stuck my
	   finger in the man's eye."

Hattak akayoppa'cho sashkin
   okaabaafatokootok<u>o</u>.
	"I don't like the man because he
	   stuck his finger in my eye."

Aachompa' ayala'chi paska
   chompa sabannahootokoot.
	"I am going to go to the store because
	   I want to buy bread."

Anchipotaat aachompa' aya'chi
   paska chompa'ni sabannahootok<u>o</u>.
	"My child is going to go to the store
	   because I want her to buy bread."

The "because" sentences **satikahbi, omba, ishkin okaabaafalitok, sashkin okaabaafatok, paska chompa sabanna,** and **paska chompa'ni sabanna** have the "because" endings **±hootokoot** and **±hootoko** (**±ootokoot** and **±ootoko** after a consonant). As with other switch-reference endings, you use the **t** ending (**±hootokoot**) when the subject of the dependent "because" sentence is the same as that of the main sentence, and you use the nasal vowel ending (**±hootoko**) when those subjects are different.

Thus, in the first example, the "because" sentence is **satikahbi** and the main sentence is **nosila'chi.** These both have the same subject, "I" (even though one "I" is indicated by the prefix **sa+** and the other by the ending **+li**), so the same-subject "because" ending **±hootokoot** is used. In the second example, the two sentences have different subjects (**omba** has no real subject in Chickasaw, while **nosila'chi,** again, has the subject "I"), so the different-subject "because" ending **±hootoko** is used.

As these examples show, the "because" sentence may either precede or follow the main sentence. Thus, another way to say the first sentence above would be

Nosila'chi satikahbihootokoot.   "I'm going to sleep because I'm tired."

Something a little more complicated happens in both the Chickasaw sentence and the English translation when you turn around the two parts of a sentence like the last example in the group above:

Anchipotaat paska chompa'ni
 sabannahootoko aachompa' aya'chi.

"Because I want my child to buy bread
 she is going to go to the store."

Anchipotaat is part of both sentences here. It makes sense for it to appear in whichever sentence is at the beginning. Here's another pair of examples:

Anchipotaat hopobahootoko
 paska inchompala'chi.
Anchipota paska inchompala'chi
 hopobahootoko.

"Because my child is hungry
 I will buy him bread."
"I will buy my child bread
 because he is hungry."

Once again, the child is part of both sentences—the object in the main sentence and the subject in the "because" sentence. Here again, it is clearer if the speaker puts the "child" word earlier in the sentence.

Exercise 18F. Connect the following pairs of Chickasaw sentences by deciding which one is more likely to be the reason for the other and adding an appropriate "because" ending to the verb of the reason sentence, as in the example. Then translate your sentences.
 Example. Chipotaat malit kaniyatok. Holiss-aapisa' ikayoppa'cho.
 Answer. Chipotaat malit kaniyatok holiss-aapisa' ikayoppa'chohootokoot.
 "The child ran away because he doesn't like school."
 Notice that the reason sentence may come either before or after the main sentence.
 1. Ahattakat lhabanka. Iksano'so. 2. Hattakat fani' abitok. Apa banna. 3. Ta'oss-aa-alhto' honkopatok. Ta'osso banna. 4. Chipota tiikat ayoppa. Ishkaat tashpishofa iksaachi. 5. Ihooat chokma'si. Holbachilitok.

Lesson 18.5: The Y Grade

Y grades of stative verbs. As you know, Chickasaw verbs have grades, accented forms that change in regular ways to express differences in meaning. You learned about the HN grade in unit 8 and the N grade in unit 15. Below are some verbs in the Y GRADE:

Basic verb	Y grade form
losa "to be black"	lóyyo'sa
litiha "to be dirty"	litíyyi'ha
hopoba "to be hungry"	hopóyyo'ba
okchamali "to be blue, to be green"	okchamáyya'li
kosoma "to stink"	kosóyyo'ma
champoli "to taste good"	champóyyo'li
tikahbi "to be tired"	tikáyya'hbi
kawaski "to be hard"	kawáyya'ski
ilbashsha "to be poor"	ilbáyya'shsha
chonna "to be skinny"	chóyyo'nna

chokma "to be good"	chóyyokma
lakna "to be brown, to be yellow"	láyyakna
chaaha "to be tall"	cháyya'ha
mas<u>o</u>fa "to be bald"	masóyy<u>o</u>'fa
lhinko "to be fat"	lhíyy<u>i</u>'ko

As you can see, Y grades contain a double **y** following an accented vowel, plus two additional syllables.

Stative Y grades, like those in the examples above, generally add the meaning "very" or "really" to the meaning of the basic verb. Thus, **lóyyo'sa** means "very black", **chóyyokma** means "very good", and so on. They are used in sentences just like the basic verbs from which they are derived, except that, as you know from lesson 10, **ik±** negatives of grade forms are usually expressed as **ik±** negatives of the basic verbs.

Therefore, speakers might consider that sentences like those in the following pair were equivalent:

Paskaat champóyyo'li.	"The bread tastes very good."
Paskaat kan<u>i</u>hk<u>a</u> champoli.	"The bread tastes very good."

It might seem easier to use **kan<u>i</u>hk<u>a</u>** to say "very", but using a Y grade will make you sound more like a fluent Chickasaw speaker and may help express your meaning with more emotion.

Forming Y grades. Here's the process for forming a Y grade.

First, identify the changing vowel in the basic verb. For forming a Y grade, this is always the next-to-last vowel.

Then, add an accented copy of the changing vowel followed by **yy** before the changing vowel. If the changing vowel is long or nasalized, the copy should be a short, plain vowel.

Next, look at the changing vowel. If it is followed by **f, h, l, lh, m, n, s, sh, w,** or **y** or by any single consonant, add **'** (a glottal stop) between the changing vowel and that following consonant. If it is followed by anything else, don't add the **'**. Check out how this works in the following examples. The first group of examples contain a short, non-nasal changing vowel followed by a single consonant. The Y grades contain an accented copy of the changing vowel followed by **yy** plus the changing vowel plus **'**. The **'** is added before the final consonant of the basic form.

losa "to be black"	lóyyo'sa
litiha "to be dirty"	litíyyi'ha
hopoba "to be hungry"	hopóyyo'ba
okchamali "to be blue, to be green"	okchamáyya'li
kosoma "to stink"	kosóyyo'ma
champoli "to taste good"	champóyyo'li

The next examples have a changing vowel followed by two consonants, of which the first is **f, h, l, lh, m, n, s, sh, w,** or **y**. Again, an accented copy of the changing vowel is followed by **yy** plus the changing vowel plus **'**.

tikahbi "to be tired"	tikáyya'hbi
kawaski "to be hard"	kawáyya'ski
ilbashsha "to be poor"	ilbáyya'sha
chonna "to be skinny"	chóyyo'nna

If the changing vowel is followed by any other sequence of two consonants, the ' does not appear. The Y grade still has an accented copy of the changing vowel followed by **yy** and the changing vowel:

chokma "to be good"   chóyyokma
lakna "to be brown, to be yellow"   láyyakna

Exercise 18G. Tell what the Y grade is for each of the following verbs. Then tell the meaning of each of the new forms. 1. abika. 2. akmi. 3. bashafa. 4. imilhlha. 5. hichito. 6. inchokmishto. 7. lawa. 8. kapassa. 9. palhki. 10. tohbi.

If the changing vowel is long, shorten it. If the changing vowel is nasal, it should remain nasal. Here are some examples:

chaaha "to be tall"   cháyya'ha
masofa "to be bald"   masóyyo'fa

If the the basic form has **mb, mp, nch, nk,** or **nt** after the changing vowel, you should make the changing vowel nasal, add a ', and drop the **m** or **n** after the ':

lhinko "to be fat"   lhíyyi'ko

Y grades of verbs ending in long vowels. Here are some examples of what happens with verbs that end in long vowels:

falaa "to be long"   faláyya'ha / faláyya'a
hashaa "to be angry"   hasháyya'ha / hasháyya'a
hopoo "to be jealous"   hopóyyo'ha / hopóyyo'wa

Y grades of these verbs end in a short accented copy of the final vowel of the verb, plus **yy**, plus that vowel followed by **'ha**. Some speakers may drop the **h** after the '. If the preceding vowel is **o**, these speakers use a **w** after the '.

As you learned in lesson 8, the changing vowel of a verb that ends in a long vowel or a long nasal vowel is the first part of that long or nasal vowel. The Y grades of verbs like **falaa** and **hashaa** suggest that it makes sense to think of these verbs as **falaha** and **hashaha** (and indeed, some speakers use these pronunciations). If we think of these as the basic forms of "to be long" and "to be angry", their Y grade formation is completely regular. (**Hopoo** works more as if its basic form was **hopoha** or **hopowa**.)

Exercise 18H. Put each of the following Chickasaw sentences into the Y grade, then translate each one. 1. Hattak yammat wiiki. 2. Issoba hasimbishat falaa. 3. Hachihashaa. 4. Holisso yappat holiitopa. 5. Kiihopoo. 6. Ihoo yammakoot sipokni. 7. Waakat waaka. 8. Chinkowi'at lhinko.

Y grades of active verbs. Most active verbs are not commonly used in the Y grade, although sometimes they may be used with the meaning "really". However, there are some active verbs that have a different meaning in the Y grade. Here are some examples:

Basic Verb	Y Grade
achaknaski "to turn on one's side"	achaknáyya'ski "to lie on one's side"
achokmilhka "to kneel down"	achokmíyyi'lhka "to be kneeling"
anchi "to cover oneself with"	áyya'chi "to be covered with"
fokha "to put on (clothes)"	fóyyokha "to wear (clothes)"
holo "to put on (shoes)"	hóyyo'lo "to wear (shoes)"
okcha "to wake up"	óyyokcha "to be awake"

Compare the meanings of the verbs in the two columns. The basic verbs have an active meaning. The Y grades have a stative meaning—they refer to the state that a subject is in after it has performed the action of the basic verb.

These Y grade stative verbs have "surprising subjects", as discussed in lesson 3—although their meaning is stative, they have the same kind of subject marker as the basic verb (A, in these cases). You can see this in the following examples:

Naachi kiláyya'shtok.	"We were covered with a quilt."
Sholosh hóyyo'loli.	"I am wearing shoes."
Achóyyokchataa?	"Are you awake?"

These examples show that endings like **+tok**, **+taa**, and **+li** are not included in the basic verb from which the Y grade is formed, as you learned concerning HN grade formation in unit 8.

Summary of Y grade formation. Below is a summary of the facts about Y grade formation you have learned in this lesson.

- The Y grade is made by adding **yy** after an accented, short copy of the changing vowel of a basic verb (which may include **+chi** but not other endings).
- If the changing vowel is followed by a single consonant or by two consonants, of which the first is **f, h, l, lh, m, n, s, sh, w,** or **y**, a ' is added after the changing vowel.
- If the changing vowel is long, it is shortened.
- If the last vowel of the basic verb is long, the Y grade ends with a short, accented copy of this vowel, plus **yy**, plus the vowel followed by **'ha**. With a long nasal vowel, the vowel before the **'ha** is nasalized.
- Since the next-to-last syllable of a Y grade is always heavy, the vowel drop rule can apply when the last consonant of a Y grade verb is **s, sh, lh,** or (with the ch/sh rule) **ch** and the Y grade is followed by the ending **+li, +tok, +taa,** or **+taam**.

By following these rules, you can put almost any verb into the Y grade. Try forming the Y grade of other verbs you know. You may find, however, that Chickasaw speakers think some verbs don't sound too good in this form.

Exercise 181. Translate the following Chickasaw sentences into English. 1. Chipota nakni' yappat sholosh hóyyo'la' ki'yo. 2. Kow-oshi'at óyyokcha. 3. Tii'at páyya'llihootoko ishko iksabanno. 4. Paska' champoli'at champóyyo'li. 5. Holisso yappa ayoppáshli, chóyyokmahootoko. 6. Kiitoksalihootokoot potikáyya'hbi.

| **Lesson 18.6:** Exclamations | A speaker uses an EXCLAMATION to express strong emotion. Here are some examples of Chickasaw exclamations: |

Ofi'at ishtoho!   "Wow, the dog is big!", "The dog is so big!"

Hashtilhaaha!   "Wow, you guys are running!"

Holisso hayooshlihi!   "Wow, I found the book!"

Anchipotaat choka'to' apaha!   "Wow, my child is eating the tomatoes!"

We've translated these exclamations with "wow!" here to indicate the type of emotional statement that they express. That's not a necessary part of the translation, however. The exclamation point (!) at the end of the exclamation reminds you to pronounce them with feeling.

If you compare the exclamations above with the corresponding statements, you'll see how they are formed. In each case the verb of the exclamation is followed by **h** plus a nasalized copy of the last vowel of the verb word. We'll represent this ending as ±h**V**, where "V" indicates a nasalized copy of the vowel before the **h**.

Listen as your teacher reads the exclamations above. You'll hear that they have the same kind of rhythm as a question: the last syllable of their verbs (the **h** plus nasal vowel syllable) is not stressed; instead, the stress goes on the heavy syllable preceding that syllable. Thus, the exclamation verbs above have the following stress (double-underlined): **ishtoho!**, **hashtilhaaha!**, **hayooshlihi!** Practice these and other exclamations so that you feel comfortable using them.

Exclamations are only made from verbs ending in vowels. This means you can't make an exclamation from a verb ending in the past endings +**tok** or ±**ttook**, and verbs with other endings (other than the A ending +**li**, which you can see in the third example above), including future ±**a'achi**, may not sound too good in exclamations either. There are also no negative exclamations.

Listen as speakers use exclamations. You'll find that usually the word order they use is the basic subject—object—verb order you learned in unit 5. Occasionally a speaker may change this order, but it's not common, so it's probably best to keep your exclamations in this basic order.

Exercise 18J. Here are some Chickasaw sentences. Make each one into an exclamation, then translate it. (You can use "wow!" in your translation if you like, or just write a "!") 1. Abikaat illi. 2. Pali' kiipisa 3. Chichokma'si. 4. Hattak yammat lhinko. 5. Chomak howasa. 6. Chimamboohaat hashtahli. 7. Chipotaat kaniya. 8. Hilhali.

Terms and Concepts

COMPOUND, COMPOUND ACCENT, Y GRADE, EXCLAMATION.

VOCABULARY

abika' sick person
aboowoshi' bathroom, outhouse
achaknaski to turn on one's side (A)
achaknáyya'ski to lie on one's side (A)
achokmíyyi'lhka to be kneeling (A)
alhchifa to be washed (S)

anchi to cover oneself with (A,Noun)

ani' produce, crop, fruit

ashana to be locked (Noun)

áyya'chi to be covered with (A,Noun)

aahashtahli' window

aahilha' dance hall

aaholloppi' graveyard, cemetery

bo'wa to be hammered (Noun)

chomak tobacco

hashshok-ishtamo' grass cutter, scythe

hashtahli to be bright, light (Noun)

hattak-abi' man killer, murderer

hattak-apa' man-eater, cannibal

hilha' dance; dancer

hilha'chi' top (toy)

holloppi to be buried (S)

howasa to chew (A,Noun)

impa' food

ishbashli' kitchen knife

ishchokoshkomo' toy

ishfama' switch, whip (noun)

ishholbachi' camera

ishliichi' plow (noun)

ishtalhchifa' soap

ishtasha'na' lock

ishtiwa' key

kosoma to stink (S)

kawaski to be hard, solid (Noun)

liichi to plow (A,Noun)

okaabaafa to stick one's finger in (someone's eye) (A,Noun)

oshi' little (used as the second part of a compound)

piha to be swept (Noun)

pofa to smoke (tobacco) (A,Noun)

takafa to be dipped up (Noun)

taloowa' song, hymn, singer

ta'oss-aa-alhto' (small) bank, money box

READING AND SPEAKING

Ponayyo'cha and Linho' Filli'ta'

This true story was told by the late Mina Christie. About one hundred years ago, two sisters were left well-off by their father, so they didn't have to depend on men. The "hack" referred to in the story is a type of carriage. (The translation is provided in Appendix C.)

Ponayyo'cha' Linho' Filli'ta' táwwa'at tánno'wacha issoba ombiniilikat imponnoot tánno'wacha ilaapilla'oot inchokka' aháshwacha—

(. . . hattakat lhiyohlikya sakka' ki'yo. Kanahookya sakka' ki'yo aachikya chaffookano sakka'hi bíyyi'ka mi'hacha aashtokoot okkisa' yamma takchit táyyahcha híkki'yatoko ootayat tahahma, "Kanahoot hachisakka' ki'yo, aachihminattookya, hachisakkili!" aachihma—pílla' nanna ki'yo . . .)

—pitabaanablit itto'lacha tilhaat tamowattook.

Kaniya' ayakmat ofi' kánnohmiho ishtittánno'wahminattook.

Hack aachika albi'hacha tánno'wahminattook.

Issoboot hallalittook.

Kaniya' ootalbinachikmat topa tashkit tahakmat naafkishto' cho'mi fokhattookmat akka' yamma impatalikma ayya'sht nosittookma onnat tahakma aya'chikmat Linho' Filli'ta'akoot—

(. . . holhchifo ishtaalhi'at Filli'ta' attook . . .)

—Linho'akoot issoba shaapolisht itti' chanaa halallichit tahlikma ofi' cho'mat chokkowat tahakma anowa' Ponayyo'cha' chokkowakma ayat tahahminattook inchokka'.

SUPPLEMENTARY VOCABULARY

akka' floor; down
albiha to get inside (dl. subj.) (A,Noun)
halallichi to make (someone) pull (something): to hitch up (a horse) to (a wagon) (A,S,Noun)
impatali to spread (something) out for (someone) on (A,D,Noun,Noun)
imponna to know how; to know how (to do something) well (D) (see note 1 below)
ishtaalhi to be last (A)
ishtittánno'wa to take (dl. subj.) (A,S) (includes preverb **isht±**)
ittola to fall (A / S)
kánnohmi some; to be some (A)
miha, miya to say about oneself (A)
naafkishto' coat
ombiniili to ride (a horse); to sit down on (A,S)
onna to be the next day; to dawn (—)
ootalbinachi to go and stay over in (a place) (A,Noun) (includes preverb **oot±**)
ootaya to go by, to pass by (A) (includes preverb **oot±**)
pitabaanabli to go over (A,S) (includes preverb **pit±**)
shaapolichi to harness (A,S)
tánno'wa, ittánno'wa to walk, pass by, go by, travel around (dl. subj.) (A)
tannohówa, ittannohówa to walk, pass by, go by, travel around (tpl. subj.) (A)
tashki to lie down; to go to bed (A)
táyyahli (Y grade of **tahli**)

NOTES

1. **Imponna** "to know how (to do something); to know how (to do something) well" is used with a preceding verb plus ±**kat**.

2. ±**Hoot** / ±**ho** can be a short form of the "because" ending ±**hootokoot** / ±**hootoko̱**.

3. Mrs. Christie includes several long parenthetical remarks in the middle of her story. Thinking of it this way helps us to understand how she uses the same-subject and diffferent-subject markers.

4. **Chaffookano** contains the ±**hookano** ending. In **Chaffookano sakka'hi bíyyi'ka miha**, this means something like "there was one" ("One said he could catch up with them").

5. ±**Tokoot** and ±**toko̱** are used for background information. You might express this with "having done . . ." in English. Thus, **aachitokoot okkisa' yamma̱ takchit táyyahli** means "Having said it, he tied up that gate". Another translation of these endings is to say someone "was doing" something at the same time as another event, as in **Híkki'yatoko̱ ootayat taha** "He was standing there when they went by".

6. As you'll learn in unit 19, **taha** is used as a triplural subject auxiliary with motion verbs like **aya**. But in the sentence just referred to, only Ponayyo'cha' and Linho' are going by—isn't this dual, not triplural? Probably Mrs. Christie was also thinking of the dogs who always traveled with the sisters, although they probably weren't along on this trip.

7. Sometimes speakers use different endings on n-words from those presented in unit 17. **Kanahoot hachisakka' ki'yo** means "No one ever caught you".

8. **Pitabaanablit itto'lacha tilhaat tamowattook** means "Going over it, they fell and went running on". In other words, the sisters jumped their horses over the gate and rode on.

9. **Naafkishto' cho'mi fokhattookmat akka' yamma̱ impatali** means "They spread out the coats and things they had been wearing for them [the dogs] on that floor".

10. The last sentence of Mrs. Christie's story is surprising, because she uses an object noun after the verb, but there's no object ending on it. This is the kind of thing that a speaker knows when to do—but it's pretty uncommon, and as a learner you shouldn't do it until you've had more practice, since normally speakers regard such sentences as incorrect.

ADVANCED CHICKASAW GRAMMAR 8: MORE TYPES OF COMPOUNDS

Compound Verbs. Most Chickasaw compounds are nouns, but there are some compound verbs that have a noun at the front which is part of the verb word. Many compound verbs are formed from the noun **oka'** "water". Here are some examples:

> **ok-aailli** "to drown" (from **oka'- aa**± **illi**)
> **ok-aa-abi** "to drown (someone)" (from **oka'- aa**± **abi**)
> **ok-aayopi** "to swim" (from **oka'- aa**± **yopi**)

Like **illi**, **ok-aailli** is a one-place (S) verb; **ok-aayopi** is an (A) verb, and **ok-aa-abi** is a two-place (A,S) verb. **Ok-aa-abi** is a word with two hyphens—one to separate the two parts of a compound and one to keep apart two similar vowels (lesson 1). Pronounce each word after your teacher. Each one contains the **aa**± location prefix, as well as **ok-**. **Ok-aailli** might be explained as "to die in water". Can you give an explanation of the meaning of the other two words?

The new verbs work like any other o-verb:

Ishok-aa-abitok.	"You drowned him."
Asok-aailla'chi!	"I'm going to drown!"
Kilok-aayo'pokitok.	"We didn't swim."

As you can see, the **ok**- in these words doesn't work like any other noun, since the verb prefixes come in front of it. It really is just a part of the verb.

Noun-noun compounds. In English we have a lot of compounds made with two simple nouns put together—in other words, noun-noun compounds. Some examples are *apple pie, river rat,* and *ice cream.* (These are usually not written with a hyphen.) In every case the first noun is interpreted as a modifier of the second noun—*apple pie* is a type of pie, not a type of apple (in fact, *pie apple* would probably mean a type of apple grown especially for pies).

Here are some Chickasaw noun-noun compounds:

foshi' hishi' ishholissochi'	"quill pen (bird feather pen)"
holisso amposhi'	"paper plate"
shokhoshi' ta'oss-aa-alhto'	"piggy bank"

As you can see, these compounds follow the same order as English noun-noun compounds, with the modifying noun before the main noun.

Some Chickasaw noun-noun compounds aren't as easy to figure out, though:

hattak shawi'	"monkey"

Is a monkey a person-raccoon or a raccoon-person?

And some Chickasaw compounds may occur in either order, as in these examples:

sinti' bala' / bala' sinti'	"snake beans (type of beans)"
tiyak itti' / itti' tiyak	"pine tree"

Listen for compounds, and you will hear many more.

Unit 19

"And" More about Plurals

You learned in unit 2 that Chickasaw does not indicate plural the way English does. This lesson presents a number of new ways to express plural concepts in Chickasaw.

Lesson 19.1 introduces a number of verbs that change to show the difference between singular and plural subjects, as well as some verbs referring to breaking that show other concepts. Lesson 19.2 presents the use of auxiliary **taha** to show triplural subjects of motion verbs. Lesson 19.3 concerns **alhiha'** "a bunch". The use of **táwwa'a** to express "and" is explained in lesson 19.4. Lesson 19.5 shows how n-words plus ±**hookya** are used to say "every". The Advanced Chickasaw Grammar lesson presents more Chickasaw grade forms.

| **Lesson 19.1:**
Verbs That Indicate Plural | Most Chickasaw verbs do not change to indicate singular versus plural subjects. The difference between singular "I" and plural "we" or singular "you" and plural "you guys" is shown with different A, S, D, or N subject |

markers. A speaker normally interprets a Chickasaw sentence without one of these subject markers on the verb as having a singular subject. The first two sentences below could refer to a plural "they" subject, but speakers would normally guess that they have a singular subject:

Taloowa.	"She is singing." (could mean "They are singing.")
Ihooat taloowa.	"The woman is singing. (could mean "The women are singing.")

As you learned in lesson 2.7, however, when the verb includes the prefix **hoo±**, the subject must be "they" or a plural noun:

Hootaloowa.	"They are singing."
Ihooat hootaloowa.	"The women are singing."

Some verbs have different forms for different numbers of subjects. In unit 10 you learned that positional verbs have separate forms for singular, dual, and triplural subjects (for example, singular **bínni'li** "to be sitting", dual **chí'ya**, triplural **binoht máa**), and you've learned a few other verbs that make a distinction between singular and plural subjects (such as singular **ishto** "to be big", plural **hichito**, or singular **iskanno'si** "to be little", plural **sawa'si**). A number of verbs that refer to motion also have different forms for singular and plural subjects. You already know the first pair below:

> **malili** "to run (sg. subj.)"—**tilhaa** "to run (pl. subj.)"
> **biniili** "to sit down, get into a sitting position (sg. subj.)"
>   —**binohli** "to sit down, get into a sitting position (pl. subj.)"
> **kaniya** "to go away (sg. subj.)"
>   —**tamowa** "to go away (pl. subj.)"
> **wakaa** "to fly; to blow away (sg. subj.)"
>   —**wakowa** "to fly; to blow away (pl. subj.)"

Biniili and **binohli**, incidentally, refer to the action of sitting down, not the state of being seated—for that, use the positional verbs **bínni'li**, **chí'ya**, or **binoht máa**. The comparable word for getting into a standing position is **hika**. **Tashki** means "to lie down" or "to get into a lying position". Neither of these two verbs has separate singular and plural subject forms.

Some verbs tell you about plural objects instead of plural subjects. Here are some examples:

> **halhabli** "to kick (sg. obj.); to kick once"
> **halhlhi** "to kick (pl. obj.); to kick more than once"
>
> **sholaffi** "to scratch (sg. obj.); to scratch once"
> **sholli** "to scratch (pl. obj.); to scratch more than once"

When you hear these verbs used, you'll know whether the object is singular or plural or, sometimes, how many times the action was done.

It can get more complicated. Consider the Chickasaw words for "break". First, here are a V1-V2 pair that involve a singular item breaking:

> **kobafa** "to break, to be broken (of a sg. long subj.)"
> **kobaffi** "to break (a sg. long obj.)"

The item in question must be long (or longish), such as a stick, a pencil, or a bone. Here are some examples:

> Sayyaat kobafa.   "My leg is broken."
> Ishholissochi' kobaffilitok.   "I broke the pencil."

Both verbs are used about a single item breaking, but with **kobafa** that item is the subject of the verb, while with **kobaffi** the item is the object.

When you're talking about more than one long item breaking, you use the following verbs:

> **kobahli** "to break (of pl. long subj.)"
> **kobbi** "to break (pl. long obj.)"

To talk about an item breaking that is not long, but rather round or compact, such as a dish, Chickasaw speakers use a different set of verbs:

kowa "to break (of a sg. compact subj.)"
kooli "to break (a sg. compact obj.)"
kookowa "to break (of pl. compact subj.)"
kookoli "to break (pl. compact obj.)"

Here are some examples:

Amposhi' kiikootok.	"We broke the dish."
Amposhi' kiikookolitok.	"We broke the dishes."

So, with a "break" verb you have to think about the shape of the item that is breaking, as well as how many of these items you're talking about. The number of people doing the breaking doesn't change which verb you choose.

Exercise 19A. i. Look at each of the following Chickasaw sentences. If the sentence has a plural subject, change the sentence so that the subject will be interpreted as singular. If the sentence has a singular subject, change the sentence so that the subject is plural. Translate the new sentences.
   Example. Foshi'at wakaa.
   Answer. (The example has a singular subject.)
   Foshi'at wakowa. "The birds are flying."
   1. Kiitilhaa. 2. Minkaat kaniya. 3. Chipotaat hootashki. 4. Holissaat wakowa. 5. Hashbinohtaam?
6. Akankoshi'at iskanno'si. 7. Issobaat hattak halhlhi. 8. Kowi'at chipota sholaffitok.

   ii. Translate each of the following "break" sentences into Chickasaw. 1. The dish broke. 2. I broke the dish. 3. The stick broke. 4. The monkey broke the sticks. (**hattak shawi'** = "monkey") 5. You broke the dishes. 6. The sticks broke. 7. The dishes broke. 8. We broke the stick.

Lesson 19.2:
Triplural Subject Motion Verbs with the Auxiliary **Taha**

A PLURAL subject or object includes more than one participant. In Chickasaw, as you know, we sometimes distinguish between two categories of plural, DUAL (meaning exacty two participants) and TRIPLURAL (meaning more than two participants).

number of participants	1	2	3, 4, 5, . . .
category	singular	dual	triplural
		plural	

Some Chickasaw verbs that refer to motion can be used with the auxiliary **taha** when they have a triplural subject (in other words, when the subject includes more than two participants). Here are some examples:

Kilonat tahatok.	"We got there."
Hashiyyat tahataam?	"Did you guys go?"
Mintit ta'hacha impatok.	"They came and ate."

In sentences like these, the motion verb is a t-verb preceding the auxiliary in the following pattern:

SUBJECT + VERB + **t**   **taha**
PREFIX
TRIPLURAL SUBJECT PATTERN FOR MOTION VERBS WITH **TAHA**

With a "they" subject, as in the last example above, there is no subject prefix, of course.

This pattern probably reminds you of the stative completion pattern you learned about in lesson 14.5. It's very similar. The difference is that this pattern is used to indicate a triplural subject, not completion, and the verbs involved are not stative. The completion pattern can be used with singular subjects, but the triplural subject pattern, obviously, cannot.

When a motion verb like **ona** "to get there", **aya** "to go", and **minti** "to come" is used without the **taha** auxiliary, then, speakers will normally interpret its subject as either singular or dual (referring to exactly two participants), not triplural. If there is a plural subject prefix on the verb, like the A prefix **hash±** "you guys" in the next two examples, then the sentence without **taha** has a dual subject and the sentence with **taha** has a triplural subject.

Hashiyyataam?	"Did you guys [dual] go?"
Hashiyyat tahataam?	"Did you guys [triplural] go?"

If there is no subject prefix on the verb, then the sentence without **taha** could have either a singular or a dual subject:

Hattakat anchokka' onatok.	"The man came to my house.", "The men [dual] came to my house."
Hattakat anchokka' onat tahatok.	"The men [triplural] came to my house."

In addition to **ona** "get there", **aya** "go", and **minti** "come", several other verbs can be used in the same pattern to indicate a triplural subject. These include **ala** "get here", **kochcha** "go out", **akkowa** "go down", and **chokkowa** "go in". You might hear speakers use other motion verbs this way, too.

> *Exercise. 19B.* Translate the following Chickasaw sentences. If two translations are possible, give both. 1. Ihooat akkowa. 2. Kilakkowa'chi. 3. Hashla. 4. Alikchaat chokkowattook. 5. Kiliyyat taha'ni. 6. Chokfaat kochchat ikta'ho. 7. Alikchaat chokkowat tahattook. 8. Hashlat taha. 9. Kilakkowat taha'chi. 10. Ihooat akkowat taha. 11. Chokfaat ikkochcho. 12. Kiliyya'ni.

The same **taha** triplural subject pattern is used with motion verbs that have separate forms for singular and plural subjects, like those you saw in lesson 19.1. Here's how this works. With a singular subject, you use the singular form of the verb. With a dual subject, you use the plural subject form of the verb in the normal way. With a triplural subject, you use the t-verb of the plural subject form with **taha**.

Ishkaniya.	"You go away."
Hashtamowa.	"You guys [dual] go away."
Hashtamowat taha.	"You guys [triplural] go away."

Issoba-at malili.	"The horse is running."
Issoba-at tilhaa.	"The horses [dual] are running."
Issoba-at tilhaat taha.	"The horses [triplural] are running."
Biniilili.	"I sit down."
Kiibinohli.	"We [dual] sit down."
Kiibinoht taha.	"We [triplural] sit down."

(The **li** at the end of **binohli** drops before the **+t** ending, because of **li** deletion.) With these verbs, then, you always know whether the subject is singular, dual, or triplural.

Exercise 19C. Translate the following Chickasaw sentences into English. 1. The chiefs [dual] went away. 2. The duck is flying. (**fochosh** = "duck") 3. Are you guys [triplural] running? 4. The chiefs [triplural] went away. 5. Did you guys [dual] come? 6. Are you [singular] running? 7. The ducks [triplural] are flying. 8. The chief went away. 9. We [dual] got here yesterday. 10. They [dual] went to town. 11. We [triplural] got here yesterday. 12. Are you guys [dual] running? 13. The ducks [dual] are flying. 14. Did you guys [triplural] come? 15. They [triplural] went to town.

Occasionally, speakers will use motion verbs without the **taha** auxiliary even when they have a triplural subject. Listen to what the speakers you know say.

Lesson 19.3:
Alhiha' "A Bunch"

As you learned in lesson 2, Chickasaw nouns don't have plural forms comparable to English plurals, like *women* or *dogs*. So sentences like the following can be interpreted as referring to one dog or many, one woman or several:

Ihooat hilha.	"The woman is dancing.", "The women are dancing."
Ofi' píslitok.	"I saw the dog.", "I saw the dogs."

Earlier in this unit you learned some ways to show that a noun refers to more than one individual by changing the verb. Another way to show that you mean more than one dog or woman is to include a number, as in

Ihoo toklohoot hilha.	"Two women are dancing."
Ofi' toklohǫ píslitok.	"I saw two dogs."

(As you know, modifying verbs, like numbers, are generally used with the focus subject and object markers **±hoot** and **±ho**.) Often, though, you might not know the number, or you might just want to indicate a larger quantity. In that case you might use the verb **lawa** "to be a lot, to be many" and say, for example,

Ihoo lawahoot hilha.	"A lot of women are dancing."
Ofi' lawahǫ píslitok.	"I saw a lot of dogs."

There's another way to refer to a "bunch" of people, however, as in

---

Ihoo-alhihaat hilha.   "A bunch of women are dancing."
Chipot-alhiha' píslitok.   "I saw a bunch of kids."

These sentences use the word **alhiha'** "bunch". This word can be used after any noun referring to a person, forming a compound noun (like those you learned about in lesson 18.2)—**ihoo-alhiha'** means "bunch of women" and **chipot-alhiha'** means "bunch of kids". (Notice that the last vowel or vowel-plus-' of the noun may drop when **alhiha'** is used.) An **alhiha'** noun usually refers to a group of at least three people and may suggest a group that would be somewhat smaller than the group you'd refer to with **lawa** (thus, it's not necessarily "many").

Alhiha' is usually not used by itself, which is why it makes sense to think of it as part of a compound. Although speakers generally translate **alhiha'** as "bunch", it doesn't necessarily refer to people all acting or being together in a group. Thus, the sentence

Chipot-alhihaat aaittanaa ayatok.   "A bunch of children went to church."

can be used even if the children went separately to different churches from different homes.

Alhiha' is only used about groups of people. You can't use this word to talk about a "bunch" of animals or nonliving things.

Exercise. 19D. One noun is italicized in each of the following sentences. Change that noun to specify a "bunch" of people by forming an **alhiha'** compound and then translate the sentence, as in the example.
Example. Chikashshaat ayat tahatok.
Answer. Chikashsh-alhihaat ayat tahatok. "A bunch of Chickasaws went."
1. *Chipotaat* amposhi' kookolitok. 2. *Chalakki'* ishpístaam? 3. *Alikchi'* inchokkaat lowat tahatok. (**lowa** = "to burn, to burn down") 4. *Ihoo* yammat binoht tahatok. 5. Minkaat *hattak* yappa imanompoli banna. 6. *Nannimaabachi'at* chipota tiika ibaatoksala'chi. 7. Nannimaabachi'at *chipota tiika* ibaatoksala'chi. 8. Ankaat *Chahta' iminko'* ishtanompolitok.

You might also hear the word **bíyyi'ka** used to express the same idea as **alhiha'** in sentences like

Ihoo bíyyi'kahoot hilha.   "Several women are dancing."
Chipota bíyyi'kaho píslitok.   "I saw several children."

Bíyyi'ka does not form a compound with the preceding noun as **alhiha'** does. Instead, it works like an ordinary stative verb and is used with the focus endings, subject ±**hoot** and object ±**ho**. We've used the word "several" to translate it in these examples, but the meaning is actually somewhere between "several" and "many".

Lesson 19.4:
"And"

You've probably been wondering how to say things like "the man and the woman" in Chickasaw. It's more complicated than it is in English. The "and" in phrases like this is expressed with a form of **táwwa'a**, as in

Ihoo hattak táwwa'at hilha.   "The woman and the man are dancing."
Hattak ihoo táwwa'a píslitok.   "I saw the man and the woman."

How does this work? You put the two nouns you want to link with "and" (let's call them NOUN-1 and NOUN-2) before either the subject "and" word **táwwa'at** or the object "and" word **táwwa'a**. Here are the patterns:

NOUN-1	NOUN-2	**táwwa'at**	
ihoo	hattak	táwwa'at . . .	(subject "and" pattern with nouns)

NOUN-1	NOUN-2	**táwwa'a**	
ihoo	hattak	táwwa'a . . .	(object "and" pattern with nouns)

You might also hear another version of the subject "and" pattern, with subject marking on the first noun, as in

Ihooat hattak táwwa'at hilha.   "The woman and the man are dancing."

This is the pattern:

NOUN-1±at	NOUN-2	**táwwa'at**	
ihoo	hattak	táwwa'at . . .	(subject "and" pattern 2)

More commonly, though, there is no ending on either noun.

Exercise 19E. The Chickasaw sentences with **+cha** below are somewhat awkward and repetitious. Combine them into a sentence with just one verb by using **táwwa'a**, as in the examples. Read your new sentences out loud and then translate them.

Example. Ihooat aachompa' a'yacha hattakat aachompa' aya. (This means "The woman goes to town and the man goes to town.")

Answer. Ihoo hattak táwwa'at aachompa' aya. "The woman and the man are going to town."

Example. Sashkaat minko' afa'macha alikchi' afama'chi. (This means "My mother will meet the chief and she will meet the doctor.")

Answer. Sashkaat minko' alikchi' táwwa'a afama'chi. "My mother will meet the chief and the doctor."

1. Johnat amposhi' ko'cha Maryat amposhi' kootok. 2. Chipota naknaat kowi' lhiyohcha ofi' lhiyohtok. 3. Nannimaabachi'at hattak ilbashshahaho api'lacha alikchaat hattak ilbashshaho apilatok. 4. Chinkaat ta'osso honko'pacha chinkaat holisso honkopataam? 5. Ihooat paska ikbicha chipota tiikat paska ikba'chi. 6. Ihooat paska ikbicha paska champoli' ikba'chi.

Have you figured out what **táwwa'a** is? It's actually a verb meaning something "to be together with" (or, sometimes, "to live in sin with, to shack up with"). So the "and" patterns above are actually like short dependent sentences—just as the subject and object normally come before the verb in an ordinary sentence, NOUN-1 and NOUN-2 come before **táwwa'a** in these "and" phrases, and NOUN-1 can have subject marking (even though this is not required). Unlike nouns in an ordinary sentence, however, the nouns that come before **táwwa'a** cannot be moved around—they can't come following **táwwa'a**, and they never use object endings.

It's easier to believe that **táwwa'a** is a verb when you consider sentences with "and" in which the two linked items are not both nouns. Here are some examples:

Ihoo kiitáwwa'at kiihilha.	"The woman and I are dancing."
Ihoo hashtáwwa'at hashhilha.	"The woman and you are dancing."
Ihoo táwwa'at hilha.	"The woman and he are dancing."
Ishno' kiitáwwa'at kiihilha.	"You and I are dancing."

(A special word for "you", **ishno'**, is used here. This word is much less common than the contrastive pronouns **ishnaakoot** and **ishnaako** that you learned in unit 9, but it's the best one to use in this type of sentence.)

When one or both of the items you want to link are singular pronouns ("I", "you", "he", "she"), you need to be aware of some combinations. To start with, let's consider combinations of subjects. If you do something alone, you use "I" for the subject. But if you do something with another person, that other person plus you yourself makes a "we" subject. Whenever you combine two people, you make a plural pronoun. Here is a table of other equivalences of the same type. Make sure you understand all of them:

NOUN + "I" = "we"
NOUN + "you" = "you guys"
NOUN + "he" = "they"
NOUN + "she" = "they"
"you" and "I" = "we"
SUBJECT PRONOUN COMBINATIONS

As the examples above show, to express these combinations in Chickasaw, you use special forms of subject "and" **táwwa'at** with an A prefix indicating the combination:

NOUN "and I"= NOUN **kiitáwwa'at** ("we" subject)
NOUN "and you" = NOUN **hashtáwwa'at** ("you guys" subject)
NOUN "and he" = NOUN **táwwa'at** ("they subject)
NOUN "and she" = NOUN **táwwa'at** ("they subject)
"you and I" = **ishno' kiitáwwa'at** ("we" subject)
SUBJECT PRONOUN COMBINATIONS WITH **táwwa'at**

When using these combination phrases, you also have to pay attention to two additional things. First, since the whole phrase is a subject, you have to use the subject form **táwwa'at**, as in the chart. Second, the main verb of the sentence must have the right form to match the combination given in parentheses in the table—thus, with a phrase that expresses a "you guys" subject, the main verb must have a "you guys" subject prefix, and so on. Consider the following example:

Alikchi' hashtáwwa'at hassapísa. "The doctor and you see me."

Here, the combination is NOUN "and you": **alikchi'** is the noun, and the combination is expressed with a sequence of the noun plus the "you guys" A prefix on the verb. The whole phrase is a "you guys" subject, so there must also be a "you guys" S prefix on the following main verb.

There's one more point about the translations. In English it might sound better to say *You and the doctor . . .* rather than *The doctor and you . . .*—sometimes we feel that it is more polite to begin with one word rather than the other. In Chickasaw, however, the word order in **táwwa'a** phrases is quite fixed. You should only use the patterns given in the tables above. With these combinations, you never use ±**at** on the first noun.

> *Exercise 19F*. Each of the following Chickasaw sentences has a singular subject. Add the additional subject given in parentheses after the sentence, using the appropriate form of **táwwa'a** and changing the verb as necessary, as in the example. Translate the new sentences.
>   *Example*. Hilhali. (alikchi')
>   *Answer*. Alikchi' kiitáwwa'at kiihilha. "The doctor and I are dancing."
>   1. Amposhi' kookolitok. (hattak) 2. Ishtashka'chi? (chipota tiik) 3. Sachaaha. (ishno')
>   4. Holisso habinalitok. (minko') 5. Sapontaki' ishbi. (Chahta') 6. Chipota nakna ta'osso imalitok oblaashaash. (ishno')

With object pronouns ("me", "you", "him", "her"), there are also special combinations, as with subjects. If someone does something just to you, you use "me" for the object. But if someone does something to you plus another person, then the object is "us". Below are the rest of the combinations (which are really sort of like little addition problems). Make sure you understand each of them.

NOUN + "me" = "us"
NOUN + "you" = "you guys"
NOUN + "him" = "them"
NOUN + "her" = "them"
"you" and "me" = "us"
OBJECT PRONOUN COMBINATIONS

There's nothing to memorize here—you already use these same ideas all the time when you speak English.
    Now, here are some Chickasaw sentences using object combinations with pronouns:

Hattak kiitáwwa'a ishpopístaam?   "Did you see the man and me?"
Hattak hashtáwwa'a hachipíslitok.   "I saw you and the man."
Hattak táwwa'a ishpístaam?   "Did you see the man and her?"
Ishno' kiitáwwa'a popístok.   "He saw you and me."

As these examples show, to express these combinations in Chickasaw, you use special forms of **táwwa'a** with an A prefix indicating the combination:

NOUN "and me" = NOUN **kiitáwwa'a** ("us" object)
NOUN "and you" = NOUN **hashtáwwa'a** ("you guys" object)
NOUN "and him" = NOUN **táwwa'a** ("them" object)
NOUN "and her" = NOUN **táwwa'a** ("them" object)
"you and me" = **ishno' kiitáwwa'a** ("us" object)
OBJECT PRONOUN COMBINATIONS WITH **táwwa'a**

These are the same phrases that you used for combined subjects. The only thing that is different about them is the English translation. When using these combination phrases, once again, you need to pay attention to two things. First, since you want to use these phrases as objects, you have to use the object "and" form **táwwa'a**. Second, the main verb of the sentence must have the right form to match the combination given in parentheses in the table—thus, with a phrase that expresses an "us" object, the main verb must have an "us" object prefix, and so on.

Consider the following example:

Alikchi' hashtáwwa'a hachipísli.   "I see the doctor and you."

Here, the combination is NOUN "and you": **alikchi'** is the noun. The combination is expressed with a sequence of the noun plus the "you guys" A prefix on the verb. The whole phrase is an object, however, so there must be a "you guys" S prefix on the following main verb. With these combinations, you never use ±**at** on the first noun.

Exercise 19G. Translate the following sentences into Chickasaw using an appropriate form of **táwwa'a**. 1. That man gave his car to you and me. 2. Do you see the woman and me? 3. The book and the money burned up. 4. I know the doctor and you. 5. Where did you and the chief go? 6. The old man tied up the horse and the dog. 7. Don't tie up the boy and me! 8. The chief and I sat down. 9. The chief and you are sitting down (in a sitting position). 10. The teacher sent the doctor to you and me.

All the "and" examples presented so far use combinations of two participants. When your combination includes three or more participants, the "and" word is not **táwwa'a**, but rather **cho'mi**. Basically, things work just the same as with **táwwa'a**—you use the subject form **cho'maat** and the object form **cho'ma**. Here are some examples with three nouns:

Ihooat hattak chipota cho'maat hilha.   "The woman, the man, and the child are dancing."

Ihoo hattak chipota cho'ma píslitok.   "I saw the woman, the man, and the child."

These examples show that you use the same pattern—three nouns before **cho'mi** (in the appropriate subject or object form) plus the verb. As before, when the **cho'mi** phrase is a subject, you can choose to use ±**at** on the first of the three nouns, or not.

Once again, pronouns will combine in the same ways as you saw earlier: any combination of three participants will add up to "they", "we", or "you guys" (as a subject) or "them, us", or "you guys" (as an object).

Here are the subject combinations, used with the subject form **cho'maat**:

NOUN NOUN "and I"= NOUN NOUN **kiicho'maat** ("we" subject)
NOUN "and we"= NOUN **kiicho'maat** ("we" subject)
NOUN NOUN "and you" = NOUN NOUN **hashcho'maat** ("you guys" subject)
NOUN "and you guys" = NOUN **hashcho'maat** ("you guys" subject)

NOUN NOUN "and he" = NOUN NOUN **cho'maat** ("they" subject)
NOUN NOUN "and she" = NOUN NOUN **cho'maat** ("they" subject)
NOUN "and they" = NOUN **cho'maat** ("they" subject)

"you and we" = **ishno' kiicho'maat** ("we" subject)
"you guys and I" = **hachishno' kiicho'maat** ("we" subject)
"you guys and we" = **hachishno' kiicho'maat** ("we" subject)
SUBJECT PRONOUN COMBINATIONS WITH **cho'maat**

The chart shows, for example, that you can use one noun plus "we" or two nouns plus "I" and still come up with three participants. Another new special pronoun, **hachishno'** "you guys", is used in the last two combinations. In these combinations you never use ±**at** on the nouns.

Now, here are the object combinations, used with the object form **cho'm<u>a</u>**:

NOUN NOUN "and me" = NOUN NOUN **kiicho'm<u>a</u>** ("us" object)
NOUN "and us" = NOUN **kiicho'm<u>a</u>** ("us" object)

NOUN NOUN "and you" = NOUN NOUN **hashcho'm<u>a</u>** ("you guys" object)
NOUN "and you guys" = NOUN **hashcho'm<u>a</u>** ("you guys" object)

NOUN NOUN "and him" = NOUN NOUN **cho'm<u>a</u>** ("them" object)
NOUN NOUN "and her" = NOUN NOUN **cho'm<u>a</u>** ("them" object)
NOUN "and them" = NOUN **cho'm<u>a</u>** ("them" object)

"you and we" = **ishno' kiicho'm<u>a</u>** ("us" object)
"you guys and me" = **hachishno' kiicho'm<u>a</u>** ("us" object)
"you guys and us" = **hachishno' kiicho'm<u>a</u>** ("us" object)
OBJECT PRONOUN COMBINATIONS WITH **cho'm<u>a</u>**

Pretty complicated, but these combinations all work regularly once you understand the patterns. In these object combinations, once again, you never use ±**at** on the nouns.

Here are some examples:

Ishno' kiicho'maat kiihilhatok.	"You and we danced."
Hachishno' kiicho'maat kiihilhatok.	"You guys and I danced.",
	"You guys and we danced."
Ihooat ishno' kiicho'm<u>a</u> pop<u>í</u>stok.	"The woman saw you and us."
Ihooat hachishno' kiicho'm<u>a</u> pop<u>í</u>stok.	"The woman saw you guys and me.",
	"The woman saw you guys and us."
Ihooat hattak hashcho'm<u>a</u> hachip<u>í</u>stok.	"The woman saw the man and you guys."

Here too, you need to keep in mind whether the **cho'mi** phrase is a subject or an object in the main sentence (use **cho'maat** if it's a subject, **cho'm<u>a</u>** if it's an object), and you need to remember that the verb of the main sentence will have a subject or object marker that indicates the combination. In the first example above, the combination is "we", so there is an A "we" prefix on the verb. In the third example, the combination is "us", so there is a an S "us" prefix on the verb.

Obviously, the prefix you choose will depend on the verb, as these examples show:

Ishno' kiicho'maat potikahbi.	"You and we are tired."
Ihooat hachishno' kiicho'm<u>a</u> p<u>o</u>hollo.	"The woman loves you and us."

The verb in the first example, **tikahbi**, takes an S subject, so the subject prefix is the S prefix for "we", **po+**. The verb in the second example, **ihollo**, takes a D object.

> *Exercise 19H*. Translate these Chickasaw sentences into English. 1. Hattak hashcho'maat hashittibi. 2. Alikchi' minko' nannimaabachi' cho'ma imanompoli sabanna. 3. Ishno' kiicho'maat minko' kilimanola'chi. 4. Chipota naknaat hachishno' kiicho'ma pobo'tok. 5. Chipota tiik chipota nakni' kiicho'maat kiichokoshkomo. 6. Chahta' Chalakki' Mashkooki' cho'maat ittibitok. 7. Chahta' Chalakki' hashcho'maat hashittibitok. 8. Hattak yammat ishno' kiicho'ma popist ala'chi.

Remember that **táwwa'a** and **cho'mi** are only used for linking nouns or groups of nouns with "and". To link sentences, you should use switch-reference.

Lesson 19.5:
"Every" and (Not) "Any" Words

Here are some Chickasaw sentences that express "every":

Ihooat kanahookya ihollo.	"The woman loves everyone."
Imofi'at nannahookya apa.	"Their dog eats everything."
Chipota kaniya'ookya ishtaya.	"She takes the child everywhere."

These sentences use the following new words:

kanahookya "everyone" (or "everybody")
kaniya'ookya "everywhere" (or "everyplace")
nannahookya "everything"

These words are formed from the n-words **kana**, **kaniya'**, and **nanna**, which you learned in lesson 17.7, with the ending ±**hookya** (±**ookya** after a consonant). Sometimes these words have a shorter pronunciation: you may also hear speakers say **kanookya** or **nannookya**. The **kya** in this ending may sound to you like <kiya> or <giya>; the ending is usually pronounced with an echo vowel between the **k** and the **y**.

The new "every" words don't change, whether they are subjects or objects:

Kanahookya ihoo yamma ihollo.	"Everyone loves that woman."
Nannahookya champoli.	"Everything tastes good."
Ankaat kanahookya anhínchi.	"My father likes everyone."
Nannahookya apa'chi.	"She'll eat everything."

Words with the ±**ookya** ending don't have separate subject and object endings. (**Anhínchi** is another way to say "like".)

> *Exercise. 19I*. Translate the following sentences into Chickasaw. 1. I want to buy everything! 2. Everyone likes the girl and the boy. 3. Everything burned up. 4. Everybody kissed my mother. 5. We stole money from everyone. 6. Everyone found a book. 7. Everyone's books got lost. 8. Can you write everything? 9. Everyone tells lies. (**loshka** = "to lie, to tell lies") 10. He tells lies about everything. (**oloshka** = "to lie about, tell lies about")

The same new words are used to express "not . . . any" in negative sentences, as in the following examples:

Kanahookya akpi'sokitok. "I didn't see anyone."
Chipotaat nannookya ikpo. "The child isn't eating anything."
Kaniya'ookya ikiyyoka'chi. "They aren't going to go anywhere."

These words can also be translated with English "no" words:

Kanahookya akpi'sokitok. "I saw no one."
Chipotaat nannookya ikpo. "The child is eating nothing."
Kaniya'ookya ikiyyoka'chi. "They are going to go nowhere."

"No" words are also used as subjects.

Nannookya iksakisi'lokitok. "Nothing bit me."
Kanahookya hattak shawi' ikisso. "No one is hitting the monkey.", "Nobody is hitting the monkey."
Kanahookya asayoppánchi. "Nobody likes me."

Once again, these verbs don't need subject markers. They don't change, even if they are used as subjects. Thus, **nannookya** can be either a subject, as in **Nannookya iksakisi'lokitok**, or an object, as in **Chipotaat nannookya ikpo**.

Look at the examples again, and you'll see an important difference between these English sentences with "no" words and the Chickasaw sentences. The Chickasaw sentences have negative verbs, and the English sentences don't. In Chickasaw, if you use an n-word to express a negative idea with ±**hookya**, you have to use a negative verb with it, as in the examples.

Exercise 19J. Each of the following Chickasaw sentences uses a "some" form made with an n-word like those in lesson 17.7. Make each sentence negative—you'll have to change both the form of the n-word in each sentence and the form of the verb. Then translate both sentences. The example shows how this works.

 Example. Kanahmat sassotok. "Someone hit me."
 Answer. Kanahookya iksassokitok. "No one hit me."
 1. Kanahm<u>a</u> ta'osso imalitok. 2. Kaniya'm<u>a</u> aya pobanna. 3. Nannimaabachi'at kanahm<u>a</u> imanompolitok. 4. Nannahmat lowatok. 5. Nannahm<u>a</u> kiikootok. 6. Nannahmat kobafatok. 7. Nannahm<u>a</u> kiikobaffitok. 8. Nannahmat kowatok. 9. Kaniya'm<u>a</u> ta'osso fokhilitok. 10. Kanahmat impa.

VOCABULARY

akkowa to go down (A)
alhiha' bunch (of people) (used as the second element of a compound)
anhínchi to like (A,S)
biniili to sit down, get into a sitting position (sg. subj.) (A)
binohli to sit down, get into a sitting position (pl. subj.) (A)

bíyyi'ka several, many (used as a stative verb following a noun)

cho'mi to be (more than two) together with (A)

chokkowa to go in (A)

fochosh duck

hachishno' you guys

halhabli to kick (sg. obj.); to kick once

halhlhi to kick (pl. obj.); to kick more than once

hattak shawi' monkey

ishno' you

kanahookya everyone, everybody

kaniya to go away (sg. subj.)

kaniya'ookya everywhere, everyplace

kobafa to break, to be broken (sg. long subj.) (Noun)

kobaffi to break (sg. long obj.) (A,Noun)

kobahli to break (pl. long subj.) (Noun)

kobbi to break (pl. long obj.) (A,Noun)

kowa to break (sg. compact subj.) (Noun)

kookoli to break (pl. compact obj.) (A,Noun)

kookowa to break (pl. compact subj.) (Noun)

kooli to break (sg. compact obj.) (A,Noun)

loshka to lie, tell lies (A)

lowa to burn, to burn down) (Noun)

minti to come (A)

nannahookya, nannookya everything

oloshka to lie about, tell lies about (A,S)

sholaffi to scratch (sg. obj.); to scratch once

sholli to scratch (pl. obj.); to scratch more than once

taha triplural subj. auxiliary for motion verbs

tashki to lie down, get into a lying position (A)

tamowa to go away (pl. subj.) (A)

táwwa'a to be together with (used to say "and") (A); to live in sin with, shack up with (A,S)

tilhaa to run (pl. subj.) (A)

wakaa to fly (sg. subj.) (A); to blow away (sg. subj.) (Noun)

wakowa to fly; to blow away (pl. subj.) (A)

READING AND SPEAKING

Rabbit and Buzzard

This traditional Chickasaw story was told by the late Lizzie Frazier. (The translation is provided in Appendix C.)

Chiiki pilla' áyya'shakaash Chokfiat okpolottook miya. Kolo'fana impállammicha tí'wana kaniya'mat imalikcha'nika hoyokat áyya'sha. Iksho. Hayoocha' ki'yo.

Yahna Shiikiako hayoochihma Shiiki yammat imalikcha'hi bíyyi'ka mi'yana Shiiki yamma ishtonat tahahma Shiiki yammat aachihmat, "Abooha aashachakla mómaka pilla' okshittat hashtáyyahna kanookya ikpi'sokmako imalikchila'ni," a'shna, abooha cho'ma aashachakla yamma okshittat táyyahna abooha okshitat tahna Shiiki yammat Chokfi yamma imalikchi.

Yahmina Chokfi yammat yaa.

Yahna kochcha' yamma áyya'shtokoot, "Katihmihaat yaat ánchi?" aachihma, "Imalikchilikat: aaoppolo yammako ittish imaabilikako hottopakakoot ánchi," aashtoko anowa' mahma Chokfi yammat sámma'tatok mi'yana kochcha' áyya'sha yammat, "Katihmihaat sámma'ta?" aachihma, "Ittish yamma imaaiksaashlikako hottopa yammat pitnampílana nosi," aachittook miya.

Haatoko alhchímbat tahahma Shiikiaashoot, "Anowa' amalhtaha. Okkisa' tiwwi!" a'shna okkisa' tiwwihma Shiikiaashoot pilla' wakaat kochchana abooha imonat tahahma *Rabbit*mat foni' íllaat áyya'shattook miya—apat tahna.

SUPPLEMENTARY VOCABULARY

aashachakla to be cracked in (a place) (Noun, Noun) (see note 2 below)
alhchímbat tahahma after awhile
ánchi (N grade of **aachi**)
chiiki pilla' áyya'shakaash once upon a time
foni' bone (SP)
hottopa 1. to hurt, to get hurt, to be in pain (S) (works like <ittopa> with S prefixes—sattopa, chittopa, pottopa); 2. hurt, pain (noun)
ílla just, only
imalikchi to doctor (A,D)
imalhtaha to be ready (D)
imaabi to put (medicine) on (someone) (A,D,Noun)
imaaiksaachi to use (medicine) on (A,D,Noun)
impállammi to have a serious condition (D)
katihmihaat why
kolofa to be cut with a knife; to be wounded (S)
mahma then (dffierent subject)
miya, miha they say
oppolo, okpolo to be broken, messed up, ruined; to have something wrong (S)
pitnampíla to get better (Noun) (includes preverb **pit±**)
sámma'ta to get quiet (A)
shachakla to be cracked (Noun)
yahna and then (different subject)

NOTES

1. Mrs. Frazier's use of switch-reference marking in this story is quite complex. For example, at the beginning she says **kolo'fana impállammicha tí'wana**—each of these dependent sentences has Rabbit as the subject, but they have a different relationship. **Impállammicha** is dependent on the following sentence, **tí'wana**, but both **kolo'fana** and **tí'wana** are dependent on the following sentence, **kaniya'mat imalikcha'nika**. Sometimes it's interesting to look at each sentence and try to figure out all these relationships.

2. **Abooha aashachakla mómaka** means "all the places where it is cracked in the house".

3. **Hottopakoot ánchi** means "so he's saying that it hurts".

4. **Rabbitmat foni' illaat áyya'shattook** means "Only Rabbit's bones were there". This sentence uses a possessor/subject sentence pattern (as in the Advanced Chickasaw Grammar section of unit 14) with two subject-marked nouns.

5. In this last example, **ílla** is used the same way the noun ending **±akilloot** (unit 20) is used.

ADVANCED CHICKASAW GRAMMAR 9: MORE CHICKASAW GRADES

You've already learned about three Chickasaw grades: the HN grade in unit 8, the N grade in unit 15, and the Y grade in unit 18. You've probably guessed by now that there are still other Chickasaw grade forms, which are used to change the meanings of verbs in order to express shades of meaning that would be indicated in English with separate words. Some of these meanings are so subtle that speakers have trouble explaining them!

The G grade. The most common additional grade is the G GRADE. Here are some examples of G grades of stative verbs:

basic verb	G grade
litiha "to be dirty"	lítti'ha
hopoba "to be hungry"	hóppo'ba
okchamali "to be blue, to be green"	okchámma'li
chofata "to be clean"	chóffa'ta
kosoma "to stink"	kósso'ma
tikahbi "to be tired"	tíkka'hbi
kawaski "to be hard"	káwwa'ski
masofa "to be bald"	másso'fa

Speakers vary in their opinion as to the best translation for G grades, which are most common for stative verbs. Sometimes they have a meaning similar to that of Y grades—they include the meaning "very" or "really". On the other hand, sometimes the meaning of a G grade is more like "kind of". G grades are also sometimes used to express the meaning "finally get". Thus, **lítti'ha** might mean "finally get dirty", as well as "be really dirty" or "be kind of dirty", depending on the speaker and the occasion. See what your teacher thinks.

G grades of active verbs most commonly also express a "finally" meaning:

ipita "to feed"	íppi'ta "finally feed"
apila "to help"	áppi'la "finally help"

These "finally" expressions are most commonly used with the word **kaniht** "finally".

The changing vowel for a G grade is the third vowel from the end of the word, rather than the second, as with other grade forms. Thus, for **litiha** it's the first **i**, and for **chofata** it's the **o**. The changing vowel is accented, and the consonant after it is doubled. (The name "G grade" comes from the word GEMINATE, a technical name for a doubled consonant.) Then, if the vowel after the doubled consonant is followed by **f, h, l, lh, m, n, s, sh, w,** or **y** or by any single consonant, add **'** (a glottal stop) between the vowel and that following consonant. If it is followed by anything else, don't add the **'**.

In verbs with only two syllables, the first vowel is the changing vowel and the added **'** goes after that vowel:

losa "to be black"	ló'sa "be kind of black", "finally get black"
ani "to pour"	á'ni "finally pour"

If you have a verb with only two syllables and two consonants before the last vowel, where the first conso-
nant is **'**, **b**, **ch**, **k**, **p**, or **t**, you won't add the **'**. Instead, the changing vowel gets a CIRCUMFLEX accent, as in
the following examples:

haklo "to hear, listen to"   hâklo "finally hear, finally listen to"
kochcha "to go out"   kôchcha "finally go out"
lakna "to be brown, yellow"   lâkna "be kind of brown, kind of
                                           yellow", "finally get brown, yellow"

sakki "to catch up with"   sâkki "finally catch up with"

Vowels with a circumflex accent start out with a strong rise in pitch and then have a fall in pitch; you may
hear what almost sounds like a **'** sound after these vowels.

Many positional verbs are G grades, with stative meanings and "surprising subjects". Here's one example
you already know:

biniili "to sit down"   bínni'li "to be sitting down (sg. subj.)"

Although the active basic verb **biniili** can have either a singular or a plural subject, the subject of **bínni'li**
must be singular.

Other Chickasaw grade forms. There are other Chickasaw grade forms that haven't been described in this
book. The best way to learn more of these special verbs is to listen for them when you hear Chickasaw speakers
talking and to try to incorporate them into your own spoken and written Chickasaw.

Unit 20

Saying a Lot

This lesson explains how to tell who said something and presents several ways to make noun phrases in sentences more precise, as well as how to express wishes and wonderings.

Lesson 20.1 shows how to use the frame pattern to report a quotation. Lesson 20.2 presents the "too" ending ±**akookya**. Several types of modifying phrases are explained in lesson 20.3. Lesson 20.4 concerns three different sentence patterns that say "only". Lessons 20.5 and 20.6 are about wishing and wondering.

Here are some new vocabulary words that will be used in this lesson.

áa to go along, to be going along (A)
fala crow
fóyyokha to wear (A,Noun)
hottopa to hurt; to get hurt; to be in pain (S) (works like <ittopa> after an S prefix—thus, sattopa is "I hurt", chittopa is "you hurt", etc.)
hottopachi to hurt, injure (someone or something) (A,S) (works like <ittopachi> with an S prefix—thus, sattopachi is "he hurt me", etc.)
imanoli to tell (someone) (A,D)
ittola to fall (A / S)
imalhata to be scared of (A,D)
imiha to bawl out (A,D)
masofa to be bald (S)
naafka lombo' shirt
nannokchamali' vegetable
niha to be greasy (S)
toba to become (A,Noun)
woochi to bark (A)
yaalhipa hat

As the entries above show, **hottopa** and the causative verb **hottopachi** are slightly irregular. When an S prefix is used with these verbs, they work as if they were <ittopa> and <ittopachi>. (Some speakers use the word **ittopa** instead of **hottopa**, though we will not use that word in this book. You should follow your teacher's usage, of course.)

Lesson 20.1:
Who Said It?

Reporting exact quotations with the frame pattern. In English there are several ways to give an exact quote of what someone has said. You can put the quote first—as in *"Let's go," said John.*—or you can put the quote at the end—as in *John said, "Let's go."* With a longer quotation, you can even put the *John said* part in the middle.

There are several ways to do this in Chickasaw, too. Here are two examples of the most natural and complete way:

Paulineat aachikat, "Kiliyya'," aashtok.   "Pauline said, 'Let's go.'"
Aashlikat, "Ihoo yammat haksi,"   "I said, 'That woman is crazy.'"
    aashlitok.

How does this work? First there's a dependent sentence ending in ±**kat** that introduces the speaker and gives the "say" verb. Then comes the quotation. Finally, you end with the main "say" verb. In this way the two "say" verbs, "say"-1 and "say"-2, make a FRAME for the quote in the following pattern:

SUBJECT "say"-1 ±**kat,**   "QUOTATION"   "say"-2
DEPENDENT SENTENCE   MAIN SENTENCE

frame pattern for reporting speech

The two "say" verbs in the frame pattern have the same subject (**Pauline** and "I", in the examples above), which explains why the same-subject ending ±**kat** is used on the first "say"-1 verb. (No matter what the subject of the quotation sentence is, you always use a same-subject ending on the first "say" verb.) Both "say" verbs need to be in the right form for their subject. Thus, in the second example above, both "say" verbs include the A ending for "I", +**li**. Any ending that applies to the whole pattern, such as the past +**tok** endings in these examples, goes at the end of the "say"-2 verb. Of course, the subject (if you use one) must have ±**at** or another subject ending.

You might think of the frame pattern as corresponding to an English sentence like *John said, "Let's go," he said.* But unlike the English sentence, which probably sounds repetitious or awkward to you, the Chickasaw pattern is completely natural.

Here are some more examples:

Sashkaat amaachikat, "Nittak   "My mother said, 'I'm going
    yamma ayala'chi," aashtok.   tomorrow,' to me."
Hattak yamma ishimaachikat,   "Did you say, 'You eat too much,'
    "Ishimpa' salami," ishaashtaam?   to that man?"

These examples show that the first "say"-1 verb can also include things that the second "say"-2 verb doesn't. In the examples above, the "say"-1 verbs include a dative prefix and a dative object. The "say"-2 verbs repeat the same subject marking as the "say"-1 verbs. (**Nittak yamma** is another way to say "tomorrow".)

Suppose you want to use a different verb with your quotation, such as **asilhha** "to ask" or **imanoli** "to tell (someone)". Any other verb that makes sense with a quotation can be used for the "say"-1 in the frame, but the "say"-2 should always be **aachi.**

Chimasilhhakat, "Ishiyya'chitaa?" aashtok.   "He asked you, 'Are you going to go?'"

Hattakat aman<u>o</u>likat, "Chikashsha   "The man told me, 'I'm a Chickasaw.'"
     saya," aashtok.

Exercise 20A. i. Translate the following sentences into Chickasaw using the frame pattern. 1. Mary said, "I want to go to town." 2. The teacher said, "Copy this word." 3. "I can help you," I said to the man. 4. Are you going to say, "I love you"?

     ii. Now, translate the following sentences into English. 1. Chimasilhhalikat, "Sabaa-aya chibannataa?" aashlitok. 2. Chikashsha <u>I</u>minkaat chimaachikat, "Yamma ishholissochinna!" aashtaam? 3. Sashkaat aman<u>o</u>likat, "Kan<u>i</u>hka chichokma'si!" aashtok. 4. Ishaachikat, "Chink<u>a</u>na' saya ki'yo," ishaashtok. 5. Alikchaat ihoo imasilhhakat, "Chittopataam?" aashtok. 6. Hattak yammat aachikat, "Iksamas<u>o</u>'fo," aashtok. 7. Chipota naknaat aachikat, "Minko' toba sabanna," aashtok. 8. Ofi' kilimaachikat, "Ki'yo!" kilaashtok.

Variations on the frame pattern. Speakers occasionally use variants of the frame pattern. Sometimes they omit the "say"-2 verb:

Johnat aachikat, "Kiliyya'!"   "John said, 'Let's go!'"
Aashlikat, "Ihoo yammat haksi."   "I said, 'That woman is crazy.'"

This pattern seems to follow a word order like that of English, but it's very unusual for Chickasaw. Do you see why? These sentences use a switch-reference marker (same-subject ±**kat**) that doesn't refer to anything!

     Another variant you may hear omits the "say"-1 verb, as in

Johnat, "Kiliyya!" aashtok.   "John said, 'Let's go!'"
"Ihoo yammat haksi," aashlitok.   "I said, 'That woman is crazy.'"

If you think of the quotation as a kind of object of the "say"-2 verb, this pattern may also seem sensible to you, since it has the object right before the "say" verb. But Chickasaw speakers often feel that this pattern, like the first variant, is incomplete—the complete frame pattern is usually better.

     You may hear both these variants, but it's probably best to learn to use the frame pattern when you're reporting the exact words someone used.

Other ways to tell what someone said. Verbs that tell who said something can also be used with the switch-reference markers ±**kat** and ±**ka** as follows:

Hattak yammat aya'chikat aashtok.   "That man said that he was going."
Ankaat aman<u>o</u>likat,   "My father told me that I was
     ayala'chitok<u>a</u> aashtok.   supposed to go."

Sentences like these don't report exact quotations. Just as in the English translations, they give the general idea that was conveyed by the speaker, but they don't give the speaker's exact words. (Think about it. If the man said he was going, he probably said, **Ayala'chi** "I am going"—but there is no "I" in the sentence above. If my father told me I was supposed to go, he might have said **Ishiyya'chitok** "You were supposed to go"— but there is no "you" in the sentence above.)

     This kind of report uses a dependent sentence with the same-subject switch-reference marker ±**kat** or the different-subject switch-reference marker ±**ka**, depending on whether the subject of what was said is the same as the speaker.

The second sentence above shows that you can still use a frame pattern for this type of report, though it's not necessary to have two "say" verbs.

Exercise 20B. Take the sentences in exercise 20A, part ii, and turn them into nonexact reports. Here's an example:

Example. Chimasilhhalikat, "Sabaa-aya chibannataa?" aashlitok.

Answer. (i) Sabaa-aya chibannak̲a chimasilhhalitok.

(ii) Chimasilhhalikat sabaa-aya chibannak̲a aashlitok.

(ii) uses a frame pattern, and (i) doesn't. Try to use both types in your answers.

1. Chikashsha I̲minkaat chimaachikat, "Yammaak̲o ishholissochinna!" aashtaam? 2. Sashkaat amano̲likat, "Kani̲hk̲a chichokma'si!" aashtok. 3. Ishaachikat, "Chink̲ana' saya ki'yo," ishaashtok. 4. Alikchaat ihoo imasilhhakat, "Chittopataam?" aashtok. 5. Hattak yammat aachikat, "Iksamaso̲'fo," aashtok.

Lesson 20.2:
±Akookya "Too"

Here are some examples of Chickasaw "too":

Coke ishkolikmat
  Pepsiakookya ishkola'chi.

"When I drink a Coke
  I'm going to drink a Pepsi too."

Ofi'at sakisilitok.
  Kowi'akookya sakisilitok.

"The dog bit me.
  The cat bit me too."

Tii' ayoppáshli.
  Kaafi'akookya ayoppáshli.

"I like tea.
  I like coffee too."

Alikchi' yappat chokma—
  chaffo' yammakookya chokma.

"This doctor is good—
  that other one is too."

(**Chaffo'**, a word related to **chaffa** "one", means "other one".) When we use *too* in English, we usually mean that some subject performed an action or was in some state in addition to another one, or that some action was performed on some object in addition to some other one. The Chickasaw ending **±akookya** works the same way. You can use this ending on either a subject or an object to indicate that it works the same way relative to some verb as one you've mentioned earlier. The **kya** in this ending may sound to you like <kiya> or <giya>; the ending is usually pronounced with an echo vowel.

Do you see what's unusual about these sentences? When **±akookya** goes on a subject, there is no subject ending, and when it goes on an object, there is no object ending. You never use a subject or object ending on a "too" noun marked with **±akookya**. (You may hear some speakers use **±akya** instead of **±akookya**.)

Exercise 20C. Translate the following sentences into Chickasaw. 1. I went to the store. I went to school, too. 2. The chief knows me; the teacher knows me, too. 3. This book is good. Is that book good, too? 4. Mary's hand hurts. Her foot hurts, too. 5. I saw a monkey, and I saw a flying squirrel, too. 6. You gave me a dress and you gave me a hat, too. 7. The doctor is bald and the teacher is bald, too. 8. The meat is greasy and the dishes are greasy, too.

---

*Endings containing **ookya**.* The "every"/"any"/"no" words in lesson 19.5 use the same ending, ±**hookya**, that you saw meaning "but" on verbs in lesson 16.4. The same ending seems to be part of the "too" ending ±**akookya** introduced in this lesson. Is there some connection between "every"/"any"/"no" and "but" or between these ideas and "too"? (There's no right answer to this one.) However, even if we can't see the connection, all these endings do have one thing in common—they aren't used with other endings, even if we would expect them to be. Thus, both the "every"/"any"/"no" ending ±**hookya** and the "too" ending ±**akookya** don't change, whether they go on subjects or objects (unlike every other type of Chickasaw noun ending). Similarly, the "but" ending ±**hookya** doesn't indicate switch-reference (unlike almost every other type of Chickasaw dependent verb ending).

Lesson 20.3:
Modifying Phrases

In unit 12 you learned how to use modifying verbs in sentences like

Ihoo chokma'sihoot hilha.	"The pretty woman is dancing."
Amposhi' litihaho achifalitok.	"I washed the dirty dish."
Folosh tochchí'naho honkopatok.	"He stole three spoons."

The modifying verb pattern is most commonly used with stative verbs. As you know, it is most common for modifying verbs to have focus subject or object endings, ±**hoot** or ±**ho**.

With active verbs it is most common to use a MODIFYING PHRASE pattern. A modifying phrase is a type of dependent sentence that speakers use to help listeners identify who or what is being referred to. Two English examples of modifying phrases are in *the man who stole the spoon* and *the woman who is dancing*. Such expresssions help tell which man or which woman is being referred to.

Here are two examples of Chickasaw sentences containing modifying phrases:

Hattak folosh honkopakaashoot kaniyatok.	"The man who stole the spoon went away."
Ihoo hilhakaashoot amaompolitok.	"The woman who is dancing spoke to me."

These sentences contain the modifying phrases **hattak folosh honkopakaash** "the man who stole the spoon" and **ihoo hilhakaash** "the woman who is dancing". The verbs of these modifying phrases end in the modifying phrase ending ±**kaash**. Since these phrases are subjects in their main sentences, the modifying phrases have the focus subject ending ±**oot** (in the form used following a consonant, since this ending comes after ±**kaash**). The noun that these modifying phrases identify is called the MODIFIED NOUN: **hattak** is the modified noun in **hattak folosh honkopakaash** and **ihoo** is the modified noun in **ihoo hilhakaash.**

Now, here are sentences containing the same modifying phrases used as objects, followed by the focus object ending ±**o** (the form of the focus object used following a consonant, since they are used after ±**kaash**):

Hattak folosh honkopakaasho ishitháfinataa?	"Do you know the man who stole the spoon?"
Ihoo hilhakaasho ayoppáshli.	"I like the woman who is dancing."

Hattak folosh honkopakaash "the man who stole the spoon" and **ihoo hilhakaash** "the woman who is dancing" are SUBJECT MODIFYING PHRASES, because in each case the modified noun is the subject of the verb marked with ±**kaash**; for example, **hattak** is the subject of "stole the spoon" and **ihoo** is the subject of "is dancing".

Here's the pattern for forming the modifying phrase.

SUBJECT (MODIFIED NOUN)	(REST OF SENTENCE)	VERB±**kaash**
hattak	*folosh*	*honkopa±kaash*
ihoo		*hilha±kaash*

SUBJECT MODIFYING PHRASE PATTERN

If the modifying phrase contains a one-place verb like **hilha**, there probably won't be anything between the subject and the verb, as in **ihoo hilhakaash**. If the modifying phrase contains a two-place verb like **honkopa** or other material, there may be additional words (like the object **folosh**, in the first example) between the subject and the verb. Finally, ±**oot** or ±**o** is added, depending on whether the modifying phrase is a subject or an object in the main sentence.

Do you see what's important (and very unusual) about the subject modfying phrase pattern? The subject in this phrase pattern does not have a subject ending. Usually, there is no object ending on the object, either.

A subject modifying phrase works like a noun phrase within the main sentence. As you saw in the examples above, a subject modifying phrase can be used either as a subject or as an object in the main sentence. Subject modifying phrases are used both as subjects and as objects, as in the examples above, with either focus subject ±**oot** or focus object ±**o** added after ±**kaash**, depending on whether the subject modifying phrase is used as a subject or an object in the main sentence.

Here is another pair of examples, with the same subject modifying phrase used as both a main sentence subject and a main sentence object:

Ihoo alikchi' apilakaashoot ittolatok.	"The woman that helped the doctor fell down."
Chipotaat ihoo alikchi' apilakaasho iholissochitok.	"The child wrote to the woman that helped the doctor."

In both cases the subject modifying phrase is **ihoo alikchi' apilakaash. Ihoo** is the modified noun, the subject of the verb **apila**. The modifying phrase ending is ±**kaash**: in the first sentence, the modifying phrase subject ending ±**kaashoot** (±**kaash** plus ±**oot**) is used; the second sentence uses the modifying phrase object ending ±**kaasho** (±**kaash** plus ±**o**).

Exercise 20D. Translate each of the sentences below into English. They contain subject modifying phrases, which are italicized to help you identify them. 1. *Alikchi' asapilakaashoot* kanihka chaaha. 2. *Chipota tiik cholhkan imalhatakaasho* ishithánataa? 3. Ihooat *hattak naafka lombo' fóyyokhakaasho* ittihaalalla'chi. 4. *Hattak áakaashoot* anki'. 5. Nannimaabachi'at *chipota nakni' mahli haklokaasho* imanompolitok. 6. *Ofi' woochikaashoot* fala lhiyohli banna.

OBJECT MODIFYING PHRASES, in which the modified noun is an object within the modifying phrase, correspond to English phrases like *the spoon that the man stole* and *the doctor that the woman helped*. In these phrases the modified noun is an object, not a subject, of the verb of the modifying phrase. Don't be confused by the English translations. In English modifying phrases you'll hear *who*, sometimes *that*, sometimes even *whom*. These differences aren't relevant for what we say in Chickasaw.

Here are some Chickasaw examples:

Hattakat folosh honkopakaashoot litiha.	"The spoon that the man stole is dirty.
Ihooat alikchi' apilakaashoot illitok.	"The doctor that the woman helped died."

The modifying phrases here are **hattakat folosh honkopakaash** "the spoon that the man stole" and **ihooat alikchi' apilakaash** "the doctor that the woman helped". The modified nouns are **folosh** and **alikchi'**. Both phrases are used as subjects of the main sentences, so they have the modifying phrase subject ending ±**kaashoot**.

Here's the pattern used for the new modifying phrases:

SUBJECT±**at**	OBJECT (modified noun)	(REST OF SENTENCE)	VERB±**kaash**
hattakat	*folosh*		*honkopa±kaash*
ihoo	*at*	*alikchi'*	*apila±kaash*

OBJECT MODIFYING PHRASE PATTERN

One unusual thing here is that the modified noun doesn't come at the beginning of the phrase (as in *the spoon that the man stole*). Instead, it comes in the normal Chickasaw object position, right before the verb. Another unexpected difference from the subject modifying phrase pattern is that the subjects of these modifying phrases have subject endings.

As you can see, this pattern looks very similar to the subject modifying phrase pattern, except that the subject is marked with ±**at**. Once again, the object usually doesn't have an object ending.

As before, however, ±**oot** or ±**o** is added at the end of the modifying phrase, depending on whether the modifying phrase is a subject or an object in the main sentence. Here are some examples with the same phrases as above used as main sentence objects:

Chipotaat hattakat folosh honkopakaash<u>o</u> ishtimpatok.	"The child ate with the spoon the man stole."
Ishkaat ihooat alikchi' apilakaash<u>o</u> afamatok.	"My mother met the doctor that the woman helped."

Since the modifying phrases are objects in the main sentence here, their verbs have the modifying phrase object ending ±**kaasho.**

The subject in the modifying phrase doesn't have to be a noun. Here are some additional examples:

Chipotaat folosh ishhonkopakaash<u>o</u> ishtimpatok.	"The child ate with the spoon you stole."
Ishkaat alikchi' apilalikaash<u>o</u> afamatok.	"My mother met the doctor that I helped."

In these cases there is no subject word, but you can tell who the subject is from the marker on the verb.

> *Exercise 20E.* Below are sets of two Chickasaw sentences that each include the same noun. Form an object modifying phrase from the second sentence to modify the noun repeated in the first sentence, as in the example. Translate the sentences you make up.
>
>   *Example.* Fala-at amilhlhali. Chipotaat fala pístok.
>
>   *Answer.* Chipotaat fala písakaashoot amilhlhali. "The crow that the child saw scares me."
>
>   Remember, the subject or object marking on the modified noun in the first (main) sentence will tell you whether to use **±oot** or **±o** on **±kaash**. In the example above, for example, we use **±kaashoot**, because **fala** is a subject in the main sentence.
>
>   1. Hattakat áa. Ihooat hattak ittihaalalli banna. 2. Ihooat nannimaabachi' toba banna. Ihoo ayoppáshli. 3. Minkaat alikchi' imihatok. Alikchi' ishapilatok. 4. Paska champoli' kiipatok. Sashkaat paska champoli' ikbitok. 5. Issoba-at malit kaniyatok. Hattak sipoknihoot issoba honkopatok. 6. Shalaklak ishhoyotaa? Hattak yammat shalaklak nalhlhitok.

You've now seen two different types of modifying phrases—subject modifying phrases and object modifying phrases, depending on the role of the modified noun within the modifying phrase—each used in two ways (as subjects and objects of their main sentences). The table below summarizes the differences among these four modifying phrase patterns.

	modifying phrase used as main sentence subject	*modifying phrase used as main sentence object*
subject modifying phrase: modified noun is a subject within the phrase	*no subject ending on subject; verb ends in **±kaashoot*** EXAMPLE: Hattak folosh honkopakaashoot kaniyatok. "The man who stole the spoon went away."	*no subject ending on subject; verb ends in **±kaasho*** EXAMPLE: Hattak folosh honkopakaasho ishithánataa? "Do you know the man who stole the spoon?"
object modifying phrase: modified noun is an object within the phrase	*subject ending on subject; verb ends in **±kaashoot*** EXAMPLE: Hattakat folosh honkopakaashoot litiha. "The spoon that the man stole is dirty."	*subject ending on subject; verb ends in **±kaasho*** EXAMPLE: Chipotaat hattakat folosh honkopakaasho ishtimpatok. "The child ate with the spoon the man stole."

In forming the modifying phrase, then, you first need to think about whether the modified noun is the subject or object within the phrase. If the modified noun is the subject, then it won't have a subject ending; if the modified noun is not the subject, the subject of the modifying phrase will have a subject ending. Next, you need to think about whether the modified noun is the subject or object of the main sentence. This determines whether you use **±kaashoot** (for subjects) or **±kaasho** (for objects) on the verb of the modified phrase. This seems like a lot to keep track of, but the more you practice using modifying phrases, the easier it will become for you to do it. Chickasaw speakers put together sentences containing modifying phrases automatically (as you do in English), without thinking about these questions at all.

In conversation, speakers often leave the subject and object focus endings off of modifying phrases whose verbs end in ±**kaash**, saying things like

Hattak folosh honkopakaash kaniyatok.	"The man who stole the spoon went away."
Hattakat folosh honkopakaash litihatok.	"The spoon that the man stole is dirty."
Hattak folosh honkopakaash ishithánataa?	"Do you know the man who stole the spoon?"
Chipotaat hattakat folosh honkopakaash ishtimpatok.	"The child ate with the spoon the man stole."

As you can see, you can still tell the difference between subject modifying phrases and object modifying phrases (the object modifying phrases have ±**at** on their subject noun), but there's nothing about the ending of the phrase itself that tells you if it is a subject or an object.

In the examples above, it's always possible to tell whether the modifying phrase is a subject or object in the main sentence. If the main sentence is a one-place verb like **kaniya** or **litiha**, you know that the modifying phrase must be a subject. If the main sentence already has a subject, like **chipotaat** in the fourth sentence or "you" in the third one, you know that the modifying phrase must be an object.

If the main sentence is a two-place verb that already has an object, as in the following example, then (once again) you know that the modifying phrase must be a subject:

Hattak folosh honkopakaash minka ikayoppa'cho.	"The man who stole the spoon doesn't like the chief."
Hattakat folosh honkopakaash sayya onittolatok.	"The spoon that the man stole dropped on my foot."

Exercise 20F. Translate the following sentences into Chickasaw, following the patterns in this lesson and using either ±**kaashoot** (for modifying phrases used as subjects) or ±**kaasho** (for modifying phrases used as objects) on the verb of the modifying phrase. Then, for each new sentence, form a second sentence with the same meaning by dropping the ±**oot** and ±**o** endings. Read all your new sentences out loud.

1. I don't like the man who hurt the dog. 2. The man who hurt the dog doesn't like me. 3. The dog that the man hurt is barking. 4. My brother wants to buy the dog that the man hurt. 5. My brother wants to buy the dog that was barking. 6. Did the dog that was barking scared you? 7. The chief bawled out the woman we talked to. 8. The woman we talked to ran away. 9. Do you know the woman that talked to us? 10. The woman that talked to us does not eat vegetables.

As you listen to Chickasaw conversation, you'll hear many other types of subject and object modifying phrases. Occasionally, things can be more confusing—but listeners can usually tell what another speaker means without any trouble by the context in which the modifying phrase is used.

Lesson 20.4:
Saying "Only"

Here are some Chickasaw "only" sentences:

Maryakilloot sapístok.	"Only Mary saw me."
Maryakillo píslitok.	"I saw only Mary."
Hattakakilloot folosh honkopatok.	"Only the man stole a spoon."
Hattakat foloshakillo honkopatok.	"The man stole only a spoon."

These sentences use a new set of endings: subject ±**akilloot** and object ±**akillo**. These endings tell you that the marked subject or object is the only subject or object that the sentence is true of. "Only" is modifying either the subject or object noun in these sentences.

These new endings work like all the other subject and object endings that you've learned. If you want to say "only" with a noun, you need one of these endings at the end of the noun phrase.

Sometimes in English we put *only* in a different position in the sentence. So you may well feel that *The man only stole a spoon* sounds better than *The man stole only a spoon*. If the sentence means that all the man stole was a spoon, then you can assume that "only" is modifying "spoon", so you should put the object "only" ending ±**akillo** on the object noun. In this book we'll put "only" next to the object in the translations, just to make things a little clearer.

As with some other endings, you use a different form of the "only" endings after a vowel-loss noun. The subject vowel-loss "only" ending is ±**aakilloot**; the object vowel-loss "only" ending is ±**aakillo**. Here are some examples:

Chokfaakilloot illitok.	"Only the rabbit died."
Chokfaakillo abitok.	"He killed only the rabbit."

The final vowel (or vowel plus ') of a vowel-loss noun like **chokfi** (see unit 5) is replaced by these vowel-loss endings.

You can also use the "only" endings with pronouns, as follows:

anaakilloot "only I"	anaakillo "only me"
ishnaakilloot "only you (subj.)"	ishnaakillo "only you (obj.)"
poshnaakilloot "only we"	poshnaakillo "only us"
haposhnaakilloot "only we (special)"	haposhnaakillo "only us (special)"
hachishnaakilloot "only you (pl. subj.)"	hachishnaakillo "only you (pl. obj.)"

These words are used like the contrastive pronouns you learned in unit 9, in sentences like

Anaakillo sapístok.	"He saw only me."
Poshnaakilloot kiliyyatok.	"Only we went."

As you would expect, even when you use these "only" pronouns, you still need to have the corresponding subject or object markers on the verb, as in the examples.

Exercise 20G. i. Add "only" to the italicized noun or noun phrase in each of the following Chickasaw sentences, as in the example. Translate the new sentences.

Example. Anchipotaat *nannokchamali'* apa.

Answer. Anchipotaat nannokchamali'akillo̲ apa. "My child eats only vegetables."

1. *Minkaat* alikchi' i̲mihatok. 2. Minkaat *alikchi'* i̲mihatok. 3. *Ankaat* maso̲fa. 4. *Naafka lombo'* fóyyokhali. 5. *Ihoo hilhakaashoot* sapi̲stok.

ii. Use an "only" pronoun to add the meaning in parentheses to each of the following Chickasaw sentences, as in the example. Translate the new sentences.

Example. Hattakat hachibo'li banna. ("only you guys")

Answer. Hattakat hachishnaakillo̲ hachibo'li banna.

"The man wants to hit only you guys."

1. Ihoo hilhakaasho̲ kiipi̲stok. ("only we") 2. Chahta' ihooat paska champoli' amatok. ("only me") 3. Yaalhipa chompalitok. ("only I") 4. Ofi'at woochika̲ hashhánglotok. ("only you guys") 5. Nannimaabachi' ishithánataa? ("only you")

"Only" can also modify a verb, with two different meanings. Think about the English sentence *He only eats vegetables* or *She's only going to dance.* These sentences can have two meanings. One is that you're saying that the action happens instead of some other action (*He only eats vegetables, he doesn't grow them; She's only going to dance, not sing*). Alternatively, they can mean that the action is all that the person does, period (*He only eats vegetables, he doesn't do anything else; She's only going to dance, that's all she'll ever do*). In Chickasaw these two ideas are expressed differently.

The first meaning, where you contrast the verb with other possible activities, can be expressed with **pilla'**, as in

Asoshi'at pilla' taloowa'chi.	"My son is only going to sing (he won't dance, for instance)."
Ofi'at kowi'a̲ pilla' lhiyohtok.	"The dog only chased the cat (it didn't kill it, for instance)."
Pilla' i̲holissochili.	"I only write to him (I don't call him, for example)."

Sentences with **pilla'** plus a verb usually indicate that you are saying that only the action you're mentioning happens, rather than some other action—my son is only going to sing, he's not going to dance; the dog only chased the cat, it didn't do anything else to it. **Pilla'** is an ADVERB, a special type of verb modifier that usually goes immediately before a Chickasaw verb.

The second meaning is expressed with an auxiliary verb, **ílla**, as shown in the following sentences:

Asoshi'at taloowa ílla'chi.	"My son is only going to sing (that's all he'll do)."
Ofi'at kowi'a̲ lhiyohli íllatok.	"The dog only chased the cat (it didn't do anything else)."
I̲holissochili ílla.	"I only write to him (that's all I do)."

Sentences with **ílla** say that the action is the only thing the subject does at all. As the first example suggests, another way to translate these sentences is with "all [the subject] is going to do is . . ." (or "all [the subject]

does is . . ." or "all [the subject] did was . . ."). **Ílla** goes after the main verb. Subject and object marking go on the main verb, but endings like ±**a'chi** and +**tok** follow **ílla**.

Another English translation for these "only" expressions is "just". All three types of "only" sentence use words or endings containing **ílla**—the noun ending ±**akilloot** / ±**akillo**, the adverb **pilla'**, and the auxiliary **ílla** itself. Some speakers use other forms containing **illa** or **ílla**, which you'll pick up if you listen to more Chickasaw conversation. In English we don't make the same distinctions among all these "only" words that Chickasaw does. It's tricky, but practice will help you feel comfortable with the differences.

> *Exercise 20H.* Translate the following sentences into Chickasaw using **pilla'** or **ílla**. The meanings in parentheses are for clarification only; don't try to include them in your translations. 1. I only want to dance (not sing). 2. I only want to dance (that's all). 3. The woman only cooked the meat (she didn't eat it). 4. The woman only cooks meat (she does nothing more). 5. We only talked to the chief (we didn't yell at him). 6. We only talked to the chief (we didn't do anything else).

Lesson 20.5: Wishing

Anhi "to wish". The word for "to wish" is **anhi**. Here are some examples of how you use this verb:

Chipotaat chokoshkomohookmano anhi.	"The child wishes he could play."
Chipotaat ishkaat ibaachokoshkomohookmano anhi.	"The child wishes his mother would play with him."

Like **banna** "to want" (unit 9), **anhi** does not use switch-reference marking on its dependent verb. Instead, the dependent verb used with **anhi** is marked with the ending ±**hookmano**. You always use ±**hookmano** on the dependent verb, whether the subject of the dependent sentence is the same as the subject of **anhi** (as in the first sentence) or different (as in the second). ±**Hookmano** is often translated into English with "would" or "could", but not always, as you'll see in the examples below.

The dependent verb can have any subject, and it can be positive or negative. Here are three more examples of "wish" sentences using **anhili** "I wish":

Chipotaat chokoshomohookmano anhili.	"I wish the child would play.", "I wish the child was playing."
Ishiyyahookmano anhili.	"I wish you would go.", "I wish you were going."
Akayyohookmano anhilitok.	"I wished I wasn't going."

The wish expressed in a dependent verb with ±**hookmano** is always something that is not currently true but that the subject of **anhi** wishes would happen. As you can see, in English we sometimes express this in different ways. *I wish you would go* is just a simple wish for something that's not currently true. *I wish you were going* and *I wish I wasn't going* suggest that the speaker believes that the opposite is true (you aren't going, I am going) but wishes that it was not.

Dependent verbs with ±**hookmano** never include endings like +**tok** or ±**a'chi**.

"I wish". The last set of examples express "I wish" with **anhili**, but there's another way to say this. You can leave off the **anhili**. The following sentences mean the same as the first two above, with **anhili**:

Chipotaat chokoshomohookmano.	"I wish the child would play.", "I wish the child was playing."
Ishiyyahookmano.	"I wish you would go.", "I wish you were going."

When you put **±hookmano** on a verb and use it by itself, the resulting sentence means "I wish . . .". Obviously, there is no "I" in these last two sentences—the subject of the first one is **chipotaat** "the child", and the subject of the second is "you". The word **anhili** "I wish" is not expressed, but is implied. Chickasaw speakers feel that **Ishiyyahookmano anhili** and **ishiyyahookmano** mean the same thing.

As before, you can't put **±hookmano** on a sentence that contains a past or future ending. Also, a negative verb with **±hookmano** but without **anhili** does not form a complete sentence (so by itself, <akayyohookmano> will sound incomplete).

Exercise. 201. i. Translate the following "wish" sentences into Chickasaw using **anhi**. 1. I wish that man would marry my sister. 2. Do you wish we could go to town? 3. That girl wishes that the teacher would like her. 4. The boy I know wishes he could become a teacher. 5. I wish that the meat wasn't greasy. 6. Do you guys wish that man would go? 7. I wish that bad man was dead. 8. The woman wished that she could find money.

ii. Now, take all the positive "I wish" sentences and shorten them by dropping **anhili** from the end. The new shorter sentences mean the same thing. (Remember, you can't drop the **anhili** if the preceding wish is negative.) Read all your sentences aloud.

One more thing about wishing. You may occasionally hear "wish" sentences like

Chipotaat anokfillikat chokoshkomohookmano anhi.	"The child wishes he could play."
Chipotaat anokfillikat ishkaat ibaachokoshkomohookmano anhi.	"The child wishes his mother would play with him."
Anokfillilikat chipotaat chokoshomohookmano anhili.	"I wish the child would play.", "I wish the child was playing."
Anokfillilikat ishiyyahookmano anhili.	"I wish you would go.", "I wish you were going."
Anokfillilikat akayyohookmano anhilitok.	"I wished I wasn't going."
Ishanokfillikat ishiyyahookmano ishanhitaa?	"Do you wish you weren't going?"

These sentences mean something like "The child thinks about it and wishes he could play", or "Thinking about it, I wish I wasn't going", or "If you think about it, do you wish you weren't going?" But usually the "think" verbs at the beginning of these sentences wouldn't be translated into English.

These sentences use a form of **anokfilli** "to think" in a sentence pattern that may remind you of the frame quotation pattern you learned about in lesson 20.1:

SUBJECT **anokfilli ±kat,**   DEPENDENT SENTENCE **±hookmano**   **anhi**
"THINK" PLUS "WISH" SENTENCE PATTERN FOR WISHING

Both **anokfilli** and **anhi** have the same subject, which explains why the same-subject ending **±kat** is used on **anokfilli**. (No matter what the subject of the dependent **±hookmano** sentence is, you always use a same-subject ending on **anokfilli**.) Both **anokfilli** and **anhi** need to be in the right form for their subject (thus, in the next-to-last example above, both verbs include the A ending for "I", **+li**, while in the last example, both verbs have the A prefix for "you", **ish±**). Any ending that applies to the whole pattern, such as the past **+tok** and question **+taa** endings in these examples, goes at the end of **anhi**.

Lesson 20.6:
Saying "I Wonder If" or "Maybe"

Speakers use the ending **±hchi** (**±chi** after a consonant) to express doubt about a statement. Here are some examples:

Intiikat taloowahchi.	"I wonder if his sister is singing.", "Maybe his sister is singing."
Ayala'chihchi.	"I wonder if I'm going to go.", "Maybe I'm going to go."
Kaar yamma chompatokchi.	"I wonder if he bought the car.", "Maybe he bought the car."
Shookola' ikcho'pokitokchi.	"I wonder if she didn't buy sugar.", "Maybe she didn't buy sugar."

This ending can be used after either a positive or a negative statement, as the examples show. The usual translation is either "I wonder if . . ." or "maybe . . ." (or even "I wonder if maybe . . ."). Sometimes speakers feel that using a **±hchi** sentence is like asking a question, so another translation for **Ayala'chihchi** might be "Will I (maybe) go?"

Listen as your teacher reads the sentences above. As in Chickasaw questions, the final syllable of a **±hchi** verb is not stressed. Instead, the stress goes on the syllable before the ending, so the verbs above are pronounced **taloowahchi, ayala'chihchi, chompatokchi,** and **ikcho'pokitokchi,** with a double underline marking the stressed syllable.

±Hchi only expresses the speaker's doubt, though—you can't use this ending to say "she wonders" or "you wonder". And although we might translate it with "I wonder . . .", the "I" meaning is just the speaker's feeling—the subject of the sentence is still whoever is the subject of the verb; thus, "I" is the subject of **Ayala'chihchi,** but "his sister" is the subject of **intiikat taloowahchi,** and so on. These sentences are somewhat similar to the **±hookmano** "I wish" sentences you saw in lesson 20.4, since they include an "I" idea without expressing this in words. But unlike the **±hookmano** sentences, these **±hchi** sentences are not shorter versions of any longer sentences—there's no way to put the "I wonder" into words here.

Sometimes a **±hchi** sentence means about the same thing as a **±ha'ni** "must" sentence (unit 16). Either of the following sentences could be said by a speaker who unpacks her shopping and can't find a certain item in the bag:

Akcho̱'pokitoka'ni.	"I must not have bought it.",
	"Maybe I didn't buy it."
Akcho̱'pokitokchi.	"I wonder if I didn't buy it.",
	"Maybe I didn't buy it."

Exercise 20J. Read each of the sentences below out loud, taking care to stress the right vowel in the ±**hchi** verbs. Each Chickasaw sentence can have several English translations. Try to think of at least two different translations for each sentence. 1. Kanahmat a̱holisso a̱honkopatokchi. 2. Chi̱hattakat Naahollo I̱yaakni' ayatokchi. 3. Tishohminkaat daala' talhipa chaffaho̱ ishittookchi. (See reading at the end of unit 14.) 4. Chipotaat hattak folosh i̱'shikaasho̱ honkopa'chihchi. 5. Ihooat amaachikat, "Anchipota chiyahchi!" amaashtok. 6. Kanahmat ponta'osso hayooshtokchi. 7. Chihoowa iki̱yimmohchi. 8. Hattak yammat ponka̱na' a'chi'hchi.

Terms and Concepts

FRAME, MODIFYING PHRASE, MODIFIED NOUN, SUBJECT MODIFYING PHRASE, OBJECT MODIFYING PHRASE, ADVERB.

VOCABULARY

anaakillo̱ only me
anaakilloot only I
anhi to wish (A)
áa to go along, to be going along (A)
chaffo' other one
fala crow
fóyyokha to wear (A,Noun) (Y grade of **fokha**)
hachishnaakilloot only you (pl. subj.)
hachishnaakillo̱ only you (pl. obj.)
haposhnaakilloot only we (special)
haposhnaakillo̱ only us (special)
hottopa to hurt; to get hurt; to be in pain (S) (works like <ittopa> after an S prefix—thus, sattopa is "I hurt", chittopa is "you hurt", etc.)
hottopachi to hurt, injure (someone or something) (A,S) (works like <ittopachi> with an S prefix—thus, sattopachi is "he hurt me", etc.)
ílla only (auxiliary—see lesson 20.4)
imano̱li to tell (someone) (A,D)
imasilhha, imasilhlha to ask (someone) (A,D)
i̱malhata to be scared of (A,D)
i̱miha to bawl out (A,D)
ishnaakillo̱ only you (obj.)
ishnaakilloot only you (subj.)
maso̱fa to be bald (S)
naafka lombo' shirt
nannokchamali' vegetable
niha to be greasy (S)

pilla' only (adverb—see lesson 20.4)
poshnaakillo only us
poshnaakilloot only we
toba to become (A,Noun)
woochi to bark (A)
yaalhipa hat

READING AND SPEAKING

The Christmas Story

Mrs. Willmond (assisted by the late Eloise Pickens) retold the Christmas story based on Luke 2: 1, 3–20. The small raised numbers correspond with verses in the original. (A translation of this retelling is provided in Appendix C.)

[1]Yahmihma nittak yamma fokhaka, yaakni' mómakat holisso toba'chika Caesar Augustusakoot naalhpisa' bohólittook. [3]Yahmihma mómat falamat ayat tahattook ilaapo' aaittapiha' ittibaaholissa'chihoot.

[4]Josephat falamat Galilee Nazareth aachikako ayattook. [5]Josephat Marya ittihaalalla'chit ishtayattook chipotaat ikshokíshaka.

[6]Haatoko ootaháshwa tánglahma chipotaat imahántattok. [7]Yahmihmat kaniya' aabohla'nikat ikshohmat issoba aaipita' piini'ako fokhit bohlittook.

[8]Yahmihma chokfalhpooba' apiisachi'-alhihaat oklhilika chokfalhpooba' apiisachikat áyya'shattook.

[9]Haatoko Chihoowaat *angel* oshtinchaffi'shna *angel*at imallattook. Oshoppalalittook. Mómakat imilhlhattook. [10]*Angel*at aachihmat, "Hachimilhlhanna," imahánchittook, "anompa nanna ishtachiyoppa'chiho ishchimallali, hattak mómakat nannishtilayoppa'chiho. [11]Chihoowa Oshi'oot yaakni' yappa atahántatok, hattak móma okchaalíncha'chihoot. [12]Chihoowa Oshi'a hashhayoochikma naalhilafa' aboknóyyo'hahoot issoba aaipita' piini'ako fóyyokhat tí'wa'chi."

[13]*Angel*at a'lacha atpisahma *angel* ílakat aba' aamintikat, lawahoot a'lacha Chihoowa ootibaa-ayoppahánchittook. [14]"Chihoowa nannishtimaaholitto'pa' aba' chaaha' móma immayyakat yaakni' nanna aya chokmakat hattak mómaka imalla."

[15]*Angel*at falamat aba' yaakni' ayat tahattook. Chokfalhpooba' apiisachi'akilloot áyya'shattook. Yahmicha ittimahánchihmat, "Bethlehemako kilooayyacha Chihoowaat nannaho hapomoktanihínchikma iloopisa'shki."

[16]Toshpat ayyacha onahmat Mary Joseph táwwa'a hayoochittook chipotaat issoba aaipita' piini'ako fóyyokhat tí'wana. [17]Ootpisahmat chipota tí'waka kaniya' móma annoyachittook.

[18]Haatoko chokfalhpooba' apiisachi'-alhihaat ootimanolihma kanihmilchi anhit ishtanokfihíllittook.

[19]Maryat nanna anokfillikat imichonkash finha ishtanokfihíllittook.

[20]Nanna háyyaklocha pihístok mómakat anohólihmat holiitoblichit Chihoowa ayoppahánchit falamat ayat tahattook chokfalhpooba' apiisachi'-alhihaat.

SUPPLEMENTARY VOCABULARY

aboknóyyo'ha to be wrapped in (S,Noun)

anhit ishtanokfilli to wonder about (A,S) (inclues preverb **isht±**)

annoyachi to make (something) known (A,Noun)

apiisachi to take care of, watch over (A,S)

atahánta to come and be located in, to come and be born in (A) (includes preverb **at±**)

atpisa to come and see (A,S) (includes preverb **at±**)

aaittapiha' group

chipotaat imánta to have a baby, to give birth (D)

chokfalhpooba' sheep

chokfalhpooba' apiisachi' shepherd

finha just

fokhaka (in **nittak yamma fokhaka**)

háyyaklo hear (A,S) (Y grade of **haklo**)

holisso toba to be recorded on paper, to be enumerated (A)

holiitoblichi to glorify (A,S)

ilaapo' himself, herself, themselves; his own, her own, their own (see note 2 below)

imichonkash heart (DP)

imoktanichi to reveal to (A,D,Noun) (HN grade **imoktanihínchi**)

issoba aaipita' piini' horse trough

ittibaaholisso to be recorded together (A)

kanihmihchi how could it be

kaniya' somewhere

kaniya' móma everywhere

móma to be the whole (A)

nanna what (see note 6 below)

nanna aya peace

nannishtilayoppa to rejoice (Noun) (includes preverbs **nanna** and **isht±**)

nannishtimaaholitto'pa' glory

naalhilafa' rags

nittak yamma tomorrow

nittak yamma fokhaka at about that time

okchaalínchi to save (A,S)

oshtinchaffichi to send (someone or something) to (A,D,Noun) (includes preverb **osht±**)

shoppalali to shine (Noun)

tángla while (auxiliary)

toshpat aya to go fast, go quickly (A)

yahmicha and then (same subject) (see note 1 below)

yahmihma it happened that (different subject) (see note 1 below)

yahmihmat it happened that (same subject) (see note 1 below)

NOTES

1. You've previously seen several paragraph connectors that include switch-reference endings, such as **haatokoot** and **haatoko**. This story adds different-subject **yahmihma** and same-subject **yahmihmat** and **yahmicha**. As you read and hear more Chickasaw stories, you'll get a better understanding of when speakers choose to use these words. (The English translations given here are just approximations.)

2. **Ilaapo'** is an emphatic way to say "self" (listen to how Chickasaw speakers use this word before you try it). Before a possessed noun, it can add the meaning "own", as in **ilaapo' aaittapiha'** "their own group".

3. Usually, **ishtaya** "begin" is preceded by a t-verb formed from a verb plus +t, but **Ittihaalalla'chit ishtayattook** uses a t-verb containing ±a'chi. This means "he was about to marry her".

4. **Chipotaat imánta** means "she has a baby" or "she gives birth". "Mary had a baby" is **Maryat chipotaat imántattook**. This sentence uses the same pattern as the "have" sentences in unit 12, with the subject followed by an object marked with ±at.

5. This story uses a lot of preverbs. New verbs formed with the preverbs **isht±** "with, about" and **oot±** "go to, go and" and new verbs already in the vocabulary are not listed above, but less regular meanings or formations and verbs with the new preverbs **at±** "come and" and **osht±** (similar to **oot±**) are included. Chickasaw speakers use preverbs to help show the relationship of actions in a story or conversation. You can get a feeling for how they work by comparing the verbs **atpisa** and **ootpisa** used here.

6. Verse 14 is difficult: **Chihoowa nannishtimaaholitto'pa' aba' chaaha' móma immayyakat yaakni' nanna aya chokmakat hattak mómaka imalla** "God's glory in the highest heaven and good peace on earth have come to all people".

ADVANCED CHICKASAW GRAMMAR LESSON 10: THINGS YOU CAN LEARN FROM THE CHICKASAW DICTIONARY

In the Beyond the Grammar section of unit 10, you learned the basics of using the Chickasaw dictionary by the authors of this book (*Chickasaw: An Analytical Dictionary*, University of Oklahoma Press, 1994). The dictionary uses exactly the same spelling system you have learned to use in this book, but some of the abbreviations used in it are different from the ones we use here. Instead of A markers, *Chickasaw: An Analytical Dictionary* refers to I markers; S prefixes are called II prefixes; and D prefixes are called III prefixes. Knowing these correspondences should make it easy for you to use the dictionary to look up new words and check the meanings of familiar ones.

The dictionary entries for many verbs contain a good deal of other information, expressed with coded abbreviations. The meanings of several of these abbreviations are presented below, and all of them are explained briefly in the dictionary itself.

[PR] and [CPR] verbs. In *Chickasaaw: An Analytical Dictionary* and other technical writing, possessor/subject sentences are called *possessor raising* sentences. As you learned in unit 14, there are two different possessor/subject patterns, exemplified by sentences like the following:

Ihooat ofi'at imillitok.	"The woman's dog died."
Ihooat imofi'at illitok.	"The woman's dog died."

Different verbs vary in terms of how they work in these types of sentences. Usually, only one-place verbs may be used in possessor/subject sentences. For some verbs, only the first pattern can be used; for others, only the second; for others, both may be used; and for yet others, neither may. But there is usually no difference in meaning between different possessor/subject sentences.

One-place verbs that can be used in the first possessor/subject pattern shown above are marked [+PR] in the dictionary. One-place verbs that can be used in the second pattern are marked [+CPR]. "PR" stands for "possessor raising". "CPR" stands for "color possessor raising". As explained in unit 14, the second pattern is always used with color verbs.

(III;3-at) verbs. As you know, "have" verbs and possessor/subject sentences may have two nouns or noun phrases that have subject endings. For example, in a sentence like

> Ihooat ofi'at iwáyya'a. "The woman has a dog."

both the subject "woman" and the "have" object "dog" have the subject ending ±at, as you learned in unit 12. The same is true of possessor/subject sentences like the examples in the previous section.

Chickasaw has other verbs that work the same way, but that don't include "have" or a possessive idea in their translations. Here's an example:

> Chipotaat holissat imittolatok. "The child dropped the book."

Imittola "to drop" is a verb whose subject looks like a normal subject but whose object works like a "have" object, since it, too, must be followed by the subject ending ±at. This verb includes the dative prefix **im±** (added onto the verb **ittola** "fall") and takes a D subject, so you will also hear sentences like

> Holissaat amittolatok. "I dropped the book."

Verbs ike **imittola** have the following type of entry in the dictionary:

> **imittola** to drop (something) (III;3-at)

The "III" in the parentheses means that the verb takes a D subject. "3-at" is an abbreviation meaning that the object of this verb can only be a noun and that this object noun has to have a subject ending. In the vocabulary at the end of this book, "have" verbs and other verbs like this are listed as "(D,Noun±at)".

[-SC] verbs. You learned in unit 6 that when the final vowel of a verb drops between **ch** and another consonant, that **ch** will turn into a **sh**, as in these examples:

> **aachi** "say" +**tok** > **aashtok** "he said it"
> **aachi** "say" +**li** > **aashli** "I say it"

As you know, these final vowels drop if the previous syllable is a heavy syllable ending in a vowel, **h**, or **'**.

The same thing happens with verbs that include the causative ending ±**chi**, as in

> **hilha** "dance" +**chi** > **hilhachi** "to make (someone) dance",
> "he makes her dance"
> **hilhachi** +**tok** > **hilhashtok** "he made her dance"
> **hilhachi** +**li** > **hilhashli** "I make her dance"

> **toksali** "work" +**chi** > **toksalichi** "to make (someone) work",
> "she makes him work"
> **toksalichi** +**tok** > **toksalishtok** "she made him work"
> **toksalichi** +**li** > **toksalishli** "I make him work"

This process interacts with the **li** deletion rule, explained in unit 8, in a way that has not been covered in this book. The last two syllables of **malichi** "to make (someone or something) run", "to start (a car)" sound like the last two syllables of **toksalichi**, since both end in a **li** syllable, with its vowel rhythmically lengthened, followed by the causative ending **+chi**.

There's a difference in how these two verbs work, however. Look at these additional forms of **malichi**:

> **malichi +tok > malichitok** "she made him run", "he started it"—*not* <malishtok>
> **malichi +li > malichilitok** "I make him run", "I start it"—*not* < malishli>

In these words the final **i** of **malichi** does not drop, so the **ch** before it does not become **sh**. If you compare these forms of **malichi** with those of **toksalichi** (and especially if you listen as your teacher pronounces them), you can see how different they sound. The **chi** syllables in the last two words have a lengthened vowel.

Why does this happen? **Malichi** is derived from **malili** "to run" plus **+chi**, with the **li** at the end of **malili** dropped because of the **li** deletion rule. (Review this in lesson 8.7 if you need to do so.) Although the last **li** of **malili** is not pronounced in forms of **malichi** (because of **li** deletion), its syllable counts in the rhythmic lengthening sequence and explains why these **chi**'s have lengthened vowels (which keeps them from dropping). Here's a diagram that shows how this works:

> ma lī l̶i̶-chī tok
>   1 2 1 2
> ———————————
> ma lī l̶i̶ chī li
>   1 2 1 2

What's unusual here is that words like **malīchītok** and **malīchīli** contain two lengthened vowels in a row. These are the only type of words that work this way in Chickasaw!

In the dictionary, verbs that work like **malichi** are marked [-SC], indicating that the **sh-ch** rule does not operate normally in these words.

If you listen to Chickasaw speakers, you may find that some of them do not use **malichi** and other similar verbs as we describe here. Listen to your teacher!

Appendix A

Rhythmic Lengthening in Chickasaw

This appendix is a summary of all the information presented about the Chickasaw rhythmic lengthening rule and related pronunciation rules in the book, with references to the sections where each concept is originally presented. Only section RL5 contains new material not already covered in the units. This summary may help you relate what you have learned about Chickasaw rhythmic lengthening to what you know about English spelling.

RL1 (Rhythmic Lengthening section 1) describes the basic operation of the rule. RL2 describes other rules that change the pronunciation of Chickasaw words because of rhythmic lengthening. RL3 covers cases where the rhythmic lengthening rule works in a special way. RL4 explains the pronunciation in words with ± markers. Finally, RL5 discusses the way rules like the rhythmic lengthening rule and other patterns of vowel alternation interact with a language's spelling system.

RL1: THE RHYTHMIC LENGTHENING RULE

Understanding how the rhythmic lengthening rule works requires an understanding of what lengthened vowels sound like, how words are divided into syllables, how short syllables are identified, and the difference between + and ± markers. This sounds complicated, but you'll find that once you practice saying words in which the rhythmic lengthening rule applies, lengthening the right vowels will become automatic.

RL1.1: Lengthened vowels (unit 4)

Three different types of vowel sounds are written in our Chickasaw spelling system, but there are actually four types of vowel sounds in Chickasaw: ordinary short vowels (**a, i, o**), long vowels (**aa, ii, oo**), nasal vowels (**a̱, i̱, o̱**), and lengthened vowels. Lengthened vowels sound longer and more prominent than short vowels but are not normally written any differently from the short vowels, because it is predictable which vowels in any word will be lengthened. In discussing lengthened vowels, we often write them with macrons ("long marks" over the vowels)—ā ī ō—but once you understand the rules, you won't have to write them in a special way.

Lengthened vowels are very common in Chickasaw. They sound longer than ordinary short vowels but generally not quite so long as long vowels. Syllables that contain lengthened vowels are heavy syllables. Like other heavy syllables, they receive more emphasis and give a special rhythm to the words in which they occur. Because of vowel lengthening, you almost never hear two light syllables in a row in a Chickasaw word.

The pronunciation of lengthened vowels, like that of long vowels, varies less than that of short vowels. Lengthened **ā** always sounds like the *a* of the English word *father* (though nonlengthened short **a** can sound like the *a* of English *sofa*). Lengthened **ī** always sounds like the *i* of the word *police* (but nonlengthened **i** can sound like the *i* of *bit* or the *e* of *bet*). Lengthened **ō** always sounds like the *o*'s in *Ohio*, never like the *oo* of *cook* (which is often the sound of nonlengthened **o**).

RL1.2: Rhythmic patterns in Chickasaw (unit 4)

The following pairs of words illustrate how the rhythmic patterns of Chickasaw words containing lengthened vowels (written with macrons: **ā, ī, ō**) often change from one form of the same word to another:

Chofāta. "It is clean."   Sachōfata. "I am clean."
Tikahbi. "He is tired."   Potīkahbi. "We are tired."
Hopōba. "He is hungry."   Chihōpoba. "You are hungry."
Hofahya. "She is ashamed."   Sahōfahya. "I am ashamed."
Sachōfata. "I am clean."   Sachōfatātok. "I was clean."
Chihōpoba. "You are hungry."   Chihōpobātok. "You were hungry."
Mallili. "I jump."   Mallilītok. "I jumped."
Impali. "I eat."   Impalītok. "I ate."

It is possible to predict exactly which vowels in a Chickasaw word will be lengthened, so they need not be written in a special way, except as a learning aid. Doing this requires a clear understanding of heavy, light, and short syllables.

RL1.3: Chickasaw syllables (units 1, 4)

Dividing a Chickasaw word into syllables is not difficult.

- First, notice how many separate vowel sounds (different short, long, and nasal vowels) the word has. This is its number of syllables.
- Second, look at each vowel in turn. It is best to begin at the right (ending) side of the word. If it has a consonant in front of it, that consonant also belongs to the syllable containing the vowel you are looking at.
- Third, see whether there are any other consonants in front of the consonant you just identified. Those consonants are part of the preceding syllable.

For instance, consider the word **impalītok**. It has four vowels, so there are four syllables. The last vowel is **o**, and the consonant in front of it is **t**, so the last syllable is **tok**: **impalī/tok**. The next syllable from the end contains the lengthened **ī** and the consonant **l**: **impa/lī/tok**. The next syllable from the end contains **a** plus the consonant in front of it, **p**; when you mark the beginning of this syllable with a slash before the **p**, **im/pa/lī/tok**, you can see that the first syllable ends in **m**. The first vowel has no consonant in front of it, so the first syllable starts with **i** (the beginning of a word is always the beginning of a syllable).

Here are some other examples of how words are broken into syllables:

ho/poo/tok   chi/chaa/ha   mal/li/li   ish/toy/ya/tok

The syllable break (/) comes between the two **l**'s in **mallili** and the two **y**'s in **ishtoyyatok**. Letter combinations that represent a single sound (such as **ch**, **lh**, and **sh**) count as just one consonant. Long vowels (such as

aa) each count as just one vowel, not two. Never break a syllable in the middle of a letter combination or a long vowel. The second syllable of **chi/chaa/ha** begins with the letter combination **ch**, not with **h**.

Words like **hoo/ilh/po/kon/na** show that if two vowel sounds come together in a word, the syllable division comes between them.

Syllables that end in a consonant or that contain long, nasal, or lengthened short vowels are heavy syllables. Short syllables are nonfinal syllables containing a single consonant plus a short vowel or just a short vowel by itself. The vowels of some short syllables are lengthened, so these are heavy syllables. Short syllables whose vowels are not lengthened are light syllables. Final syllables can be either light o0r heavy, but they are never considered short syllables.

RL1.4: The rhythmic lengthening rule (unit 4)

Many Chickasaw words contain rhythmic lengthening sequences of two or more short syllables. The short syllables in these sequences can be numbered, starting from the first short syllable on the left, as in the examples below.

cho/fā/ta	sa/chō/fa/ta	sa/chō/fa/tā/tok	toy/ya/lī/tok
1 2	1 2 3	1 2 3 4	1 2

im/pa/lī/tok	ho/põ/bi	po/hō/po/bi	po/hō/po/bī/tok
1 2	1 2	1 2 3	1 2 3 4

These examples demonstrate the Chickasaw rule of rhythmic lengthening:

THE VOWEL OF EVERY SECOND SHORT SYLLABLE IN A RHYTHMIC LENGTHENING SEQUENCE IS LENGTHENED.

The vowels of even-numbered short syllables get lengthened. Some words contain as many as four (or more) short syllables in a row, so they may have several lengthened vowels. Rhythmic lengthening is a regular rule, and speakers apply it automatically while pronouncing Chickasaw words. With practice, you can learn to do this too.

RL1.5: Changing rhythmic patterns with changing word structure (unit 4; see also units 5, 7, 9, 10)

The rhythmic lengthening rule works automatically in rhythmic lengthening sequences within unchanged original words or in words with added ordinary plus (+) markers, such as S prefixes (whether they mark subjects or objects), the A ending **+li**, the past ending **+tok**, the question endings **+taa** and **+taam**, and so on. Adding or taking away one of these markers can change the count of short syllables within a rhythmic lengthening sequence, so that different vowels are lengthened as the word is pronounced.

On the other hand, plinus (±) markers, such as the A, D, and N prefixes and other prefixes such as **on±**, are not included in rhythmic lengthening sequences.

ish/o/kaa/mi	il/a/chok/milh/ka	hash/a/nom/po/li
1	1	1 1

The **sh** of the prefix **ish±** is not included with the **o** in the second syllable in the first example: you don't say <i/sho/kaa/mi>. The final consonant of an A prefix is not part of the following syllable. ± markers are almost always heavy syllables. Usually ± prefixes are pronounced as separate syllables, though ± endings may form syllables with the preceding word. However, adding a ± marker to a word never results in vowel lengthening. (See also RL4 below.)

Prefixes and endings that are joined to a plain verb with + create increasingly longer words and often increasingly longer rhythmic lengthening sequences. Adding a + marker to the word can result in new lengthened vowels. But although prefixes and endings joined to a word with ± make a word longer, they don't change rhythmic lengthening sequences. Adding a ± marker to a word never results in new rhythmically lengthened vowels.

RL2: RULES THAT DEPEND ON THE RHYTHMIC LENGTHENING RULE

Several rules that determine how Chickasaw verbs are pronounced depend on whether vowels in those verbs are lengthened or not.

RL2.1: The vowel drop rule and the ch/sh rule (unit 6)

According to the vowel drop rule, a nonlengthened vowel at the end of a verb drops between **s**, **sh**, or **lh** and the endings **+li**, **+tok**, **+taa**, or **+taam** as long as the **s**, **sh**, or **lh** is preceded by a vowel, **h**, or '.

Hostaam?	"Did he shoot at it?" (not <hosataam>)
Hihílhtok.	"She danced all the time" (not <hihílhatok>)

The syllable before any vowel that drops in this way is always a heavy syllable.

When a verb ends in a heavy syllable plus **ch** plus a nonlengthened vowel followed by **+li**, **+tok**, **+taa**, or **+taam**, the final vowel of that verb drops and the **ch** becomes **sh**:

Pilashtok.   "He sent it." (not <pilachitok> or <pilachtok>)

When a verb ends in a vowel plus **nch** plus a nonlengthened vowel followed by **+li**, **+tok**, **+taa**, or **+taam**, the final vowel of that verb drops, **ch** becomes **sh**, and the preceding vowel-plus-**n** becomes the corresponding nasal vowel:

Ayoppáshli.   "I like it." (not <ayoppánchili> or
<ayoppánchli> or <ayoppánshli>)

RL2.2: The li deletion rule (unit 8; also, unit 13)

A **li** syllable at the end of a basic verb whose vowel is not lengthened is dropped before the endings **+tok**, **+taa**, and **+taam** if that **li** syllable is preceded by a vowel, **h**, or ':

Tahtok.	"He finished it." (not <tahlitok>)
Ishtoksahátok.	"You worked all the time." (not <ishtoksahálitok>)

This rule does not affect the A ending **+li**: this ending is not dropped by the rule, and other **li**'s are not dropped before this ending.

Li deletion only works before + endings, and ±**ttook** is not a + ending. Although ±**ttook** starts with **t**, just like **+tok** and **+taa**, the **li** deletion rule only works before certain + endings that start with a single **t**, **ch**, or **n**. ±**Ttook** starts with a double **t**.

RL3: THE RHYTHMIC LENGTHENING RULE AND SOME SPECIAL WORD FORMS

The rhythmic lengthening rule works in a special way in words with S prefixes containing **ha**, verbs with future ±**a'chi**, and a-verbs with S prefixes.

RL3.1: Rhythmic lengthening with the S prefixes hapo+ and hachi+ (unit 4)

The **ha** syllable of the S prefixes **hapo+** and **hachi+** is never part of a rhythmic lengthening sequence. So when counting short syllables on words with these two prefixes, start counting with the syllable after **ha**:

ha/<u>chi</u>/ch<u>ō</u>/<u>fa</u>/t<u>ā</u>/tok   ha/<u>po</u>/lh<u>ā</u>/<u>yi</u>/ta
     1   2 3 4   1 2   3

One way to remember this fact about **ha** prefixes is to think of them as **ha±chi+** and **ha±po+**. Then, if **ha±** is a ± marker, this syllable cannot be part of a rhythmic lengthening sequence of short syllables. Alternatively, you can remember to exclude the **ha** syllable from your short syllable count. The syllable after **ha** (**po** or **chi**) can begin a rhythmic lengthening sequence.

RL3.2: Rhythmic lengthening with the ±a'chi future ending (unit 5)

The **i** of the ±**a'chi** ending is always lengthened when it occurs before a + ending like +**taa**:

Mallila'ch<u>ī</u>taa?   "Am I going to jump?"

Because this vowel is lengthened, it never drops before an ending; the future question combination is never pronounced <±a'shtaa>. Because the last heavy syllable before +**taa** is stressed, as explained in unit 4, the **i** of ±**a'chi** is always stressed in +**taa** questions.

Most likely the reason for the special pronunciation of this ending is that ±**a'chi** was originally <±a'lichi> (related forms containing **li** occur in Choctaw). The **lichi** of this earlier ending formed a rhythmic lengthening sequence, so the vowel of **chi** was lengthened when it was not final, while the **li** dropped because of **li** deletion (unit 8). If this explanation seems too complicated, just memorize the special pronunciation ±**a'chītaa** and remember that other + endings will work the same way following ±**a'chi**.

RL3.3: Rhythmic lengthening with S prefixes on a-verbs (unit 6; also, unit 9)

An S prefix is added after the **a** at the beginning of an A verb, and (if the initial **a** of the verb is followed by only one consonant) its vowel is lengthened by the regular rule:

Ach<u>ī</u>pila.   "He helps you."
Ap<u>ō</u>bika.   "We are sick."

When an A or N prefix is used in combination with an S prefix on an a-verb, the **a** vowel drops. But the vowel of the S prefix is still lengthened, as in forms with no A or N prefix:

Kiich<u>ī</u>pila.   "We help you."
Iks<u>ā</u>pi'lo.   "He doesn't help me."
Ikp<u>ō</u>bi'ko.   "We aren't sick."

You can simply memorize combinations like **kiichī**+, **akchī**+ if you like, but here's how this actually works:

kiiᴀchīpila
1 2 3

ikᴀsāpi'lo
1 2

The A and N ± prefixes do not count as part of the rhythmic lengthening sequence, which starts with the initial **a** of the a-verb. The following S prefix is an even-numbered short syllable, so its vowel is lengthened. Then the **a** drops (there's a line through it, ᴀ, above).

Notice that when the **a** of an a-verb is followed by two consonants, an S prefix vowel is never lengthened, because in such verbs it is in a heavy syllable:

Achikmi.   "You are frozen."

RL3.4: Rhythmic lengthening in [-SC] verbs (unit 20, Advanced Chickasaw Grammar Lesson)

A few verbs with the **+chi** causative ending derived from verbs ending in li—such as **malichi** "to make (someone or something) work", "to start (a car)"—work in an unexpected way. Here are some examples:

Malichitok.   "He started it.", "She made him run."
Malichili.   "I start it.", "I make him run."

The **chi** in these verbs is lengthened. This is unusual, because normally the syllable before a syllable containing a lengthened vowel must be a short syllable. Because **malichi** derives from **malili** "run" plus **+chi**, however, the **+chi** syllable is preceded by a short syllable—the **li** syllable at the end of the verb, which, however, gets dropped by the **li** deletion rule. Here's how it works:

ma lī l̶i̶-chī tok
1 2 1 2

ma lī l̶i̶ chī li
1 2 1 2

In *Chickasaw: An Analytical Dictionary,* entries for verbs like **malichi** include the abbreviation [-SC]. These forms of **malichi** and similar verbs are the only Chickasaw words in which there can be two rhythmically lengthened syllables in a row.

RL4: SPECIAL SYLLABLES IN WORDS WITH ± MARKERS

Many Chickasaw words contain rhythmic lengthening sequences four or more syllables long, usually with some syllables part of a basic verb and others added with + markers. Dividing these words into syllables follows the regular rules whereby a consonant in front of any vowel is included in that vowel's syllable (see RL1.3 above).

When words are built up with ± markers, syllable division may work differently. Frequently a consonant next to or near a ± is included in a syllable with the vowel that precedes it, not with the vowel that follows it. Such consonants often sound somewhat lengthened.

RL4.1: Syllable division and consonant lengthening with ± prefixes (unit 4; also, units 6, 7, 9, 10)

Consonant lengthening sometimes occurs in words containing ± markers. Unlike vowel lengthening, consonant lengthening is not required. Speakers sometimes pronounce words with slightly lengthened or emphasized consonants, as described below, but just as often they do not. Listen, and you'll hear many examples of this process.

The word **Ishanompoli** "You talk" consists of the A prefix **ish±** added to the verb **anompoli**. This word is divided into syllables as follows: **ish/a/nom/po/li** (never like <i/sha/nom/po/li>, because an added ± marker never creates a rhythmic lengthening sequence). When the syllable after an A prefix starts with a vowel and is not itself a heavy syllable, the pronunciation of the final consonant of the A prefix may be emphasized or slightly lengthened. Thus, sometimes "You talk" may sound almost like <ishshanompoli>. The same thing can happen with D or N prefixes or another ± prefix, such as the **on±** "on" prefix.

RL4.2: Syllable division and consonant lengthening with noun endings (unit 4; also, unit 5)

The noun subject ending **±at** and object ending **±a** are never included in rhythmic lengthening sequences. Adding **±at** or **±a** to a Chickasaw noun never results in new rhythmically lengthened vowels, because these are ± endings.

Pronunciation changes can occur with nouns whose next-to-last syllables are light, all of which are non-vowel-loss nouns. You might guess that **foshi'at** would he be divided into syllables as <fo/shī/'at> and that **folosha** would be <fo/lō/sha>, with the second syllables of each word lengthened. But this is not correct: adding **±at** or **±a** does not change the syllable division, and there are no lengthened vowels in these words. Careful pronunciations of such words may sound like **fo/shi'/at** and **fo/losh/a**, with the endings pronounced as completely separate syllables.

More commonly, subject and object forms of non-vowel-loss nouns with light next-to-last syllables, like **foshi'** and **folosh**, have a special pronunciation. Speakers often pronounce the subject form of "bird" as **fosh/i/'at** and the object form of "spoon" as **fol/o/sha**. In this common pronunciation, the consonant before the last vowel of the noun's basic form is pronounced at the end of the syllable preceding it. When this happens, the last consonant of the noun (if there is one) is pronounced in the syllable with the noun ending. Speakers who use this pronunciation may emphasize or slightly lengthen the consonant before the final vowel of the basic form of the noun, so these words may sound almost like <foshshi'at> or <follosha>.

RL4.3: Syllable divisions and consonant lengthening in HN grades (unit 8)

Many HN grades have two alternative pronunciations:

Basic verbs	*HN grades*
cho/fā/ta	cho/fa/hán/ta *or* chof/a/hán/ta
i/pī/ta	i/pi/hín/ta *or* ip/i/hín/ta
chi/nō/si	chi/no/hó/si or chin/o/hó/si

The changing vowel of an HN grade is never lengthened. In each of the examples above, the next-to-last vowel is lengthened in the basic verb but not in the corresponding HN grade. In fact such HN grades are often pronounced with the consonant before the changing vowel at the end of the preceding syllable. This happens when the syllable before the changing vowel syllable is a light syllable, as in the examples. You may even feel that the consonant before the changing vowel sounds emphasized or slightly lengthened, almost like <choffahánta> or <ippihínta>.

These syllable changes do not occur when the syllable before the changing vowel is heavy. Examples like the following show that HN grade verbs can even contain lengthened vowels:

Sachōfahánta.   "I get clean all the time."

The important thing to remember is that changing vowels of HN grades are never lengthened.

RL4.4: Negatives of verbs ending in long vowels (unit 9)

Verbs that end in a long vowel form their negatives in a special way. The verbs change their last (single) vowel to ±o and then add ' right before the ±o:

Hopoo. "He's jealous."   Ikhopo'o. "He's not jealous."
Yaa. "He cries."   Ikya'o "He does not cry."
Tilhaa. "They run."   Iktilha'o. "They don't run."

There are no lengthened vowels in these negative verbs. Adding a ± ending (like the ' plus ±o combination) can never change a rhythmic lengthening sequence. The syllable divisions sound as follows:

ik/ho/po'/o *or* ik/hop/o/'o   ik/ti/lha'/o *or* ik/tilh/a/'o

The second version of each pair is the more common pronunciation, with the consonant before the ' pronounced at the end of a syllable. You may feel that such words sound as though the middle consonant in the verb is doubled—almost like <ikhoppo'o> or <iktilhlha'o>. Listen to the way your teacher says these words:

This unusual pronunciation is only used in verbs with a single short syllable before the final long vowel of the basic verb. In cases like the following, where there are two short syllables before the long vowel, syllable division and lengthening work just as you'd expect:

Iksahōpo'o.   "He's not jealous of me."

RL4.5: Syllable division and consonant lengthening with ± verb endings (units 11, 13)

When a word ending in an even-numbered short syllable comes before a ± ending that starts with a consonant, like **±hmat**, you may hear a different rhythmic pattern from what you expect. **Hilhahmat** may be pronounced **hi/lhah/mat**, according to the regular rules of syllable division you learned in units 1 and 4. Alternatively, it may be pronounced as **hilh/ah/mat**, with the consonant before the ± ending pronounced at the end of the preceding syllable, perhaps even sounding double, almost like <hilhlhahmat>. Other ± verb endings, such as the long past **±ttook**, work the same way.

Similarly, because **±kat** and **±ka** are ± endings, they cannot be part of a rhythmic lengthening sequence (even though they begin with a single consonant). A dependent verb like **hilhakat** doesn't have any lengthened syllables and may even sound like <hilhlhakat> to you.

RL5: VOWEL PRONUNCIATIONS AND VOWEL SPELLINGS

In some other spelling systems people have suggested for Chickasaw, many short, nonlengthened **a** sounds have been spelled with the letter *u*. This seems to make sense when you first think about it, since about the same sound is written with *u* in English words like *but* (although, of course, *a* can also be used to spell this sound in English words like *sofa*). In the same systems for writing Chickasaw, the letter *a* (or sometimes *ah*) has been used to spell both long **aa** and lengthened **ā**, as well as final **a**. (Most of these earlier systems do not consistently indicate the difference between long and short vowel sounds in spelling.)

Any system will work as long as it is used consistently, so there is nothing wrong with writing the short **a** sound with *u*. A spelling system is hard to learn, however, if it works inconsistently, so every instance of short **a** would have to be written *u* for this system to be consistent. The problem with writing nonlengthened short **a** with *u* and lengthened short **a** with *a* is that if this system is used consistently, the same word must be spelled in different ways on different occasions. Thus, **bashafa** "he is cut" (**bashāfa**) would be spelled *"bushafa"*, but **sabashafa** "I am cut" (**sabāshafa**) would be spelled *"subashufa"*. Similary, the S prefix **sa+** would be spelled as *"su"* in the previous example, where its vowel is not lengthened, but as *"sa"* in a word like **asapila** "I am sick" (**asāpila**), which might be spelled *"usapila"*. Spelling variations like these make it harder to see the connections between related uses of the same word or prefix, and also make it difficult to see the connection among all the vowels of the **a** family: **a** (short or lengthened), **aa**, and **a̱**. It is not hard to learn the rhythmic lengthening rule, and once you learn it, Chickasaw spelling and reading actually become a good deal simpler.

Chickasaw is not the only language that has different pronunciations for related vowel sounds. English does too! The use of the macron to represent Chickasaw lengthened vowels probably reminds you of the way English "long vowels" are written in grade-school reading materials and in some English dictionaries. (Chickasaw lengthened vowels are not the same as English long vowels, of course—in each case, the macron is just used to help make things easier for people learning to read.) Part of learning how to read and write English is understanding the idea that the same letter can have very different pronunciations in different words. For instance, the English letter *i* has a "short" pronunciation in *pin* but a "long" pronunciation in *pine*. The first part of these words is spelled the same way, but the letter *i* represents two different sounds, depending (as all readers of English know) on whether there is a "silent *e*" at the end of the word. Sometimes, in fact, the different "long" and "short" sounds are used in related forms of the same English word. For example, the words *divine* and *divinity* are related. The underlined *i* is "long" (as in *pine*) in the first word but "short" (as in *pin*) in the second word. Yet the two *i*'s are written the same way, so English speakers have to learn how to read and pronounce them.

English spelling is quite complex and full of exceptions. Chickasaw spelling is much more regular, especially when you know the rules. The main reason for this difference between English and Chickasaw spelling is that Chickasaw spelling was developed very recently and doesn't reflect centuries of changing use by many different people, as English spelling does. People learning to read English have to memorize the spellings of many more words than people learning to read Chickasaw do.

However, English and Chickasaw share the feature of having regular rules that explain why related vowels are pronounced differently in different words. In order to read either language, then, you have to learn its spelling rules. The rules of one language don't necessarily apply to the other language, because each language has its own system.

Appendix B

Stories of Old Times: Original Versions of Readings in Units 5–10

Units 5–10 include simplified versions of reminiscences of old days in Oklahoma composed by Mrs. Willmond. Her original stories are given below, followed by English translations.

UNIT 5: KOSHIBBA'

Sashkaat abokkoli' ayyacha koshibba' ayowahminattook. Ayowat tahcha ishtalakmat hopo'nina kiipahminattook.

UNIT 6: FANI'

Hopaakikaashookano fani'at lawahminattook. Ankaat abokkoli' ayyacha fani' abihminattook. Fani' abit ishta'lana sashkaat anakshoot tahlikmakoot hopo'nina kiipahminattook.

UNIT 7: AAITTANAA'

Hopaakikaashookano aaittanaa' iliyyakma Hattak Api' Hommaat lawahminattook. Aaittanaa' áyya'shakmat Chahta' intaloowa' taloowahminattook. Holisso Holitto'pa' ittimanompolikmat Chahta' iholissoho ittimanompolihminattook. Chikashshookano holissaat ikimikshokittook. Aba' anompa ishtanompoli'at Chahta' imanompa'o toshoolihminattook. Yahmikmat Chahta' intaloowa'o taloowahminattook. Himmaka' nittakookano naahollo intaloowa' bíyyi'ka.

UNIT 8: NITTAK HOLLISHTO'

Hopaakikaash Nittak Hollishto' ookma Appo'si' inchokka' ilonatokmat aaittanaa' kiliyyahminattook. Nittak Holiishto' ookma nanna habinachihminattook. Itti'chanaa ilaalhtocha iliyyahminattook. Ilonatokmat onnakmako falamat kiimintihminattook.

UNIT 9: TASHPISHOFA

Hopaakikaashookano Chikashshaat áyya'shakat tanchi' waachikmat ilaapakáynit tanchi' hosihminattook. Hosit tahlikmat yammak<u>o</u> t<u>a</u>shpishofa ikbihminattook. Shokha' abikmat shokha' nipi' ibaanihminattook. Ittiba'ncha hopoont tahlikmat yammak<u>o</u> t<u>a</u>shpishofa hochifohminattook. Himmaka' áyya'shookano nannakat pilla' alhtaha bíyyi'ka. Tanchi' ishchompakmat, nipi' ishchompakmat, aaholhponi' ishchompakmat yammak ishaahopoon'achi. Lowak nannakya ishoota'chi ki'yo. Tali' palli' bíyyi'ka. Ishaahopoona'chi himmaka' nittakookano.

UNIT 10. ITTI' ITTABAANA' ABOOHA

Hopaakikaashookano hattakat ilaapakaynit chokka' ikbihminattook. Itti' ittabaana' abooha ikbihminattook. Ilaapakaynit itti' hoocha'lihminattook. Abokkoli' anonka'<u>a</u> itti' aa-ayowahminattook. Katolhlhit tahlikmat itti'chanaa a'nicha shaat ishtayyahminattook. M<u>ó</u>m<u>a</u> shaat ishtonat táyyahlikmat yammak<u>o</u> chokka' ikbihminattook. Chokka' ikbit tahlikmat aahashtahli' chompat abihlihminattook. Mishsha' fónkha áyya'shookano aahashtahli'<u>a</u> amposhi' shokawwa'li' nannakya ikabihlokihminattook. Okkisoshi'<u>o</u> ikbihminattook. Himmaka' nittakookano itti' ittabaana' abooha nannakya iksho. Itti' basha' abooha bíyyi'ka yahmikmat lokfi' nona' abooha bíyyi'ka—yammakilla himmaka' nittakookano.

ENGLISH TRANSLATIONS

UNIT 5: POKE SALAD

My mother would go to the woods and gather poke salad. After having gathered it, she would bring it home and cook it, and we would eat it.

UNIT 6: SQUIRREL

Long ago there were lots of squirrels. My father would go to the woods and kill squirrels. After killing a squirrel he would bring it home, and when my mother had singed it she would cook it and we would eat it.

UNIT 7: CHURCH

Long ago when we went to church there would be a lot of Indians. When they were in church, they would sing Choctaw hymns. When they read the Bible, they would read the Choctaw book. The Chickasaws didn't have a book. The preacher would explain it in Choctaw. And then they would sing Choctaw hymns. Nowadays it's all white people's hymns.

UNIT 8: CHRISTMAS

Long ago on Christmas, when we were going to Granny's house, we would go to church. On Christmas they would give things. We would be in the wagon and we would go. After we had gotten there, the next morning we would come back.

UNIT 9: PISHOFA

Long ago the Chickasaws were there, and when they grew corn they would pound the corn themselves in a mortar. After they pounded it, they would make it into pishofa. When they killed a hog, they would add the pork to it. They added it, and when they had cooked it, they named that pishofa. These days things are just already prepared all the time. You buy the corn, you buy the meat, you buy the pot, and you'll cook it in that. You won't kindle any fire. It's all appliances. You cook on them nowadays.

UNIT 10: LOG HOUSES

Long ago people would build houses themselves. They would build log houses. They would chop trees down themselves. They would get trees in the woods. When they had cut them up, they would put them in wagons and haul them there. After they had hauled them all, they would make them into a house. When they had finished the house, they would buy windows and put them in. In still earlier times they didn't put any glass in windows. They would make little doors. Nowadays there aren't any log houses. It's all frame houses and it's all brick houses—there are just those nowadays.

Appendix C

Translations of Readings in Units 11–20

These readings include short reminiscences, true and made-up stories, and retellings of things originally expressed in English. If you're studying Chickasaw, you should try your best to understand the reading for each unit based on the vocabulary and notes provided, in the context of the current unit. However, if you need more help, or if you are interested in the readings primarily as a window on Chickasaw culture, you can use the translations below.

UNIT 11: A TRIP TO TEXAS

Well, I'm going to tell you this now.
In about 1983 or '84 Pam and I went to Texas.
And then when we got there it was all Indians there.
We went there to talk to the ones they call the Alabamas. The Chickasaws call them a "Lost Tribe".
They were talking five languages there!
We went to church with them.
This is all I'm going to say. This is enough.

UNIT 12: THE HAGGADAH IN CHICKASAW

Why is tonight different from other nights?
On other nights we eat both leavened bread and unleavened bread but tonight we will eat only unleavened bread.
On other nights we eat all kinds of greens but tonight we will eat only bitter weeds.
On other nights we do not dip them but tonight we will dip them twice.
On other nights we eat sitting any old way but tonight we will eat sitting leaning back against the chairs.
On other nights we eat any old way but tonight we will eat at a holy table.

UNIT 13: THERE ARE MANY DIFFERENT INDIAN TRIBES

A long time ago God made lots of people. All the people were Chickasaw: they spoke Chickasaw, they understood each other. Those people came out of the earth, and they were made out of yellow clay. There were no other people.

One day they all looked at the sky, and they asked each other what this was. Because they wanted to reach the sky, they brought rocks and started to build a mountain. But that night while they were sleeping, the wind knocked the rocks down onto the people.

The people were not dead, but in the morning they started to talk to each other and they were scared—all of a sudden they were speaking different languages, and they could not understand each other.

Some were talking Chickasaw: those were Chickasaws, and they became the Chickasaw nation. Some were speaking almost the same language: those were Choctaws, and they became the Choctaw nation. The others who were there did not understand that language and began to fight each other.

All the people separated from each other. The Chickasaws and Choctaws were close to each other, but the others went far away—some went north, some went east, some went west. They all became different nations. This is why there are so many different Indian tribes.

UNIT 14: TISHOMINGO

Tishomingo was a Chickasaw chief. He lived in Mississippi. His name means "chief's assistant".

When Tishomingo was old, white people conquered the Chickasaws. In 1832 the white people said that the Chickasaws had to sign a treaty at Pontotoc. Tishomingo signed the treaty with various other chiefs.

Article 12 of the treaty said that every year Tishomingo was supposed to receive one hundred dollars, but the treaty also said that the Chickasaws were to leave their land and go west.

A while later many Chickasaws left their homes and went to Oklahoma. They passed by crying. English calls it the "Trail of Tears". In 1840 Tishomingo died before reaching Oklahoma. (I wonder if he got the hundred dollars?)

The first capital of the Chickasaw Nation was Tishomingo. It was called Tishomingo, named after Tishomingo. Tishomingo County, Mississippi, was also named after Tishomingo. Tishomingo's picture is on the Great Seal of the Chickasaw Nation. People still remember Tishomingo.

UNIT 15: THE LORD'S PRAYER IN CHICKASAW

Our Father who sits above, your name will be holy.
Your kingdom will come.
The way it will be on earth will be the same as the way it will be in Heaven.
So that we can eat today you will keep feeding us.
You will forgive us our debts, and the way we forgive others around for any debts will be the same.
You will not wish for us to go where things are bad.
You will save us from where things are bad.
The kingdom and the power and the glory will be yours forever and ever.
It will be like that.

UNIT 16: THE SCOTT FAMILY COMES HOME

Emile Scott with his wife and all had gone to the store, they came back, they arrived home, and they were about to go into the house, but it seemed like someone was inside, and they wanted to see him, so they stood outside, and because he was right inside the room, they heard him banging around, and they were outside, and they were about to send for the police, but they hadn't sent for the police yet—and it was a chicken in there!

A rooster was in there! It jumped up and came out the window and crowed! (they say).

They realized, "Ah, it was a chicken in there. There wasn't anyone," they said, and they opened up the house and went in (they say).

UNIT 17: SELECTIONS FROM THE UNIVERSAL DECLARATION OF HUMAN RIGHTS

The Document of All People

WHERE THE DOCUMENT FIRST BEGINS [PREAMBLE]

All the people in the world are truly equal. The laws belong to all the people. All people should be happy about their being enacted. . . .

All the people of the nations must agree about that, about what is going to be truly right. . . .

Article 1

. . . All people are truly equal and they must agree with all this.

Article 2

No matter how different people look or where they come from, they are are all truly equal.

No matter what kind of country people come from, they are truly equal.

Article 3

People do not have the right to imprison or kill people. People are truly sacred.

Article 4

There should be no slaves.

. . . Article 8

If someone has done something wrong to a person the lawmakers should help that person.

. . . Article 16

1. Men and women have the right to get married if they want to marry someone.
2. If they don't want to marry someone, they never have to marry anyone . . .

. . . Article 18

The things people believe in may truly be different from each other, but if they want to worship something, they can worship it.

Article 19

If you want to think something, you can think it. If you want to write something, you can write it. If you want to read some document, you can read it.

. . . Article 26

All children have the right to go to school, even if they don't have any money. Everyone who wants to go to an educational institution should be able to go.

. . . Article 29

1. Everyone should help each other.
2. People make laws because they want to help people. They should never break the laws.
3. These articles should never be forgotten.

UNIT 18: PONAYYO'CHA' AND LINHO' FILLI'TA'

Ponayyo'cha' and Linho' Filli'ta' traveled around and because they knew how to ride well and traveled around; they lived alone—

(. . . men would chase them, but they never caught up with them. No one ever caught up with them, they say, but one said he could catch them, and having said it, he tied the gate and was standing there when they got there. "No one ever caught you, they used to say, but I caught you!" he said—it was nothing . . .)

—going over it they fell and went running on.

When they went somewhere they used to take several dogs.

They got in what they call a hack and they used to go around.

Horses pulled it.

When they would stay over somewhere, they would lie down on the bed, they would spread out the coats or something that they had been wearing for them on the floor, they would sleep there, and the next morning when they were about to go, Linho' Filli'ta'—

(. . . their last name was Filli'ta' . . .)

—Linho' would harness the horses and hitch them up to the wagon, and she and the dogs would get in, and then Panayyo'cha'would get in, and they would go home.

UNIT 19: RABBIT AND BUZZARD

Ideas that are not stated explicitly in the story are written in brackets here.

Once upon a time Rabbit had something wrong with him (they say). He was wounded, and he had it so bad that he was lying down, so they were looking for someone to doctor him. There wasn't one. They never found one.

Then they found Buzzard, and Buzzard said he could cure him, and so they brought Buzzard, and Buzzard said, "If you just close up all the cracks in the house so that no one can see, I can doctor him," he said, and they closed up all those cracks that were in the house, they closed the house all up, and Buzzard doctored Rabbit.

Then Rabbit cried out.

Then the ones who were outside [said], "Why is he crying and saying that?" they said, and [he said],"I'm doctoring him: where he's wounded, I'm putting medicine on it, so he said he hurts,"he said, and then Rabbit got quiet (they say), and those who were outside [said], "Why did he get quiet?" they said, and [he said], "I'm using medicine on him, and so the pain has gone away, and he's sleeping," he said (they say).

Then, a little later, Buzzard (the one we've been speaking about) [said], "Now I'm ready. Open the door!" he said, and they opened the door, and Buzzard (the very one) flew out, and they went back in to him: only Rabbit's bones were there (they say)—he had eaten him up.

UNIT 20: THE CHRISTMAS STORY

It happened that, at about that time, Caesar Augustus laid down a law that all the world had to be recorded. So it happened that they all went back to be recorded along with those of their own group.

Joseph went back to Galilee, to the place called Nazareth. Joseph was about to marry Mary, and there wasn't a baby yet.

Then while they were there she had the baby. It happened that there was no place for her to put him, so she put him down to lie in a horse trough.

It happened that there were shepherds watching sheep at night.

Then God sent an angel to them, and the angel came to them. Light shone on them. They were all afraid. The angel said, "Don't be afraid," saying to them, "I bring you some news that will make you happy about which all people will rejoice. The Son of God has come to this land to save all people. When you find the Son of God, he will be wrapped in rags and laid down to lie in a horse trough."

The angel came and saw that other angels had come from the heavens: many of them had come, to praise God together. "God's glory in the highest heaven and good peace on earth have come to all people."

The angels went back to heaven. Only the shepherds were there. And then they were saying to each other, "Let's go to Bethlehem—we should see what God has revealed to us."

They went quickly, and when they got there, they found Mary and Joseph, and the baby lying there, laid down in the horse trough. Having seen the child lying there, they made it known everywhere.

Then those whom the shepherds had gone and told wondered about how it had happened.

Mary thought about these things; she thought about them in her heart.

Having told about all the things they had heard and seen, the shepherds went back, glorifying and praising God.

Chickasaw Verb and Noun Markers for "I", "me", "my", "you", "your", "we", "us", and "our"

Four sets of Chickasaw markers are added to verbs to express the involvement of "I", "me", "you", "we", and "us" participants.

	A	S	D with **im±**	N substitute for **ik±**
"I", /"me", "my"	+li	sa+	a+	ak±
"you", "your"	ish±	chi+	chi+	chik±
"we", "us", "our"	kii±, ii±, kil±, il±	po+	po+	kii±, kil±
special "we", "us", "our"	kiloo±, iloo±	hapo+	hapo+	kiloo±
"you", "your" (plural)	hash±	hachi+	hachi+	hachik±

NOTES

1. For more about the use of A and S markers, see units 3 and 5. For D markers, see units 7 and 8. For N markers, see unit 9.

2. The special "we" / "us" markers express inclusive triplural participants, as explained in unit 3.

3. A and S markers are added directly to verb stems. D markers combine with the dative prefix **im±** (and its variants) on dative verbs (unit 8). N markers substitute for the unaccomplished prefix **ik±** on negative verbs (unit 9).

4. Combinations of A and S markers are described in unit 5, combinations of A and D plus dative markers in unit 8, combinations of N and S markers and N and D markers in unit 9.

5. S and D markers may not both be used on the same verb; smilarly, A and N markers may not both be used on the same verb.

6. S markers work in exceptional ways with i-verbs (unit 3), a-verbs (unit 6), and o-verbs (unit 10).

7. S and D markers are used on nouns to indicate possession (unit 7).

Prefixes and Endings

These lists of the prefixes and endings that can be used with Chickasaw verbs and nouns are arranged alphabetically, in the same alphabetical order that is used in the Chickasaw-English Vocabulary.

- Each prefix and ending is identified with a translation, if appropriate; a brief description; and a reference to the units in which its use is described. Unit numbers followed by RS indicate prefixes or endings introduced in Reading and Speaking sections of those units.
- The lists distinguish three types of elements: + prefixes and endings, ± prefixes and endings, and other elements that are not ordinary prefixes or endings, such as combinations of ordinary prefixes or endings with other elements. The difference between + and ± markers is explained in unit 4 and in appendix A: Rhythmic Lengthening in Chickasaw.
- The lists do not include elements added to verbs as part of grade formation (which cannot clearly be identified as either prefixes or endings), as described in units 8 and 15.
- The lists also don't include parts of words that are mentioned in various units but not considered regular prefixes or endings, such as the **li** at the end of many verbs, discussed in unit 8, and the elements of V1's and V2's discussed in unit 16.

CHICKASAW PREFIXES AND OTHER INITIAL ELEMENTS

a : first part of a-verbs—followed by S prefixes (6)

a+ "I"/"me"/"my" D prefix (used with dative **im±**; becomes **sa+** after A or N prefix): possessive (7), object (8), subject (8)

ach · form of **chi+** S prefix on o-verbs and other words that work similarly (10)

ak± "I" N prefix; replaces **ik±** on negative verbs (9)

ap : form of **po+** S prefix on o-verbs and other words that work similarly (10)

as : form of **sa+** S prefix on o-verbs and other words that work similarly (10)

at± "come and" preverb (20RS)

awa± used in forming higher numbers (11ACG)

aa± "in", "at" prefix (10); "with, out of" prefix (13); inanimate "from" prefix (16)

chi+ "you"/"your" S prefix: subject (3), object (5), possessive (7); "you"/"your" D prefix (used with dative **im±**): possessive (7), object (8), subject (8)

chik± "you" N prefix; replaces **ik±** on negative verbs (9)

ha± part of **hachi+**, **hachim±**, **hapo+**, and **hapom±**

hachi+ "you all", "you guys"/"your all", "you guys's" S prefix: subject (3), object (5), possessive (7); "you all", "you guys"/"your all", "you guys's" D prefix (used with dative **im±**): possessive (7), object (8), subject (8)

hachik± "you all" N prefix; replaces **ik±** on negative verbs (9)

hapo+ special "we"/"us"/"our" inclusive triplural S prefix: subject (3), object (5), possessive (7); special "we"/"us"/"our" inclusive triplural D prefix (used with dative **im±**): possessive (8), object (9), subject (9)

hassa+ "you all", "you guys" A subject, "me" S object prefix combination (5)

hassa-aasa+ "you guys" A subject, "me" S object, plus **aa±** prefix combination (10)

hassam±, hassan±, hass<u>a</u>± "you all", "you guys" A subject, "me" D object plus dative prefix combination (8)

hassamaa± "you guys" A subject, "me" D object plus dative plus **aa±** prefix combination (10)

hash± "you all", "you guys" A subject prefix (3)

hoo± "they" plural subject (2), plural command (2)

ibaa± "with" (accompanying) verb prefix (10)

ik± unaccomplished prefix, used on negative verbs that, if non-negative, would not have A subject prefixes (9)

il± variant of **ii±** used before vowels (3)

ili+ reflexive verb prefix (5)

iloo± special "we" inclusive triplural A subject prefix (3)

im±, in±, <u>i</u>± dative verb prefix; possessive (7), object (8), subject (8)

imaa± animate "from" prefix (16)

issa+ "you" A subject, "me", S object prefix combination (5)

issa-aasa+ "you" A subject, "me" S object, plus **aa±** prefix combination (10)

issam±, issan±, iss<u>a</u>± "you" A subject, "me" D object plus dative prefix combination (8)

issamaa± "you" A subject, "me" D object plus dative plus **aa±** prefix combination (10)

ish± "you" A subject prefix (3)

isht± "with", "about" preverb (13)

itti+ reciprocal verb prefix (10) (often shortened to **ti+** after an A, N, or D prefix; see unit 10)

ii± "we" A subject prefix (3)

kil± variant of A subject, N subject "we" prefixes **kii±** used before vowels (3, 9)

kiloo± special "we" inclusive triplural A subject prefix (3); N subject prefix; replaces **ik±** on negative verbs (9)

kii± "we" A subject prefix (3); N subject prefix; replaces **ik±** on negative verbs (9)

naa± (sometimes **n<u>a</u>±**) compound form of **nanna** "something"

okaa± "in", "into" verb prefix (18)

on±, om±, <u>o</u>± "on" verb prefix (10)

osht± "that way" preverb (7RS, 20RS)

oot± "go to", "go and" preverb (11RS)

po+ "we"/"us"/"our" S prefix: subject (3), object (5), possessive (7); "we"/"us"/"our" D prefix (used with dative **im±**): possessive (7), object (8), subject (8)

sa+ "I"/"me"/"my" S prefix: subject (3), object (5), possessive (7); "I" / "me" D prefix used (with dative **im±**) after any A or N prefix

CHICKASAW ENDINGS AND OTHER FINAL ELEMENTS

±' "too much" ending (on verbs used with auxiliary **salami**) (16); noun-forming ending (18)

±a'chi future ending (5)

±a'chitokak<u>o</u> "be about to" (different subject) (17RS)

±a'hi "can" ending (on verbs used with auxiliary **bíyyi'ka**) (5)

±**a'ni** "may", "can" ending (5)

±**a'ntaa** "may", "can" question ending (5)

±**a'ntok** "could have, might have" ending (16)

±**a'si** "just", "only" number verb ending (12)

±**a'shki** positive hortative ending (15)

±**ak** special object ending (10)

±**akilloot** subject "only" ending (20)

±**akill͟o** object "only" ending (20)

±**akm͟a** nonpast ending on time words (8RS, 17)

±**akookya** "too" ending (20)

±**akoot** contrastive subject ending (9)

±**ak͟o** contrastive object ending (9)

±**akya** variant "too" ending (20)

±**at** noun subject ending (4), "have" object ending (12)

±**aak** special object ending used after vowel-loss nouns (10)

±**aakilloot** subject "only" ending used after vowel-loss nouns (20)

±**aakill͟o** object "only" ending used after vowel-loss nouns (20)

±**aakoot** contrastive subject ending used after vowel-loss nouns (9)

±**aak͟o** contrastive object ending used after vowel-loss nouns (9)

±**aash** past ending on time words (8RS, 11RS, 17)

±**aat** noun subject ending used after vowel-loss nouns (4); "have" object ending used after vowel-loss nouns (12); question subject ending used after consonants (17)

±**a͟** object ending (5)

+**cha** used in forming higher numbers (11ACG); same-subject "and" switch-reference ending (13RS, 15)

+**chi** causative verb ending (6)

+**chichi** variant of +**chi** (6)

±**ch͟i** "I wonder" ending used after consonants (20)

±**ha'ni** "must" conclusion ending (16)

±**haat** question subject ending (17)

±**hch͟i** "I wonder" ending (20)

±**hmat** same-subject "after"/"when"/"if" switch-reference ending used for completed events (11); subject "some" ending (17)

±**hm͟a** different-subject "after"/"when"/"if" switch-reference ending used for completed events (11); object "some" ending (17)

±**hmano** "where is", "where are" noun question ending used after vowels (4RS, 12ACG, 17)

+**hminatok** nonremote habitual ending (12RS)

+**hminatookya** combination of remote habitual ending and ±**hookya** "but" (12RS)

+**hminattook** remote habitual ending (5RS)

+**hnattook** variant of remote habitual ending +**hminattook** (5RS)

±**hookano** ending used to show that a noun or noun phrase is of continuing importance in a conversation (11RS, 18RS)

±**hookmaka'chi** "must" ending (17RS)

±**hookmano** ending on verbs used with **anhi** "to wish"; "I wish" ending (20)

±**hookya** "but" ending (12RS, 16); "every" ending on n-words (19); "even if" ending (17RS)

±**hoot** subject focus and modifying verb ending (12); short form of ±**hootokoot** "because" (18RS)

±**hootokoot** same-subject "because" ending (13RS, 18)

±**hootoko** different-subject "because" ending (18)

±**ho** object focus and modifying verb ending (12); short form of ±**hootoko** "because" (18RS)

±**hta**, ±**hta** question object ending (17)

±**hto** "is it" noun question ending used after vowels (17)

±**hV** exclamation ending ("V" is a nasalized copy of the vowel before the **h**) (18)

±**ísha** "(not) yet" ending (14)

±**ka'chi** negative future ending used after negative ±**o** (9)

±**kat** same-subject "that" switch-reference ending (13)

±**kaash** modifying phrase ending (20)

±**ka** different-subject "that" switch-reference ending (13); used on object modifying verbs (12RS)

+**ki** special negative ending used between negative ±**o** and a following ending (9)

±**kmaka'chi** "has to" ending (16)

±**kmakilla** "should" ending (17RS)

±**kmakoot** same-subject switch-reference ending used for noncompleted events (12RS)

±**kmat** same-subject "after"/"when"/"if" switch-reference ending used for noncompleted events (11)

±**kma** different-subject "after"/"when"/"if" switch-reference ending used for noncompleted events (11)

+**li** "I" A ending: subject (3)

+**lit** "I" A ending plus +**cha** same-subject "and" (15)

+**li** "I" A ending plus +**na** different-subject "and" (15)

±**m** past focus verb question ending (17)

±**mano** "where is", "where are" noun question ending used after consonants (4RS, 12ACG, 17)

±**ma** variant of object "some" ending ±**hma** (17)

+**na** different-subject "and" switch-reference ending (15)

±**nna** negative hortative ending (15)

±**o** negative verb ending (9)

±**ot** negative verb ending plus +**cha** same-subject "and" (15)

±**ookya** "but" ending used after consonants (16); "every" ending on n-words used after consonants (19)

±**oot** subject focus and modifying verb ending used after consonants (12)

±**o** object focus and modifying verb ending used after consonants (12); negative verb ending plus +**na** different-subject "and" (15)

+**t** dependent verb (t-verb) ending (12RS, 13)

±**ta** question object ending used after consonants (17)

+**taa** verb question ending (4)

+**taam** past verb question ending (4)

±**ta** question object ending used after consonants (17)

+**tok** past verb ending (4)

+**tokat** past same-subject "that" switch-reference ending combination (13)

+**toka** past different-subject "that" switch-reference ending combination (13)

+**tokchincha** past verb ending indicating a conclusion (17RS)

±**tokoot** background information verb ending (same-subject) (18RS)

±**toko** background information verb ending (different-subject) (18RS)

±**to** "is it" noun question ending used after consonants (17)

±**ttook** remote (long) past ending (11RS, 13) be answered with "yes" or "no" (4)

Glossary of Grammatical Terms

All the grammatical terms introduced throughout this book in SMALL CAPITAL LETTERS are defined below, with references to the units in which they are first used indicated by a number in parentheses following the definition: "RL" indicates appendix A, Rhythmic Lengthening in Chickasaw; "ACG" indicates the Advanced Chickasaw Grammar section of certain units; "RS" indicates Reading and Speaking sections. In many cases the definitions use other terms in the glossary, which are themselves given in capital letters in the definition. The glossary also includes some technical linguistic terms that are given for reference but not used in the book; these words are listed in *italics*. If you have difficulty understanding any other terms used in the book or in these definitions, check them in a standard English dictionary.

A MARKER. A PREFIX or ENDING used to indicate the SUBJECT of certain VERBS. (3)

A SUBJECT. A SUBJECT that can be marked by an A MARKER on a VERB. (3)

ACCENT. A rise in the pitch of the voice on the VOWEL of the next-to-last SYLLABLE or the syllable before that one in a Chickasaw VERB, which may appear to be emphasized even more strongly than the final vowel of the word (the one with STRESS). Accented vowels usually have the same sound as the corresponding LONG VOWELS. These vowels are written with an accent mark (´) in Chickasaw spelling. A second type of accented vowel is written with a special CIRCUMFLEX accent mark (^). Chickasaw GRADE forms contain accented vowels. COMPOUND words may have a special COMPOUND ACCENT pattern. (1, 8)

ACTION. An event characterized by activity. VERBS or SENTENCES that tell about actions are generally ACTIVE. (2)

ACTIVE. Characterizing a VERB or SENTENCE that refers to an ACTION. (2)

ADVERB. A special type of VERB modifier. Chickasaw has very few adverbs; most ideas that are expressed with adverbs in other languages are expressed with verbs or AUXILIARIES in Chickasaw. (20)

ANIMATE. Referring to a living creature (most commonly, a person). (16)

ASPIRATION. The slight puff of air that follows the English CONSONANT sounds *p*, *t*, *k*, and *ch*, particularly at the beginning of a word. The corresponding sounds have less aspiration in Chickasaw than in English. (1)

AUXILIARY. A type of Chickasaw VERB used after another verb to MODIFY or help tell more about or clarify its meaning. Auxiliaries are sometimes called "helping verbs". (5)

A-VERB. A Chickasaw VERB starting with **a** or **aa**. (6)

BASIC VERB. A Chickasaw verb without an ACCENT, from which a GRADE FORM may be derived. (8)

CAUSATIVE. A VERB form or SENTENCE used to say that a SUBJECT (the CAUSER) makes someone or something (the CAUSEE) perform some ACTION or be in some STATE. An action that is caused to occur may have an ORIGINAL OBJECT. Thus, for example, in the sentence *The woman made the man hit the dog*, *woman* is the

341

causer, *hit* is the caused action, *man* is the causee, and *dog* is the original object. Causative sentences have an additional PARTICIPANT in comparison with corresponding noncausative sentences (like *The man hit the dog*). Chickasaw causative verbs generally include the ending **+chi**. (6)

CAUSEE. The OBJECT of a CAUSATIVE VERB, the one who is made to perform some ACTION or be in some STATE. Thus, for example, in the sentence *The woman made the man hit the dog*, *man* is the causee. (6)

CAUSER. The SUBJECT of a CAUSATIVE VERB, the added PARTICIPANT who makes the CAUSEE perform some ACTION or be in some STATE. Thus, for example, in the sentence *The woman made the man hit the dog*, *woman* is the causer. (6)

CHANGING VOWEL. The VOWEL of a BASIC VERB that is altered in the formation of a GRADE FORM. Usually, the changing vowel is the next-to-last vowel of a verb, but in some G grades it is the vowel before that one. Changing vowels have an ACCENT. (8, 19ACG)

CIRCUMFLEX. An uncommon type of ACCENT used instead of the normal accent in a very small number of Chickasaw VERBS (G grades). VOWELS with a circumflex accent start out with a strong rise in pitch, then have a fall in pitch; you may almost hear what sounds like a GLOTTAL STOP (') sound after these vowels. (1, 19ACG)

COMMAND. An order to do something—specifically, a VERB form used to order someone to do something. (2)

COMPARATIVE. A SENTENCE that compares one thing to another (describing its qualities as more "than" those of the other) or a VERB form that expresses a relatively greater quality. (15)

COMPARED VERB. The VERB in a COMPARATIVE sentence that expresses the quality being compared. (15)

COMPLETION. Finishing an action completely or affecting all the objects of the action. In Chickasaw, completion is expressed using the auxiliaries **tahli** and **taha** following a t-verb. (14)

COMPOUND. A word formed by combining two or more separate words into a single word. (7RS, 18)

COMPOUND ACCENT. A special ACCENT pattern used in COMPOUND words (especially those whose first part ends in a VOWEL or a vowel plus GLOTTAL STOP), in which the next-to-last SYLLABLE of the first part of a compound is pronounced as a heavy syllable. (18)

CONSONANT. A SOUND in which the steady passage of air through the mouth is interrupted at some point by contact or constriction between two parts of the mouth, such as the two lips (as in a sound like **p** or **m**) or the tongue and the roof of the mouth (as in **t** or **l**). This constriction can even be at the glottis, the opening at the top of the larynx (as in the sounds ' and **h**). (1)

CONTRASTIVE. A special ENDING on a NOUN or PRONOUN used to emphasize that noun or pronoun as opposed to others that someone might think of. Chickasaw contrastive forms are often roughly equivalent to words pronounced with heavy emphasis in English and include the endings ±**akoot** or ±**ak̲o**. (9)

CONTROLLED. Referring to an ACTION that is done deliberately or on purpose, in contrast with one that just happens, that is said to be not controlled. (3)

COPY VOWEL. A VOWEL sound that is not part of a Chickasaw word but that is added to that word in rapid speech—especially between the CONSONANTS **k** or **h** and a following consonant like **l** or between a GLOTTAL STOP and a following consonant. Copy vowels are never written in Chickasaw spelling and do not count as SYLLABLES of a Chickasaw word. (1)

D OBJECT. An OBJECT marked by a DATIVE or D PREFIX on a VERB. D object verbs always include a dative prefix and are usually related to verbs that can be used without D objects. (8)

D PREFIX. A PREFIX that replaces the DATIVE prefix, indicating the POSSESSOR of a POSSESSED NOUN or the SUBJECT or OBJECT of a VERB. (7, 8)

D SUBJECT. A SUBJECT marked by a D PREFIX on a VERB. D subject verbs always include a DATIVE prefix and often cannot be used without it. (8)

DATIVE. Referring to the PREFIX **im±**, which normally indicates the involvement of an additional PARTICIPANT, such as an added POSSESSOR of a NOUN or an added OBJECT of a verb). (7, 8)

DEPENDENT VERB. A VERB in a SENTENCE with more than one verb that is not the MAIN VERB and could not form a complete sentence by itself. Usually, a dependent verb in a Chickasaw sentence comes before the main verb. Often it will be marked, through SWITCH-REFERENCE, to show whether its SUBJECT is the same as or different from that of the main verb. (11)

DITRANSITIVE. See THREE-PLACE.

DOUBLE CONSONANT. A sequence of two instances of the same Chickasaw CONSONANT sound, such as **pp** or **lhlh**. Double consonants seem longer than single consonants and take longer to say. They do not occur at the beginnings or ends of words in Chickasaw. (In technical linguistic terminology, double consonants are referred to as *GEMINATE*.) (1, 19ACG)

DROP. To delete or eliminate a sound in forming a new word. ("Drops" is sometimes replaced by "is dropped" in this use. For instance, you can say either "The i of an i-verb drops after an S prefix" or "The i of an i-verb is dropped after an S prefix," whichever seems better to you.) When a sound drops in this way, it is neither written nor pronounced in the new word. (3)

DUAL. Referring to exactly two, as opposed to SINGULAR and TRIPLURAL. These opposing concepts normally refer to the SUBJECTS or OBJECTS of certain types of Chickasaw VERBS. (10)

ENDING. An element added to the end of a VERB or NOUN to change its grammatical meaning or function. Endings are not words themselves and cannot be used alone. (3) There are two types of endings in Chickasaw, + (PLUS) endings and ± (PLINUS) endings. (4)

EXCLAMATION. A SENTENCE used to indicate strong emotion (indicated by a !). (18)

FINAL. Last in a word; at the end of a word. (1)

FOCUS. 1. A special ENDING on a NOUN used to emphasize its identification. Focus endings are also used on MODIFYING VERBS. 2. To use a focus ending to emphasize a noun. (12)

FOCUS QUESTION. A type of YES-NO QUESTION in which either the SUBJECT or the OBJECT noun is FOCUSED, using the subject and object QUESTION ENDINGS. (17)

FRAME. A special SENTENCE pattern used for expressing an exact quotation, with a "say" verb on either side of the words someone said. (14RS, 20)

FUTURE. The time following the PRESENT, including events that have not yet taken place. (5)

G GRADE. A GRADE FORM that includes a double consonant following a CHANGING VOWEL. (19ACG)

GEMINATE. See DOUBLE CONSONANT. (19ACG)

GLOTTAL STOP. A CONSONANT sound, or what may strike the hearer as an absence of sound, produced when the vocal folds of the glottis (the opening at the top of the larynx) come into contact during speech. Glottal stops are used in both Chickasaw and English, but they are meaningful only in Chickasaw. The Chickasaw glottal stop is written with a ' (apostrophe). (1)

GRADE FORM (or GRADE). A Chickasaw VERB with an ACCENT on its CHANGING VOWEL. Some grade forms are listed in the Chickasaw-English Vocabulary, but most are derived from BASIC VERBS by regular processes, with an accompanying change in meaning. Grade forms covered in this book include the HN grade (8), the N grade (15), the Y grade (18), and the G grade (19ACG). (8)

HABITUAL. Referring to an event or situation that is not a one-time occurrence, but something that happens regularly, as a normal part of life. (5RS)

"HAVE" OBJECT. The OBJECT of any "HAVE" VERB; the noun possessed in a "have" SENTENCE. Unlike other Chickasaw objects, "have" objects are marked with the ending ±**at**. The "have" object must occur immediately before the "have" verb. (12)

"HAVE" VERB. A Chickasaw VERB used in a SENTENCE that expresses "have". Chickasaw "have" verbs include number verbs and POSITIONAL verbs of existence, among others. A "HAVE" OBJECT, unlike other OBJECTS, is marked with ±**at**. Usually, "have" verbs have D SUBJECT prefixes. (12)

HEAVY SYLLABLE. A SYLLABLE that contains a LONG VOWEL, a LENGTHENED VOWEL, or a NASAL VOWEL or whose VOWEL is followed by a sequence of two or more CONSONANTS, including a DOUBLE CONSONANT. Any syllable in which a vowel is followed by a consonant which is part of that syllable is a heavy syllable. All heavy syllables are pronounced with extra emphasis or prominence in a Chickasaw word and sometimes may seem louder than the final vowel, which has STRESS. Any syllable that is not a heavy syllable is a LIGHT SYLLABLE. (1, 4)

HN GRADE. A GRADE FORM that includes an **h** before the CHANGING VOWEL, which is NASAL or followed by a NASAL CONSONANT. (8)

HORTATIVE. A VERB that expresses the speaker's wish that something should or should not be allowed to happen. In Chickasaw, negative hortatives are expressed with ±**nna** and positive hortatives are expressed either with ±**a'shki** or with the unaccomplished prefix **ik**± (or an N prefix). (15)

IDENTIFICATIONAL SENTENCE. A SENTENCE used to identify its SUBJECT with some NOUN or name (as in "He is a doctor" or "That woman is Mary"). In Chickasaw, an identificational sentence can consist simply of a noun, or of a subject and that noun, with no equivalent of "is" or "are". (2)

INANIMATE. Referring to a nonliving thing or to an institution. (16)

INCLUSIVE. Including the hearer as well as the speaker (used to refer to "we", "us", or "our"). In Chickasaw, the special prefixes **kiloo**±, **iloo±, hapo+,** and **hapom**± are inclusive TRIPLURAL prefixes—they refer to a group that includes the hearer as well as the speaker, plus at least one additional person. (3)

INITIAL. At the beginning of a word. (1)

INSTRUMENT. Something with which an action is accomplished. Verbs specifying instruments in Chickasaw begin with **isht**±. (13)

INTONATION. The rhythm of the voice when saying a PHRASE or SENTENCE. Different types of sentences (such as statements, COMMANDS, QUESTIONS, and so on) have characteristically different intonation patterns. (2)

INTRANSITIVE. See ONE-PLACE.

IRREGULAR. Not following the usual (regular) pattern for the use of PREFIXES and ENDINGS or for the interpretation of meaning. (5RS, 6, 11)

I-VERB. A Chickasaw VERB starting with **i**. (3)

LENGTHENED VOWEL. A SHORT VOWEL in a SHORT SYLLABLE that follows a single additional such syllable or an odd number of such syllables, lengthened by the rule of RHYTHMIC LENGTHENING. Lengthened vowels are intermediate in length, between ordinary (nonlengthened) short vowels and LONG VOWELS, and they have the same quality (sound) as the corresponding long vowels. All the even-numbered short syllables in a RHYTHMIC LENGTHENING SEQUENCE are lengthened. Syllables containing lengthened vowels are HEAVY SYLLABLES. Lengthened vowels need not be written any differently from ordinary short vowels, because the rules that tell you where to pronounce them are regular. If desired, language learners can write them in a special way—in this book, they are often written with a MACRON. (4, RL)

LETTER COMBINATION. A sequence of two letters used to write a single sound in Chickasaw or English ORTHOGRAPHY. **Ch** is an example of a letter combination in both English and Chickasaw; **lh** is a Chickasaw letter combination that does not occur in English. (1)

LIGHT SYLLABLE. A SYLLABLE consisting of a short vowel that is not a LENGTHENED VOWEL, with or without a preceding consonant. A light syllable is a SHORT SYLLABLE whose vowel is not lengthened by the RHYTHMIC LENGTHENING rule. Any syllable that is not a HEAVY SYLLABLE is a light syllable. (1)

LOCATIONAL NOUN. A NOUN that specifies the part or area of another noun relative to which a location is specified. (10)

LONG NASAL VOWEL. A sequence of a NASAL VOWEL followed immediately by a SHORT non-nasal version of the same VOWEL. While both vowels in such sequences can usually be distinguished, the sequence may seem like a single SYLLABLE, especially in rapid speech. (1)

LONG VOWEL. A VOWEL that is longer (taking nearly twice as long to pronounce) as the corresponding SHORT VOWEL sound. Long vowels are written with two instances of the short vowel letter. All syllables containing long vowels are HEAVY SYLLABLES. (1)

MACRON. A horizontal line over a VOWEL letter, used to indicate some type of "long" pronunciation. The macron is used in this book to represent Chickasaw LENGTHENED VOWELS; in English, it is used for "long vowels". (4, RL)

MAIN VERB. The VERB of a SENTENCE containing more than one verb that looks just like the verb of a sentence with only one verb; thus, a verb that is part of a sentence with more than one verb but that could be used by itself as a complete sentence. Most often the main verb is the last one in a Chickasaw sentence with more than one verb, coming after the DEPENDENT VERBS. In a sense the verbs of all sentences with just one verb can also be considered main verbs. (11) (See also SWITCH-REFERENCE.)

MARKER. A PREFIX or ENDING added to a VERB or NOUN to indicate some additional meaning. Chickasaw has four sets of SUBJECT and OBJECT markers: the A markers, the S prefixes, the D prefixes, and the N prefixes. (3)

MODIFIED NOUN. The NOUN within a MODIFYING PHRASE that is identified or specified by that phrase. (20)

MODIFY. To identify, clarify, or tell more about the meaning of something. Chickasaw has both MODIFYING VERBS and MODIFYING PHRASES to modify the meaning of NOUNS. Chickasaw AUXILIARIES and ADVERBS are used to modify the meanings of VERBS. (5, 12)

MODIFYING PHRASE. A type of DEPENDENT SENTENCE that speakers use to help listeners identify who or what is being referred to, the MODIFIED NOUN within the phrase. There are both SUBJECT MODIFYING PHRASES and OBJECT MODIFYING PHRASES. (20)

MODIFYING VERB. A VERB used to identify, specify, or tell more about a preceding NOUN with which it forms a PHRASE. SUBJECT and OBJECT FOCUS endings referring to the whole phrase go on the end of the modifying verb. (12)

MOTION VERB. A VERB that expresses movement by its subject. (13)

N GRADE. A GRADE FORM in which the CHANGING VOWEL is NASAL or followed by a NASAL CONSONANT. (15)

N PREFIX. A PREFIX that replaces the UNACCOMPLISHED PREFIX **ik±** on a NEGATIVE or HORTATIVE verb, indicating a SUBJECT of that verb that on a corresponding non-negative, nonhortative form would be shown by an A MARKER. (9, 15)

NASAL CONSONANT. A CONSONANT produced with air released through the nose, as with a NASAL VOWEL. The Chickasaw nasal consonants include **m** and **n** and also the rare consonant sound **ng**. (1)

NASAL VOWEL. A VOWEL produced with the mouth and tongue in position for an ordinary vowel but with air released through the nose rather than just through the mouth. In Chickasaw and Choctaw ORTHOGRAPHY, nasal vowels are written underlined (as in this book) or occasionally in *italics*. Chickasaw nasal vowels are about as long as long vowels. SYLLABLES containing nasal vowels are always HEAVY SYLLABLES. (1)

NEGATIVE. A SENTENCE used to report that some ACTION did not take place or that some STATE does not hold. (7, 9)

NEGATIVE VERB. A VERB containing the NEGATIVE ENDING **±o**. Such verbs also include the UNACCOMPLISHED PREFIX **ik±** or an N prefix and may have changes in the verb. (9)

NOUN. A word that is used to name or refer to a person, place, or thing (some concrete item, in other words) or to an idea or concept. (2)

N-WORD. A word related to a T-WORD (a QUESTION WORD used in a QUESTION WORD QUESTION), with an **n** substituted for the **t**. N-words are used to express "some"/"any" words and question words in DEPENDENT SENTENCES. (17, 17ACG)

OBJECT. The one or ones that receive or are affected by the action of the VERB of a SENTENCE. Often, a statement of the object is necessary to complete the idea expressed by a verb. A NOUN word or some other element (often a verb prefix) may be used in Chickasaw to name the object of a sentence, or the object may be UNDER-STOOD—clear to both the speaker and the hearer but not explicitly named. Some Chickasaw sentences may have more than one object. (5) (There are several types of object: see also CAUSEE, D OBJECT, "HAVE" OBJECT, ORIGINAL OBJECT, S OBJECT.)

OBJECT MODIFYING PHRASE. A MODIFYING PHRASE in which the MODIFIED NOUN is the OBJECT. (20)

ONE-PLACE. Referring to a VERB that has a SUBJECT but no OBJECT. (In technical linguistic terminology, one-place verbs are generally referred to as *INTRANSITIVE*.) (5)

ORIGINAL. The form of a word one starts with before adding a PREFIX or ENDING, making a GRADE FORM, or changing the form by a RULE, for example. (4)

ORIGINAL OBJECT. The OBJECT of a TWO-PLACE VERB that is made CAUSATIVE. Thus, for example, in the sentence *The woman made the man hit the dog*, *hit* is the two-place caused action and *dog* is the original object. (6)

ORTHOGRAPHY. Spelling system (an alphabet and the rules needed to interpret it). The orthography for any given language is generally different from that for any other language, and some languages have more than one recognized orthography that speakers or scholars use. (1)

O-VERB. A Chickasaw VERB starting with **o**, **oo**, or **o̲**. All Chickasaw verbs starting with VOWELS other than **i**, **a**, or **aa** work like o-verbs. (10)

PARTICIPANT. One of those involved or concerned with an ACTION or STATE and mentioned in a SENTENCE. A VERB always has at least one participant, its SUBJECT, and may include several others; a NOUN may have an added participant involved with it, a POSSESSOR. (5, 7, 8)

PASSIVE. A VERB whose SUBJECT is on the receiving end of the action. In English, passive sentences include a form of *to be* plus a verb usually ending in *–ed*, as in *The governor <u>was</u> elect<u>ed</u> by the people*. Chickasaw verbs that express a passive meaning are usually V1's containing **l** or **lh**, but there's no way to specify a "by" meaning with them. (15)

PAST. Referring to a time prior to the time of speaking. In Chickasaw, there are two past TENSE forms, the normal past (indicated with **+tok**) and the REMOTE PAST (indicated with **±ttook**). There is also a REMOTE PAST HABITUAL. (4)

PHRASE. A word or group of words with a single grammatical use—**issi' yammat** "that deer" is a Chickasaw subject noun phrase, for instance. (2)

PLAIN. With no added PREFIXES or ENDINGS. The plain form of a VERB or NOUN is listed in the Chickasaw-English Vocabulary. (2)

PLINUS. The "plus/minus" sign (±), used to join PREFIXES or ENDINGS to another word. Prefixes or endings joined to a word with a plinus do not count as part of a RHYTHMIC LENGTHENING SEQUENCE. (2, 4)

PLURAL. Referring to two or more items; not SINGULAR. Most English NOUNS change their form when they are plural, but Chickasaw nouns do not, and their plural status is UNDERSTOOD within a particular conversational situation rather than being explicitly marked. (2) (See also TRIPLURAL.)

PLUS. The ordinary plus sign (+), used to join PREFIXES or ENDINGS to another word. Prefixes or endings joined to a word with a plus sign can count as part of a RHYTHMIC LENGTHENING SEQUENCE. (2, 4)

POSITIONAL. A special type of Chickasaw VERB that specifies the bodily position or orientation that the subject is in. Positional verbs have SINGULAR, DUAL, and TRIPLURAL forms. With D PREFIXES, many positional verbs are used as "HAVE" VERBS. (10, 12)

POSSESSED. Referring to a noun that is owned by or in a relationship with another noun, the POSSESSOR, with which the possessed noun forms a POSSESSIVE PHRASE. *Mother* and *house* are possessed in the possessive phrases *the girl's mother* and *the bird's house*. In these English examples and in all Chickasaw possessive phrases, the possessed noun follows the possessor noun. (5RS, 7)

POSSESSED FORM. The form of a NOUN that allows it to be interpreted as having a "his", "her", "its", or "their" POSSESSOR. Possessed forms of many nouns are made by adding a DATIVE prefix. Other nouns only occur in possessed form. (7)

POSSESSION. A relationship like ownership or kinship between a POSSESSED noun and its POSSESSOR. (7)

POSSESSIVE PHRASE. An expression containing more than one word that specifies POSSESSOR and POSSESSED NOUNS. (7)

POSSESSOR. The person or thing with regard to which POSSESSION is viewed; usually, the owner. (7)

POSSESSOR/SUBJECT. A POSSESSOR that is also a SUBJECT in possessor/subject "have" sentences. (14)

PREFIX. An element added to the front of a VERB or NOUN to change its grammatical meaning or function. Prefixes are not words themselves and cannot be used alone. There are two types of prefixes in Chickasaw, + (PLUS) prefixes and ± (PLINUS) prefixes. (2, 4)

PRESENT. Referring to the time of speaking or writing; referring to now, neither the PAST nor the FUTURE. (2)

PREVERB. A type of PREFIX that must be the first item in its word, before any prefixes that indicate SUBJECTS and OBJECTS. Preverbs end in a **t**, which drops between two consonants. (7RS, 11RS, 13, 19)

PRONOUN. A word like "I", "you", or "we" that refers to one of the PARTICIPANTS in the conversation (either the speaker or the hearer). A pronoun is always a separate word in the sentence. (3, 7RS, 9)

QUESTION. A SENTENCE used to ask for confirmation or information. There are a number of different types of questions in Chickasaw, including YES-NO QUESTIONS, QUESTION WORD QUESTIONS, and others. (4)

QUESTION WORD. A WORD used in a QUESTION asking for specific information, not just a "yes" or "no" answer (these questions are called QUESTION WORD QUESTIONS). Chickasaw examples of question words include **kata** "who", **nanta** "what", and many others, including question VERBS. All Chickasaw question words used in question word questions include a **t** sound in the middle (hence, they may be called T-WORDS), and most begin with **kat**. N-WORDS are used to express question words in DEPENDENT SENTENCES. (17, 17ACG)

QUESTION WORD QUESTION. A QUESTION that includes (but need not begin with) a QUESTION WORD, used to ask for specific information, not just a "yes" or "no" answer. (17)

RECIPROCAL. A SENTENCE containing a TWO-PLACE VERB with a PLURAL SUBJECT whose members act on each other. *They killed each other* is an English reciprocal sentence. Chickasaw reciprocal verbs include the PREFIX **itti+**. (10)

REFLEXIVE. A SENTENCE containing a TWO-PLACE VERB whose SUBJECT acts on itself and which thus has only one PARTICIPANT. *They killed themselves* is an English reflexive sentence with a PLURAL subject; *He loves himself* is one with a SINGULAR subject. Chickasaw reflexive verbs include the PREFIX **ili±**. (5)

REMOTE PAST. A TENSE of a VERB referring to a time that is not just the PAST, but an occasion definitely remote from the PRESENT. The remote past is used for any time more than a few years back and certainly to refer to events that took place before the speaker was born. In Chickasaw, the remote past is marked with the ENDING **±ttook**. (13)

REMOTE PAST HABITUAL. A PAST TENSE of a VERB specifying regular situations or events in a long-ago time remote from the PRESENT. Such events or situations are not a one-time occurrence, but something that used to happen as a normal part of life. Chickasaw verbs in the remote habitual end in **+hminattook** or **+hnattook**. These ENDINGS include the REMOTE PAST ending **±ttook**. (5RS)

RHYTHMIC LENGTHENING. The RULE that produces LENGTHENED VOWELS in even-numbered SHORT SYLLABLES within a RHYTHMIC LENGTHENING SEQUENCE. (4)

RHYTHMIC LENGTHENING SEQUENCE. A sequence of SHORT SYLLABLES in which the even-numbered syllables get LENGTHENED VOWELS by the RHYTHMIC LENGTHENING RULE. MARKERS attached to an ORIGINAL form of a NOUN or VERB with a + (PLUS) may create longer rhythmic lengthening sequences; markers attached with a ± (PLINUS) never change the word's original rhythmic lengthening sequence. (4)

RULE. A statement of regular grammatical processes. (4)

S OBJECT. An OBJECT that can be marked by an S PREFIX on a VERB. Generally, only D OBJECTS marked with D prefixes are referred to with a special name; the term "object" usually indicates an S object. (8)

S PREFIX. A PREFIX used to mark the SUBJECT of an S subject VERB, the OBJECT of a verb that takes S objects, or the POSSESSOR of a NOUN that uses S POSSESSION. (3, 7, 8)

S SUBJECT. A SUBJECT that can be marked by an S PREFIX on a VERB. (3)

SENTENCE. A word or group of words used to express a complete thought—most often, reporting an ACTION or describing a situation or STATE of events. Most sentences have at least one VERB and at least one SUBJECT. (2)

SHORT SYLLABLE. A SYLLABLE containing a single consonant and a short vowel. Even-numbered short syllables (counting from the beginning of any RHYTHMIC LENGTHENING SEQUENCE) have their VOWELS LENGTHENED. Any short syllable whose vowel is not lengthened is a LIGHT SYLLABLE. (4)

SHORT VERB. A Chickasaw VERB whose PLAIN form consists of a SHORT VOWEL plus a single CONSONANT plus another short vowel. All such verbs are IRREGULAR in Chickasaw. (11)

SHORT VOWEL. A VOWEL sound that is shorter (takes less time to pronounce) than the corresponding LONG VOWEL sound written with two instances of the same letter. Short vowels have more variations in pronunciation than long vowels. Short vowels may be LENGTHENED. (1, 4)

SIGN. See PLINUS SIGN, PLUS SIGN.

SINGULAR. Referring to only one; not PLURAL. (2) In certain groups of Chickasaw VERBS, singular is also opposed to the concepts of DUAL and TRIPLURAL. (10)

SOUND. A VOWEL or CONSONANT. Every language has its own set of different speech sounds. (1)

SPECIAL "we". A short way of referring to the INCLUSIVE TRIPLURAL "we" PREFIXES. (3)

STATE. A condition rather than an activity. A VERB or SENTENCE that describes a state is generally STATIVE. (2)

STATIVE. Characterizing a VERB or SENTENCE that refers to a STATE of being rather than to an action. (2)

STOP. See GLOTTAL STOP.

STRESS. The increase in loudness or intensity of the voice on certain VOWELS or SYLLABLES in a word—for instance, the English word *English* has the stress on the first (*Eng*) syllable. In Chickasaw, words generally have the stress on the last vowel. (1)

SUBJECT. The one or ones who perform the action of or may be characterized by a VERB or that a particular SENTENCE is used to describe. A NOUN word or some other element may be used in Chickasaw to name the subject of a SENTENCE, or the subject may be UNDERSTOOD—clear to the speaker and hearer but not explicitly named. (2) (There are several types of subject: see also A SUBJECT, CAUSER, D SUBJECT, POSSESSOR/SUBJECT, S SUBJECT, as well as SWITCH-REFERENCE.)

SUBJECT MODIFYING PHRASE. A MODIFYING PHRASE in which the MODIFIED NOUN is the SUBJECT. (20)

SWITCH-REFERENCE. A system by which a DEPENDENT VERB in a Chickasaw SENTENCE is marked to show whether its SUBJECT is the same as or different from that of the MAIN VERB of that sentence. (11)

SYLLABLE. A unit in the pronunciation of a word that contains a VOWEL and, often, a preceding CONSONANT and one or more following consonants. Every vowel (long, short, or nasal) in a Chickasaw word constitutes a separate syllable. Syllables may be either LIGHT SYLLABLES or HEAVY SYLLABLES. Light syllables are one type of SHORT SYLLABLES. Identifying the syllables in Chickasaw words is very important for pronunciation, especially RHYTHMIC LENGTHENING. A sequence of a NASAL VOWEL plus a following SHORT VOWEL may be pronounced like a single syllable, called a LONG NASAL VOWEL. Added COPY VOWELS that are not present in the ORIGINAL form of a word (and are never written) do not increase the number of syllables in that word. (1, 4)

TENSE. The time of a sentence, the time that an action takes place or that a state is true. In Chickasaw, verbs can indicate PAST, REMOTE PAST, and FUTURE with different endings; verbs without endings refer to the PRESENT. (4)

THREE-PLACE. Referring to a VERB that has a SUBJECT, an OBJECT, and a second object which may be specified by a NOUN. (In technical linguistic terminology, three-place verbs are generally referred to as *DITRANSITIVE*.) (6)

TRANSITIVE. See TWO-PLACE.

TRIPLURAL. Referring to three or more, as opposed to SINGULAR or DUAL. These concepts normally refer to the SUBJECTS or OBJECTS of certain types of Chickasaw VERB; triplural is also used to refer to inclusive triplural "we" prefixes on verbs. (See also PLURAL.) (3, 10)

T-VERB. A DEPENDENT VERB with a +t ending. (13)

TWO-PLACE. Referring to a VERB that has both a SUBJECT and an OBJECT. (In technical linguistic terminology, two-place verbs are generally referred to as *TRANSITIVE*.) (5)

T-WORD. A word used to express a QUESTION WORD in a QUESTION WORD QUESTION. T-words contain a **t**; with an **n** substituted for the **t**, they become N-WORDS. (17, 17ACG)

UNACCOMPLISHED. Referring to an ACTION that has not taken place or a STATE that does not hold, such as a NEGATIVE. (9)

UNDERSTOOD. Not explicitly mentioned, but clear to the people in a conversation—in other words, to you (the speaker) and to your hearer or hearers. An understood SUBJECT of a SENTENCE, for example, is a subject that is not explicitly named but is known to both speaker and hearer through the previous conversation or the situation in which they are speaking. A NOUN may be understood as PLURAL without any change in its form, for instance, if it is used as the subject of a VERB marked as having a plural subject. (2)

V1, V2. See VERB PAIR.

VERB. A word that reports an ACTION or a STATE of events. Most SENTENCES have at least one verb. A verb has a SUBJECT. (2) (See also A-VERB, BASIC VERB, COMPARED VERB, DEPENDENT VERB, "HAVE" VERB, I-VERB, MAIN VERB, MOTION VERB, NEGATIVE VERB, O-VERB, SHORT VERB, T-VERB.)

VERB PAIR. A pair of VERBS related in meaning, appearance, and use, referred to as the V1 and V2 of the pair. Usually the V1 is a ONE-PLACE verb, most commonly with an S SUBJECT, and the V2 is a TWO-PLACE verb used to say that its A subject causes someone to experience the V1. (16)

VOWEL. A SOUND produced with the mouth open and no interruption in the flow of the airstream by the tongue or other speech organs. In Chickasaw, vowels may be either SHORT, LONG, or NASAL; short vowels may be LENGTHENED. Each Chickasaw vowel sound forms a separate SYLLABLE. (1) (See also COPY VOWEL.)

VOWEL-LOSS NOUN. A NOUN ending in a HEAVY SYLLABLE followed by a SHORT VOWEL, with or without a following GLOTTAL STOP. This final vowel or vowel-plus-glottal stop is lost before ENDINGS that start with vowels. (4)

Y GRADE. A GRADE FORM in which the CHANGING VOWEL is followed by **yy**. (18)

YES-NO QUESTION. A QUESTION that can be answered with "yes" or "no". (4)

Chickasaw-English Vocabulary

This vocabulary includes all the basic words introduced in this book, except for a few complex expressions introduced in the Reading and Speaking sections. Generally, only plain forms of verbs and nouns are included; therefore, if you are trying to find a word in the vocabulary, make sure you take all prefixes and endings off it before you begin. Prefixes and endings are listed in a special index of their own, earlier in this book.

Often you will find it helpful to consult the English-Chickasaw Vocabulary before looking a word up here. More information is given in this Chickasaw-English Vocabulary than in the English-Chickasaw one, however, and it's best to check this vocabulary to be sure how a word will behave in a sentence.

In general words are listed in their basic form, without added prefixes or endings. The numbers of the units in which a word is first introduced or in which it is extensively discussed follow its English definition in parentheses. This information may be important: often the lessons in that unit provide important information on how to use the word in sentences. Words from the Reading and Speaking sections of the units are identified with the unit number plus RS; words from Advanced Chickasaw Grammar sections are identified with the unit number plus ACG. Full cross-references are not given for all the numbers in 11ACG.

All verbs have an English definition beginning with "to". Verbs introduced in unit 2 and following units are listed with grammatical information, including a following abbreviation that explains which sets of Chickasaw markers are used to indicate their subjects and objects, as explained in units 3, 5, 6, and 8, as well as providing information on irregular and related forms. This information is not given for verbs that only appear as examples in unit 1. Representative prefixed forms of irregular verbs (short verbs and the verb <ya> "be", as discussed in unit 11) are listed following the definitions of these verbs.

Regular grade forms (units 9, 15), negatives (unit 9), reflexives (unit 5), reciprocals (unit 10), and most verbs formed with the ending +chi (unit 6) or the prefixes im± (unit 7) or on±, ibaa±, and aa± (unit 10) are not listed, unless there is something irregular about their form or meaning or they do not have a corresponding basic form. When such forms are listed, they have their own main entries in the vocabulary, but there is a cross-reference to them under the entry for the basic form of the verb if one exists.

Nouns are assumed to have possessed forms made by adding the dative prefix im±, as explained in unit 7, unless they are followed by the abbreviation SP (meaning that the noun takes S prefixes in the possessive form) or DP (meaning that the noun includes a dative prefix in the basic form listed in the vocabulary and is always possessed). Irregular possessed forms of certain nouns are listed in the vocabulary. See unit 7.

A few words that cannot be used alone but must have markers attached to be pronounced are listed in angles (<>'s) in the vocabulary. Variant pronunciations for words in the vocabulary are listed following the main entry. If these would come at a different point in the alphabet, they are listed there, too, with a cross-reference to the main entry. (Not all variant pronunciations used by every speaker of Chickasaw are listed here, of course. Your teacher may use a somewhat different pronunciation for some of the words in this vocabulary, and you should always follow your teacher's pronunciation.) Words that are used in this book only as parts of longer expressions are listed with a reference to those other expressions.

Chickasaw words are listed in this vocabulary according to the following alphabetical order: ', a, aa, a̱, b, ch, (d), (e), (g), f, h, i, ii, i̱, (j), k, l, lh, m, n, ng, o, oo, o̱, p, (r), s, sh, t, (v), w, y, (z) (parenthesized sounds occur only in rare loan words). There are no words in Chickasaw that begin with ' or ng and no words in this vocabulary that begin with e, g, ii, j, r, or z. Accents and hyphens are ignored in alphabetizing. Letter combinations are alphabetized separately. Thus, for example, **aabachi** comes after **abi** and all other words starting with **a**, because **aa** (long **a**) is a different letter combination from **a** (short **a**).

The following abbreviations are used in the vocabulary: A = A marker, aux. = auxiliary, cntr. = contrastive, D = D prefix, dl. = dual, DP = D possession, Ggr. = G grade, HNgr. = HN grade, loc. n. = locational noun, N = N prefix, neg. = negative, Ngr. = N grade, obj. = object, pl. = plural, poss. = possessed form, S = S prefix, sg. = singular, SP = S possession, subj. = subject, tpl. = triplural, Ygr. = Y grade. Numbers after an entry refer to the units in which that entry was introduced. As explained above, RS, BG, and ACG refer to the Reading and Speaking, Beyond the Grammar, and Advanced Chickasaw Grammar sections of those units.

a

aba' above (15RS)

aba' anompa ishtanompoli' preacher (7RS)

Aba' Yaakni' Heaven (15RS)

abi to kill (A,S) (short verb: ishbi, kiibi; ikbo, akbo, chikbo, kiibo; sabi; imambi) (1, 6RS, 11)

abihli to put (two or a small number of obj.) in (a container) (10RS)

abika to be sick (S) (6)

  imambiika to be sick for

abika' sick person (18)

abokkoli' woods, thicket (5RS)

aboknóyyo'ha to be wrapped in (S,Noun) (20RS)

abooha, aboowa house; building; room (DP = imambooha, imamboowa) (1, 7)

  aaimpa' abooha dining room

  itti' basha' abooha frame house

  itti' ittabaana' abooha log house, log cabin

  lokfi' nona' abooha brick house

aboowoshi' bathroom, outhouse (18)

achaknaski to turn on one's side (A) (18)

achaknáyya'ski to lie on one's side (A) (18)

achokmilhka to kneel down (A) (4)

achokmíyyi'lhka to be kneeling (A) (18)

afama to meet (A,S) (6)

afammi year (9RS)

ahi' potato (12)

ahiika to incur a debt; to go into debt (A) (15RS)

aholhchi'fo to be named after (A,S) (14RS)

ahooba to look like, resemble, seem like (A,S) (16RS)

akanka' chicken (4)

aka̱nakni' rooster (11)

akiilawa to belch, burp (S / A) (15)

akka' floor; down (18RS)

akkowa to go down (A)

akmi to be frozen (S) (6)

ala to arrive, to get here, to be here (A), to arrive at (a place here) (A,Noun) (short verb: ishla, kiila; iklo, aklo, chiklo, kiilo; imalla) (1, 11); to be born (A) (17)

  ishtala to bring (here)

alba weed (12RS)

alba homi' bitter weed (12RS)

Alibaamo' Alabama Indian (11RS)

albí'ha, albí'ya to be inside (A,Noun) (dl. subj.) (12ACG)

albiha to get inside (dl. subj.) (A,Noun) (18RS)

albihat máa, albiyat máa to be inside (A,Noun) (tpl. subj.) (12ACG)

alikchi' doctor (2)

almo to be mowed (Noun) (16AACG)

alhchifa to be washed (S) (18)

alhchímbat tahahma̱ after a while (19RS)

alhiha' bunch (of people) (used as the second element of a compound) (17RS, 19)

alhkaniya to be forgotten (S) (17RS)

  imalhkaniya to forget (D,Noun)

alhpí'sa to be enough (Noun) (11RS)

alhtaha to be ready, to be already prepared (of a food, for example) (Noun) (9RS)

alhtoka to be elected (S) (16)

ámmo'na to be first (A) (14RS)

Ammo'na' part of **Nittak Ammo'na'**

amo to mow, cut, harvest (grass) (A, Noun); to give a haircut to (A,S) (short verb: ishmo/ishammo, kiimo/kilammo; ikmo/ikammo, akmo/akammo, chikmo/chikammo, kiimo/kilammo; imammo) (1, 11)

amposhi' dish, plate (12)

  holisso amposhi' paper plate

amposhi' shokawwa'li' glass (10RS)

anakshooli to singe, burn the hair off (A,S) (6RS)

anaakilloot only I (20)

anaakillo̱ only me (20)

anaakoot I (cntr.) (9)

anaako̱ me (cntr.) (9)

anchi to cover oneself with (A,Noun) (18)

ánchi (Ngr. of **aachi**) (19RS)

anchokma I'm fine (1RS)

anhi to wish (A) (1, 20)

  inanhi to wish something for (someone) (A,D)

  anhínchi to like (A,S) (Ngr.) (19)

anhit ishtanokfilli to wonder about (A,S) (inclues preverb **isht±**) (20RS)

ani to put (many obj.), pour (liquid) into (a container) (A,Noun,Noun); to bear, set fruit, have fruit on it (of a plant) (Noun) (short verb: ishanni, kilanni; ikanno, akanno, chikanno, kilanno; imanni) (1, 10RS, 11)

  á'ni (Ggr.)

ani' fruit, crop, produce (noun) (1, 18)

annoyachi to make (something) known (A,Noun) (20RS)

anokfilli to think (A) (13)

  anhit ishtanokfilli to wonder about (A,S) (inclues preverb **isht±**)

anompa word; language (6)

anompoli to speak, to talk (A) (1,4); to speak (a language) (A,Noun) (5)

anonka' inside (SP); in, inside (loc. n.) (SP) (10)—*see* **anonkaka'**

anonkaka' inside—form of anonka' usually used with S prefixes or to refer to locations relative to a person (S) (10)

ano̱wa' also; again (7RS, 14)

ánta to stay (sg. human or living subj.) (A) (3, 9); to be located in, live in (a place) (sg. human or living subj.) (A,Noun) (10, 12ACG) (neg. ikánto)

  imánta to have (a relative) (sg. human obj.)

apa to eat (something) (A,S) (short verb: ishpa, kiipa; ikpo, akpo, chikpo, kiipo; sapa; imappa) (1, 5RS, 11)

apat pisa to taste (A,Noun) (13)

Api' part of **Hattak Api' Homma'**

apila to help (A,S) (6)

  áppi'la (Ggr.)

apiisachi to take care of, watch over (A,S) (20RS)

  chokfalhpooba' apiisachi' shepherd

apootaka' side; beside, next to (loc. n.) (10)

Appo'si' Grandmother (refers to the speaker's grandmother) (8RS)

ashana to be locked (Noun) (18)

ashiila soup (13)

atahánta to come and be located in, to come and be born in (A) (includes preverb **at±**) (20RS)

atáyya'at leaning back against (12RS)

atobbi to pay (A,Noun) (8)

  imaatobbi to pay to

Atochchi'na' part of **Nittak Atochchi'na'**

Atokla' part of **Nittak Atokla'**

atookoli to elect (A,S) (16)

atpisa to come and see (A,S) (includes preverb **at±**) (20RS)

awa-chaffa eleven (10RS)

awa-chakká'li nineteen (10RS)

awa-hanná'li sixteen (10RS)

awa-ontochchí'na eighteen (10RS)

awa-ontoklo seventeen (10RS)

awa-oshta fourteen (10RS)

awa-talhlhá'pi fifteen (10RS)

awa-tochchí'na thirteen (10RS)

awa-toklo twelve (10RS)

aya to go (A), to go to (a place) (A,Noun) (short verb: ishiyya, kiliiya; ikiyyo, akiyyo, chikiyyo, kiliyyo; imayya) (1, 5RS, 11); part of **hoot aya!, nani' hoot aya!**

  ishtaya to begin; to bring, take

  nanna aya peace

  pist aya to go see

ayoppa to be happy (S) (1, 6)

ayoppachi to worship, to praise (A,S) (17RS)

ayoppánchi to like (A,S) (6)

ayowa to gather, get (food plants, for example) (A,Noun) (5)

áyya'sha to stay, be there (A); to be located in (a place) (A,Noun) (tpl. subj.) (1, 11RS, 12)

  himmaka' áyya'shookano these days

  imáyya'sha to have (relatives) (tpl. human obj.)

  mishsha' fónkha áyya'shookano in still earlier times

  chiiki pilla' áyya'shakaash once upon a time

áyya̱'chi to be covered with (A,Noun) (18)

Ayyoshta' part of **Nittak Ayyoshta'**

aa

aa oh (16RS)

aabachi to point at (A,S) (6)

aabi to paint, to smear (A,S) (1, 6)

  aahámbi (HNgr.)

aachi to say (something) (A,Noun) (6); to call (someone something) (A,Noun,Noun) (11RS); to mean (something) (Noun,Noun) (14RS); they say (16RS)

  ánchi (Ngr.)

aachompa' store, town (1, 10)
aahámbi (irregular HNgr. of **aabi**) (8)
aahashtahli' window (10RS, 18)
aahilha' dance hall (18)
aahobachi to copy (something) from (a thing) (A,Noun,Noun) (16)
aaholloppi' graveyard, cemetery (18)
aaholhponi' pot (9RS), kitchen (10)
aahonkopa to steal (something) from (an institution) (A,Noun,Noun) (16)
aahopooni to cook (something) in, cook (something) on (A,Noun,Noun) (9RS)
Aaiklanna' part of **Nittak Hollo' Aaiklanna'**
aaiksaa to be made from (A,Noun) (13RS)
aaimpa' restaurant (10)
aaimpa' abooha dining room (10)

aaipita' in **issoba aaipita' piini'**
aaissachi to leave (A,S) (14RS)
aaittanaa' church (7RS, 10)
aaittapiha' group (20RS)
aai̱'pa' table (10)
aai̱'pa' holiito'pa' holy table (12RS)
aalhakoffichi to save from (A,S)
aalhpí'sa to be right, be correct; to do the right thing (A) (6)
aalhponi' kitchen (10)
aaminti to come from (A,Noun)
aanosi' bedroom (10)
aaombiniili' chair (12)
aapihlichika' kingdom (DP) (15RS)
aaponta to borrow (something) from (an institution) (A,Noun,Noun) (16)
aayimmi to believe in (something) (S;Noun) (17RS)

a

áa to go along, to be going along (A) (1, 20)
alhínchi to be enacted, made true (Noun) (17RS)
ashaka', ashka' behind, rear, back (SP); in back of (loc. n.) (SP) (10)

áshwa to stay, be there (A); to be located in (a place) (A,Noun) (dl. subj.) (12)
  imáshwa to have (relatives) (dl. human obj.)

b

bala' bean (2)
  sinti' bala' / bala' sinti' snake bean
balaafokha' / balaafka' pants (14)
banna to want (S,Noun) (9)
basha to be cut, to be operated on (S) (6)
  itti' basha' abooha frame house
bashafa to be cut (of a long subj.) (S) (16)
bashaffi to cut (a long obj., usually with a knife) (A,S) (5)
bashli to operate on, to cut (A,S) (5)
bashpo knife (1, 7)
baafa to stab (A,S) (9)
bila to melt, to be melted (S) (1, 4)
biliili to melt (something) (A,S) (16)
bílli'yacha bílli'ya forever and ever (15RS)
bini'cha loshka sit down and tell lies! (an invitation to gossip) (3)
biniili to sit down, get into a sitting position (sg. subj.) (A) (12RS, 19)
bínni'li to sit, be seated, be in a sitting position (A); to sit in, to be located (sitting) in (a place) (A,Noun) (sg. subj.) (8, 10)

binohli to sit down, get into a sitting position (pl. subj.) (A) (19)
binohmáa to sit, be seated, be in a sitting position (A); to sit in, be located (sitting) in (a place) (A,Noun) (tpl. subj.) (10)
bíyyi'ka all the time, always (aux.) (1, 8); (aux. used with ±a'hi "can" verbs) (5); it's all, it was all (7RS); truly (17RS); several, many (used as a stative verb following a noun, with focus endings) (18)
bo'li to hit (more than once); to beat up; to pound; to hit (pl. subj.) (A,S) (1, 13)
bo'wa to be hammered (Noun) (18)
bohli to lay down, put down (sg. long obj.) (A,S) (1, 13)
  ishtombohli to accuse, blame; to accuse about, blame for [isht ombohli]
  ombohli to lay (something) down on, put (something) down on

ch

chaffa one (3RS); to be one in number (A) (12); part of **awa-chaffa, holhtina' chaffa**
  inchaffa to have one

  nittak chaffaka one day
chaffo' other one (20)
Chahta' Choctaw (1, 2)

Chahta' Iyaakni' Choctaw Nation (13RS)
Chahtanompa, Chahtanompa', Chahta imanompa
    Choctaw language (7RS)
chakká'li nine (3RS); to be nine in number (A) (12); part
    of **awa-chakká'li, holhtina' chakká'li**
    inchakká'li to have nine
Chalakki' Cherokee (11)
champoli to be sweet, taste good (S) (12)
    paska champoli' cake, cookie, pie
chaaha to be tall (S) (1, 3)
cha'li to chop, chop down (A,Noun) (10RS)
chi'ya to sit, be seated, be in a sitting position (A); to sit
    in, be located (sitting) in (A place) (A,Noun) (dl.
    subj.) (10)
Chihoowa God (8)
    Pinki' Chihoowa God our Father
Chikashsha Chickasaw (2)
Chikashsha Iminko' the Chickasaw governor (the gover-
    nor of the Chickasaw Nation) (17)
Chikashsha Iyaakni' Chickasaw Nation (7RS, 16)
Chikashshanompa, Chikashshanompa', Chikashsha
    imanompa Chickasaw language (5)
Chikashshihoo, Chikashshihoo' Chickasaw woman (2)
chimmi' yours (7)
chinchokma, chinchokmataa, chokma, chokmataa
    how are you? (greeting) (1RS)
chinoffi to pinch (A,S) (5)
chínto to be bigger (S)—irregular Ngr. of **ishto** (15)
chipota child; baby (4)
    inchipota child, offspring (son or daughter)

chipota nakni' boy (4)
chipota tiik girl (4)
chipotaat imánta to have a baby, to give birth (D) (20RS)
chiiki pilla' áyya'shakaash once upon a time (19RS)
cho'mi to be (more than two) together (A) (16RS, 19)
chofak fork (9BG, 13)
chofalli to clean (A,S) (16)
chofata to be clean (S) (4)
    chóffa'ta (Ggr.)
chohmi part of **ittihooba chohmi**
chokaano fly (13)
chokfalhpooba' sheep (20RS)
chokfalhpooba' apiisachi' shepherd (20RS)
chokfi rabbit (1, 14)
chokfiyammi to hiccup (S / A) (3)
chokka' house, home (7)
chokkíllissa to be quiet (A) (3)
chokkowa to go in (A) (16RS, 19)
choklhan. See **cholhkan**
chokma 1. to be good, nice (S) (1, 2); to be good, act
    good (A) (3); see **chinchokma**
    inchokma to feel good
chokma'si to be pretty (S) (6)
chokmataa. See **chinchokma**
chokoshkomo to play (A) (4)
cholhkan, choklhan spider (1, 13)
chomak tobacco (18)
chompa to buy (A,Noun) (5)
chonna to be skinny (S) (2)
chowaala', chowahala' cedar (1, 2)

d

daala', taala' dollar (1, 14RS)

f

fala crow (1, 20)
falama to return, go back (A) (7RS)
falamat minti to come back (A) (8RS)
falammi north (13RS)
falammichi to return (something), to bring (something)
    back, take (something) back (A,S) (7RS)
falaa to be long (S) (1, 8)
faliili to make long, lengthen (A,S) (16ACG)
fama to be whipped (S) (1, 16)
fammi to whip (A,S) (1, 15)
fanalhchi' wings (SP) (14)
fani' squirrel (4)
finha just (20RS)
fochosh duck (19)
fohi' bee (8)
fokha to put on (clothing, like a dress or pants) (A,Noun)
    (1, 16ACG)

    nittak yamma fokhaka at about that time (20RS)
fokhakaash, fokhakma part of **katiya fokhakaash,**
    katiya fokhakma
fokhakaasho in about (a time in the past) (11RS)
fokhi to put (sg. obj.) inside (A,S,Noun) (16)
foni' bone (SP) (19RS)
fónkha part of **mishsha' fónkha áyya'shookano**
folosh spoon (4)
foshi' bird (4)
foshi' hishi' feather (of a bird) (14)
foshi' hishi' ishholissochi' quill pen (18ACG)
foyopa to breathe (A) (4)
fóyyokha to be inside (Ygr.) (A,Noun) (sg. subj.)
    (12ACG); to wear (A,Noun) (16ACG)
footi. See **vooti**

h

habina to get (something) as a present (A,Noun) (17)

habinachi to give (something) to (someone), usually as a present (A, S,Noun) (8RS)

habishko to sneeze (S / A) (15)

hachimmi' yours (pl.), you all's (7)

hachinchokmataa hello, how are you (addressed to many) (1RS)

hachishnaakilloot only you (pl., subj.) (20)

hachishnaakillo only you (pl., obj.) (20)

hachishnaakoot you (pl., cntr. subj.) (9)

hachishnaako you (pl., cntr. obj.) (9)

hachishnaato and you all? (response to greeting) (3)

hachishno' you (pl.), you guys (19)

haklo to listen to, to hear (A,S) (1, 9)
  hâklo (Ggr.)
  hánglo to hear (A,S) (9) (Ngr.)
  háyyaklo hear (A,S) (Ygr.)

haknip body (1)

haksi to be drunk, get drunk; to be crazy (S) (8, 15)

hakson cheekbone area (1)

haksibish ear (SP) (14)

hakshop skin, outer covering (SP) (14)
  itti' hakshop bark (of a tree)

halalli to pull (A,S) (5)

halallichi to make (someone) pull (something): to hitch up (a horse) to (a wagon) (A,S,Noun) (18RS)

halili to touch (A,S) (8)

hallito hello (1RS)

haloppa to be sharp (S) (12)

halhabli to kick (sg. obj.); to kick once (A,S) (19)

halhlhi to kick (pl. obj.); to kick more than once (A,S) (19)

hanná'li six (3RS); to be six in number (A) (12); part of
  awa-hanná'li, holhtina' hanná'li

ihanná'li to have six

hánglo to listen to (A,S) (1, 9)—Ngr. of haklo

hapommi' ours (special) (7)

haposhnaakilloot only we (special) (20)

haposhnaakillo only us (special) (20)

haposhnaakoot we (special pl.—cntr. subj.) (9)

haposhnaako us (special pl.—cntr. obj.) (9)

hashaa to be angry (S) (1, 8)
  ishhashaa to be angry about [isht hashaa]
  ihashaa to be angry at

hashaakochcha' east (13RS)

hashaaobya', hashaaobyaka' west (13RS)

hashi' sun (4)

hashi' kanalli katohmi? what time is it? (10RS)

hashi' kanalli (plus a number) it's (number) o'clock (10RS)

hashshok grass (11)

hashshok-ishtamo' grass-cutter, scythe (18)

hashtahli to be bright, light (Noun) (18)

hatip hip; backside (SP) (7RS)

hattak man; person (2)
  ihattak husband

hattak yoka' slave, prisoner (17RS)

hattak-abi man killer, murderer (18)

hattak-apa' man-eater, cannibal (18)

Hattak Api' Homma', Hattak Nipi' Homma' Indian (7RS, 11)

hattak losa' black person, African American (6)

hattak nakni' man (2)

hattak shawi' monkey (18ACG, 19)

Hattak Yoshoba' Lost Tribe, Lost People (11RS)

hattak-abi man killer, murderer (18)

hattak-apa' man-eater, cannibal (18)

hayowani' worm (1)

háyyaklo hear (A,S) (Ygr. of **haklo**) (20RS)

haatokma well, OK (used to begin a story) (11RS)

haatokmat go ahead, OK (in "let" hortative sentences) (15)

haatokoot and then (same-subj.) (11RS)

haatoko and then (different-subj.) (11RS)

hichito to be big (pl. subj.) (S) (12)

hí'li to stand, be in a standing position (A); to stand in, be located (standing) in (a place) (A,Noun) (dl. subj.) (10)

hika to stand up, get into a standing position; to step (A) (1, 4)

híkki'ya to stand, be in a standing position (A); to stand in, be located (standing) in (a place) (A,Noun) (sg. subj.) (10)

hilha to dance (A) (1, 4); to dance (a dance) (A,Noun) (5)

hilha' dance (noun); dancer (1, 18)

hilha'chi' top (toy) (18)

himitta to be young (S) (12)

himmaka' now (11RS)

himmaka' áyya'shookano these days (9RS)

himmaka' nittakookano nowadays (7RS)

himmaka' oklhili tonight (12RS)

himonha to wait (A) (15)
  ihimonha to wait for

himónali' suddenly (13RS)

hishi' fur; body hair (SP) (as "body hair", usually follows the name of the body part whose hair is referred to) (14)
  foshi' hishi' feather (of a bird)
  foshi' hishi' ishholissochi' quill pen
  itti' hishi' leaf (of a tree)

hitokla' twice (12RS)

hiyohmáa to stand, be in a standing position (A); to stand in, be located (standing) in (a place) (A,Noun) (tpl. subj.) (10)

hobachi to copy, imitate (A,S) (16)
  aahobachi to copy from (a thing)
  imaahobachi to copy from (a person)

hochifo to name (A,S); to name (someone or something) (a name) (A,S,Noun) (9RS, 16)

hofahya to be ashamed (S) (1, 4)
  ihofahya to be ashamed of

holba' picture (SP; DP = iholba') (7)

holbachi to photograph, take a picture of (A,S) (9)

holiss-aapisa' school (10)

holisso book, paper, letter, document (or other paper item, such as a newspaper) (5)

holisso amposhi' paper plate (18ACG)

Holisso Holitto'pa' Bible (7RS)

holisso toba to be recorded on paper, to be enumerated (A) (20RS)

holissochi to write (A,Noun) (5)

Holitto'pa' part of **Holisso Holitto'pa'**

holiitobli to make sacred, consider precious (A,S) (16)

holiitoblichi to glorify (A,S) (20RS)

holiitopa to be sacred, precious, holy (S) (16)
  aai'pa' holiito'pa' holy table
  holliittó'pa to be precious, holy, sacred (S) (Ggr.) (15RS)

Hollishto' part of **Nittak Hollishto', Nittak Hollishto' ookma**

Hollo' part of **Nittak Hollo', Nittak Hollo' Aaiklanna', Nittak Hollo' Nakfish**

holloppi to be buried (S) (18)

holhchifo name (SP) (1, 2RS, 7); to be named (S); to be named (a name) (S,Noun) (16)

holhponi' part of **koshibba' holhponi'**

holhtina' number (6RS)

holhtina' chaffa ace (6RS)

holhtina' chakká'li nine (in cards) (6RS)

holhtina' hanná'li six (in cards) (6RS)

holhtina' ontochchí'na eight (in cards) (6RS)

holhtina' ontoklo seven (in cards) (6RS)

holhtina' oshta four (in cards) (6RS)

holhtina' pokoli ten (in cards) (6RS)

holhtina' talhlhá'pi five (in cards) (6RS)

holhtina' tochchí'na three (in cards) (6RS)

holhtina' toklo two (in cards) (6RS)

homi to be bitter (Noun) (12RS)
  alba homi' bitter weed

homma to be red (S) (3)
  Hattak Api' Homma', Hattak Nipi' Homma' Indian

honkopa to steal, kidnap (A,S) (16)
  aahonkopa to steal from (an institution)
  imaahonkopa to steal from (a person)
  ihonkopa to steal for; (for some speakers) to steal from (a person)

hopaakichi to go far off (A) (13RS)

hopaakikaashookano long ago (6RS)

hopoba to be hungry (S) (4)
  hóppo'ba (Ggr.)

hopoo to be jealous (A) (1, 3); to be jealous of (A,S) (5)
  hopohówa (HNgr.)

hopooni to cook (A,S) (5RS, 8)

hoppi to bury (A,S) (5)

hosi to pound (corn) in a wooden mortar (A,Noun) (9RS)

hotihna to count (A,S) (5)

hotolhko to cough (S / A) (15)

hottopa to hurt, to get hurt, to be in pain (S) (works like <ittopa> with S prefixes—sattopa, chittopa, pottopa) (19RS, 20); hurt, pain (noun) (19RS)

hottopa to hurt, injure (someone or something) (A,S) (works like <ittopachi> with S prefixes—sattopachi, chittopachi, pottopachi) (20)

howasa to chew (A,Noun) (18)

howita to vomit (S / A) (15)

hoyahno to sweat (S) (15)

hoyo to look for (A,S) (1, 5) (irregular neg. ikhoyyo)

hoyya to drip (1)

hookay (word used at the end of a formal statement) (1)

Hooki' Pooki' Hokey Pokey (7RS)

hookmat go ahead, OK (in "let" hortative sentences) (15)

hoot aya! go look for it! (6RS); part of **nani' hoot aya!**

hosa to shoot at (A,S) (6)

i

ibaani to add (something) to (something) (A,Noun,Noun) (9RS)

ibichchala' nose (SP) (14)

ichchokwa to be cold (of a person) (S) (2)

ihoo woman (1, 2)
  imihoo wife

ikalhchibo'soka not too long after, a while later (14RS)

ikánto neg. of ánta (9)

ikayyo'bo to be bad (includes N ik±) (S) (9)

ikbi to make (A,S) (1, 8)

ikimalhpi'so to be sad, unhappy (includes N ik±) (D) (9)

iknokhánglo neg. of nokhánglo (9)

ikpassáo neg. of passáa (9)

Iksa' Christian (17)

iksho not to exist, not to be there, not to be around (includes N ik±) (S) (irregular verb: iksaksho, ikchiksho) (9, 10)
  nannakya iksho not to exist at all (S) (13RS)—*see* unit 13RS

iláyyo'ka to be various, separate, different (A) (12RS)

ilaapakáyni by himself, by herself, by themselves (1)
  ilaapakáynit by himself, by herself, by themselves (sentence form) (9RS)
ilaapo' himself, herself, themselves; his own, her own, their own (20RS)
ilbak hand, arm (SP) (1, 7)
ilbakchosh fingernail (SP) (14)
ilbashsha to be poor, pitiful (S) (6)
ilifilito'chi to turn (oneself) around (A) (7RS)
ílla only (auxiliary) (12RS, 20); just, only (19RS)
illi to be dead, to die (S) (3)
ilhko'chi to shake (something), to move (something) (A,S) (7RS)
ilhko'li to shake (oneself), move (oneself) (A) (7RS)
ilhpokonna to dream (S) (3)
ishtilhpokonna to dream about
ima to give to (A,D,Noun) (short verb: imātok, imāli, ishīma, kilīma—D and A ±prefixes work like + prefixes) (1, 11)
imalikchi to doctor (A,D) (19RS)
imalhkaniya to forget (D,Noun) (13)
imalhtaha to be ready (D) (19RS)
imambiika to be sick for (A,D) (8)
imambooha house (poss.) (DP) (7)—poss. of abooha
inanhi to wish something for (someone) (A,D) (15RS)
imanompa kanihmo'si article (of a document) (DP) (14RS)
imaoli to tell (someone) (A,D)
imánta to have (a relative) (sg. human "have" obj.) (D,Noun±at) (12)
  chipotaat imánta to have a baby, to give birth (D)
imasilhha; imasilhlha to ask (someone something) (A,D) (20)
  ittimasilhha to ask each other (A)
imáyya'sha to have (relatives) (tpl. human "have" obj.) (D,Noun±at) (12)
imaabachi to teach (someone) (A,D); to teach (something) to (A,D,Noun) (1, 8)
imaabi to put (medicine) on (someone) (A,D,Noun) (19RS)
imaahobachi to copy (something) from (a person) (A,D,Noun) (16)
imaahonkopa to steal (something) from (a person) (A,D,Noun) (16)
imaaiksaachi to use (medicine) on (A,D,Noun) (19RS)
imaaishi to take (something) from (a person) (A,D,Noun) (16)
imaalhpí'sa to have the right to (D) (17RS)
imaaponta to borrow (something) from (a person) (A,D,Noun) (16)
imaatobbi to pay (something) to (A,D,Noun) (8)
imáshwa to have (relatives) (dl. human "have" obj.) (D,Noun±at) (12)

imichonkash heart (DP)
imihoo wife (DP) (7)
imilhlha to be scared; to be wild (D) (8)
imilhlhali to scare (A,D) (15)
ikimiksho not to have (D,Noun±at) (12)
imissikopa to be mean to (A,D) (8)
imishto to be big for (sg. subj.) (Noun,D) (8)
imittimanompoli to read to (A,D); to read (something) to (A,D,Noun) (10)
imittola to drop (something) (D,Noun±at) (20ACG)
ímmayya to be ahead of (A,D); to be more than (preceded by compared verb plus ±kat) (A,D) (9BG, 15)
immi' possession, belonging (DP) (6, 7); his, hers, theirs (7); (used to say "belong to") (17RS)
imoktanichi to reveal to (A,D,Noun) (HNgr. **imoktanihínchi**) (20RS)
imontochchí'na to have eight (D,Noun±at) (12)
imontoklo to have seven (D,Noun±at) (12)
imoshta to have four (D,Noun±at) (12)
impa to eat, to have a meal (A) (1, 3)
impa' food (18)
impállammi to have a serious condition (D) (19RS)
impalli to feel hot (D) (15)
impalhki to be fast for, to go fast for (A,D) (8)
impatali to spread (something) out for (someone) on (A,D,Noun,Noun) (18RS)
impokkó'li to have ten (D,Noun±at) (12)
imponna to know how; to know how (to do something) well (D)—*see* unit 18RS
inchaffa to have one (D,Noun±at) (12)
inchakká'li to have nine (D,Noun±at) (12)
inchipota child, offspring (son or daughter) (DP) (7)
inchokma to feel good (D) (8)
inchokmishto to be healthy (D) (8)
inkapassa to feel cold (D) (15)
inkashoffi to forgive (A,D); to forgive (someone) for (A,D,Noun) (15RS)
inkana' friend (DP) (11)
inki' father (DP) (6RS, 7)
intakho'bi to be lazy (D) (8)
intálla'a to have (D,Noun±at) (sg. "have" obj. thought of as having an opening on the top) (12)
intállo'wa to have (D,Noun±at) (dl. "have" obj. thought of as having an opening on the top) (12)
intalowat máa to have (D,Noun±at) (tpl. "have" obj. thought of as having an opening on the top) (12)
intalhlhá'pi to have five (D,Noun±at) (12)
intikba' older sibling of the same sex as the possessor: older brother, big brother (of a man); older sister, big sister (of a woman) (DP) (7)
intiik sister (of a male) (DP) (7)
intochchí'na to have three (D,Noun±at)

intoklo to have two (D,Noun±at)

ipashi' hair of the head; mane (of a horse) (SP) (14)

ipita to feed (A,S) (5); to feed (something) to (someone) (A,S,Noun) (6)

  íppi'ta (Ggr.)

  issoba aaipita' piini' horse trough

iskanno'si to be little, small (sg. subj.) (12)

issi' deer (2)

issikopa to be mean (S) (3)

  imissikopa to be mean to

isso to hit (A,S) (mainly sg. subj.) (5)

issoba horse (DP = i̲soba) (7)

issoba aaipita' piini' horse trough (20RS)

issochichi to make hit (A,S,Noun) (6)

isso̲sh bug, insect (1, 7)

istokchank watermelon (1)

ishbashli' kitchen knife (18)

ishchokoshkomo' toy (18)

ishfama' switch, whip (noun) (18)

ishhashaa to be angry about (S,Noun) [isht hashaa] (13)

Ishhanna'li' part of **Nittak Ishhanna'li'**

ishholbachi' camera (18)

ishholissochi' pen, pencil (13)

  foshi' hishi' ishholissochi' quill pen

ishi to take, to get, to pick up (A,S); to take (medicine) (A,N) (short verb: ishi̲'shi, kili̲'shi; iki̲'sho—with A and N prefixes, i̲'shi replaces ishi; imi̲shi—D ± prefixes work like + prefixes) (1, 11)

ishki' mother (SP) (5RS, 7)

ishkin eye (SP) (7)

ishko to drink (A,S) (1, 5)

ishkobo' head (SP) (7RS, 14)

ishliichi' plow (noun) (18)

ishnaakilloot only you (sg., subj.) (20)

ishnaakillo̲ only you (sg., obj.) (20)

ishnaako and you? (response to greeting) (1RS)

ishnaakoot you (sg. cntr. subj.) (1, 7RS, 9)

ishnaako̲ you (sg. cntr. obj.) (9)

ishno' you (sg.) (9BG, 19)

ishpiha' broom (13)

ishtalhchifa' soap (18)

ishtasha'na' lock (18)

ishtaka'fa' cup (DP = i̲shtaka'fa') (10)

ishtala to bring (here), to bring home (A,S) [isht ala] (short verb—*see* ala) (5RS, 13)

ishtalakchi' rope, leash (DP = ishtalakchi') (5)

Ishtalhlha'pi' part of **Nittak Ishtalhlha'pi'**

ishtaya to begin (used with preceding t-form) (A); to bring, take (A,S) [isht aya] (short verb—*see* **aya**; ishtayyali "I begin, I take") (8RS, 13)

Ishtaa-aya Ámmo'na Holisso Preamble (17RS)

ishtaalhi to be last (A) (18RS)

ishtilhpokonna to dream about (A,S) [isht ilhpokonna] (13)

ishtittánno'wa to take (dl. subj.) (A,S) (includes preverb **isht**±) (18RS)

ishtiwa' key (18)

ishto to be big (sg. subj.) (S) (1, 3)

  chínto to be bigger (S)—irregular Ngr. (15)

  imishto to be big for

ishtochichi to make (sg. obj.) big (A,S) (6)

ishtombohli to accuse, blame (A,S) [isht ombohli] (13)

ishtona to take (over there) (A,S) [isht ona] (short verb—*see* ona) (13)

Ishtontoklo' part of **Nittak Ishtontoklo'**

ithana to get to know (A,S); to realize, learn (A, N) (15)

  nanna aaithana' educational institution, place to learn (17RS)

ithána to know (A,S) (5)—Ngr. of ithana

  ittimithána to understand each other (A)

ittanaha, ittanaa to have a church service (A) (11RS)

tánno'wa, ittánno'wa to walk, pass by, go by, travel around (dl. subj.) (A)

tannohówa. *See* **tannohówa**; part of **yaháat ittanohówa**

iti mouth (SP) (1, 4)

ittabaana' part of **itti' ittabaana' abooha**

ittakoba' stomach, belly (SP) (14)

itti' tree; wood; stick, log (1, 2)

tiyak itti' / itti' tiyak pine tree

itti' basha' abooha frame house (10RS)

itti' hakshop bark (of a tree) (14)

itti' hishi', itti'shi' leaf (of a tree) (14)

itti' ittabaana' abooha log house, log cabin (10RS)

itti'chanaa wagon (DP = inti'chanaa) (7)

itti'shi'. *See* **itti' hishi'**

ittialbi', ittihalbi' lips (1)

ittibaachaffa to agree with each other about (A,Noun) (17RS)

ittibaaholisso to be recorded together (A) (20RS)

ittibaapishi brother, sister; sibling (SP) (4RS, 7)

ittibi to fight, to fight with (A,S); to fight (A) (11)

ittihalbl'. *See* **ittialbi'**

ittihaalalli to marry, to be married to, to get married to (A,S) (5); to get married (A) (10)

ittihaalallichi to marry, perform a marriage ceremony for (A,S) (6)

ittihooba chohmi to be just about the same (A) (13RS)

ittikalhalha'chi to bang around, to make a banging noise (A) (16RS)

ittíllawwi to be equal to, to be the same as (A,S) (15RS)

ittimanompoli to read (A); to read (something) (A,Noun) (7RS, 10)

  imittimanompoli to read to (A,D)

ittimasilhha to ask each other (A) (13RS)
ittimithána to understand each other (A) (13RS)
ittimíla to be different from (A,S) (12RS)
ittifilamo'li to separate from each other (A) (13RS)
ittimilinka'si to be close to each other (A) (13RS)
ittish medicine (7)

ittola to fall (A / S) (18RS, 20)
   imittola to drop (something) (D,Noun±at)
iyyakchosh toenail (SP) (14)
iyyi' foot, leg (SP) (7)
iyyinto'lhka' knee (SP) (14)

i

í'ma to be located on (something) as an integral part (for instance, of a picture painted on a wall) (A,Noun) (14RS)
í'shi to keep, to hold, to have in one's hand (A,Noun) (*see also* **ishi**) (6RS, 11)
ifilammi to leave behind (A,D) (14RS)
ihanná'li to have six (D,Noun±at) (12)
ihashaa to be angry at (A,D) (8)
ihattak husband (DP) (7)
ihimonha to wait for (A,D) (15)
ihofahya to be ashamed of (A,D) (8)
iholba' picture (owned) (DP) (7)—*see* **holba'**
ihollo to love (A,D) (8)
ihonkopa to steal (something) for; (for some speakers) to steal (something) from (A,D,Noun) (16)
ii yes (1, 4)
íla to be different, other (S) (1, 12RS, 10)
ilawa to have many; to have a lot of (D,Noun±at) (12)
ilhafi to sign (a document) (A,Noun) (14RS)
imalhata to be scared of (A,D)

imiha to bawl out (A,D)
inakfi' brother (of a female) (7)
inokhánglo to be sorry for (A,D) (8)
isoba horse (poss.) (DP) (7)—poss. of issoba
ihanná'li to have six (D,Noun±at) (12)
ilawa to have many, to have a lot (D,Noun±at) (12)
Iminko' part of **Chikashsha Iminko'**
iwayowat máa to have (D,Noun±at) (tpl. "have" obj. thought of as having an opening on the bottom) (12)
iwáyya'a to have (D,Noun±at) (sg. "have" obj. thought of as having an opening on the bottom) (12)
iwáyyo'wa to have (D,Noun±at) (dl. "have" obj. thought of as having an opening on the bottom) (12)
iyahmohmi to do (something) to (someone) (A,D,Noun) (17RS)
Iyaakni' part of **Chahta' Iyaakni', Chikashsha Iyaakni', Naahollo Iyaakni'**
iyimmi to believe (human or living obj.), to believe in (someone) (A,D) (8)

k

kahat máa to lie, be in a lying position (A); to lie in, be located (lying) in (a place) (A,Noun) (tpl. subj.) (10)
kalakshi to be degraded (S) (1, 6)
kamoshli to tickle (A,S) (5)
kana someone, somebody (17)
   kana móma everyone (17RS)
kanahookya, kanookya everyone, everybody; (in a neg. sentence) no one, nobody (16RS, 19)
kanalli
   hashi' kanalli katohmi? what time is it?
   hashi' kanalli (plus a number) it's (number) o'clock
kanchi to sell (A,Noun) (1, 6)
kani'mi to be some, to be several (A) (13RS)
kanihmihchi how could it be (20RS)
kanihmit somehow, any old way (12RS)
kaniya to go away (sg. subj.) (A) (13, 19)
   malit kaniya to run away (sg. subj.)
kaniya' somewhere (17); someone (16RS)
kaniya' móma everywhere (20RS)
kaniya'ookya everywhere, everyplace; (in a neg. sentence) nowhere, no place (19); everyone, anyone (17RS)
kaniyaak somewhere (17)

kaníhka really, very (3)
kánnohmi some; to be some (A) (18RS)
kanookya. *See* **kanahookya**
kapassa to be cold, get cold (S) (15)
   inkapassa to feel cold
katolhlhi to cut, cut up (A,Noun)
kasbi yard (1, 10)
kata who (17)
katihchi to do what to (A;S); to do (what) to (A;S;Noun = nanta) (17)
katihkaash / katihkaasht / katihkaashta / katihkaashta when (past) (17)
katihkmak when (nonpast) (17)
katihmi to happen (Noun = **nantahaat**); to happen to, be wrong with (Noun = **nantahaat**; S); to do (what) (A;Noun = **nanta**) (becomes **katih-** before endings starting with **t** or **ch**) (17)
katihmihaat how (17); why (19RS)
katihmihta why (12RS, 17)
katihsht / katihchihaat how, in what way (*see* lesson 17.6) (17)
katiht how, how on earth (*see* lesson 17.6) (17)

katimpi which; to be which one, to be which ones (A) (17)

katiya fokhakaash / katiya fokhakaasht / katiya fokhakaashta / katiya fokhakaashta when (past) (17)

katiya fokhakmak when (nonpast) (17)

katiya' / katiyaak where (17)

katohmi how many; to be how many (A) (17)

  hashi' kanalli katohmi? what time is it?

kawaski to be hard, solid (Noun) (18)

  káwwa'ski (Ggr.)

  kawáyya'ski (Ygr.)

kawwi to break (sticks) for kindling (1)

kayya to be full (1)

káyya'a, káyya'ha to lie, be in a lying position (A); to lie in, be located (lying) in (a place) (A,Noun) (dl. subj.) (10)

kaar, kaa car (1, 10)

ki'yo no (4); not (auxiliary) (7, 9)

kiliha, kiliya to growl (A) (1, 2)

kisili to bite (A,S) (8)

kitoba bottle (16)

kii oh! (1)

kobafa to break, to be broken (of sg. long subj.) (Noun) (19)

kobaffi to break (sg. long obj.) (A,Noun) (19)

kobahli to break (of pl. long subj.) (Noun) (19)

kobbi to break (pl. long obj.) (A,Noun) (19)

kochcha to go out (A) (1, 8)

  kôchcha (Ggr.)

kochcha' outside (16RS)

kola to be dug (Noun) (1, 16)

kolli to dig (A,Noun) (1, 16)

kolofa to be cut with a knife; to be wounded (S) (19RS)

koni skunk (4)

konta to whistle (A) (3)

kosoma to stink (S) (18)

  kósso'ma (Ggr.)

  kosóyyo'ma (Ygr.)

koshibba' poke salad, pokeweed (5RS)

koshibba' holhponi' cooked poke salad (5RS)

kowa to break (of a sg. compact subj.) (Noun) (19)

kowi' cat (5)

kookoli to break (pl. compact obj.) (A,Noun) (19)

kookowa to break (of pl. compact subj.) (Noun) (19)

kooli to break (a sg. compact obj.) (A,Noun) (1, 19)

l

lakna to be yellow; to be brown (S) (1, 2)

  lâkna (Ggr.)

lapoht máa, lapoot máa to be sticking onto (A,Noun) (tpl. subj.) (12ACG)

láppa'li to be sticking onto (A,Noun) (sg. subj.) (12ACG)

láppohli to be sticking onto (A,Noun) (dl. subj.) (12ACG)

lawa to be many, to be numerous, for there to be a lot of (A) (1, 6RS, 12)

  ilawa to have many, to have a lot

laa to be plowed (1)

litiha, litiya to be dirty (S) (4)

  lítti'ha (Ggr.)

  litíyyi'ha (Ygr.)

liichi to plow (A,Noun) (18)

lohmi to hide (A,S) (1, 5)

lokfi' mud (13RS)

lokfi' nona' abooha brick house (10RS)

losa to be black (S) (1, 6)

  hattak losa' black person, African American

loshka to lie, tell lies (A) (19)

  oloshka to lie about, tell lies about (A,S)

lowa to burn, to burn down) (Noun) (19)

lowak fire (1, 9RS)

lh

lhabanka to snore (A) (1, 3)

lhabocha to be mashed (S) (16)

lhaboshli to mash (A,S) (16)

lhayita to be wet (S) (4)

lhilaffi to tear, rip (sg. obj.) (A,S) (14)

lhinko to be fat (S) (2)

lhiyohli to chase (A,S) (8)

m

mahli wind (noun) (1, 10); to be windy (—); to have wind (of a location) (Noun) (10)

malichi to make (sg. obj.) run (A,S); to start (a car) (A,Noun) (ACG20)

malili to run (sg. subj.) (A) (8, 19)

malit kaniya to run away (sg. subj.) (A) (13)

malli to jump (A) (2)

mallittakaali to jump back, jump off (A) (16RS)

masofa to be bald (S) (1, 20)
  másso'fa (Ggr.)
  masóyyo'fa (Ygr.)
Mashkooki' Creek (11)
máa part of **binohmáa, hiyohmáa, intalowat máa, iwayowat máa, kahat máa, talowat máa, wayowat máa**
mahma then (dffierent subj.) (19RS)
micha' and—*see 15RS*
miha, miya to try (1); to say about oneself (A) (18RS); they say (19RS)
  imiha to bawl out

mikmat go ahead, OK (in "let" hortative sentences) (15); and (15RS)—*see 15RS*
minko' chief (2); king (in cards) (6RS)
minko' imihoo queen (in cards) (6RS)
minko' oshi' jack (in cards) (6RS)
minti to come (A) (8RS, 19)
  falamat minti to come back (falamat kiiminti "we come back") (A) (8RS)
Missipi' Mississippi (14RS)
mishsha' fónkha áyya'shookano in still earlier times (10RS)
móma to be all (A) (12RS, 14); to be the whole (A) (20RS)

n

nakfish younger sibling of the same sex as the possessor: younger sister, little sister (of a woman); younger brother, little brother (of a man) (SP) (1, 7)
  Nittak Hollo' Nakfish Saturday
nakni' male; man (2)
  chipota nakni' boy
nalha to be shot (S) (1, 6)
nalhlhi to shoot (A,S) (1, 5)
nampakali' flower (14)
nani' fish (6RS)
nani' hoot aya! go fish! (6RS)
nanna something (6, 17); what (n-word) (17); some, any (17RS)
nanna aya peace (20RS)
nanna aaithana' educational institution, place to learn (17RS)
nanna ikaachokmoka where things are bad (15RS)
nanna ikchokmo something bad (17RS)
nannabli to swallow (A) (5)
nannahookya, nannookya everything; (in a neg. sentence) nothing (19)
nannakat things (subj.) (9RS); what (subj.) (n-word) (17RS)
nannakya any (9RS) *see unit 9RS*
nannakya iksho not to exist at all (S) (13RS) *see unit 13RS*
nannalhpisa' holisso treaty (14RS)
nannalhpooba' animal (typically, a domesticated animal) (2)
nannaayámmohmi to be some way in (a place) (A,Noun) (n-word; includes **nanna** "things", as a preverb) (15RS)
nannimaabachi' teacher (11)
nannishtaaholiitó'paka' glory (15RS)
nannishtaayalhlhi' power (15RS)
nannishtilayoppa to rejoice (Noun) (includes preverbs **nanna** and **isht±**) (20RS)
nannishtimaaholitto'pa' glory (20RS)

nannokaachi to say something; to say how (n-word) (A,Noun) (17ACG)
nannokchamali' vegetables, greens (12RS, 20)
nannookya. See **nannahookya**
nanta what (2RS, 16, 17) *see unit 2RS*
nantokaachi to say how (A, Noun); to say what (A) (17)
nashoba wolf (14)
naaishbo'wa' hammer (13)
naafka. See **naafokha**
naafka lombo' shirt (20)
naafkishto' coat (18RS)
naafokha, naafka dress (1, 8)
Naahollimanompa' English (14RS)
naahollo white person, non-Indian; white man (2)
Naahollo Iyaakni' Texas (10)
naalhilafa' rags (20RS)
naalhpisa' law (17RS)
naalhtoka' policeman (11)
naapiisa' lawmaker (17RS)
niha to be greasy (1, 20)
nipi' flesh (SP); meat (7)
  Hattak Nipi' Homma' Indian
  shokha' nipi' pork
nita' bear (4)
nittak day (8RS)
Nittak Ammo'na' Monday (8RS)
Nittak Atochchi'na' Wednesday (8RS)
Nittak Atokla' Tuesday (8RS)
Nittak Ayyoshta' Thursday (8RS)
nittak chaffaka one day (13RS)
Nittak Hollishto' Christmas (8RS)
Nittak Hollishto' ookma on Christmas (8RS)
Nittak Hollo' Sunday (8RS)
Nittak Hollo' Aaiklanna' Wednesday (8RS)
Nittak Hollo' Nakfish Saturday (8RS)
Nittak Ishhanna'li' Saturday (8RS)
Nittak Ishtalhlha'pi' Friday (8RS)
Nittak Ishtontoklo' Sunday (8RS)

nittak yamma tomorrow (20)
nittak yamma fokhaka at about that time (20RS)
nittaki in the morning (13RS)
nittakookano part of **himmaka' nittakookano**
nokchito to rest, behave oneself (S) (1, 3)
nokfónkha to remember (S,Noun) (13)
nokfóyyokha to really remember (A,S) (Ygr.) (14RS)

nokhánglo to be sad (S) (1, 3, 9) (neg. iknokhánglo)
  inokhánglo to be sorry for
nona' part of **lokfi' nona' abooha**
nosi to fall asleep, be asleep (S); to go to sleep, to sleep
  (A) (1, 6)
nota' underside, bottom; (loc. n.) under (SP) (10)
nowa to walk (A) (1, 2)

o

oblaashaash yesterday (4)
ofi' dog (1, 2)
oka' water (5)
ok-aa-abi to drown (someone) (A,S) (18ACG)
okaabaafa to stick one's finger in (someone's eye)
  (A,Noun) (18)
ok-aailli to drown, get drowned (18ACG)
okaami to wash one's face (A) (1, 4)
okaamichi to wash (someone's) face (A,S) (10)
okaapisa to stare at (A,S) (18)
ok-aayopi to swim (A) (18ACG)
okcha to be awake, wake up (S) (10)
okchaalínchi to save (A,S) (20RS)
okchali to wake (someone) up (A,S) (10)
okchamali to be blue, to be green (S) (10)
  okchámma'li (Ggr.)
  okchamáyya'li (Ygr.)
okcháa to be alive (S) (10)
okkisa' door; gate (15)
okkisoshi' little door (10RS)
okla town (1, 2)
Oklahomma' (10)
okloshi' tribe (13RS)
oklhili night; to be night (12RS)
  himmaka' oklhili tonight
oklhilika at night (13RS)
okommo to mix (A,Noun) (16ACG)
okpolo, oppolo to be broken, messed up, ruined; to have
  something wrong (S) (18RS)
oksop bead (1)
okshitta to close (1, 8)
okti' snow (16)
oktosha to snow (—); to have snow (of a place) (—,Noun)
  (10)
ola to crow, to make a noise (A) (short verb: ishōa, imōla—
  A and D ± prefixes work like + prefixes; ishimōla—A
  prefix before D prefix works normally) (11)

ollali to laugh (A); to laugh at (A,S) (10)
olhkomo to be mixed (Noun) (16ACG)
omba to rain (—) (1, 2); to have rain (of a location)
  (Noun) (10)
ombiniili to ride (a horse); to sit down on (A,S) (18RS)
ombohli to lay (sg. obj.) down on, put (sg. obj.) down on
  (A,S,Noun) (13)
ona to get there (A), to get to (a place there) (A,Noun)
  (short verb: ishōna, imōna—A and D ± prefixes work
  like + prefixes; ishimōna—A prefix before D prefix
  works normally) (11)
  ishtona to take (over there)
onchaba mountain (13RS)
onkof persimmon (1, 17)
onna to be the next day; to dawn (—) (18RS)
  onnakma tomorrow (3, 5)
  onnakmako the next day (8RS)
ontochchí'na eight (3RS); to be eight in number (A)
  (12); part of **awa-ontochchí'na, holhtina'**
  ontochchí'na
imontochchí'na to have eight
ontoklo seven (3RS); to be seven in number (A) (12);
  part of **awa-ontoklo, holhtina' ontoklo**
  imontoklo to have seven
oppolo. *See* **okpolo**
oshi' son (SP) (10); little (used as the second part of a
  compound) (18)
oshiitiik daughter (SP) (10)
Oshpaani' Mexican, Chicano, Hispanic person (11)
oshta four (1, 3RS); to be four in number (A) (12); part
  of **awa-oshta**
  imoshta to have four
oshtinchaffichi to send (someone or something) to
  (A,D,Noun) (includes preverb **osht±**) (20RS)
owwatta to hunt (A) (3)

oo

<oo>. *See* **<ya>**
oochi to draw water (1)
ookma part of **Nittak Hollishto' ookma**

oopa owl (1)
ootalbinachi to go and stay over in (a place) (A,Noun)
  (includes preverb **oot±**) (18RS)

ootaya to go by, to pass by (A) (includes preverb **oot±**) (18RS)

ooti to kindle (a fire), start (a fire) (A,Noun) (1, 9RS)

ootimanompoli to go to talk to (A,D) (includes preverb **oot±**)

ootímmayya'chi to beat, conquer (A,D) (includes preverb **oot±**) (14RS)

o

oloshka to lie about, tell lies about (A,S) (19)

osi' eagle (4)

oyilhlhichi to knock (something) down on (someone or something) (A,S Noun) (13RS)

p

pakali to bloom (1)

pakna' top (SP); on, on top, on top of (loc. n.) (SP) (10)

pali' flying squirrel (1, 17)

palli to be hot (S) (15)

  impalli to feel hot

  tali' palli appliance

palhki to be fast (S); to go fast (A) (1, 3)

  impalhki to be, go fast for

Pantatak Pontotoc, Mississippi; Pontotoc, Oklahoma (14RS)

paska bread (1, 2)

paska champoli' cake, cookie, pie (12)

paska shatabli' bread made with yeast (light bread, leavened bread) (12RS)

paskikshatablo' bread made without yeast (unleavened bread) (12RS)

passáa to spank (A,S) (1, 5, 9) (neg. ikpassáo)

patkachit máa to be lying spread out on the floor (A); to be lying spread out on the floor in (a location) (A,Noun) (tpl. subj.) (12ACG)

patkáyya'chi to be lying spread out on the floor (A); to be lying spread out on the floor in (a location) (A,Noun) (dl. subj.) (12ACG)

pátta'a to be lying spread out on the floor (A); to be lying spread out on the floor in (a location) (A,Noun) (sg. subj.) (12ACG)

páa to whoop (A) (15)

pichchaa barn (1, 10)

piha to be swept (Noun) (18)

pihli to sweep (A,Noun) (13)

pilachi to send (A,S) (6)

pilla' just, only (9RS, 20)

  chiiki pilla' áyya'shakaash once upon a time

Pinki' Chihoowa God our Father (15RS)

pinti' mouse (2)

pisa to look at, to catch sight of, to see (A,S) (1, 9)

  apat pisa to taste

pistaya, pist aya to go see

  písa to see (Ngr.)

pisa ittimilayyokha to look different from each other (A) (17RS)

pistaya, pist aya to go see (A,S) [pist aya] (13)

piini' boat (16)

  issoba aaipita' piini' horse trough

piini' wakaa' airplane, plane (16)

písa to see (A,S) (9)—Ngr. of pisa

pitabaanabli to go over (A,S) (includes preverb **pit±**) (18RS)

pitnampíla to get better (Noun) (includes preverb **pit±**) (19RS)

pofessa', pofissa' professor (1)

pokkó'li ten (3RS); to be ten in number (A) (12)

  impokkó'li to have ten

pokoli (used in decade numbers like **pokoli toklo, pokoli tochchí'na, pokoli oshta,** etc.) (11ACG); part of **holhtina' pokoli**

pokoli hanná'li awa-hanná'li sixty-six (11ACG)

pokoli ontoklo awa-oshta seventy-four (11ACG)

pokoli oshta forty (11ACG)   forty

pokoli tochchí'na thirty (11ACG)

pokoli tochchí'na awa-chaffa thirty-one (11ACG)

pokoli toklo twenty (10RS)

pommi' ours (7)

ponta to borrow (A,Noun) (1, 16)

  aaponta to borrow from (an institution)

  imaaponta to borrow from (a person)

poshnaakilloot only we (20)

poshnaakillo only us (20)

poshnaakoot we (cntr.) (9)

poshnaako us (cntr.) (9)

Pooki' part of Hooki' Pooki'

pofa to smoke (tobacco) (1, 18)

r

riidi, riiti to read (1)

s

sakki to catch up with (A,S) (1, 5)
sâkki (Ggr.)
salakha' liver (7)
salami too much (aux.) (16)
sámma'ta to get quiet (A) (19RS)
sapontaki' mosquito (17)

sawa'si to be little, small (pl. subj.) (12)
sipokni to be old (S) (1, 12)
sinti' snake (11)
sinti' bala' / bala' sinti' snake bean (type of bean) (18ACG)
sishto rattlesnake (1)

sh

shachakla to be cracked (Noun) (19RS)
shakba' upper arm (SP) (14)
shanti' rat (16)
shawi' raccoon (1, 13)
  hattak shawi' monkey
shaali to haul (A,Noun)
shaapolichi to harness (A,S) (18RS)
Shimmanooli' Seminole (11)
sho'li to carry (A,S) (14)
shoha to stink, smell bad (S) (12)
shokawwa'li' part of **amposhi' shokawwa'li'**
shokcha sack, bag (13)
shokha' hog (9RS, 11)

shokha' nipi' pork (9RS)
shokhoshi' pig (13)
shokhoshi' ta'oss-aa-alhto' piggy bank (18ACG)
sholaffi to scratch (sg. obj.); to scratch once (A,S) (19)
sholli to scratch (pl. obj.); to scratch more than once (A,S) (19)
sholosh shoe (1, 17)
shoppalali to shine (Noun) (20RS)
shotik sky (13RS)
shooli to hug (A,S) (1, 8)
sho'ka to kiss (A,S) (5)
sho'kachichi to make kiss (A,S,Noun) (6)

t

ta'oss-aa-alhto' (small) bank, money box (18)
  shokhoshi' ta'oss-aa-alhto' piggy bank
ta'osso money (9)
tabli to cut off the top of, cut in two (A,S) (16ACG)
taha to be all gone, used up; to be finished; to be worn out (for instance, no longer wearable), all raggedy (S) (1, 14); completely (auxiliary) (14); (tpl. subj. auxiliary for motion verbs) (16RS, 19)
tahli to finish (A); to finish (something) (A,Noun) (8); completely (auxiliary) (13RS, 14) (Ygr. **táyyahli** (18RS))
takafa to be dipped up (Noun) (18)
takaali to get caught or hung up on (1)
takaffi to dip (something) (A,Noun) (12RS)
takchi to tie; to tie up (A,S) (13)
tákka'li to be hanging, be crouched down, be squatting (A); to be hanging, be crouched down, be squatting in (a location) (A,Noun) (sg. subj.) (12ACG)
tákkohli to be hanging, be crouched down, be squatting (A); to be hanging, be crouched down, be squatting in (a location) (A,Noun) (dl. subj) (12ACG)
takoht máa to be hanging, be crouched down, be squatting (A); to be hanging, be crouched down, be squatting in (a location) (A,Noun) (tpl. subj.) (12ACG)
takolo peach (8, 11)
talakchi to be tied up, be tied (S) (16)

tali' rock, stone (5)
tali' palli' appliance (9RS)
tálla'a to exist, to be there (Noun) (10); to be located in (a place) (Noun,Noun) (sg. subj. thought of as having an opening on the top) (10)
intálla'a to have (D,Noun±at) (sg. "have" obj. thought of as having an opening on the top)
tállo'wa to exist (Noun); to be located in (a place) (Noun,Noun) (dl. subj. thought of as having an opening on the top) (12)
  intállo'wa to have (D,Noun±at) (dl. "have" obj. thought of as having an opening on the top)
talowat máa to exist (Noun); to be located in (a place) (Noun,Noun) (tpl. subj. thought of as having an opening on the top) (12)
  intalowat máa to have (D,Noun±at) (tpl. "have" obj. thought of as having an opening on the top)
taloowa to sing (A) (1, 3); to sing (a song) (A,Noun) (5)
taloowa' song, hymn; singer (1, 7RS, 18)
talhipa hundred (3RS)
talhipa chaffa one hundred (11ACG)
talhipa chakká'li nine hundred (11ACG)
talhipa ontochchí'nacha pokoli oshta eight hundred forty (11ACG)
talhipa oshtacha pokoli toklo awa-hanná'li four hundred twenty-six (11ACG)
talhipa sipokni' thousand (11ACG)

talhipa sipokni' chaffa one thousand (11ACG)

talhipa sipokni' chakká'li nine thousand (11ACG)

talhipa sipokni' chakká'licha talhipa ontochchí'nacha pokoli toklo awa-talhlhá'pi nine thousand eight hundred twenty-five (11ACG)

talhipa sipokni' talhlhá'picha pokoli hanná'li awa-oshta five thousand sixty-four (11ACG)

talhipa sipokni' toklo two thousand (11ACG)

talhipa talhlhá'pi five hundred (11ACG)

talhipa toklocha awa-tochchí'na two hundred thirteen (11ACG)

talhlhá'pi five (3RS); to be five in number (A) (12); part of **awa-talhlhá'pi, holhtina' talhlhá'pi**

intalhlhá'pi to have five

talhpak basket (1, 2)

tamowa to go away (pl. subj.) (A) (19)

tanchi' corn (9RS)

tánno'wa, ittánno'wa to walk, pass by, go by, travel around (dl. subj.) (A) (18RS)

tannohówa, ittánnohówa to walk, pass by, go by, travel around (tpl. subj.) (A) (18RS)

tángla while (auxiliary) (20RS)

tapa to be cut; to have the end or head cut off (S) (14)

tashki to lie down; to go to bed (A) (18RS)

tawáa both (to be both together) (12RS)

táwwa'a to be (two) together (used to say "and") (A) (11RS, 13RS, 19); to live in sin with, shack up with (A,S) (19)

táyyahli (Ygr. of **tahli**) (18RS)

taala'. See **daala'**

tashpishofa pishofa (Chickasaw dish made from corn and pork) (9RS, 17)

tí'wa to lie, be in a lying position (A); to lie in, be located (lying) in (a place) (A,Noun) (sg. subj.) (10)

tikahbi to be tired (S) (4)

　tíkka'hbi (Ggr.)

tili'ko' flour (13)

tilhaa to run (pl. subj.) (A) (3)

tisho assistant (usually, to an Indian doctor or shaman) (old word) (14RS)

Tishohminko', Tishominko' Tishomingo (Chickasaw chief); Tishomingo, Oklahoma (1, 14RS)

tiwa to open (of a door) (Noun) (1, 16)

tiwwi to open (something) (A,Noun) (1, 16)

tiyak itti' / itti' tiyak pine tree (18ACG)

tii', tii tea (1, 9)

tiik female (used after an animal name; not used alone) (2)

　chipota tiik girl

to'li to play ball (A) (15)

to'wa' ball (12)

toba to become (A,Noun) (13RS, 20)

tochchí'na three (3RS); to be three in number (A) (12); part of **awa-tochchí'na, holhtina' tochchí'na**

intochchí'na to have three

tofa to spit (A) (4)

tohbi to be white (in color) (S) (1, 3)

tokfol dogwood (1)

toklo two (1, 3RS); to be two in number (A) (12); part of **awa-toklo, holhtina' toklo**

intoklo to have two

toksali to work (A) (1, 4)

topa bed (10)

toshooli to explain something in (a language), to translate (something) (A,Noun)

toyya to climb (A) (3)

toomi to shine (Noun) (4)

toshpat aya to go fast, go quickly (A) (20RS)

v

vooti, footi to vote (1)

w

wakaa to fly (A) (sg. subj.) (1, 3, 19); to blow away (sg. subj.) (Noun) (19)

wakiili to make (something) fly (A,S) (16)

wakowa to fly; to blow away (pl. subj.) (A)

wayowat máa to exist (Noun); to be in (a place) (Noun,Noun) (tpl. subj. thought of as having an opening on the bottom) (12)

　iwayowat máa to have (D,Noun±at) (tpl. "have" obj. thought of as having an opening on the bottom)

wáyya'a to exist, be there (Noun); to be located in (a place) (Noun,Noun) (sg. subj. thought of as having an opening on the bottom) (10) [Note: may be used by some speakers with a human A subj. to tell a person's location; however, this sounds rude to many people, so such sentences should probably be avoided by language learners.]

　iwáyya'a to have (D,Noun±at) (sg. "have" obj. thought of as having an opening on the bottom)

wáyyo'wa to exist (Noun); to be located in (a place) (Noun,Noun) (dl. subj. thought of as having an opening on the bottom) (12)

　iwáyyo'wa to have (D,Noun±at) (dl. "have" obj. thought of as having an opening on the bottom)

waa to be ripe (1)

waachi to grow, cultivate (a plant) (A,Noun) (9RS)
waaka to be spotted (S) (1, 8)
waaka' cow (1, 8)
wihli to hold (something) out (A,S) (7RS)

winda' window (1, 16RS)
wiiki to be heavy (S); to weigh oneself (A) (1, 3)
woochi to bark (A)

y

<ya>, <oo> to be (S) (irregular verb—used only with a prefix or ending; <ya> used with S prefixes, <oo> with endings but no prefix) (11)
yaháat ittanohówa to go crying (pl. subj.) (A) (traditional way to refer to the journey on the Trail of Tears) (14RS)
yahmi to do (A,Noun) (7RS)
yahmicha and then (same subj.) (20RS)
yahmihma it happened that (different subj.) (20RS)
yahmihmat it happened that (same subj.) (20RS)
yakhookay thank you (1, 3)
yammak there; that one, that (10)
yammakaatooko that's why (13RS)
yammakílla just that, just those
yammakoot that, those, he, she, it, that one, they (cntr. subj.) (9)
yammako that, those, him, her, it, that one, them (cntr. obj.) (9)
yammat that, those, that one (subj.) (2)
yamma that, those, that one (obj.) (5)
　nittak yamma tomorrow
　nittak yamma fokhaka at about that time
yámmohmi to be like that (A) (15RS)
　nannaayámmohmi to be some way in (a place) (A,Noun) (includes **nanna** "things", as a preverb)
yanha to have a fever (S) (15)

yappa here it is (said when holding something out) (6RS)
yappak here; this one, this (10)
yappakílla only this (11RS)
yappakoot this one, these, this (cntr. subj.) (9)
yappako this one, these, this (cntr. obj.) (7RS, 9)
yappat this, these, this one (subj.) (2)
yappa this, these, this one (obj.) (9)
yaa to cry (A) (1, 2)
yaalhipa hat (20)
yaakni' land; world (10)
　Aba' Yaakni' Heaven
　Chahta' Iyaakni' Choctaw Nation
　Chikashsha Iyaakni' Chickasaw Nation
　Naahollo Iyaakni' Texas
yahna and then (different subj.) (19RS)
yimmi to believe it, to think so (S) (3); to believe (something) (S,Noun) (8)
　iyimmi to believe (a human obj.), to believe in
yokachi to catch, grab (pl. obj.) (A,S) (15); to imprison (A,S) (17RS)
yokli to catch, grab (sg. obj.) (A,S) (15)
yollichi to shake, shiver, tremble (S) (15)
yopi to swim, to take a bath (A) (6)
yopichi to bathe (someone), to make (someone) swim (A,S) (6)
yoshoba' part of **Hattak Yoshoba**

English-Chickasaw Vocabulary

This section is primarily an index to the Chickasaw-English Vocabulary, since it does not include as much information as is provided there.

When you find a word in this vocabulary, especially a verb, you should always be sure to check its entry in the Chickasaw-English Vocabulary in order to learn more about how the word is used in Chickasaw sentences. This is especially important when more than one translation is given in the index for a Chickasaw word: the Chickasaw-English Vocabulary will usually make the differences among such different translations clearer. Also, the Chickasaw-English Vocabulary lists the number of the unit in which the word was introduced. Often that unit contains additional important information about using the word in sentences.

There are a number of entries in the Chickasaw-English Vocabulary that are not indexed here. These include many of the numbers in 11ACG and many grade forms, for example.

As you know, many English concepts are expressed in Chickasaw with prefixes and endings attached to nouns and verbs or are not expressed at all. Some of these important concepts appear in the English-Chickasaw Vocabulary with references to appropriate units where they are discussed, but these references provide only a rough guide.

The main entries in this vocabulary are arranged in standard English alphabetical order.

a

a lot, to be lawa
  to have a lot of ilawa
about
  at about that time nittak yamma fokhaka
  in about (a time in the past) fokhakaasho
above aba'
accuse, to ishtombohli
ace holhtina' chaffa
act good, to chokma
add to, to ibaani
African American hattak losa'
after a while alhchímbat tahahma
again anowa'
ago, long hopaakikaashookano
agree with each other about, to ittibaachaffa
ahead of, to be ímmayya

airplane piini' wakaa'
Alabama Indian Alibaamo'
alive, to be okcháa
all
  it's all, it was all bíyyi'ka
  to be all móma
  to be all gone taha
all the time bíyyi'ka
along, to go; to be going along áa
also anowa'
always bíyyi'ka
and. *See* units 15, 19
  and then (same-subject) haatokoot
  and then (different-subject) haatoko
  and you? ishnaato
  and you all? hachishnaato

and (*continued*)
    to be (more than two) together with cho'mi
    to be (two) together with táwwa'a
    and micha', mikmat—*see* unit 15 RS
angry, to be hashaa
    to be angry about ishhashaa
    to be angry at ihashaa
animal (typically, a domesticated animal) nannalhpooba'
any nannakya, nanna
any old way, doing it kanihmit
appliance tali' palli'
arm ilbak
    upper arm shakba'

around, not to be iksho
arrive, to ala
article (of a document) imanompa kanihmo'si
ashamed, to be hofahya
    to be ashamed of ihofahya
assistant tisho
ask
    to ask (someone something) imasilhha
    to ask each other ittimasilhha
asleep, to be; asleep, to fall nosi
awake, to be okcha

b

baby chipota
    to have a baby chipotaat imánta
back; in back of ashaka'
    to bring back falammichi
    to go back falama
    to take back falammichi
backside hatip
bad, to be ikayyo'bo
    something bad nanna ikchokmo
    where things are bad nanna ikaachokmoka
bad, to smell shoha
bag shokcha
bald, to be masofa
ball to'wa'
    ball, to play to'li
bang around, to; to make a banging noise ittikalhalha'chi
bank (small) ta'oss-aa-alhto'
    piggy bank shokhoshi' ta'oss-aa-alhto'
bark
    bark of a tree itti' hakshop
    to bark woochi
barn pichchaa
basket talhpak
bathe (someone), to yopichi
bathroom aboowoshi'
bawl out, to imiha
be. *See* the vocabulary entry under the word that would
    follow *be* in your English sentence
    how could it be kanihmihchi kanihmihchi
    to be <ya>
    to be like that yámmohmi
bead oksop
bean bala'
    snake beans sinti' bala'
bear nita'
bear fruit, to ani

beat
    to beat ootímmayya'chi (includes preverb **oot±**)
    to beat up bo'li
become, to toba
bed topa
    to go to bed tashki
bedroom aanosi'
bee fohi'
begin, to ishtaya
behave oneself, to nokchito
behind ashaka'
belch, to akiilawa
believe, to iyimmi, yimmi
    to believe in (someone) iyimmi
    to believe in (something) aayimmi
    to believe it yimmi
belly ittakoba'
belonging immi'—*see also* unit 17RS
beside apootaka'
better, to get pitnampíla
Bible Holisso Holitto'pa'
big for, to be imishto
big, to be ishto (sg. subj.), hichito (pl. subj.)
    to make big ishtochichi
bigger, to be chínto
bird foshi'
bird's feather foshi' hishi'
birth, to give chipotaat imánta
bite, to kisili
bitter, to be homi
bitter weed alba homi'
black person hattak losa'
black, to be losa
blame, to ishtombohli
bloom, to pakali
blue, to be okchamali

boat piini'
body haknip
body hair hishi'
bone foni'
book holisso
born, to be ala
   to come and be born in atahánta
borrow, to ponta
   to borrow from aaponta, imaaponta
both tawáa (*see* 12RS)
bottle kitoba
bottom nota'
box, money ta'oss-aa-alhto'
bread paska
   bread made with yeast; light bread; leavened bread
      paska shatabli'
   bread made without yeast; unleavened bread
      paskikshatablo'
break for kindling, to kawwi
break, to kobafa, kobaffi, kobahli, kobbi, kowa, kookoli,
   kookowa, kooli

breathe, to foyopa
brick house lokfi' nona' abooha
bright, to be hashtahli
bring, to ishtala, ishtaya
   to bring back falammichi
   to bring home ishtala
broken, to be oppolo
broom ishpiha'
brother inakfi', ittibaapishi
   older brother intikba'
   younger brother nakfish
brown, to be lakna
bug issosh
building abooha
bunch (of people) alhiha'
buried, to be holloppi
burn, to lowa
   to burn the hair off anakshooli
burp, to akiilawa
bury, to hoppi
buy, to chompa

c

cabin, log itti' ittabaana' abooha
cake paska champoli'
call (someone something), to aachi
camera ishholbachi'
can *see* unit 5
cannibal hattak-apa'
car kaar
care of, to take apiisachi
carry, to sho'li
cat kowi'
catch, to yokachi, yokli
   to catch sight of pisa
   to catch up with sakki
caught up on, to get takaali
cedar chowaala'
cemetery aaholloppi'
chair aaombiniili'
chase, to lhiyohli
cheekbone area hakson
Cherokee Chalakki'
chew, to howasa
Chicano Oshpaani'
Chickasaw Chikashsha
   Chickasaw governor Chikashsha Iminko'
   Chickasaw language Chikashshanompa,
      Chikashshanompa', Chikashsha imanompa
Chickasaw Nation Chikashsha Iyaakni'
Chickasaw woman Chikashshihoo
chicken akanka'

chief minko'
child chipota, inchipota
Choctaw Chahta'
   Choctaw language Chahtanompa, Chahtanompa',
      Chahta imanompa
   Choctaw Nation Chahta' Iyaakni'
chop, to cha'li
Christian Iksa'
Christmas Nittak Hollishto'
   on Christmas Nittak Hollishto' ookma
church aaittanaa'
   to have a church service ittanaha
clean, to chofalli
clean, to be chofata
climb, to toyya
close, to okshitta
close to each other, to be ittimilinka'si
coat naafkishto'
cold, to be ichchokwa, kapassa
   to get cold kapassa
   to feel cold inkapassa
come, to minti
   to come and be located in; to come and be born in
      atahánta
   to come back falamat minti
   to come from aaminti
completely taha, tahli
condition, to have a serious impállammi
conquer, to ootímmayya'chi (includes preverb oot±)

consider precious, to holiitobli
container, to put into a ani
cook, to hopooni
   to cook on, to cook in aahopooni
cooked poke salad koshibba' holhponi'
cookie paska champoli'
copy, to hobachi
   to copy from aahobachi, imaahobachi
corn tanchi'
correct, to be aalhpí'sa
cough, to hotolhko
could it be, how kanihmihchi
count, to hotihna
cover oneself with, to anchi
covered with, to be áyya'chi
covering, outer hakshop
cow waaka'
cracked, to be shachakla
crazy, to be haksi

Creek Mashkooki'
crop ani'
crouched down, to be tákka'li (sg. subj.), tákkohli (dl. subj.), takoht máa (tpl. subj.)
crow fala
crow, to ola
cry, to yaa
   to pass by crying yaháat ittanohówa
cultivate, to waachi
cup ishtaka'fa'
cut, to bashaffi, bashli, katolhlhi, tabli
   to be cut basha, bashaffi, tapa
   to be cut with a knife kolofa
   to cut (grass) amo
   to cut the top off, to cut in two tabli
   to cut up katolhlhi
   to have the end or head cut off tapa
cutter, grass hashshok-ishtamo'

d

dance hilha'
dance hall aahilha'
dance, to hilha
dancer hilha'
daughter oshiitiik
dawn, to onna
day nittak
   nowadays himmaka' nittakookano
   one day nittak chaffaka
   these days himmaka' áyya'shookano
   to be the next day onna
dead, to be illi
debt, to go into; to incur a debt ahiika
deer issi'
degraded, to be kalakshi
die, to illi
different
   to be different íla, iláyyo'ka
   to be different from ittimíla
   to look different from each other pisa ittimilayyokha
dining room aaimpa' abooha
dip, to takaffi
dipped up, to be takafa
dig, to kolli
dirty, to be litiha
dish amposhi'
do
   doing it somehow, doing it any old way kanihmit
   to do yahmi

   to do (something) to (someone) iyahmohmi
   to do the right thing aalhpí'sa
   to do (what) katihmi
   to do what to; to do (what) to katihchi
doctor alikchi'
   to doctor imalikchi'
dog ofi'
dogwood tokfol
dollar daala'
domesticated animal nannalhpooba'
door okkisa'
   little door okkisoshi'
down akka'
   to go down akkowa
   to put down; to lay (something) down bohli
draw water, to oochi
dream, to ilhpokonna
   to dream about ishtilhpokonna
dress naafokha, naafka
drink, to ishko
drip, to hoyya
drop (something), to imittola
drown, to ok-aailli
   to drown (someone) ok-aa-abi
drunk, to be; to get drunk haksi
duck fochosh
dug, to be kola

e

each other. *See* unit 10
eagle osi'
ear haksibish
earlier times, in still mishsha' fónkha áyya'shookano
east hashaakochcha'
eat, to impa
  to eat (something) apa
eater, man- hattak-apa'
educational institution nanna aaithana'
eight; eight in number, to be ontochchí'na
  eight (in cards) holhtina' ontochchí'na
  to have eight ontochchí'na
eighteen awa-ontochchí'na
elect, to atookoli
elected, to be alhtoka
eleven awa-chaffa
enacted, to be alhínchi

end
  to have the end or head cut off tapa
English Naahollimanompa'
enough, to be alhpí'sa
enumerated, to be holisso toba
equal to, to be ittíllawwi
ever, forever and bílli'yacha bílli'ya
everybody; everyone kanahookya; kaniya'ookya
everyplace kaniya'ookya
everything nannahookya
everywhere kaniya'ookya, kaniya' móma
exist, to tálla'a, tállo'wa, talowat máa, wayowat máa, wáyya'a, wáyyo'wa
  not to exist iksho
explain something in, to toshooli
eye ishkin

f

face, to wash one's okaami
  to wash (someone's) face okaamichi
fall, to ittola
  fall asleep, to nosi
far off, to go hopaakichi
fast, to be; fast, to go palhki
  to be fast for; to go fast for impalhki
fat, to be lhinko
father inki'
  God our Father Pinki' Chihoowa
feed (something) to (someone), to; feed, to ipita
feel
  to feel cold inkapassa
  to feel good inchokma
  to feel hot impalli
female tiik (used after an animal name)
fever, to have a yanha
fifteen awa-talhlhá'pi
fight, to; to fight with ittibi
fine, I'm anchokma
finger in (someone's eye), to stick one's okaabaafa
fingernail ilbakchosh
finish (something), to; finish, to tahli
finished, to be taha
fire lowak
first, to be ámmo'na
fish nani'
  go fish! nani' hoot aya!
five; five in number, to be talhlhá'pi
  five (in cards) holhtina' talhlhá'pi
  to have five intalhlhá'pi

flesh nipi'
floor akka'
  to be lying spread out on the floor pátta'a (sg. subj.), patkáyya'chi (dl. subj.), patkachit máa (tpl. subj.)
flour tili'ko'
flower nampakali'
fly (insect) chokaano
  fly, to wakaa
  to make fly wakiili
flying squirrel pali'
foot iyyi'
for. *See* unit 8
forever and ever bílli'yacha bílli'ya
forget, to imalhkaniya
forgive, to; to forgive (someone) for inkashoffi
forgotten, to be alhkaniya
fork chofak
forty pokoli oshta
four; four in number, to be oshta
  four (in cards) holhtina' oshta
  to have four imoshta
fourteen awa-oshta
frame house itti' basha' abooha
Friday Nittak Ishtalhlha'pi'
friend inkana'
frozen, to be akmi
fruit ani'
fruit, to bear ani, waa
full, to be kayya
fur hishi'

g

gate okkisa'
gather (food plants), to ayowa
get, to ishi
  to get as a present habina
  to get better pitnampíla
  to get caught up on takaali
  to get cold kapassa
  to get drunk haksi
  to get (food plants) ayowa
  to get here ala
  to get hung up on takaali
  to get hurt hottopa
  to get inside albiha
  to get into a lying position tashki
  to get into a sitting position biniili, binohli
  to get into a standing position hika
  to get married to ittihaalalli
  to get quiet sámma'ta
  to get (something) as a present habina
  to get there ona
  to get to ala, ona
  to get to know ithana
give to, to ima
  to give a haircut to amo
  to give birth chipotaat imánta
  to give (something) to (someone), usually as a present habinachi
glass amposhi' shokawwa'li'
glorify, to holiitoblichi
glory nannishtaaholiitó'paka', nannishtimaaholitto'pa'
go ahead (in "let" hortative sentences) haatokmat, hookmat, mikmat
go, to aya
  go fish! nani' hoot aya!
  go look for it! hoot aya!
  to go along áa

to go and stay over in (a place) ootalbinachi
to go away kaniya, tamowa
to go by ootaya, tánno'wa, tannohówa
to go down akkowa
to go far off hopaakichi
to go fast palhki
to go fast for impalhki
to go in chokkowa
to go into debt ahiika
to go out kochcha
to go over pitabaanabli
to go see pistaya
to go to bed tashki
to go to sleep nosi
to go to talk to ootimanompoli (includes preverb oot±)
God Chihoowa
God our Father Pinki' Chihoowa
going along, to be áa
gone, to be all taha
good, to be chokma
  to feel good inchokma
  to be good tasting champoli
governor, Chickasaw Chikashsha Iminko'
grab, to yokachi, yokli
grandmother ippo'si'
Grandmother, Granny Appo'si
grass hashshok
grass cutter hashshok-ishtamo'
graveyard aaholloppi'
greasy, to be niha
green, to be okchamali
greens nannokchamali'
group aaittapiha'
grow (a plant), to waachi
growl, to kiliha

h

hair
  body hair hishi'
  head hair ipashi'
  to burn the hair off anakshooli
haircut to, to give a amo
hall, dance aahilha'
hammer naaishbo'wa'
hammered, to be bo'wa
hand ilbak
  to have in one's hand í'shi
hanging, to be tákka'li (sg. subj.), tákkohli (dl. subj.), takoht máa (tpl. subj.)

happen, to; to happen to katihmi
  it happened that yahmihmat (same subject), yahmihma (different subject)
happy, to be ayoppa
hard (solid), to be kawaski
harvest (grass), to amo
hat yaalhipa
haul, to shaali
have
  not to have ikimiksho
  to have intálla'a, intállo'wa, intalowat máa, iwayowat máa, iwáyya'a, iwáyyo'wa—*see also* unit 12

to have a baby chipotaat imánta
to have a church service ittanaha
to have a fever yanha
to have a lot of ilawa
to have a meal impa
to have (a relative) imánta
to have a serious condition impállammi
to have eight imontochchí'na
to have five intalhlhá'pi
to have four imoshta
to have fruit on it ani
to have in one's hand í'shi
to have many ilawa
to have nine inchakká'li
to have one inchaffa
to have rain omba
to have (relatives) imáyya'sha, imáshwa
to have seven imontoklo
to have six ihanná'li
to have snow oktosha
to have something wrong oppolo
to have ten impokkó'li
to have the end or head cut off tapa
to have the right to imaalhpí'sa
to have three intochchí'na
to have two intoklo
to have wind mahli
he yammakoot—*see also* units 2, 3, 8, 9
head ishkobo'
   to have the end or head cut off tapa
head hair ipashi'
healthy, to be inchokmishto
hear, to hánglo, haklo, háyyaklo
heart imichonkash
Heaven Aba' Yaakni'
heavy, to be wiiki
hello hallito; chinchokmataa, hachinchokmataa
help, to apila
her yammako—*see also* units 5, 7, 8
   her own ilaapo'—*see also* unit 16RS
here yappak
   here it is (said when holding something out) yappa
   to be here; to get here ala
hers immi'
herself ilaapo'—*see also* unit 5
   by herself ilaapakáynit

hiccup, to chokfiyammi
hide, to lohmi
him yammako—*see also* units 5, 7, 8
himself ilaapo'—*see also* unit 5
   by himself ilaapakáynit
hip hatip
his immi'—*see also* unit 7
   his own ilaapo'
Hispanic person Oshpaani'
hit, to isso
   to hit more than once bo'li
   to hit (plural subject) bo'li
   to make hit issochichi
hitch up (a horse) to (a wagon), to halallichi
hog shokha'
Hokey Pokey Hooki' Pooki'
hold, to í'shi
   to hold (something) out wihli
holy table aai'pa' holiito'pa'
holy, to be holiitopa, holiittó'pa
home chokka'
   to bring home ishtala
horse issoba
horse trough issoba aaipita' piini'
hot, to be palli
   to feel hot impalli
house abooha, chokka'
   brick house lokfi' nona' abooha
   frame house itti' basha' abooha
   log house itti' ittabaana' abooha
how
   how are you? chinchokma, hachinchokmataa
   how could it be? kanihmihchi
   how (in what way) katihsht, katihchihaat
   how many; to be how many katohmi
   how (how on earth) katiht, katihmihaat
   to say how nantokaachi, nannokaachi
hug, to shooli
hundred talhipa
hung up on, to get takaali
hungry, to be hopoba
hunt, to owwatta
hurt hottopa
   to hurt; to get hurt hottopa
   to hurt (someone) hottopachi
husband ihattak

i

I anaakoot—*see also* units 3, 8, 9
   I'm fine anchokma
   only I anaakilloot
imitate, to hobachi
imprison, to yokachi

in anonka', anonkaka'
   in about (a time in the past) fokhakaasho
   in back of ashaka'
   in still earlier times mishsha' fónkha áyya'shookano
incur a debt, to ahiika

Indian Hattak Api' Homma'
injure, to hottopachi
insect iss<u>o</u>sh
inside anonka', anonkaka'
    to be inside fóyyokha (sg. subj.), albi'ha (dl. subj.),
        albihat m<u>á</u>a (tpl. subj.)
to get inside albiha
    to put inside fokhi

institution, educational nanna aaithana'
it yammakoot, yammak<u>o</u>—*see also* units 2, 3, 5
it's (number) **o'clock** hashi' kanalli (number)
    it was all bíyyi'ka
its. *See* unit 7
it's all bíyyi'ka
itself. *See* unit 5

j

jealous of, to be; jealous, to be hopoo
jump
to jump malli
    to jump back; to jump off mallittakaali
just pilla', finha, ílla

just that; just those yammakílla

k

keep, to í'shi
key ishtasha'na'
kick, to halhabli (sg. obj.), hallhi (pl. obj.)
    to kick more than once halhlhi
    to kick once halhabli
kidnap, to honkopa
kill, to abi
killer, man hattak-abi'
kindle, to ooti
kindling, to break for kawwi
kingdom aapihlichika'
kiss, to sh<u>o</u>'ka
    to make kiss sh<u>o</u>'kachichi
kitchen aalhponi'

kitchen knife ishbashli'
knee iyyinto'lhka'
kneel down, to achokmilhka
    to be kneeling achokmíyyi'lhka
knife bashpo
    kitchen knife ishbashli'
    to be cut with a knife kolofa
knock (something) down on, to <u>o</u>yilhlhichi
know, to ith<u>á</u>na
    to get to know ithana
    to know how; to know how (to do something) well
        imponna
known, to make annoyachi

l

land yaakni'
language anompa
last, to be ishtaalhi
later, a while ikalhchibo'sok<u>a</u>
laugh at, to; laugh, to ollali
law naalhpisa'
lawmaker naapiisa'
lay down, to bohli
    to lay (something) down on ombohli
lazy, to be intakho'bi
leaf (of a tree) itti' hishi'
leaning back against atáyya'at
learn, to ithana
    place to learn nanna aaithana'

leash ishtalakchi'
leave
    to leave aaissachi
    to leave behind <u>i</u>filammi
leavened bread paska shatabli'
leg iyyi'
lengthen, to faliili
letter holisso
lie down, to tashki
lie, to
    to lie; to be lying down tí'wa (sg. subj.), káyya'a (dl.
        subj.), kahat m<u>á</u>a (tpl. subj.)
    to lie; to tell lies loshka
    to lie about; to tell lies about <u>o</u>loshka
    to lie on one's side achaknáyya'ski

lies
  to tell lies loshka
  to tell lies about oloshka
light, to be hashtahli
like
  to be like that yámmohmi
  to like anhínchi; ayoppánchi
  to look like; to seem like ahooba
lips ittialbi'
listen to, to haklo
little
  (used as the second part of a compound) oshi'
  little, to be iskanno'si (sg. subj.), sawa'si (pl. subj.)
live in (a location), to ánta (sg. subj.), áshwa (dl. subj.), áyya'sha (tpl. subj.)
live in sin with, to táwwa'a
liver salakha'
loaded with fruit (of a plant), to be waa
located, to be; to be located in (a place) ánta (sg. subj.), áshwa (dl. subj.), áyya'sha (tpl. subj.)
  to be located in (a place) tálla'a (sg. subj.), tállo'wa (dl. subj.), talowat máa (tpl. subj.), wáyya'a (sg. subj.), wáyyo'wa (dl. subj.), wayowat máa (tpl. subj.)—*see* unit 10
  to be located (lying) in (a place) tí'wa (sg. subj.), káyya'a (dl. subj.), kahat máa (tpl. subj.)
  to be located on (something) as an integral part í'ma
  to be located (sitting) in (a place) bínni'li (sg. subj.), chí'ya (dl. subj.), binohmáa (tpl. subj.)

to be located (standing) in (a place) híkki'ya (sg. subj.), hí'li (dl. subj.), hiyohmáa (tpl. subj.)
  to come and be located in atahánta
lock ishtasha'na'
locked, to be ashana
log itti'
log house; log cabin itti' ittabana' abooha
long
  not too long after ikalhchibo'soka
  to be long falaa
long ago hopaakikaashookano
look
  go look for it! hoot aya!
  to look at pisa
  to look different from each other pisa ittimilayyokha
  to look for hoyo
  to look like ahooba
Lost People; Lost Tribe Hattak Yoshoba'
lot of, for there to be a lawa
love, to ihollo
lying
  to be in a lying position tí'wa (sg. subj.), káyya'a (dl. subj.), kahat máa (tpl. subj.)
  to be lying spread out on the floor pátta'a (sg. subj.), patkáyya'chi (dl. subj.), patkachit máa (tpl. subj.)
  to get into a lying position tashki

m

made
  to be made from aaiksaa
  to be made true alhínchi
make, to ikbi—*see also* unit 6
  to make a banging noise ittikalhalha'chi
  to make a noise ola
  to make big ishtochichi
  to make fly wakiili
  to make hit issochichi
  to make kiss sho'kachichi
  to make known annoyachi
  to make run malichi
  to make sacred holiitobli
  to make (someone) pull (something) halallichi
  to make swim yopichi
male nakni'
man hattak, hattak nakni', nakni'
man-eater hattak-apa'
man killer hattak-abi'
mane ipashi'

many
  how many katohmi
  to be many lawa
  to be how many katohmi
  to have many ilawa
  many (used as a stative verb following a noun) bíyyi'ka
married to, to be ittihaalalli
marry, to ittihaalalli, ittihaalallichi
mash, to lhaboshli
mashed, to be lhabocha
may. *See* unit 5
me anaako—*see also* units 5, 8
  only me anaakillo
meal, to have a impa
mean
  to be mean issikopa
  to be mean to imissikopa
  to mean (something) aachi
meat nipi'

medicine itt̲ish
meet, to afama
melt, to bila
   to melt (something) biliili
melted, to be bila
messed up, to be oppo̲lo
Mexican Oshpaani'
mine ammi'
Mississippi Missipi'
mix, to okommo
mixed, to be olhkomo
Monday Nittak Ammo'na'
money ta'osso
money box ta'oss-aa-alhto'
monkey hattak shawi'
more than, to be ímmayya
morning, in the nittaki

morning, the next onnakmako̲
mortar, to pound in a wooden hosi
mosquito sapontaki'
mother ishki'
mountain onchaba
mouse pinti'
mouth iti
move
   to move (oneself) ilhko'li
   to move (something) ilhko'chi
mow, to amo
mowed, to be almo
mud lokfi'
murderer hattak-abi'
my. *See* unit 7
myself. *See* unit 5

n

nail
   fingernail ilbakchosh
   toenail iyyakchosh
name holhchifo
   to name hochifo
named
   to be named holhchifo
   to be named after aholhchi'fo
Nation
   Choctaw Nation Chahta' I̲yaakni'
   Chickasaw Nation Chikashsha I̲yaakni'
needle naaishtalhcho'wa'
next
   next to apootaka'
   the next morning onnakmako̲
   to be the next day onna
nice, to be chokma
night oklhili
   at night oklhilik̲a
   to be night oklhili
   tonight himmaka' oklhili
nine; nine in number, to be chakká'li
   nine (in cards) holhtina' chakká'li
   to have nine inchakká'li

nineteen awa-chakká'li
no ki'yo
no one kanahookya (in a negative sentence)
no place kaniya'ookya (in a negative sentence)
nobody kanahookya (in a negative sentence)
noise
   to make a banging noise ittikalhalha'chi
   to make a noise ola
non-Indian naahollo
north falammi
nose ibichchala'
   not ki'yo—*see also* unit 9
   not to be around; not to be there; not to exist iksho
   not to exist at all nannakya iksho—*see also* unit 13RS
   not to have ikimiksho
   not too long after ikalhchibo'sok̲a
nothing nannahookya (in a negative sentence)
now himmaka'
nowadays himmaka' nittakookano
nowhere kaniya'ookya (in a negative sentence)
number holhtina'
numerous, to be lawa

o

o'clock
   it's (number) o'clock hashi' kanalli (number)
offspring inchipota
oh! kii, aa

OK
   (in "let" hortative sentences) haatokmat, hookmat, mikmat
   (used to begin a story) haatokm̲a

Oklahoma Oklahomma'
old, to be sipokni
older sibling intikba'
on; on top; on top of pakna'—*see also* unit 10
once upon a time chiiki pilla' áyya'shakaash
one chaffa
    to have one inchaffa
one day nittak chaffaka
one in number, to be chaffa
oneself. *See* unit 5
    to say about oneself miha
only ílla—*see* unit 20
    only (adverb) pilla'
    only (auxiliary) illa
    only I anaakilloot
    only me anaakillo
    only us poshnaakillo
    only we poshnaakilloot

only this yappakílla
only you hachishnaakilloot, hachishnaakillo,
    ishnaakilloot, ishnaakillo
open, to tiwa
    to open (something) tiwwi
operate on, to bashli
operated on, to be basha
other
    other one chaffo'
    to be other íla
our. *See* unit 7
ours pommi', hapommi'
ourselves. *See* unit 5
outer covering hakshop
outside kochcha'
outhouse aboowoshi'
owl oopa

p

pain; to be in pain hottopa
paint, to aabi
pants balaafokha'
paper holisso
    paper plate holisso amposhi'
    to be recorded on paper holisso toba
pass
    to pass by ootaya, tánno'wa, tannohówa
    to pass by crying yaháat ittanohówa
pay, to atobbi
    to pay (something) to imaatobbi
peace nanna aya
peach takolo
pen; pencil ishholissochi'
    quill pen foshi' hishi' ishholissochi'
People, Lost Hattak Yoshoba'
perform a marriage ceremony for, to ittihaalallichi
persimmon onkof
person hattak
photograph, to holbachi
pick up, to ishi
picture holba'
    to take a picture of holbachi
pie paska champoli'
pig shokhoshi'
piggy bank shokhoshi' ta'oss-aa-alhto'
pinch, to chinoffi
pine tree tiyak itti'
pishofa tashpishofa
pitiful, to be ilbashsha
place to learn nanna aaithana'
plane piini' wakaa'

plate amposhi'
    paper plate holisso amposhi'
play, to chokoshkomo
    to play ball to'li
plow ishliichi'
    to plow liichi
plowed, to be laa
point at, to aabachi
poke salad koshibba'
    cooked poke salad koshibba' holhponi'
pokeweed koshibba'
policeman naalhtoka'
Pontotoc Pantatak
poor, to be ilbashsha
pork shokha' nipi'
possession immi'
pot aaholhponi'
potato ahi'
pound, to bo'li
    to pound in a wooden mortar hosi
pour into a container, to ani
power nannishtaayalhlhi'
praise, to ayoppachi
preacher aba' anompa ishtanompoli'
Preamble Ishtaa-aya Ámmo'na Holisso
precious, to be holiitopa, holiittó'pa
    to consider precious holiitobli
prepared, to be already alhtaha
present, to get (something) as a habina
pretty, to be chokma'si
prisoner hattak yoka'
produce ani'

professor pofessa'
pull, to halalli
   to make (someone) pull (something) halallichi
put, to
   to put down bohli

to put in (a container) abihli, ani
to put inside fokhi
to put (medicine) on (someone) imaabi
to put on (clothes) fokha
to put (something) down on ombohli

q

quiet, to be chokkíllissa
   to get quiet sámma'ta

quill pen foshi' hishi' ishholissochi'

r

rabbit chokfi
raccoon shawi'
rags naalhilafa'
raggedy, to be all taha
rain, to; rain, to have omba
rat shanti'
rattlesnake sishto
read, to ittimanompoli, riidi
to read to imittimanompoli
ready, to be alhtaha, imalhtaha
realize, to ithana
really kaníhka
rear ashaka'
recorded
   to be recorded on paper holisso toba
   to be recorded together ittibaaholisso
red, to be homma
rejoice, to nannishtilayoppa
remember, to nokfónkha
   to really remember nokfóyyokha
resemble, to ahooba

rest, to nokchito
restaurant aaimpa'
return, to falama
   to return (something) falammichi
reveal to, to imoktanichi (Hngr. **imoktanihínchi**)
ride, to ombiniili
right
   to be right (correct) aalhpí'sa
   to do the right thing aalhpí'sa
   to have the right to imaalhpí'sa—*see also* unit 17RS
rip, to lhilaffi
ripe, to be waa
rock tali'
room abooha
   dining room aaimpa' abooha
rooster akanakni'
rope ishtalakchi'
ruined, to be oppolo
run, to malili (sg. subj.), tilhaa (pl. subj.)
to make run malichi
to run away malit kaniya

s

sack shokcha
sacred, to be holiitopa, holiittó'pa
   to make sacred holiitobli
sad, to be ikimalhpi'so, nokhánglo
same
   to be just about the same ittihooba chohmi
   to be the same as ittíllawwi
Saturday Nittak Hollo' Nakfish, Nittak Ishhanna'li'
save, to okchaalínchi
save from, to aalhakoffichi
say, to aachi
   they say aachi, miha
   to say about oneself miha
   to say how; to say what nantokaachi
scare, to imilhlhali

scared
   to be scared imilhlha
   to be scared of imalhata
school holiss-aapisa'
scratch, to sholaffi (sg. obj.), sholli (pl. obj.)
   to scratch more than once sholli
   to scratch once sholaffi
scythe hashshok-ishtamo'
seated, to be binohmáa, bínni'li, chí'ya
see, to písa, pisa
   to go see pistaya
seem like, to ahooba
sell, to kanchi
Seminole Shimmanooli'
send, to pilachi

separate
  to be separate iláyyo'ka
  to separate from each other ittifilamo'li
serious condition, to have a impállammi
service, to have a church ittanaha
set fruit, to ani
seven; seven in number, to be ontoklo
  seven (in cards) holhtina' ontoklo
  to have seven imontoklo
seventeen awa-ontoklo
several
  several, to be kani'mi
  several (used as a stative verb following a noun)
    bíyyi'ka
shack up with, to táwwa'a
shake, to yollichi
  to shake (oneself) ilhko'li
  to shake (something) ilhko'chi
sharp, to be
she yammakoot—*see also* units 2, 3, 8, 9
sheep chokfalhpooba'
shepherd chokfalhpooba' apiisachi'
shine, to shoppalali, toomi
shirt naafka lombo'
shiver, to yollichi
shoe sholosh
shoot, to nalhlhi
  to shoot at hosa
shot, to be nalha
sibling ittibaapishi
  older sibling intikba'
  younger sibling nakfish
sick, to be abika
  to be sick for imambiika
sick person abika'
side apootaka'
  to lie on one's side achaknaski
  to turn on one's side achaknáyya'ski
sign (a document), to ilhafi
sight of, to catch pisa
sin with, to live in táwwa'a
sing, to taloowa
singe, to anakshooli
singer taloowa'
sister intiik, ittibaapishi
  older sister intikba'
  younger sister nakfish
sit down, to biniili (sg. subj.), binohli (pl. subj.)
  sit down and tell lies! bini'cha loshka
  to sit down on ombiniili
sit, to; sitting position, to be in a bínni'li (sg. subj.),
  chí'ya (dl. subj.), binohmáa (tpl. subj.)

sitting position
  to be in a sitting position bínni'li (sg. subj.), chí'ya (dl.
    subj.), binohmáa (tpl. subj.)
  to get into a sitting position biniili (sg. subj.), binohli
    (pl. subj.)
six; six in number, to be hanná'li
  six (in cards) holhtina' hanná'li
  to have six ihanná'li
sixteen awa-hanná'li
skin hakshop
skinny, to be chonna
skunk koni
sky shotik
slave hattak yoka'
sleep, to nosi
small, to be iskanno'si (sg. subj.), sawa'si (pl. subj.)
smear, to aabi
smell bad, to shoha
smoke (tobacco), to pofa
snake sinti'
snake beans sinti' bala'
sneeze, to habishko
snore, to lhabanka
snow okti'
  to snow; to have snow oktosha
soap ishtalhchifa'
solid, to be kawaski
some nanna, kánnohmi
  to be some kani'mi, kánnohmi
  to be some way in (a place) nannaayámmohmi
    (includes **nanna** "things" as preverb)
somebody; someone kana; kaniya'
somehow, doing it kanihmit
something nanna
somewhere kaniya'
son oshi'
song taloowa'
sorry for, to be inokhánglo
soup ashiila
spank, to passáa
speak, to anompoli
spider cholhkan
spit, to tofa
spoon folosh
spotted, to be waaka
spread out
  to be lying spread out on the floor pátta'a (sg. subj.),
    patkáyya'chi (dl. subj.), patkachit máa (tpl. subj.)
  to spread (something) out for (someone) on
    impatali
squatting, to be tákka'li (sg. subj.), tákkohli (dl. subj.),
  takoht máa (tpl. subj.)

squirrel fani'
  flying squirrel pali'
stab, to baafa
stand up, to hika
stand, to híkki'ya (sg. subj.), hí'li (dl. subj.), hiyohmáa
  (tpl. subj.)
standing position
  to be in a standing position híkki'ya (sg. subj.), hí'li
  (dl. subj.), hiyohmáa (tpl. subj.)
  to get into a standing position hika
stare at, to okaapisa
start
  to start (a car) malichi
  to start (a fire) ooti
stay, to ánta, áyya'sha, áshwa
  to go and stay over in ootalbinachi
steal, to honkopa
  to steal for ihonkopa
  to steal from aahonkopa, imaahonkopa
stick itti'
  to stick one's finger in (someone's eye) okaabaafa

sticking onto, to be láppa'li (sg. subj.), láppohli (dl.
  subj.), lapoht máa (tpl. subj.)
still (auxiliary) ímmo'ma
stink, to kosoma, shoha
stomach ittakoba'
stone tali'
store aachompa'
suddenly himónali'
sun hashi'
Sunday Nittak Hollo', Nittak Ishtontoklo'
swallow, to nannabli
sweat, to hoyahno
sweep, to pihli
sweet, to be champoli
swept, to be piha
swim, to yopi, ok-aayopi
  to make swim yopichi
switch ishfama'

t

table aai̱'pa'
  holy table aai̱'pa' holiito'pa'
take, to ishi, ishtaya, ishtona, ishtittánno'wa
  to take a bath yopi
  to take a picture of holbachi
  to take care of apiisachi
  to take from imaaishi
  to take (something) back falammichi
talk, to anompoli
  to go to talk to ootimanompoli (includes preverb **oot±**)
tall, to be chaaha
taste, to apat pisa
tasting, to be good champoli
tea tii'
teach (something) to, to imaabachi
teacher nannimaabachi
tear, to lhilaffi
tell
  to tell (someone) imano̱li
  to tell lies loshka
  to tell lies about o̱loshka
ten; ten in number, to be pokkó'li
  ten (in cards) holhtina' pokoli
  to have ten impokkó'li
Texas Naahollo I̱yaakni'
thank you yakhookay
that; that one yammak, yammakoot, yammako̱, yammat,
  yamma̱

  just that yammakílla
  to be like that yámmohmi
that's why yammakaatoko̱
their. *See* unit 7
  their own ilaapo'
theirs immi'
them. S*ee* units 5, 8
themselves ilaapo'—*see also* unit 5
  by themselves ilaapakáynit
then mahma̱ (different-subject)
  and then (same-subject) haatokoot, yahmicha
  and then (different-subject) haatoko̱, ya̱hna
there yammak—*see also* unit 10
there, to be ánta, áyya'sha, á̱shwa, tálla'a, wáyya'a
  not to be there iksho
these yappakoot, yappako̱, yappat, yappa̱
these days himmaka' áyya'shookano
they yammakoot—*see also* units 2, 3, 8, 9
thicket abokkoli'
things nannakat—*see also* unit 9RS
  something nanna
think, to anokfilli
  to think so yimmi
thirteen awa-tochchí'na
thirty pokoli tochchí'na
this; this one yappak, yappakoot, yappako̱, yappat,
  yappa̱
  only this yappakílla

those yammakoot, yammak<u>o</u>, yammat, yamm<u>a</u>
  just those yammakílla
thousand talhipa sipokni'
three; three in number, to be tochchí'na
  three (in cards) holhtina' tochchí'na
  to have three intochchí'na
Thursday Nittak Ayyoshta'
tickle, to kamoshli
tie, to; to tie up takchi
time
  at about that time nittak yamm<u>a</u> fokhak<u>a</u>
  chiiki pilla' áyya'shakaash once upon a time
  what time is it? hashi' kanalli katohmi?
times, in still earlier mishsha' fónkha áyya'shookano
tired, to be ikahbi
Tishomingo Tishohminko'
to. *See* units 8, 10
tobacco chomak
together
  to be (more than two) together with cho'mi
  to be (two) together with táwwa'a
tomorrow onnakm<u>a</u>; nittak yamm<u>a</u>
tonight himmaka' oklhili
too much salami
top
  lid, top of (something) pakna'
  toy top hilha'chi'

under; underside nota'
understand each other, to ittimith<u>á</u>na
unhappy, to be ikimalhpi'so
unleavened bread paskikshatablo'
upper arm shakba'

various, to be iláyyo'ka
vegetable nannokchamali'

wagon itti'chanaa
wait, to himonha
  to wait for <u>i</u>himonha
wake (someone) up, to okchali
wake up, to okcha
walk, to n<u>o</u>wa, tánno'wa, tannoh<u>ó</u>wa
want, to banna
wash one's face, to okaami
  to wash (someone's) face okaamichi
washed, to be alhchifa
watch over, to apiisachi

touch, to halili
town aachompa', okla
toy ishchokoshkomo'
translate, to toshooli
travel around, to tánno'wa, tannoh<u>ó</u>wa
treaty nannalhpisa' holisso
tree itti'
  bark (of a tree) itti' hakshop
  leaf (of a tree) itti' hishi'
  pine tree tiyak itti'
tremble, to yollichi
tribe okloshi'
  Lost Tribe Hattak Yoshoba'
trough, horse issoba aaipita' piini'
true, to be made <u>a</u>lhínchi
truly bíyyi'ka—*see* unit 17RS
try, to miha
Tuesday Nittak Atokla'
turn
  to turn on one's side achaknaski
  to turn (oneself) around ilifilito'chi
twelve awa-toklo
twenty pokoli toklo
twice hitokla'
two; two in number, to be toklo
  two (in cards) holhtina' toklo
  to have two toklo

u

us haposhnaak<u>o</u>, poshnaak<u>o</u>—*see also* units 5, 8
  only us poshnaakill<u>o</u>, haposhnaakill<u>o</u>
use (medicine) on, to imaaiksachi
used up, to be taha

v

very kan<u>í</u>hk<u>a</u>
vote, to vooti

w

water oka'
water, to draw oochi
watermelon istokchank
way
  doing it any old way kanihmit
  in what way kat<u>i</u>hsht; katihchihaat
  to be some way in (a place) nannaayámmohmi
    (includes **nanna** "things" as preverb)
we poshnaakoot, haposhnaakoot—*see also* units 3, 8, 9
  only we poshnaakilloot, haposhnaakill<u>o</u>
wear, to fóyyokha

Wednesday Nittak Atochchi'na', Nittak Aaiklanna'
weed alba
   bitter weed alba homi'
weigh oneself, to wiiki
well (used to begin a story) haatokma
west hashaaobya'
wet, to be lhayita
what nanta; nanna; nannakat—*see* units 2, 17, 17ACG
   in what way (how) katihsht; katihchihaat
   to do (what) katihmi
   to do what to; to do (what) to katihchi
   to say what nantokaachi
   what time is it? hashi' kanalli katohmi?
when
   when (nonpast) katiya fokhakmak; katihkmak
   when (past) katiya fokhakaash; katihkaash
where katiya'; katiyaak; kaniya'—*see* unit 17, 17ACG
where is. *See* units 4, 17
where things are bad nanna ikaachokmoka
which; to be which one; to be which ones katimpi
while tángla (auxiliary)
   after a while alhchímbat tahahma
whip ishfama'
   whip, to fammi
whipped, to be fama
whistle, to konta
white (in color), to be tohbi
white man; white person naahollo
who kata; kana—*see also* unit 17, 17ACG
whole, to be the móma
whoop, to páa
why katihmihta, katihmihaat
   that's why yammakaatoko

wife imihoo
wild, to be imilhlha
will. *See* unit 5
wind mahli
   to be windy; to have wind mahli
window aahashtahli', winda'
windy, to be mahli
wings fanalhchi'
wish, to anhi
   to wish something for (someone) imanhi
with. *See* unit 10
wolf nashoba
woman ihoo
   Chickasaw woman Chikashshihoo
wonder about, to anhit ishtanokfilli
wood itti'
woods abokkoli'
word anompa
(word used at the end of a formal statement) hookay
work, to toksali
world yaakni'
worm hayowani'
worn out, to be taha
worship, to ayoppachi
wounded, to be kolofa
wrapped in, to be aboknóyyo'ha
write, to holissochi
wrong
   to be wrong with katihmi
   to have something wrong oppolo

y

yard kasbi
year afammi
yeast
   bread made with yeast paska shatabli'
   bread made without yeast paskikshatablo'
yellow, to be lakna
yes ii
yesterday oblaashaash
you ishnaakoot, ishnaako, hachishnaakoot, hachishnaako, ishno'—*see also* units 3, 5, 8, 9
   how are you? chinchokmataa?, hachinchokmataa?
   only you ishnaakilloot, ishnaakillo
you all hachishnaakoot, hachishnaako, hachishno'—*see also* units 3, 5, 8, 9
   only you all, only you guys hachishnaakilloot, hachishnaakillo

you all's chimmi', hachimmi'—*see also* unit 7
you guys hachishnaakoot, hachishnaako, hachishno'—*see also* units 3, 5, 8, 9
   only you all hachishnaakilloot, hachishnaakillo
young, to be himitta
younger sibling nakfish
your. *See* unit 7
yours chimmi', hachimmi'
yourself; yourselves. *See* unit 5

Bibliography

WORKS CITED

Bushnell, David I., Jr. 1909. *The Choctaw of Bayou Lacomb, St. Tammany Parish, Louisiana.* Smithsonian Institution, Bureau of Ethnology Bulletin 48. Washington, D.C.: Government Printing Office.

Byington, Cyrus. 1978. *A Dictionary of the Choctaw Language.* Edited by J. R. Swanton and H. S. Halbert. Smithsonian Institution, Bureau of American Ethnology Bulletin 46. Washington, D.C.: Government Printing Office, 1915. Reprint, 1973, Oklahoma City Council of Choctaws; St. Clair Shores, Mich.: Scholarly Press.

Haag, Marcia, and Henry Willis. 2001. *Choctaw Language and Culture: Chahta Anumpa.* Norman: University of Oklahoma Press.

Humes, Rev. Jesse, and Vinnie May (James) Humes. 1973. *A Chickasaw Dictionary.* Ada, Okla.: Chickasaw Nation.

Jacob, Betty, Dale Nicklas, and Betty Lou Spencer. 1977. *Introduction to Choctaw.* Durant, Okla.: Choctaw Bilingual Education Program, Southeastern Oklahoma State University.

Munro, Pamela, and Catherine Willmond. 1994. *Chickasaw: An Analytical Dictionary.* Norman: University of Oklahoma Press.

Swanton, John R. 1984. *The Indians of the Southeastern United States.* Smithsonian Institution, Bureau of American Ethnology Bulletin 137. Washington, D.C.: Bureau of American Ethnology, 1946. Reprint, 1979, Washington, D.C.: Smithsonian Institution Press.

Wright, Allen. 1880. *Chahta Leksikon: A Choctaw in English Definition for the Choctaw Academies and Schools.* St. Louis: Presbyterian Publishing.

SELECTED ADDITIONAL SCHOLARLY WORKS ON CHICKASAW GRAMMAR

Gordon, Lynn. 1987. "Relative Clauses in Western Muskogean languages." In *Muskogean Linguistics,* edited by Pamela Munro. UCLA Occasional Papers in Linguistics 6, 66–80.

Gordon, Matthew. 1999. "The Intonational Structure of Chickasaw." *Proceedings of the 14th International Congress of Phonetic Sciences,* 1993–96.

Gordon, Matthew, Pamela Munro, and Peter Ladefoged. 2000. "Some Phonetic Structures of Chickasaw." *Anthropological Linguistics* 42: 366–400.

———. 2001. "Chickasaw." *Journal of the International Phonetics Association* 31: 287–90.

Munro, Pamela. 1984. "The Syntactic Status of Object Possessor Raising in Western Muskogean." In *Proceedings of the Tenth Annual Meeting of the Berkeley Linguistics Society,* edited by Claudia Brugman and Monica Macaulay, 634–49. Berkeley: BLS.

———. 1987. "Some Morphological Differences between Chickasaw and Choctaw." In *Muskogean Linguistics*, edited by Pamela Munro. UCLA Occasional Papers in Linguistics 6, 119–33.

———. 1998. "Chickasaw Expressive 'Say' Constructions." In *Studies in American Indian Languages: Description and Theory*, edited by Leanne Hinton and Pamela Munro. University of California Publications in Linguistics 131: 180–86.

———. 1999. "Chickasaw Subjecthood." In *External Possession,* edited by Doris L. Payne and Immanuel Barshi, 251–89. Amsterdam/Philadelphia: John Benjamins.

———. 2000. "The Leaky Grammar of the Chickasaw Applicatives." In *The Proceedings from the Main Session of the Chicago Linguistic Society's Thirty-Sixth Meeting,* edited by Arika Okrent and John P. Boyle. Vol. 36-1, 285–310. Chicago: CLS.

———. "Chickasaw." 2005. *The Native Languages of the Southeastern United States*, edited by Janine Scancarelli and Heather Hardy, 114–86. Studies in the Anthropology of North American Indians. Lincoln: University of Nebraska Press.

Munro, Pamela, and Lynn Gordon. 1982. "Syntactic Relations in Western Muskogean: A Typological Perspective." *Language* 58: 81–115.

Munro, Pamela, and Charles H. Ulrich. 1984. "Structure-Preservation and Western Muskogean Rhythmic Lengthening." In *Proceedings of the Third Annual West Coast Conference on Formal Linguistics*, edited by Mark Cobler, Susannah MacKaye, and Michael T. Wescoat, 191–202. Stanford, Calif.: Stanford Linguistics Association.

Payne, Doris L. 1982. "Chickasaw Agreement Morphology: A Functional Explanation." In *Studies in Transitivity*, edited by Paul J. Hopper and Sandra A. Thompson, 351–78. Syntax and Semantics 15. New York–London: Academic Press.

Pulte, William. 1975. "The Position of Chickasaw in Western Muskogean". In *Studies in Southeastern Indian Languages*, edited by James M. Crawford, 251–56. Athens: University of Georgia Press.

Index

In this index **boldface** type indicates Chickasaw sounds, words, prefixes, or endings. Quotation marks enclose the English translations of the Chickasaw. Numbers in parentheses following an entry reference the unit. If you do not find an item in this index, check the list of prefixes and endings and the glossary.

Contents of the Accompanying Audio CD